Church, State, and Society

CATHOLIC MORAL THOUGHT

General Editor: Romanus Cessario, O.P.

Church, State, and Society

An Introduction to Catholic Social Doctrine

J. Brian Benestad

The Catholic University of America Press
Washington, D.C.

Nihil Obstat:
The Very Reverend David M. O'Connell, C.M.
Censor Deputatus

Imprimatur:
The Most Reverend Donald W. Wuerl
Archbishop of Washington

January 27, 2010

The *nihil obstat* and the *imprimatur* are declarations that a work is considered to be free from doctrinal or moral error. It is not implied that
those who have granted the same agree with the contents, opinions, or
statements expressed.

The paper used in this publication meets the minimum requirements of
American National Standards for Information Science—Permanence of
Paper for Printed Library Materials, ANSI Z39.48-1984.
∞

Library of Congress Cataloging-in-Publication Data
Benestad, J. Brian.
Church, state, and society : an introduction to Catholic social doctrine /
J. Brian Benestad.
p. cm.
Includes bibliographical references and index.
ISBN 978-0-8132-1800-7 (cloth : alk. paper) —
ISBN 978-0-8132-1801-4 (pbk. : alk. paper)
1. Christian sociology—Catholic Church.   2. Catholic Church—
Doctrines.   I. Title.   II. Title: Introduction to Catholic social doctrine.
BX1753. B435 2011
230'.2—dc22
2010035471

To my wife, Janet, and my children,
Katherine, Christopher, Elizabeth, and Brian,
with love and gratitude

❖

With gratitude to Pope Benedict XVI, preeminent
theologian and teacher of the Catholic faith

"Charity is at the heart of the Church's social doctrine. Indeed, all the responsibilities and all the duties spelled out by that doctrine are derived from charity. . . . [C]harity in its turn needs to be understood, confirmed, and practiced in the light of truth.

If we love others with charity, then first of all we are just to them. . . . [J]ustice is inseparable from charity, and intrinsic to it."

(*Caritas in veritate*, nos. 2, 6.)

"[T]here can be no justice without a resurrection of the dead. . . . I am convinced that the question of justice constitutes the essential argument, or in any case the strongest argument, in favor of eternal life. . . . [O]nly in connection with the impossibility that the injustice of history should be the final word does the necessity for Christ's return and for new life become fully convincing."

(*Spe salvi*, nos. 42, 43.)

Contents

Acknowledgments

The University of Scranton gave me a sabbatical and some released time from teaching in order to do research and to write my book on Catholic social doctrine. For this alloted time I am grateful to the provost, Dr. Hal Baillie, to two former deans of the College of Arts and Sciences, Drs. Joseph Dreisbach and Paul Fahey, and to those faculty who approved my sabbatical application. I am much in debt to my first teacher of Catholic social doctrine, Rev. Ernest Fortin, A.A., and to Marie Gaughan, the secretary of the Department of Theology and Religious Studies, for the various kinds of help that she so promptly and generously gave me. In addition, I want to express my heartfelt thanks to Rev. Joseph Tylenda, S.J., Professors Mary Keys and Joseph Capizzi for their helpful comments on my entire manuscript, my copy editor, Aldene Fredenburg, my proof reader and daughter, Elizabeth Benestad, and above all my wife, Janet, who engaged me in serious conversation on Catholic social doctrine and read every chapter with a critical eye. I say with gratitude that she always loved truth more than her husband.

I would be remiss not to offer special thanks to David McGonagle and Fr. Romanus Cessario, O.P., for their invitation to write this book and for their patience in waiting for its completion. For their encouragement and counsel I thank Bishop John Dougherty and my friends Rev. Matthew Lamb, Drs. Edward Capestany, Robert Hueston, Marc Guerra, and Greg Burke.

In writing this book I made ample use of material that I have previously published elsewhere. The chapters in which these articles appear, in whole or in part, are listed below. Publication data and permissions are indicated.

Introduction

"Understanding the Opposition to Pope John Paul II's *Evangelium Vitae* in the Light of Alexis de Tocqueville's *Democracy in America*," in *Proceedings of the Pontifical Academy for Life*, edited by Juan Correa and Elio Sgreccia (Vatican City: Libreria Editrice Vaticana, 2001), 502–12. By permission

of the Pontifical Academy for Life. "Do Today's Catholics Know Anything about the Church's Social Teachings?" in *Keeping Faith*, edited by
Patrick G. D. Riley (Front Royal, Va.: Christendom Press, 2000), 31–61. By
permission of Christendom Press.

Chapter 1

Janet P. Benestad and J. Brian Benestad, "Human Dignity: The Heart
of Catholic Social Teaching," in *The Great Life: Essays on Doctrine and Holiness
in Honor of Father Ronald Lawler, O.F.M. Cap* (Steubenville, Ohio: Emmaus
Road Publishing, 2005), 63–85. By permission of Emmaus Road Publishing. "Do Today's Catholics Know Anything About the Church's Social
Teachings?" By permission of Christendom Press.

"The Distorted Understanding of Human Dignity in Liberal Re-
gimes," in *The Dignity of the Dying Person: Proceedings of the Fifth Assembly of the
Pontifical Academy for Life*, edited by Juan Correa and Elio Sgreccia (Vatican
City: Libreria Editrice Vaticana, 2000), 368–72. By permission of the Pontifical Academy for Life. "Henry George and the Catholic View of Morality and the Common Good I," *American Journal of Economics and Sociology*
44, no. 3 (1985): 365–78. By permission of Blackwell Publishing. "Philosophy, Political Philosophy and Historicism in Pope John Paul II's *Fides et
Ratio*," In *Gladly to Learn and Gladly to Teach: Essays on Religion and Political Philosophy in Honor of Ernest L. Fortin, A.A.*, 53–67 (Lanham, Md.: Rowman and
Littlefield, 2002). By permission of Rowman and Littlefield.

"Review essay on Leon Kass's *Life, Liberty and the Defense of Dignity: The
Challenge for Bioethics*," in *Etica Della Ricerca Biomedica: Per Una Visione Cristiana*,
edited by Juan Correa and Elio Sgreccia, 22–30 (Rome: Pontifical Academy for Life, 2004). By permission of the Pontifical Academy for Life.
"Review Essay on Leon Kass's *Life, Liberty and the Defense of Dignity: The Challenge for Bioethics* and *Toward a More Natural Science: Biology and Human Affairs*,"
National Catholic Bioethics Quarterly 5, no. 3 (Autumn 2005): 631–45. By permission of the National Catholic Bioethics Center.

Chapter 3

"Ordinary Virtue as Heroism," in *Seedbeds of Virtue*, edited by Mary
Ann Glendon and David Blankenhorn, 221–52 (Lanham, Md.: Madison
Books, 1995). By permission of Rowman and Littlefield.

Chapter 4

"The Catholic Concept of Social Justice: A Historical Perspective," *Communio* 11, no. 4 (1984): 364–81. By permission of *Communio*.

Chapter 5

"Review essay on Leon Kass's *Life, Liberty and the Defense of Dignity: The Challenge for Bioethics*," in *Etica Della Ricerca Biomedica*. By permission of the Pontifical Academy for Life. "Review Essay on Leon Kass's *Life, Liberty and the Defense of Dignity: The Challenge for Bioethics* and *Toward a More Natural Science: Biology and Human Affairs*," *National Catholic Bioethics Quarterly*. By permission of the National Catholic Bioethics Center. "Review essay on *Beyond Therapy: Biotechnology and the Pursuit of Happiness* by the President's Council on Bioethics," in *La Dignitá Della Procreazione Umana E Le Tecnologie Riproduttive: Aspetti Antropologici Ed Etici*, edited by Juan Correa and Elio Sgreccia (Rome: Pontifical Academy for Life, 2005), 7–17. By permission of the Pontifical Academy for Life.

Chapter 6

"The Statement of the U.S. Catholic Bishops on Faithful Citizenship: A Missed Opportunity," *Fellowship of Catholic Scholars Quarterly* 27, no. 3 (Fall 2004): 3–12. By permission of the Fellowship of Catholic Scholars. "The Theology of the Laity," *The Newman Rambler* 7, no. 1 (Summer 2003): 7–13. By permission of the Newman Centre at McGill University.

Chapter 8

"Reflections on the Santa Clara Address of Father Peter-Hans Kolvenbach, S.J. *Fellowship of Catholic Scholars Quarterly* 24, no 3 (2001): 12–20. By permission of the Fellowship of Catholic Scholars.

Chapter 9

"Welfare Reform and the Catholic Church: A Round Table Discussion," *Notre Dame Journal of Law, Ethics and Public Policy* 2, no. 2 (1997): 697–700, 727–28. By permission of *Notre Dame Journal of Law, Ethics and Public Policy*.

Chapter 11

"Dignity in the United Nations Declaration of Human Rights," in *Natura e Dignita Della Persona Umana a Fondamento Del Diritto Alla Vita. Le Sfide Del Contesto Culturale Contemporaneo*, edited by Juan Correa and Elio Sgreccia, 143–52 (Rome: Pontifical Academy for Life, 2003). By permission of the Pontifical Academy for Life.

Chapter 12

"Just War Principles," in *The Catholic Citizen: Debating the Issues of Justice*, proceedings of the 26th Annual Convention of the Fellowship of Catholic Scholars, edited by Kenneth Whitehead (South Bend, Ind.: St. Augustine's Press, 2004). By permission of the Fellowship of Catholic Scholars.

Conclusion

"The Liberal Insistence That Religion Is a Private Affair," in *Die Bedeutung der Religion für die Gesellschaft: Erfahrungen und Problemen in Deutschland und den USA*, edited by Anton Rauscher, 109–26 (Berlin: Duncker & Humblot, 2004). By permission of Dunker and Humblot GMbh.

Catholic Social Doctrine and Political Philosophy

Learning More about Catholic Social Doctrine

Do contemporary Catholics know the social teachings of the Church? Otherwise stated, can the typical member of a Catholic parish give an account of Catholic social doctrine (CSD)?[1] In a 1998 statement, the United States Catholic Bishops answer this question in the negative through their episcopal conference.[2] The bishops say, "Our social heritage is unknown by many Catholics. Sadly our social doctrine is not shared or taught in a consistent and comprehensive way in too many of our schools, seminaries, religious education programs, colleges and universities."[3] The Pontifical Council for Justice and Peace sounded the same alarm in its *Compendium of the Social Doctrine of the Church*, published in 2004. "[The Church's social doctrine] is neither taught nor known sufficiently, which is part of the reason for its failure to be suitably reflected in concrete behavior."[4]

1. In the United States the terms "Catholic social teaching" and "Catholic social thought" are more frequently used than "Catholic social doctrine." I will usually use the term "Catholic social doctrine" in keeping with the title of the book published in 2004 by the Pontifical Council for Justice and Peace, *Compendium of the Social Doctrine of the Church* (Vatican City: Libreria Editrice Vaticana), and with the usage adopted by Pope Benedict XVI.

2. The conference of Catholic bishops was previously two conferences, the National Conference of Catholic Bishops (NCCB) and the United States Catholic Conference (USCC), from 1966 until July 1, 2001. At that time these two conferences merged to become the United States Conference of Catholic Bishops (USCCB). Between 1919 and 1966 the bishops' conference was named the National Catholic Welfare Council (1919–1922) and then the National Catholic Welfare Conference (1922–1966); see www.usccb.org for more information about the history of the bishops' conference.

3. U.S. Catholic Bishops, *Sharing Catholic Social Teaching: Challenges and Directions* (Washington, D.C.: United States Catholic Conference of Bishops, 1998), 3.

4. Pontifical Council for Justice and Peace, *Compendium of the Social Doctrine of the Church* no. 528.

To address the problem, the bishops call for sweeping changes in the curriculum of seminaries and in Catholic schools from kindergarten through college. Besides suggesting curriculum revisions, the bishops themselves offer guidance to Catholics by providing a summary of the principles and themes of CSD under the following headings: the sacredness of life and the dignity of the human person; the social character of the human person ("call to family, community, and participation"); rights and responsibilities; option for the poor and vulnerable; the dignity of work and the rights of workers; international solidarity; and care for creation. The bishops also mention subsidiarity and the common good.[5]

The summary presented by the bishops in 1998 reiterates all they said in *A Century of Social Teaching*, published in 1990 to commemorate the 100th anniversary of *Rerum novarum*. The more recent statement differs, however, from the earlier one in three respects: in the order of the themes presented, the recommendation to exercise stewardship over creation, and the introduction of two teachings crucial to a proper understanding of CSD. The first addition appears in the last paragraph of the introduction, which reads, "Our commitment to the Catholic social mission must be rooted in and strengthened by our spiritual lives. In our relationship with God we experience the conversion of heart that is necessary to truly love one another as God has loved us."[6] This really means that understanding and living CSD depends upon living the whole Christian faith. This obvious fact is hardly ever mentioned in typical presentations of CSD in the United States. Yet it cannot be emphasized enough, since it is from their faith that most people begin to learn about the meaning of virtue and justice. The education of the minds and hearts of people in the truths of the faith is the first, and most basic, contribution that the family, Catholic school, and the Church make to the common good.

"We shall reach justice through evangelization," said Pope John Paul II

5. To supplement their presentation, the bishops direct their readers to the new *Catechism of the Catholic Church* (Vatican City: Libreria Editrice Vaticana, 1994); the *Guidelines for the Study and Teaching of the Church's Social Doctrine in the Formation of Priests*, published by the Vatican Congregation for Catholic Education (Vatican City: Polyglot Press, 1988); their own pastoral message entitled *A Century of Social Teaching: A Common Heritage, A Continuing Challenge* (Washington, D.C.: United States Catholic Conference of Bishops, 1990); and a report included in *Sharing Catholic Social Teaching: Challenges and Directions* (Washington, D.C.: United States Catholic Conference of Bishops, 1998), issued by a task force set up by the bishops' conference.

6. U.S. Catholic Bishops, *Sharing Catholic Social Teaching*, 2.

to the Latin American bishops early in 1979. Otherwise stated, people who have truly embraced the faith act justly in all that they do. Vatican Council II's *Dignitatis humanae* (*Declaration on Religious Freedom*) says that "society itself will benefit from the goods of justice and peace which result from people's fidelity to God and his holy will."[7] In other words, the Church can't expect to transform society by issuing debatable policy statements or even brief summaries of CSD if great numbers of Catholics are no longer committed to understanding and practicing their faith. So, the Church believes that there will be more social reform if it does not neglect individual reform.

Catholics who understand and live their faith put into practice all that is taught in the *Catechism of the Catholic Church* on doctrine, morality, the sacraments, and prayer. They know that their work for justice and the common good depends on receptivity to the grace of Christ and the inspiration of the Holy Spirit, both in themselves and in those they serve. In their quest for holiness, the common good, and the salvation of their neighbors, Catholics desiring to observe the social doctrine of the Church open the door when Christ comes knocking. Otherwise stated, they respond wholeheartedly to Pope John Paul II's resounding exhortation in the first homily of his pontificate given on October 22, 1978: "Do not be afraid. Open, better still, open wide the doors for Christ." Openness to Christ is the precondition for attaining greater union with Christ, without which Catholic social doctrine cannot be adequately grasped or lived.

The second significant addition in the bishops' 1998 statement occurs under the heading of the "life and dignity of the human person." The text mentions the evils of abortion, assisted suicide, the death penalty, cloning, and proposals to "perfect" human beings by genetic engineering. Including these items in the 1998 statement sends an important message about what cannot be tolerated in any society that aspires to promote human dignity, and implies that the whole realm of bioethics must be considered in the light of the Church's teaching on the dignity of the human person, and of Catholic social doctrine as a whole. In other words, the life issues cannot be separated from the work for justice.

While most Catholics could not list or discuss in any detail the themes mentioned by the bishops in their account of CSD, many are aware of

---

7. Vatican Council II, *Dignitatis humanae* (*Declaration on Religious Freedom*), no. 6. All 16 documents of Vatican Council II are found in Walter M. Abbott, ed., *The Documents of Vatican II* (New York: Guild Press, America Press, and Association Press, 1966).

the spiritual and corporal works of mercy and are influenced by them in the conduct of their daily lives. They visit the sick, contribute to the relief of the poor, comfort the afflicted, forgive offenses; they do, therefore, live in accordance with important social teachings. What many Catholics, however, are unable to do is to perceive all the implications of the themes mentioned by the bishops. For example, they are unable to see all that CSD requires of them in the neighborhood, in the workplace, and in their social and political lives. Many Catholics are genuinely puzzled that Catholic citizens and politicians are expected to act according to a well-formed Catholic conscience in the public square; many don't understand why the Church teaches that there should be laws against abortion, embryonic stem cell research, euthanasia, and same-sex marriage; they fail to grasp the Church's welcoming attitude toward immigrants, or its teaching on the importance of ethics in all of one's business dealings; they don't grasp the implications of natural law for public life or see that the exercise of rights must be guided by the insights of a person with a virtuous character; they don't know what the principles of subsidiarity and solidarity require in a society; and, they don't see all the good that can accrue to society if more Catholics lived in accord with God's will.

While the brief, authoritative introduction to CSD by the U.S. bishops is helpful, the inquiring mind will naturally raise some further questions. Where is CSD found in Church teaching, and to whom is it addressed? Does it encourage dialogue with non-Catholics on all matters pertaining to the common good? Is CSD a relatively recent phenomenon, or does it go back to the beginning of the Church? Is it based on faith *and* reason? Is it both a teaching of the Church and discipline to be studied on its own? Does the discipline of Catholic social teaching simply reflect the Church's social doctrine, or does it usually contain additional subject matter? Does CSD contain both permanent principles and contingent judgments? Does it fall under the rubric of moral theology, and is it part of the evangelizing mission of the Church? Why is CSD so important, both for the life of the Church and the well-being of society? Does the implementation of CSD have the potential of promoting unity in a country? Is living according to CSD an act of patriotism? What role do the lives of the saints play in promoting the understanding and acceptance of CSD?

Various Church documents give answers to these questions. Let us first take a look at one part of the *Instruction on Christian Freedom and Liberation*, issued by the Congregation for the Doctrine of the Faith (CDF) in 1986 under the signature of Joseph Cardinal Ratzinger. The *Instruction* says that Catholic social doctrine necessarily had to emerge from the practice of the Christian faith. "The Church's social teaching is born of the encounter of the Gospel message and of its demands (summarized in the supreme commandment of love of God and neighbor in justice) with the problems emanating from the life of society."[8] CSD then gives valuable guidance by helping people come to know what love and justice require in the various circumstances of life, knowledge that would escape many people without instruction. St. Augustine also underscores the difficulty of carrying out the commandment to love one's neighbor: "From this commandment arise the duties pertaining to human society, about which it is difficult not to err."[9] For example, many Catholics have difficulty seeing that love requires that their faith should affect the way they do business and that all people should refrain from killing embryos by extracting embryonic stem cells for research purposes. Since CSD seeks to overcome the split between Christian teaching and daily life, it is addressed not just to scholars and other well-educated people, but to the whole people of God and even to all people of good will. The latter can be addressed because many elements of CSD can be grasped and appreciated by reason alone.

The CDF *Instruction* calls social teaching a doctrine because it uses "the resources of human wisdom and the sciences."[10] More precisely, it discerns the permanently valid ethical principles in the treasury of human wisdom and applies these principles to the many and varied situations arising in the life of any society. CSD is also a doctrine, in my opinion, because it relies upon the truths of the faith in conjunction with right reason to make ethical judgments on human affairs. That CSD can be rightly based on both faith and reason is confirmed by the teaching of Vatican Council II's *Dignitatis humanae*: "For the Church is, by the will of Christ, the teacher of the truth. It is her duty to give utterance to, and authoritatively to teach, that truth which is Christ Himself, and also to declare and confirm by her authority those principles of the moral order which have their origins in human nature itself."[11] Pope Benedict XVI has been

---

8. Ibid., no. 72. I inserted the parentheses to make the sentence more clear.

9. St. Augustine, *The Catholic and Manichaean Ways of Life (De Moribus Ecclesiae Catholicae et de Moribus Manichaeorum)* (Washington, D.C.: The Catholic University of America Press, 1966), no. 49:40.

10. Congregation for the Doctrine of the Faith, *Instruction on Christian Freedom and Liberation* (1986), no. 72.

11. Vatican Council II, *Dignitatis humanae*, no. 14.

particularly eloquent on the Church's role in promoting the use of reason. Addressing the Muslim community of Cameroon, he said, "My friends, I believe a particularly urgent task of religion today is to unveil the vast potential of human reason, which is God's gift and which is elevated by revelation and faith."[12]

Given the heavy reliance on reason in CSD, no one should be surprised that it encourages Catholics to dialogue and cooperate on matters pertaining to the common good with non-Catholic Christians, with members of the world's religions, and with civil and political authorities.[13] The assumption, of course, is that Catholics have reason in common with everyone else on the planet. Pope Benedict, not surprisingly, touched on this theme in his trip to Africa. "May the enthusiastic cooperation of Muslims, Catholics, and other Christians in Cameroon be a beacon to other African nations of the enormous potential of an interreligious commitment to peace, justice and the common good."[14]

The *Instruction* next makes the very important point that CSD contains both permanently valid principles and "contingent judgments." The latter is the case because, "being essentially oriented towards action, [CSD] develops in accordance with the changing circumstances of history." Of course, it will not always be easy to discern what is permanent and what is contingent in CSD. For example, there are disputes among scholars about whether some things affirmed by Pope Leo XIII in *Rerum novarum* remain permanently valid.

In addition to the permanently valid principles, the Church's social doctrine also presents "criteria for judgment" and "directives for action."[15] The Vatican *Compendium of the Social Doctrine of the Church* says these three aspects of CSD "are the starting point for the promotion of an integral and solidary humanism."[16] The CDF's *Instruction* mentions as examples of fundamental principles the dignity of the human person, solidarity, and subsidiarity, and then adds that these principles "are the basis

12. "Meeting with Representatives of the Muslim Community of Cameroon," March 19, 2009.

13. Pontifical Council for Justice and Peace, *Compendium of the Social Doctrine of the Church*, nos. 534–37.

14. "Meeting with Representatives of the Muslim Community of Cameroon," March 19, 2009.

15. Congregation for the Doctrine of the Faith, *Instruction*, no. 72; Cf. Pope Paul VI, *Octogesima adveniens* (*Apostolic Letter on the Eightieth Anniversary of Rerum novarum*, 1971), no. 4, where the pope speaks of "norms of judgment."

16. *Compendium*, no. 7.

of *criteria for making judgments* on social *situations, structures* and *systems.*"[17] Correct judgments, however, cannot be made unless people keep in mind that "the first thing to be done is to appeal to the spiritual and moral capacities of the individual and to the permanent need for inner conversion, if one is to achieve the economic and social changes that will truly be at the service of man."[18] Otherwise stated, a society will not be just unless individuals are virtuous. This point is the leitmotiv of CSD and of my book.[19] Of course, virtues can only be true and effective if supported by divine grace.[20]

As for the guidelines for action, the *Instruction* says that "means of action must be in conformity with human dignity and facilitate education for freedom."[21] While violence must be rejected as a path to liberation, prudent action to achieve the constitutional protection of individual and social rights is applauded. Furthermore, the guidelines for action encourage individuals both to acquire technical and scientific skills and to make progress in their life of virtue. The *Instruction* concludes by emphasizing that the knowledge of CSD "does not dispense from education in the political prudence needed for guiding and running human affairs."[22]

While relying on reason, CSD begins from faith, as Pope John Paul II argued in *Centesimus annus.*[23] This cannot be otherwise if CSD is an attempt to show how the two love commandments (love of God and love of neighbor) are lived out in one's daily life. John Paul II also teaches that CSD is a branch of moral theology because it aims "to guide Christian behavior," and "the teaching and spreading of her social doctrine are part of the Church's evangelizing mission."[24] In fact, "The 'new evangelization,' which the modern world urgently needs...must include among its essential ele-

17. *Instruction,* No. 74.

18. Ibid., no. 75.

19. *Compendium,* no. 19. The humanism of Catholic social doctrine "can become a reality if individual men and women and their communities are able to cultivate moral and social virtues in themselves and spread them in society."

20. Vatican Council II, *Gaudium et spes* (Pastoral Constitution on the Church in the Modern World, 1965), no. 30: "Thus, with the needed help of divine grace, men who are truly new and artisans of a new humanity may be forthcoming."

21. *Instruction,* no. 76.

22. Ibid., no. 80.

23. Pope John Paul II, *Centesimus annus* (On the Hundredth Anniversary of Rerum novarum), no. 54: "man's true identity is only fully revealed to him through faith, and it is precisely from faith that the Church's social teaching begins."

24. *Pope John Paul II, Sollicitudo rei socialis (On Social Concern), no. 41.*

ments *a proclamation of the Church's social doctrine."*[25] This is the case, argues John Paul II, because CSD "points out the direct consequences of [the Christian message] in the life of society."

To understand the importance of implementing CSD for the life of individuals, let us listen respectively to Pope Pius XI and Vatican Council II. "The whole scheme of social and economic life is now such as to put in the way of vast numbers of people most serious obstacles which prevent them from caring for the one thing necessary, namely, their eternal salvation."[26] Thirty-four years later *Gaudium et spes* (*Pastoral Constitution on the Church in the Modern* World) affirms that "people are often diverted from doing good and spurred toward evil by the social circumstances in which they live and are immersed from birth."[27] Of course, the implementation of CSD not only facilitates the attainment of eternal life, but also generates a political and social order respectful of human dignity, the common good, solidarity, and subsidiarity, and thereby promotes unity among the citizens of a nation. In the measure that these goals are attained, people have a greater chance of attaining happiness in this life. In his meeting with the bishops of Cameroon, Pope Benedict XVI emphasized this point: "Moreover, through her social doctrine, the Church seeks to awaken hope in the hearts of those left by the wayside. So it is the duty of Christians, particularly lay people with social, economic and political responsibilities, to be guided by the Church's social teaching, in order to contribute to the building up of a more just world where everyone can live in dignity."[28] To do the work of justice is, of course, a good way to love one's country.

The immediate sources of CSD are the social encyclicals, from Pope Leo XIII's *Rerum novarum* to those of Pope Benedict XVI, all of which deal with CSD in some way, and other encyclicals not classified as social, such as Pope John Paul II's *Evangelium vitae* (*The Gospel of Life*). Other sources include the Christmas messages of Pope Pius XII; synod documents; papal responses to the work of the synods, such as Pope John Paul II's *Familiaris consortio;* Vatican Council II, especially *Gaudium et spes* and *Dignitatis humanae;*[29] the *Catechism of the Catholic Church;* and documents issued by Vatican

25. *Centesimus annus,* no. 5.
26. Pope Pius XI, *Quadragesimo anno (On Reconstruction of the Social Order),* no. 130.
27. Vatican Council II, *Gaudium et spes,* no. 25.
28. "Meeting with the Bishops of Cameroon," March 18, 2009.
29. *The Pastoral Constitution on the Church in the Modern World* and the *Declaration on Religious Freedom;* see Abbott, ed., *The Documents of Vatican II.*

congregations and councils, such as those put out by the Congregation for the Doctrine of the Faith and the Pontifical Council for Justice and Peace.

To this list must be added the Bible, the fathers of the Church (especially St. Augustine, St. Thomas Aquinas, St. Thomas More), the lives of the saints, and the tradition of political philosophy. It is hard to understand the full meaning of the papal social encyclicals without some familiarity with these great saints and political philosophers. The application of CSD to the contemporary scene requires a good knowledge of the society, government, and the history of one's country, as well as the problems in the nations of the world. A good deal of dialogue will have to take place between Catholic authorities on CSD and all those who think about and address the problems of society. To say the least, a complete education in CSD is a daunting task, requiring a thorough liberal education in addition to serious education and formation in the faith as a whole.

While most Catholics will never be experts in CSD (or in dogmatic theology or fundamental moral theology), they will certainly be able to grasp some fundamental principles on their own through study and observation, and even acquire more knowledge if helped by their bishop, parish priests, and Catholic associations to which they belong. In addition, in the measure that Catholic students receive instruction in Catholic theology as an integral part of a genuine Catholic liberal education, they will be more able both to give an account of CSD and to live it more completely in every aspect of their lives.[30] Familiarity with the lives of the saints will also help Catholics understand CSD and be a source of inspiration in the difficult work of upholding human dignity and living for the common good.

The Plan of the Book

It is the purpose of this book to give an accurate account of the Church's social doctrine for the inquiring Catholic and non-Catholic on the basis of authoritative Church sources—for example, papal encyclicals,

30. In writing this section, I benefitted from two foreign sources: Joseph Cardinal Höffner, *Christian Social Teaching* (Cologne: Ordo Socialis, 1983), and Juan Souto Coelho, coordinator, *Doctrina Social de la Iglesia, Manual Abbreviado* (Madrid: Biblioteca De Autores Cristianos, 2002). The latter book has a whole team of authors.

Vatican Council II, statements of Vatican congregations (such as those made by the Congregation of the Doctrine of the Faith), and statements of the United States bishops. In dealing with the statements of the United States Conference of Catholic Bishops (USCCB), I will make distinctions between their authoritative doctrinal teaching on justice and the common good and their advocacy of political opinions with which the Catholic laity may legitimately agree or disagree. I will also occasionally bring out more explicitly points not fully developed in the authoritative sources of CSD. In addition, I will make use of both Catholic and non-Catholic scholars to place CSD in a context that makes it more understandable.

In twelve chapters and a conclusion I will give a reasonably complete presentation of Catholic social doctrine, understood as a part of Church teaching on morals. Except for the *Compendium of the Social Doctrine of the Church*, no other single volume attempts to do this in recent times. I have written the book in such a way as to be a resource for pensively reflecting on CSD and subsequently teaching it to others. As popes John Paul II and Benedict XVI have indicated, knowledge of CSD is crucial for the life of the Church and the well-being of the political and social order.

As a part of Church teaching on morals, CSD is most effective when Catholics also accept the Church's doctrinal teachings on faith, such as the Nicene Creed. For example, belief in the Incarnation and the Paschal mystery are the foundation for a life of love and justice in response to God's love. Christ's death and resurrection are the proof that God loves his people. However, because many teachings of CSD are attainable by reason alone, they can be embraced in various degrees by people who do not share the Church's teachings on faith, the sacraments, and prayer.

The book is divided into four parts, the first of which is the longest. Titled "The Human Person, the Political Community, and the Common Good," this first part contains five chapters dealing with the dignity of the human person, human rights, natural law, and the common good. The subjects of the virtues, grace, law, and public policy will be discussed as means of seeking the common good. Part 2 focuses on the three principal mediating institutions of civil society: the family, the Church, and the Catholic university. Part 3 covers the subjects of the economy, work, poverty, immigration, and the environment, while part 4 focuses on the international community and just war principles. The conclusion discusses the tension between CSD and liberal democracy.

In order to facilitate the understanding of the principles and themes of

Catholic social thought, the rest of my introduction will discuss some of Pope Benedict XVI's teaching on CSD and conscience, and then briefly explain some of the main differences between classical and modern political philosophy (dialogue partners of CSD), and conclude by discussing a few of the subjects in Tocqueville's *Democracy in America* that affect the application of Catholic social doctrine in the United States.

Pope Benedict XVI on Catholic Social Doctrine

Pope Benedict XVI has touched on CSD in his first two encyclicals and devoted the third exclusively to Catholic social teachings.[31] In addition, in all his travels and in not a few speeches, he has directed attention to points that, if understood and accepted, could have deep and lasting effects on the study and the practice of CSD.[32] My goal in this section is to continue this introduction to CSD by explaining the *gist* of Pope Benedict's approach to political and social matters, including his engagement with political philosophers. Of course, the pope's comprehensive thought on CSD cannot be fully understood without studying the themes discussed in this book, especially the dignity of the human person and the common good.

First, the pope has continually and consistently told the world that the laws ought to proscribe abortion, euthanasia, embryonic stem cell research, and same-sex marriage. In addition, the laws should allow religious liberty and never force anyone to act against his conscience. In his meeting with President Obama on July 10, 2009, Pope Benedict discussed the protection of life and the right of all to abide by their conscience. He even gave President Obama a copy of the most recent statement of the CDF on bioethics, *Dignitas personae (The Dignity of the Person)*. The president promised to read it on his way to Africa.

In his trip to Brazil in May of 2007, Benedict XVI takes up the question of the relation of the Catholic faith as a whole to the work for justice, and thereby further explains and develops what the USCCB said in

31. I will thoroughly analyze Pope Benedict XVI's third encyclical, *Caritas in veritate (On Integral Human Development in Charity and Truth)*, in the appendix.

32. This section on Pope Benedict XVI doesn't attempt to give a complete presentation of his perspective on Catholic social doctrine, but simply summarizes the basics that the pope presented during his recent trip to Brazil and in his first two encyclicals, *Deus caritas est (God Is Love)* and *Spe salvi (On Christian Hope)*. Pope Benedict's approach to CSD corresponds to the emphasis of this book.

its 1998 statement on Catholic social teaching, Benedict said, "Wherever God and his will are unknown, wherever faith in Jesus Christ and in his sacramental presence is lacking, the essential element for the solution of pressing social, political problems is also missing." Catholics, he adds, must have a thorough knowledge of their faith, as presented in the *Catechism of the Catholic Church* and its abbreviated *Compendium*. They must also receive an "[e]ducation in Christian personal and social virtues" as well as an education in social responsibility. One example of this kind of education is the formation of "a genuine spirit of truthfulness and honesty among the political and commercial classes."[33] In short, the work for justice requires that the minds and the hearts of Catholics must be educated and formed to know and practice the whole faith.

Anticipating a likely objection to his emphasis, he asks how one can justify "the priority of faith in Christ and of 'life' in him" when there are so many pressing political, economic, and social problems in Latin America. He answers that both Marxism and capitalism promised that just structures, an indispensable condition for promoting justice in society, could be established and maintained without "individual morality"—without individuals formed by the virtues. Benedict XVI implies that people now see that both political and economic systems failed to live up to their promises. In fact, he argues, just structures depend on a moral consensus in the body politic and lives lived by citizens in accord with the virtues. Benedict XVI further holds that the necessary moral consensus cannot develop where God is not acknowledged. So, a great effort is constantly needed to maintain belief in God. "In other words, the presence of God, friendship with the Incarnate Son of God, the light of his word: these are always fundamental conditions for the presence of justice and love in our societies."[34] This, of course, is the teaching of St. Augustine and St. Thomas Aquinas, as well as that of the social encyclicals from Pope Leo XIII to Pope John Paul II.

It is not up to the Church to tell the state what particular measures it should adopt in order to achieve justice. The Church must not identify herself "with a single political path and with debatable partisan posi-

---

33. Pope Benedict XVI, "Meeting and Celebration of Vespers with the Bishops of Brazil," May 11, 2007. All of Pope Benedict's speeches can be found on the Vatican website, http://www.vatican.edu; search under the category of Pope Benedict XVI's travels outside of Italy.

34. Pope Benedict XVI, "Address at the Inaugural Session of the Fifth General Conference of the Bishops of Latin America and the Caribbean," May 13, 2007.

tions." On the contrary, "respect for a healthy secularity—including the pluralism of political opinion—is essential in the Christian tradition."[35] In other words, both the clergy and the laity are to refrain from identifying their debatable political opinions with the Gospel. Vatican II's *Gaudium et spes* and Pope John Paul II also made this point in the light of the tendency of Catholics not to make nuanced distinctions between Catholic social doctrine and political options that may or may not be a good application of CSD to a particular situation.[36]

In his first encyclical, *Deus caritas est* (*God Is Love*, December 25, 2005), Pope Benedict indicates that the very nature of the Church requires Catholics to take most seriously their obligation to help the poor. "The Church cannot neglect the service of charity any more than she can neglect the sacraments and the word."[37] In his personal words to the Brazilian bishops the pope urges them to preach the faith to the poor, attend to their material needs, and make them "feel truly loved." "The poor living in the outskirts of the cities or the countryside need to feel that the Church is close to them, providing for their most urgent needs, defending their rights and working together with them to build a society founded on justice and peace."[38]

The question naturally arises whether the Church's love of the poor should lead it to participate in the political process. *Deus caritas est* begins to answer this question by reflecting on the roles of the Church and state in promoting justice. Pope Benedict XVI says, "The just ordering of society and the state is a central responsibility of politics." This work, always a political battle, is not the responsibility of the Church. What, then, is the role of the Church and its social doctrine with respect to justice? The aim of that doctrine "is simply to help purify reason and to contribute, here and now, to the acknowledgment and attainment of what is just." Because people are blinded by their interests and love of power, they have difficulty reasoning about justice and seeing what it requires in particular instances. To be an effective instrument, reason "must undergo constant purification." As a part of the work of purifying reason, the Church forms the conscience of people, builds their character, and mo-

---

35. Ibid.

36. Chapter six contains a detailed account of the difference between Catholic social doctrine and ordinary partisan politics.

37. Pope Benedict XVI, *Deus caritas est*, no. 22.

38. Pope Benedict XVI, "Meeting and Celebration of Vespers with the Bishops of Brazil," May 11, 2007.

tivates them to act justly. Still otherwise stated, the Church has a significant role in bringing about "openness of mind and will to the demands
of the common good."[39] In this perspective the Church *indirectly* but powerfully contributes to the realization of justice in society and the state.

In a subsequent section of the encyclical, Pope Benedict does add that
the "*direct* duty to work for a just structuring of society, on the other hand,
is proper to the lay faithful" (my emphasis).[40] Under the influence of love
they have the responsibility to work for the policy that will best contribute to the realization of the common good. For example, on the basis of
more or less limited knowledge, the lay faithful will endorse various positions on health care, taxes, immigration policy, decisions about the wisdom of going to war. The Church as Church will not endorse debatable
policy options as the laity must do to fulfill their responsibilities as citizens. The laity will also contribute to the just structuring of society by
practicing the virtues in their family life, at work, and in their relations
with neighbors by engaging in the spiritual and corporal works of mercy.

The pope explicitly connects what he says about the purification of
reason and virtue to the establishment of just structures in society. He
argues that "just structures are neither established nor proven effective in
the long run" unless the Church helps to purify reason and moves people
to act ethically in all areas of their lives.[41] This is exactly the same point
Benedict XVI made in his speeches to the Brazilian bishops. In other
words, a just society is not possible unless individuals are just. The corollary is that there will be as much injustice in the structures of society as
there is injustice in the souls of individual citizens.

Pope Benedict XVI's most general point about Catholic social doctrine is that it provides a set of guidelines for Catholics and non-Catholics alike in their work for justice. These CSD guidelines, however, "need
to be addressed in the context of dialogue with all those seriously concerned for humanity and for the world in which we live."[42] The pope
doesn't elaborate on this point, but it can be understood in the light of
my initial comments about the necessity of connecting CSD with other
disciplines and with the problems of one's own society.

The last major point that Benedict XVI makes in his encyclical is
about the relation between justice and charity.

39. *Deus caritas est*, no. 28.   40. Ibid., no. 29.
41. Ibid.   42. Ibid., no. 27.

Love—*caritas*—will always prove necessary, even in the most just society.... There will always be suffering which cries out for consolation and help. There will always be loneliness. There will always be situations of material need where help in the form of concrete love of neighbor is indispensable.[43]

Benedict XVI implies that those arguing for the sufficiency of justice in society do not really understand the nature of a human being, who does not live "by bread alone." Men and women need to give and receive love in order to be happy. A society where people only receive their due would indeed be a cold place. By these remarks the pope is responding to the Marxist objection that with the establishment of a just social order people would "no longer have to depend on charity."

Spe salvi (*On Christian Hope*) reiterates his basic argument that the attainment of a just society depends on the practice of virtue by individuals. So he says with emphasis, "Are we not perhaps seeing once again, in the light of current history, that no positive world order can prosper where souls are overgrown?"[44] Just as a garden can be overgrown with weeds, so souls can be overgrown with sins and vices. In the measure that this happens, the prospects for a decent world order diminish.

Pope Benedict then discusses attempts in the modern period to have a reasonably just society, as well as comfort and health, without overcoming the problems of overgrown souls and the absence of solidarity among people. Originally, "the recovery of what man had lost through the expulsion from Paradise was expected from faith in Jesus Christ: herein lay redemption. Now this Redemption is no longer expected from faith, but from the newly discovered link between science and praxis."[45] Faith is not denied, but is relegated to private affairs and to the other world. Hope for the future is now derived from faith in progress, which results from the Baconian project, the conquest of nature by science in view of man's comfort and health.

Reliance on science and technology for hope, however, proved to be insufficient. So, there was a turn to politics. Benedict explains this turn by summarizing what Marx expected from the political process. "Progress towards the better, towards the definitively good world, no longer comes from science but from politics—from a scientifically conceived politics that recognizes the structure of history and society and thus points out the road towards revolution, towards all encompassing change."[46] The

---

43. Ibid., no. 28.
45. Ibid., no. 16.
44. *Spe salvi*, no. 15.
46. Ibid., no. 20.

key change for Marx was, of course, socializing the means of production as the way to bring about the new Jerusalem, a society in which people would no longer be unjust to each other.

Pope Benedict dismisses the exaggerated hopes from science and politics with commonsense observations. He mentions Theodore Adorno's point that progress brought about by science and technology is always ambiguous because it can produce both good and evil. "If technical progress is not matched by corresponding progress in man's ethical formation, in man's inner growth…, then it is not progress at all, but a threat for man and the world."[47] (Think of nuclear weapons in the hands of terrorists.) While we can reasonably expect continuous progress in the areas of science and technology, we cannot reasonably expect similar progress in moral behavior. Why not? Every human being and every generation have the choice either "to draw upon the moral treasury of the whole of humanity" or to reject that treasury. This means that scientific and technological progress will always be a two-edged sword. Some individuals or some generations may lose contact with the moral treasury or may simply choose to ignore it. This is, indeed, happening today in the area of biotechnology.

Because the moral treasury of humanity "is present as an appeal to freedom and a possibility for it," "[t]he right state of human affairs, the moral well-being of the world can never be guaranteed simply through structures alone, however good they are."[48] Not that structures are unimportant! But they have to be animated by people with wisdom and virtue. Since each generation has to produce enough of those people to make a difference, "the kingdom of good will never be definitively established in the world."[49] Every generation must seek to understand the moral treasury of humanity and make it accessible to more and more people. That is exactly what Catholic social doctrine attempts to do for the citizens and nations of the world.

Pope Benedict's response to Marx's reliance on politics to bring about the definitively just society by socializing the means of production, of course, logically follows from his understanding of human freedom. Marx's error, the pope argues, is not recognizing that man's freedom to do good or evil remains, no matter what shape the structures of society take.

47. Ibid., no. 22.   48. Ibid., no. 24.
49. Ibid., no. 24.

He forgot that man always remains man. He forgot man and he forgot man's freedom. He forgot that freedom always remains also freedom for evil. He thought that once the economy had been put right, everything would automatically be put right. His real error is materialism: man, in fact, is not merely the product of economic conditions, and it is not possible to redeem him purely from the outside by creating a favorable economic environment.[50]

Pope Benedict's reflection on the potential of freedom for good or ill is both a summons to use freedom well and to recognize that people's bad use of freedom will deny justice and love to many people while they are living on this earth. The only hope for the latter is the Last Judgment, belief in which is fading today. Belief in the Last Judgment moves Christians to love and to work for justice with all their heart and soul, and offers the hope that people not helped by their efforts will receive justice in the afterlife. This is a consoling thought when Christians fail to overcome the injustice in their midst; it sustains them amidst their failures, for example, to protect the life of the unborn from abortion. The victims of injustice especially draw hope from belief in the resurrection of the flesh. Pope Benedict movingly explains:

There is justice. There is an "undoing" of past suffering, a reparation that sets things aright. For this reason, faith in the Last Judgment is first and foremost hope—the need for which was made abundantly clear in the upheavals of recent centuries. I am convinced that the question of justice constitutes the essential argument, or in any case the strongest argument, in favor of faith in eternal life.[51]

Christ must return as judge if the injustices of this life are not to be the "final word."

I would like to conclude this brief overview of Pope Benedict's thought on CSD by going back to the day before Joseph Cardinal Ratzinger became pope, April 18, 2005. On that day the cardinal gave the homily at the Mass for the election of the new pope. He captured the attention of many with his striking comments on the "dictatorship of relativism."

Having a clear faith, based on the creed of the Church, is often labeled today as fundamentalism. Whereas, relativism, which is letting oneself be tossed and "swept along by every wind of teaching" [Eph 4:14], looks like the only attitude in line with the times today. We are moving toward establishing a dic-

50. Ibid., no. 21.
51. Ibid., no. 42.

tatorship of relativism, which does not recognize anything as definitive, and which has as its highest measure one's own ego and one's own desires.

Back in 1997 Cardinal Ratzinger had already pointed out in his *Salt of the Earth* that a "dictatorship of opinion" was growing. By this phrase he means that people are marginalized and excluded if they do not go along with the reigning opinions. Today's pervasive relativism and its endorsement by opinion leaders intimidates Christians either to give up their "controversial" beliefs or to remain silent about them when these beliefs contradict the reigning opinions.

I discern two forms of relativism in today's society. One form is a complete or almost complete ignorance or rejection of the moral treasury of humanity. The more common form of relativism, especially targeted by Cardinal Ratzinger, emerges from the influence of the principle of autonomy and the sway of politically correct opinions. People choose which tenets of the natural law or the Christian faith that they will reject. They defend drunkenness and promiscuity, greed, the right to abortion, same-sex marriage.

The dictatorship of relativism undermines not only Christian morality and doctrine, but also the foundations of democracy. When the appeal to truth can play only a diminished role in the life of a democratic society, all that is left is the will of the majority, against which there can be no compelling claim. There is no reasonable protest against injustice unless one can invoke some truth regarding the nature of justice.

Pope Benedict XVI on Conscience and Catholic Social Doctrine

Pope Benedict XVI has told us that the Church "wishes to help form consciences in political life" as an indirect contribution to the establishment of justice. Before he became Pope Benedict XVI, Joseph Cardinal Ratzinger addressed the issue of conscience in relation to all aspects of life in a justly famous essay entitled "Conscience and Truth."[52] Turning briefly to that essay, we can see more clearly why Pope Benedict believes

52. Joseph Ratzinger, "Conscience and Truth," in *Crisis of Conscience*, edited by John M. Haas (New York: Crossroad, 1996), 1–20; this essay was originally published in *Catholic Conscience Foundation and Formation: Proceedings of the Tenth Bishops' Workshop*, ed. Russell E. Smith (Braintree, Mass.: Pope John XXIII Medical-Moral Research and Education Center, 1991). It is also available in Polish, Czech, French, Spanish, Italian, and in

that the correct formation of consciences by the Church is so impo\
for making CSD a reality in people's lives.[53]

Many believe, Cardinal Ratzinger argues, that you have to mak\
choice between a morality of conscience and morality of authority. Within the Church "two notions of 'Catholic' are set in opposition to each
other." The so-called "pre-conciliar" view is understood to require un-
critical submission to Church teaching on faith and morals and is, thus,
insufficiently respectful of human freedom. The new view is that the
Magisterium presents Church teaching as material to be considered in
conscientious decisions. After input from the Magisterium, "[c]onscience
would retain, however, the final word."[54] Some would even argue that
conscience is infallible. The cardinal, of course, rejects these views as contrary to Catholic doctrine.

Cardinal Ratzinger persuasively makes the point that you can't really
speak of conscience and free decisions of conscience if there is no truth
by which it takes its bearing. This is true, he argues, for everyone, whether
believer or nonbeliever. Consequently, a person's judgment of conscience
can be wrong if he doesn't know the truth or if he chooses not to follow
the accurate judgment of his conscience. Think of the argument about
whether the Nazis could justify their atrocities by arguing that they were
following their consciences. Could an erroneous conscience excuse their
behavior? Cardinal Ratzinger noted that at German universities scholars
have answered both yes and no to this question. Those who excused the
Nazis because they acted morally in following their mistaken consciences said that people "should not doubt their eternal salvation."[55] A view of
conscience that would lead to such conclusions, argues the cardinal, has
to be wrong.

By way of first response to the claim of the infallible conscience, Car-
dinal Ratzinger quotes Psalm 19:12–13. "But who can discern his errors?
Clear thou me from my unknown faults."[56] A literal translation of the
Septuagint reads, "Who understands his own faults? Cleanse me of my

numerous German publications, the last of which is *Werte in Zeiten des Umbruchs: Die Her-ausforderungen der Zukunft Bestehen* (Freiburg: Herder, 2005), 100–122. I mention the many translations to show that this essay has been well received in various parts of the world.

53. There certainly is no reason to believe that Joseph Ratzinger has changed his mind on the nature of conscience since becoming pope.

54. Ratzinger, "Conscience and Truth," 1–2.

55. Ibid., 5.

56. Ibid.

secret sins." The Vulgate has, of course, the well-known *ab occultis munda me* (*Ps. 18:13*). This Old Testament text communicates a wisdom discernible by all men and women. People can choose to do evil, but refuse to acknowledge any guilt; they can remain inattentive to the depth of their own soul. Not being willing or able (because of ignorance) to discern one's own sins remains a possibility and a great danger for human beings. "He who no longer recognizes that killing is a sin has fallen further than the one who still recognizes the shamefulness of his actions, because the former is further removed from the truth and conversion."[57] The cardinal's point is that the erroneous conscience can become a screen behind which one chooses to hide in order to avoid self-knowledge.

In Eastern Europe under communist rule people lost sight of fundamental moral principles because of intellectual deformation and spiritual starvation. Consciences fell silent in the face of outrageous acts of injustice. "The silencing of conscience," argues Cardinal Ratzinger, "leads to the dehumanization of the world and to mortal danger, if one does not work against it."[58] In working against the silencing of conscience one must keep in mind that the invocation of conscience can become simply a rationalization for what one wants to do and a mere reflection of the prevailing opinions of society. There is no real exercise of conscience if there is no "co-knowing with the truth," if the individual simply creates his own moral standards.

Cardinal Ratzinger says that "two standards become apparent for ascertaining the presence of a real voice of conscience. First, conscience is not identical to personal wishes and taste. Second, conscience cannot be reduced to social advantage, to group consensus, or to the demands of political and social power."[59] Conscience requires individuals to ask not what they can do, but what they should do. This is what both Socrates and Jesus Christ taught. The martyrs, in fact, are "the great witnesses of conscience, of that capability given to man to perceive the 'should' beyond the 'can' and thereby render possible real progress, real ascent."[60] Ultimately, it doesn't make any sense to speak of conscience if there is no ascertainable truth by which to live. Without truths to live by, the best society can do is to set up a framework that allows individuals to exercise their liberty in any way they see fit, as long as they don't infringe on other people's liberty or break the law.

57. Ibid.
59. Ibid., 10.

58. Ibid., 7.
60. Ibid., 12.

In order to help modern men and women recognize that there are discernible truths to guide them in the exercise of their freedom, Cardinal Ratzinger discusses the two levels of conscience: *anamnesis* (remembrance) and *conscientia* (the act of judgment and decision that makes concrete applications). He calls *anamnesis* the ontological level of conscience. Thomas Aquinas, says the cardinal, called it "an inner repugnance to evil and an attraction to the good."[61] The cardinal further identifies *anamnesis* with what St. Paul says in the Letter to the Romans 2:14–15a: "When Gentiles, who do not have the law, do by nature what the law requires, they are a law unto themselves, even though they do not have the law. They show that what the law requires is written on their hearts while their conscience also bears witness."[62]

St. Basil, the cardinal further explains, sheds more light on the concept of *anamnesis* by arguing that we are instilled with the knowledge that love for God requires the observance of such divine commandments as the Ten Commandments. Divine commandments "are not something imposed from without," writes Basil.[63] The cardinal also quotes St Augustine, who adds, "We could never judge that one thing is better than another if a basic understanding of the good had not already been instilled in us."[64] Cardinal Ratzinger's summary of these points is so lucid and penetrating that it must be quoted in its entirety.

This means that the first so-called ontological level of the phenomenon of conscience consists in the fact that something like an original memory of the good and the true (both are identical) has been implanted in us, that there is an inner ontological tendency within man, who is created in the likeness of God, toward the divine. From its origin man's being resonates with some things and clashes with others. This *anamnesis* of the origin, which results from the godlike constitution of our being, is not a conceptually articulate knowing or a store of retrievable contents. It is, so to speak, an inner sense, a capacity to recall, so that the one whom it addresses, if he is not turned in upon himself, hears its echo from within. He sees: "That's it! That is what my nature points to and seeks."[65]

In this perspective people will give a sympathetic hearing to the truths of the faith and *recta ratio* (right reason) if they have not previously chosen to shut out the truth or to hate it. In fact, argues Cardinal Ratzinger, "the

61. Ibid., 16.
63. Ibid., 13.
65. Ibid.

62. Ibid., 12.
64. Ibid.

anamnesis instilled in our being needs, one might say, assistance from without so that it can become aware of itself."[66] What this means in practice is that people need to come into regular contact with the truths of faith and with those truths accessible to reason. Let us recall that striking sentence from his *Christianity and the Crisis of Cultures*: "Christianity is this remembrance of the look of love that the Lord directs to man, this look that preserves the fullness of his truth and ultimate guarantee of his dignity."[67]

The Church keeps alive the Christian memory of the *magnalia Dei*, of all the wonders that God has accomplished for humanity, and reminds everyone to be attentive to God's commandments out of gratitude for gifts received. The pope, for example, doesn't arbitrarily impose commandments on Catholics, but calls to mind the basic Christian truths, especially those in danger of being neglected. Without this reminder many Catholics are liable to be misled by the reigning opinions of the day. When the whole faith is not taught in the churches, schools, and families, it will be very hard for Catholics to remain wholly in the truth. Besides the competent exercise of Church authority, liberal education also reminds students of attitudes and behavior reflective of human dignity. For example, in teaching the novels of Jane Austen I have noticed that students readily identify and admire the good characters and blame the bad ones for their immoral attitudes or behavior. These correct judgments are even made by students who may be engaging in the same unchaste or unjust behavior that they blame in Austen's characters. Something in their being responds to Austen's appealing presentation of the true and the good.

If Cardinal Ratzinger is right on target in his reflections on conscience, how do we explain the Nazis, totalitarian communists like Stalin, and those people in liberal regimes who defend the right to choose abortion for the whole nine months of pregnancy, the destruction of the embryo for research purposes, or euthanasia? One explanation, of course, is the decision of the will to reject the truth, as mentioned by the cardinal. The other, in my judgment, is that the *anamnesis* of individuals has not been sufficiently assisted by education, or by the timely exercise of the Church's teaching mission on the local level, or by the beneficent influence of the laws and customs.

---

66. Ibid., 14.

67. Joseph Cardinal Ratzinger, *Christianity and the Crisis of Cultures*, trans. Brian Mc-Neil (San Francisco: Ignatius Press, 2006), 71.

The Quarrel between the Ancients and the Moderns

In order to put Pope Benedict XVI's explanation of CSD in a clarifying context, I am now going to explain briefly the distinction between the ancients and the moderns, one of the helpful categories reintroduced into the contemporary discussion of political philosophy. The distinction has not been an explicit theme of CSD, although Pope Benedict XVI's encyclicals, *Deus caritas est* and *Spe salvi,* speak of Nietzsche, Marx, Bacon, Kant, Adorno, and Horkeimer in a way to remind us that aspects of modern thought diverge sharply from, say, the emphasis on virtue in the political thought of Aristotle, Plato, Augustine, and Aquinas. Scholars who talk about the ancients and the moderns usually see a sharp distinction between the political philosophy in ancient and modern periods. (Not all scholars, of course, accept this distinction, seeing rather continuity in the development of thought between the two periods.) Ernest Fortin,[68] theologian and political philosopher, argues for making this distinction not to create nostalgia for the ancient city or medieval Christendom, but to shed light on contemporary problems. The distinction helps make sense of the emphasis in CSD on the priority of individuals embracing a life of virtue over the modern emphasis on the simple change of structures, or the protection of rights as the best way to seek reform. For example, Marx taught that the establishment of communism would bring about a just society. My contention is that understanding why Aristotle and Plato stressed the importance of virtue in their political thought helps people understand why there is a similar emphasis in CSD and why the exclusive emphasis on rights, to the neglect of duties emanating from a life of virtue, cannot possibly bring about a just society. People need a reason to respect rights besides fear and self-interest.

Modernity has been remarkably successful in providing health, prosperity, democracy, and freedom, but has generated a host of social problems, such as the erosion of religious belief and practice, the breakup of the family, greed, drug and alcohol abuse, the culture of death, and the celebration of individual autonomy to the detriment of character and vir-

---

68. Ernest Fortin was a professor of theology for many years at Boston College. While well known by many professors of political philosophy, he is not yet a household name in the Catholic theological community. In my judgment, however, there is a hardly any American theologian who has reflected as deeply as Fortin on the relation between Christianity and political philosophy. I hope that my book makes him more well-known and appreciated.

tue. The language of rights—the moral language of America—is not able to describe all the problems, much less come up with solutions. The language of values has been used to pick up the slack, but with mixed success. How can a word that implies the subjectivity of belief about good and evil address real human problems? Is there any precise meaning to such terms as family values or Gospel values?

Against the widespread scholarly opinion that Western thought is continuous from Socrates to the nineteenth century, I defend the view that modernity represents a break with classical philosophy and Christianity. "Classical philosophy," writes Fortin, "studies human behavior...in the light of virtue, and it claims to be able to show the way to these goals. It culminates in a discussion of the best life and, on the political level, of the best 'regime' or the type of rule that is most conducive to the best life."[69] The best life is the life of virtue, and the best regime promotes the practice of virtue in the lives of citizens. Good government, then, makes for good human beings. Of course, the converse is also true: the predominance of good human beings, especially among those who set the tone for society, makes for good government. Plato and Aristotle were well aware that the best regime would exist only in speech, as a model for actual regimes to imitate as closely as possible. They knew that a great number of circumstances would have to be favorable for the emergence of good regimes, much less the "best regime."

Machiavelli was the first philosopher to break with the classical view. A passage from chapter 15 of *The Prince* reveals his quarrel with the classical orientation:

And many have imagined republics and principalities that have never been seen or known to exist in truth: for it is so far from how one lives to how one should live that he who lets go of what is done for what should be done learns his ruin rather than his preservation. For a man who wants to make a profession of good in all regards must come to ruin among so many who are not good.[70]

What has never existed in reality is, for example, the best regime as described by Plato in the *Republic*. The ideal cannot be realized, because

69. Ernest Fortin, *Human Rights, Virtue, and the Common Good: Untimely Meditations on Religion and Politics*, vol. 3 of *Collected Essays*, ed. J. Brian Benestad (Lanham, Md.: Rowman and Littlefield, 1996), 148.

70. Niccolo Machiavelli, *The Prince*, trans. Harvey C. Mansfield, Jr. (Chicago: University of Chicago Press, 1985), 61.

most people do not seek excellence as they ought. Claiming to see things the way they are, Machiavelli proposes a political philosophy that abandons the ideal and takes its bearings by the way most people tend to behave most of the time. In line with his new orientation, Machiavelli proposes a new "ought." Henceforth, rulers should not rule in such a way as to help people live as they ought in some ideal sense. Rather, leaders ought to be good or bad according to the needs of the situation. In other words, they should not hesitate to use evil means in order to achieve decent political goals.

The form in which the trend inaugurated by Machiavelli became respectable and attractive was through the invention of universal natural rights by Thomas Hobbes and their elaboration by John Locke. The latter proposed a beguiling alternative to the classical position that only the practice of virtue could bring about harmony between the individual and society or between self-interest and the common good. Locke held that things could be so arranged in society that "unlimited appropriation with no concern for the need of others [would be] true charity."[71] The key is to unleash people's acquisitive passions. Even if entrepreneurs are focused exclusively on their well-being, their genius creates many well-paying jobs for others. In Locke's perspective, unlimited acquisitiveness is more effective in promoting the common good of society than moderation or charity, because it is more reliable. Simply by pursuing their own selfish goals, people automatically contribute to the realization of the common good.

Locke's political philosophy is largely responsible for the acceptance of natural rights doctrines. Locke convinced people that they are by nature free and equal and have rights to life, liberty, and property. Looking at life exclusively through the prism of rights initiated a quiet revolution in the way people understood the purpose of their own lives as well as the end of society. It was a quiet revolution, because many citizens do not realize that rights are not simply another way of talking about classical virtue or the teaching of Jesus Christ. In fact, the doctrine of rights presupposes an understanding of human nature that assumes that people cannot really rise above preoccupation with their own interests. The language and perspective of rights, then, constitutes a sharp break with the idealism of the ancients, who stressed the practice of virtue and the fulfillment of duties. According to natural-law teaching, when individuals

71. Leo Strauss, *Natural Right and History* (Chicago: University of Chicago Press, 1953), 243.

fulfill duties to family, friends, and society, they perfect their human nature and act in accordance with their dignity as human persons.[72]

Liberalism and liberal democracy, the contemporary offspring of modernity, incline Americans to think about morality almost exclusively in
terms of rights. This in turn leads to a preoccupation with choice and
freedom as ends in themselves, and about the sovereignty of the individual and the goods of the body: safety, health, pleasure, and prosperity. The
liberal temper is anything but neutral in the moral tone it sets for citizens. It does not encourage the practice of virtue, but rather an unprecedented openness to all human possibilities. Fortin explains: "What this
leads to most of the time is neither Nietzschean creativity, nor a noble
dedication to some pregiven ideal, nor a deeper religious life, nor a rich
and diversified society, but easygoing indifference and mindless conform-
ism."[73] In other words, today's version of openness encourages not the
pursuit of truth, but rather subservience to public opinion, preoccupation
with material things, and a reshaping of religion to suit the temper of the
times. In other words, religions are tempted to ascribe normative character to the spirit of the age. For example, the emphasis on autonomy today
inclines Christians to redefine their faith in terms of what the culture ap-
proves. Many Catholics now accept the right to abortion and believe that
same-sex marriage should be legal.

Papal social teaching and Vatican Council II have labored to put rights
into a teleological framework so that they are ordered to the fulfillment
of duties and less subject to a purely individualistic interpretation. Part of
chapter 1 will recount how the Church has approached this intellectual
challenge.

If my kind readers do not find the distinction between the ancients
and moderns to be persuasive or helpful, put it aside, but do try to make
sense of the unmodern emphasis in CSD on the priority of individual
conversion and the practice of all the virtues. CSD does not, of course,
expect governments to take the lead in promoting the acceptance of moral norms and the practice of virtue. This is the primary responsibility of
the various associations in civil society, especially the family, the Church,

---

72. Cf. John Hittinger, *Liberty, Wisdom, and Grace: Thomism and Democratic Political Theory*
(Lanham, Md.: Lexington Books, 2002); see especially "Why Locke Rejected an Ethics
of Virtue and Turned to Utility," 87–96. For an understanding of Locke that rejects the
interpretation put forth by Strauss, Fortin, Hittinger, Benestad, et al., see John Dunn,
Locke (New York: Oxford University Press, 1984).

73. Fortin, *Human Rights, Virtue, and the Common Good*, 20.

and the educational institutions. Governments (including liberal democracies) will, nevertheless, have some limited role in promoting a public morality.

Alexis de Tocqueville's *Democracy in America*

The study of ancient and modern political philosophy helps students of CSD to understand the theoretical framework established by liberal political principles, in which Catholics attempt to apply their social teaching. Alexis de Tocqueville's *Democracy in America* does a brilliant job of showing how liberal political principles have, in fact, both affected the way Americans live and the way they understand and practice their faith. Even though Alexis de Tocqueville wrote his masterwork in the 1830s, it is still widely regarded as one of the most profound books ever written on democracy and the shape of the democratic regime in America. While Tocqueville admires America's rights-based democracy, he is not blind to the kinds of problems the American regime will always have to address. By revisiting Tocqueville to learn important truths about the effect of democracy on individuals, society, and especially Christianity, Catholics will be in a better position both to preserve Catholicism and to promote and improve democracy in the United States. My intention is to analyze parts of Tocqueville's *Democracy in America*, especially through the eyes of Pierre Manent's *Tocqueville and the Nature of Democracy*. "Pierre Manent's elegant and profound work," writes Professor Harvey Mansfield of Harvard University, "is the best introduction I know to the greatness of Tocqueville."[74]

One of Tocqueville's main points is that democracy is not a neutral regime. By its nature it promotes both a certain way of looking at things and even a way of life. For example, Tocqueville argues that the power of the majority is "not only predominant but irresistible." Once the majority makes up its mind on any particular question, "there are, so to say, no obstacles which can retard, much less halt, its progress and give it time to hear the wails of those it crushes as it passes. The consequences of this state of affairs are fate-laden and dangerous for the future."[75] Americans believe, according to Tocqueville, that "there is more enlightenment and

74. Pierre Manent, *Tocqueville and the Nature of Democracy*, foreword by Harvey C. Mansfield, trans. John Waggoner (Lanham, Md.: Rowman and Littlefield, 1996), vii; Manent is a Catholic political philosopher and the director of studies at the École des Hautes Études en Sciences Sociales in Paris.

75. Alexis de Tocqueville, *Democracy in America* (New York: Harper Collins, 1988), 248.

wisdom in a numerous assembly than in a single man."[76] But they also assume that each individual is "as educated, virtuous, and powerful as any of his fellows."[77] Given this view of the individual, it is no wonder that Americans can place such faith in an association of people who think the same way. If everyone knows what is important for the guidance of his life, is there any reason to seek out the wisdom of superior individuals or the guidance of the Church?

While Tocqueville doesn't systematically lay out his arguments for asserting that irresistible majority opinion is dangerous for the future of America, he does suggest various reasons for this observation. He fears that Americans will give up thinking, even accept their religion as a common opinion rather than as revealed by God, and ultimately conform their way of thinking and acting to the reigning public opinions. In other words, they will be tempted to take their bearings by what is powerful in the culture and regard it as normative for their lives. In a section entitled "The power exercised by the majority in America over thought," Tocqueville makes one of the most shocking statements of his book: "I know no country in which, speaking generally, there is less independence of mind and true freedom of discussion than in America."[78] Then, he adds, "there is no freedom of the mind in America."[79] Of course, these statements logically follow from Tocqueville's observations about the power and influence of majority opinion. How can there be independent and free minds when majority opinion dictates how individuals are to look at things? How can freedom be assured when untutored subjective wills are more likely to give rise to majority opinion than objective truth? Not that truth cannot enter into the formation of majority opinion and thus guide the exercise of freedom, but that depends especially on the success of religious leadership, real religious conversion, and various kinds of political and civic initiatives.

How religion guides and moderates is neatly summarized in this oft-quoted sentence from Tocqueville's *Democracy:* "Religion, which never intervenes directly in the government of American society, should therefore be considered as the first of their political institutions, for although it did not give [the American people] the taste for liberty, it singularly facilitates their use thereof." Even though the law allows them to do most everything, "these are things which religion prevents them from imagining

---

76. Tocqueville, *Democracy in America*, 247.   77. Ibid., 66.
78. Ibid., 254–55.   79. Ibid., 256.

and forbids them to dare."[80] In particular, religion moderates the love of material things and the desire to be sovereign, encourages its adherents to have common bonds and to be in solidarity with others. It regulates family life, especially through the influence of the woman, and thereby has an immense influence on society and the state. So, religion is very useful for the preservation of democracy, but, as Manent rightly notes, "the religion of the Americans loses its utility proportional to their attachment to it for reasons of utility."[81] So far, it looks as though there is a perfectly natural fit between democracy and religion, especially Christianity.

Tocqueville's honesty, however, compels him to say things about religion in America that should raise a red flag for serious Christians. Toward the beginning of volume 2 Tocqueville comes back to the influence of the majority in "supplying the individual with a quantity of ready-made opinions" and then makes a statement disquieting for Christian believers. "So there are many theories of philosophy, morality, and politics which everyone adopts on the faith of public opinion. And if one looks very closely into the matter, one finds that religion is strong less as revealed doctrine than as part of common opinion."[82] Of course, he doesn't say that religion is not at all believed as divine revelation, but that its power comes from being part of public opinion, or more precisely majority opinion. In hearing that religion can be accepted as common opinion, I immediately thought of a citation from St. Augustine quoted by Pope John Paul II in *Fides et ratio*: "To believe is to think with assent.... Believers are also thinkers: in believing they think and in thinking they believe.... If faith does not think, it is nothing."[83] People must think not only to understand the Christian faith (*intellectus fidei*), but also even to hear it correctly (*auditus fidei*).

While Tocqueville's analysis of American democracy is very perceptive and still most relevant, Catholicism, in some important ways, doesn't fit his description of religion in America. Tocqueville believes that all religions are necessarily transformed by democracy, so as to suffer some significant loss. I and many others would grant that Catholicism in America is affected by public opinion, the political correctness of the opinion

---

80. Ibid., 292.

81. Manent, *Tocqueville and the Nature of Democracy*, 91.

82. Toqueville, *Democracy in America*, 435–36.

83. John Paul II, *Fides et ratio*, no. 79, quoting St. Augustine, *De praedestinatione sanctorum*, 2, 5: PL 44, 963.

molders, and the deviations of contemporary philosophy previously mentioned. To see that influence, an interested observer could simply note the following: the resistance in Catholic universities to *Ex corde ecclesiae* in the name of academic freedom and institutional autonomy, the generation of a dissenting moral theology partially grounded in historicism and modern philosophies of will, the widespread ignorance of the contents of the faith, especially among the young, resistance to the new *Catechism of the Catholic Church* because of its emphasis on content as opposed to experience, fairly widespread acceptance of abortion, euthanasia, contraception and divorce, and abuses in the liturgy.

As bad as these trends are, they are by no means the inexorable by-product of life in American democracy. Tocqueville errs by implying that Catholicism is inevitably received more as "common opinion" than as revealed religion. One is forced to conclude that Tocqueville exaggerates the irresistible force of public opinion. With divine help, Catholicism can take its bearings by scripture, tradition, and the Magisterium. With more effective hierarchical and lay leadership in the United States, coupled with serious liberal education in Catholic universities, the problems besetting Catholicism in America would diminish. American Catholicism can preserve its soul and *can* be even more effective than Tocqueville thought in moderating democracy.

Conclusion

Although Americans tend to understand freedom more in relation to rights than to truth, they are not at all impervious to the Catholic argument that real freedom depends on knowing and living the truth about God and man. We must grant that the common understanding of rights in America is not usually linked to a teaching on natural or supernatural ends and, therefore, not to truth. As Professor Daniel Mahoney puts it, "human beings are rights-bearing individuals and hence worthy of respect. This is the unchallenged faith of modern democracy. We speak endlessly about human rights but have difficulty saying very much about the nature of man, of this human being whose dignity we must respect."[84] Nevertheless, even though the self-understanding of many Americans

---

84. Daniel J. Mahoney, "The Moral Foundations of Liberal Democracy," in *Public Morality, Civic Virtue and the Problem of Modern Liberalism*, ed. T. William Boxx and Gary M. Quinlivan (Grand Rapids, Mich.: Eerdmans, 2000), 25.

doesn't easily link rights to truth, their practice, so to speak is better than their theory. In their daily lives Americans will exercise their freedom in the light of some truths, although not always self-consciously. Because of the split in the American soul I would affirm the following with Professor Mahoney:

> It is to be expected that the two notions of liberty, that we have discussed, the "self-sovereignty" of man [or the exercise of autonomy without the *summum bonum* or highest good as the lodestar] and "liberty under God," will continue to compete for the loyalty of democratic citizens and for the souls of individual men and women. This division is what is ultimately at stake in our "culture wars."[85]

Many Americans think that the separation of church and state in the United States means that the Catholic Church really has no business making suggestions for governance of the political order or even shaping the customs of life in society. But on the other hand, there is some explicit and much latent receptivity to the concept of liberty under God, which can be achieved with the help of God's grace. The great popularity of the poem and hymn "America the Beautiful," written respectively by Katherine Lee Bates in 1893 and Samuel A. Ward shortly afterward, shows that many respond not only to the physical beauty of America, but also to the moral beauty of American heroes and moral ideals. Let us recall the first three stanzas of this poem set to music.

> O beautiful, for spacious skies,
> For amber waves of grain,
> For purple mountain majesties
> Above the fruited plain!
> *America! America! God shed his grace on thee,*
> *And crown thy good with brotherhood, from sea to shining sea.*
>
> O beautiful, for pilgrim feet
> Whose stern, impassioned stress
> A thoroughfare for freedom beat
> Across the wilderness!
> *America! America! God mend thine ev'ry flaw;*
> *Confirm thy soul in self-control, thy liberty in law!*

85. Mahoney, "The Moral Foundations of Liberal Democracy," 39.

O beautiful for heroes proved
In liberating strife,
Who more than self their country loved
And mercy more than life!
America! America! May God thy gold refine
Till all success be nobleness, and ev'ry gain divine.

In the first stanza, after paying tribute to the beauty of the Midwest plains and the Rocky Mountains in Colorado, Bates asks God's help in establishing brotherhood throughout the land. She then pays tribute in the second stanza to those early American pilgrims who prepared the way for the establishment of a regime dedicated to the protection of liberty. Knowing that liberty can degenerate into license, Bates asks God for help in guiding the American effort, both to shape the character of its citizens and to make laws that guide the use of liberty. Finally, in the third stanza Bates pays tribute to those soldiers who, in their sacrifices for liberty, loved their country and mercy more than their own lives. Bates concludes by reminding Americans that they should look to God to ennoble everything they do. In sum, on their own, Americans cannot hope to live on the high level celebrated in this moving poem.

The enthusiastic reception of "America the Beautiful" indicates that there is the potential in America for receptivity to the beauty of Catholic social doctrine. If American Catholic universities could eventually find a way to educate their graduates to think intelligently about the moral and legal requirements of democratic regimes, then there could be enthusiastic responses to the proposals of CSD for the constitution of a good democracy or liberty under God. The prospects for that kind of education on a wide scale may still not be bright at the present moment. My hope is that *Ex corde ecclesiae* (Pope John Paul II's *Apostolic Constitution on Catholic Universities*) will eventually be the catalyst to bring about the renewal of Catholic liberal education.

PART I

The Human Person,
the Political Community, and the
Common Good

The Dignity of the Human Person, Human Rights, and Natural Law

The Dignity of the Human Person

Introduction

The practice of courtesy revels that people have an innate sense of the dignity of the human person. Even toward perfect strangers, many people will behave with good manners. We all know that the practice of courtesy makes civil life much more enjoyable.

C.S. Lewis provides us with an apt introduction to our reflection on the theme of human dignity in the comparison he makes between individuals and civilizations, noting that the former have an eternal destiny of happiness or misery, while the latter will one day perish.

There are no *ordinary* people. You have never talked to a mere mortal. Nations, cultures, arts, civilizations—these are mortal, and their life is to ours as the life of a gnat. But it is immortals whom we joke with, work with, marry, snub, and exploit—immortal horrors or everlasting splendors.[1]

Lewis also reminds us that by our actions we are "helping each other to one or other of these destinations." I would also note that the character of the civilizations and cultures in which we live helps or hinders us in achieving a blessed eternal life. That is why Catholic social doctrine (CSD) on the dignity of the human person, human rights, and natural law is so important. Human dignity, properly understood, requires the kind of culture and political community in which it can thrive—in other words, the right kind of mores and laws. In fact, as Cardinal Höffner writes, "The ultimate purpose of all sociality is the perfection of person-

---

1. C.S. Lewis, *The Weight of Glory and Other Addresses*, rev. ed. (New York: Macmillan, 1980), 18–19; I found this reference in Peter Kreeft's book *The Philosophy of Tolkien: The Worldview Behind* The Lord of the Rings (San Francisco: Ignatius Press, 2005).

hood."[2] That is to say, the reason that people live together in community
is to achieve the perfection of human dignity, the integral development of
the human person. As Pius XI says, "In the plan of the Creator, society is
a natural means which man can and must use to reach his destined end.
Society is for man and not vice versa."[3]

The contemporary culture of liberalism, unfortunately, disposes citizens to have an incomplete understanding of human dignity. It inclines
or tempts Americans, including Catholic Americans, to exercise their
rights without taking into account what Catholicism teaches about the
proper use of freedom or the right attitude toward the possession and
use of material things. Persons are said to have dignity because they are
autonomous and are capable of making choices. According to the most
common opinion in contemporary society, the dignity of the human person is especially secured by ensuring the protection of rights. The initial and primary emphasis on rights is, of course, a logical step, since the
autonomous exercise of choice requires the possession of rights. Catholic social doctrine certainly agrees that the dignity of the human person
needs the protection of rights, but stresses that Catholics should exercise their rights in the light of faith and natural law, or they will diminish their dignity. This kind of emphasis is nearly absent in a liberal democracy.

Another consequence of understanding dignity as constituted by human autonomy is linking the assessment of human dignity to a person's
quality of life, especially the capacity to make autonomous choices. It is
now commonly thought that a person's dignity diminishes with his declining quality of life. Physical and mental deterioration, as well as suffering, supposedly diminish human dignity. In *Quill v. Vacco* (1997) the Second Circuit Court of Appeals even went so far as to make an ominous
statement about legal obligations toward the terminally ill: "The state's
interest lessens as the potential for life diminishes."[4] The presence of this
statement in a decision of an appeals court surely indicates a trend toward

2. Joseph Cardinal Höffner, *Christian Social Teaching*, 2nd ed. (Bratislava: Lúc, 1997), 48.
3. Pope Pius XI, *Divini redemptoris*, no. 29, quoted from Höffner, *Christian Social Teaching*, 48.
4. Quoted from Frances X. Hogan and Marianne Rea-Luthin, "Exporting Death or
Offering Compassion: Vignettes of the American Experience with Physician-assisted
Suicide," in *The Dignity of the Dying Person: Proceedings of the Fifth Assembly of the Pontifical Academy for Life*, edited by Juan Correa and Elio Sgreccia (Vatican City: Librereia Editrice
Vaticana, 2000), 378.

regarding those persons with diminished physical capacity as less than fully human. Some argue that they are not entitled to the same rights as healthy individuals. The Terri Schiavo case showed that the courts and many people gave their approval to the withdrawing of food and water from a person because of her poor quality of life.

Pope John Paul II makes reference to the contemporary assault on the traditional understanding of human dignity in his *Evangelium vitae (Gospel of Life)*. He writes,

We must also mention the mentality which tends to *equate personal dignity with the capacity for verbal and explicit,* or at least perceptible *communication.* It is clear that on the basis of these presuppositions there is no place in the world for anyone who, like the unborn or the dying, is a weak element in the social structure, or for anyone who appears completely at the mercy of others and radically dependent on them, and can only communicate through the silent language of a profound sharing of affection.[5]

This way of understanding the human person is highly individualistic and fails to appreciate the rhythm of life, in which a person moves from the weakness and dependence of the unborn to the strength of adulthood, to the weakness of old age. Even during the time of people's strength, they are dependent in various ways for their physical, intellectual, and spiritual care. In the Catholic mind, human beings retain their dignity when they are receiving care and may even grow in dignity. Think of the person who accepts his dependence and suffering as a way of identifying with the passion of Christ.

Discussion of human dignity naturally leads into discussion of human rights, because people readily understand that rights can afford some protection to the dignity of the human person. What is less clear to people is how to think about the exercise of rights in the light of some objective moral standard. The relation of natural law to human dignity is unclear these days, because few are conversant with natural law, and the subtle Catholic concept of human dignity has not been sufficiently explained in the United States. In order to advance the discussion in Catholic circles on these subjects, the first section of this chapter draws upon both Catholic and non-Catholic sources to bring out the essential aspects of the Catholic concept of the dignity of the human person. The next section reflects on human rights and natural law in the light of that Catholic con-

---

5. Pope John Paul II, *Evangelium vitae (The Gospel of Life)*, no. 19.

cept of human dignity. This second section explains why Catholic social doctrine both defends and criticizes contemporary understandings of human rights and insists on the importance of natural law for public life in the United States.

The Nature and Basis of Human Dignity

Careful education is necessary for Catholics to understand that the dignity of the human person is not essentially constituted by the ability to make choices. According to Catholic teaching, people have dignity because they are created in the image and likeness of God, redeemed by Jesus Christ, and destined for eternal life in communion with God. In Pope John Paul II's words,

The dignity of the person is manifested in all its radiance when the person's origin and destiny are considered: created by God in his image and likeness as well as redeemed by the most precious blood of Christ, the person is called to be a "child in the Son" and a living temple of the Spirit, destined for eternal life of blessed communion with God.[6]

The threefold foundation for human dignity is both unshakable and instructive. No act of the human person can remove this foundation. Even when people commit the worst sins and crimes and suffer diminished physical and spiritual capacities, they retain human dignity. While this Christian teaching about the permanent character of human dignity is often mentioned and acknowledged by informed Christians, rarely do Catholics hear that human dignity is also a goal or an achievement. But this is the clear implication of the threefold foundation of human dignity and the explicit teaching of Vatican Council II and John Paul II.

As Vatican Council II puts it, "The principal cause of human dignity lies in the call of human beings to communion with God."[7] Being created in the image of God and redeemed by Jesus Christ makes it possible for everyone to respond to God's invitation to communion with him. Because it is the actual communion with God that perfects the dignity of human beings, Vatican II says, that the "dignity of man...is rooted and perfected

6. Pope John Paul II, *Christifideles laici* (*On the Vocation and Mission of the Lay Faithful in the Church and the Modern World*), no. 37.

7. Vatican Council II, *Gaudium et spes* (*Pastoral Constitution on the Church in the Modern World*), no. 19, "Dignitatis humanae eximia ratio in vocatione hominis ad communionem cum Deo consistit"; for all Vatican II documents see Walter M. Abbott, ed., *The Documents of Vatican II* (New York: Guild Press, America Press, and Association Press, 1966).

in God" (*in ipso Deo fundetur et perficiatur*).[8] It is important to note that only through the mystery of the Incarnation and the redemption do human beings fully understand themselves, especially their call to communion with God. During his pontificate Pope John Paul II kept reminding us of this point by quoting a sentence from *Gaudium et spes* (*Pastoral Constitution on the Church in the Modern World*), no. 22: "Christ the new Adam, in the very mystery of the Father and his love, *fully reveals man to himself* and brings to light his most high calling." In other words, Jesus Christ makes known to man his eminent dignity, a being destined for communion with his Creator, and the means to realize it every day: avoidance of sin and the practice of all the virtues, especially charity. Still otherwise stated, human beings are true to their dignity when they imitate the love of Jesus Christ, the love he showed for every single human being by dying on the cross.

Given the foundation of human dignity and the reality of sin, it logically follows that all will have to strive and strain to reach their ultimate goal, communion with the triune God. All human beings are able to do this because God "willed to leave man 'in the power of his own counsel' (cf. Sir 15:14), so that he would seek his Creator of his own accord and would fully arrive at full and blessed perfection by cleaving to God."[9] Given God's action, "human dignity requires that a person act according to a conscious and free choice," in seeking what is good. The council describes the effect of such human action on human dignity in the language of achievement.

Man realizes such dignity [that of "full and blessed perfection"] when emancipating himself from all captivity to passion, he pursues his goal in a spontaneous choice of what is good, and procures for himself through effective and skillful action, apt means to that end. Since man's freedom has been damaged by sin, only by the help of God's grace can he bring such a relationship with God to full flower.[10]

It is, of course, true to note that very few will succeed in freeing themselves from all captivity to passion. Nevertheless, everyone has the capacity, with the help of God's grace, of moving toward the dignity of perfection.

---

8. Ibid., no. 21.

9. Pope John Paul II, *Veritatis splendor* (*Splendor of Truth*), no. 34, quoting *Gaudium et spes*, no. 17.

10. *Gaudium et spes*, no. 17.

The council makes the same point when discussing the obligation of all to obey their conscience. "Man has a law in his heart inscribed by God, to obey which is his very dignity, and according to which he will be judged."[11] The text implies that people diminish their dignity by not obeying their conscience. Everyday speech captures this human possibility in the expression "to act beneath one's dignity." In sum, all people continually *achieve* or realize their dignity by seeking the truth, obeying conscience, resisting sin, practicing virtue, and repenting when they succumb to temptation. In other words, dignity is not just a permanent possession, unaffected by the way they live. All people have to obey their informed conscience, both to avoid acting beneath their dignity and to develop it.

So, there is a sense in which dignity may be continually diminished by a life of sin or progressively appropriated over a lifetime by seeking perfection, as John Paul II said. In *Rerum novarum*, Pope Leo XIII made the same point using language characteristic of Thomas Aquinas: "true dignity and excellence in men resides in moral living, that is, in virtue."[12] Saint Leo the Great's famous Christmas sermon states this point in a memorable way: "Christian, recognize your dignity, and now that you share in God's own nature, do not return by sin to your former base condition."[13] It is significant that this quotation stands as the first sentence in the section on morality in the new *Catechism of the Catholic Church*. It immediately directs attention to the necessity of achieving human dignity by living without sin.

Pope John Paul II argues that "genuine freedom is an outstanding manifestation of the divine image in man."[14] By genuine freedom the pope means freedom that takes its bearing by what is true and good, not the freedom that is indistinguishable from license. In other words, people who understand freedom as license will diminish their dignity by committing sin. On the other hand, people increase their dignity by living virtuously. Pope John Paul II goes so far as to say that martyrdom is "the supreme glorification of human dignity."[15] This statement makes eminent sense, because martyrs achieve the summit of human dignity by laying down their lives for God and neighbor. This is the reason martyrs are held in such high regard by Christians.

11. Ibid., no. 16.   12. Pope Leo XIII, *Rerum novarum*, no. 37.
13. *Catechism of the Catholic Church* (Vatican City: Libreria Editrice Vaticana, 1994), no. 1691.
14. *Veritatis splendor*, no. 34.
15. Pope John Paul II, *Dominum et vivificantem* (On the Holy Spirit in the Life of the Church and the World), no. 60.

The Vatican *Guidelines for the Study and Teaching of the Church's Social Doctrine in the Formation of Priests* says that human advancement depends on "ennobling the human person in all the dimensions of the natural and supernatural order" and that "man's true dignity is found in a spirit liberated from evil and renewed by Christ's redeeming grace."[16]

The recent *Compendium of the Social Doctrine of the Church* also implies that human dignity is not just a given, but also a goal of the individual and the Church. "By her preaching of the Gospel, the grace of the sacraments, and the experience of fraternal communion, the Church 'heals and elevates the dignity of the human person,...consolidates society and endows the daily activity of all people with a deeper sense and meaning.'"[17] If the human dignity of the individual person necessarily receives healing and elevation by the activity of the Church, then it is not simply a given, needing only the protection of rights. Human beings cooperate with their healing and ennobling by repenting of their sins, avoiding them in the future, and contributing to the common good by practicing virtue in every area of their lives.

In its section on the human person the *Compendium* makes much of the fact that sin and its effects offend the dignity of the human person. When people act beneath their dignity by sinning, the consequences are "alienation, that is the separation of man not only from God, but also from himself, from other men and from the world around him."[18] This separation or alienation, caused by sin, is an assault on human dignity because it is an obstacle to communion with God and to communion among human beings through their union with him. The piling up of personal sins produces structures of sin in society or the kind of twisted culture that becomes "sources of other sins, conditioning human conduct."[19] In other words, the personal sins of enough individuals produce the kind of culture that will lead others into temptation and sin. So, when individuals act beneath their dignity, they harm the life of society.

16. Congregation for Catholic Education, *Guidelines for the Study and Teaching of the Church's Social Doctrine in the Formation of Priests* (Rome: Congregation for Catholic Education, 1988); reprinted in *Origins*, vol. 19, no. 1 (1988): 182, 174.

17. Pontifical Council for Justice and Peace, *Compendium of the Social Doctrine of the Church* (Vatican City: Libreria Editrice Vaticana, 2004), no. 51, quoting Vatican Council II, *Gaudium et spes*, no. 40.

18. *Compendium of the Social Doctrine of the Church*, no. 116.

19. Ibid., no. 119.

Two Different Explanations of the Dignity
of the Human Person

In *Centesimus Annus (On the Hundredth Anniversary of Rerum novarum)* Pope
John Paul II provides a perfect commentary on the importance of human
dignity. "The guiding theme of Pope Leo's Encyclical, [*Rerum novarum*],
and of all of the Church's social doctrine, is a *correct view of the human person*
and of his unique importance, inasmuch as 'man...is the only creature on
earth which God willed for itself.'"[20] On the basis of faith and reason the
Church proclaims the dignity of the human person as the foundation of
Catholic social doctrine. There is no real disagreement on this teaching.
Nor is there any disagreement on the threefold foundation of human dignity: creation in the image of God, redemption by Jesus Christ, and the
call to eternal life in communion with God.

But there is an apparent disagreement in the explanation of this key
concept. Consider the following statements made by the U.S. Bishops in
1990 and 1998.

In a world warped by materialism and declining respect for human life, the
Catholic Church proclaims that human life is sacred and that the dignity of
the human person is the foundation of a moral vision for society [and]...the
foundation of all the principles of our social teaching....We believe that every
person is precious, that people are more important than things, and that the
measure of every institution is whether it threatens or enhances the life and
dignity of the human person.[21]...Each person possesses a basic dignity that
comes from God, not from any human quality or accomplishment, not from
race or gender, or age, or economic status.[22]

These explanations point out important tenets of CSD—especially the
understanding of human dignity as a permanent endowment—but do
not mention that human dignity is in any way a quality or accomplishment. The bishops rightly focus on the permanent character of human
dignity in order to protect vulnerable human beings from being declared
unworthy of respect or of the law's protection because of poor quality of

20. Pope John Paul II, *Centesimus annus (On The Hundredth Anniversary of Rerum Novarum)*
no. 11, quoting *Gaudium et Spes*, no. 24.
21. U.S. Catholic Bishops, *Sharing Catholic Social Teaching: Challenges and Directions* (Washington, D.C.: United States Conference of Catholic Bishops, 1998), 4.
22. U.S. Catholic Bishops, *A Century of Social Teaching: A Common Heritage, A Continuing Challenge* (Washington, D.C.: United States Conference of Catholic Bishops, 1990), 4.

life. The unborn child is particularly vulnerable, because people can argue that he or she cannot make choices and therefore lacks dignity. The bishops undoubtedly choose not to draw attention to the full range of Catholic teaching on the subject for fear of endangering the weak and vulnerable in society. This is a reasonable decision, given the climate in which we live. Yet, it may be more reasonable to proclaim both the permanent character of human dignity as well as the obligation to ennoble one's dignity by a life of holiness, *with the help of divine grace.*[23]

Without teaching the twofold character of human dignity, the very keystone of CSD is not accurately described and therefore not quite up to the task of informing the elaboration of other important themes in the discipline. As John Paul II said in *Centesimus annus,* "from the Christian vision of the human person there necessarily follows a correct picture of society."[24] That picture is one in which all elements of society should find ways to help people perfect their dignity. *Gaudium et spes,* in fact, says at the beginning of its conclusion that the *whole conciliar program* for all people is to help them "so that perceiving more clearly their integral vocation, they may conform the world more to the surpassing dignity of the human person."[25] A world so conformed would not only reflect the eminent dignity of human beings, but also be an instrument in helping people to achieve that dignity. A world not so conformed leads people astray, making the achievement of dignity more difficult.

Every element of society should promote respect for human dignity and its perfection. As Vatican Council II specifically says, "it devolves on humanity to establish a political, social, and economic order which will to an even better extent serve man and help individuals as well as groups to affirm and perfect the dignity proper to them" (*ad dignitatem sibi propriam affirmandam et excolendam*).[26] This means that the family, mediating institutions, the law, and the Church all have a role to play in helping individuals perfect their dignity. For example, the education a mother and father give to their children in the family will help them recognize and

23. The argument in this chapter is not about the achievement of dignity with the *indispensable* help of divine grace, but about making known the importance of achieving holiness by living daily in accordance with one's dignity. This important aspect of dignity is too often omitted in presentations of CSD.

24. Pope John Paul II, *Centesimus annus,* no. 65.

25. *Gaudium et spes,* no. 91: "ut, suam integram vocationem clarius percipientes, mundum praecellenti dignitati hominis conforment."

26. *Gaudium et spes,* no. 9, modified translation and my emphasis.

achieve their dignity. Schools, a primary mediating institution, to a greater or lesser extent, form the character of students so that they might be inclined to act in accordance with their dignity. The law encourages people not to act beneath their dignity by driving while drunk or acting in a discriminatory manner toward racial minorities. In *Centesimus annus* Pope John Paul II says that the Church contributes to the enrichment of human dignity when she "proclaims God's salvation to man, when she offers and communicates the life of God through the sacraments, when she gives direction to human life through the commandments of love of God and neighbor."[27] These examples show that a correct conception of the human person provides guidance to all educators and to legislators, and also enables all people to recognize that they must strive to perfect their dignity in order to be good persons and even good democratic citizens.

Because of his vision of the human person, the pope said the following about the democratic way of life:

Democracy cannot be sustained without a shared commitment to certain moral truths about the human person and the human community. The basic question before a democratic society is "How ought we live together?" In seeking an answer to this question, can society exclude moral reasoning?…Every generation of Americans needs to know that freedom consists not in doing what we like, but in having the right to do what we ought.[28]

Clearly, Pope John Paul II's reflections on democracy are inspired by his understanding of human dignity. People perfect their dignity by using their freedom to live as they ought, and by so doing they contribute to the smooth functioning of a healthy democracy.

CSD needs more clarity about its foundational principle, and therefore must return to the basic questions: "What is a person?" and "what is human dignity?" A good way to approach these subjects is to reflect on the primacy of receptivity in the achievement of human dignity and on the high calling of the human person.

Receptivity and Exhortation

Many years ago Professor Joseph Ratzinger, now Pope Benedict XVI, alerted me to the theme of receptivity in his justly famous *Introduction to Christianity*. He writes, "From the point of view of the Christian faith, man

27. *Centesimus annus*, no. 55.
28. Pope John Paul II, "Homily at Camden Yards," Baltimore, Md., Oct. 8, 1995.

comes in the profoundest sense to himself not through what he does but through what he receives (or accepts)....And one cannot become *wholly* man in any other way than by being loved, by letting oneself be loved."[29] Otherwise stated, Mary's fiat is the model for the person who wants to live as a Christian: "Let it be done to me according to your word." Persons who desire to realize their dignity must be receptive to instruction, exhortation, and grace in the various communities in which they live. Especially important are the family, Church, and school. But voluntary associations and even the law also play a role in creating and developing receptivity in people.

In various places of his autobiography Msgr. George Kelly captures the laborious struggle of the nuns in Catholic schools to educate young people to act in accord with their God-given dignity. At the very beginning of his story he tells of a meeting that he had with twenty-five of his former altar boys after addressing the New York City Police Holy Name Society. The police commissioner surprised Msgr. Kelly by bringing him into a VIP room to meet the twenty-five men who had become cops, even lieutenants and captains. "As I approached them," Kelly wrote, "the best I could muster up, as a response to their warm greeting, was: 'And to think that Sister De Padua and I expected most of you to end up in jail.'"[30] After finishing his book I understood Msgr. Kelly's humorous hyperbole as a way of capturing all the time and effort that once went into forming the character of the young in a typical New York Catholic parish.

Regarding human dignity as an arduous achievement in a community characterized by receptivity and exhortation is not exclusively a Catholic teaching. Consider "Wasps' Nest," a short story written by Agatha Christie. It seems to be about the poisoning of a wasps' nest with potassium cyanide. It turns out that John Harrison discovers that he is terminally ill and devises a plan to poison himself in such circumstances that another man, Claude Langton, will surely be blamed for his death and hanged. The terminally ill man is suddenly overcome with a desire for revenge against Monsieur Langton, who has won the heart of his former fiancée, a woman he still loves. Hercule Poirot realizes what is happening and tries to make his old friend come to his senses and give up his desire to commit murder.

29. Joseph Ratzinger, *Introduction to Christianity*, tr. J. Foster (New York: Crossroad, 1988), 202. (This book is now published by Ignatius Press.)

30. George A. Kelly, *Inside My Father's House* (New York: Doubleday, 1989), 18.

[Poirot] advanced to his friend and laid a hand on his shoulder. So agitated was he that he almost shook the big man, and as he did so, he hissed into his ear: "Rouse yourself, my friend, rouse yourself. And look—look where I am pointing. There on the bank, close by that tree root. See you, the wasps returning home, placid at the end of the day? In a little hour, there will be destruction and they know it not. There is no one to tell them. They have not, it seems, a Hercule Poirot."[31]

John Harrison resists the instruction and exhortation. Poirot then finds a way to substitute washing soda for the poison and confronts his friend after the failed suicide. Harrison moans when he realizes that Poirot has thwarted his suicide and saved Langton from being hanged for murder. Harrison asks, "Why did you come? Why did you come?" Poirot replies, of course, that he wanted to prevent a murder, and then adds:

"Listen, *mon ami*, you are a dying man; you have lost the girl you loved, but there is one thing you are not: you are not a murderer. Tell me now: are you glad or sorry that I came?" There was a moment's pause and Harrison drew himself up. There was a *new dignity* in his face—the look of a man who had conquered his own baser self. He stretched out his hand across the table. "Thank goodness you came," he cried. "Oh! Thank goodness you came."[32]

The story is both an example of the education and transformation of a person's disordered desire by the prudent behavior and exhortation of his friend and, of course, an account of the achievement of dignity.

The receptivity of persons to instruction and exhortation is a most important element in the realization of their dignity. The ultimate end of a Christian community is both to educate the faithful to the love of God and neighbor with their whole heart and soul and to be a living witness to that love. If Christians enhance their dignity by growing in love for their neighbors, then there should be no doubt that human dignity is both a given and an end, a high goal to be achieved by laborious efforts with the help of God's grace.

Human Dignity as a High Calling

Christian dignity is a high calling toward which a person walks with the support of fellow Christians. The patristic theme of *epektasis* presents

31. Agatha Christie, "Wasps' Nest," in *Hercule Poirot's Casebook* (New York: Dodd, Mead, 1984), 814.
32. Ibid., 818, my emphasis.

an accurate image of this reality. The patristic scholar Professor Ernest Fortin explains, "The life of the soul, as the Church Fathers saw it, is characterized by unceasing progress, indeed, not just an *extasis* or going out of oneself but an *epektasis* or perpetual going beyond oneself in the direction of an ever more perfect God-likeness."[33] In Philippians 3:12–14 St. Paul spoke in the same way: "One thing I do, forgetting what lies behind and straining forward (*epekteinomenos*) to what lies ahead I press on toward the goal for the prize of the upward call of God in Jesus Christ."

Epektasis, of course, not only requires an individual effort, but also depends decisively on continuous instruction and exhortation in a Christian community. In Galatians 4:19 St. Paul says, "My children, for whom I again suffer birth-pangs until Christ be formed in you." The language of birth pangs is a moving image conveying all that we have to do in order to help our brothers and sisters rouse themselves to put on Christ. For example, in the latter moments of life—especially in times of weakness, suffering, and depression—family members, friends, and health-care personnel play a crucial role in exhorting and sustaining the dying person. By giving and receiving loving exhortation Christians sustain one another's dignity. Where there is a failure to give and receive, the dignity of human persons is diminished. Otherwise stated, physicians who don't dissuade their patients from thinking of suicide diminish their own dignity, as do family members who abandon relatives to fear and loneliness. The proper understanding of a person's dignity would help Catholics resist the rhetoric of the euthanasia movements and move them to appreciate Christian teachings on the redemptive value of suffering and solidarity with the dying person.

Bioethics and the Dignity of the Human Person

The Christian teaching that dignity is both a given and a high calling (or an achievement) can be appreciated by non-Christians and even by nonbelievers. Leon Kass's thinking on human dignity, as expounded in his book *Life, Liberty and the Defense of Dignity: The Challenge for Bioethics*, will illustrate this point and further deepen our insight into the Catholic concept of human dignity. It may seem odd to rely on a Jewish intellectual to clarify Catholic teaching, but Kass does offer helpful clarifications by his

33. Ernest L. Fortin, *The Birth of Philosophic Christianity: Studies in Early Christian and Medieval Thought*, vol. 1 of *Collected Essays*, ed. J. Brian Benestad (Lanham, Md.: Rowman and Littlefield, 1996), 322.

discussion of the limitations of Kant's thought on human dignity. Kass is one of the nation's leading bioethicists and often a wonderful example of right reason in action.[34]

The most common understanding of human dignity in the contemporary period, Kass rightly argues, is that inspired by Immanuel Kant. The German philosopher attempts to supply a foundation for universal human dignity by his doctrine of respect for persons. Kass explains Kant's approach: "Persons—all persons or rational beings—are deserving of respect not because of some realized excellence of achievement, but because of a universally shared participation in morality and the ability to live under the moral law."[35] This is the view that persons have dignity because they can reason and make choices. While Kass applauds Kant's efforts and his influence on promoting the respect for persons in contemporary canons of ethics, he finally judges Kant's view of human dignity as *"inhuman."*

Precisely because it dualistically sets up the concept of "personhood" *in opposition* to nature and body, it fails to do justice to the concrete reality of our embodied lives—lives of begetting and belonging no less than willing and thinking....Precisely, because "personhood" is distinct from our lives as embodied, rooted, connected, and aspiring beings, the dignity of rational choice pays no respect at all to the dignity we have through our loves and longings—central aspects of human life understood as grown togetherness of body and soul. Not all human dignity consists in reason or freedom.[36]

Under the influence of Kant even many Catholics look at human dignity simply as a given and not also as an end to be achieved by avoiding serious sin, loving one's family, friends, and neighbors, and seeking to realize communion with God. Catholics rightly look to God's creation of man in his image and likeness as the foundation of dignity, but then fail to see that living in accord with God's image is the way of realizing their dignity in their everyday life. It should be obvious that our longings and loves either increase or diminish our dignity, but this is not always the case.

34. For my critical reflections on the compatibility of Kass's thought with Catholic teaching, see J. Brian Benestad, "Review Essay on Leon Kass's *Life, Liberty and the Defense of Dignity: The Challenge for Bioethics* and *Toward a More Natural Science: Biology and Human Affairs*," *National Catholic Bioethics Quarterly* 5, no. 3 (Autumn 2005): 631–45.

35. Leon Kass, *Life, Liberty and the Defense of Dignity: The Challenge for Bioethics* (San Francisco: Encounter Books, 2002), 16.

36. Ibid., 17.

Kass makes his most extensive comments on dignity in his chapter on "Death with Dignity and the Sanctity of Life." The roots of the English and Latin words for dignity are indicative. "The central notion etymologically, both in English and in its Latin root (*dignitas*), is that of worthiness, elevation, honor, nobility, height—in short excellence or virtue."[37] If dignity is understood as various kinds of excellence, then it cannot be provided or claimed as a right. It makes as little sense to assert a right to dignity as to claim a right to wisdom or courage. Realizing that this description may strike his readers as a denial of man's special dignity, Kass reaffirms his position that human beings have dignity because they are created in God's image and likeness, and that the sanctity of life is based on human dignity. "Yet," he adds, "on further examination this universal attribution of dignity to human beings pays more tribute to human potentiality, to the *possibilities* for human excellence. *Full* dignity, or dignity properly so-called, would depend on the *realization* of these possibilities."[38] So, the dignity of human beings is realized when they live a moral life.

Kass is right to say that full dignity depends on virtuous achievements. Why else would people say in ordinary speech, "That attitude or behavior is beneath your dignity?" I remain puzzled, however, why Kass doesn't make more of the permanent character of human dignity, even in those who choose to live badly. In a footnote he does say that "it may be salutary to treat people on the basis of their capacities to live humanly, despite great falling short or willful self-degradation."[39] Still, he doesn't seem to go far enough. Because people are created in God's image, it *is* right and salutary to treat them on the basis of their inherent dignity and their capacities to live humanly.

Kass further argues that "the *sanctity* of human life rests absolutely on the *dignity*—the god-likeness—of human beings."[40] Kass arrives at this conclusion after examining the Ten Commandments, the story of Cain and Abel, and especially the covenant with Noah subsequent to the flood. Kass believes that murder is not wrong simply because God says so. Echoing Thomas's natural-law teaching, Kass says, "The entire second table of the Decalogue is said to propound not so much divine law as natural law, law suitable for man as man, not only for Jew or Christian."[41] Cain's remark "Am I my brother's keeper?" shows that he senses the wrongness of

37. Ibid., 246.
39. Ibid., 247.
41. Ibid., 239.

38. Ibid., 247.
40. Ibid., 242.

murder. Otherwise, he could have responded to God's question regarding the whereabouts of Abel with the straightforward answer, "I killed him." Kass explains, "If there was nothing wrong with murder, why hide one's responsibility? A 'proto-religious' dread accompanies the encounter with death, especially violent death."[42]

Kass finds the best evidence for his position in the story about the new order of things after the flood. God issues a prohibition enjoining all mankind to refrain from murder and explains why. Genesis 9:6 reads, "Whoever sheds the blood of man, by man shall his blood be shed; for God made man in his own image." Kass comments, "The fundamental reason that makes murder wrong—and that even justifies punishing it homicidally!—is man's divine-like status. Not the other fellow's unwillingness to be killed, not even (or only) our desire to avoid sharing his fate, but *his*—any man's—*very being* requires that we respect his life."[43] Kass goes to Genesis I to elucidate the meaning of God-like. It means that man speaks, reasons, contemplates, exercises freedom, makes judgments, distinguishes good from bad, and "lives a life freighted with moral self-consciousness." All these qualities give human beings a dignity that engenders and requires respect.

Kass believes the achievement of dignity is possible when people have the proper models to imitate and the right kind of education. He shows that this achievement is frequently noticed in the ordinary routine of life. "In truth, if we know how to look, we find evidence of human dignity all around us, in the valiant efforts ordinary people make to meet necessity, to combat adversity and disappointment, to provide for their children, to care for their parents, to help their neighbors, to serve their country."[44] Of course, people need various virtues to make these kinds of valiant efforts, which is still another indication that we have to strive day in, day out to realize our dignity. The achievement of dignity is really the most ordinary occurrence, but not a common phrase in everyday speech. The absence of appropriate language keeps us from accurately perceiving all aspects of dignity.

What does get talked about is death with dignity. By that term people mean both good and bad things. The good side is the belief that people should not be dehumanized at the end of life by unnecessary or burdensome medical treatments, or subject to unnecessary institutionalization.

42. Ibid., 239.   43. Ibid., 241.
44. Ibid., 248.

The chilling side of death with dignity is the argument that euthanasia or physician-assisted suicide will assure the dignity of a terminally ill patient whose quality of life has diminished. Kass calls euthanasia "undignified and dangerous." The assault on human dignity, he argues, comes not from the declining quality of life, but from improper treatment and care by hospital staff, relatives, and friends. "Withdrawal of contact, affection and care is probably the greatest single cause of the dehumanization of dying. Death with dignity requires absolutely that the survivors treat the human being at all times as if full god-likeness remains, up to the very end."[45] Encouragement by "many small speeches and deeds" will shore up the courage of the dying and help them to face their physical and emotional pain.[46] By bearing up in the face of suffering, the dying person, argues Kass, maintains and increases his dignity, as do his loving relatives and friends. There is no dignity in asking for lethal injections from relatives and friends. Placing such a burden on people is not dignified action.

Kass's reflection on Kant, bioethics, and the everyday events of daily life has confirmed Catholic teaching on dignity as a permanent endowment and an achievement. What remains to be done is to flesh out and make intelligible the full meaning of human dignity through conversations in both private and public places. Otherwise, dignity will not be able to provide a secure foundation for human rights. Rights will be respected when people both realize that it is beneath their dignity to violate them and acquire the virtues that will enable them to live a dignified life. Of course, this means that rights will frequently not be respected, since people will not always make the effort to live a dignified life. Catholics could make even more of a contribution to the well-being of the United States if they were able to persuade American citizens that human dignity is both a given and an achievement. But that teaching has to be more fully recovered from papal encyclicals and the documents of Vatican Council II by the Catholic Church in the United States. When recovered, that twofold teaching will shore up respect for human rights.

Human Rights and Natural Law

One need hardly make an argument that the themes of human dignity and human rights are closely linked. Scholars and nonscholars readily say that because human beings have dignity, they deserve the protection and

45. Ibid., 249.   46. Ibid., 253.

enjoyment of their many rights. What is not so clearly seen is the prob-
lematic side of commonly accepted human rights in the contemporary
period. Some ways of conceiving and invoking rights are actually an affront to human dignity. Catholic social doctrine recognizes that the protection of rights upholds human dignity as long as people exercise them
in the light of an objective moral standard.

The association of human dignity and natural law is not that common. Many would ask what the precise connection is between the two
themes, not imagining that people could enhance their dignity by observing the natural law, as Catholic social doctrine holds. Under the influence
of positivism, relativism, consequentialism, and historicism, many doubt
that there is even such a thing as natural law. Catholic social doctrine
teaches this hard-to-imagine truth and further holds that rights are based
on the duties taught by the natural law.

The second half of this chapter will first summarize the Church's nuanced embrace of rights and then briefly explain what it means to speak
of the natural law and how the observance of the natural law upholds human dignity. I will conclude this section with an explanation of historicism, the greatest threat to the acceptance of natural law, and then offer some thought on overcoming the lure of historicism by transcending
the limits of one's culture through faith and reason. According to historicism, truth is simply a function of the time period in which you live.
What is true for one culture may not be true for another. For historicists,
truth is culture-bound; no one escapes the limits of one's culture.

Human Rights

Between 1891 and the present the Catholic Church has developed an
impressive body of teachings on human rights. In addition to Vatican
Council II, popes Leo XIII, Pius XI, Pius XII, John XXIII, Paul VI,
John Paul II, and Benedict XVI have all addressed the subject of human
rights. Leo XIII's *Rerum novarum* introduced the language of rights into
Catholic social doctrine, John XXIII's *Pacem in terris* has been called a human rights encyclical, and, as Avery Cardinal Dulles pointed out, John
Paul II has placed more emphasis on human rights than any of his pre-
decessors.[47] On several occasions John Paul II has lavished fulsome praise

---

47. Avery Cardinal Dulles, "Human Rights: The United Nations and Papal Teaching," in *Church and Society: The Lawrence J. McGinley Lectures 1988–2007* (New York: Fordham
University Press, 2008), 278.

on the United Nations' Universal Declaration of Human Rights. For example, at the very beginning of his address to the UN on October 5, 1995, the late pope said that the 1948 Declaration is "one of the highest expressions of the human conscience of our time."[48]

The Catholic emphasis on rights is readily understandable. The language of rights gives the Church a way to communicate with people in the present age. The language of virtue and duty is not always clear to people and sometimes raises fears of impending impingements on their freedoms. Respect for rights honors the dignity of the human person and promotes justice in society. When human rights are respected, people's lives are safe and secure and they enjoy a whole panoply of religious, economic, cultural, and political freedoms. The right to religious freedom is crucial for the mission of the Church and the well-being of the state. The Church needs freedom to bring its message of salvation, and individuals need freedom to practice their faith, from which flows justice and peace.

The language of rights, in addition, gives people a common idiom to discuss and recognize justice and injustice, and it accords with the emphasis in modernity on freedom. Where people enjoy the protection of rights, especially the right to religious liberty, governments cannot act in a tyrannical fashion. Rights can even be invoked when there is no agreement on their philosophical and theological foundation. What problems, then, can the protection of rights actually pose?

The simple answer is that, unlike virtue, rights can be misused. They have been increasingly invoked to justify abortion, euthanasia, suicide, physician-assisted suicide, and marriage between people of the same sex. People can appeal to their rights as a justification for not making any contributions to the communities in which they live. For example, people could say they have a right to their wealth and have no obligation to share it with others. Resolving conflicting rights claims can be difficult or impossible if there is no shared understanding of human dignity. In the United States there is no commonly accepted moral standard to resolve the dispute between those who advocate a right to life and those who insist on a right to choose abortion.

As mentioned in the introduction, natural rights (now called human rights) had an unsavory origin. Hobbes put forth his rights teachings as an alternative to the natural right and natural law of the premodern pe-

---

48. Pope John Paul II, "Address to the United Nations," October 5, 1995, no. 2; cf. Vatican website under the travels of Pope John Paul II.

riod. Hobbes famously said there is no *summum bonum* (highest good) to
which people can look for guidance in the exercise of their rights. While
Locke may have softened Hobbes's formulation, he still ratified the break
with the ancients and left people without a *summum bonum* as the moral
standard for their rights. Many scholars recognize that Locke's writings
on rights had a deep influence on the American founding, but it wasn't
exclusive, since the Christian convictions of the early Americans influenced the way they exercised their rights. It is only in recent times that
rights have become more and more detached from Christianity and natural law standards, especially under the influence of historicism, relativism,
and Nietzschean autonomy. These philosophical approaches actually call
into question the foundation of rights and lead people to create their own
values by an act of the will.

In order to understand more exactly the problem of rights in the United States, it is helpful to examine parts of a book written by one of the
great defenders of the Universal Declaration of Human Rights, Mary
Ann Glendon.[49] Her book *Rights Talk: The Impoverishment of Political Discourse*
is an excellent introduction to thinking about the understanding and exercise of rights in America.

Rights Talk

Mary Ann Glendon's *Rights Talk* should help American citizens understand why the preoccupation with creating and asserting rights undermines public morality. Glendon explains that the pervasive presence of
rights talk in political, social, and cultural life causes difficulty in defining critical questions, finding common ground for discussion, and arriving at compromises in the face of intractable differences. Rights talk is
silent "with respect to personal, civic, and collective responsibilities."[50]
Furthermore, "simplistic rights talk," says Glendon, "simultaneously reflects and distorts American culture. It captures our devotion to individualism and liberty, but omits our traditions of hospitality and care for
the community."[51] Glendon, of course, doesn't argue for abandoning the
American rights tradition. Rather, she is in favor of supplementing the

---

49. Cf. Mary Ann Glendon, *A World Made New: Eleanor Roosevelt and the Universal Declaration of Human Rights* (New York: Random House, 2001).

50. Glendon, *Rights Talk: The Impoverishment of Political Discourse* (New York: Free Press,
1991), x.

51. Ibid., xi–xii.

language of rights with that of duty and responsibility in the law, public life, culture, and everyday life. This is not a utopian task, according to Glendon, because Americans already use the language of responsibility, such as duty and character, at home, in school, and at the workplace.

Glendon notes that legal concepts, especially rights talk, have permeated popular culture and political speech. She explains, "There is no more telling indicator of the extent to which legal notions have penetrated both popular and political discourse than our increasing tendency to speak of what is important to us in terms of rights, and to frame nearly every social controversy as a clash of rights."[52] These two tendencies lead Americans to misperceive the social dimension of the human person. Under the influence of the rights paradigm people fail to recognize personal and collective duties.

Our experience with abortion and property rights illustrates to me what Glendon is getting at. Focusing on the "absolute" right to property and to abortion, Americans may neglect their duty *both* to put their talents and material goods at the service of others *and* to avoid improper sexual relations. Otherwise stated, rights talk can impair self-knowledge. The assertion of rights often takes the place of giving reasons for attitudes, actions, or omissions. Describing social issues as a clash of rights, such as a woman's "right to choose abortion versus the fetus's right to life," exacerbates conflict and inhibits perception of the alternatives to abortion as well as the gravity of the option for abortion. The duty to avoid killing is hardly discussed.

"Public rhetoric," says Glendon, "regularly gloss[es] over the essential interplay between rights and responsibilities, independence and self-discipline, freedom and order[.]"[53] American public officials and citizens often talk about rights as if they had no intrinsic relation to duties. Glendon astutely notes that even our founding documents, such as the Declaration of Independence and the Bill of Rights, have nothing comparable to the statements on duties in the Universal Declaration of Human Rights. The United Nations' Declaration says that "Everyone has duties to the community," and that it is appropriate to place limitations on everyone's rights "for the purposes of securing due recognition and respect for the rights and freedoms of others and of meeting the just requirements of morality, public order, and the general welfare in a democratic society."[54]

---

52. Ibid., 3–4.   53. Ibid., 10.
54. Ibid., 13, quoting UN General Assembly, *Universal Declaration of Human Rights* (Lake

Glendon contends that the pervasiveness of rights talk and the virtual absence of appeals to duty are weakening people's sense of responsibility. She goes so far as to say that simplistic rights talk "corrodes the fabric of beliefs, attitudes and habits upon which life, liberty, and all other individual and social goods ultimately depend."[55] A liberal regime dedicated to the protection of rights depends on the presence of certain virtues in parents, workers, volunteers, citizens, and public officials.

Glendon next seeks to explain "the persistence of absoluteness in our property rhetoric, and in our rights rhetoric in general[.]"[56] In addressing this question she shows how the American way of life has been profoundly affected by the fascination with property and privacy or the right to be left alone. Glendon traces our love affair with property ultimately to John Locke, and more proximately to Blackstone's influence on those who drafted the Declaration of Independence, the Constitution, the *Federalist Papers,* and the seminal decisions of the Marshall court. Locke taught that people own their bodies as "a God-given right" and that governments are instituted to protect life, liberty, and property (actually, under the term "property" Locke included life and liberty). Locke saw the natural right to property as a way of delegitimating the monarchy and of limiting government. For Blackstone, whose *Commentaries* educated countless American lawyers, property was an end unto itself, an absolute.

The American fascination with property caused two important legal issues to be mishandled by the Supreme Court in the second half of the nineteenth century — one dealing with slavery, the other with the attempt to shape an American welfare state.

In 1856, Dred Scott, who had entered federal court in Missouri as a man, left it as a piece of property, when the Missouri Compromise (prohibiting slavery in the territories) was held unconstitutional. From the latter years of the century up to the 1930s, the Supreme Court repeatedly invoked property rights (in an expansive form) to strike down a series of laws that, taken together, might have served to ease the transition here, as similar legislation did in Europe, to a modern mixed economy and welfare state.[57]

Success: UN Department of Public Information, 1949), Art. 29; UN General Assembly, *Universal Declaration of Human Rights,* Final Authorized Text (New York: UN Department of Public Information, 1952).

55. *Rights Talk,* 15.   56. Ibid., 20.
57. Ibid., 26.

The Supreme Court invoked the right of employers and employees freely to make contracts and to control their property as a reason "for invalidating statutes that attempted to promote health and safety in the workplace, to protect female and child laborers, and to encourage the nascent labor movement."[58] As is well known to students of constitutional law, the Supreme Court began a retreat from its exaggerated constitutional protection of property rights in the 1930s by upholding New Deal legislation.

After the Court abandoned the notion of absolute property rights, it eventually began to find absoluteness in the realm of personal rights. Glendon explains: "Much of the attention the Supreme Court once lavished on a broad concept of property, including the freedom of contract to acquire it, it now devotes to certain personal liberties that it has designated as 'fundamental.'"[59] The rhetoric of absolute property rights is now used in the area of personal liberties with the all-too-familiar result: lack of common sense in working out principled limitations on the exercise of personal liberties. As an example, Glendon mentions the extreme interpretations of the First and Second Amendments. One group of people does not want any restrictions on free speech and other forms of expression; another group favors "an absolute or nearly absolute, individual right" to bear and keep arms. Glendon notes, however, an intriguing irony: "many of the same people who claim that the right of free expression trumps a community's interest in regulating pornography, [argue] that the right to keep and bear arms has to be regulated for the sake of the general welfare."[60] On the other hand, I would note that many people defending the absolute right to bear arms, such as semi-automatic weapons, are likely to defend the duty of the community to regulate pornography. Understanding the First Amendment or Second Amendment rights as absolutes causes substantial harm to the general welfare.

Finally, I want to mention Glendon's explanation for the American tendency to absolutize rights. First, she suggests that the stark formulation of rights in the Declaration of Independence and the Bill of Rights has strongly influenced the American mind. Secondly, the Lockean story about property and Blackstone's "flights of fancy about property as absolute dominion stuck in American legal imaginations."[61] Thirdly, Glendon mentions Tocqueville's observation that we are a lawyer-ridden society,

58. Ibid., 26.   59. Ibid., 40.
60. Ibid., 43.   61. Ibid., 43.

greatly affected by the omnipresent legal culture. The "strategic exagger-ation" and "overstatement" characteristic of lawyers in their adversarial roles have had an effect on most citizens. Citizens came to think about rights the way lawyers talk about them.

The question naturally arises whether the Catholic Church has suffi-ciently taken into account all the problems that the emphasis on rights can cause. In order to see how the Church initially arrived at the positions on rights articulated by Vatican II, John XXIII, et al., let us go back to the Church's first embrace of human rights in Pope Leo XIII's 1891 encyc-lical, *Rerum novarum*.

Rerum Novarum

As the Church's solution to the penurious condition of workers, Pope Leo XIII urged the acceptance of four general proposals: the protection of the right to private property; reliance on religion and the Church to teach and practice virtue; reliance on the state to assume responsibility for the common good; and cooperation among employers and associa-tions for the material and spiritual well-being of workers and their fam-ilies. Through these four proposals Leo XIII attempted to explain that the common good of a nation requires the protection of rights and the practice of virtue by all the citizens of the nation.

Anyone steeped in the theological and political thought of Augustine and Aquinas will be somewhat startled to find Leo XIII begin his en-cyclical with a defense of the right to private property. Leo's ringing en-dorsement of a natural and sacred right to property was a response to socialists who were proposing the abolition of private possessions in fa-vor of state administration of all goods. Leo XIII and the socialists were in agreement on the problem—the penurious condition of the working class. Leo, however, believed that the socialist solution would ultimately harm workers by causing disorder in society, "a harsh and odious enslave-ment of citizens," and a low economic standard of living for all.[62] As an explanation of this last point Leo writes:

If incentives to ingenuity and skill in individual persons were to be abolished, the very fountains of wealth would necessarily dry up; and the equality con-jured up by the socialist imagination would, in reality, be nothing but uni-form wretchedness and meanness for one and all without distinction.[63]

62. *Rerum novarum*, no. 22.
63. Ibid., no. 22.

What's more, the socialist remedy is "openly in conflict with justice, inasmuch as nature confers on man the right to possess things privately as his own."[64] Leo affirms a true and perfect right for a worker "to demand his wage" and "to spend it as he wishes." A worker may also exercise full control over any land he may buy with his wages. Workers, says Leo, need the freedom to dispose of their own wages and land in order to have "the hope and the opportunity of increasing their property and securing advantages for themselves."[65] Leo XIII clearly implies that society must rely on the self-interest of individuals to procure the necessities of life.

According to Leo XIII, the foundation of the right to private property is the law of nature and also divine law, which forbids us from even desiring what belongs to another. Civil laws have protected this right—even by force—and the practice of all ages points to "private possession as something best adopted to man's nature and to peaceful and tranquil living together."[66] The Italian version of *Rerum Novarum* actually locates the existence of rights in the Gospel (*"Ecco l'ideale dei diritti e doveri contenuto nel vangelo.* [sic]" Behold the ideal of rights and duties contained in the Gospel [sic].) The official Latin text reads *Christiana philosophia* (Christian Philosophy), and not Gospel.[67]

Both natural law and divine law, according to Leo XIII, teach that the individual *qua* individual has a right to property. Leo emphasizes this point by affirming that rights "have much greater validity when viewed as fitted into and connected with the obligations of human beings in family life."[68] Leo XIII's initial position on the right to private property bears a striking resemblance to the teaching of John Locke, who is justly regarded as one of the fathers of capitalism. Leo *sounds* Lockean, especially in affirming that an individual may dispose of his wages and land as he wishes (*"uti velit"*)[69] and by holding that individual rights are well grounded and solid apart from any connection to individual duties. But this is far from the pope's last word on the use of property. He goes on to affirm that the father of a family has a duty to provide for his offspring: "It is a most sacred law of nature that the father of a family see that his offspring are provided with all the necessities of life."[70]

Leo XIII's grounding of the right to private property in natural law

64. Ibid., no. 10.
66. Ibid., no. 17.
68. Ibid., no. 18.
70. Ibid., no. 20.

65. Ibid., no. 9.
67. Cf. ibid. no. 39.
69. Ibid., no. 9.

is a new development in the Catholic tradition. There simply is no statement about the right to property in the natural law teaching of Thomas
Aquinas. Thomas Aquinas never argued that anyone had a natural right
to property, much less "a sacred right." He did say that "the division of
possessions is not according to natural right but rather arose from human agreement.... Hence, the ownership of possessions is not contrary
to natural right but an addition thereto devised by human reason."[71]
Aquinas defended private ownership not as a right, but simply as an efficient means of promoting industry, order, and peace. (It is important to
note that Aquinas's reference to natural right is not at all a synonym for
natural rights or human rights. The latter concepts refer to the subjective claims of the individual against other individuals and governmental power, while natural right refers to moral principles that have validity apart from the claims and opinions of individuals. Aquinas, in fact,
never spoke of natural or human rights. The concept of universal natural rights, as we have seen, only emerged in the seventeenth century in the
writings of Thomas Hobbes.)

Leo cites from Deuteronomy 5:21 to prove that divine law undergirds
the right to property. That text reads: "Thou shall not covet thy neighbor's wife, nor his house, nor his field, nor his maid-servant, nor his ox,
nor his ass, nor anything that is his." The text affirms the duty of all not
to desire the property or wife of another, and thus implies that people
have a right to their lawful possessions. If the duty is observed, the people
will enjoy the right to their property without disturbance.

The first section of *Rerum Novarum* is, of course, not the whole story on
Leo XIII's view of property. In subsequent sections Leo puts forth the
traditional Catholic teaching on property as expressed by Thomas Aquinas. Citing Thomas Aquinas, he writes that "man ought not regard external goods as his own but as common so that, in fact, a person should
readily share them when he sees others in need. Wherefore, the apostle
says: 'Charge the rich of this world...to give readily to others.'"[72] According to Leo, then, there really is no absolute right to dispose of wages, land, and personal property as one wishes (*uti velit*). Rather, Christians
have an obligation to use their property and talents for their own good
and the good of others:

71. Thomas Aquinas, *Summa theologiae*, II-II, qu. 66, a. 2, reply to obj. 1.
72. *Rerum novarum*, no. 36.

whoever has received from the bounty of God a greater share of goods, whether corporeal and external, or of the soul, has received them for this purpose, namely, that he employ them for his own perfection, and likewise, as a servant of Divine Providence, for the benefit of others.[73]

In the section on the role of the state Leo XIII clearly says that duties owed to God take precedence over rights belonging to human beings. In this Leonine perspective it makes no sense to speak of individual rights to property apart from obligations to love God, self, and neighbor. *Rerum Novarum* teaches that nothing in life is more important than virtue. Those examining the example given by Jesus, says Leo, cannot fail to understand these truths:

The true dignity and excellence of human beings consist in moral living, that is in virtue; virtue is the common inheritance of man, attainable equally by the humblest and the mightiest, by the rich and poor; and the reward of eternal happiness will follow upon virtue and merit alone, regardless of the person in whom they may be found.[74]

Rerum novarum also teaches that the attainment of the common good—including the material relief of the working class—can only be attained if people practice virtue at home, in the marketplace, and in positions of political and civic leadership. "Wherefore, if human society is to be healed, only a return to Christian life and practices will heal it" (*Rerum novarum*, no. 41), (*revocatio vitae institutorumque Christianorum; il ritorno alla vita e ai costumi Christiani*).[75]

[S]ince religion alone, as we said in the beginning, can remove the evil root and branch, let all reflect upon this. First and foremost, Christian morals must be re-established, without which even the weapons of prudence, which are considered especially effective, will be of no avail to secure well being.[76]

Pope Leo XIII's attempt to use and tame the modern teaching on rights was a grand effort. Leo really tried to integrate the premodern virtue tradition with the modern rights tradition stemming from Thomas Hobbes and John Locke. This is an immense task, since the originator

73. Ibid., no. 36.

74. Ibid., no. 37.

75. Ibid., no. 41; Latin and Italian texts included to justify my modification of the English translation. The Italian *costumi* correctly translates *institutorum*, whereas the English should be practices or customs, instead of institutions.

76. Ibid., no. 82.

of rights doctrines, Thomas Hobbes, as previously mentioned, completely divorced rights from any notion of a *summum bonum.* In other words, for
Hobbes, the exercise of rights was not guided by the highest good. Ernest
Fortin discusses the difference between the premodern tradition of virtue
and the modern tradition of rights in this most illuminating paragraph:

> The passage from natural law to natural rights and later (once "nature" had
> fallen into disrepute) to "human" rights represents a major shift, indeed *the*
> paradigm shift in our understanding of justice and moral phenomena gener-
> ally. Prior to that time, the emphasis was on virtue and duty, that is to say, on
> what human beings owe to other human beings or to society at large rather
> than on what they can claim from them.[77]

According to a prevalent understanding of rights, individuals are free
to create their own values. In one of their abortion cases, *Planned Parenthood
v. Casey* (1992), the U.S. Supreme Court said, "At the heart of liberty is the
right to define one's own concept of existence, of meaning, of the universe
and of the mystery of human life." Fortin rightly notes that this much-
cited sentence has striking implications.

> The only just society is the one that grants to each individual as much free-
> dom as is compatible with the freedom of every other individual. It has noth-
> ing to say about the good life and is not concerned with the promotion of
> virtue. Its sole function is to insure the safety of its members and provide for
> their comfort.[78]

These theoretical observations, as well as the experience of living in
America, show that rights are not that easily integrated into the premodern virtue tradition. Rights tend to be understood and lived as though
they are divorced from the highest good. Not that everyone understands
them that way!

For many years I have been asking my students—who are mostly Catholic—why they respect the rights of others. They invariably respond, "So
that other people will respect mine." They hardly ever say because it is
the right or virtuous thing to do. Yet, I believe that many of them do respect rights because it is the right or virtuous thing to do, but they cannot
speak in the language of virtue.

---

77. Ernest L. Fortin, *Human Rights, Virtue, and the Common Good: Untimely Meditations on Religion and Politics,* vol. 3 of *Collected Essays,* ed. J. Brian Benestad (Lanham, Md.: Rowman and
Littlefield, 1996), 20.

78. Ibid., 23.

Vatican Council II did place rights in a context where they could be integrated into the premodern virtue tradition. *Gaudium et spes* says:

Therefore, by virtue of the gospel committed to her, the Church proclaims the rights of man. She acknowledges and greatly esteems the dynamic movements of today by which these rights are everywhere fostered. Yet these movements must be penetrated by the spirit of the gospel and protected against any kind of false autonomy. For we are tempted to think that our personal rights are fully insured only when we are exempt from every requirement of divine law. But in this way the dignity of the human person is by no means saved; on the contrary, it is lost.[79]

This approach would put rights in the kind of framework—teleological, to be exact—that would enable Catholics to integrate rights doctrines with traditional teachings on virtue. This passage clearly reveals the Church's awareness that people are tempted to invoke rights as a way to justify an autonomy independent of objective moral norms. This false autonomy would include the kind promoted by relativism and historicism.

In *Pacem in terris* Pope John XXIII insists on grounding human rights in the natural law and keeping them linked to duties.

For every fundamental human right draws its indestructible moral force from the natural law, which in granting it imposes a corresponding obligation. Those, therefore, who claim their own rights, yet altogether forget or neglect to carry out their respective duties, are people who build with one hand and destroy with the other.[80]

By teaching that the foundation of human rights is natural law and that a person's duties remain in the age of rights, John XXIII reveals that his understanding of rights differs from that of Hobbes and Locke. Until these teachings of Vatican Council II and of Pope John XXIII find their way into local catechisms, Sunday homilies, and subsequent Church documents, most Catholics will most likely not understand their full import.

People with a secular perspective on rights would have a great deal of difficulty accepting that rights are subordinate to the divine law, or otherwise stated, the highest good. The Church could perhaps persuade some non-Catholics and nonreligious people that rights must be exercised in

---

79. *Gaudium et spes*, no. 41.
80. Pope John XXIII, *Pacem in terris (Peace on Earth)*, no. 30.

the light of some shared understanding of the good, however minimal. The understanding and observance of the natural law is an excellent way of coming to an agreement on common standards.

Natural Law

"The expression 'natural law,'" explains Ernest Fortin, "is often loosely applied to any theory that holds to objective standards of morality. In its proper sense, it designates a moral law that both exists by nature and is known by nature to be binding on everyone."[81] Many people believe that there is a law higher than the civil law to which people owe allegiance and to which they can be held accountable. Consider the conviction of war criminals at the Nuremberg International War-Crimes Trials in 1945–46. Defendants could not claim that they were simply obeying the law in Nazi Germany. They were judged to be guilty for not following a higher law, a natural law that had to take precedence over unjust Nazi laws.

In his famous "Letter from Birmingham City Jail" Martin Luther King, Jr., notes Fortin, cited Thomas Aquinas "in support of the view that a human law not rooted in eternal and natural law is an unjust law."[82] The Reverend King, of course, was protesting against laws mandating segregation and other forms of racial injustice. King composed this letter on April 16, 1963, in response to a letter written on April 12 by eight white Alabama clergymen. They argued that King and others should seek relief in the courts, avoiding any demonstrations in the streets against unjust laws, however peaceful. In my judgment, King's invocation of Thomas Aquinas's thought was wholly justified and remains a reminder that all human laws should be evaluated in the light of the eternal and natural law.

The description of racism and its effects in Dr. King's "Letter" is actually a proof that the natural law is a reality. Every person of good will senses that legally enforced racism must contradict a higher law. Just let us listen to Dr. King's words explaining why African-Americans are tired of waiting to be treated justly and decently:

I guess it is easy for those who have never felt the stinging darts of segregation to say, "Wait." But when you have seen vicious mobs lynch your mothers and fathers at will and drown your sisters and brothers at whim; when

81. Fortin, *Human Rights, Virtue, and the Common Good*, 159.
82. Ibid., 163; King's exact words are as follows: "To put it in terms of St. Thomas Aquinas: An unjust law is a human law that is not rooted in eternal law and natural law."

you have seen hate-filled policemen curse, kick, brutalize and even kill your black brothers and sisters with impunity; when you see the vast majority of your twenty million Negro brothers in an airtight cage of poverty in the midst of an affluent society; when you suddenly find your tongue twisted and your speech stammering as you seek to explain to your six-year-old daughter why she can't go to the public amusement park that has just been advertised on television, and see tears welling up in her little eyes when she is told that Funtown is closed to colored children, and see the depressing clouds of inferiority begin to form in her little mental sky, and see her begin to distort her little personality by unconsciously developing a bitterness toward white people; when you have to concoct an answer for a five-year-old son asking in agonizing pathos: "Daddy, why do white people treat colored people so mean?"; when you take a cross-country drive and find it necessary to sleep night after night in the uncomfortable corners of your automobile because no motel will accept you; when you are humiliated day in and day out by nagging signs reading "white" and "colored"; when your first name becomes "nigger" and your middle name becomes "boy" (however old you are) and your last name becomes "John," and when your wife and mother are never given the respected title "Mrs."; when you are harried by day and haunted by night by the fact that you are a Negro, living constantly at tiptoe stance never quite knowing what to expect next, and plagued with inner fears and outer resentments; when you are forever fighting a degenerating sense of "nobodiness"; then you will understand why we find it difficult to wait.[83]

In order to clarify further the meaning of the natural law, I will turn now to Thomas Aquinas and to John Paul II's *Veritatis splendor*. Aquinas argues that God governs the whole universe by divine reason and divine providence. "This mode of ordering things (*ratio ordinis rerum*) toward an end is...in God called providence."[84] God's providential government has the nature of law, because law is "nothing else but a dictate of practical reason from the ruler who governs a perfect community."[85] This law is called eternal because God "is not subject to time."

The rational creature participates in this eternal law by having a "natural inclination to its proper act and end."[86] It is God's providence that gives man his end and a natural inclination thereto. Because man is free,

---

83. Martin Luther King, Jr., "Letter From Birmingham City Jail," in *A Testament of Hope: The Essential Writings of Martin Luther King, Jr.*, edited by James Melvin Washington (San Francisco: Harper and Row, 1986), 292–93.

84. *Summa theologiae*, I, qu. 22, a. 1.   85. Ibid., I-II, qu. 91, a. 1.

86. Ibid., I-II, qu. 91, a. 2.

he shares further in God's providence by providing for himself and others in accordance with his natural inclinations. That is to say, he can make moral choices and laws on the basis of his God-given natural end. Otherwise stated, "Since law is a rule or measure, there are two ways it can be in someone: in one way, as the one ruling and measuring; in the other way, as the one ruled and measured, since a thing is ruled or measured, insofar as it partakes of the rule or measure."[87] Aquinas is saying that human beings are ruled or measured by God; he imprints on them their end and natural inclinations to that end. They, in turn, can rule or measure on the basis of who they are as a result of God's providential government. Human beings don't create an end for themselves, as Nietzsche and Sartre maintained.

Aquinas holds that a human being has three natural inclinations, which he immediately perceives as good: to stay alive, to procreate and educate children, and both to seek the truth and to live in community. The first inclination is common to all living beings, the second to animals and man, and the third is proper to man. As the first precept of the natural law is that "good is to be done and pursued, and evil is to be avoided,"[88] a human being tends to act in accordance with his natural inclinations and to avoid acting against them. A person naturally steps out of the way of a car about to hit him, a mother naturally feeds her baby, and human beings naturally seek the company of others. Behaving in such a way, of course, upholds and enhances the dignity of human persons.

We all have noticed, however, that human beings don't always act according to their natural inclinations. Mothers sometimes kill their babies, people kill themselves or take unjustifiable risks showing little regard for their life or health, parents neglect the education of their children, and nearly everyone shows some disregard for the truth to a greater or lesser degree. As a response to this obvious fact, Aquinas points out that "in some the reason is perverted by passion, or evil custom, or an evil natural disposition (*ex mala habitudine naturae*); thus formerly, theft, although it is expressly contrary to the natural law, was not considered wrong among the Germans, as Julius Caesar relates (*De Bello Gallico*, VI)."[89] Today, abortion, euthanasia, "hooking up" or fornication, pornography, and same-sex marriage are not considered wrong by many people, although they are forbidden by the fifth and sixth commandments. They may have come to

87. Ibid., I-II, qu. 91, a. 2.   88. Ibid., I-II, qu. 94, a. 2.
89. Ibid., I-II, qu. 94, a. 4.

this opinion under the influence of passion or of bad mores receiving approval in the culture. A pronounced disposition to excess in the area of sex or anger, not corrected by education, could lead people to fornication, adultery, or to aggressive behavior toward one's family, friends, and neighbors.

It is not hard to understand that the passions and habits generated by the culture could induce people to disregard the commandments on the second table of the Decalogue (commandments four through ten). Unjustifiable killing, such as abortion and euthanasia, and various forms of unchastity can become so routine under the influence of the culture that their wrongness is only dimly perceived or not at all. If this can and does happen, how can Aquinas still speak of a natural law impressed on the mind and heart of all human beings? Despite all the deviations, people still tend to act in accordance with their three natural inclinations, and the first precept of the natural law, do good and avoid evil, is rarely denied, though people disagree about the meaning of good and evil. Aquinas recognizes that the perception and observance of the natural law sometimes depend on instruction by the wise and the practice of the virtues. In other words, wisdom and the habit of virtue offer protection against the onslaught of disordered passions and bad habits that find approval in the culture.[90]

Virtue is not foreign to a human being, because "there is in every man a natural inclination to act according to reason: and this is to act according to virtue. Consequently, considered thus, all acts of virtue are prescribed by the natural law, since each one's reason naturally dictates to him to act virtuously."[91] Aquinas qualifies this statement by adding that "many things are done virtuously, to which nature does not incline at first; but which through the inquiry of reason, have been found by men to be conducive to well-being."[92] Aquinas seems to be saying that inquiries carried out by the wise over the centuries will further increase knowledge of virtuous acts in the less learned majority. In a later discussion of the moral precepts of the Old Law, including the Ten Commandments, Aquinas says that everyone can recognize the validity of the fourth, fifth, and seventh commandments, but some aspects of the law of nature are only known by the wise and those taught by the wise.[93] But, as we have already seen, people may even fail to recognize the validity of the seventh com-

90. Cf. Ibid., I-II, qu. 100, a. 2.
92. Ibid., I-II, qu. 94, a. 3.
91. Ibid., I-II, qu. 94, a. 3.
93. Ibid., I-II, qu. 100, a. 1.

mandment and presumably the other commandments on the second table of the Decalogue. Aquinas, nevertheless, thinks that all seven commandments on the second table of the Decalogue are part of the natural law.

In short, to act fully in accord with their natural inclinations, human beings need instruction and training in virtue. It is possible, but very difficult, for human beings to know the truths about God, including the truth that God is the author of the natural law; thus they need instruction by divine revelation. Aquinas explains:

Even as regards those truths about God which human reason could have discovered, it was necessary that man should be taught by a divine revelation; because the truth about God such as reason could discover, would only be known by a few, and that after a long time, and with the admixture of many errors.[94]

Aquinas believes training in virtue is also necessary because the effects of sin inhibit perception of the natural law. In other words, the law of nature is opposed by the law of concupiscence, that disordered desire caused by original sin and personal sin. Toward the end of his life Aquinas went so far as to say, "Since then the law of nature was destroyed by concupiscence, man needed to be brought back to works of virtue, and to be drawn away from vice: for which purpose he needed the written law."[95]

A contemporary author, J. Budziszewski, has an insightful way of explaining what is needed for an accurate perception of the natural law.

Even insights into "what we can't not know" require the assistance of others, for a good deal of what we know is latent; we may not realize *what it is* that we know, and we are certainly unlikely to know all its presuppositions and implications. Most of the "others" on whose assistance we rely will belong to previous generations, because people of our own time are likely to have the same blind spots that we do.[96]

This means, of course, that the grand tradition of learning, found especially in great texts or masterworks, will be indispensable for those seeking knowledge of the natural law. For example, Aristotle's *Ethics* and

94. Ibid., I, qu. 1, a. 1.

95. Thomas Aquinas, *Collationes in Decem Praeceptis*, I, line 27, édition critique avec introduction et notes par Jean-Pierre Torrell, in *Revue des sciences philosophiques et théologiques* 69 (1985): 5–40, 27–63; cited from Russell Hittinger, *The First Grace: Rediscovering the Natural Law in a Post-Christian World* (Wilmington, Del.: ISI, 2003), 11.

96. J. Budziszewski, *What We Can't Not Know* (Dallas: Spence, 2003), 25.

St. Augustine's *Confessions* have insights into the effect of good and bad habits on the perception and acceptance of truth that most individuals could not hope to discover on their own.

A second point made by Budziszewski is that "bad living" can blot out moral truths derived from first principles. In other words, the mind and the character work together. The mind of people who live badly will be hindered in its perception of the natural law—hence the importance of the tradition in the form of moral education. This kind of education not only instructs, but also exhorts. Budziszewski explains,

Moral education serves at least five purposes. It reinforces what we know, because the mere fact that we know something is wrong is not enough to keep us from doing it. It elicits what we know, because we know many things without noticing that we know them. It guards what we know, because although deep conscience cannot err, surface conscience can err in all too many ways. It builds upon what we know, because only the most general and basic matters of right and wrong are known to us immediately, and second knowledge must be added to first. Finally, it confronts us about what we know, because sometimes we need to be told "You know better."[97]

This combination of instruction and exhortation corresponds to the New Testament's approach to moral matters. St. Paul, for example, is always instructing and exhorting his listeners.

Budziszewski's distinction between deep conscience (what Aquinas called *synderesis*) and surface conscience (*conscientia*) also helps to explain why people have difficulty accurately perceiving the natural law. Surface conscience misses the mark, argues Budziszewski, because of insufficient experience, poor reasoning ability, unwillingness to reason because of sloth, corrupt customs, disordered passions, fear of discovering the truth, misleading ideologies, and stubborn desire to do what one wants despite its wrongness. Deep conscience gives everyone "knowledge of basic goods, of formal norms, and of everyday rules."[98]

Deep conscience is the reason why even a man who tells himself there is no right and wrong may shrink from committing murder; why even a man who murders may suffer the pangs of remorse; and why even a man who has deadened himself to remorse shows other symptoms of deep-buried guilty knowledge.[99]

97. Ibid., 114–15.   98. Ibid., 80.
99. Ibid., 81.

Budziszewski does concede that people still can frustrate deep conscience by lying to themselves, by denying that they know what they really do. How often this may happen Budziszewski does not presume to say.

Despite the perception problems caused by imperfect reason and disordered desire, at least the seeds of the natural law are instilled in the human mind. Human beings can usually see that "the natural condition of man is one of participation in a higher norm. Man has liberty to direct himself because he is first directed by another." In other words, to use Thomistic language, "The human reason is a measured measure (*mensura mensurata*) not a measuring measure (*mensura mensurans*). Having received a law the human mind can go on to judge and command according to that law."[100] In simple language, a human being naturally has a sense that he doesn't make up the rules he lives by, but knows intuitively that he is not his own god. He discovers rather than creates or invents the principles on the basis of which he will direct and live his life. Because people no longer see this point clearly, one of the things the Church needs to do is to show that being commanded by God is the natural condition of a human being and not a teaching strategy invented by the Church in order to control people.[101]

Genesis 2:17 teaches human beings that their natural condition is one of receiving instruction in how to live. In *Veritatis splendor* John Paul II comments on Genesis 2:17 as follows:

by forbidding man to "eat of the tree of the knowledge of good and evil," God makes it clear that man does not originally possess such "knowledge" as something properly his own, but only participates in it by the light of natural reason and of Divine Revelation, which manifests to him the requirements and the promptings of eternal wisdom.[102]

So, revelation reinforces the teaching given by the law that God impresses on every mind about the necessity of achieving perfection in a prescribed way.

The pope is well aware that today's cultural climate encourages people to "*exalt freedom to such an extent that it becomes an absolute, which would then be the source of values.*"[103] Following in the footsteps of Nietzsche, individuals would "*determine what is good or evil.*" Otherwise stated, people are encouraged to think that their moral judgments are necessarily true because

100. Hittinger, *The First Grace*, 97.   101. Ibid., 25.
102. *Veritatis splendor*, no. 41.   103. Ibid., no. 32.

they stem from their conscience. In this perspective, conscience becomes a kind of oracle that makes pronouncements instead of a herald, which announces the message transmitted by reason and divine revelation. In other words, "there is a tendency to grant to the individual conscience the prerogative of independently determining the criteria of good and evil and then acting accordingly.... Taken to its extreme consequences, this individualism leads to a denial of the very idea of human nature."[104] Having a human nature means that you can't simply create your own values, but you must live in accordance with your nature. For example, you can't decide to love no one without doing harm to yourself, no matter how "sincere" you are. In other words, the human mind is not a measuring measure, but a measured measure.

Reason has to discern the moral law and then apply it to situations. All moral law has its origin in God, but the natural moral law can be discerned by the human heart. Quoting Aquinas, the pope says it "'is nothing other than the light of understanding infused in us by God, whereby we understand what must be done and what must be avoided. God gave this light and this law to man at creation.'"[105] When our practical reason grasps this natural law, it participates "in the wisdom of the divine Creator and Lawgiver."[106] What Aquinas and John Paul II are saying is that the natural condition of human beings is to obey the divine Lawgiver because he prescribes what is good for them. The only other real alternative, as mentioned, is to reject guidance by natural law and divine revelation in favor of an autonomy that entitles one to create values out of whole cloth. The choice is either participated theonomy or unbounded freedom.

The pope describes God's wisdom as providence because he "cares for man not 'from without,' through the laws of physical nature, but 'from within,' through reason, which, by its natural knowledge of God's eternal law, is consequently able to show man the right direction to take in his free actions."[107] There is a right direction because the rational creature has "'its proper act and end.'"[108] In other words, not just any attitude or act perfects the human agent, but only those attitudes and acts in accord

104. Ibid., no. 32.
105. Ibid., no. 40, citing Thomas Aquinas, *In Duo Praecepta Caritatis et in Decem Legis Praecepta. Prologus, Opuscula Theologica*, II, no. 1129, edited by Raymundi A. Vercudo and Raymundi M. Spiazzi (Torino: Marietti, 1954), 245.
106. Ibid., no. 40.
107. Ibid., no. 43.
108. Ibid., quoting *Summa theologiae*, I-II, qu. 91, a. 2.

with the image of God that man is. God created human beings to seek truth, not falsehood; virtue, not vice; holiness, not depravity. We abuse our freedom if we reject our participation in the eternal law, that is to say, the natural law.

Natural law is called a law because it is "'the reason or the will of God, who commands us to respect the natural order and forbids us to disturb it.'"[109] It would not be called a law unless God had authority over us as our Creator and lawgiver. It could not be called law if we were our own supreme legislators who decided what is good or bad without any guidance from a higher reason.

Two reasons that the teaching on natural law seems wrongheaded to people, according to John Paul II, are contemporary convictions about the nature of the body and the cultural conditioning of all norms. The pope explains:

A freedom which claims to be absolute ends up treating the human body as a raw datum, devoid of any meaning and moral goods [or values] until freedom has shaped it in accordance with its design. Consequently, human nature and the body appear as *presuppositions or preambles*, materially *necessary* for freedom to make its choice, yet extrinsic to the person, the subject and the human act.[110]

This means, for example, that the human body gives no indication as to the morality or immorality of contraception, direct sterilization, or homosexual relations. Only the person matters, and the body is not considered to be an essential part of the person. In addition, if all moral norms are culturally conditioned, then human beings can't make decisions on the basis of some universal norm. Joseph Fuchs is one of those Catholic moral theologians who has taken this position. He writes, "Neither the Hebrew Bible nor the New Testament produces statements that are independent of culture and thus universal and valid for all time; nor can these statements be given by the church or its Magisterium."[111] Human beings must freely determine the meaning of their behavior without any guidance from the body, human nature, moral norms that transcend time and place, or revelation. What this means in practice is that most people will

109. Ibid., quoting *Dignitatis humanae (Declaration on Religious Freedom)*, 3; see Abbott, ed., *The Documents of Vatican II.*

110. Ibid., no. 48.

111. Hittinger, *The First Grace*, 23, quoting Joseph Fuchs, *Moral Demands and Personal Obligations*, trans. Brian McNeil (Washington, D.C.: Georgetown University Press, 1995), 55.

adopt the mores taught by the opinion makers of the contemporary culture, as Tocqueville noted.

The position that Joseph Fuchs and others have advocated can be understood in the light of what John Paul II said about historicism in *Fides et ratio*. "The fundamental claim of historicism…is that the truth of a philosophy is determined on the basis of its appropriateness to a certain period and a certain historical purpose. At least implicitly, therefore, the enduring validity of truth is denied. What was true in one period, historicists claim, may not be true in another."[112] So what the Bible said in the past was true for its time period, but not for all time. Furthermore, historicist theologians such as Fuchs claim that the Magisterium or the teaching authority of the Church can never definitively settle any moral issue with authoritative teaching. This is because reality supposedly doesn't allow such a thing.

The Practical Effect of Historicism

Given the situation in the universities and in the culture, John Paul II's comments on historicism are especially noteworthy. If historicism is true, then it does not make sense to read classic texts of the past in order to find perennial wisdom about important matters. The acceptance of historicism really leads people to accept either the opinions of the majority or the reigning opinions of the movers and shakers in society. It is also a form of historicism to "think that truth is born of consensus and not of consonance between intellect and objective reality."[113] Consensus would obviously depend on locale and the time period.

C.S. Lewis captured the effect of historicism on scholarship in a passage from his *Screwtape Letters*. Screwtape explains to his nephew that scholars can be deterred from seeking truth in old books by inculcating in them what is called the historical point of view.

The Historical Point of View, put briefly, means that when a learned man is presented with any statement in an ancient author, the one question he never asks is whether it is true. He asks who influenced the ancient writer, and how far the statement is consistent with what he said in other books and what phase in the writer's development or in the general history of thought it illustrates, and how often it has been misunderstood (especially by the learned man's colleagues) and what the general course of criticism on it has been for

112. Pope John Paul II, *Fides et ratio*, no. 87.
113. Ibid., no. 56.

the last ten years, and what is the "present state of the question." To regard
the ancient writer as a possible source of knowledge—to anticipate that what
he said could possibly modify your thoughts or your behavior—this would be
rejected as unutterably simple-minded.[114]

With this kind of approach "scholarship becomes an immunization
against the truth,"[115] since it is unscholarly to ask whether Dante or
Shakespeare have actually seen something that is true for all time.

The effect of historicism on people's attitude toward the culture in
which they live is visible in the common opinion that all cultures are to
be respected. In other words, value judgments are to be avoided. A historicist mentality, then, leads people to bow down before what becomes authoritative in a culture, simply because it is experienced as imposing and
powerful. Historicism reinforces the persuasiveness of the old adage: "to
get along, go along." A philosophical principle now supports the all-too-
human tendency to adapt to one's surroundings, even if that means giving
up or blunting the love of truth and living immorally.

In order to clarify further the meaning and implication of historicism
for everyday life, I will present Pope John Paul II's alternative way of
appreciating and evaluating any particular culture. The pope says that
Christians always experience their faith as imbued in a culture, and their
faith, in turn, forms the local culture over a period of time. His fundamental conviction, however, is that cultures are a mixture of truth and
error. "When cultures are deeply rooted in human nature [natura humana,
mistranslated as 'experience' in the Vatican translation] they show forth
the human being's characteristic openness to the universal and the transcendent."[116] When grounded in human nature, cultures "offer different
paths to truth" and thereby are able to incline human beings to live well,
that is, in the truth. But with respect to God's revelation every culture
falls short. "No one culture can ever become the norm of judging, much
less the ultimate norm of truth with regard to God's revelation."[117] The
Gospel message, in fact, "is the true form of liberation from all the disorders caused by sin and is likewise the call to the fullness of truth."[118]

---

114. C. S. Lewis, *The Screwtape Letters* (New York: Macmillan, 1961), 139–40, partially
quoted in Joseph Cardinal Ratzinger, "Culture and Truth: Reflections on the Encyclical," *Origins* 28, no. 36 (1999): 627.

115. Ratzinger, "Culture and Truth: Reflections on the Encyclical," 627.

116. *Fides et ratio*, no. 70.   117. Ibid., no. 71.

118. Ibid., no. 71.

Otherwise stated, John Paul II is saying that every culture will have some-thing missing and, therefore, must remain open to correction and fulfill-ment. So, even the very best cultures imaginable, those rooted in human nature, will fall short of the full truth.

While appreciating the valuable contributions that rich cultures can offer to humanity, he still says that no "particular cultural tradition should remain closed in its difference and affirm itself by opposing oth-er traditions."[119] In making this statement John Paul II shows his aware-ness that cultures have the tendency to love their own way more than the truth. Today, of course, some prevailing opinions justify this kind of complacency by urging a general respect for all cultures, whatever their characteristics. What else is there to do if it is impossible to arrive at truth by philosophical inquiry and acceptance of revelation? People ad-versely affected by closed-minded cultures will not be open to learn from the great writers of the past, to perceive the truths in other religious tra-ditions, or to hear the Gospel message of salvation. To illustrate the im-plications of his thought, the pope says that "at this time it is the duty of Christians, especially Indian Christians, to draw from the rich heritage [of the religious and philosophical thought in the nation of India] those elements compatible with their faith in order to enrich Christian doc-trine."[120] This means that Christians living in any culture should be open to whatever truth is found in the prevailing mores, or in any particular philosophy or religious tradition.

Transcending Culture through Faith and Reason

John Paul II is fully aware how difficult it is for people to give up their erroneous opinions and practices. Even the Bible shows that the ancient Israelites had to engage in a laborious struggle to overcome the limita-tions of their own culture. In commenting on *Fides et ratio,* Cardinal Ratz-inger nicely clarifies John Paul II's thought in the following paragraph:

The Bible is not simply the expression of the culture of the people of Isra-el but rather manifests a constant conflict with the completely natural de-sire of the people of Israel to be only themselves, to shut themselves in their own culture. Faith in God and their yes to the will of God are wrested from them against their own wishes....Israel's faith requires a continual self-transcendence, an overcoming of its own culture, in order to open itself and

119. Ibid., no. 72.
120. Ibid., no. 72.

enter into the expansiveness of a truth common to all. The books of the Old Testament…possess their own originality in this struggle of faith against particularity, the process of taking leave of what is their own, which begins with Abraham's departure on his journey.[121]

To understand more fully this wonderfully illuminating paragraph, think of the people's inclination to make and worship idols shortly after the exodus from Egypt or the continuous efforts of the prophets to call Israel back to the God of Abraham, Isaac, and Jacob. The struggle of the Israelites to avoid error and sin is continuous and difficult, but possible and partially successful, according to Biblical teaching.

The Bible is more sanguine about the possibility of Israel's faith overcoming the limits of its culture than Plato is about widespread emergence from the cave. The Greek philosopher taught that every culture is a cave, from which only the few could emerge into the light. John Paul II seems to be telling all people that they may live in a more or less dark cave, from which there is a possibility of emerging with the help of philosophical inquiry and religious faith. He knows that even the Christian faith and theology can be affected by the erroneous opinions and practices of the cave. That is why he exhorts Christians to respect philosophical inquiry, even to study the erroneous opinions of philosophers as a path to light.

In the New Testament, "all peoples are invited to join in the process of self-transcendence of their own particularity, the process which first began in Israel."[122] In other words, the New Testament teaches that all can overcome the love of their own and be liberated for communion with God and one another. Cardinal Ratzinger puts it this way: "Faith in Jesus Christ is of its nature a continual opening of the self: it is God breaking into the world of human beings and the response of human beings breaking out toward God, who at the same time leads them to one another."[123] With the advent of Christianity no one is destined to remain in the cave because of inferior intellectual abilities. Christianity, in principle, frees Christians from the pervasive influence of the regime. In other words, people are not simply the product of the culture in which they live.

This transcending of the particular also took place in the Greek world prior to the coming of Jesus Christ. This is what made possible the fruitful encounter between Greek philosophy and the fathers of the Church.

121. Ratzinger, "Culture and Truth: Reflections on the Encyclical," 629.
122. Ibid.
123. Ibid.

"The Fathers...did not simply mix an autonomous Greek culture into the Gospel," writes Cardinal Ratzinger. "They were able to take up the dialogue with Greek philosophy and use it as an instrument for the Gospel, because in the Greek world a form of auto-criticism of their own culture...was already underway." In other words, Greek philosophers were able to rise above limitations in their own culture and arrive at knowledge that is true for all time. As a result, when the Church brought the Christian faith to Asia, Africa, and America, she "introduced these people not to Greek culture as such, but rather to its capacity for self-transcendence which was the true connecting point for interpreting the Christian message."[124] So, it is not the Hellenization of the faith that took place in the early Church, but an encounter between a faith and a philosophy, both of which transcended the cultures in which they emerged. That encounter, one of the great themes of Ernest Fortin's writing, became a guide and an exhortation to overcome love of one's own, particularity, the cave of one's culture.

Pope John Paul II believes that the Church's encounter with Greek philosophy gave the Church a heritage that can never be forgotten. He says,

In engaging great cultures for the first time, the Church cannot abandon what she has gained from her inculturation in the world of Greco-Latin learning. To reject this heritage would be to deny the providential plan of God, who guides his Church down the path of time and history. This criterion is valid for the Church in every age.[125]

For example, the concepts of person and nature, as well as the Greek and Latin languages, can never be forsaken by the Church. So much of the Church's patrimony is in Greek or Latin, such as the New Testament, the original formulation of the Christological doctrines, and the writings of Augustine and Aquinas. While John Paul affirms the permanent validity of the Greco-Latin heritage in the Church, "this hardly means that other approaches are excluded."[126] He is open to the possibility that people in other cultures will transcend their limits and provide humanity with eternal truths. To illustrate the drift of his thought, he says, "a great spiritual impulse leads the Indian mind to seek an experience which might attain absolute good, when the spirit is free from the shackles of time

124. Ibid.   125. *Fides et ratio*, no. 72.
126. Ibid.

and space."[127] He also says that he expects the Church of the future to be enriched by its encounter with Eastern cultures. Like St. Paul, he urges Christians always to be open to whatever is true and good.

Finally, John Paul II affirms that the Gospel truth can be "grasped across all boundaries of culture and time" and that it "can be expressed faithfully in many different languages." Otherwise, Jesus's command to go and make disciples of all nations would make no sense. That the New Testament is written in a language different from that spoken by Jesus already shows, right from the beginning, that an accurate translation is possible.

Because many people believe that a universal truth is an empty concept, a new notion of conscience has arisen. It is no longer generally regarded as a judgment of reason on the basis of an objective truth. "In what concerns morality and religion," writes Cardinal Ratzinger in his German commentary on the encyclical, "the subject is the last authority. This is logical, if truth as such is inaccessible. So in recent times the concept of conscience is the canonization of relativism, the impossibility of common ethical and religious standards."[128] Conscience has become a synonym for the absolute authority of the individual to create his own values.[129]

Cardinal Ratzinger makes clear that Christianity claims to speak the truth about God, man, and the world. "The fundamental claim of the Christian faith is expressed in the word of Christ from the gospel of John, 'I am the way, the truth and the life.'"[130] Today, the objection is raised that neither Christianity nor any other religion can rightfully claim to be the *religio vera*, the true religion or the religion of truth. At the beginning of this century the Protestant theologian Ernst Troeltsch made this point by arguing that religion was the offshoot of a culture. He regarded Christianity as "a European affair" that cannot be exported to other lands. In looking at things this way, "the question of truth," writes Ratzinger, "is in practice given up, the boundaries of cultures cannot be crossed."[131] In an address given in French at the Sorbonne on November 27, 1999, Ratzinger described Troeltsch's position in slightly different terms. The cardinal said, "[Troeltsch] had arrived at the conviction that cultures are un-

127. Ibid.
128. Ratzinger, "Glaube, Wahrheit und Kultur: Reflexionen im Anschluss an die Enzyklika *Fides et Ratio*," unpublished text made available to the public, 18.
129. See *Veritatis splendor*, nos. 54–64.
130. Ratzinger, "Glaube, Wahrheit und Kultur," 2.
131. Ibid., 9.

surpassable and that religion is linked to cultures. Christianity is then only the side of God's face turned toward Europe."[132] If this is so, what is to prevent changes in European culture that render Christianity unsuitable for Europeans, at least in their minds? Consequently, Ratzinger logically raises this question: "Is it perhaps necessary even to take one step more than Troeltsch, who still considered Christianity as the religion adapted to Europe, taking into account that Europe itself doubts that it is now suitable?"[133] In other words, on the basis of Troeltsch's reasoning, which is a historicist approach, there really is no compelling argument that Christianity can claim a permanent validity as the religion of Europe. If the culture changes and becomes, for example, relativist, then religion may and will follow suit, because "religion is linked to cultures."

In trying "to rehabilitate the question of truth in a world marked by relativism," the encyclical not only had to discuss the universal truth claims of faith and philosophy, but, according to Ratzinger, also had to ask "whether there can at all be a communion of cultures in one truth."[134] In other words, is there a truth to which all cultures can look for guidance in recognizing erroneous opinions and bad morals? As we saw, the Old Testament teaches that the people of Israel had to overcome the limits of their own culture in order to have faith. They took their bearings by a transcendent truth. The New Testament invites everyone to overcome "love of their own," to use the idiom of Plato. The implicit premise of the Bible is that every person can transcend the limits of his own culture by rising to the contemplation of truth on the wings of faith and/or reason. It is also the teaching of much philosophy that some measure of truth can be apprehended despite the limits of the culture in which one lives. So in John Paul II's mind, there is no doubt that there can be a communion of cultures in one truth, but not without great effort and a persevering love of truth.

If it is possible to arrive at truths that transcend culture, then it is certainly not impossible for the Church to put forth both negative and positive precepts as universally binding. The command to love God and neighbor is always valid, but may be carried out in various ways, because circumstances may change. Universally negative commandments are easier to state because there are certain kinds of actions that are always in-

132. Ratzinger, "Vérité du Christianisme," *La documentation catholique*, no. 2217 (January 2, 2000): 29.

133. Ibid., 3–4.

134. Ratzinger, "Glaube, Wahrheit und Kultur," 9.

compatible with human dignity, such as murder, adultery, fornication, homosexual activity, stealing, bearing false witness. Everyone in principle can come to see this, because the Ten Commandments forbidding these actions are part of the natural law.

Conclusion

I have tried to show that the dignity of the human person must be understood both as a permanent endowment and an ongoing achievement. Because of the constant temptation to act beneath our dignity, we must strive and strain to avoid sin and practice virtue. The family, educational institutions, the Church, mediating institutions, and the state help people in various ways to live in accordance with their dignity.

Because of their great dignity, human beings have both duties and rights. To act in accordance with their dignity, they must practice the virtues required by the natural law. In obeying the natural law, people will necessarily respect the rights of their fellow human beings. Not to respect the genuine rights of others is to act beneath one's dignity. Hence, Mary Ann Glendon declared,

From a Christian point of view,...[it] may be that human rights are grounded in the obligation of everyone to perfect one's own dignity, which in turn obliges one to respect the "given" spark of dignity of others whatever they may have done with it. In other words, it may be our own quest for dignity (individually and as a society) that requires us to refrain from inflicting cruel punishments on criminals, or from terminating the lives of the unborn and others whose faculties are underdeveloped or dormant.[135]

For the sake of safeguarding human rights, human dignity must not be understood to require only the protection of rights. Only when people are intent on perfecting their own dignity will they both attain their end in life and necessarily respect the rights of others. (Of course, people may respect the rights of their neighbors out of self-interest or fear, but such motives are inherently unreliable.) So, the best way of advancing the cause of rights is to promote a correct understanding of human dignity. People must first think about what they owe to others, rather that what claims they can make on them by asserting their rights.

---

135. Mary Ann Glendon, *Traditions in Turmoil* (Ann Arbor, Mich.: Sapientia Press, 2006), 346.

CHAPTER 2

The Meaning of the Common Good

Recent Catholic social doctrine still holds that the highest purpose of the political community is to promote the common good.[1] This seems clear enough until one asks what Church documents mean by the term. Echoing John XXIII's *Mater et magistra (On Christianity and Social Progress)* and *Pacem in Terris (Peace on Earth)*, and quoting Vatican Council II's *Gaudium et spes (Pastoral Constitution on the Church in the Modern World)*, the *Catechism of the Catholic Church* describes the common good as "the sum total of the conditions of social life which allow people, either as groups or individuals, to reach their own perfection more fully and more easily."[2] In a more specific paragraph the *Catechism* adds, "The common good consists of three elements: respect for and promotion of the fundamental rights of the person; prosperity, or the development of the spiritual and temporal goods of society; the peace and security of the group and its members."[3] Except for the reference to "spiritual goods," this seems to be a purely instrumental description of the common good. The term "instrumental"

1. Vatican Council II, *Gaudium et spes (Pastoral Constitution on the Church in the Modern World)*, no. 74, formulates the traditional teaching as follows: "Hence the political community exists for that common good in which it finds its full justification and meaning, and from which it derives its pristine and proper right"; quotations from the documents of Vatican Council are taken from Walter M. Abbott, ed., *The Documents of Vatican II* (NewYork: Guild Press, America Press, and Association Press, 1966). I will, however, often modify the translation in the light of the authoritative Latin text.

2. *Catechism of the Catholic Church* (Vatican City: Libreria Editrice Vaticana, 1994), no. 1906 (summam eorum vitae socialis condicionum quae tum coetibus, tum singulis membris permittunt ut propriam perfectionem plenius atque expeditius consequantur); cf. John XXIII, *Mater et Magistra (On Christianity and Social Progress)*, no. 65; John XXIII, *Pacem in terris (Peace on Earth)*, no. 58; *Gaudium et spes*, nos. 26 and 74; and Vatican Council II, *Dignitatis humanae (Declaration on Religious Freedom)*, no. 6.

3. *Catechism*, no. 1925; bonum commune tria elementa implicat essentialia: iurium fundamentalium personae observantiam et promotionem; prosperitatem seu bonorum spiritualium et temporalium societatis incrementum; pacem et securitatem coetus eiusque membrorum.

refs to goods that facilitate the attainment of our proper end as human beings, but are not part of that end, such as food, clothing, shelter, a transportation system, and civil liberties. Instrumental goods would not include such important civic goods as the practice of faith, character formation in schools, forgiveness and reconciliation among racial and ethnic groups, the promotion of fidelity in marriage, courtesy, the prohibition of euthanasia, or the promotion of a commitment to the poor.

In both *Mater et magistra* and *Pacem in terris* Pope John XXIII described the common good as "the sum total of the conditions of social life, by which people may reach their perfection more fully and easily."[4] So, John XXIII's encyclicals are clearly the source of the definition found in Vatican Council II's *Gaudium et spes* and the *Catechism*. The only difference is that Pope John XXIII speaks of "people" (*homines*) instead of individuals and groups, but this doesn't change the substantial identity of the two definitions.

Writing on Christian social doctrine, Oswald von Nell-Breuning, the well-known architect of Pius XI's *Quadragesimo anno* (*On Reconstruction of the Social Order*), referred to Pope John's definition of the common good as an "organizational and organizing value," what we would call the common welfare or instrumental goods.[5] These would include the whole panoply of rights described in *Pacem in terris*. Nell-Breuning says that Pope John's understanding of the common good differs from the traditional view articulated by Thomas Aquinas. For Aquinas the highest purpose of politics is to promote virtue in the body politic. Therefore, the common good in a Thomistic perspective includes not only instrumental goods, but also goods that perfect the human soul. God is the common good, par excellence. Nell-Breuning says that Thomistic authors understand by the term "common good" the perfection of human nature in all citizens. In summing up the differences between the Thomistic understanding of the common good and Pope John's view, he writes: "The common welfare is a most important value in the service of the good, whereas the common good is a value in itself."[6] Germain Grisez also interprets the papal documents to mean that "the Church's teaching treats the common

4. "Summam complecti earum vitae socialis condicionum, quibus homines suam ipsorum perfectionem possent plenius atque expeditius consequi"; *Mater et magistra*, no. 65, and *Pacem in terris*, no. 58.

5. Oswald von Nell-Breuning, "Social Movements," in *Sacramentum Mundi: An Encyclopedia of Theology*, vol. 6, edited by Karl Rahner, et al. (New York: Herder and Herder, 1970), 110.

6. von Nell-Breuning, "Social Movements," 110.

good of political society as instrumental to the full good of persc

It *appears* that Pope John XXIII, Vatican Council II, and the new echism have officially endorsed a limited notion of the common good, thereby quietly putting aside the longstanding Catholic teaching that the political community, with the help of the Church, intermediary associations, and individuals, should attempt to describe and pursue a substantive common good—that is to say, a common good that has as its ultimate focus the perfection of individual citizens.

The purpose of this chapter is first to show that neither Pope John XXIII nor Vatican Council II, nor, by logical inference, the *Catechism*, has adopted a purely instrumental understanding of the common good, appearances notwithstanding. Because the *Catechism* relies on the beloved pope and the Council for its definition of the common good, its proper interpretation logically depends on the correct understanding of their teaching. The refutation of the instrumental interpretation of both John XXIII's and the Council's definition of the common good paves the way, and also inchoately begins to realize, the second purpose of this chapter: a presentation of the substantive understanding of the common good put forth by Catholic social doctrine in popes John XXIII, John Paul II, and Benedict XVI, and in Vatican Council II. I will show that the Church's social doctrine still holds that the attainment of the common good requires the political community, the institutions of civil society, and individuals both to restrain evildoers and remedy unjust situations, and to promote the practice of virtue in the lives of every individual, while preserving or establishing good mores and institutions.

What's more, the Church could not embrace an instrumental notion of the common good without endangering the mission of the Church—the salvation of all human beings. To bishops making their ad limina visits Pope John Paul II kept asking, "What have you done to change the culture?" The pope obviously thought that the Church would have more difficulty preaching the faith in a culture hostile to Christian teaching. This is not a new thought. "Aquinas," writes Mary Keys, "indicates that the moral evil and confusion of one's society, of one's forebears and contemporaries, can infect and blind even those with fundamentally good hearts and wills (cf. I-II 94, 6)."[8] For example, in the United States to-

7. Germain Grisez, *The Way of the Lord Jesus*, vol. 2, *Living a Christian Life* (Quincy, Ill.: Franciscan Press, 1993), 340.

8. Mary Keys, *Aquinas, Aristotle, and the Promise of the Common Good* (New York: Cambridge University Press, 2006), 211.

day the overwhelming influence of relativism and a utilitarian approach in bioethical matters are serious obstacles to the reception and practice of the whole Christian faith. The Church, therefore, encourages its members and all people of good will to work for better laws and healthier mores as a good in itself and as a preparation for the reception of Jesus Christ.

The key to understanding the common good in Catholic social doctrine is to keep in mind that responsibility for seeking it falls upon individuals, voluntary associations, the Church, and the political community.[9] Civil society and the political order together seek the full common good. In a liberal democratic society, with its focus on liberty and equality, the various elements of civil society will do more, and the state through its laws will do less.

In a democratic society the specific responsibilities of the state and civil society for the common good will always be under discussion, but the state must play a role of leadership. Listen to the words of the *Compendium of the Social Doctrine of the Church:*

The State, in fact, must guarantee the coherency, unity and organization of the civil society of which it is an expression, in order that the common good may be attained with the contribution of every citizen. The individual person, the family or intermediate groups are not able to achieve their full development by themselves for living a truly human life. Hence, the necessity of political institutions, the purpose of which is to make available to persons the necessary material, cultural, moral and spiritual goods. The goal of life in society is in fact the historically attainable common good.[10]

So, the *Catechism* and the *Compendium of the Social Doctrine of the Church* hold that cultural, moral, and spiritual goods are a necessary part of the common good. The *Compendium* further argues that it is Catholic social doctrine that "political institutions" have a role to play with respect to spiritual and moral goods.[11]

In the paragraph cited above, the *Compendium* also points out that without state intervention for the sake of the common good, individuals, families, and intermediary institutions will not be able to achieve their ends.

9. Pontifical Council for Justice and Peace, *Compendium of the Social Doctrine of the Church* (Vatican City: Libreria Editrice Vaticana, 2004), nos. 168, 417.

10. *Compendium,* no. 168.

11. The question posed by political theorists and analysts, of course, is how the state could promote moral and spiritual goods without endorsing some religion or without being repressive of democratic liberties.

This latter position is not new. In his *Summa theologiae* Thomas Aquinas also spoke in the same vein in affirming that "the individual good is impossible without the common good of the family, state, or kingdom."[12] This is so because every individual depends on many others for his physical, intellectual, and moral development.

With this brief introduction in mind, let us turn to John XXIII's *Pacem in terris*, Vatican Council II's *Gaudium et spes* and *Dignitatis humanae (Declaration on Religious Freedom)*, and Pope John Paul II's *Evangelium vitae*. Even my incomplete examination of these writings will show that the two popes and the Council have not abandoned the traditional understanding of the common good, but have, in fact, ratified it. I will complete this chapter by first summarizing the basic elements of the common good and then explaining the two reasons the Church must have a teaching on a substantive common good.

Pope John XXIII

Pope John's 1963 encyclical, *Pacem in terris*, is justly well known for presenting a synthesis of Catholic teaching on human rights. Less noticed is John XXIII's teaching on duties. Having listed the rights of the human person, John XXIII affirms that there are just as many corresponding duties. He adds that "rights as well as duties find their source, their sustenance and their inviolability in natural law which grants or enjoins them."[13] For example, to the right to life corresponds the duty to preserve it; to the right of having a worthy standard of living corresponds the duty of living in a suitable manner; with the right of freely investigating truth goes the duty of seeking it with all one's ability. A person also has the natural duty to acknowledge and respect all the natural rights of others and to contribute to a civic order in which the exercise of rights and the fulfillment of duties are a reality.[14] If we ask what is the precise relation between rights and duties, Pope John answers: "The chief concern of civil authorities...must be to ensure that these rights are acknowledged, respected, coordinated with other rights, defended and promoted, so that in this way each one may more easily carry out his duties."[15]

---

12. Thomas Aquinas, *Summa theologiae*, qu. 47, a. 10, reply to obj. 2.
13. *Pacem in terris*, no. 28.
14. Ibid., nos. 29–31.
15. Ibid., no. 60 ("ut hinc iura agnoscantur, colantur, inter se componantur, defen-

When the passage is cited in *Evangelium vitae (Gospel of Life)* by John Paul II, there is a new translation that reads: "the chief concern of civil authorities must...be to ensure that these rights are recognized, respected, co-ordinated, defended and promoted *and* that each individual is enabled to perform his duties more easily."[16] The translation in *Evangelium vitae* seems to be literally accurate, while the first translation captures what Pope John is trying to say—namely, we have rights so that we can more easily fulfill our duties. That Pope John clearly places rights in a teleological framework is the only reasonable conclusion to draw. The context itself points to this interpretation.

Right after speaking in his own name, Pope John XXIII quotes the famous 1941 Pentecost address of Pius XII: "To safeguard the inviolable rights of the human person, and to take care that each may more easily fulfill his duties, should be the chief duty of every public authority."[17] All through his Pentecost radio address Pius XII indicates that people have rights for the sake of duties. One example will have to suffice: "The native right to the use of material goods, intimately linked as it is to the dignity and other rights of the human person...provides man with a secure material basis of the highest import, on which to rise to the fulfillment, with reasonable liberty, of his moral duties."[18] The logic of Catholic social doctrine also requires the ordering of rights to duties or to the divine law. The clearest statement of that position that I have found is in the *Gaudium et spes* passage quoted in chapter 1, which says, "For we are tempted to think that our personal rights are fully ensured only when we are exempt from every requirement of divine law. But in this way the dignity of the human person is by no means saved; on the contrary, it is lost."[19] Pope John XXIII would have judged this Vatican II formulation to be fully in accord with his *Pacem in terris*.

If we ask John XXIII what is the relationship of rights and duties

---

dantur, provehantur, illinc suis quisque officiis facilius fungi possint"). In this translation published by the National Catholic Welfare Conference, the translator took *"illinc"* as a particle indicating result after verbs of effecting.

16. John Paul II, *Evangelium vitae (The Gospel of Life)*, no. 71.

17. *Pacem in terris (Peace on Earth)*, no. 60, quoting Radio Message of Pius XII, Pentecost, June 1, 1941, *Acta Apostolicae Sedis* 33 (1941): 200.

18. Pius XII, *Acta Apostolicae Sedis* 33 (1941): 221.

19. *Gaudium et spes*, no. 41, "Tentationi enim subiicimur, iudicandi nostra iura personalia tunc tantum plene servari, cum ab omni norma Legis divinae solvimur. Hac autem via, personae humanae dignitas, nedum salvetur, potius perit."

to the common good, he responds: "In our time, the common good is thought to be especially guaranteed when rights and duties are maintained."[20] Even if the government did all it could to protect rights, that would not be sufficient to realize the common good of a community. John XXIII clearly says that the attainment of the common good depends on citizens' performing their duties. In other words, the government can't achieve its proper end if citizens are not moved to carry out their duties by such institutions as families, churches, schools, other mediating institutions, and the state. It almost goes without saying that the ruling authorities would also have to perform their duties. If the performance of duties by government authorities and ordinary citizens is necessary for the attainment of the common good, then Pope John is surely not proposing a purely instrumental common good. But why, then, does he propose what sounds like a misleading definition?

I used to think that Nell-Breuning was correct in his interpretation of John's definition of the common good as the sum total of instrumental goods needed by human beings. I was impressed by Nell-Breuning because he recognizes that modern Catholic social doctrine really does endorse a substantive common good, even though, in his mind, it proposes only instrumental definitions on several important occasions. He doesn't attempt to explain why Church documents would only define a "subordinate sense" of the common good and leave undefined the Church's more complete understanding of this term. In his commentary on *Gaudium et spes* he writes:

> When ecclesiastical documents give a definition of the common good, it usually concerns this second and subordinate sense. This is the case with reference to John XXIII (*Mater et magistra*, 65). On the other hand, if mention is simply made of the common good, the term denotes or implies the value in itself.[21]

As a "value in itself" Nell-Breuning means all the goods "which belong to fully developed humanity, the full exercise and realization of all the potentialities and faculties inherent in man in society."[22] These comments don't explain why the Church would, without explanation, pres-

---

20. *Pacem in terris,* no. 60.

21. Herbert Vorgrimler, ed., *Commentary on the Documents of Vatican II,* vol. 5 (New York: Herder and Herder, 1969), 318.

22. *Commentary on the Documents of Vatican II,* 318.

ent contradictory definitions of the common good. Without falling into self-contradiction the Church cannot be advocating both an instrumental and a substantive view of the common good. My judgment is that Pope John's definition of the common good just doesn't seem to capture what he really means, as is more clearly evident from a look at other parts of *Pacem in terris*.

Just before he reiterates his *Mater et magistra* definition, Pope John XXIII says, "The common good touches the whole man, the needs of both of his body and soul." Then, he adds, "Therefore it follows that the civil authorities are to endeavor [*spectent*] to effect [*assequandum*] the common good by ways and means proper to them, that is, while respecting the right order of things, they are to procure for citizens along with goods of the body, goods of the soul as well."[23] (It is noteworthy that John XXIII uses the Latin expression *bona animi* (goods of the soul) in spelling out the responsibilities of government. It is the same expression used by Pope Leo XIII in *Rerum novarum*.) In the very next sentence and paragraph of his text he links his statement on the responsibility of civil authorities for the souls of citizens to the teaching of *Mater et magistra* and to the now-famous definition of the common good. Then he argues that the common good ought to be procured in such a way as to contribute to the eternal salvation of all.[24]

There are still other comments in *Pacem in terris* indicating that Pope John didn't intend to propose a mere instrumental notion of the common good. When discussing the subject of law he says, "It is unquestionable that a legal structure in conformity with norms of the just and right and corresponding to the level of development of the state is of great advantage for achieving common advantages for all."[25] This implies that the law aims at the common good by embodying what is just and right, both substantive goods.

---

23. This is the Latin original of the citation from *Pacem in terris*, no. 57: "bonum commune ad integrum hominem attinere, hoc est ad eius tam corporis quam animi necessitates. Ex quo consequens est, ut rei publicae rectores ad bonum illud idoneis viis gradibusque assequendum spectent: ita scilicet ut, recto rerum ordine servato, cum bonis corporis bona pariter animi civibus suppeditent." The two qualifications on the extent of public authority ("by ways and means proper to them" and "while respecting the right order of things or values") show that Pope John XXIII is not endorsing socialism or abandoning the principle of subsidiarity.

24. *Pacem in terris*, no. 59.

25. Ibid., no. 70.

Later on, while discussing relations between Catholics and non-Catholics in social and economic affairs, he suggests that the virtue of prudence is important for the achievement of the common good. "Prudence...is the guiding light of the virtues that regulate life, both individual and social."[26] He further adds that the virtue of prudence is exercised in the light of the natural law, the social doctrine of the Church, and the Magisterium of the Church.

Finally, when discussing the conditions for the establishment of peace, the pope says, "In fact, there can be no peace among men unless there is peace within each one of them, unless each one builds up within himself the order wished by God."[27] Then, he explains what he means by quoting from St. Augustine. The meaning of the quotation is that peace depends on order in the soul, which can only be achieved by adhering to God's will through the practice of the virtues. As peace has to be one of those conditions of social life of which Pope John speaks, then the practice of the virtues by individuals has to be an integral part of the common good.

There is another very revealing statement on the meaning of the common good in *Pacem in terris* that is quoted at length by the *Catechism* in the section on conversion and society and by the *Compendium of the Social Doctrine of the Church* in a section on the "Foundation and Purpose of the Political Community."[28] I didn't fully appreciate the significance of this text until I examined the Latin original. Here is a literal translation:

Human society must primarily be considered something pertaining to the soul [*res quaedam ad animum presertim pertinens*]. Through life in society, in the bright light of truth, men should communicate their knowledge to one another, be able to exercise their rights and fulfill their duties, be inspired to seek the goods of the soul [*bona animi*]; mutually derive a true pleasure from the beautiful, of whatever order it may be; always be readily disposed to pass on the best of themselves to others; and eagerly strive to make their own the *bona animi* of others. These goods of the soul not only influence, but at the same time give aim and scope to all that has bearing on cultural expressions, economic life, the union of citizens, the progress and governing of regimes, laws and lastly all other parts, which outwardly constitute and continuously develop the human community.[29]

26. Ibid., no. 160.   27. Ibid., no. 165.
28. *Compendium*, no. 386.
29. *Catechism of the Catholic Church*, no. 1886, quoting *Pacem in terris*, no. 36, modified translation.

This passage really prepares the way for the *Catechism*'s treatment of the common good, which follows in the next section. John XXIII's *bona animi* must, at least, include conversion, the virtues (especially charity), and knowledge or wisdom, and be among the spiritual goods (*bonorum spiritualium*) that the *Catechism* describes as one of the three elements of the common good.[30] What seems so significant in John XXIII's thought is that every part of civil society and the government must be guided in some way by an understanding of the *bona animi.*

In the light of all of Pope John XXIII's teaching pertaining to the common good, it is reasonable to conclude that he didn't realize that his definition of the common good would be understood as endorsing an instrumental understanding of the common good. Otherwise, he would have formulated it differently. He must have thought that social conditions, allowing for a full and expeditious attainment of a person's perfection, could not be understood as mere instrumental goods. That he is now misunderstood can be traced to several causes, such as the ignorance of political philosophy in Catholic circles and the influence of political liberalism.

Given the misunderstanding of John XXIII's definition of the common good, permit me to summarize the gist of what we have gleaned from his thought. In order to attain the common good, the civil authorities must ensure the protection of rights as an end in itself and so that individuals may fulfill their duties. Rights must be exercised in the light of the natural law and the divine law. Pope John XXIII clearly says that the common good cannot be attained unless rights are respected and duties fulfilled. The pope also supports the traditional understanding of the common good by saying that everyone, every institution, and the government itself must keep in mind the *bona animi* (the goods of the soul). *Pacem in terris*, no. 57, says, "The common good touches the whole man, the needs of both his body and soul." Since the goods of the soul include the practice of the virtues, the aims of the public authorities, the family, and the Church must in some way include the practice of the virtues. The pope specifically says that the law is to aim at what is just and right.

Vatican Council II: *Gaudium et Spes*

I only look at enough of the Council document to make my case that Vatican II has not abandoned the traditional understanding of the com-

30. *Catechism*, no. 1924.

mon good, and to indicate the basic elements of a substantial common good.

Part 1, Chapter 2: "The Community of Mankind"

Like Pope John XXIII, *Gaudium et spes* sees the *bona animi* (the goods of the soul) as an essential part of the common good. The chapter on "The Community of Mankind" reviews "some of the more basic truths" of Catholic social doctrine on human society in the light of revelation. It first calls to mind the constant teaching of the Church about the social nature of the human person and the concomitant duty of all to "treat one another in a spirit of brotherhood." The text then points out that in John 17:21–22 Jesus "implied a certain likeness between the union of the divine Persons and the union of God's children in truth and charity. This likeness reveals that man...cannot fully find himself except through a sincere gift of himself."[31] In other words, men and women can only attain their perfection by loving God and their neighbor in the proper way. Just as loving oneself badly is possible, so people can love each other in a harmful way. The union among human beings, therefore, can only be realized if they love each other in accordance with the *truth* about God and man.

While not going into much detail, the Council points out that the perfection of human persons through self-giving love depends on the family, the political community, and various voluntary associations. (*Gaudium et spes* mentions the role of the Church in leading people to perfection in part 1, chapter 4). The Council then quickly adds that "men are often diverted from doing good and spurred toward evil by the social circumstances in which they live and are immersed from their birth."[32] In other words, the way of life of the community has deep effects on the lives of individuals. In the United States the culture or regime induces not a few people to bow down before the dictatorship of relativism. For example, many young people see nothing wrong with cohabitation or losing control of their reason through drunkenness. The Supreme Court's abortion decisions have moved many citizens to believe that abortion should be legal. That is probably why Pope John Paul II kept asking bishops in Rome for their *ad limina* visits what they had done to change the culture of their countries.

The Council further adds that the defects of the social order, mani-

31. *Gaudium et spes*, no. 24, modified translation.
32. Ibid., no. 25.

fested in private associations and government, originate primarily in the pride and egoism of individual citizens. It is, then, sin that perverts culture or the regime. Once the regime is perverted by the effect of individual sins, then, as a whole, it coaxes individuals to do more evil. In the words of the Council, "When the order of things is affected by the consequences of sin, man, born with an inclination toward evil, thereafter finds new inducements to sin, which cannot be overcome without strenuous efforts and the assistance of grace."[33] The Council is really highlighting the deep and pervasive influence of the regime in a manner reminiscent of Plato and Aristotle. These philosophers also recognized the important role of the virtues and vices of individuals in bringing about a particular regime and the role of the latter in determining what kind of character individual citizens would acquire.

A recovery of the concept of regime, as elaborated in the political philosophy of Plato and Aristotle, would clarify the deep impact that "social conditions" can have on the minds and hearts of citizens. The regime or *politeia* is the whole political and social order. Leo Strauss's explanation of what the classical political philosophers meant by regime is succinct and revealing:

The cause of the laws is the regime. Therefore the guiding theme of political philosophy is the regime rather than the laws....Regime is the order, the form, which gives society its character. Regime is therefore a specific manner of life. Regime is the form of life as living together, the manner of living of society and in society, since this manner depends decisively on the predominance of human beings of a certain type, on the manifest domination of society by human beings of a certain type. Regime means that whole, which we today are in the habit of viewing primarily in a fragmentized form: regime means simultaneously the form of life of a society, its style of life, its moral taste, form of society, form of state, form of government, spirit of laws.[34]

In this perspective the regime has a crucial influence in the lives of most individuals. Only the few, such as the philosophers, could escape its pervasive influence. With the emergence of Christianity the regime is no longer *necessarily* as decisive in the lives of individuals. God's word and grace, mediated through a faithful Church, can be wholeheartedly embraced

---

33. Ibid., modified translation.

34. Leo Strauss, *What Is Political Philosophy? And Other Studies* (Glencoe, Ill.: Free Press, 1959), 34.

even in the midst of bad regimes. Yet, experience shows that many Christians are unduly influenced by the negative aspects of the culture and the social conditions—hence the importance of Church teaching on a substantive common good, which would move individuals to live in accordance with their dignity.

In arguing that individuals must be good if society is going to be good, the Council is really siding with the ancients in their quarrel with the moderns about the main source of justice in a society. Kant argued in his *Perpetual Peace* that a just society is possible even in a nation of devils, provided people intelligently organize the order of things in social and political life.[35] Marx said that injustice could be overcome by doing away with private property and establishing communism. Plato, Aristotle, Augustine, Aquinas, and Thomas More said that the attainment of justice in society always depends on the wisdom and virtue of individual citizens.

The kind of regime or social order favored by the Council is one that makes possible the attainment of the common good—that is, "the sum of those conditions of social life which allow social groups and their individual members to attain their proper perfection more fully and more quickly."[36] For this to happen, a continual effort must be made to establish a social order respectful of freedom, "founded on truth, built on justice and animated by love."[37] This project, of course, will require educating citizens to virtue so that they will fulfill their duties and respect rights. It also requires establishing the kind of society where families and religious groups can effectively pursue their mission.

The Catholic Church keeps trying to persuade people that seeking the common good requires attention to truth, justice, love, virtue, and duty in the social order. What specific initiatives should be taken by the various elements of the social order, such as the family, the Church, and the various levels of government, are not specified here, but are addressed in chapter 4 of part I and in part II of *Gaudium et spes*. The council document does say that the political community exists on account of the common good. Thus, the government should try to make possible the attainment of the common good, substantively understood, through its own action and by relying on the various elements of the social order.

35. Cf. Immanuel Kant, *Perpetual Peace and Other Essays* (Indianapolis, Ind.: Hackett, 1983), 124.

36. *Gaudium et spes*, no. 26, modified translation.

37. Ibid.

Here are some examples of how government could properly promote a substantive common good, which I judge to be in accordance with the teaching of *Gaudium et spes*. Public schools, which are agents of government, necessarily inculcate diligence and teach students to respect one another and not to cheat on exams. The law prohibits murder, rape, and robbery. It may properly give people incentives to stay married, erect obstacles to divorce, and pass laws protecting the life of the unborn and forbidding euthanasia, and even teach through the laws that marriage can only take place between a man and a woman. By making use of the "bully pulpit" the president may invite citizens to volunteer services to their country, as John Kennedy famously did.

One of the reasons many have not grasped the full teaching of *Gaudium et spes* is that the Council doesn't specify clearly enough what its definition of the common good means. When it gives specific examples of the common good, it lists things that would be the object of any procedural republic:

[F]ood, clothing, and shelter; the right to choose a state of life freely and to found a family, the rights to education, to employment, to a good reputation, to respect, to appropriate information, to activity in accord with the upright norm of one's conscience, to protection of privacy and to rightful freedom in matters religious too.[38]

The requirements of human dignity, and therefore, of the common good, entail much more than this list indicates, as we have previously indicated. The Council, however, did spell out what the dignity of the human person requires in and from the social order, as we have seen in the previous chapter, thereby shedding more light on the shape of the common good.

Because of the dignity of the human person, *Gaudium et spes* implies that neither the mores should support, nor the law allow, any of the following:

[A]ny type of murder, genocide, abortion, euthanasia, or voluntary suicide; whatever violates the integrity of the human person, such as mutilation, torments inflicted on body or mind, attempts to coerce the will itself; whatever offends human dignity, such as subhuman living conditions, arbitrary imprisonment, deportation, slavery, prostitution, the selling of women and children; as well as ignominious working conditions...and other disgraceful things of this sort.[39]

38. Ibid.
39. Ibid., no. 27, modified translation.

While this list is obviously not meant to be exhaustive, it is sufficiently inclusive to indicate what kinds of things should receive no support from the law or the mores. The obvious reason is that the practice of these things is an assault on human dignity. The less obvious reason is that such behavior "defiles those who do them more than those who suffer the injustice."[40] In other words, the doers of evil deeds act beneath their own dignity. This fact indicates that the common good must include concern for the character of citizens. In some instances, then, the law should not only protect citizens from being the victims of injustice, but also prevent others from being perpetrators of injustice. This approach of the Council brings to mind a statement of St. Augustine on the justification for the use of force against evildoers. "He whose license for wrongdoing is wrested away is usefully conquered, for nothing is less prosperous than the prosperity of sinners, which nourishes punishable impunity and strengthens the evil will, which is, as it were, an enemy within."[41]

After reading the last section of the chapter on community, one cannot but notice that the Council fathers leave the realm of politics and civil society and focus on the life of the Church. While most of the chapter focuses on the common good of civil society, this last section exclusively discusses sanctification, solidarity, and social unity in the Church. These goals must always be pursued by the Church, whatever the state of civil society and the political order. When the Church fulfills its salvific mission, it will make significant contributions to the common good of civil society. Even when civil society fails to be a place of solidarity among citizens, the Church can still provide a haven for its members who seek sanctification in a community bound together by solidarity. Their holiness and solidarity with their fellow citizens will necessarily promote the common good.

Part I, Chapter 3: "Human Action in the World"

Through good human action people change the world for the better and ennoble themselves. The ennobling or perfection is, of course, the ultimate end of human action. For "a man is more precious for what he is than for what he has. Similarly, all that men do to obtain greater jus-

40. Ibid., modified translation.
41. "Letter 138 to Marcellinus," in Augustine, *Political Writings*, translated by Michael W. Tkacz and Douglas Kries, edited by Ernest Fortin and Douglas Kries (Indianapolis, Ind.: Hackett, 1994), 209.

tice, wider brotherhood, and a more humane ordering of social relationships has greater worth than technical advances."[42] The Council is surely implying that it is not science and technology that will bring about a
just society, but the new commandment of love Christ taught us, which is
"the basic law of human perfection and hence of the world's transformation."[43] This latter statement is still another way the Council expresses
its agreement with the teaching of Augustine and Aquinas: the common
good of society depends on the perfection of individual souls.

The Council injects a note of realism in pointing out that human action in view of individual perfection and the world's transformation will
always be engaged in a "monumental struggle against the powers of dark-
ness."[44] People will encounter opposition in themselves and in the world
when they work for peace and justice out of love for God and neighbor.
The only solution is for human beings, constantly threatened by pride
and disordered self-love in their activity, to be "purified and perfected by
the power of Christ's cross and resurrection"[45] and to be nourished by
the body and blood of Christ, the viaticum for the journey back to God.
By these remarks the Council is surely implying that the Church plays a
major role in helping individuals to achieve perfection in their action to
transform the world.

Part II, Chapter 1, "On Fostering the Dignity of Marriage and the Family"

While the subject matter of chapter 1 of the first part of *Gaudium et spes*
is the dignity of the human person, the first chapter of the second part is
entitled "On Fostering the Dignity of Marriage and the Family." This is
a fitting parallelism. The key text reads, "The well-being [*salus*] of the person and of human and Christian society is intimately connected with the
healthy condition of marriage and the family."[46] It is in the family that
parents ennoble themselves by bringing children into the world and educating them in the faith. Children first learn to practice virtue and become aware of their duties toward others. Because so many great goods
flow from domestic well-being, *Gaudium et spes* urges both civil society and
the government to promote the good of marriage and the family. The
specific recommendation to government is instructive. "Public authority

---

42. *Gaudium et spes*, no. 35.   43. Ibid., no. 38.
44. Ibid., no. 37.   45. Ibid.
46. Ibid., no. 47, modified translation.

should regard it as a sacred duty to recognize, protect, and promote their authentic nature, to shield public morality, and to favor the prosperity of domestic life."[47] Since "the political community exists for [the]common good,"[48] the latter must include the protection of public morality and efforts by the government to promote the mission of the family.

Part II, Chapter 4, "The Life of the Political Community"

In chapter 4, on the life of the political community, the Council fathers say that the political-juridical order should protect personal rights in order to show respect for human dignity and to make possible the participation of citizens at all levels of government. It is through participation in government and in the life of civil society that citizens are able to contribute to the realization of the common good through the fulfillment of their legal and moral duties. Ultimately, government protects rights so that people will be able to achieve perfection through the practice of the virtues in the service of the common good. The priority of virtues and duties over rights is clearly indicated by the following statement: "No better way exists for attaining a truly human political life than by fostering an inner sense of justice, benevolence, and service for the common good."[49] In other words, the virtues of love and justice contribute to a human political life and therefore to the common good of the political community.

This section of *Gaudium et spes* also sheds light on the meaning of the common good by what it says about the role of the Church in the political order. "For she is at once a sign and a safeguard of the transcendence of the human person....She also has the right to pass moral judgments, even on matters touching the political order, whenever basic personal rights or the salvation of souls make such judgments necessary."[50] The Church is faithful to this conciliar teaching when it defends life, traditional marriage, religious freedom, and public morality. By exercising these roles, the Church is necessarily contributing to the realization of a substantive common good.

Part II, Chapter 5, "The Fostering of Peace and the Promotion of a Community of Nations"

In the next chapter *Gaudium et spes* teaches that peace is "'a work of justice' (Is 32:17)" and "likewise the fruit of love, which goes beyond what

47. Ibid., no. 52.   48. Ibid., no. 74.
49. Ibid., no. 73.   50. Ibid., no. 76.

justice can provide."[51] No one can doubt that peace is an important element of the common good. If peace depends on the practice of charity and justice, then these virtues are an essential part of the common good. It is also not surprising to find in this same section a general statement about the common good, which reads: "The common good of the human race is in its basic sense governed by the eternal law."[52] As the eternal law is not focused on instrumental goods, this is surely another indication that the common good of political communities must include the *bona animi*, the goods of the soul.

Conclusion: The Mission of the Church and the Common Good

By proposing a high, substantive notion of the common good, the Church is asking a lot of the political community—more than it can deliver most of the time. Even though the mission of the Church is not political, but religious, it still is able to offer valuable help to the political community in its work for the common good by remaining faithful to its salvific mission. *Gaudium et spes* explains: "But out of this religious mission itself comes a duty [*munus*], a light, and forces which can serve to structure and consolidate the human community according to the divine law."[53] The Church tries to persuade the world that a "genuine external social union has its origin in the union of minds and hearts," especially by faith and love. But the Church does more than teach. "The force which the church can inject into modern society consists in that faith and charity put into vital practice, not in any external dominion exercised by merely human means."[54] In other words, the Church provides citizens to nations who have the wisdom and courage to work for the common good.

The Church also teaches lay Christians that they have an obligation in conscience "to see that the divine law is inscribed in the life of the earthly city."[55] Again, this is practically an impossible task to accomplish throughout society, but feasible in selected instances. For example, maintaining the legal prohibition of euthanasia in the United States is not yet out of reach. The Council, of course, recognizes that the people of the world need encouragement to face the challenge of working for a high-level, common good. Hence, the Council implies that the life and words of all members of the Church must continually show that "the Church,

51. Ibid., no. 78, modified translation.   52. Ibid., modified translation.
53. Ibid., no. 42, modified translation.   54. Ibid.
55. Ibid., no. 43.

by her presence alone and by all the gifts which she possesses, is the inexhaustible source of those virtues which the modern world most needs."[56]

I would like to conclude my brief review of points in *Gaudium et spes* by citing a passage that sums up the contribution of the Church to the common good of civil society: "When the Church, in pursuit of its divine mission, preaches the gospel and imparts the treasures of grace to all, it is contributing throughout the world to the strengthening of peace and helping to lay what is the firm foundation of community among individuals and peoples, namely, knowledge of the divine and natural law."[57] Observance of the natural law, the divine law, and the reception of grace are all necessary for realizing an elevated common life in the nations of the world.

Vatican Council II: *Dignitatis Humanae*

Turning now to Vatican Council II's *Dignitatis humanae*, we find several statements that further clarify the meaning of the common good and the nature of the government's responsibility toward the political community. In this document Vatican Council II declares that all people have a right to religious freedom and recognizes the right of all churches and religious communities to immunity from coercion in what concerns religious belief, worship, practice, or observance, public testimony, and the internal autonomy of the Church itself. The Council states that the "freedom of the Church is the fundamental principle in what concerns the relations between the Church and the public powers and the whole civil order."[58] The Church must be free from government interference to bring Christ's message of salvation to all.

The government's role, according to *Dignitatis humanae*, is to make religious freedom a civil right by the appropriate constitutional guarantees. The government does not have the power to command or inhibit the performance of religious acts by individuals or associations. Of course, it cannot prescribe or proscribe religious beliefs or forms of worship, nor can government require attendance in a school from which all religion is excluded or force children to attend any kind of religious instruction that is contrary to their religious beliefs. What the government can and

56. Ibid., modified translation.
57. Ibid., no. 89, modified translation.
58. *Dignitatis humanae*, no. 13, modified translation.

should do "through just laws and other suitable means" is "to create conditions favorable to the fostering of religious life."[59] The Council fathers go so far as to say that civil authority "should certainly recognize and promote the religious life of its citizens" as a way of providing for the "temporal common good" (*bonum commune temporale*) of the political community.[60] Because of government action people will be able to exercise their religious rights and observe duties, and as a result "society itself will benefit from the goods of justice and peace which result from people's fidelity to God and his holy will."[61] Since *Dignitatis humanae* affirms that the common good of society "especially consists in the protection of the human person's rights and the performance of duties,"[62] then the fulfillment of religious duties is an integral part of the common good.

Dignitatis humanae doesn't make clear exactly what the government could or should do to promote conditions favorable to religion. One could argue persuasively that the government cannot fulfill its responsibilities toward religion without promoting a public morality, including the practice of various virtues. A legally enforced public morality sets a tone in a society and a culture that facilitates the development and preservation of faith in the life of citizens. At the very least, the government should not be neutral toward religion, but convey in various ways that it is important for the well-being of the regime. "If the state is indifferent to religion...," argues Ernest Fortin, "chances are most of its citizens will be indifferent as well."[63] As things stand in American liberal democracy, the state often claims to provide a neutral framework "within which each individual is allowed to choose his own goal and find his own way to it."[64] When the

---

59. Ibid., no. 6; several English translations don't make crystal clear that the Vatican Council is recommending the use of law "to create conditions favorable to the fostering of religious life." The pertinent Latin text is as follows: Debet igitur potestas civilis per iustas leges et per alia media apta suscipere tutelam libertatis religiosae omnium civium, ac propitias suppeditare condiciones ad vitam religiosam fovendam, ut cives revera religionis iura exercere eiusdemque officia adimplere valeant et ipsa societas fruatur bonis iustitiae et pacis, quae proveniunt ex fidelitate hominum erga Deum eiusque sanctam voluntatem.

60. *Dignitatis humanae*, no. 3, modified translation.

61. Ibid., no. 6, modified translation.

62. Ibid., no. 6, modified translation.

63. Ernest L. Fortin, *Human Rights, Virtue, and the Common Good: Untimely Meditations on Religion and Politics*, vol. 3 of *Collected Essays*, edited by J. Brian Benestad (Lanham, Md.: Rowman and Littlefield, 1996), 11.

64. Ibid., 11.

state denies religion any intrinsic claim to respect, people have more difficulty in living up to the stringent demands of their faith, especially when
those demands are countercultural.

The Council fathers also introduce the concept of public morality as
a part of the public order, which also includes "the effective protection
of rights for all citizens and the peaceful settlement of conflicts of rights
and a sufficient care of an honorable public peace which is an ordered living together in true justice." Then the text says that these three "constitute a fundamental part of the common good and they come under the
rubric of the public order."[65] If the common good of a society requires a
public morality and citizens living together in true justice, then instrumental goods cannot constitute the whole of the common good. There
has to be a sharing in substantive goods.

There are still other indications that the Council is recommending a
substantive common good for society. In speaking of education, the Vatican document "urges all, and especially those who have charge of educating others, to do their utmost to form people who, while respecting the
moral order obey legitimate authority and are lovers of genuine liberty."[66]
In making this exhortation the Vatican Council does not distinguish between public and private authorities. All educators are expected to form
character in a way that is appropriate to their position. All the educated
are expected to use their own judgment "to make decisions in the light
of truth." The Council also expresses the hope that "religious freedom,
therefore, ought to have this further purpose and aim, namely, that people may act with greater responsibility in fulfilling their duties in community life."[67]

Finally, the Council says, "among those things which concern the good
of the Church and indeed the good of the earthly city...this certainly is
preeminent, that the Church enjoy so much liberty of action as caring for
the salvation of all requires."[68] What the Church does for the salvation of
all is the preeminent contribution to the common good of civil society.
This reminds me of a leitmotif of John Paul II's social teaching: "We will
reach justice through evangelization." In other words, civil society cannot
achieve the common good unless individuals are good. It is the work of
evangelization that forms individuals according to the mind and heart of

65. *Dignitatis humanae*, no. 7, modified translation.
66. Ibid., no. 8, modified translation.   67. Ibid., modified translation.
68. Ibid., no. 13, modified translation.

Christ. The state, of course, doesn't do the work of evangelization, but, as we have seen, it should favor religious life so that the Church can fulfill its proper mission. Only if the Church is successful in its work will the state have a chance of realizing the common good. The state is not limited to providing instrumental goods for the Church, but prepares the way for the work of the Church by upholding various moral norms through the laws. It is also true that favoring the religious life of citizens is not an instrumental good. If the state limited itself to the promotion of instrumental goods, it would be neutral toward the churches and the practice of religion.

Pope John Paul II

In *Evangelium vitae (The Gospel of Life)* Pope John Paul II argues that the law in democratic societies ought to promote public morality and the common good. He rejects the view that ethical relativism is "an essential condition of democracy." On the contrary, the moral quality of democracy "depends on conformity to the moral law to which it like every other form of behavior, must be subject." The pope doesn't spell out all that he means, but does give revealing indications that dovetail with the teachings of Vatican II and John XXIII. A democracy in conformity with the moral law would promote the dignity of the human person, protect human rights, and have the common good as an end. The basis of these principles cannot be majority opinion, "but only the acknowledgment of an objective moral law which, as the moral law written in the human heart, is the obligatory point of reference for civil law itself." (John Paul seems to be referring to the natural law in this context.) The pope further argues that "the democratic system would be shaken to its foundations" if people come to doubt the existence of an objective moral law that can provide the foundation for the civil law.[69]

Paraphrasing *Dignitatis humanae*, John Paul II adds that the aim of the civil law, "more limited in scope than that of the moral law," is "that of ensuring the common good of people through the recognition and defense of their fundamental rights, and the promotion of peace and public morality."[70] The pope doesn't explain in detail all that this means, but does say that the legalization of abortion and euthanasia is "radically op-

69. John Paul II, *Evangelium vitae*, no. 70.
70. Ibid., no. 71.

posed" to the common good of the political community. He even adds that all members of civil society should be most solicitous "to make unconditional respect for human life the foundation of a renewed society."[71]

On October 5, 1995, shortly after the publication of *Evangelium vitae*, John Paul II delivered an address to the United Nations. He certainly did not use this occasion to tell the nations of the world that they could achieve the common good of their political communities simply by providing instrumental goods to their citizens. Instead, he directs his listeners' attention to the limitations of modern autonomy as a sufficient guide for individual and political life by suggesting that people build a "civilization of love, founded on the universal goods of peace, solidarity, justice and liberty. And the 'soul' of the civilization of love is the culture of freedom: the freedom of individuals and the freedom of nations lived in self-giving solidarity and responsibility."[72] When freedom takes its bearings by truth, the result is order in the soul as well as the civilization of love and solidarity.

Throughout his papacy Pope John Paul II spoke often and passionately of solidarity. In *Sollicitudo rei socialis (On Social Concern)* he defines it as "*a firm and persevering determination* to commit oneself to the *common good;* that is to say to the good of all and of each individual, because we are all really responsible *for all.*"[73] He goes on to describe solidarity as a Christian virtue, which inclines individuals to overcome sources of division within themselves and in society. "Structures of sin" and personal sins, in which the sinful structures are rooted, cause disorder in the soul and disunity in society. Order in the soul, of course, requires the practice of all the virtues.

Toward the very end of his speech John Paul II emphasizes that the Church must promote solidarity in addition to proposing her message of salvation: "the church asks only to be able to propose respectfully this message of salvation and to be able to promote, in charity and service, the solidarity of the entire human family."[74] In this speech to the nations of the world John Paul quite appropriately doesn't explain that the Church's work for the salvation of all peoples necessarily promotes solidarity with-

71. Ibid., no. 77.
72. "The Fiftieth General Assembly of the United Nations: Address of His Holiness John Paul II," *Origins* 25, no. 18 (October 19, 1995): 299.
73. Pope John Paul II, *Sollicitudo rei socialis (On Social Concern)*, no. 38.
74. *Origins* 25, no. 18 (October 19, 1995): 299.

in and among nations. It is also fitting that John Paul II doesn't explicitly say how radical his vision of solidarity is for liberal regimes. He is actually inviting people to be morally transformed in order to be capable of solidarity. The moral transformation of citizens is, then, an essential part of the common good.

Why does John Paul II say that the Church desires the freedom both to deliver the message of salvation and to promote solidarity among people in every nation? If he just spoke of salvation, people might not realize that the Church is interested in promoting the temporal common good of society. Not everyone realizes that the evangelization of peoples in view of salvation will promote the moral transformation of citizens and solidarity in civil society in the measure that people are willing to receive and live the truth proclaimed to them. Solidarity is a word that suggests connections among citizens in any civil society, even solicitude for one another. By using the word "solidarity," the pope is exhorting people to direct their practice of the virtues toward the realization of the common good.

I think there is still another reason for the distinction that John Paul draws between salvation and solidarity or the common good. Resting in God along with other human beings is the highest common good. The common good of the political community prepares and disposes individuals for the attainment of such a lofty goal. It is, then, a subordinate, though substantive, common good that takes various shapes in different sectors of society. For example, it is helpful to speak of the common good of families, associations, cities, and the nation.

The very beginning of Vatican II's *Lumen gentium (Dogmatic Constitution on the Church)* has a powerful statement on the centrality of the highest common good in the life of the Church: "By her relationship with Christ the Church is a kind of sacrament of intimate union with God, and of the unity of all mankind, that is, she is a sign and instrument of such union and unity."[75] In other words, the Church's mission of salvation is to help people seek and achieve forgiveness of their sins so that they might be free for greater and greater union with God and with one another through Christ. The Church will carry out this salvific work in whatever regime it happens to find itself.

No person properly seeks salvation for himself alone. He wants all people to share his liberation from sin and his union with God. To affirm the primacy of the highest common good is to desire that all human be-

75. Vatican Council II, *Lumen gentium (Dogmatic Constitution on the Church)*, no. 1.

ings participate in the life of God and that all are united in that participation. To will the end is to will the means. Therefore, those desirous of
salvation pray that everyone's trespasses will be forgiven and that all live
virtuously in the eyes of God. It may seem ironic that seeking God as the
highest common good leads to the greatest respect for the dignity of every human person. That dignity, as we saw in chapter 1, consists not in
simply having reason and the power of choice, but in actually reaching
God through the practice of the Christian virtues. So, respecting people's
dignity is to pray and work for their salvation. The whole message of salvation proclaimed by the Church teaches people that, as parts of a whole,
they are ordered to the greatest of all goods, union with God.

While the Church will always be successful in helping individuals to
achieve salvation or the highest common good, it can only reasonably
hope to be partially successful in transforming society. There may or may
not be a critical mass of transformed individuals to have a noticeable effect on the structures or institutions of society. What success the Church
has in getting a hearing for its message of salvation may not be enough
to be that visible in society. Besides, visible transformations of society are
never definitively possessed and can be lost for a time or indefinitely. Pope
John Paul II, however, certainly agrees with Augustine's view that a significant Christian impact is always possible in society:

Hence, let those who say that the teaching of Christ is contrary to the republic
give us an army of the sort of soldiers that the teaching of Christ commands.
Let them give us such provincial subjects, such husbands, wives, parents, children, masters, servants, kings, judges, and finally such taxpayers and collec-
tors of public taxes of the sort commanded by Christian teaching, and then let
them dare to say that this teaching is contrary to the republic; indeed let them
even hesitate to confess that it is, if observed, a great benefit for the republic.[76]

If Christian teaching is observed, then great benefits ensue. There are no
guarantees that the teaching of Christ will be widely accepted. The idea
of inevitable progress is alien to Christian doctrine.

The end of the political community is to establish a suitable order by
aiming at a subordinate common good. We have seen that neither Pope
John XXIII nor Vatican Council II's *Gaudium et spes* and *Dignitatis humanae*
understand the common good to be simply a list of instrumental goods.
Pope John Paul II's *Evangelium vitae* shows familiarity with John XXIII's

---

76. "Letter 138, to Marcellinus," in Augustine, *Political Writings*, 209–10.

thought and yet still argues that a society needs more than instrumental goods to achieve its common good. John Paul II's speech to the UN offers helpful guidance by distinguishing the Church's mission of salvation from her work to promote solidarity.

Pope Benedict XVI's First Encyclical and First Apostolic Exhortation

While the first section has discussed Pope Benedict's thought on Catholic social doctrine in general, this short section will explicitly focus on Benedict's contribution to thinking about the common good. In his first encyclical, *Deus caritas est* (DCE), Pope Benedict briefly summarized what the Church can do to promote the common good. As mentioned, he points out that the aim of Catholic social doctrine is to help purify reason so that people are more able to see what justice requires in every situation.[77] This is an indispensable task, since people, blinded by interests and power, often cannot perceive the requirements of justice. The Church also has the potential for contributing to the attainment of the common good by forming consciences and inspiring individuals to take action in the political and social order. Pope Benedict explains, "The Church wishes to help form consciences in political life and to stimulate greater insight into the authentic requirements of justice as well as greater readiness to act accordingly, even when this might involve conflict with situations of personal interest."[78] (Chapter 4 will present the comprehensive teaching of Catholic social doctrine on the various meanings of justice: distributive, commutative, legal, or social justice.)

Pope Benedict also reminds his readers that the common good not only requires justice, but also the practice of love. If "the just ordering of society and the State is a central responsibility of politics,"[79] the service of love belongs to individuals, the Church, and other mediating institutions. Pope Benedict argues that justice, however perfectly realized, is never sufficient, because human life always requires the giving and receiving of love. The service of charity is as important to the Church as the preaching of the Word and the administration of the sacraments, and it is crucial for the happiness of citizens in every country. (Pope Paul VI and Pope John Paul II kept speaking of the civilization of love.)

---

77. Benedict XVI, *Deus caritas est (God is Love)*, no. 28.
78. Ibid.   79. Ibid.

In his first apostolic exhortation, *Sacramentum caritatis* (*On the Eucharist as the Source and Summit of the Church's Life and Mission*), made public on March 13, 2007, Pope Benedict shed more light on his view of the government's role in promoting the common good in the following statement on Catholic politicians:

Here it is important to consider what the synod fathers described as eucharistic consistency, a quality which our lives are objectively called to embody. Worship pleasing to God can never be a purely private matter, without consequences for our relationships with others: it demands a public witness to our faith. Evidently, this is true for all the baptized, yet it is especially incumbent upon those who, by virtue of their social or political position, must make decisions regarding fundamental values, such as respect for human life, its defense from conception to natural death, the family built upon marriage between a man and a woman, the freedom to educate one's children and the promotion of the common good in all its forms. These values are not negotiable. Consequently, Catholic politicians and legislators, conscious of their grave responsibility before society, must feel particularly bound, on the basis of a properly formed conscience, to introduce and support laws inspired by values grounded in human nature. There is an objective connection here with the Eucharist (cf. 1 Cor 11:27–29). Bishops are bound to reaffirm constantly these values as part of their responsibility to the flock entrusted to them.[80]

In this paragraph the pope is clearly implying that the common good requires laws prohibiting abortion and euthanasia, upholding traditional marriage, and defending the religious freedom of parents. He also calls on Catholic politicians to support these kinds of laws and others that will likewise promote the common good. There is no room in this perspective for Catholics to say that they are personally opposed to abortion, but would on principle not seek legislation prohibiting its widespread practice.

Cardinal Bertone on the Common Good

The new Vatican Secretary of State, Cardinal Tarcisio Bertone, recently addressed the theme of love and the common good in a 2007 publication, *L'Etica del bene commune* (*The Ethics of the Common Good*), reinforcing the

---

80. Benedict XVI, *Sacramentum caritatis* (*On the Eucharist as the Source and Summit of the Church's Life and Mission*), no. 83.

teaching of Pope Benedict XVI on the same subject. Cardinal Bertone argues that it is not enough to aim at a free and just society; "the Christian aims at the fraternal society," by which Cardinal Bertone means a society characterized by love. To promote a fraternal society Christians "must be in a position to show that the principle of fraternity is capable of inspiring concrete options on the political agenda."[81] He then refers to the *Compendium of the Social Doctrine of the Church* to buttress his point. The *Compendium* argues that it is not enough for living together in civil and political society to draw up an inventory of rights and duties. "Such living together acquires its whole significance if based on civil friendship and on fraternity."[82] That friendship entails detachment from material goods, the generous gift of one's own goods and service, and the interior inclination to respond to the needs of others. Cardinal Bertone goes so far as to quote an early writing of Jacques Maritain, who wrote, "Fraternity in society requires the most noble and generous of the virtues to enter into the very order of political life."[83] The cardinal concludes by pointing out that "the central message that Benedict XVI's encyclical sends to us is that of considering gratuity, that is to say fraternity, as a point of reference of the human condition."[84] Without the practice of fraternity or love, neither the state nor the market will be able to function in view of the common good. Even in a simply just society, unless citizens are generous toward one another, "persons will not be aided to realize the joy of living."[85]

Concluding Reflections on the Understanding and Pursuit of the Common Good

Let us call to mind Pope John XXIII's famous definition of the common good, as slightly reformulated by the *Catechism of the Catholic Church:* "the sum total of the conditions of social life which allow people, either as groups or individuals, to reach their own perfection more fully and more easily." In the explanation of this definition the following clarifications have become necessary. The perfection of each citizen is the goal of

81. Cardinal Tarcisio Bertone, *L'Etica del Bene Commune nella Dottrina Sociale della Chiesa* (Vatican City: Libreria Editrice Vaticana, 2007), 39.
82. Ibid., 40, quoting the *Compendium of the Social Doctrine of the Church*, no. 390.
83. Bertone, *L'Etica del Bene Commune*, 27; quoting Jacques Maritain, *I Believe* (New York: Simon and Schuster, 1939), 10.
84. *L'Etica del Bene Commune*, 55.
85. Ibid., 56.

civil society and is, therefore, an essential part of the common good. The various social conditions helpful for the pursuit of perfection making up the common good should be listed and described. Establishing the requisite social conditions and educating individuals to perfection are the shared responsibility of government, the Church, voluntary associations, and individuals themselves. In other words, the government must not attempt to realize all elements of the common good, but respect the principle of subsidiarity. When that principle is observed, there is less chance of improper intrusion on the part of the government and more chance of success in the combined efforts to achieve the common good. And the common good is only rightly conceived when it is understood to be the good of every individual in a society. CSD recommends that certain social conditions be established so that individuals will be able to seek perfection without too many obstacles and with appropriate help.

The term "perfection" does not, of course, have a univocal meaning, especially in a liberal society. Catholics would necessarily understand perfection as the imitation of Jesus Christ and union with God, but would recognize other religious and philosophic understandings of perfection as a preparation for, or partial realization of, the way taught by Jesus. Some understandings of perfection would surely be at odds with the Catholic view. Be that as it may, Catholics are always bound by the ideal of Christian perfection and would rely on the family, Church, educational institutions, other voluntary associations, and the law to promote perfection as they understand it. What the law could and should achieve in a liberal society will always be a subject for debate, in which Catholics have the right and duty to participate. In accord with their understanding of the common good, Catholics would also support efforts by individuals, voluntary associations, and the government to promote sound but incomplete understandings of perfection.

The social conditions "which allow people...to reach their proper perfection" may, at first glance, seem too difficult to name or describe. Perfection is not a common term in a liberal society. Citizens and theorists would more readily speak of social conditions conducive to the attainment or preservation of liberty and equality. The attainment of perfection would require a special set of social conditions, hardly limited to instrumental goods. According to Catholic social teaching some of these conditions are as follows: respect for life (e.g., no abortion, euthanasia, or destruction of embryos), religious freedom, the fidelity of the Catholic Church to its salvific mission, fidelity in marriages, sound family life, character education in families and schools, comprehensive liberal education in the universities, high ethical principles in places of work (the trades, business and the professions), true friendships, concord or harmony among citizens, forgiveness of injuries and reconciliation among citizens who have committed and suffered wrong, education and care for the poor. How these goals could be attained through persuasion and law is beyond the scope of this chapter.

My final comment is on the practicality of the Church's teaching on the necessity of pursuing a substantive common good in every society. This teaching doesn't mean that Christians have to engage in utopian political reform. St. Augustine indirectly offers us some timely advice on how to proceed in his reflections on the nature of a republic. In *De civitate Dei* Augustine comments on the definition of a republic given by Scipio in Cicero's *De re publica*. Scipio says that a republic is "the affair of a people." He then defines people as a "fellowship of a multitude united through a consensus concerning right and a sharing of advantage."[86] Augustine then explains that there can be no "consensus concerning right" without justice. In Augustine's radical formulation justice requires order in the soul of citizens. Reason rules the vices and, in turn, is subject to God through the practice of the Christian virtues. If there is no justice in individuals, "without doubt neither is there any in a fellowship of human beings which consists of such men." So, without justice so understood there can be no consensus concerning right and, thus, no real republic. This seems to be a description of a common good that would be as close to communion with God as one can imagine on this earth.

Augustine's second and more realistic definition of a republic is "a fellowship of a multitude of rational beings united through a sharing in and agreement about what it loves....It is a better people if it agrees in loving better things; a worse one if it agrees in loving worse things."[87] Otherwise stated, there can be various levels of solidarity or forms of a subordinate good in any particular regime. Citizens inspired by a Catholic vision of the common good have a paradigm in Augustine's first definition of a republic by which to take their bearings in prudently working to refine and elevate the agreement about what the political community loves.

86. Augustine, *Political Writings, The City of God*, book XIX, chap. 21, 160.
87. Ibid., chap. 24.

Reasons for Catholic Teaching on the Common Good

Why does the Church even have a teaching on the common good of the political community? The answer to that question is not complicated. The realization of the common good facilitates the attainment of salvation. Since good laws and mores dispose people to receive Christian teaching and live a Christian life, and bad laws and mores do the opposite, the Church attempts to persuade political communities to establish and maintain good laws and mores, or in the language of classical political philosophy, a good regime. Pius XII made this point in his 1941 Pentecost message, in which he says that the Church "must take cognizance of social conditions, which, whether one wills it or not, make difficult or practically impossible a Christian life in conformity with the precepts of the Divine Lawgiver."[88] He says that people need to "breathe the healthy vivifying atmosphere of truth and moral virtue" and not "the disease laden and often fatal air of error and corruption." As a precedent and proof of his position, Pius XII cites Leo XIII's encyclical to the world, *Rerum novarum*, which "pointed out the dangers of the materialist Socialism conception, the fatal consequences of economic Liberalism, so often unaware, or forgetful, or contemptuous of social duties." Around the time that Pius XII was thinking about the significance of social conditions for the faith, a famous French theologian, Yves de Montcheuil, S.J., addressed the same subject in an essay entitled "Christian life and Temporal Action." He wrote: "The repercussions of political and social conditions in the lives of individuals can, in fact, render easier or more difficult the birth and development of religious life in humanity. It is therefore the duty of the Christian to create in this world conditions favorable to Christian life."[89] He also told his readers that *Rerum novarum* reminded Catholics of this obligation. Montcheuil and Pius XII clearly do not limit their understanding of social conditions to instrumental goods. They have to be talking about those substantive elements of the common good that dispose people to be receptive to the gift of salvation.

The second reason for the Church's social teaching is that the realization of a subordinate common good is a partial expression of the way human beings ought to live together. The dignity of the human person

---

88. *Acta Apostolicae Sedis* 33 (1941): 218–19.

89. Yves de Montcheuil, S.J., *Problèmes de Vie Spirituelle* (Paris: Editions de L'Epi, 1961), 199.

not only requires freedom for each individual, but a life dedicated to the practice of virtue and harmony among people based on truth. The Church's teaching on the common good provides guidelines not only for political authorities and the mediating institutions of civil society, but also for individuals living in every kind of regime. The latter can always practice virtue in view of the common good, even if they live under a corrupt government.

CHAPTER 3

Seeking the Common Good through
Virtue and Grace

Virtue in Augustine and Aquinas

While many things contribute to the attainment of the common good, virtue (including wisdom) and grace deserve special mention. The *Catechism* sets the proper tone in the section on the human community with the following statement: "It is necessary, then, to appeal to the spiritual and moral capacities of the human person and to the permanent need for his *inner conversion,* so as to obtain social changes that will really serve him."[1] Otherwise stated, conversion leading to love of God and neighbor and the practice of all the virtues is the necessary condition for obtaining social reform. So that there is no misunderstanding in the meaning of the text, the *Catechism* adds,

The acknowledged priority of the conversion of heart in no way eliminates but on the contrary imposes the obligation of bringing the appropriate remedies to institutions and living conditions when they are an inducement to sin, so that they conform to the norms of justice and advance the good rather than hinder it.[2]

In other words, it is not really possible to bring about the reform of institutions and living conditions unless people really know and want to do the right thing, and the desire to do the right thing must include efforts to reform institutions and establish societal conditions favorable to virtue. Recall the discussion of this matter at the end of the previous chapter.

Finally, the *Catechism* links conversion, love (namely, the theological virtue of charity), and social reform to grace. The text reads,

---

1. *Catechism of the Catholic Church* (Vatican City: Libreria Editrice Vaticana, 1994), no. 1888.
2. *Catechism of the Catholic Church*, no. 1888.

Without the help of grace, men would not know how "to discern the often narrow path between the cowardice which gives in to evil, and the violence which under the illusion of fighting evil only makes it worse." This is the path of charity, that is of the love of God and neighbor. Charity is the greatest social commandment. It respects others and their rights. It requires the practice of justice, and it alone makes us capable of it. Charity inspires a life of self-giving.[3]

To put this in Augustinian terms, grace is the true bond of society because it makes possible genuine love of God and neighbor, not to mention respect for human rights. The *Catechism* clearly implies that rights are not the primary moral counter. Having rights doesn't transform the soul and, therefore, doesn't necessarily incline a person to love God and neighbor. Charity, on the other hand, transforms people and causes them to respect the genuine rights of fellow human beings. This catechetical teaching, with roots in the grand Catholic tradition, has enormous implications for the way rights are conceived and approached, and for the place of virtue and grace in Catholic social doctrine (CSD). The proclamation of rights cannot deliver all that seekers of social justice expect unless individuals have order in their soul produced by charity and the other virtues. The virtues and grace, therefore, deserve a place in the line-up of major themes of CSD, whether in scholarly studies or episcopal statements.

Pope Benedict XVI's *Salt of the Earth* has a nice statement on the theme of social problems caused by disorder in the soul or lack of virtue. He says,

[T]he pollution of the outward environment that we are witnessing is only the mirror and consequence of the pollution of the inward environment, to which we pay too little heed. I think this is also the defect of the ecological movements. They crusade with an understandable and also a legitimate passion against the pollution of the environment, whereas man's self-pollution of his soul continues to be treated as one of the rights of his freedom. There is a discrepancy here. We want to eliminate the measurable pollution, but we don't consider the pollution of man's soul....As long as we retain this caricature of freedom, namely, of the freedom of inner self-destruction, its outward effects will continue unchanged.[4]

3. *Catechism of the Catholic Church*, no. 1889, quoting Pope John Paul II's *Centesimus annus*, no. 25.

4. Joseph Ratzinger, *Salt of the Earth: The Catholic Church at the End of the Millenium—An Interview with Peter Seewald* (San Francisco: Ignatius Press, 1997), 230–31.

Environmental problems are caused by disorder in people's souls, as are all other social problems in one way or another.

A detailed explanation of the cardinal and theological virtues is important in order to see in detail why the common good depends on their practice. The Latin derivation of the word "cardinal" tells us a lot about the function of the cardinal virtues. It derives from the Latin word *cardo*, which means hinge. The moral life and the common good hinge on the practice of these virtues. As Pope John Paul II was leaving the United States in the fall of 1995, he said,

Today the challenge facing America is to find freedom's fulfillment in the truth....I say this to the United States of America: Today, in our world as it is, many other nations and peoples look to you as the principal model and pattern for their own advancement in democracy. But democracy needs wisdom. Democracy needs virtue, if it is not to turn against everything that it is meant to defend and encourage.[5]

Given the all-too-common view that virtue is a private affair, it is not superfluous to point out that Aquinas refers to the cardinal virtues as social virtues. "Since man by nature is a social animal, these cardinal virtues, insofar as they are in him according to the condition of his nature, are called social virtues; since it is by reason of them that man behaves well in the conduct of his affairs."[6]

After listening to Pope John Paul II's speeches any thoughtful person will ask himself, what does the pope understand by virtue, and could he reasonably expect segments of American culture to become inquisitive and enthusiastic about his understanding of virtue, especially given the fascination with autonomy and the predominance of rights talk in America? In this chapter I will present an account of the Catholic understanding of the virtues so as to make clear how living a life of virtues would contribute to the common good of the United States. "Virtue in General" gives a theoretical presentation of the theological and cardinal virtues (except for justice, which will be treated in the next chapter), based especially on the writings of Augustine and Aquinas. Using two famous novels, Jane Austen's *Persuasion* (1818) and Alessandro Manzoni's *The Betrothed* (1840), "Virtue in Two Novels" shows how these virtues manifest themselves in everyday life and transform the lives of ordinary people.

5. Pope John Paul II, "The Fiftieth General Assembly of the United Nations Organization: Address of His Holiness John Paul II," *Origins* 25, no. 18 (1995): 314.

6. Thomas Aquinas, *Summa theologiae*, I-II, qu. 61, a. 5.

Virtue in General

The use of the word "virtue" has not been heard in public until very recently. People more readily speak of values, rights, good character, moral or ethical conduct, fairness, and integrity. Even in Catholic circles virtue is no longer a familiar word. Asking a freshman theology class at a Catholic university to name a virtue is usually a conversation stopper. In response to silence, I usually ask students to take a guess, to say something. On one occasion a student said "cleanliness," no doubt thinking of the proverb "cleanliness is next to godliness." On another occasion a student came closer to the mark by saying "patience." I couldn't help but think that the source of this answer was not some kind of religious instruction, but the maxim "patience is a virtue." In all my years of teaching no one ever responded "prudence, justice, temperance, and fortitude," or "faith, hope, and charity." This is not to say that many students and other Americans don't practice these virtues in their everyday lives. Most simply can't describe their thoughts, desires, words, and deeds in terms of virtue.

Nevertheless, publications such as Alasdair MacIntyre's *After Virtue* have given rise to "virtue talk" and "virtue theory" in academic circles. The emphasis on social justice among Catholics has gradually increased interest in the older concepts of the common good and virtue. The revival of core curricula in universities has, in many instances, led to the rediscovery of older books in which virtue is a common theme.

In Christian theologians such as Ambrose, Augustine, and Aquinas, some common descriptions of virtue are as follows: order in the soul, well-ordered reason, the proper control of the passions by reason, the good use of free choice, living according to nature, living according to reason, compliance with God's will or the divine law, love of God and neighbor, and friendship of man for God.

St. Augustine defines virtue as "the perfect love of God." He then refines this definition by adding that virtue is fourfold:

Temperance is love giving itself wholeheartedly to that which is loved, fortitude is love enduring all things willingly for the sake of that which is loved, justice is love serving alone that which is loved, and thus ruling rightly, and prudence is love choosing wisely between that which helps it and that which hinders it.[7]

7. St. Augustine, *Catholic and Manichaean Ways of Life* (*De Moribus Ecclesiae Catholicae et de Moribus Manichaeorum*) (Washington, D.C.: The Catholic University of America Press, 1966); hereafter *De moribus ecclesiae catholicae*, chap. 15, no. 25.

This love of God, for Augustine, is an attitude and activity that engages a person's whole mind, heart, and soul. He goes so far as to say, "when the divine majesty has begun to reveal itself in the measure proper to man while an inhabitant of earth, then, such ardent charity is engendered, and such a flame of divine love bursts forth that all vices are burned away and man is purged and sanctified."[8] The fervor of charity consumes vices such as envy, gluttony, drunkenness, avarice, and anger. In other words, a passionate love of God and neighbor gives a person motivation to overcome sinful habits, always, of course, with the necessary help of God's grace.

Thomas Aquinas says that nothing in the Gospel is taught that does not pertain to virtue.[9] Aquinas continually points out that virtue makes people good and their work good. His precise definition of virtue is as follows: "Virtue is a good quality of the mind, by which we live rightly, of which no one can make bad use, which God works in us without us." Aquinas affirms that this definition, originally put forward by Peter Lombard, "expresses perfectly the whole nature of virtue," because it includes all the causes of virtue. The formal cause of virtue is a good quality or, more appropriately stated, a "good habit." The object of virtue or "the matter about which it is concerned" does not appear, because Aquinas wants to present a general definition of virtue. Specification of the object would require a reference to the function of each particular virtue. Consequently, Aquinas only mentions the ultimate subject of virtue or "the matter in which" virtue is found, that is, the mind or reason. Virtue can only be in the concupiscible or irascible appetites insofar as they participate in reason by following its commands. That the end of virtue is a good operation is expressed by the words "by which we live rightly." That virtue consists of habits continually inclining a person to the good is indicated by the words "of which no one can make bad use." The efficient cause of virtue is God, indicated by the clause "which God works in us without us." Both the theological and cardinal virtues (respectively, faith, hope, and charity; prudence, justice, temperance, and fortitude) can be infused by God "without acts on our part, but not without our consent." In other words, free will must cooperate with divine grace.[10] The cardinal virtues can also be acquired by habituation with the help of divine grace.

Possession of the cardinal or principal virtues gives not only the ability

8. Ibid., chap. 30, no. 64.
9. Aquinas, *Summa theologiae*, II-II, qu. 117, a. 1.
10. Ibid., I-II, qu. 55, a. 4.

to be good, "but also causes the performing of a good action." The cardinal virtues exhibit the perfect notion of virtue because they bring about "rectitude of appetite."[11] Intellectual virtue, on the contrary, simply gives an ability to perform a good action. A person in possession of intellectual virtues, except for prudence, may choose to use them or not. The theological virtues are similar to the moral virtues, since they also cause "the performing of a good action." Like Augustine, Aquinas also stresses the involvement of heart and mind in the practice of virtue. He explains, "But if a passion follows a judgment of reason as commanded by reason, the passion helps in the carrying out of the command of reason."[12] This means that virtue at its height causes the enthusiastic performance of good deeds.

Theological Virtues

Every human action is good, according to Aquinas, because it "attains reason or God Himself," the twofold rule or measure of human acts. The theological virtues, according to Aquinas, are principles that order human beings to supernatural happiness—that is, God. These principles or habits are designated theological for three reasons: "first, because they have God as their object, inasmuch as by them we are rightly ordered to God; secondly, because they are infused in us by God alone; and finally, because these virtues are made known to us only by divine revelation in Sacred Scripture."[13] The ordering of human beings to God requires a raising and transformation of both intellect and will.

The Epistle to the Hebrews says that "faith is the substance of things to be hoped for, the evidence of things not seen" (Heb 11:1). Aquinas explains this biblical definition describing faith as a habit of the intellect whose act is to believe truths which are not seen, at the command of the will and under the influence of grace. In the words of Aquinas, "Faith is a habit of the mind, whereby eternal life is begun in us, making the intellect assent to what is non-apparent."[14] Faith assents to truths about God because they are revealed by God. Truths about Christ, the Church, the sacraments also come under faith "insofar as by them we are directed to God, and inasmuch as we assent to them on account of the Divine Truth."[15] In other words, things that order us to eternal life are the object of faith.

11. Ibid., I-II, qu. 61, a. 1.
13. Ibid., I-II, qu. 52, a. 1.
15. Ibid., I-II, qu. 1, a. 1.
12. Ibid., I-II, qu. 59, a. 2, reply to obj. 3.
14. Ibid., II-II, qu. 4, a. 1.

Faith is a virtue because it inclines the intellect infallibly to seek its object "which is the truth," and living faith also directs the will to its last end "on account of which it assents to the true." For faith to be living, a person must possess the virtue of charity, the effect of which is always to direct the soul toward a good end. Aquinas also describes faith as the first of the virtues, "since the end is the principle [or starting point] in matters of action.... [T]he last end must, of necessity, be present to the intellect before it is present to the will, since the will has no inclination for anything except insofar as it is apprehended by the intellect."[16]

Hope is the habit by which we regard as possible the attainment of eternal happiness by means of God's assistance. It is the virtue that causes us to tend toward our final end by means of an appetitive movement of the will, which is the so-called intellective appetite. Hope is a theological virtue because God is its principal object. More precisely, "hope makes us adhere to God as the source whence we derive perfect goodness, i.e., insofar as by hope, we trust to the Divine assistance for obtaining happiness."[17]

Augustine's definition of all virtue as "the perfect love of God" is also the proper definition of charity. Aquinas says "charity is friendship of man for God made possible by a gift of the Holy Spirit."[18] The intensity of man's love for God is "not according to our natural capacity, but according as the Spirit wills to distribute his gifts."[19] Charity, then, is an infused virtue by which people love themselves and their neighbor for the sake of God. In other words, love of God is the reason for love of neighbor. In the words of Aquinas, "the aspect under which our neighbor is to be loved, is God, since what we ought to love in our neighbor is that he may be in God."[20] Augustine makes the same point. Right after his conversion he expresses the strong desire to lead others to what he has understood about the proper relation to God: "Oh if they would only see that eternal light, which I had tasted. I was sore grieved because I was not able to show it to them, even if they brought me their heart in those eyes of theirs that looked away from you."[21]

Saying that charity is the love of God says everything, but in so general a way as to provide insufficient guidance for most people. Aquinas clari-

16. Ibid., II-II, qu. 4, a. 7.   17. Ibid., II-II, qu. 17, a. 6.
18. Ibid., II-II, qu. 23, a. 1.   19. Ibid., II-II, qu. 24, a. 3.
20. Ibid., II-II, qu. 25, a. 1.
21. St. Augustine, *The Confessions* (Indianapolis, Ind.: Hackett, 1993), book 9, chap. 4.

fies the meaning of love of God in a number of ways, only a few of which
can be mentioned. Human love of God not only includes love of neighbor, but also love of self and love of one's body. Aquinas reports Augustine's view that "however much a man may stray from the truth, the love
of himself and of his own body always remains in him."[22] Hence, with
respect to these two requirements of love, separate precepts were not required. Aquinas argues that some do not understand that love of God includes the love of neighbor. Consequently, in the formulation of precepts
about charity, love of neighbor is presented as a separate precept. The
purpose of precepts, says Aquinas, is to specify "acts of virtue."[23]

The meaning of charity becomes clearer by noting that all the precepts of the Decalogue or Ten Commandments are directed to the love of
God and of our neighbor. More specifically, through the Decalogue God
lays the groundwork for friendship with himself and for harmony among
human beings. The presence of eight negative precepts in the Decalogue
indicates the minimum we must avoid not to offend God and harm our
neighbor. The two positive precepts regarding God and parents are included, says Aquinas, because it is a primary dictate of reason to make a
suitable return for kindnesses received. We are most in debt to God and
our parents, whose gifts we cannot repay, "Therefore, it is that there are
only two affirmative precepts: one about honor due to parents, the other
about the celebration of the Sabbath in memory of the divine favor."[24] In
sum, the Decalogue clearly shows that the practice of charity requires the
renunciation of certain desires, words, and deeds.

An example of positive ways to love one's neighbor is found in the traditional works of mercy. The seven corporal works of mercy are: to feed
the hungry, to give drink to the thirsty, to clothe the naked, to give shelter to the homeless, to visit the sick, to visit the imprisoned, and to bury
the dead. The spiritual works of mercy include the following: to instruct
the ignorant, to counsel the doubtful, to comfort the sorrowful, to re-
prove the sinner, to forgive injuries, to bear with those who do us wrong,
and to pray for the living and the dead.

Finally, according to Aquinas, the love of God and neighbor includes
the practice of moral virtues. This should become clear after the discussion of each moral virtue and the connection among all the virtues.

22. Aquinas, *Summa theologiae*, II-II, qu. 44, a. 3.
23. Ibid., II-II, qu. 44, a. 2.
24. Ibid., I-II, qu. 100, a. 7, reply to obj. 1.

St. Augustine offers insightful reflections on the difficulty of avoiding harm and doing good for one's neighbor. "But here good will alone does not suffice, for it is a work demanding great understanding and prudence, which none can exercise unless they be given to him by God, the fountain of all good."[25] Augustine, of course, cannot mean that every kind of harm to neighbor is difficult to understand, but unintentional harm is hard to avoid on every occasion. Quite logically, he believes that the commandment to love one's neighbor entails duties toward society, "about which it is difficult not to err."[26] Errors are likely because a person needs self-knowledge, the ability to understand the needs of a particular community, as well as adequate information and education. Consequently, positive duties are even more difficult to state than negative precepts. This is so because positive duties will vary according to a person's talents, opportunities, and the requirements of the community in which one is living.

Cardinal Virtues

Augustine says that the role of prudence is "to keep a constant watch so that we are not led astray by the imperceptible working of an evil influence."[27] Aquinas quotes Augustine describing prudence as "the knowledge of what to seek and what to avoid," and as "love discerning aright that which helps from that which hinders us in tending to God."[28] Aquinas says that "love is said to discern because it moves the reason to discern."[29] In fact, prudence is "in the reason" and may be properly characterized as right reason applied to action. Otherwise stated, it is the function of prudence to apply right reason to action with the help of an ordered appetite. In applying reason to action, prudence doesn't appoint the ends of the moral virtues, but chooses the means appropriate for realizing these ends.[30] The virtue of prudence necessarily relies on the moral virtues to order the appetites, because seeing clearly requires well-ordered passions or feelings—not their absence.

To see clearly a person must also take counsel or think things over, with the help of others when necessary, discern the relevant factors, make a judgment, and then act. Seeing clearly requires docility or open-mindedness,

25. Augustine, *De moribus*, chap. 26, no. 5.
26. Ibid., chap. 26, no. 49.   27. Ibid., chap. 24, no. 45.
28. Aquinas, *Summa theologiae* II-II, qu. 47, a. 1 and reply to obj. 1.
29. Ibid., II-II, qu. 47, a. 1.
30. Cf. ibid., II-II, qu. 47, a. 6.

which is often a difficult trait to acquire. Even St. Augustine was not al-ways open-minded or docile as a young man before his conversion. On one occasion a bishop refused a request from Augustine's mother, Monica, that he talk to her son. The bishop simply said, he lacks docility as of yet and therefore will not listen.[31] At the time of the bishop's refusal Augustine was enthusiastic about Manicheanism.

Counsel and judgment are necessary because the exercise of prudence requires not only knowledge of universal principles, but also familiar-ity with a host of "singulars," or the relevant factors in a situation. It be-longs to counsel to discern the pertinent singulars from the great num-ber present to a person's mind. We take counsel in order to grasp what needs to be known about a particular situation. This ability to see is en-hanced by long experience and the possession of various qualities desig-nated by Aquinas as the quasi-integral parts of prudence. *Experience* helps us discover "what is true in a majority of cases." Since "experience is the result of many memories…memory is fittingly accounted a part of pru-dence."[32] *Docility* is another aspect of prudence, since we have a "very great need of being taught by others, especially by old folk who have acquired a sound understanding of the ends in practical matters."[33] It is docility that makes us open-minded and thus disposed to learn from others. *Shrewdness,* says Aquinas, is the disposition "to acquire a right estimate by oneself."[34] The quality of *foresight* enables us to take contingent future events into ac-count.[35] Still other parts of prudence mentioned by Aquinas are under-standing, the ability to use reason well, circumspection, and caution. All these qualities enable us to come into contact with reality.

I have always been impressed by Joseph Pieper's statement about the role of prudence in enabling us to see things the way they are:

> The pre-eminence of prudence means that the realization of the good presup-poses knowledge of reality. He alone can do the good who knows what things are like and what their situation is. The pre-eminence of prudence means that so-called "good intention" and so-called "meaning well" by no means suf-fice.[36]

---

31. Augustine, *Confessions,* book III, chap. 12.

32. Aquinas, *Summa theologiae,* II-II, qu. 49, a. 1.

33. Ibid., II-II qu. 49, a. 3.   34. Ibid., II-II qu. 49, a. 4.

35. Ibid., II-II qu. 49, a. 6.

36. Joseph Pieper, *The Four Cardinal Virtues* (Notre Dame, Ind.: University of Notre Dame Press, 1966), 10.

We often praise people for being well-intentioned and meaning well, and rightly so, to a point. Some of my freshmen students no doubt mean well when they party too much in their first semester. Nevertheless, there is always a price to be paid for not seeing things the way they are, even if we have the best intentions in the world. Being in the truth always matters.

Everyone in the state of grace has sufficient prudence or diligence to work out his own salvation. But there is another kind of diligence "which is more than sufficient, whereby a man is able to make provision both for himself and for others, not only in matters necessary for salvation, but also in all things relating to human life, and such diligence as this is not in all who have grace."[37] In other words, not everyone can be a lawgiver or a statesman, a civil leader, or a leader of private organizations that distribute common goods.

Fortitude is the virtue that enables a person to face death and hardship or toil for the sake of achieving a good in accordance with reason and/or God's will. Fortitude "is chiefly about fear of difficult things, which can withdraw the will from following the reason" or God.[38] In *De officiis (On Duties)*, St. Ambrose uses the concept of fortitude in a very broad sense to indicate a form of resolve in the face of every kind of temptation. As a limited virtue, with the specific task of facing death, the principal act of fortitude is endurance, "that is to stand immovable in the midst of dangers rather than to attack them."[39]

A virtue closely associated with fortitude is patience. It occupies an important place in the thought of St. Ambrose, St. Gregory the Great, St. Augustine, and St. Thomas. St. Gregory the Great goes so far as to affirm that charity cannot exist without patience. He further says, "The less patient a man proves to be, the less instructed does he show himself to be and he cannot truly impart by instruction what is good, if in his own way of life he does not know how to bear with equanimity the evils that others do."[40] Aquinas says patience safeguards "the good of reason against sorrow lest reason give way to sorrow."[41] The moderation of sorrow is important, both to obviate the temptations to such vices as anger and hatred and to prevent loss of enthusiasm for the practice of virtue. According to

37. Aquinas, *Summa theologiae*, II-II, qu. 47 a. 14.

38. Ibid., II-II, qu. 123, a. 3.

39. Ibid., II-II, qu. 123, a. 6.

40. Gregory the Great, *Pastoral Care* (New York: Newman Press, 1978, 1950), part III, chap. 9.

41. Aquinas, *Summa theologiae*, II-II, qu. 136, a. 2.

scripture, "because wickedness is multiplied, the love of many will grow cold" (Mt 24:12). Giving way to sorrow because of personal suffering or societal injustice not only takes up valuable time, but also decreases zeal for accomplishing whatever good is possible.

Not surprisingly, Aquinas argues that patience is caused by charity, which no one attains without the help of grace. A strong desire to love God and neighbor gives the strength to bear adversity and everyday difficulties. To make his point Aquinas quotes Augustine's *De patientia:* "The strength of desire helps a man to bear toil and pain; and no one willingly undertakes to bear what is painful save for the sake of that which gives pleasure."[42] Pleasure arises from the practice of charity and all other virtues.

In the *Summa theologiae* Aquinas argues that the virtues that restrain the impetuosity of the emotions are reckoned as parts of temperance.[43] In *De moribus* Augustine says the function of temperance "is to restrain and still the passions which cause us to crave the things that turn us away from the laws of God and the enjoyment of His goodness, that is to say, from the happy life."[44] As examples of these passions Augustine first mentions covetousness, bodily pleasures, desire for human glory, and desire of vain knowledge. The problem with these desires is that "each man is conformed to the thing he loves." In addition, disordered cravings cause us to lose our freedom and to become slaves of the objects we crave. For example, desire for popular acclaim makes one a slave of others' opinions and desires. This passion for public acceptance and affection leads people in positions of authority (whether public or private, civil or religious) to neglect the real good of those for whom they have responsibility. In his book on the priesthood John Chrysostom warns priests and bishops that desire for affection could induce them to dilute or omit part of Christ's teaching.

[T]hrough his passion for praise [the priest or bishop] aims to speak more for the pleasure than the profit of his hearers.... The man who is carried away with the desire for eulogies may have the ability to improve the people, but chooses instead to provide nothing but entertainment.... His soul, being unable to bear the senseless criticism of the multitude, grows slack and loses all earnestness about preaching.[45]

42. Ibid., II-II, qu. 136, a. 3.   43. Ibid., II-II, qu. 161, a. 4.
44. Augustine, *De moribus*, chap. 19, no. 35.
45. St. John Chrysostom, *Six Books On the Priesthood* (Crestwood, N.Y.: St. Vladimir's Seminary Press, 1984), 128, 133.

In *De officiis* Ambrose's discussion of temperance focuses on the control of anger. He says "each one ought to take care not to be disturbed when wrong is done him."[46] We should become like children who never keep an injury in mind. Otherwise,

indignation is a terrible incentive to sin. It disorders the mind to such an extent as to leave no room for reason. The first thing, therefore, to aim at, if possible, is to make tranquility of character our natural disposition by constant practice, by desire for better things, by fixed determination.[47]

To make his point about the danger of indignation, Ambrose tells the story of Nabal, Abigail, and David. While David and his men were in the wilderness they gave protection to the shepherds of the rich man, Nabal. David sent some of his men to Nabal to request assistance. When Nabal sent them away empty-handed, David resolved to take revenge by killing Nabal and his men. Hearing of Nabal's rebuff of David, Abigail, Nabal's wife, went to David and made a peace offering and then persuaded him not to harm himself by taking revenge. David listened to Abigail, praised her discretion, and thanked her for saving him from sin (1 Sm: 25).

Ambrose suggests several ways to control anger. The first thing to do is to educate ourselves "to allow reflection on good things to enter the mind."[48] The knowledge and desire of what is fine and noble are powerful incentives to allay indignation at the wrong done to us or others. Giving way to indignation leaves less time and energy to do what is right. For Ambrose, knowledge of the good things would come both from the kind of reasoning Cicero exhibited in his own *De officiis* and from faith.

When the soul's tranquility is inordinately disturbed, Ambrose says, "First calm your mind. If you can't do this, put a restraint upon your tongue. Lastly, omit not to seek for reconciliation."[49] Ambrose puts so much emphasis on the control of speech that he begins his book on duties with an exhortation to silence. He says, "He is wise who knows how to keep silent."[50] He is wise "who has received of the Lord to know when he ought to speak."[51] And, he adds, "[I]t was a mark of divine protection for a man to be hid from the scourge of his own tongue."[52] As a model of

---

46. St. Ambrose, *De officiis* (Oxford and New York: Oxford University Press, 2001), book I, no. 23.

47. Ibid., book I, no. 90.
48. Ibid., book I, no. 98.
49. Ibid., book I, no 92.
50. Ibid., book I, no. 2.
51. Ibid., book I, no. 5.
52. Ibid., book I, no. 6.

prudent reserve, Ambrose cites the example of David's reaction to the verbal abuse of Shimei. David "was not disturbed by insults, for he had full knowledge of his own good works."[53]

Aquinas argues that anger is moderated by meekness, a virtue that forms part of temperance. Like Ambrose, Aquinas recognizes that anger can be very harmful. It leads one to take revenge on others and is "a very great obstacle to man's free judgment of truth." Because of its impetuousness, anger often leads an individual to contradict what is true. Consequently, Aquinas favorably quotes Augustine's observation, "To be meek is not to contradict Holy Writ, whether we understand it, if it condemn our evil ways, or understanding it not, as though we might know better and have a clearer insight of the truth."[54] In his main discussion of temperance Aquinas doesn't discuss anger or love of money, or desire for fame, but focuses on the role of temperance in moderating the pleasures of touch and taste, namely, those pleasures associated with sex, food, and drink. Aquinas calls these the greatest pleasures. "If a man can control the greatest pleasures, much more can he control lesser ones. Wherefore, it belongs chiefly and properly to temperance to moderate desires and pleasures of touch, and secondarily other pleasures."[55]

Connection among the Virtues

Aquinas quotes Gregory the Great as support for his view on the connection of the virtues with each other: "[T]here is no true prudence without justice, temperance, and fortitude." Aquinas also points out that Augustine and Aristotle hold the same opinion. The reason, as previously mentioned, is simple and logical. Virtue is the good use of choice; choice requires "not only an inclination to an appropriate end, which arises directly from the habit (justice, fortitude and temperance) but also the correct choice of means to an end, which is made by prudence, which deliberates, judges and commands in regard to the means."[56] The converse, of course, is also true: "Likewise one cannot have prudence without having the moral virtues since prudence is right reasoning about what is to be done, whose starting point is the end of the action to which we are rightly disposed by the moral virtues."[57]

53. Ibid., book I, no. 21; See 2 Samuel 16:6ff.
54. Aquinas, *Summa theologiae*, qu. 157, a. 4, reply to obj. 1.
55. Ibid., II-II, qu. 141, a. 4.   56. Ibid., II-II, qu. 65, a. 1.
57. Ibid., I-II, qu. 65, a. 1.

Aquinas further notes that the practice of all the moral virtues must be guided by the virtue of charity. He explains, "Now for the right reasoning of prudence it is much more necessary that man be well disposed to the ultimate end, which is the result of charity, than that he be well disposed to other ends which is the result of moral virtue."[58] It logically follows that justice, fortitude, and temperance cannot exist without charity, either, since they depend on prudence, which ultimately takes its bearings by charity. On the other hand, charity cannot be complete without the assistance of the moral virtues to facilitate the performance of "each kind of good work." For example, temperance restrains the passions—such as the desire for gain or pleasure—which might lessen or blot out our love of God. Fortitude gives strength to overcome fear of dangers or hardships that could deter us from loving our neighbor by conscientiously fulfilling responsibilities in the family or on the job outside the home. With respect to the relation between prudence and charity, Joseph Pieper says that "the highest and most fruitful achievements of Christian life depend upon the felicitous collaboration of prudence and charity."[59] The practice of charity requires the infused virtue of prudence. Charity inclines an individual to love God, and prudence chooses the various means to realize that end, taking into account such things as one's state in life, talents, and opportunities, as well as the needs of the church and the requirements of the common good.

Finally, the theological virtues themselves are connected with each other. There can be no charity or hope without faith, but "there can be faith and hope without charity, but without charity they are not virtues properly speaking."[60] Charity depends on faith, since "we cannot tend to something by appetitive movement, whether by hope or love, unless it is apprehended by sense or intellect. Now the intellect apprehends by faith what we hope for and love."[61] This point rests on the anthropology that Thomas lays out in his so-called treatise entitled *De homine*.[62] In that part of the *Summa* he elaborates at length on his understanding of the relation between the intellect and the will, which understanding is based largely on Aristotle's *De Anima*. The dependence of charity on faith means that the proper practice of virtue depends on belief in the Nicene Creed.

58. Ibid., I-II, qu. 65, a. 1.
59. Pieper, *The Four Cardinal Virtues*, 37.
60. Aquinas, *Summa theologiae*, I-II, qu. 65, a. 4.
61. Ibid., I-II, qu. 62, a. 4.   62. Ibid., I, questions 75–102.

Belief in the truths of salvation not only gives knowledge of man's ultimate end, but also provides motivation to seek it by practicing all the virtues.

Virtue and Happiness

Aristotle defines "the happy man as one whose activities are an expression of complete virtue, and who is sufficiently equipped with external
goods, not simply at a given moment but to the end of his life."[63] Self-in-
flicted unhappiness necessarily results from absence of virtue. Some degree of unhappiness is, however, also caused by chance misfortunes such
as ill health, extreme poverty, loss of liberty, the death of family members
and friends, hunger, and war. Aristotle clearly teaches that even the most
dedicated practice of virtue is no guarantee against "the outrageous slings
of fortune." In Christian terms, even the most prudent and innocent conduct is sometimes not enough to keep troubles away.

Virtue in Two Novels

In the second half of this chapter I rely on two works of literature to
reveal the practice of virtues in real-life situations. They are Jane Austen's
Persuasion (1818) and Alessandro Manzoni's *I Promessi Sposi,* or *The Betrothed*
(1840). Although the latter book is well-known in Europe and is one of
the Harvard Classics, it is still relatively unknown in the United States. I
don't expect to do justice to Austen and Manzoni, but do hope to draw
enough from these works to show how the virtues transform the lives of
particular individuals.

Persuasion

A helpful way to approach Jane Austen's *Persuasion* is to examine the
two crucial scenes in the novel in which the outcome depends on the willingness to be persuaded. The first scene depicts a decisive moment that
took place eight years before the events being narrated in the story. At
the age of nineteen Anne Elliot falls in love with Frederick Wentworth,
an intelligent, spirited, charming naval officer. Anne, says Jane Austen,
was "an extremely pretty girl, with gentleness, modesty, taste and feeling. Half the sum of attraction, on either side, might have been enough,

---

63. Aristotle, *Nicomachean Ethics,* tr. Martin Ostwald (New York: Macmillan, 1962),
book 1, chap. 10.

for he had nothing to do, and she had hardly anybody to love."[64] Anne's father, Sir Walter Elliot, opposed the marriage because Frederick was not wealthy and had no connections to ensure his advancement in the navy. Anne's friend Lady Russell also opposed the marriage because of her low opinion of Frederick. In her mind, he was brilliant, headstrong, and poor, with no certain prospect of attaining the requisite affluence for marriage. She advised Anne to break off the engagement. Since the death of her mother five years before, Anne had come to rely on the judgment of the well-meaning Lady Russell. In response to her godmother's tender, confident advice, "she was persuaded to believe the engagement a wrong thing—indiscreet, improper, hardly capable of success, and not deserving it."[65] Jane Austen notes that Anne was not motivated by "selfish caution," but saw her painful self-denial as contributing to Frederick's true interest. Frederick is bitterly disappointed, leaves the country, and harbors resentment against Anne and Lady Russell.

The other scene occurs eight years later when Anne is 27. Frederick, still unmarried, returns to Anne's neighborhood because of family ties. He develops an interest in Louisa Musgrove, to whom he explains his view of good character, which Anne inadvertently overhears without Frederick's knowledge. After Louisa explains that she is never easily persuaded, Frederick praises Louisa for her firmness and says, "It is the worst evil of too yielding and indecisive character, that no influence over it can be depended on. You are never sure of a good impression being durable. Everybody may sway it; let those who would be happy be firm."[66] Frederick has obviously drawn a very clear lesson from his experience with Anne's change of mind.

Shortly after Frederick's impassioned defense of firmness, he is out for a walk near the seashore with Louisa, Anne, and others. Louisa insists on jumping down to the pavement from a height. She jumps once and insists upon doing so again. In vain, Frederick attempts to dissuade Louisa. She smiles and says, "I am determined I will."[67] Frederick holds out his hands; Louisa jumps, but trips and falls on the pavement, unconscious. In the face of general consternation Anne keeps her composure and suggests what should be done to care for Louisa and then attends to her distraught friends, including Captain Wentworth. After proper care is arranged,

---

64. Jane Austen, *Persuasion* (New York: Viking Penguin, 1986), 55.
65. Ibid., 56.   66. Ibid., 110.
67. Ibid., 129.

Jane Austen gives us a glimpse of Anne's thoughts about Frederick's opinion of a good character:

Anne wondered whether it ever occurred to him now to question the justness
of his own previous opinion as to the universal felicity and advantage of firmness of character, and whether it might strike him, that, like all other qualities
of the mind, it should have its proportions and limits. She thought it would
scarcely escape him to feel that a persuadable temper might sometimes be as
much in favor of happiness as a very resolute character.[68]

During her convalescence, Louisa falls in love with a Captain Benwick.
Frederick and Anne eventually get back together and decide to marry.
Anne then casually explains her decision to Frederick not to marry him
eight years before. While both are admiring green lawn plants, Anne says:

I have been thinking over the past and trying impartially to judge of the right
and wrong, I mean with regard to myself; and I must believe that I was right,
much as I suffered from it, that I was perfectly right in being guided by the
friend whom you will love better than you do now. To me she was in the place
of a parent. Do not mistake me, however, I am not saying that she did not err
in her advice. It was perhaps one of those cases in which advice is good or bad
only as the event decides; and for myself, I certainly never should, in any circumstance of tolerable similarity, give such advice. But I mean that I was right
in submitting to her, and that if I had done otherwise I should have suffered
more in continuing the engagement than I did even in giving it up, because I
should have suffered in my conscience. I have now, as far as such a sentiment is
allowable in human nature, nothing to reproach myself with; and if I mistake
not, a strong sense of duty is no bad part of a woman's portion.[69]

Student reaction to Anne's explanation is generally quite negative. My
students contend that Anne was weak because she followed Lady Russell's advice. That, of course, was Frederick's judgment at the time, too.

As is well known, Jane Austen believes that a person needs good judgment in order to do the right thing. The young need to listen attentive-
ly to parents and other adults in order to become ever better observers
of people and situations. Because they are subject to various and sundry
disordered passions, such as pride, vanity, and immoderate love of money and pleasure, young men and women may not heed wise counsel. Jane
Austen would have readily understood a bishop's statement to Monica

68. Ibid., 136.
69. Ibid., 248.

that her son, the future St. Augustine, was not yet willing to heed wise
counsel. Various passions and mistaken religious opinions held sway over
him. Even well-meaning, good adults may not always be wise counselors.
While Lady Russell usually gave Anne and her family good advice, she
wrongly discouraged Anne from marrying Frederick because of prejudices on her part. Lady Russell didn't appreciate Frederick's intelligence, wit,
optimistic temper, and fearlessness. Jane Austen seems to imply that even
the most teachable young person can be misguided by imprudent adults.
She also implies that human beings cannot grow up well in communities
and families where good advice is not forthcoming.

I would add that all young people must learn how to see reality, and
all need guidance, especially from family members and close friends, and
even from authoritative traditions that are very much alive, at least in the
Church, if not in the culture. To choose between a "persuadable temper" and a "resolute character" is an ongoing task. Youth is a time when
docility to authoritative guidance is especially necessary. In this time of
misplaced compassion, choice without requisite information, and an exaggerated sense of independence, Jane Austen's vision of persuasion in a
community is an appealing alternative. There are things common to all
human lives that must and can be understood before choices are made.
Not will, but understanding, is primary in Jane Austen's world. Being
open to persuasion is a mark of good judgment, which is an abiding characteristic of Anne Elliot.

To her own chagrin, Anne recognizes that her father, Sir Walter, was
extremely vain about his appearance, a spendthrift, a lover of rank, unaf-
fectionate, and not respectful of her opinions. Jane Austen is very critical
of Sir Walter's attitude toward his daughter. "Anne, with an elegance of
mind and sweetness of character, which must have placed her high with
any people of real understanding, was nobody with either father or sister
[i.e., her older sister Elizabeth]."[70] Anne perceives her situation but neither
complains nor grows bitter. She seems to understand intuitively that being resentful or bearing grudges is harmful to one's character.

Anne also displays unerring judgment about the character of people
in her surroundings. She knows that Mrs. Clay, the companion of her
sister Elizabeth, always says what pleases others and is probably schem-
ing to become Sir Walter's wife. Anne is unerring in her judgment about
the worth of her own suitors. At the age of twenty-two, contrary to the

70. Ibid., 37.

advice of Lady Russell, she rejects a marriage offer from Charles Musgrove, "whose landed property and general importance were second in
that county, only to Sir Walter's."[71] Lady Russell wanted Anne to marry
Charles, not only to benefit from Charles's money and importance, but
also to secure a respectable removal "from the partialities and injustice
of her father's house, and settled so permanently near herself."[72] While
Charles was a pleasant fellow and very patient with the whining of Mary,
the sister of Anne, whom he eventually marries, he is lazy and boring and
hardly a suitable match for Anne. Jane Austen sums up his life by saying
that "he did nothing with much zeal but sport and his time was otherwise trifled away, without benefit from books or anything else."[73]

At the age of twenty-seven Anne comes to the judgment that her cous-
in, William Elliot, would not make a suitable marriage partner. While
not prying into the details of his disreputable past—which she eventually discovers—Anne, nevertheless, picks up from conversation that at one
period of his life he had been "careless on all serious matters."[74] Although
he was agreeable and expressed good opinions, Anne remained skeptical.

Mr. Elliot was rational, discreet, polished—but he was not open. There was
never any burst of feeling, any warmth of indignation or delight, at the evil or
good of others. This, to Anne, was a decided imperfection. Her early impressions were incurable. She prized the frank, the open-hearted, the eager character beyond all others. Warmth and enthusiasm did captivate her still. She felt
that she could so much more depend upon the sincerity of those who sometimes looked or said a careless or a hasty thing, than of those whose presence
of mind never varied, whose tongue never slipped.[75]

Another aspect of Anne's character and Jane Austen's vision of a good
person is revealed in the encounters between Anne and Mrs. Smith, the
former Miss Hamilton. Anne accidently discovered that her former
schoolmate was living nearby, "who had the two strong claims on her attention, of past kindness and present suffering."[76] During the course of a
year, Miss Hamilton had graciously softened Anne's grief over the premature loss of her mother. Now, thirteen years later, Mrs. Smith was a wid-
ow, poor, sickly, and "almost excluded from society."[77] Against the judgment of her father and sister, Elizabeth, Anne visits and consoles her old

71. Ibid., 57.   72. Ibid., 57.
73. Ibid., 70.   74. Ibid., 173.
75. Ibid., 173.   76. Ibid., 106.
77. Ibid., 165.

friend in a section of town where Sir Walter would never be seen. Anne discovers a woman displaying a patience in the face of suffering that is truly extraordinary.

[N]either sickness nor sorrow seemed to have closed her heart or ruined her spirits....A submissive spirit might be patient, a strong understanding would supply resolution, but here was something more: here was that elasticity of mind, that disposition to be comforted, that power of turning readily to good, and of finding employment which carried her out of herself, which was from Nature alone. It was the choicest gift of heaven.[78]

It is, of course, not surprising to find that Anne appreciates the beauty of patient endurance. She herself was patient, despite suffering from her separation from Frederick Wentworth on account of Lady Russell's mistaken advice. She bore with equanimity slights from her father and sister Elizabeth. She put up with the constant complaints of her sister Mary and even responded with kindness both to her and her children. Anne rallied her spirits by gladly embracing the duties available in her state of life. She genuinely showed love to her family and acquaintances, and— Jane Austen notes in passing—she regularly distributed alms to the poor.

Anne's patient endurance in the face of personal sufferings protects her from the debilitating effects of sadness and self-pity. Anne maintains her enthusiasm for life and is kind to her family and acquaintances, even when they don't respond. Anne's good judgment enables her to love wisely by giving good counsel to her father and sister Elizabeth. While Anne's prudence and patient endurance are the most striking aspects of her character, no less noteworthy is her temperance.[79] Unlike her father and sister Elizabeth, Anne is not inordinately fond of money, rank, personal appearance, or the good opinion of "important" people. If attached to the opinion of those in her father's social circle, she could never have shown gratitude and friendship to Mrs. Smith. Desire for property and security probably would have led Anne to accept Charles Musgrove's proposal of marriage. Anne's detachment from inordinate desires also removed temptation to any kind of hypocrisy. Anne was never angling for recognition or money. She was always straightforward and candid.

78. Ibid., 166–67.

79. The function of this virtue, says St. Augustine, is to restrain and still the passions that cause us to crave the things that turn us away from the laws of God and the enjoyment of his goodness. As examples of these passions, Augustine mentions covetousness, bodily pleasures, desire for human glory, and vain knowledge.

It is interesting to note how Anne's life displays the connection among the virtues so often discussed by theologians. Anne's prudence, patience, and temperance all facilitate the practice of charity or beneficence toward others. Jane Austen makes clear that real kindness toward others depends on the virtues Anne possesses.

The Betrothed

Alessandro Manzoni's *The Betrothed* (1840) is a historical novel set in the seventeenth century in what is now northern Italy. Manzoni's scenes and characters nicely reveal the meaning of virtue as well as the dependence of the common good on the practice of virtue. The novel opens on November 7, 1628, when two bravoes of a local nobleman by the name of Don Rodrigo order Don Abbondio, a simple parish priest, not to marry two peasants by the names of Renzo Tramaglino and Lucia Mondello. Don Rodrigo wanted Lucia for himself. Don Abbondio is thoroughly intimidated, complies with the order, and thereby sets in motion the subsequent events.

Don Abbondio had not become a priest for religious reasons. Seeing himself as an "earthenware jar...in the company of many iron pots," Don Abbondio willingly followed his parents' command to enter the priesthood. "To win the means of living with some degree of comfort, and to join the ranks of a revered and powerful class seemed to him more than sufficient motive for such a course."[80] Manzoni briefly sums up the years of Abbondio's priesthood. He got along by not taking sides in the frequent conflicts "between clergy and lay authorities, between military and civilians, between noble and noble—right down to quarrels between two peasants arising from a hasty word, and settled with fists or knives."[81] If forced to take sides, Don Abbondio "always sided with the stronger of two adversaries" in such a way as to avoid offending the weaker party.

He kept away from bullies when he could, he pretended not to notice passing, capricious acts of arrogance, and greeted those that arose from a serious and deliberate intention with total submission....But above all he used to declaim against those of his colleagues who took the risk of supporting the weak and the oppressed against a powerful bully.[82]

80. Alessandro Manzoni, *The Betrothed* (New York: Viking Penguin, 1987), 38.
81. Ibid., 38.
82. Ibid., 38–39.

In response to the difficult situation caused by Don Abbondio's cowardly behavior, Lucia decides to ask for help from Father Cristoforo, a Capuchin priest, "a man of great authority, both within the monastery and
outside of it." Before becoming a Capuchin friar, Fr. Cristoforo's name
was Lodovico. As the son of a rich merchant, he used his resources "to set
himself up as a protector of the downtrodden and a righter of wrongs."[83]
On one occasion Lodovico, accompanied by his servant Cristoforo, lets
himself be provoked into a quarrel with a tyrannical nobleman. Manzoni's narrative shows that the pride and blazing temper of Lodovico sucks
him into a useless sword fight, thereby, unjustifiably putting both himself
and Cristoforo at risk of being harmed and of inflicting harm on others. As things turn out, Cristoforo dies trying to protect his master and
Lodovico kills the nobleman. To make amends for his deed, Lodovico
gives all his property to Cristoforo's wife and eight children and resolves
to become a Capuchin and to take the name of his servant, Cristoforo.
He then humbles himself before the relatives of the man he killed and
actually frees them from their anger and hatred toward him. As a Capuchin friar "his two official duties were those of preaching and of tending
the dying which he carried out willingly and conscientiously, but he never
missed a chance of performing two other duties, which he had set himself—the composing of quarrels and the protection of the oppressed."[84]
He tries to save people from immoderate anger and finds ways of protecting the oppressed without doing anything unjust himself.

   Given his mission in life, Father Cristoforo willingly agrees to help Lucia and Renzo. He goes to Don Rodrigo and offers a face-saving way to
let the two young people marry. When Don Rodrigo refuses, Father Cristoforo opposes him to his face and then arranges safe passage for Renzo
and Lucia to another part of the country. Cristoforo acts both to save the
young peasants respectively from Don Rodrigo's anger and desire and to
protect Renzo from the effects of his own anger against Don Rodrigo.
Cristoforo consequently suffers a transfer to another locale for his courageous deed, because Don Rodrigo is well-connected through his relatives
with the Capuchin authorities. Manzoni indicates that Rodrigo's uncle, a
member of the nobility, has no trouble manipulating the Capuchin provincial, who was wise as a serpent, but not as innocent as a dove. He does
the bidding of Rodrigo's relative in order not to have any unpleasant con-

83. Ibid., 79.
84. Ibid., 90.

sequences. Like many of his Capuchin confreres, Cristoforo volunteers to take care of plague victims and eventually dies from the plague. Before succumbing, Cristoforo looks after the dying Don Rodrigo, another victim of the plague, and succeeds in persuading Renzo to give up his hatred for Don Rodrigo and even to forgive him.

At a convent in Monza where Lucia takes refuge, Manzoni introduces the reader to Gertrude, also known as the Signora or the nun of Monza. Her father had forced her to enter the convent. Upon first meeting Lucia, Gertrude importunately asks the young girl whether Don Rodrigo was indeed a "hateful persecutor" or not. When pressed to give an answer, Lucia reluctantly says that she would "rather die than fall into his clutches."[85] She also says of Renzo, "I chose him for my husband of my own free will."[86] Lucia's invocation of free choice sets the stage for the story of Gertrude, who tyrannizes over herself in response to the tyranny of her father. She has never known interior freedom. In his two chapters on the nun of Monza, Manzoni reveals how important freedom is for human flourishing.

Along with a number of other girls, Gertrude was placed in the convent at the age of six to receive an education. Most left at the age of 14 to take their place in the world. At an early age Gertrude knew that she was expected to become a nun when she turned fourteen. During her eight-year residence in the convent as a lay person, Gertrude would often tell her companions how she would freely decide to become a nun or get married. She desperately wanted to live in the world, but couldn't bear the thought of opposing the will of her father. Manzoni says she lost all sense of real religion and became subject to an unreal image of religion.

Then poor Gertrude would be overcome by confused terrors and oppressed by confused ideas of duty until she imagined that her repugnance toward the cloistered life and her resistance to the subtle influence of her elders in the matter of a future choice constituted a sin, which she would resolve to expiate by voluntarily taking the veil.[87]

She submits an application to become a nun but, according to Church law, she must wait a year and then be examined by a priest known as the vicar of nuns. His duty is to make certain that her decision to enter the convent is "of her own free choice." At the end of the year Gertrude de-

85. Ibid., 173–74.   86. Ibid., 173.
87. Ibid., 180.

cides not to enter the convent and informs her father by letter. After suffering verbal abuse from her father and imprisonment in her own home, Gertrude again changes her mind and agrees to enter the convent. When undergoing the requisite questioning by the vicar of nuns, she makes up her mind to deceive the priest and succeeds. Unable to break free of the tyranny in her life, Gertrude serves twelve months as a novice and then takes her final vows.

Manzoni's comment on Gertrude's final decision is a reflection on the power of the Christian religion to offer help in any circumstance.

If there is a remedy for what is past, she prescribes it and gives us the vision and strength to carry it out, whatever the cost. If there is no remedy, she shows us how to make a literal reality of the proverbial expression "to make a virtue of necessity." She teaches us to continue wisely in the course we entered upon out of frivolity. She chastens our heart to accept gladly that which is imposed on us by tyranny, she gives a reckless but irrevocable choice, all the sanctity, all the wisdom, all the—let us say,—all the joyful happiness of true vocation.[88]

Gertrude doesn't try to become religious, but instead tortures the young pupils placed in her charge out of envious revenge for the happiness they will one day enjoy outside the convent. She begins an affair with Egidio, a low-level criminal living near the convent, who works for a powerful criminal whom Manzoni calls the Unnamed. Gertrude even becomes an accomplice in the murder of a lay sister because of her threat to tell the authorities about Gertrude's relation with Egidio. It was a year after the murder that Lucia sought asylum in the convent, giving Gertrude a chance to begin her own redemption by taking care of the unfortunate Lucia.

Manzoni reports that Gertrude suffered great interior torments because of her way of life, such that even her physical appearance manifested the pain and disorder in her soul. Her situation worsened when the Unnamed gave Egidio the order to kidnap Lucia and bring her to his castle for delivery to Don Rodrigo. Gertrude took pleasure in Lucia's company, and helping her was even an act of expiation for her sins. She didn't want to sacrifice an innocent girl but, as usual, acting against her better judgment, complied with Egidio's demand to give up Lucia. Complicity in kidnapping was of a piece with her acceptance of bloodshed and other crimes. As Manzoni writes, "Crime is a rigid, unbending master, against

88. Ibid., 203–4.

whom no one can be strong except by total rebellion. Gertrude did not make up her mind to this—and so she did what she was told."[89]

Manzoni introduces the Unnamed to his readers just before the kidnapping of Lucia takes place. He is a man who "had outdistanced the ordinary crowd of evil doers and left them far behind." Around the age of sixty he begins to feel "not remorse but a sort of disquiet at the thought of his past crimes. The numerous offenses which had piled up in his memory, if not on his conscience, seemed to come to life again whenever he committed a new one."[90] Manzoni reports that feelings of repugnance first arose when he initially embarked on a life of crime. He was able to overcome the pangs of conscience with thoughts of his own strength and the long future ahead of him, as well as by the excitement of his life. "In earlier times," writes Manzoni, "the non-stop spectacle of violence, revenge and murder had filled him with a ferocious competitive spirit and also served as a sort of counterweight to his conscience."[91] But now the thought of a God to whom he was responsible kept intruding into his consciousness—"and yet I am."[92] He was still laboring to expel thoughts of repentance when Nibbio brings Lucia to his castle and, totally out of character, talks to the Unnamed about the feeling of compassion he felt for Lucia. The frightened girl pleads with him and says, "God will forgive so many things, for a single act of mercy."[93] He begins to wonder why he ever agreed to help Don Rodrigo kidnap this girl, but can't come up with an answer. At this point, Manzoni offers an interpretation of the Unnamed's motivation: "His willingness to take that action had not been the fruit of a deliberate decision, but rather the instantaneous response of a mind trained to follow long-standing—habitual ideas— the consequences of a thousand previous events."[94] The Unnamed was just acting in character according to his settled habits. Upon further self-examination, the Unnamed begins to realize the enormity of his crimes, "an enormity which the passions had previously concealed."[95]

Manzoni's reference to the blinding effect of passions calls to mind the long-standing Christian tradition on this theme. Freely willed personal sin causes a lack of self-knowledge and an inability to appreciate the attractiveness of virtue. In *The Confessions* St. Augustine eloquently describes

89. Ibid., 372.   90. Ibid., 369.
91. Ibid., 370.   92. Ibid., 370.
93. Ibid., 386.   94. Ibid., 393–94.
95. Ibid., 394.

his self-willed ignorance. He accuses himself of not wanting to know the truth about God and himself. Commenting on his tendency to ask questions with the wrong attitude, Augustine writes, "I sought an answer to the question 'Whence is evil?' but, I sought it in an evil way, and did not see the evil in my search."[96] In book 8, Augustine explains at length how bad habits voluntarily assumed become a despot and a burden. For example, he says: "For in truth lust is made out of a perverse will, and when lust is served it becomes habit, and when habit is not resisted, it becomes necessity."[97] The Unnamed's habit of crime had become a necessity in his life. Augustine also explains how God's grace gave him the opportunity to see his mistake and the strength to change course. As the Unnamed begins to see the horror of his life, he first feels despair and even contemplates suicide, but then finds some relief in Lucia's words "heard more than once, only a few hours before, 'God will forgive so many things, for an act of mercy.'"[98] The final stage of the Unnamed's conversion takes place in front of a man as famous for his virtue as the Unnamed was notorious for his vice. He is Cardinal Federigo Borromeo, the Archbishop of Milan.

Upon first meeting Cardinal Borromeo, the Unnamed doesn't speak:

The Unnamed had been driven there by the compelling force of a mysterious inner tempest, rather than led there by a reasoned decision; and it was the same force that made him stand there, tormented by two contrary passions— on the one hand, a powerful longing and a confused hope of finding relief from his internal torture, and on the other, wrath and shame at the idea of coming like a penitent, an underling, a vulgar wretch, to admit himself in the wrong, and implore the help of a fellow man.[99]

In a few moving pages, Manzoni reports the conversation between the two "great" men and conveys the emotions felt by both. Manzoni clearly shows that the Cardinal's insight into the soul of the Unnamed, as well as his virtue, especially humility, facilitate the last stages of the Unnamed's conversion. The Unnamed once again understands the depth of his iniquities but this time is able to say: "and yet I feel a comfort, a joy...yes, yes,...a joy such as I have never known during all this repugnant life of mine."[100]

96. Augustine, *Confessions*, book 7, ch. 5.   97. Ibid., book 8, ch. 5.
98. Manzoni, *The Betrothed*, 395.   99. Ibid., 413.
100. Ibid., 418.

The Cardinal's interpretation of the joy felt by the Unnamed echoes perennial Christian wisdom. He says, "That is a foretaste of joys to come…which God gives you to make you love his service, and to hearten you to enter resolutely into the new life in which you will have so much evil to undo, so many acts of reparation to perform, so many tears to shed."[101] The Unnamed responds to the Cardinal by telling him about the outrage to which Lucia had been subject. Then both the Unnamed and the Cardinal set about to restore Lucia to her former way of life.

Manzoni's description of Federigo Borromeo gives still another angle on virtue. "He was one of those few men—rare in any age—who devote the resources of an exceptional intellect, of vast wealth, and of a privileged position in society in an unbroken effort to seek out and practice the means of making the world a better place."[102] As a young boy Borromeo was able to accept the constant teaching of his religious tradition on humility, the vanity of pleasure, and the injustices of pride, even though the diametrically opposed teachings were often professed and lived by the very people who taught the authentic Christian doctrine. He came to believe that everyone has a duty to perform so that life is not "a treadmill for the majority and unending holidays for the few."[103] He had no interest in having a superior position so that he might enjoy superiority over others. He was content to do his duty as a simple priest, and only accepted to become Archbishop of Milan "at the express command of the Pope."[104]

While Archbishop, Borromeo was frugal in the use of resources for himself, but very generous toward others. He used his great personal wealth both to help the poor and to support learning. He did the latter on a grand scale by establishing the Ambrosian Library and paying a salary to nine scholars to work in theology, history, literature, and oriental languages. Manzoni reports that Borromeo continued his patronage of the library and scholars despite hearing criticism. When a plague was ravaging Milan, Cardinal Borromeo resisted pressure to leave the city, but stayed on, motivating his priests to offer their lives in the care of the sick.

Cardinal Borromeo's conversation with Don Abbondio shows pastoral care and an appreciation for the possibility and obligation of overcoming moral weakness. As Abbondio's bishop, Borromeo reproaches him for failing to carry out his priestly duty to marry Renzo and Lucia, but then he helps the parish priest to overcome his fear of threats, to appreciate

101. Ibid.   102. Ibid., 401.
103. Ibid.   104. Ibid.

the sufferings of the betrothed, and to grow in love for them. The bishop tells the parish priest that he should have prepared himself for his priestly duties by asking God for the requisite courage. This exhortation reminded me of Augustine's reflection on the accountability of the soul in his *On the Free Choice of the Will:* "It must be held to account for what it has not tried to know, and for what it has not taken proper care in preparing itself to perform rightly."[105] Don Abbondio clearly did not prepare himself to carry out the duties of the priesthood. In fact, he never tried to understand the meaning of being a priest.

A remarkable trait possessed by Cardinal Borromeo was his independence from the opinions of others. After describing an unusual act of kindness by Borromeo, Manzoni writes, "we would like to see more examples of a virtue so free from influence by the reigning opinions of the day—for every period has its own."[106] Despite criticism, Borromeo had given a young girl a suitable dowry so that she would not be forced into a nunnery by her father.

Manzoni makes clear that Borromeo's virtues were quite extraordinary, even for a good bishop. Despite the pressures of the culture and corruption within the Church, Borromeo was able to avoid unwise accommodation to the spirit of the age. He lived out, in truly remarkable fashion, the Biblical teaching that all men and women should find ways to live for the common good. "As each has received a gift, employ it for one another, as good stewards of God's varied grace" (1 Pt 4:10).

Manzoni is such a realistic storyteller, with an eye for revealing details, that his readers cannot but see more clearly into personal and social consequences of passions and virtues. The story of Fr. Cristoforo shows that zeal for justice requires equal attentiveness to one's own vices and imperfections, as well; Gertrude's story makes the reader *feel* that freedom is a necessary condition of genuine virtue; the conversion of the Unnamed reveals how the attainment of self-knowledge requires a person to overcome the blinding effect of passions. The description of Borromeo suggests the possibility of learning to live the Christian faith, even when religious leaders inculcate Christian and non-Christian teachings at the same time. His life also shows that the attainment of the common good depends on the practice of virtue by individuals, especially leaders.

105. St. Augustine, *On Free Choice of the Will* (Indianapolis and New York: Bobbs Merrill, 1964), book III, no. 218.

106. Manzoni, *The Betrothed*, 408.

On the last page of his novel Manzoni himself expresses agreement with the reflections of Lucia and Renzo on the meaning of the events in their lives. After being married for some indeterminate period of time, they both come to this conclusion:

Troubles may come because we have asked for them; but that the most prudent and innocent of conduct is not necessarily enough to keep them away; also that when they come, through our fault or otherwise, trust in God goes far to take away their sting, and makes them a useful preparation for a better life.[107]

Alas, this conclusion to Manzoni's novel is true for just about everyone.

107. Ibid., 720.

CHAPTER 4

Seeking the Common Good through Justice and Social Justice

The first part of this chapter relies mainly on Aquinas and Augustine to explain Catholic wisdom on justice. Such terms as justice, distributive justice, and commutative justice will be explained. In the second half of the chapter I discuss the debates about the meaning of social justice among Catholic scholars and make an argument for interpreting social justice in the light of what Aquinas said about legal and universal justice. The practice of justice in all its various forms is crucial for the attainment of the common good.

Aquinas on Justice

Many people speak endlessly of justice, especially social justice, without saying what it is or without even feeling the need to ask about its nature. In one strange respect justice is now like pornography: people say they can't give a definition, but they know it when they see it. Justice doesn't have to remain so mysterious. We can all profitably turn to Thomas Aquinas for assistance in clarifying the nature of justice and its various dimensions. He may not have said everything we need to know today, but he did make many illuminating and apt observations about justice, legal justice, distributive justice, and commutative justice.

Aquinas gets to the heart of the matter with the basic definition of justice: "a habit whereby an individual renders to each one his due (*ius*) by a constant and perpetual will."[1] This may be the most oft-quoted definition of justice. It shows that justice is about those things that have to do with our relations with one another. The word "right" in the definition, of course, is not synonymous with the modern concept of "rights," but

1. Thomas Aquinas, *Summa theologiae*, II-II, qu. 58, a. 1.

143

refers to "the just thing itself." While justice, properly speaking, governs the relations of one person or entity to another, it can also be understood in a metaphorical sense as the virtue regulating "diverse principles of actions, such as the reason, the irascible [or spirited] appetite and the concupiscible [or desiring] appetite, as though they were so many agents." In other words, justice governs the relations among the various powers of the soul, "so that metaphorically in one and the same man there is said to be justice in so far as the reason commands the irascible appetite and concupiscible appetite, and these obey reason; and in general in so far as to each part of man is ascribed what is becoming to it."[2] Reason, then, would in turn be subject to God's will known through faith.

This concept of justice as order in the soul of individuals needs to be rediscovered today. There are several reasons for this. First, it enables us to understand better the meaning of justification and justice in the New Testament. Aquinas explains, "the justice which faith works in us, is that whereby the ungodly is justified: it consists in the due co-ordination of the parts of the soul....Now this belongs to justice metaphorically understood, which may be found even in a man who lives by himself."[3] We capture this sense of justice when we speak of the just person in our ordinary speech. Second, the political and social significance of justice as order in the soul can be readily perceived by turning back to Augustine's influential teaching that the attainment of justice in a political community depends on the presence of justice in the souls of individuals. And justice must be understood as order in the soul, which is only achieved by the practice of all the virtues.[4]

Today, there is a lot of talk about giving people their due, usually under the rubric of "social justice." There is not, however, a corresponding enthusiasm for achieving order in our souls, even though many people readily understand that some don't receive what is just because others don't want to give it to them. The reluctance to give, if it doesn't proceed from ignorance, is caused by disordered passions in the soul. People with disorder in their souls will not be inclined to give others their due. Ordinary speech makes this same judgment when it blames an unjust situation on the "corruption" of leaders. Thomas Aquinas clarifies this point in his

2. Ibid., II-II, qu. 58, a. 2.
3. Ibid., II-II, qu. 58, a. 2, reply to obj. 1.
4. St. Augustine, *The City of God* (Baltimore: Penguin Books, 1972; New York: Modern Library, 1950), book XIX, chap. 21.

treatment of the connection among the virtues. He makes the common-sense observation that fear and desire, if not governed by fortitude and temperance, can often lead people to injustice. He expresses this point nicely in his *Disputed Questions on Virtue*, recently translated by Ralph Mc-Inerny:

But the principles of morals are so interrelated to one another that the failure of one would entail the failure in others. For example, if one were weak on the principle that concupiscence is not to be followed, which pertains to desire, then sometimes in pursuing concupiscence, he would do injury and thus violate justice.[5]

In other words, excessive love of pleasure and money can lead people to harm others by, for example, committing adultery or defrauding them of their good. Similarly, people may have to overcome their own fears in order to protect others from being harmed in some way. For example, a young person may know that his friends are wrong to pick on a weaker boy, but hesitates to speak up for fear of being excluded from his group. An adviser to a president may hesitate to speak the truth in front of his boss about some injustice for fear of losing influence or his job. Road rage often leads to injury or death on the nation's highways. It is patience, a dimension of fortitude, that enables a person both to control his anger in the face of provocation and to persevere in the face of opposition. Without sufficient patience a person may not persevere in the struggle to make sure that others receive their due. For example, the principal of a school may lack the patience to seek out good teachers or to make sure that his school really delivers a quality education.

The connection of prudence with justice is especially pertinent. Aquinas distinguishes ordinary prudence from political prudence. He says that everyone in the state of grace has sufficient prudence to do what is required for his own salvation, but not everyone has the political prudence to discern the requirements of the common good. In Aquinas's words, "There is also another diligence which is more than sufficient, whereby a man is able to make provision both for himself and for others, not only in matters necessary for salvation, but also in all things relating to human life; and such diligence as this is not in all who have grace."[6] The acqui-

5. Thomas Aquinas, *Disputed Questions on Virtue*, trans., ed. Ralph McInerny (South Bend, Ind.: St. Augustine's Press, 1999), 120.
6. Aquinas, *Summa theologiae*, II-II, qu. 47, a. 14, reply to obj. 1.

sition of such diligence may be acquired over time with the right kind of experience and instruction. "In matters of prudence man stands in very great need of being taught by others, especially elders who have acquired a sane understanding of the ends in practical matters."[7] In Thomas's terminology much experience is necessary to become a prudent person. Wise older people with much experience of the world are apt instructors of the young. It logically follows that understanding books written by those who have wisdom on matters pertaining to the common good is an excellent way of seeking political prudence.

The Old Testament story of David and Abigail, to which we briefly referred in the previous chapter, sheds a clear light on the relation of prudence and justice. While David and his men were living in the wilderness, they had shown respect for the property of Nabal and even protected his sheep and goats. On a feast day David sent ten young men to ask Nabal to give them what he could spare. Nabal refused and even insulted David. The latter resolved to take vengeance on Nabal and his men. When Abigail, Nabal's wife, discovered what happened she brought a great quantity of food to David and persuaded him to forgive Nabal's offense. She explained to David that he would have "pangs of conscience" and cause for grief if he "shed blood without cause" and indulged a desire for personal vengeance. She also reminded David that he had duties to fulfill to the Lord before and after he became king of Israel. She clearly implied that behaving unjustly would be an obstacle to his God-given mission. David responded to Abigail in these words: "Blessed be the Lord, the God of Israel, who sent you this day to meet me! Blessed be your prudence, and blessed be you, who have kept me from bloodguilt and from avenging myself with my own hand" (1 Sm 25:33). David avoided doing an injustice because he was able to accept the counsel of a wise woman. On another occasion, when King David does behave unjustly both by committing adultery with Bathsheba and having her husband Uriah killed, he is able to repent when the prophet Nathan reproaches him for his sins. David has sufficient docility to accept wise counsel.

Understanding justice as what is due to another *and* as order in the soul, brought about by the practice of the virtues, is the most important starting point of any inquiry into the nature of justice, but is still only a beginning. Virtuous persons are inclined and able to give others their due if they have acquired sufficient knowledge of what, in fact, is the just

7. Ibid., II-II, qu. 49, a. 3.

thing to do. Knowledgeable people without virtue are not likely to act justly toward others, unless it happens to be in their self-interest. Virtuous individuals, without knowledge of what is due to others, will not be able to make much of a contribution, although they will be inclined to seek out the requisite knowledge. That knowledge cannot be acquired by simply adopting, say, the prevailing opinions in the Republican or Democratic parties. A work of discernment is necessary, which will be facilitated by the right kind of education (see chapter 8).

Aquinas also offers us a commentary on particular justice that is directed to the private individual in two ways and, appropriately, has two different names. "The order of one private individual to another" is governed by commutative justice.[8] A $10,000 payment to a dealer for a car entitles a person to a vehicle worth the same. This form of justice is the easiest to grasp. What is owed (the *debitum*) is twofold. First, Aquinas says, "it is necessary to equalize thing with thing, so that the one person should pay back to the other just so much as he has become richer out of that which belonged to the other."[9] This form of commutative justice is also called "contract justice," because the parties agree to some fair exchange—a certain sum of money in exchange for a house or a car. Commutative justice also takes the form of restitution. Aquinas says restitution is in order when one person has what belongs to another, "either with his consent, for instance on loan or deposit, or against his will, as in robbery or theft."[10] People have a serious obligation to restore what has been taken unjustly. Such restitution is even necessary for salvation, says Aquinas. While commutative justice is mainly about buying and selling, it also deals with penal justice. Offenses against the citizens of a nation call for proportionate punishment.

It is interesting to note that Aristotle devotes more attention to commutative justice than to distributive justice. Commenting on the justice section of the *Ethics*, political philosopher Leo Strauss argues in his class notes that Aristotle describes "commutative justice as the bond of society." What Aristotle seems to mean is that fair exchange in buying and selling is crucial for the stability of society. People will not produce goods and services if they are habitually defrauded, and they will lose confidence in the fairness of their nation's economy. In the United States the dishonesty of banks and other large companies has eroded confidence

---

8. Ibid., II-II, qu. 61, a. 1.   9. Ibid., II-II, qu. 61, a. 2.
10. Ibid., II-II, qu. 62, a. 1.

in corporate America, with detrimental effects that will be felt for a long time. The economic crisis of 2008–2009 has aggravated the situation.

The other form of particular justice is called distributive. It governs "the order of the whole towards the parts to which corresponds the order of that which belongs to the community in relation to each single person."[11] Distributive justice distributes common goods proportionately. The community distributes common goods to individuals as they are deserving because of some excellence or need. There will, of course, always be arguments as to who is more entitled to receive the common goods, but at times nearly everyone will agree that a particular group of people will justly receive more material goods or services than others. Citizens agree that the political community should obviously spend much more money on the education of children than that of adults. The state and private entities provide primary and secondary education to young people between the ages of seven and eighteen or nineteen. Whether private educational institutions should receive direct or indirect aid is a disputed question.

A Supreme Court decision upholding the constitutionality of school vouchers in the city of Cleveland is, in my judgment, an example of distributive justice. With $2,250 vouchers in hand, the poor and the disadvantaged will have the opportunity to choose private schools as an attractive alternative to inadequate public schools, especially in the inner city. Most parents will choose religiously affiliated schools, since they are more numerous and affordable. Some deny, of course, that the high court's decision is an act of distributive justice, but label it a violation of the constitutional separation between church and state as well as bad policy. *The Boston Globe* made this twofold argument in an editorial, despite conceding that a state-sponsored audit revealed "that only 10 percent of Cleveland students met basic proficiency standards, and more than two-thirds dropped out or failed before graduation." The *Globe's* solution is to rely on "proven reforms in public education." The Boston paper further argues that "Private schools can pick and choose their state-subsidized enrollees, draining resources from the schools left behind and creating even greater divisions between poor students and successful ones."[12] The *Washington Post* columnist George Will, on the other hand, had high praise for the decision.

11. Ibid., II-II, qu. 61, a. 1.
12. "The price of vouchers," *Boston Globe* editorial (June 28, 2002).

The opposition to school choice for the poor is the starkest immorality in contemporary politics. It is the defense of the strong (teachers' unions) and comfortable (the middle class) against the weak and suffering—inner-city children. Happily yesterday, socially disadvantaged children had their best day in court since *Brown v. Board of Education* in 1954.[13]

The sharp disagreement between the *Boston Globe* and George Will indicates the difficulty of arriving at a consensus on the meaning of distributive justice in particular cases. Disagreements on church-state issues, of course, are always more contentious and implacable than differences of opinion on many other political issues.

The dispute between the supporters of the positions taken by Will and the *Globe* does not even raise all the pertinent issues. If religiously affiliated schools accept state money provided by the vouchers, they might be legally coerced or pressured by public opinion to water down their religious identity or to accept students who have no interest in receiving a religious formation. The existence of vouchers, furthermore, cannot be an excuse for accepting the poor performance of public schools in the inner city or elsewhere. Since many children will not be able to take advantage of vouchers, they will need better public schools in their neighborhoods.

All in all, I think vouchers could benefit a significant number of needy families, but steps must be taken both to ensure the quality of all public schools and to uphold the religious identity of private institutions. I believe the public schools will fare better if they face competition from private schools, especially in the inner city. At any rate, the failure of this nation to ensure quality education for the poor, especially minorities in the inner city, is an egregious violation of distributive justice.

Another interesting aspect of distributive justice is the manner of determining the mean. "The mean is observed, not according to equality between thing and thing, but according to proportion between things and persons: so that, namely, as one person surpasses another, so also a thing which is given to one person surpasses the thing given to another." "The equality between thing and thing" is an equality according to the arithmetic mean. It refers to the practice of commutative justice, whereby two persons exchange things of equal value. It doesn't matter who the persons are. Whether rich or poor, king or commoner, a person must give the equivalent value in a fair exchange. With respect to distributive justice, the situation of the individual person is determinative. Only cer-

13. George Will, "Implacable Enemies of Choice," *Washington Post* (June 28, 2002).

tain classes of people receive veteran's benefits, Medicaid, Medicare, social security, public education. The mean "follows geometrical proportion, wherein equality depends not on quantity, but on proportion."[14]

The attainment of distributive justice depends very much on the prudence and moral virtue of those responsible for distributing common goods. Since citizens in democratic regimes can bring pressure to bear on rulers to act justly, they share in the responsibility for distributive justice. However, electoral persuasion will not be effective without sufficient knowledge and virtue in the electorate. For that kind of transformation to happen, democratic citizens must be suitably educated by the institutions of civil society, especially by the family and the university. In other words, for distributive justice to be effective, social justice will have to be practiced on a sufficiently wide scale. Why that is the case will be explained in the next section.

Social Justice

The mark of the moral person today, both within and outside the Catholic Church, has become dedication to human rights and especially social justice. The intellectual, moral, and theological virtues are hardly mentioned in social-justice circles. (Virtue has only become a principal theme of contemporary philosophical and theological ethics in the last thirty years or so.) Social justice as presently understood has little to do with personal virtue. Two common meanings of the term are a more equitable distribution of wealth through government intervention and, especially, a reconstruction of the social and political order in view of a more equitable distribution of goods through the reform of institutions. The second meaning, of course, is not without ambiguity. Father J. Bryan Hehir, under the influence of William Ferree,[15] clarifies this meaning by arguing that "social justice is designed to evaluate and redirect those public institutions that hinder the achievement of the common good.... [It] is focused on the functioning of major public institutions of the social, legal, economic, or political orders."[16] According to this description, social justice means a state of affairs brought about by some kind of concerted

14. Aquinas, *Summa theologiae*, II-II, qu. 61, a. 2.
15. I discuss the thought of Ferree toward the end of the chapter.
16. J. Bryan Hehir, "Social Justice," in *The Harper Collins Encyclopedia of Catholicism*, ed. Richard P. McBrien (San Francisco: Harper Collins, 1995), 1204.

activity, especially by the activity of the state. Still other meanings may include progressive opinions on political and social issues, volunteer work for the needy, and the recognition of a wide variety of rights, especially for the disadvantaged. While these descriptions of social justice have their measure of truth, they do not reveal the whole concept.

The contemporary concern for social justice leads primarily to a stress on public-policy initiatives, to a reorganization of "the system," and to social reform. In addition, there is a tendency to regard social justice as a principle of rights against society rather than as a virtue inclining a person to fulfill duties toward society. There is a stress on the demand for just treatment for others rather than the duty to act justly oneself. In other words, the perspective of social justice leads to an outlook that considers things not from the just person's point of view, but from that of those citizens to whom just treatment is due. Social justice is the title in whose name individuals and groups demand things as their rights or make demands on behalf of others.

Without more clarity some good actions will not be accepted as acts of social justice, and the preconditions for its practice, namely the laborious effort to prepare one's soul for action through the cultivation of the virtues and the acquisition of knowledge, will not be recognized. I contend that some works of justice require very sophisticated knowledge and very great efforts to control pride, anger, and fear as well as love of pleasure, money, honor, and power. To achieve the requisite clarity I now take a brief look at the history of the term "social justice."

The concept of social justice is relatively new in the history of theology and political philosophy. No theologian or philosopher prior to the nineteenth century ever spoke of social justice: not Plato, not Aristotle, neither Augustine nor Aquinas. A Jesuit philosopher by the name of Luigi Taparelli D'Azeglio was the first to use the concept of social justice in his major work, *Saggio teoretico di diritto naturale appoggiato sul fatto.*[17] It was not until 1931, with the publication of Pius XI's *Quadragesimo anno*, that the concept of social justice officially and formally entered into the patrimony of papal social thought, although as early as 1923 Pius XI had already equated Thomistic legal justice with social justice.[18] Between Taparelli

17. Luigi Taparelli D'Azeglio, *Saggio teoretico di diritto naturale appoggiato sul fatto*, 2 vol. (Palermo, 1840–1843).

18. Jean Y. Calvez, "Social Justice," in vol. 13 of the *New Catholic Encyclopedia* (Washington, D.C.: The Catholic University of America Press, 1967), 319.

and Pius XI, scholars explained the concept of social justice in different ways. Crucial to an adequate appraisal of the concept is some appreciation of what happened to Aquinas's notion of legal justice in the works of his commentators.

My intention is to analyze the prevailing concepts of social justice in terms of the broader context of the Catholic philosophical and theological tradition stemming from Aquinas. I do so, not with the intention of denying the legitimacy, sincerity, or importance of the contemporary concern for social justice, but with the intention, on the contrary, of giving greater balance to that concern, precisely by retrieving a fuller sense of the concept of social justice. To this end, this chapter will proceed by considering, in turn, the meaning of social justice as found in Pius XI's *Quadragesimo anno* and the two interpretations of *Quadragesimo anno* that have shaped the American discussion of social justice. These considerations will prepare us, in conclusion, to propose a concept of social justice more faithful to the Catholic tradition than the typical contemporary understanding. That is to say, social justice should be an updated version of Thomistic legal justice.

Aquinas originally wrote that legal justice is the virtue that "directs the acts of all the virtues to the common good."[19] Legal justice inclines a person to perform actions useful to another, to the community, or to the ruler of the community. It consists in the exercise of every virtue having to do with another. Every moral virtue directed to the common good is called legal justice. Prudence, of course, is essential for the practice of legal justice, since all moral virtue is incomplete without prudence. Through examining the virtue of legal justice, Thomas Aquinas makes clear the essential link between personal virtue and justice, as well as the obligation of all citizens to find a way to contribute to the common good, either by fighting injustices and/or promoting an ever-more-just society.

Prior to the publication of Pius XI's *Quadragesimo anno* in 1931, Catholic scholars proposed different interpretations of Thomistic legal justice and the new concept of social justice. A number of Aquinas's commentators interpreted legal justice to mean simple obedience to the laws of the state.[20] With such a narrow meaning, legal justice could not play a central role in guiding the quest for a just social order. French social Catholics

19. Aquinas, *Summa theologiae*, II-II, qu. 58, a. 6.
20. Jeremiah Newman, *Foundation of Justice: A Historico-critical Study in Thomism* (Cork, Ireland: Cork University Press, 1954), 97–115.

were mainly responsible for diffusion of the term "social justice" between 1880 and 1890, but they didn't clearly distinguish the concept from distributive justice. German scholars had a tendency to reduce social justice to commutative justice.[21]

The publication of *Quadragesimo anno* (*On Reconstruction of the Social Order*) had the potential of ending the debate about the meaning of social justice, but it did not. The scholarly commentary on the so-called social justice encyclical is unevenly divided as to the meaning of sound social justice. The larger group of scholars, including Brucculeri, Calvez, Nell-Breuning, and Newman, among others, argue, correctly in my opinion, that Pius XI understood by social justice what Thomas Aquinas meant by legal justice.[22] For example, Jeremiah Newman writes, "As a virtue it is best described as that disposition of the will which inclines individuals and social groups in general to work for the common good of the community of which they are parts."[23] That means that individuals and groups can work for the common good of the family, the professions, any voluntary association, and the country as a whole. Hence everyone "can contribute directly to the common good at some level or another."[24]

After studying *Quadragesimo anno* over a period of years I can well understand why scholars could disagree about the proper interpretation of social justice. The full meaning of the concept can be discerned only by connecting various parts of the encyclical and by drawing out the implications of the connections. The most helpful interpretive aid for that work of discernment is to keep in mind the precise definition of social justice given by Pius XI in his 1937 encyclical *Divini redemptoris* (*On Atheistic Communism*).

It is of the very essence of social justice to demand from each individual all that is necessary for the common good. But just as in the living organism it is impossible to provide for the good of the whole unless each part and each individual member is given what it needs for the exercise of its proper functions, so it is impossible to care for the social organism and the good of society as a unit unless each single part and each individual member...is supplied with all that is necessary for the exercise of his social functions.[25]

---

21. Jean-Yves Calvez and Jacques Perrin, *Église and Societé économique: L'enseignment social des papes de Leon XIII à Pie XII 1878–1958* (Paris: Aubier, 1959), 543–57.

22. Aquinas, *Summa theologiae*, qu. 58, a. 3.   23. Newman, *Foundation of Justice*, 108.

24. Ibid., 109.

25. Pope Pius XI, *Divini redemptoris* (*On Atheistic Communism*), no. 51.

This means, as Newman suggested, that social justice is a virtue inclining persons and groups to work for the common good of the family, the
professions, voluntary associations, schools, neighborhoods, and the political community on the local, national, or international level. In this
understanding of social justice "the duty of making oneself a neighbor
to others and actively serving them becomes even more urgent, the more
needy people are, in whatever area this may be."[26] This Catholic perspective opens up vistas of service for individuals of widely differing talents,
but implicitly suggests that various levels of knowledge and suitable dispositions are required for effective service. Consider all that would be
necessary to be accomplished by many individuals to make sure that more
college students graduate with the ability to read well, to write correctly, and to ponder questions pertaining to the best way to live and to the
meaning of the common good. Imagine all that individuals would have to
know and do in order to help various communities address the problems
of poverty at home and abroad. Social justice, then, requires not only that
the common good be served by everyone, but also, as Pius XI implies in
the above selection from *Divini redemptoris,* that all have the requisite material goods and receive the kind of education and formation in order
to make a contribution to the common good. If individuals are not adequately prepared to work for social justice, there is no reasonable ground
to expect very much.

Turning now to the grand themes of *Quadragesimo anno,* we see that Pius
XI is striving "to restore society according to the mind of the Church on
the firmly established basis of social justice and social charity."[27] This
restoration of society can happen only if there is a Christian reform of
morals. To make his point forcefully and link it with the tradition of papal social teaching, he quotes Leo XIII: "If human society is to be healed,
only a return to Christian life and morality will heal it."[28] In such phras-

26. *Catechism of the Catholic Church* (Vatican City: Libreria Editrice Vaticana, 1994), no.
1932.

27. Pius XI, *Quadragesimo anno* (*On Reconstruction of the Social Order*), no. 126.

28. *Quadragesimo anno,* no. 129. "Si societati generis humani medendum est, revocatio
vitae institutorumque christianorum sola medebitur." The Italian translation of this
sentence reads "se ai mali del mondo v'e rimedio, questi non puo essere altro che il
ritorno alla vita e ai costumi cristiani." The word *institutorum,* the genitive plural of *in-
stitutum,* was correctly translated in the Italian version of *Rerum novarum* as "costumi,"
meaning morality. In *Quadragesimo anno* there is a new Italian translation of Leo XIII's
Latin. It reads "Se un remedio si vuole dare alla societa umana, questo non sara altro

es as "the Christian reform of morals," "correction of morals," "reform of morals," "a renewal of the Christian spirit," "the spirit of the Gospel, which is the spirit of Christian moderation and universal charity," "return...to the teaching of the gospel [and] to the precepts of [Christ]" and, of course, "a return to Christian life and morality," Pius XI stresses the correction of morals or a return to virtue as the principal means of restoring society.[29] What Pius XI says, in particular, about social justice must be understood in the light of what he says about the role of virtue or morals in bringing about the renewal of society. Virtue is so impor-

---

che il ritorno alla vita e alle istitutioni cristiane." *Institutorum* is incorrectly translated as institutions. When Pius XI means institutions he uses the Latin word *institutio*. See, for example no. 78, "When we speak of the reform of institutions" (*institutionum*, the genitive plural of *institutio*). Unfortunately, the English translations of both *Rerum novarum* and *Quadragesimo anno* have "institutions" for *institutorum*. These translations were, indeed, unfortunate, because English-speaking peoples have difficulty understanding the dependence of the reform of society upon the correction of morals. While "Christian institutions" don't suggest morals at first glance, the term could direct a discerning reader to the four main aspects of Christianity: belief, morality, sacraments, and prayer. It will more likely conjure up in the general reader an image of societal "structures" that have some kind of a Christian inspiration.

29. (1) "We deem it fitting...to lay bare the root of existing social confusion and at the same time show the only way to sound restoration: namely, the Christian reform of morals" (*christianam nempe morum reformationem*, no. 15). (2) "[t]hat even more copious and richer benefits may accrue to the family of mankind, two things are especially necessary: reform of institutions and correction of morals" (*institutionum reformatio atque emendatio morum*, no. 77). (3) "What we have taught about the reconstruction and perfection of social order can surely in no-wise be brought to realization without reform of morals (*sine reformatione morum*)," no. 97. (4) "There remains to us, after again calling to judgment the economic system now in force and its most bitter accuser, socialism, and passing explicit and just sentence upon them, to search out more thoroughly the root of these many evils and to point out that the first and most necessary remedy is a reform of morals" (in *moribus reformandis*, no 98). (5) "Yet, if we look into the matter more carefully and more thoroughly, we shall perceive that preceding this ardently desired social restoration, there must be a renewal of the Christian spirit (*spiritus christiani renovatio*), from which so many immersed in economic life have, far and wide, unhappily fallen away, lest all our efforts be wasted and our house be built not on a rock but on shifting sand" (no. 127). (6) "No genuine cure can be furnished for this lamentable ruin of souls, which, so long as it continues, will frustrate all efforts to regenerate society unless men return openly and sincerely to the teaching of the Gospel and to the precepts of Him who alone has the words of eternal life" (no. 136). (7) "Therefore, out of this new diffusion throughout the world of the spirit of the Gospel, which is the spirit of Christian moderation and universal charity (*christianae moderationis et universalis caritatis spiritus est*), we are confident there will come that longed-for and full restoration of human society in Christ" (no. 138).

tant because it "alone can provide effective remedy for that excessive care for passing things that is the origin of all vices."[30] In other words, when souls are in ruin, "all efforts to regenerate society will be ineffective."[31] The vices and souls in ruin, of course, are the main cause of societal injustice. Otherwise stated, the disordered passions in the soul—the result of original sin—are the cause of injustices in economic and social life. For example, greed leads people to seek wealth by breaking God's laws and by violating the rights of one's neighbors. The same immoderate love of riches will incline people to omit practicing almsgiving, beneficence, and munificence. This is one of the most basic political teachings of Augustine, Aquinas, Thomas More, Plato, and Aristotle.

The restoration of the social order depends not only on the correction of morals, but also on the reform of institutions. What Pius XI means by this kind of reform is really the reinvigoration of civil society through respect for the principle of subsidiarity by the state. The pope deplores the "the overthrow and near extinction of that rich social life which was once highly developed through associations of various kinds."[32] What he saw was a social order dominated by individuals and the state, with the latter overburdened by tasks once shared with the associations of civil society. He recommends the kind of institutional reform that would allow individuals and various kinds of associations to make significant contributions to the maintenance and renewal of the social order.

The supreme authority of the state ought, therefore, to let subordinate groups handle matters and concerns of lesser importance, which would otherwise dissipate its efforts greatly. Thereby the state will more freely, powerfully, and effectively do all those things that belong to it alone, because it alone can do them: directing, urging, restraining, as occasion requires and necessity demands. Therefore, those in power should be sure that the more perfectly a graduated order is kept among the various associations, in observance of the principle of "subsidiary function," the stronger social authority and effectiveness will be and the happier and more prosperous the condition of the state.[33]

These recommendations, made in 1931, are now all the rage. Just about everyone wants individuals and voluntary associations to be active and participating in the renewal of the political and social order.[34] And nearly everyone wants the state to do effectively what the institutions of civil so-

---

30. *Quadragesimo anno*, no. 129.   31. Ibid., no. 136.
32. Ibid., no. 78.   33. Ibid., no. 80.
34. The principle of subsidiarity will be discussed more thoroughly in chapter 7.

ciety are not equipped to do: for instance, protect citizens from terrorists and prosecute those business executives who disrupt economic life by dishonest practices.

When Pius XI turns to particular reflections on social justice, he doesn't make a thorough presentation, but does give several concrete examples of what it entails, thereby revealing some implications of the new concept. He says that "the norms of the common good," "this law of social justice," require that each individual should receive his share of material goods, enough "both to meet the demands of necessity and decent comfort."[35] The pope leaves undefined what would be a proper distribution of goods. He does deplore "the huge disparity between the few exceedingly rich and the unnumbered propertyless," but implies that there will always be wealthy individuals who will be bound to find ways to benefit society by means of their superfluous income.[36]

Social justice further demands that wages be neither too high nor too low and so managed that as many people as possible have suitably remunerated work. Wages should be large enough so that workers and other employees can save part of their income after necessary expenditures have been made. In addition, social justice requires that a worker receive "a wage sufficient to support him and his family," the so-called family wage, "one large enough to meet ordinary family needs adequately. But if this cannot always be done under existing circumstances," adds Pius XI, "social justice demands that changes be introduced as soon as possible whereby such a wage will be assured to every workingman."[37] This papal teaching, with enormous implications, has been warmly received by many Catholics and non-Catholics. It demands systemic or structural changes in the political, economic, and social order to make possible what individuals and groups could not possibly afford to pay on their own. Pius XI implies that the way he reasons about the family wage could be applied to many other policy issues, as well. People are drawing out the implications of his thought when they say that social justice demands this or that systemic change.

In arguing that changes should be made to allow the payment of a just wage, Pius XI was not really proposing anything not already required by Thomistic legal justice. Among the requirements of that virtue are systemic changes that would promote the common good. Pius XI's presen-

35. *Quadragesimo anno*, nos. 58 and 75.   36. Ibid., no. 58.
37. Ibid., no. 71.

tation of social justice made clear that it too sometimes requires systemic changes, but, unlike many modern advocates of social justice, Pius XI
never assumed that such changes would be possible without the practice
of virtues by citizens and their leaders. As we have already seen, Pius XI
made that point over and over again in *Quadragesimo anno*. What Pius XI
doesn't emphasize is the vast learning required to know what systemic
changes would indeed promote the common good. Today it is not un-
common for people to speak and act as though the demands of social justice were easy to see and heed because the necessity of virtue and knowledge are no longer kept in mind. The program of the Democratic Party is
often used as a substitute for the laborious struggle to acquire knowledge
of what would serve the common good. It is amazing to hear so much
talk of social justice today that is uninformed by any serious inquiry into
the meaning of the common good. Both the acquisition of knowledge and
virtue are often treated as dispensable in the work for social justice.

The practice of virtue is the principal means of realizing the common
good or social justice. Virtue is thus clearly an essential *means* to the restoring of society, but it is also an end in itself. Pius XI makes this point
in discussing the relation between material well-being and virtue: To remove any possible doubt as to the meaning of the passage, Pius XI refers
the reader to the *De regimine principum* (On Kingship) of Thomas Aquinas
and to *Rerum novarum*, which contains references and even citations from
De regimine principum. The key passage from Aquinas reads as follows:

For an individual man to lead a good life two things are required. The first
and most important is to act in a virtuous manner (for virtue is that by which
one lives well); the second, which is secondary and instrumental, is a sufficiency of those bodily goods whose use is necessary for a virtuous life.[38]

Pius XI does not have an individualistic concept of virtue. He expects
individuals in all walks of life to make a contribution to the common
good or social justice by their virtue. Pius XI concludes his encyclical
with the exhortation: "let all strive according to the talent, powers, and
position of each to contribute something to the Christian reconstruction
of human society."[39]

In short, great individual efforts, whether alone or in groups, are need-

38. Thomas Aquinas, *On Kingship, to the King of Cyprus* (Toronto: Pontifical Institute of
Medieval Studies, 1982), I, 15.
39. *Quadragesimo anno*, no. 147.

ed to implement the teachings of the Gospel and thereby save society from ruin. Moral reform is important not only to save individuals from personal disaster, but also to fight evil in society, which in turn has a devastating effect on individual lives. "To ward off such great evils from human society nothing, therefore, is left untried; to this end may all our labors turn, to this all of our energies, to this our fervent and unremitting prayers to God. For with the assistance of Divine Grace the fate of the human family rests in our hands."[40]

Two American Interpretations of *Quadragesimo anno*

With the publication of *Quadragesimo anno* two American scholars, Msgr. John A. Ryan and William Ferree, believed that people finally could attain clarity about the meaning of social justice. Msgr. Ryan, one of the most prominent architects of Catholic social thought in the United States, wrote two articles in order to clarify the concept of social justice.[41] In the 1934 article he examines the eight paragraphs (Nos. 57, 58, 71, 74, 88, 101, 110, and 126) where Pius XI uses the term. He concludes that the pope means by "social justice" both legal justice (seven times) and distributive justice (eight times), and sometimes even commutative justice (two times.). The virtue of legal justice is practiced when individuals, associations, and the state contribute to the common good, for example, by bringing about reforms that would allow workers to be paid a wage sufficient for themselves and their families. This is an example of the structural reform of which we hear so much today. Distributive justice is understood to be a part of social justice when "it requires society or the state to bring about a proper distribution of goods among all classes" and to each individual in the various classes.[42] The provision of economic opportunities by the state is also an example of distributive justice. Commutative justice is understood to be an example of social justice when it proclaims that "workers have a strict right to living wage and employers a strict obligation to pay it or to achieve such reforms as will make such payment possible."[43] Finally, Ryan argues that when Pius XI identifies social justice as

40. Ibid., no. 145.
41. John A. Ryan, "The Concept of Social Justice," *Catholic Charities Review* 18, no. 10 (1934): 313–15; and Ryan, "Social Justice and the State," *Commonweal* 30 (1939): 205–6.
42. "Ryan, The Concept of Social Justice," 314.
43. Ibid., 314.

the common good, he understands the latter not to be "the good of the community taken collectively," but "the good common to all the members of the community."[44]

In his 1939 article Msgr. Ryan quotes with approval the following definition of social justice, given by Father Andre Rocaries: "Social Justice is the virtue which governs the relations of the members with society, as such, and the relations of society with its members; and which directs social and individual activities to the general good of the whole collective community." The general or common good of the whole community signifies "the good of society as a whole" and "the good *of all and of each.*" Father Rocaries believed that Pius XI was breaking new ground in teaching that the pursuit of the common good requires commitment to the good of every single individual. The subjects of social justice, according to Rocaries, are individuals, associations, and the rulers of the state. It is the latter that bears the primary responsibility in assuring the fair distribution of goods to individual members of the society.

Rocaries believes that distributive justice, strictly speaking, binds only the state, while social justice binds individuals, associations, and the state. Rocaries maintains that social justice is the same as legal justice, in that the object of both virtues is the common good of the whole community. Social justice, in addition, "aims at promoting the well-being of each and all, particularly by a more equitable division of the wealth of the world." Finally, Ryan reports that Rocaries "makes the practice and enforcement of social justice depend to a very great extent upon the state, particularly in the realm of economics." Ryan agrees with Rocaries's emphasis on the role of the state and even says that "the state should be regarded as by far the most important agent and instrument of social justice." Ryan makes this latter statement after quoting at length from paragraphs 51, 52, and 75 of Pius XI's *Divini redemptoris.* Ryan says nothing about the key quotation from no. 51, where Pius XI gives his well-known description of social justice, already discussed earlier in this chapter: "Now it is of the very essence of social justice to demand for each individual all that is necessary for the common good."

Msgr. Ryan is right to argue that Pius XI presents social justice to mean both legal justice and distributive justice, and sometimes even commutative justice. He is not correct in arguing that the good of every single individual is a new requirement of the common good. Thomas Aquinas

44. Ibid., 315.

also understood the common good to include the proper good of individuals. In agreeing with Rocaries that "the state should be regarded as by far the most important agent and instrument of the common good," Ryan effectively downplays the important role played by individuals and groups in contributing to the common good. Recall that Pius XI put a great deal of emphasis on this in no. 51 of *Divini redemptoris*. Absent from Ryan's commentaries is an explicit comment on the laborious struggle to acquire all the knowledge and virtues needed to practice social justice.

The confusion of social justice with distributive justice was especially characteristic of French scholars, according to Calvez and Perrin.[45] There are at least two major problems with this identification. First, if social justice is identical to distributive justice, then it cannot be the criterion by which goods are distributed. Secondly, as Leo Shields argues, scholars such as Father Ryan make social justice into particular justice "because they want to guarantee rights to individuals. For this reason there is a tendency to regard social justice as the principle of rights against society rather than obligations towards society."[46]

William Ferree calls Pius XI one of the greatest social thinkers of all times, especially because of his doctrine of social justice.[47] Ferree's attempt to explain Pius XI's concept of social justice, however, is not only incomplete but even erroneous in parts. Ferree does correctly recognize that the term "social justice" is the modern equivalent of Thomas Aquinas's concept of legal justice. According to Ferree, Aquinas redefined Aristotle's legal justice as a "special virtue which has the common good for its direct object."[48] Ferree rightly adds that for Aquinas every virtue could become an act of social justice if practiced for the common good. Ferree, however, criticizes Aquinas for failing to posit for legal justice a "special and direct act of its own." He asks:

It is easy to see how acts of the other virtues could all give the common good a "lift" once this common good is already a "going concern," but is there an act of this special virtue which directly "makes" the common good—starts it off and builds it up, or rebuilds it if it happens to be destroyed?[49]

45. Jean-Yves Calvez and Jacques Perrin, *Église et societé économique*, 558–67.

46. Leo Shields, "The History and Meaning of the Term Social Justice" (Ph.D. diss., Notre Dame University, 1941), 62–63.

47. William Ferree, *Introduction to Social Justice* (New York: Paulist Press, 1948), 5.

48. Ibid., 8.

49. Ibid., 11.

Aquinas, says Ferree, did not ask, much less answer, this question. Ferree's criticism of Aquinas on this point is off the mark. As Jeremiah Newman indicated, "Whatever is necessary for the common good of society is demanded by the virtue of legal justice, according to St. Thomas."[50] The demands of the common good will, of course, vary depending on the condition of a particular society. The common good of a stable society will be different from that of disintegrating societies or from those that need to be completely rebuilt.

According to Ferree, Pius XI, at long last, discovered the specific feature or act of social justice. It is found, says Ferree, in the preamble to *Quadragesimo anno* and is widely used as the English title to the encyclical "On Reconstructing the Social Order." Ferree then explains what this title essentially means by citing two sentences from paragraph 71.

Every effort must therefore be made that fathers of families receive a wage large enough to meet common domestic needs adequately. But if this cannot be done under existing circumstances, social justice demands that changes be introduced [into *the system*] so soon as possible, whereby such a wage will be assured to every adult workingman. (My emphasis. "Into the system" does not appear in the English or in the official Latin text.)[51]

The specific object of social justice is not the family wage, but "the *reorganization of the system*"[52] in order to make possible the payment of a family wage. Employers, says Ferree, have the duty, which cannot be neglected without sin, to reorganize their industry so that they are in a position to pay a family wage. Ferree adds that social justice demands, on the part of everyone, according to capacity, "a serious and constant preoccupation with social organization in all its forms."[53] This includes not only employers, but also workers and the public authorities. Everyone must be preoccupied with perfecting situations on all levels of society. Ferree identifies a society's vast network of institutions as the common good on which everyone depends to achieve personal perfection. Social justice requires that the society be so organized as to be in fact a vehicle for human perfection. Unlike Aquinas, Ferree no longer includes human perfection as an essential part of the common good.

Social organization in the form of all kinds of institutions is of such importance that Ferree goes so far as to make the following observa-

50. Newman, *Foundation of Justice*, 114.   51. Ferree, *Introduction to Social Justice*, 11.
52. Ibid., 11.   53. Ibid., 16.

tions:...a society is not to be called good without qualification for the good individuals in it or for some great collective act of generosity or valor, but for its *good institutions,* that is, its social justice.[54] Ferree gives an example of a direct act of social justice in a society where people are in the habit of paying debts. Social justice requires, says Ferree, not an education to virtue, but the reorganization of the group into an honest community. He gives an example of how this could be done. A group of individuals should get together and lend each other money to pay back debts, join forces to take on big jobs, and thus arrive at economic security through honesty. Their example of honest success will generate imitations, and thus society will gradually be reformed.

Ferree is ebullient about the possibilities of social justice. Henceforward, nothing is impossible, he says: "No problem is ever too big or too complex, no field is ever too vast, for the methods of social justice."[55] As warrant for his optimism, Ferree applied social justice to the problem of declining moral standards in the areas of business, medicine, and law. To businessmen, lawyers, and physicians who lament the decline but say that they must engage in immoral behavior in order to support their families, Ferree replies, not so. They need not, as individuals, take a heroic stand, buck the tide, and suffer the economic consequences. All they have to do is reorganize the system, says Ferree, and establish the proper institutions. It may take time but cannot fail to succeed.

The second major point Ferree makes is that social justice cannot be sought by individuals qua individuals, but as members of a group. "The power to make all human society conform to the norms of Social Justice is vested in *institutions,* in *organizations of men,* not in men as isolated individuals."[56] Every individual, says Ferree, is directly responsible for the lower institutions that immediately impinge on his life and indirectly responsible for the welfare of his own country and the whole world. Individuals will exercise all their responsibilities through the various groups to which they belong. Ferree leaves no room, as do Thomas Aquinas and Pius XI, for great accomplishments by individuals working alone for the common good or for the nobility of a lone individual who lives virtuously in a corrupt society.

Ferree is right in arguing that Pius XI calls for a restructuring of economic life so that workers may receive a family wage. He is also right in

54. Ibid., 33.   55. Ibid., 47.
56. Ibid., 19.

drawing out the implications of this papal recommendation. Social justice may require structural changes in social, political, and economic life in order to address particular problems. But he is mistaken both to *limit* the specific act of social justice to these structural changes and to insist that individuals cannot act on their own to promote social justice.

Ferree's interpretation of *Quadragesimo anno* seems influenced by utopian longings. His expectation of overcoming dishonesty and greed by various kinds of reorganization is closer to the major theme of modern political philosophy than to Catholic social teaching. In a most enlightening paragraph, Leo Strauss briefly describes the modern orientation initiated by Machiavelli:

The political problem becomes a technical problem. As Hobbes put it, "when commonwealths come to be dissolved by intestine discord, the fault is not in men as they are the matter but as they are the makers of them." The matter is not corrupt or vicious; there is no evil in men which cannot be controlled; what is required is not divine grace, morality, nor formation of character, but institutions with teeth in them. Or, to quote Kant, the establishment of the right social order does not require, as people are in the habit of saying, a nation of angels: "Hard as it may sound, the problem of establishing the state [i.e., the just state] is soluble even for a nation of devils, provided they have the sense," i.e., provided their selfishness is enlightened; the fundamental political problem is simply one of a "good organization of the state of which man is indeed capable."[57]

In contrast with what Ferree says, Pius XI very clearly states that the reconstruction and perfection of social order cannot be brought about without the practice of virtue. Pius XI is, of course, in favor of reforming institutions, but has no expectation that they will work well or ever be established unless individuals are converted from various kinds of self-seeking to a serious concern with virtue.

Ferree's argument, that only individuals as members of groups can practice social justice, considerably diminishes the breadth of that virtue. As explained by Pius XI, social justice requires everyone to work for the common good according to capacity in private associations, through public authorities, or alone.

---

57. Leo Strauss, *Political Philosophy: Six Essays by Leo Strauss*, ed. by Hilail Gildin (New York: Bobbs Merrill, 1975), 87.

Conclusion

The Catholic concept of social justice, as elaborated by Pius XI, has been difficult to grasp, especially by American Catholic scholars in the United States. The debate in Catholic circles over the meaning of social justice took place mostly among French, German, and Italian scholars. Neither before nor after *Quadragesimo anno* was any consensus reached. In addition, the encyclical gives only a skeletal explanation of social justice. Pius XI apparently expected philosophers and theologians to explain and develop what he said about social justice. Brucculeri, Nell-Breuning, Calvez, and Perrin did explain that the pope was trying to revive the Thomistic concept of legal justice. Even knowledge of this fact would mean little to most people, including many Catholic scholars. We have already seen that many close students of Aquinas misunderstood his concept of legal justice, reducing it to obedience to the law.

As a matter of fact, the positions of Brucculeri, Calvez, Perrin, and Nell-Breuning on social justice are either not known or not accepted in the United States. The writings of John Ryan and William Ferree have been more influential; what I have argued is that their misinterpretation of Pius XI's concept of social justice persists today. We still hear Ryan's view that social justice consists primarily in a more equitable distribution of wealth, with the state as the principal agent. Ferree's argument that social justice calls for the reorganization of the system as the principal means of overcoming injustice has become a truism.

The Thomistic and papal understanding of legal/social justice is very difficult to understand, because it includes two important themes that are foreign to the prevailing modern mentality: namely, virtue and the common good. Neither of these figures prominently in the contemporary understanding of justice and the public interest. Legal/social justice imposes weighty duties on individuals, groups, and rulers; it doesn't square well with the contemporary emphasis on rights. People today are taught to know their rights and then to make demands in the light of them. There is thus a stress on the demand for just treatment rather than on the duty to act justly. Social justice has come to be the title in whose name the individual demands things as his rights. It is now widely assumed that the protection of rights is possible without worrying about educating people to virtue. The securing of rights just requires the proper framework, which is constructed by social reform, structural change, reorganization of the system, and new laws.

Once again, then, as noted at the outset, my point in calling attention to what seem to be the limitations in the contemporary understanding of rights and social justice is not to deny the legitimacy and importance of such concerns. Rather, it is merely to try to underscore the narrowness and one-sidedness of the horizon within which these concerns typically come to expression today. And in this light, my proposal is simply that a recovery of the fuller Thomistic/papal understanding of social justice would immeasurably benefit Catholic social doctrine in the United States. It would enable the bishops and priests to show the connection between the practice of virtue and the quest for justice.

Doesn't even common sense indicate that vices harm social, economic, and political life? Everyone can think of examples to show the harmful influence of pride or excessive ambition, greed, laziness, envy, anger, not to mention lust and intemperance regarding drink. Laws can and should mitigate the evil effects of these vices by such means as stiff penalties for drunk driving and child pornography. Still, it is important for the churches to inspire people to overcome their faults and vices or at least to maintain a constant struggle. This is, of course, very difficult, but it is facilitated by a focus on the positive, as Plato remarked in his *Republic:* "we surely know that when someone's desires incline strongly to some one thing, they are therefore weaker with respect to the rest, like a stream that has been channeled off in that other direction."[58] John of the Cross put the same thought in a theological context:

A love of pleasure, and attachment to it, usually fires the will toward the enjoyment of things that give pleasure. A more intense enkindling of another better life (love of one's heavenly Bridegroom) is necessary for the vanquishing of the appetites and the denial of this pleasure. By finding his satisfaction and strength in this love, a man will have the courage and the constancy to deny readily all other appetites.[59]

Many persons, both scholars and nonscholars, will likely object that the concern with virtue or the "better love" is either utopian and ineffective or excessively individualistic. However, when properly understood, the Catholic concept of virtue is on the contrary always seen as ordered to the common good. Even the desire for one's salvation and the presence

58. Plato, The *Republic*, 2nd ed., tr. Allan Bloom (New York: Basic Books, 1968), 485d.
59. St. John of the Cross, *The Ascent of Mount Carmel*, book 1, chap. 14., in *Collected Works of St. John of the Cross*, translated by Kieran Kavanaugh and Otilio Rodriquez (Washington, D.C.: Institute of Carmelite Studies, 1973), 105.

of God must always include a desire that everyone else share the same goods. Catholics have the duty to make a contribution to the common good through family life, work, and public spiritual activity. Not everyone has the same obligations, but all are bound to do what is possible. There are many small and great things that can be done by individuals in the various circumstances of their lives. To practice social justice, individuals must take initiative, sometimes heroic, in order to bring about a just social order. They cannot wait for precise instructions from bishops and priests.

Individuals do need some general guidance as to what constitutes the common good, but no one can spell it out in every detail. The virtue of prudence can guide everyone to see what he or she should do. It is incumbent on religious leaders to aid the faithful by educating them to virtue and giving an outline of the common good.

CHAPTER 5

Seeking the Common Good
through Law and Public Policy
Same-Sex Marriage, the Life Questions,
and Biotechnology

Most people readily understand that good public policy on a range of issues is a significant contribution to the common good because it provides structural solutions to problems that every society faces. Examples of such issues are the life questions (abortion, death penalty, euthanasia, cloning, creation and destruction of embryos); the delivery of health care to all the citizens of a nation; the economy (jobs, interest rates, tax policy, economic growth); the environment and sources of energy; civil liberties and anti-terrorism measures; racism, discrimination, and affirmative action; and the protection of the rights of conscience. All the pertinent issues should be evaluated in the light of Catholic teaching on the dignity of the human person and the common good. It would, of course, be impossible to discuss in a single chapter or even in a single book every relevant policy in the light of Catholic social doctrine (CSD). Besides, such a discussion would not serve the purposes of this book, which is to expound the principles of CSD. Consequently, my approach in this chapter is first to explain briefly how CSD views the role of law in a political community, and then to apply the principles of CSD to law and public policy on same-sex marriage, the life questions, and biotechnology. I chose these particular issues for several reasons. In the perspective of Catholic social doctrine, the laws upholding traditional marriage are crucial for the well-being of civilization, and laws are sorely needed to prevent the unjust taking of life and the willing or unwitting dehumanization of citizens through biotechnology.

It is usually much easier to state what evils must be forbidden by law than to suggest positive strategies to address such matters as the economy or health care. Catholics will necessarily disagree with one another on which health care policies are likely to work best; they should agree on what evils should be thwarted by the law (see chapter 6). A secondary purpose of this chapter is to persuade readers that these three areas must fall under the rubric of Catholic social doctrine.

Law and Morality

In an article on "Law and Moral Purpose," Professor Robert P. George begins with the following sentence: "The obligations and purposes of law and government are to protect health, safety, and morals, and to advance the general welfare—including, preeminently, protecting people's fundamental rights and basic liberties."[1] Then he adds some qualifications to ensure that he is not understood to be saying that government has "vast and sweeping powers." Its role is primary when it comes to maintaining public order and protecting citizens from being harmed by the attacks of other nations or from assaults by fellow citizens. Government power, however, must be limited by respect for the principle of subsidiarity. The "subsidiary" role is "to support the work of the families, religious communities, and other institutions of civil society that shoulder the primary burden of forming upright citizens, caring for those in need, encouraging people to meet their responsibilities to one another while also discouraging them from harming themselves or others."[2] I would add that the government's responsibility for the general welfare could require in some circumstances substantial intervention so as, for example, to promote economic productivity and distribution of goods when the institutions of civil society are unable to do so. The law also can act as a teacher of what promotes the good of a nation.

While the above description of the role of law is a good description of what CSD proposes to Catholics, it does not and cannot indicate precisely the exact shape of appropriate government intervention in the economy or the exact meaning of the public morality fittingly promoted by the government. The extent of appropriate government intervention in the economy is a subject of legitimate debate among Catholics, because CSD cannot resolve all the relevant issues on the level of principle. In any case, the principle of subsidiarity must always be respected. While the rest of

1. Robert P. George, "Law and Moral Purpose," *First Things*, no. 79 (2008): 22.
2. George, "Law and Moral Purpose," 22.

the chapter will shed light on morals that government should uphold, readers should keep in mind all that was said about the meaning of the common good in chapter 2. Government, the institutions of civil society, and individuals all have a role to play in promoting the common good. In a liberal society government will not have the primary responsibility for promoting the full range of the common good, as explained.

To continue our brief and sketchy presentation of CSD on law, let us now turn to chapter 3 in Pope John Paul II's encyclical *Evangelium vitae (The Gospel of Life)*, where the pope reflects on the role of law in a democracy. He begins by taking issue with the argument that "the legal system of any society should limit itself to taking account of and accepting the convictions of the majority."[3] This would mean that the moral beliefs and practices of the majority should be the norm, whatever they might be. Ironically, this way of looking at things also requires the legislature to acknowledge the autonomy of individual consciences. In other words, individuals may claim for themselves "the most complete freedom of choice," and they may "demand that the state should not adopt or impose any ethical position but limit itself to guaranteeing maximum space for the freedom of each individual with the sole limitation of not infringing on the freedom and rights of any other citizen."[4] If enough individuals think this way, they form a majority and get their way.

Some go so far as to say that public officials and professionals should set aside their own conscientious beliefs in order to accommodate the demands of citizens, which are "recognized and guaranteed by the law." For example, if euthanasia were legal, the argument runs, physicians should help people end their lives, no matter what their personal convictions are.

The pope believes that "ethical relativism which characterizes much of present-day culture" lies at the basis of the argument just presented. The pope rightly believes that people "consider such relativism an essential condition of democracy, inasmuch as it alone is held to guarantee tolerance, mutual respect between people and acceptance of the decisions of the majority, whereas moral norms considered to be objective and binding are held to lead to authoritarianism and intolerance."[5] The pope grants that crimes have been committed in the name of "truth," but they also have been authorized in the name of ethical relativism by individual tyrants and popular consensus. The legal permission to kill the unborn

3. Pope John Paul II, *Evangelium vitae (The Gospel of Life)*, no. 69.
4. Ibid., no. 69.   5. Ibid., no. 70.

is really a tyrannical decision by the strong against "the weakest and most defenseless of human beings."[6]

The pope argues that the democratic process is a means and not an end in itself. Every democracy must be evaluated by the goods and moral principles "which it embodies and promotes." A good democracy is not neutral with respect to values or principles. "The basis of these principles cannot be provisional and changeable 'majority' opinions, but only the acknowledgment of an objective moral law which, as the 'natural law' written in the human heart, is the obligatory point of reference for civil law itself."[7] The pope is not arguing that the moral law and civil law should correspond in every respect. The purpose of the latter is "more limited in scope."[8] Following Vatican II's *Dignitatis humanae (Declaration on Religious Freedom)*, the pope says that the purpose of the civil law is to ensure "the common good of the people through the recognition and defense of their fundamental rights and the promotion of peace and public morality," as well as through "an ordered social existence in true justice," which allows individuals to perform their duties and live a godly existence. The civil law, however, must never take the place of conscience or attempt to govern outside its competence.

John Paul II then quotes Pope John XXIII and Thomas Aquinas to affirm that civil laws in opposition to the moral order or right reason are unjust laws. Such are laws, for example, permitting and promoting abortion, euthanasia, and racism. These practices are not only opposed to the good of individuals but also to the common good. "Disregard for the right to life, precisely because it leads to the killing of the person whom society exists to serve, is what most directly conflicts with the possibility of achieving the common good."[9] It is most important to note that, according to John Paul II, the common good is a standard and goal of the civil law (not that individuals and mediating institutions don't also have a role in promoting the common good, as we have seen).

Some Catholic scholars say that the scope of the civil law is limited to the promotion of the public order, as described in the *Declaration on Religious Freedom.* They further dispute the authority of the government to limit freedom through law on the basis of the common good. The pope rightly disagrees with this position. As mentioned in chapter 2, *Gaudium et spes (Pastoral Constitution on the Church in the Modern World)* affirms that

6. Ibid., no. 70.
7. Ibid., no. 70.
8. Ibid., no. 71.
9. Ibid., no. 72.

the political community exists for the common good, which "embraces
the sum of those conditions of social life by which individuals, families,
and groups can achieve their own perfection in a relatively thorough and
ready way."[10] The political community, of course, relies on the law in various ways to achieve its end. It also relies on other instruments as well,
such as the mores and mediating institutions (families, schools, voluntary
associations).

In order to further clarify what Catholic social doctrine expects from
the law, I would like to examine a few parts of Mary Ann Glendon's
work *Abortion and Divorce in Western Law: American Failures, European Challenges.*
In the introduction to her book she reminds her readers of Plato's teaching in the *Laws* "that the aim of law is to lead the citizens toward virtue,
to make them noble and wise."[11] This notion of law is not popular in the
United States, where most scholars look at law as "a command backed
up by organized coercion."[12] Glendon believes that Plato's insight into
law can still help us today. She approvingly quotes James Boyd White,
who says that "'law is most usefully seen not...as a system of rules, but
as a branch of rhetoric,...as the central art by which community and culture are established, maintained and transformed.'" Glendon adds that
the law "tells stories about the culture that helped to shape it and which
it in turn helps to shape; stories about who we are, where we come from,
and where we are going."[13] Law is constitutive of society "when legal language and legal concepts begin to affect ordinary language and to influence the manner in which we perceive reality." Think of how law has conditioned Americans to think about morality more in terms of rights than
in terms of duty, or consider how the Supreme Court abortion decision
of 1973 eventually induced more people to accept abortion.

Glendon gives a wonderful example of how law is educational in her
summary of the law on marriage:

The American story about marriage, as told in the law and in much popular
literature, goes something like this: marriage is a relationship that exists primarily for the fulfillment of the individual spouses. If it ceases to perform
this function, no one is to blame and either spouse may terminate it at will.

10. Ibid., no. 74, modified translation.
11. Mary Ann Glendon, *Abortion and Divorce in Western Law: American Failures, European
Challenges* (Cambridge, Mass.: Harvard University Press, 1987), 6.
12. Ibid., 7.
13. Ibid., 8.

After divorce, each spouse is expected to be self-sufficient. If this is not possible with the aid of property division, some rehabilitative maintenance may be in order for a temporary period. Children hardly appear in the story; at most they are rather shadowy characters in the background. Other stories, of course, are still vigorous in American culture—about marriage as a union for life, for better or worse, even in sickness or poverty; stories about taking on responsibilities and carrying through; and about parenthood as an awesome commitment. But by and large, they are not the ones that have been incorporated into the law. In the continuing cultural conversation about marriage and family life, American law has weighed in heavily on the side of individual self-fulfillment. It tells us that if a marriage no longer suits our needs or if the continuation of a pregnancy would not fit in with our plans right now, we can choose to sever the relationship.[14]

In most European countries, even where there are liberalized divorce laws, citizens "still try to reinforce the idea of marriage as a serious and durable commitment."[15] These reflections by Professor Glendon should inspire us to imagine the educational role law could play in various aspects of life. Consider the effect of civil rights legislation in the 1960s. These laws made racist behavior illegal and stigmatized it as immoral, and moved people to be less racist. Even when law doesn't command, say, fidelity in marriage to death, it could still persuade people to think of marriage as permanent commitment. Tax policy could be so framed as to reward people who don't divorce or who have children. Other laws could discourage divorce, or at least make it more difficult. As things stand, there is a consensus in the United States to limit abortion on demand. That consensus cannot yet have an effect while *Roe v. Wade* is the law of the land. Roe's declaration of abortion as a constitutional right takes precedence over any other kind of law.

Law and Same-Sex Marriage

Let us now turn to the question of whether the law should allow same-sex marriage. Scholars and other citizens are now arguing that the state ought to be neutral regarding the definition of marriage. According to that view, those holding a traditional view of marriage should not attempt to use the law to impose their morality on fellow citizens, even if the

14. Ibid., 108.
15. Ibid., 109.

majority agrees to support traditional marriage, but should allow same-sex partners to be legally married, if they so desire. The state should be neutral with respect to the prevailing understandings of marriage. So, in this perspective, the state should just recognize same-sex marriage and be done with it.

Other arguments for moving in this direction stem from respect for the principle of equality and abhorrence for arbitrariness. Stephen Macedo believes that current marriage law violates "fundamental aspects of equality" by assuming that marriage is by nature heterosexual.[16] Some critics say that the law is just arbitrary in not allowing same-sex couples to marry. Sterile couples are able to marry, as can fertile couples who have no intention of having children. In addition, as Professor Gerard Bradley points out, "Many married couples today do, in fact, engage in completed sexual acts other than intercourse."[17] Many more married couples use artificial contraception. So, if heterosexual couples can take away the life-giving power of the conjugal act by means of contraception, can there be a nonarbitrary ground for refusing same-sex couples permission to marry?

Still another argument for same-sex marriage is the belief that God or nature determines the sexual orientation of persons. If people are born homosexual, then God must want them to live as practicing homosexuals. Otherwise, they would not be true to their nature. To deny marriage, it is argued, would then be an affront to homosexual persons who have decided to marry because they love each other. If the law limits marriage to heterosexual couples, then homosexual persons will be denied the stability and happiness available in the married state.

Professor Bradley points out that arguing for the neutrality of the law "is itself a moral claim" and, therefore, not morally neutral.[18] He further argues that the law should not be morally neutral, because government has a stake in the way people understand and practice marriage. Through law the government necessarily teaches citizens about the meaning of marriage. Without parameters established by marriage law, people will not only ask for the legal recognition of same-sex marriage, but also, eventually, of polygamy, of various kinds of threesomes or foursomes.

16. Gerard V. Bradley, "Same-Sex Marriage: Our Final Answer?" in *Same-Sex Attraction: A Parents' Guide*, edited by Gerard V. Bradley and J. F. Harvey (South Bend, Ind.: St. Augustine's Press, 2003), 127, quoting Stephen Macedo, note 14 in Homer H. Clark, *The Law of Domestic Relations in the United States*, 2nd ed. (St. Paul, Minn.: West Publishing, 1998), 335.

17. "Bradley, Same-Sex Marriage: Our Final Answer?" 131.

18. Ibid., 124.

Given all the benefits available for marriage partners, siblings and friends living together—though not sexually involved—will also ask for the recognition of their relationship as a marriage. Who could blame them? Why should male friends having sexual relations with each other receive marriage benefits denied to two men living together who are not sexually involved? On what objective grounds can the law say that one relationship is a marriage and one is not, once the traditional criteria for a valid marriage are dropped? The likely scenario is that the lobbies with the strongest clout will get their relationships declared a marriage by legislatures or by state courts; unpopular partnerships, such as polygamy and bisexual relationships, will eventually prevail in the courts in the name of equal protection if same-sex marriage is legalized.

Obviously, the state can't allow just any kind of partnership to qualify as a marriage. For one thing, it could not afford to do so. Secondly, the state pursues public purposes through its law on marriage. One of its main purposes is to promote the continuation of the species by providing benefits for married couples because they are the ones who do the work of begetting and educating children. Back in 1888 the U.S. Supreme Court said in *Maynard v. Hill* that "marriage creates 'the most important relation in life' and has 'more to do with the morals and civilization of a people than any other institution.'"[19] The same court further said that marriage "'is the foundation of the family and of society, without which there would neither be civilization or progress.'"[20] In 1961 Justice Harlan summarily explained why marriage between a man and a woman was so important.

[T]he very inclusion of the category of morality among state concerns indicates that society is not limited in its objects to the physical well-being of the community, but has traditionally concerned itself with the moral soundness of its people as well.... The laws regarding marriage which provide both when the sexual powers may be used and the legal and societal context in which children are born and brought up, as well as laws forbidding adultery, fornication and homosexual practices which express the negative of the proposition, confining sexuality to lawful marriage, a pattern deeply pressed into the substance of our social life form[s].[21]

19. *Maynard v. Hill*, 125 U.S. 190 (1888), quoted in "Same-Sex Marriage: Our Final Answer?" 137.
20. Ibid.
21. Justice Harlan dissenting in *Poe v. Ullman*, 367 U.S. 497, 545–46 (1961), quoted in "Same-Sex Marriage: Our Final Answer?" 137–38.

Because same-sex couples cannot contribute to the common good by bringing forth new life, they do not deserve the special benefits designated for married couples who found a family and thereby contribute to the perpetuation of a people. Even though not all married couples are able or willing to make this contribution, the state policy of providing benefits to all married couples, with something extra for those who have children, succeeds for the most part in accomplishing its minimum goals. Enough married couples have children to justify marriage benefits. As mentioned earlier in this chapter, the law on marriage in the United States could do more to promote fidelity and the care of children. Given what the law does accomplish, I think that the state acts fairly and wisely in limiting marriage to heterosexual couples.

If homosexual marriage ever becomes the law of the land, argues Mary Ann Glendon, the following claims made by the Supreme Court of Massachusetts will be endorsed: "that marriage is mainly an arrangement for the benefit of adults; that children do not need both a mother and a father; and that alternative family forms are just as good as a husband and wife raising kids together." In other words, the whole meaning of marriage would change. Marital union, the possibility of conceiving and raising children, would no longer be part of the inherent meaning of marriage. Same-sex partners may seek union, but it cannot be marital union. They may adopt children, but their love can never lead to the natural conception of a child.

Furthermore, says Glendon, "ordinary words like *husband* and *wife* will be replaced by *partner* and *spouse*. In marriage-preparation and sex-education classes, children will have to be taught about homosexual sex. Parents who complain will be branded as homophobes and their children will suffer....Every person and every religion that disagrees will be labeled as bigoted and openly discriminated against."[22] If same-sex marriage is widely legalized, the Catholic Church will be vilified in many quarters as homophobic when it presents its teaching on marriage. Some critics of traditional marriage admit that what they ultimately really want is the abolition of marriage altogether, not just the legalization of alternative forms of marriage. Marriage itself is sometimes seen as an oppressive institution, especially when it is linked to exclusivity and indissolubility.

---

22. Mary Ann Glendon, "For Better or For Worse? The federal marriage amendment would strike a blow for freedom," *Wall Street Journal*, editorial page (February 25, 2004).

The ultimate reason that same-sex partnerships should not be legally recognized as marriages is that marital union is only possible between a man and a woman. To explain this point, let us first look at the natural-law of argument of Professor George, a lawyer and professor of politics at Princeton University. He describes traditional marriage "as a two-in-one-flesh communion of persons that is consummated and actualized by sexual acts of the reproductive type."[23] George notes that, besides religious authorities, even the law has for the most part recognized that sexual intercourse, not oral sex or anal sex, consummates a marriage. Spouses realize their two-in-one-flesh communion by sexual intercourse, not by nonmarital orgasmic acts. They do not choose to engage in sexual intercourse primarily for pleasure or just as a means to procreate, but to promote their marital union. In other words, pleasure is not sought as an end in itself, but is enjoyed as the fruit of a good act, namely, the expression and promotion of marital union by sexual intercourse. George puts it this way: "Integrated with the good of marriage,...pleasure is rightly sought and welcomed as part of the perfection of marital intercourse.... However, to simply instrumentalize intercourse to pleasure (or procreation) is to vitiate its marital quality and damage the integrity of the genital acts even of spouses."[24] Because of the unitive dimension of conjugal relations, intercourse is still wholly appropriate even if a couple is not capable of conceiving a child. In George's formulation, "But if...the genital union of spouses makes them truly one-flesh, then the marital acts of spouses, fertile or not, are perfectly intelligible. They are not pointless. On the contrary, qua unitive, they are intrinsically good."[25]

Many liberals now argue that sodomitical acts can unite same-sex partners in the same way that reproductive type acts unite spouses in a marriage. The latter's marital union is supposedly not different from the union sodomitical acts produce for homosexual partners. The answer that George makes to this argument is that by engaging in nonmarital orgasmic acts people treat their bodies and those of their partners as instruments and thus damage their integrity. He further adds,

If Susan, for example masturbates John to orgasm or applies oral stimulation to him to bring him to orgasm, no real unity has been effected. That is, al-

---

23. Robert P. George, *In Defense of Natural Law* (New York: Oxford University Press, 1999), 139.
24. Ibid., 149.
25. Ibid., 147.

though bodily parts are conjoined, and so there is juxtaposition and contact, the participants do not unite biologically; they do not become the subject of a single act, and so do not literally become "one flesh."[26]

This position presupposes that the human person cannot just choose to bring about one-flesh unity by the bodily contact of his liking. That way of looking at things doesn't really respect the body, but just sees it as an instrument of the will, not an integrated part of the human person.

There is also a liberal case to be made against same-sex marriage, as, for example, that made by Professor Susan Shell. She calls "sectarian" both the traditional defense of marriage and the demand for the legalization of gay marriage. She goes back to Locke and other liberal thinkers to see how they looked at marriage.

Such thinkers have generally viewed marriage as a contractual arrangement between two individuals for the sake of mutual advantage and the generation and rearing of children to the point where they can be self-reliant (in Locke's thinking) and/or capable of exercising their individual rights in a responsible civic manner (according to Kant).[27]

She notes that most societies have actually looked at marriage this way. States have recognized that a married couple has responsibility for the children it generates. "No known government, however brutal or tyrannical, has ever denied, in fact or principle, the fundamental claim of parents to their children."[28] Shell adds that marriage and the procreation of children have always been a part of the landscape and always will be. This fact doesn't wholly depend on a particular religious belief in divine revelation or on some kind of social construction. Just as societies require a deceased person in order to call an event a funeral, so they require a man and a woman for a marriage. If marriage could be redefined with no connection to procreation, why couldn't living persons claim the right to attend their own funerals? Anticipating an objection to her position, Shell asks, what is the harm of allowing people to redefine marriage and funerals if that makes them happy? Why don't liberal societies recognize the right of individuals to exercise their autonomy in any way they see fit, as long as they don't harm others? Shell responds, "a soci-

26. Ibid., 170.
27. Susan Shell, "The Liberal Case Against Gay Marriage," *The Public Interest*, no. 156 (2004): 2.
28. Ibid., 3.

ety without the means of formally acknowledging, through marriage, the
fact of generation, like one without the means of formally acknowledging
through funeral rites the fact of death, seems impoverished in the most
basic of human terms."[29] Her judgment is that seeking the legalization of
gay marriage is more like a demand to attend one's funeral than a marriage between infertile couples.

The Life Questions, Law, and Public Policy

In our study of social justice we saw that it is the virtue that directs all
the other virtues to the attainment of the common good. Since one of the
fundamental elements of the common good is the protection of life, the
work for social justice must include efforts to protect life and to promote
a culture of life. Catholic social thought has not always recognized that
abortion and euthanasia, for example, must be included in the discipline.
Therefore, not everyone lists Pope John Paul II's *Evangelium vitae* as one of
the encyclicals containing social teachings or thinks that the opposition
to abortion can be prompted by a love of justice. But things are beginning
to change. For example, in its 34th General Congregation, the Society of
Jesus (known popularly as the Jesuits) affirmed that the Jesuit mission to
promote justice must include the life questions:

Human life, a gift of God, has to be respected from its beginning to its natural
end. Yet we are increasingly being faced with a "culture of death" which encourages abortion, suicide and euthanasia; war, terrorism, violence, and capital punishment as ways of resolving issues; the consumption of drugs; turning
away from the human drama of hunger, AIDS, and poverty. We need to encourage a "culture of life."[30]

This statement, of course, reaffirms the teaching of John Paul II in *Evangelium vitae* on the importance of promoting a culture of life. The Jesuit
statement could eventually be very helpful, since many Catholic advocates of social justice don't usually include opposition to abortion and euthanasia on their agenda. When the Jesuits, known for their advocacy of
social justice, make a point of including the life questions under the rubric of justice, you know that an important corner has been turned. Now

29. Ibid., 5.
30. Documents of the Thirty-Fourth General Congregation of the Society of Jesus
(St. Louis: Institute of Jesuit Resources, 1995), decree 3, no. 8, p. 42.

Pope Benedict XVI has emphatically linked the protection of life with
the pursuit of justice in his third encyclical, *Caritas in veritate.*

It is not just abortion, euthanasia, the death penalty, war, terrorism,
and health questions that fall under the rubric of Catholic social doctrine, but things like cloning to produce children, cloning for biomedical
research, the creation and destruction of embryos, organ donation, genetic engineering. In order to offer support for this contention, I will briefly
review parts of John Paul II's *Evangelium vitae* (*the Gospel of Life*), Leon Kass's
Life, Liberty and Defense of Dignity: Challenges for Bioethics, and the second report
of the President's Council on Bioethics, chaired by Dr. Kass, entitled *Beyond Therapy: Beyond Technology and the Pursuit of Happiness.*

First, it is important to know the law of the land with respect to abortion. In *Roe v. Wade* (1973), the U.S. Supreme Court established abortion on
demand as the law. One reading of the Supreme Court's case is that states
might impose limitations on access to abortion in the third trimester. Indeed, the court says that the state may prohibit abortion during the seventh, eighth, and ninth months unless the life or the health of the mother
is at stake. By the court's own definition, however, health includes the psychological and emotional well-being of the mother. Under this standard
any reason will suffice to fulfill the requirements of the law. The definition of health is so broad that any abortion would necessarily be justified. There are really only two restrictions on access to abortion during
the time of pregnancy. After month three a woman must use a clinic with
a license, and after month six she must find an abortionist who says that
she needs an abortion. This is abortion on demand for the whole nine
months of pregnancy.

As we begin to think about the morality of taking life deemed not
worthy of preservation, we could do worse than keep in mind a statement by Walker Percy, the distinguished Catholic novelist. In 1988 he
wrote a letter to the *New York Times,* which the paper decided not to publish. He said that "certain consequences, perhaps unforeseen, follow from
the principle of the destruction of human life for what may appear to be
the most admirable social reasons." To prove his point Percy cites the influence of a book written by Karl Bindung, a distinguished jurist, and
Alfred Hoche, a prominent psychiatrist, before Hitler's rise to power. It
was entitled *The Justification of the Destruction of Life Devoid of Value.* Bindung
and Hoche never heard of Hitler, and the latter probably didn't read this
scholarly book.

The point is that the ideas expressed in the book and the policies advocated were the product not of Nazi ideology but rather of the best minds of the pre-Nazi Weimar Republic—physicians, social scientists, jurists, and the like, who with the best secular intentions wished to improve the lot, socially and genetically, of the German people—by getting rid of the unfit and the unwanted.

It is hardly necessary to say what use the Nazis made of these ideas.

I would not wish to be understood as implying that the respected American institutions I have named, the *New York Times*, the United States Supreme Court, the American Civil Liberties Union and the National Organization of Women are similar to corresponding pre-Nazi institutions.

But I do suggest that once the line is crossed, once the principle gains acceptance—juridically, medically, socially—innocent human life can be destroyed for whatever reason, for the most admirable socioeconomic, medical, or social reasons—then it does not take a prophet to predict what will happen next, or if not next, then sooner or later. At any rate, a warning is in order. Depending on the disposition of the majority and the opinion polls—now in favor of allowing women to get rid of unborn and unwanted babies—it is not difficult to imagine an electorate or a court ten years, fifty years from now, who would favor getting rid of useless old people, retarded children, antisocial blacks, illegal Hispanics, gypsies, Jews…

Why not?—if that is what is wanted by the majority, the polled opinion, the polity of the time.[31]

Still another important statement on abortion is that made by Mother Teresa at the 1994 National Prayer Breakfast: "Any country that accepts abortion is not teaching its people to love, but to use any violence to get what they want. This is why the greatest destroyer of love and peace is abortion." Cardinal Sean O'Malley quoted these words on October 4, 2009, in a letter he wrote to those attending Mass on Respect Life Sunday at the Cathedral of the Holy Cross in Boston. He went on to say that "the work of the Church and the Respect Life Movement, is to help people experience the conversion of hearts and minds that will prompt them to call for a change in laws, to call for the protection of unborn children." Cardinal O'Malley further argued that Catholics should resist public pressure to be silent in the public arena about Catholic teaching on abortion, embryonic stem cell research, and euthanasia. To underline this

31. Walker Percy, *Signposts in a Strange Land*, ed. Patrick Samway (New York: Noonday Press, 1992), 350–51.

point he added, "On this Respect Life Sunday, let me state clearly and unequivocally that this is not an authentically Catholic position."[32]

Let us now look at some of the arguments Pope John Paul II uses in *Evangelium vitae* to effect a change in the mores and the law by promoting a culture of life and discouraging a culture of death. A review of the pope's arguments clearly reveal his view on what kinds of laws are needed and why the life questions and bioethics are a concern of Catholic social teaching.

Pope John Paul II's *Gospel of Life*

The pope begins by describing the problem: "the extraordinary increase and gravity of threats to the life of individuals and peoples especially where life is weak and defenseless."[33] He is not making reference to the usual scourges constantly afflicting humanity: poverty, hunger, disease, violence, and war. He is referring to the new cultural climate in which "broad sections of public opinion justify certain crimes against life in the name of the rights of individual freedom."[34] Consequently, people want the state to allow such things as abortion and euthanasia. Sections of the medical profession are willing to justify abortions and to do them. To make matters even worse, the conscience of many has been so darkened that they no longer recognize that euthanasia and the killing of the unborn is morally wrong. The pope's purpose in writing is to convince Catholics and all people of good will that life is a great good, to inspire the establishment of a new culture of human life "for the building of an authentic civilization of truth and love," and to inspire support for the family so that it will remain "the sanctuary of life."[35]

In chapter 1, "The Voice of Your Brother's Blood Cries to Me from the Ground," the pope tells the story of Cain's murder of Abel. This murder violates the "kinship of flesh and blood" and, like every murder, "the spiritual kinship uniting mankind in one great family."[36] Today, the kinship of flesh and blood between parents and children is violated by abortion and, frequently, by euthanasia. (Sometimes, family members may not

32. In the conclusion I will discuss at length the argument that Catholics should be silent in the public square about Catholic teaching on such things as abortion and same-sex marriage.

33. Pope John Paul II, *Evangelium vitae*, no. 3.

34. Ibid., no. 4.

35. Ibid., no. 6.

36. Ibid., no. 8.

be involved in the euthanasia of their relative.) Another aspect of Cain's murder to note is that it immediately follows the sin of Adam and Eve. "Man's revolt against God in the earthly paradise," John Paul II explains, "is followed by the deadly combat of man against man."[37] In other words, once human beings break off their relations with God, they will have no qualms about doing harm to one another.

The pope makes much of the Lord's question to Cain: "What have you done?" Just as the Lord was teaching Cain about the gravity of murdering his brother, Abel, so the pope is hoping that reflection on this question could make us aware that taking innocent human life is a very serious matter and even alert us to the causes and consequences of such killing. He is using the ancient biblical story to overcome the darkening of conscience with respect to things like abortion and euthanasia.

In the hope of bringing light to the modern conscience, John Paul II offers reasons that people regard the attacks against human life as "rights," why the state is under pressure to give or maintain these rights, and why these attacks are so easily carried out within the family and with the complicity of the family. What lies in the background as the most general explanation of these contemporary phenomena is, first, "the profound crisis of culture, which generates scepticism in relation to the very foundation of knowledge and ethics." Without access to firm ethical principles, people fall back on individual autonomy. They just create their own values out of whole cloth or more exactly just do what the culture dictates or allows. Second, there are just personal and interpersonal difficulties, exacerbated by the fact that the affected individuals and families find themselves all alone. As examples, the pope mentions some situations of acute poverty and domestic violence, especially against women, that "make the choice to defend and promote life so demanding as sometimes to reach the point of heroism."[38] A third explanation offered by John Paul II is the "structure of sin," or a prevailing ethos that denies solidarity and takes the form of a "culture of death." By the latter expression he means a kind of *war of the powerful against the weak:* a life which would require greater acceptance, love, and care is considered useless, or held to be an intolerable burden, and is therefore rejected in one way or another."[39]

The pope then proceeds to explain in detail what he means by the cul-

37. Ibid. 38. Ibid., no. 11.
39. Ibid., no. 12.

ture of death. A great amount of money is being spent to develop pharmaceutical products that will enable women to have abortions without the assistance of health-care personnel. Contraception is promoted, allegedly to diminish the number of abortions. In fact, what happens is "that the pro-abortion culture is especially strong precisely where the Church's teaching on contraception is rejected."[40] In my mind, this happens because people with a contraceptive mentality don't anticipate that the conception of a child will or should result from sexual intercourse. The pope also mentions that a number of contraceptives act as abortifacients and, therefore, directly contribute to the culture of death. While contraception alone is a violation of chastity, any kind of abortion "is opposed to the virtue of justice and directly violates the divine commandment 'You shall not kill.'"[41]

Techniques of artificial reproduction, ironically, also pose new threats to life. A number of embryos must be created for a successful in vitro fertilization; other "spare" embryos not needed for implantation are either destroyed, frozen, or used for research and then destroyed. Prenatal diagnosis, which can be used for good purposes, is also used for eugenic abortion. Some people want to abort any baby that will have handicaps or illnesses or to deny food to babies born with unacceptable limitations. Some even try to justify the practice of infanticide.

Euthanasia is openly or surreptitiously practiced and is theoretically justified for utilitarian motives or out of misguided compassion. "Thus it is proposed to eliminate malformed babies, the severely handicapped, the disabled, the elderly, especially when they are not self-sufficient, and the terminally ill."[42]

John Paul II is not only concerned about the above-mentioned attacks on life, but also by "the fact that they receive widespread and powerful support from a broad consensus on the part of society, from widespread legal approval and the involvement of certain sectors of health-care personnel."[43] The pope goes so far as to call the death-dealing practices as a "*conspiracy against life.*" Even international institutions do what they can to make widely available contraception, sterilization, and abortion. The mass media participate in this conspiracy "by lending credit to that culture which presents recourse to contraception, sterilization, abortion and even euthanasia as a mark of progress and victory for freedom, while de-

40. Ibid., no. 13.   41. Ibid.
42. Ibid., no. 15.   43. Ibid., no. 17.

picting as enemies of freedom and progress those positions which are un-reservedly pro-life."[44]

John Paul II is very understanding when people are driven by personal circumstances, such as poverty, depression, or loneliness, to seek abortion or to yield to the euthanasia temptation. He recognizes that their culpability could be significantly decreased for making choices "which are in themselves evil." He is very disturbed, however, that crimes against life have come to be regarded as legitimate expressions of freedom deserving protection as rights. He explains: "Precisely in an age when the inviolable rights of the person are solemnly proclaimed and the value of life is publicly affirmed, the very right to life is being denied or trampled upon, especially at the more significant moments of existence: the moment of birth and the moment of death."[45] The right to life is denied in the United States because the Supreme Court, as mentioned, declared in 1973 that the right to abortion was a constitutional right. The states of Oregon and Washington recognize a right to euthanasia, as do Belgium and the Netherlands.

In my mind, the failure of educated Catholics to understand the full meaning of the rights revolution initiated by Hobbes and Locke made it difficult to foresee the bad use to which rights doctrines would be put. Remember that Hobbes separated rights from the *summum bonum*. This leaves rights without a moral guide. Of course, the Church has made every effort to persuade people to exercise their rights in the light of the good. But it is hard for that teaching to be effective when the Hobbesian view permeates aspects of American culture. This is certainly not what the founders of this country intended, but the separation of rights from a notion of the good has had a great impact on the United States.

The pope is struck by the contrast between the proclamation of the rights of persons throughout the world and their denial in practice. People are allowed to use their rights to abuse the weak, the needy, the elderly, and the unborn. "These attacks go directly against respect for life and they represent a *direct threat to the entire culture of human rights*. It is a threat capable, in the end, of jeopardizing the very meaning of democratic co-existence."[46] John Paul II implies that the promise of democracy is only achieved when everyone receives protection. A regime cannot claim to be a real democracy if it allows the strong to exclude the weak from the protection of the laws.

44. Ibid.
46. Ibid.

45. Ibid., no. 18.

One reason that some people become entitled to trample on the right of others despite the formal proclamation of rights is the widespread acceptance of a new understanding of human dignity. This mentality "tends to *equate personal dignity with the capacity for verbal and explicit,* or at least perceptible, *communication.*"[47] Under this standard the unborn and the dying at some point are regarded as beings without personal dignity and, therefore, not deserving of rights on their own. Fortunately, the law still protects the dying from mercy killing in most nations, but not the unborn. Recall our discussion of dignity in chapter 1. When personal dignity is equated with the capacity for verbal and perceptible communication, the very mention of the word "dignity" in some contexts means that someone is going to die. Since the unborn can't verbally communicate and, therefore, lack dignity, their lives are expendable if they conflict with the interests of adults who can communicate.

Another reason for the denial of rights in practice is an individualistic understanding of freedom divorced from truth and solidarity with others. When individuals don't take their bearings by the truth about good and evil, they follow some subjective opinion or their selfish interest and act as though they are not by nature in solidarity with others, not their "brother's keeper." They are, then, free to take the life of the unborn or the dependent dying if their interests dictate such a course of action and the law allows it. "If the promotion of the self is understood in terms of absolute autonomy, people inevitably reach the point of rejecting one another. Everyone else is considered an enemy from whom one has to defend oneself. Thus society becomes a mass of individuals placed side by side, but without any mutual bonds."[48]

People guided by absolute autonomy do not know how to live in civil society. This kind of autonomy actually leads to the sort of government that allows the strong to take advantage of the weak. Government "is transformed into a *tyrant State,* which arrogates to itself the right to dispose of the life of the weakest and most defenseless members, from the unborn child to the elderly, in the name of a public interest which is really nothing but the interest of one part."[49]

The deepest cause of the threat to the "culture of life" by the "culture of death," which sanctions abortion and euthanasia despite noble proclamations about the right to life, is the contemporary "*eclipse of the sense of God*

47. Ibid., no. 19.   48. Ibid., no. 20.
49. Ibid.

and of man."⁵⁰ By losing their sense of God, individuals no longer understand nature, man, or the meaning of human dignity. People need a sense
of God to know that they are sinning against God and their neighbor.
"Nature itself, from being *'mater'* (mother), is now reduced to being 'matter,' and is subjected to every kind of manipulation."⁵¹ For example, instead of respecting nature as God's creation, people feel free to create embryos in a laboratory, do their research, and then destroy them. This is a
perfect example of manipulating nature.

In particular, "the eclipse of the sense of God and of man inevitably leads to a *practical materialism,* which breeds individualism, utilitarianism and hedonism." This "practical materialism" causes people to prefer
having things to being a certain kind of person, to avoid suffering at all
costs, to depersonalize sexual relations, to look at interpersonal relations
in terms of usefulness instead of "respect, generosity and service." The
pope argues that this eclipse of the sense of God and man takes place in
the conscience. It gives up its role as a herald of God's word and becomes
its own oracle. The sad result is that "the moral conscience, both individual and social, is today subjected, also as a result of the penetrating influence of the media, to an *extremely serious and mortal danger:* that of *confusion between good and evil,* precisely in relation to the fundamental right to life."⁵²

Christians can recover their sense of God and man by reflecting on the
blood of Christ, that is to say, his death and resurrection for all. Christ's
death clearly reveals that God the Father loves all human beings and that
human beings must have great dignity if Christ died for them. "Precisely
by contemplating the precious blood of Christ, the sign of his self-giving
love (cf. Jn 13:1), the believer learns to recognize and appreciate the almost
divine dignity of every human being....Furthermore, Christ's blood reveals to man that his greatness, and therefore his vocation, consists in *the
sincere gift of self.*"⁵³ If Christians could appropriate or reappropriate this
basic teaching of the Christian faith, they would not formally cooperate
in the evil of facilitating the practice of abortion.

To conclude chapter 1, John Paul II balances his condemnation of the
threats to human life by mentioning examples of respect for life on the local, national, and international levels.⁵⁴ In chapter 2 the pope systematically presents the Christian message regarding life. The most important

50. Ibid., no. 21.
52. Ibid., no. 24.
54. Ibid., cf. no. 26–28.

51. Ibid., no. 22.
53. Ibid., no. 25.

points made in this chapter are these: Life is a gift from God, which is more precious than we can imagine. "Truly great must be the good of human life if the Son of God has taken it up and made it the instrument of the salvation of all humanity."[55] It is such a great good because it is the "'place' where God manifests himself, where we meet him and enter into communion with him."[56] We show our gratitude for the gift of life by loving God and our neighbor. "Thus the deepest element of God's commandment to protect life is the *requirement to show reverence and love* for every person and the life of every person."[57] Loving our neighbors means not doing them any harm and benefiting them, especially in times of great need, such as sickness, old age, and especially in the various dangers that people face.

The mother and father who conceive a child should be grateful that with God's help they bring a person into the world made in God's image and destined for eternal life. From the moment of conception the person has very great dignity. We have confirmation of this fact from the New Testament. John Paul II explains: "the dignity of the person is celebrated in the meeting between the Virgin Mary and Elizabeth, and between the two children they are carrying in the womb."[58]

While life is a great good, it is not the absolute good. "The death of John the Baptist, precursor of the savior, also testifies that earthly existence is not an absolute good; what is more important is remaining faithful to the word of the Lord even at the risk of one's life."[59] If life is not cut short by sudden death, then people will face both the onset of old age, with its inevitable problems, and often sickness and pain, as well, at various points throughout life. The Bible invites all to have trust in God's loving plan for them in the face of sickness and their approaching death.

After presenting the Christian vision of life, John Paul says that people will not really understand and appreciate the commandment not to kill unless they grasp *"the Law as a whole."* The pope explains:

[D]etached from this wider framework, the commandment is destined to become nothing more than an obligation imposed from without, and very soon we begin to look for its limits and try to find mitigating factors and exceptions. Only when people are open to the fullness of the truth about God, man and history will the words "you shall not kill" shine forth once more as a good for man in himself and in his relations with others.[60]

55. Ibid., no. 33.   56. Ibid., no. 38.
57. Ibid., no. 41.   58. Ibid., no. 45.
59. Ibid., no. 47.   60. Ibid., no. 48.

In other words, people need a coherent framework, a divinely inspired vision of life to appreciate why they shouldn't kill innocent persons.

In chapter 3 the pope presents his detailed reflections on the commandment "you shalt not kill." He discusses the right to self-defense of individuals and the state, the death penalty, abortion, the experimentation on and the destruction of embryos, euthanasia, and suicide, and then discusses at some length the relation of the moral law to the civil law.

The pope begins by noting what we know from tradition about murder: "in the first centuries, murder was put among the three most serious sins—along with apostasy and adultery—and required a particularly heavy and lengthy public penance before the repentant murderer could be granted forgiveness and readmission to the ecclesial community."[61] This, of course, is not surprising, given the biblical teaching that God made man in his own image. It follows that the Church would recognize self-defense as legitimate because life is such a great good and because all have the duty to love themselves. While in some circumstances a person may renounce his right to self-defense out of "heroic love," legitimate defense "can be not only a right but a grave duty for someone responsible for another's life, the common good of the family or of the State."[62]

John Paul II next takes up the subject of the death penalty, pointing out that the state does have the authority to impose the death penalty, but should refrain from executing criminals "except in cases of absolute necessity: in other words, when it would not be possible otherwise to defend society. Today, however, as a result of steady improvements in the organization of the penal system, such cases are very rare, if not practically nonexistent."[63] Thus the death penalty is not an intrinsic evil like abortion and euthanasia, since it can be used in some circumstances, and a determination has to be made regarding its necessity. That determination will inevitably lead to legitimate disagreements among Catholics regarding its necessity in particular cases. It could not be otherwise. As Cardinal Joseph Ratzinger wrote, "there may be a legitimate diversity of opinion even among Catholics about waging war and applying the death penalty, but not however with respect to abortion and euthanasia."[64] While the

61. Ibid., no. 54.

62. Ibid., no. 55, quoting *Catechism of the Catholic Church*, no. 2265.

63. *Evangelium vitae*, no. 56.

64. Cardinal Joseph Ratzinger, "Worthiness to Receive Holy Communion. General Principles," memorandum sent to Cardinal Theodore McCarrick and Bishop Wilton Gregory, June 2004.

pope can't foresee circumstances that would require anything but a rare imposition of the death penalty, he implies that Catholics have the freedom to make their own determination on the basis of the principles in *Evangelium vitae* and the *Catechism of the Catholic Church*. In its final version the latter now reads: "If, however, non-lethal means are sufficient to defend and protect people's safety from the aggressor, authority will limit itself to such means, as these are more in keeping with the concrete conditions of the common good and are more in conformity with the dignity of the human person."[65] It is, of course, hard to discern circumstances in which recourse to the death penalty would be necessary to protect people from a particular aggressor, unless he were able to order murders from his prison cell.

It is interesting to note that the pope quotes the *Catechism* on the primary purpose of all punishment imposed by society, including the death penalty: it is "to redress the disorder caused by the offense." By redressing the disorder society defends the public order and the safety of persons. This means that Pope John Paul II has not changed the traditional rationale for punishment. Cardinal Ratzinger confirms this point in response to a query by Richard Neuhaus. The cardinal wrote,

You ask about the correct interpretation of the teaching of the encyclical on the death penalty. Clearly, the Holy Father has not altered the doctrinal principles which pertain to this issue as they are presented in the *Catechism*, but has simply deepened the application of such principles in the context of present-day historical circumstances. Thus, where other means for self-defense of society are possible and adequate, the death penalty may be permitted to disappear. Such a development, occurring within society and leading to the foregoing of this type of punishment, is something good and ought to be hoped for.[66]

Since the purpose of punishment hasn't changed, even the death penalty, then, should only be imposed to defend the public order and the safety of persons. What has changed is the necessity of having recourse to the death penalty in order to accomplish these purposes of punishment. They can almost always be achieved, the pope believes, by using bloodless means.

With respect to the killing of the innocent, the pope goes to the heart

---

65. *Evangelium vitae*, no. 56, citing *Catechism of the Catholic Church*, no. 2267.
66. Joseph Cardinal Ratzinger, quoted in Richard Neuhaus, "The Public Square," *First Things*, no. 56 (October 1995): 83.

of the matter by making a formal and dramatic statement. *"I confirm that the direct and voluntary killing of an innocent human being is always gravely immoral."* He justifies his authoritative stance by appealing to reason, sacred scripture, tradition, and the Magisterium. The pope summarizes his general position by quoting from the *Declaration on Euthanasia* (1980):

Nothing and no one can in any way permit the killing of an innocent human being, whether a fetus or an embryo, an infant or an adult, an old person, or one suffering from an incurable disease, or a person who is dying. Furthermore, no one is permitted to ask for this act of killing, either for himself or herself or for another person entrusted to his care, nor can he or she consent to it, either explicitly or implicitly. Nor can any authority legitimately recommend such an action.[67]

With respect to the practice of abortion, the pope notes that its "acceptance in the popular mind, in behavior, and even in law itself, is a telling sign of an extremely dangerous crisis of the moral sense, which is becoming more and more incapable of distinguishing between good and evil." By abortion the pope means "the deliberate and direct killing by whatever means it is carried out, of a human being in the initial phase of his or her existence, extending from conception to birth." The killing of the unborn at any stage of pregnancy is murder. To make clear the evil of abortion to Catholics, the Church imposes the sanction of excommunication on all those who procure an abortion and on "those accomplices without whose help the crime would not have been committed." The purpose of the excommunication is to help people realize the seriousness of what they have done and to bring about their conversion.

The pope recognizes that mothers will not always have recourse to abortion for selfish reasons. They may be seeking to protect their own health, to maintain a certain standard of living for their families, or even to prevent the birth of a child into unfavorable circumstances. But no reason, argues the pope, can justify killing an innocent human being. Besides the mother there are other people responsible in various ways for the practice of abortion, namely, the father, relatives, friends, the law, administrators of institutions where abortions are performed, and the advocates of sexual permissiveness, as well as international institutions, associations, and foundations.

---

67. *Evangelium vitae*, no. 57, quoting Congregation for the Doctrine of the Faith, *Declaration on Euthanasia* (*Iura et bona*, May 5, 1980).

Finally, with respect to the justification of abortion, John Paul II says: "Some people try to justify abortion by claiming that the result of conception, at least, up to a certain number of days, cannot yet be considered a personal human life." He acknowledges that there is no empirical way to discern the presence of a spiritual soul, but notes that science, nevertheless, tells us that life begins with the fertilization of the ovum. There should be no killing of human beings in their early stages of development. Consequently, experimentation on human embryos or fetuses which kill them "constitutes a crime against their dignity as human beings." The stem cell research that many today are demanding requires the manufacturing of embryos and then their subsequent destruction. Many seem unfazed that the potential curing of adult diseases depends on the killing of human beings in an early stage of development. About this killing Richard Doeflinger has written, "the idea of specially creating new human embryos in the laboratory solely to destroy them for research surely does add an especially cold-blooded element to research practices that are already gravely wrong."[68] This utilitarian attitude, prevalent in both the scientific community and in the public at large, is a grave threat to human dignity.

John Paul II next turns to euthanasia and suicide. *"Euthanasia in the strict sense* is understood to be an action or omission which of itself and by intention causes death, with the purpose of eliminating all suffering."[69] This is to be distinguished from the decision not to make use of extraordinary, disproportionate, or burdensome measures. As the Vatican *Declaration on Euthanasia* states, patients may "refuse forms of treatment that would only secure a precarious and burdensome prolongation of life, so long as the normal care due to the sick person in similar cases is not interrupted."[70] For example, a person could choose not to undergo chemotherapy in order to get six more months of life. Patients may use pain killers even if they hasten one's death, but they may also refuse the use of pain killers as means of sharing in the Lord's passion.

John Paul II judges euthanasia to be false mercy. "True 'compassion'

---

68. Richard Doeflinger, "Experimentation on Human Subjects and Stem Cell Research," in *Moral Issues in Catholic Health Care* (Wynnewood, Penn.: St. Charles Borromeo Seminary, 2004), 103.

69. *Evangelium vitae,* no. 65.

70. Congregation for the Doctrine of the Faith, *Declaration on Euthanasia,* IV, "Due Proportion in the Use of Remedies"; available online at http://www.vatican.va under Congregation for the Doctrine of the Faith, doctrinal statements.

leads to sharing another's pain; it does not kill the person whose suffering we cannot bear." Euthanasia is especially heinous when it is involuntary or carried out by relatives, who have a duty to love their family
members. After calling involuntary euthanasia murder, John Paul II says,
"The height of arbitrariness and injustice is reached when certain people,
such as physicians or legislators, arrogate to themselves the power to decide who ought to live and who ought to die."[71]

To dramatize the evil of euthanasia John Paul II says, "in communion
with the bishops of the Catholic Church, I *confirm that euthanasia is a grave
violation of the law of God*, since it is the deliberate and morally unacceptable killing of a human person."[72] The basis of this teaching is the natural law, scripture, tradition, and the Magisterium of the Church. Euthanasia is particularly offensive, because it challenges the biblical teaching
that "God alone has the power over life and death: 'It is I who bring both
death and life' (Dt. 32:39; cf. 2 Kg 5:7; 1 Sm 2:6)."[73] Our duty as Christians
is to wait for the Lord; to end one's life or someone else's is to challenge
the Lordship of Christ.

What John Paul II says about the evil of euthanasia applies equally to
suicide. Asking for euthanasia is really just a way of having someone facilitate or participate in your suicide. The pope does, however, offer a few
specific reflections on suicide based on the thought of Thomas Aquinas.
Suicide is gravely immoral because "it involves the rejection of love of self
and the renunciation of the obligation of justice and charity towards one's
neighbor, towards the communities to which one belongs, and toward
society as a whole. In its deepest reality, suicide represents a rejection of
God's absolute sovereignty over life and death."[74] Everyone can always
make a contribution to the community, even by bearing his suffering at
the end of life.

Despite the arguments against euthanasia, there is a movement to see
it as a way of dying with dignity. A syndicated column appearing in the
Scranton Tribune (February 14, 2003) argued that physician-assisted suicide
and euthanasia ought to be legal so that people could die with dignity.
The columnist, Joan Ryan, told a heart-rending story of a woman with
multiple problems who swallowed a lethal drug in the presence of her close
friends and relatives. The drug was prescribed by a physician in Oregon,
where euthanasia is legal. That this sort of thing should be allowed every-

71. *Evangelium vitae,* no. 66.   72. Ibid., no. 65.
73. Ibid., no. 66.   74. Ibid.

where and even encouraged is a "no-brainer," she said. Ms. Ryan wrote her column to protest the action of Attorney General John Ashcroft, who was trying to persuade the Ninth Circuit U.S. Court of Appeals that the legalization of euthanasia in Oregon violates a federal statute. The title of her column proclaimed that Ashcroft was playing God!

The justification and legalization of euthanasia and physician-assisted suicide involve more than meets the eye at first glance. I once heard a university professor make the point that he would consider suicide if he became a severe burden to his wife as a difficult terminal patient. I suggested to him that such talk in the presence of his wife was only apparently considerate, because it implied that she should consider suicide if she became a heavy burden for him. That is the kind of pressure that no family member should place on another.

Leon Kass on Euthanasia

The argument against euthanasia, based on reason alone, can readily be seen in the works of Leon Kass. "Once there looms the legal alternative of euthanasia," writes Kass in his *Life Liberty and the Defense of Dignity: The Challenge for Bioethics*, "it will plague and burden every decision made by seriously ill elderly persons—not to speak of their more powerful caretakers—even without the subtle hints and pressures applied to them by others."[75] Many older people suffer from being dependent on others and will wonder whether they should exercise the option of euthanasia. Their relatives may even subtly suggest this possibility by their way of relating to them. Of course, the insurance companies may find ways of encouraging euthanasia and assisted suicide in order to save money. Without doubt, the granting of a right to euthanasia will exert even more pressure on the aged to exercise that right so as to spare loved ones financial and emotional burdens.

We have learned from the experience of legalized euthanasia in the Netherlands that euthanasia does not remain strictly voluntary, as the law requires. Physicians alone or in collaboration with relatives decide to end the lives of patients. Kass reports that "a 1989 survey of 300 physicians disclosed that (already then) over 40 percent had performed *non*-voluntary euthanasia and over 10 percent had done so fives times or more."[76] This is

75. Leon R. Kass, *Life, Liberty, and the Defense of Dignity: The Challenge for Bioethics* (San Francisco: Encounter Books, 2002), 252.
76. Ibid., 208.

bound to happen in the United States because of misplaced compassion or a desire to save money, either on the part of the relatives or the physicians. "No one with an expensive or troublesome infirmity," says Kass, "will be safe from the pressure to have his right to die exercised."[77] If people don't respond favorably to the pressure, doctors and relatives will sometimes resort to nonvoluntary euthanasia.

Giving physicians the right to kill, even with the patient's consent, will have an enormous impact on a doctor's self-understanding and patient trust. Kass rightly says that "the medical profession's devotion to heal and refusal to kill—its ethical center—will be permanently destroyed, and with it patient trust and physicianly self-restraint."[78] Patient trust of doctors is already at a low ebb, and will certainly be eroded even more if physicians subtly or not so subtly suggest death to patients as their best option. Some patients will, of course, fear being killed without their consent, as is the case in the Netherlands.

Death with dignity depends not on the legalization of euthanasia but on the way one has lived and faces death, and by the way one is treated by friends, relatives, doctors, and nurses. Of course, patients should not be tortured by useless treatments and should receive as many pain killers as they need. Their dignity demands as much. But "withdrawal of contact, affection and care," says Kass, is probably the greatest single cause of the dehumanization of dying. Death with dignity requires absolutely that the survivors treat the human being at all times as if full godlikeness remains, up to the very end."[79] I think that full godlikeness does remain despite the failure of cognitive and physical capacities. In the beginning of 2002 I was privileged to witness the care of the Rev. William Hill, S.J., who was confined to a hospital bed with much diminished capacities for about three months before his death. His sister and brother Jesuits at the University of Scranton faithfully cared for him on a daily basis, ennobling themselves by their efforts and sustaining the elderly priest in his courageous and serene acceptance of decline and passing. The dignity of patient, sister, and brother Jesuits was much in evidence up until the very end. The kind of virtue displayed in Fr. Hill's hospice room at Mercy Hospital won't see the light of day if patients are allowed and encouraged to end their lives with the permission of the state. At any rate, "we must never allow ourselves to relieve *our own* frustrations and bitterness over

77. Ibid., 227.   78. Ibid.
79. Ibid., 249.

the lingering deaths of others," says Kass, "by pretending that we can kill them to sustain *their dignity*."[80]

Biotechnology, the Law, and Public Policy

Kass on the Prevention of Dehumanization

Another way to see that Catholic social thought must address bio-medical matters is to look at some other parts of Kass's *Life, Liberty, and the Defense of Dignity: The Challenge for Bioethics*, a book that deals extensively with the dangers of dehumanization. Leon Kass is one of the best and most prominent bioethicists in the country and was for some time the chairman of the President's Council on Bioethics. In his book he warns Americans and the rest of the world about the dangers of dehumaniza-tion posed by the contemporary biomedical project. A great admirer of the benefits made available to humanity by modern science, Kass has, nev-ertheless, come to the conclusion that new scientific developments, if not properly managed and controlled, will most likely lead to the kind of dystopia described by Aldous Huxley in *Brave New World*. Kass contends that neither scientists nor bioethicists are alert enough to "the possibility of willing dehumanization."[81] Seeing the dangers is difficult because "in the realm of bioethics the evils are intertwined with goods we so keenly seek: cures for disease, relief of suffering, preservation of life."[82] He men-tions several areas where dangers are present or looming: the legalization of euthanasia, allowing doctors to kill their patients, embryonic stem cell research, cloning, the selling of body parts, genetic engineering, the in-terest in seeking immortality through science, turning procreation into manufacturing, and even the state of modern biology. Kass notes that "our cultural pluralism and easygoing relativism make it difficult to reach consensus on what we should embrace and should oppose; and serious moral objections to this or that biomedical practice are often facilely dis-missed as religious or sectarian."[83] He is positively dismayed that neither philosophical ethics nor religious ethics is in a state to offer much help. American religious ethicists (with some notable exceptions) are not much help, because they tend to use the same language and categories as the philosophical ethicists. "Regarding the deeper matters and ultimate con-cerns that lie just beneath the surface of everyday life—the significance of

80. Ibid., 255.
82. Ibid., 3.

81. Ibid., 10.
83. Ibid., 7.

human finitude or the moral worth of suffering or the meaning of sexuality and procreation—['the theoretical and rationalist approach to ethics'] has virtually nothing to say."[84] Kass does not seem to be aware of Pope John Paul II's *Evangelium vitae* and other writings, which have a lot to say about subjects that, in Kass's mind, are neglected by religious ethicists.

Kass begins his treatment of cloning sounding like a Catholic moral theologian. "Thanks to the sexual revolution, we have been able to deny in practice, and increasingly in thought, the inherent procreative meaning of sexuality itself. But if sex has no intrinsic connection to generating babies, babies need have no necessary connection to sex."[85] Kass goes on to argue that we no longer have a common understanding of family, marriage, sexuality, and the meaning of motherhood and fatherhood. "Stable monogamous marriage as the ideal home for procreation is no longer the agreed-upon cultural norm. For this new dispensation, the clone is the ideal emblem: the ultimate 'single parent child.'"[86] Because of feminism and the gay rights movement, many have come to doubt that marriage between a male and a female is a natural norm, but now believe that it is a cultural construct. Cloning is regarded by many as simply an extension of artificial insemination donor and *in vitro* fertilization. The latter procedures were a slippery slope, as critics initially maintained. Kass stands aghast that the profundity of human procreation is no longer sufficiently appreciated. It is not just the result of our rational wills. "It is a more complete activity precisely because it engages us bodily, erotically, and even spiritually, as well as rationally."[87] Without appreciating this fact, people do not shudder at the prospect of manufacturing babies. "Whether we know it or not—and we are well on the way to forgetting it—the severing of procreation from sex, love and intimacy is inherently dehumanizing, no matter how good the product."[88]

Kass gives four reasons that cloning is dehumanizing. First, coming up with a cloning technique that doesn't produce a handicapped, deformed, or retarded human being would require unethical experiments. If only three to four percent of the attempts to clone animals succeeded, then it is likely that many, many children would be sacrificed for the sake of scientific progress. Kass, concludes, "We cannot ethically find out whether or not human cloning is feasible." Second, "if it were successful cloning

84. Ibid., 63.   85. Ibid., 143–44.
86. Ibid., 144.   87. Ibid., 157.
88. Ibid.

would create serious issues of identity and individuality."[89] For example, because his genotype has already existed, people will expect the cloned child to live his life like the original. Wouldn't there be a lot of pressure to turn out a certain way? If the child is a clone of his mother or father, then he will have a special relationship with that parent. What if the parents get divorced and mom can't stand the sight of the child, who is a clone of her former husband?

Throughout his book Kass makes much of the third reason he puts forth to show that cloning is dehumanizing. "Human cloning would also represent a giant step toward the transformation of begetting into making, of procreation into manufacture (literally making by hand), a process that has already begun with *in vitro* fertilization and genetic testing of embryos."[90] Kass is repulsed by the prospect of people paying big money to get the right genes. The artificers will stand above the child they are planning to make. "In human cloning, scientists and prospective 'parents' adopt a technocratic attitude toward human children, as their artifacts. Such an arrangement is profoundly dehumanizing, no matter how good the product."[91]

Kass's fourth argument against cloning is that it "would enshrine and aggravate a profound misunderstanding of the meaning of having children and of the parent-child relationship....Cloning is...inherently despotic, for it seeks to make one's own children after one's own image (or an image of one's choosing) and their future according to one's will."[92] Kass notes that some parents already abuse their children by trying to live their own lives through the successes of their children. Cloning will enable parents to behave even more tyrannically. But things won't be any better if their choice of genes doesn't work out as planned. Parents will have guilt feelings, and children will have grudges against their parents for their poor choice of genes. Parents who clone will have difficulty appreciating that their children aren't their possessions or their projects, but unique individuals who should have the freedom to make their way in the world. "Their genetic distinctiveness and independence are the natural foreshadowing of the deep truth that they have their own, never-before enacted life to live."[93]

With respect to organ donation, Kass worries that the way this practice is justified may eventually lead to the sale of body parts.

89. Ibid., 158.   90. Ibid., 160.
91. Ibid.   92. Ibid., 161–62.
93. Ibid., 161.

It looks as if to facilitate and to justify the practice of organ donation, we have enshrined something like the notions of property rights and free contract in the body, notions that usually include the possibility of buying and selling. This is slippery business. Once the principle of private right and autonomy is taken as the standard, it will prove difficult—if not impossible—to hold the line between donation and sale.[94]

Throughout his book Kass raises questions about the way rights and autonomy are understood these days. In this context, if rights entitle people to make a gift of their organs, they also would authorize selling them. Kass draws the larger conclusion that rights are used as a battering ram to destroy America's moral and religious traditions, because rights are often understood as having no intrinsic connection to the good. Kass is able to make this kind of generalization because of his knowledge of political philosophy. He understands the history of rights talk from Hobbes and Locke to the present day. It becomes clear from reading his book that bioethicists need a knowledge of political philosophy to do their work.

With respect to genetic engineering, Kass sounds several warnings. "Genetic engineering will, first of all, deliberately make changes that are transmissible into succeeding generations and may alter in advance specific *future* individuals through direct 'germ line' or embryo interventions. Second, genetic engineering may be able through so-called genetic enhancement, to create new human capacities and, new norms of health and fitness."[95] Practitioners of prenatal diagnosis already tell prospective parents they should abort if the unborn child has this or that genetic abnormality. In other words, some genetic defects make persons *unworthy* of life. Still another difficulty posed by genetic technology will be the blunting of aspiration and achievement in those who believe that their genetic endowment has already determined their future.

The President's Council on Bioethics and Biotechnology

Still another work that will help us see the importance of bioethical themes for Catholic social thought is *Beyond Therapy: Biotechnology and the Pursuit of Happiness: A Report by the President's Council on Bioethics*. The former chairman of the president's council, Leon Kass, says that the purpose of this report, released late in 2003, is "to clarify the relevant scientific possibilities and, especially, to explore the ethical and social implications of

94. Ibid., 192–93.
95. Ibid., 121.

using biotechnical powers for purposes beyond therapy."[96] The council believes that this topic is "arguably the most neglected topic in public bioethics."[97] The report does not aim to be a comprehensive account of all scientific possibilities, nor does it analyze all the relevant ethical literature on the subject. It doesn't even deal with the biotechnologies that could be used for terrorism and mass population control. The report, in addition, doesn't represent the full thought of the council on the subject, and not every member of the council agrees with every "scientific explanation and ethical assessment." Despite these few limitations, the report succeeds both in clarifying possible scientific developments and in offering thoughtful reflections on the pursuit of happiness through biotechnology and on the following specific subjects: better children, superior performance, ageless bodies, and happy souls. My focus is the council's ethical assessment, not its explanation of scientific developments.

In writing its report the council takes into account that many bioethicists and intellectuals don't accept that there is such a thing as human nature or that altering it raises any ethical questions. The council, however, suggests that the evaluation of biotechnologies must be carried out in the light of these two ancient philosophical questions: "What is a good life? What is a good community?"[98] The council realizes that without truthful answers to these questions people will not be able to evaluate the various possibilities offered by biotechnology. The council's implied answers to its own questions indicate that it is sympathetic to a premodern understanding of human nature and community, classical and/or Judeo-Christian. In the very first chapter the council signals its intention to pursue a "richer bioethics," an ethics that keeps in mind the dignity of the human person. For example, the council draws attention to people's worry that the new knowledge of brain function may undermine the acceptance of free will and personal responsibility, that developments in genetic engineering might induce individuals or couples to manufacture so-called designer babies (not a real possibility in the near future, argues the council), and that the use of psychotropic drugs to alleviate depression or treat attention deficit and hyperactivity may cause a loss of personal autonomy, confused personal identity, diminished ambition, and flattened aspirations.

96. President's Council on Bioethics, *Beyond Therapy: Biotechnology and the Pursuit of Happiness* (New York: Regan Books/HarperCollins, 2003), xx.
97. Ibid., 7.   98. Ibid., 11.

Chapter 2 considers "the pursuit of 'better children,' using techniques of genetic screening and selection to improve their native endowments or drugs that might make them more accomplished, attentive, or docile."[99] The council discusses three particular techniques to produce better children: prenatal diagnosis through such procedures as amniocentesis, followed by abortion of fetuses carrying genes deemed unacceptable; preimplantation genetic screening and selection of in-vitro embryos determined to have "desirable" genetic traits; and the insertion of "better" genes into in-vitro embryos via directed genetic change or genetic engineering.

The council notes with some dismay that prenatal diagnosis solves the problem of genetic abnormalities "by eliminating the prospective patient before he can be born."[100] While individuals are free to keep their babies after an unfavorable diagnosis, subtle pressure is often employed by counselors and others on parents to abort their abnormal fetus. Furthermore, the council points out that "there appears to be a growing consensus, both in the medical community and in society at large, that a child-to-be should meet a certain (for now, minimal) standard to be entitled to be born."[101] This attitude, argues the council, could subtly coerce parents to choose abortion and increase discrimination against imperfect children whose defects were or could have been diagnosed in utero. As things stand, the attitudes of parents and society may already be shifting "from seeing a child as an unconditionally welcome gift to seeing him as a conditionally acceptable product."[102]

While discounting the real possibility of directed genetic change in the near future, the council does raise questions about the practice of fertilizing a dozen or more eggs in vitro, followed by the implantation of the embryo with the most desirable traits and, then, the destruction of the other embryos. This procedure is now done for couples deemed at risk of conceiving a child with chromosomal or genetic disorders. A test called polymerase chain reaction is now available to test the genes of the embryos produced by means of IVF. The council refers to the test by the general technical term of preimplantation genetic diagnosis (PGD). IVF and PGD can be used not only to avoid disease but also to produce a child either with the desired sex or with compatible bone marrow for an ill sibling. In the future PGD may be used to select embryos for implantation with the genotype desired by the parents, even when there is no likeli-

99. Ibid., 21.
101. Ibid.

100. Ibid., 36.
102. Ibid., 37.

hood that a mother would conceive and give birth to a child with a genetic disorder. Of course, the parents may not even carry the genotype they
desire for their children. In addition, because the interaction between nature and nurture (genes and environment) is complicated and not fully
understood, there is no guarantee that a child will grow up with the desired trait.

After mentioning abortion of fetuses with genetic disorders as a benefit of IVF and PGD, the council goes on to raise a host of problems
with these procedures, including the death of the fetus and possible dangers to the woman from abortion. (It looks as though some members of
the council favor abortion and others don't.) The problems mentioned are
significant. The council first points out that the long-term effects of the
blastomere biopsy on the 4- to 10-cell embryo are unknown. There are no
real protections for the embryo, since it is not treated as a human subject.
The council asks how the parents can claim to be pursuing the best interests of the child (the governing moral norm) if they are exposing their
unborn children to unknown risks, especially when PGD is not employed
for any therapeutic benefit.

The council expresses dismay at the future prospect of IVF and PGD
becoming the preferred way of having children. This would have far-
reaching negative implications for the family and society. Still another
significant concern is the prospect of declining tolerance, both for children born with genetic disorders and for adults with disorders born before the new technology was available. The council also notes that
bringing children into the world by means of IVF and PGD looks like
"manufacturing," rather than procreation. The effects on the children
will also be huge. Children will see themselves more as products of their
parents' will rather than as gifts of their parents' love. And they will feel
pressure to live up to the expectations of their parents, who hand-picked
their genotype.

A subset of producing children with a certain genotype is sex selection.
After explaining the various methods of ensuring the birth of a child
with the desired sex (sonography or amniocentesis followed by abortion;
IVF and PGD followed by the destruction of the embryos; and "prefer-
tilization separation of sperm into X- and Y-bearing spermatozoa,")[103]
the council explains why there has not been a hue and cry about the practice of sex selection, since it usually discriminates against females. People

103. Ibid., 60.

don't want to jeopardize the liberal principles of individual autonomy, reproductive freedom, and "the right to choose" by thoroughly criticizing the practice of sex selection. The council incisively comments,

> The "pro-choice" idea of "every child a wanted child" establishes the rule in reproductive matters of the supremacy of parental "wants." Ironically, the "right to choose," which was and is defended in the name of equality for women, has in this way made permissible the disproportionate choice of aborting female fetuses. It is open to question whether the cause of equality has been well served by this development.[104]

There is the clear implication that adherence to liberal principles in this case leads to, and justifies, prejudice against females, not to mention their death via abortion.

Still another problem with sex selection is the problem it poses for males and for society at large. After mentioning the countries in which an imbalance has been created between males and females by the abortion of the latter, the council notes that males in the affected countries (e.g., Azerbaijan, Armenia, Georgia, Cuba, China, parts of India, Pakistan) have less of a chance of finding a wife.

The council concludes this section by taking note of an interesting fact and by endorsing a high moral principle on the relations between parents and children: that reproductive-assistance clinics require their clients to sign an agreement that they will accept the "product" of IVF, even if sex selection doesn't work. This way of proceeding shows that the clinics "must make into a matter of compulsory agreement what the ideal of parenthood should take for granted: that each child is ours to love and care for, from the start, unconditionally, and regardless of any special merit of theirs or special wishes of ours."[105] In enunciating such a principle this governmental council shows that it appreciates and cherishes the gratuity of unmerited love.

The last section of chapter 2 is a probing reflection on the use of psychotropic drugs such as Ritalin to make children better-behaved and more competent. The council expresses grave reservations about the policy of popping pills into children as a matter of course. "For very few behavioral disorders," the council argues, "is there likely to be a purely genetic cause."[106] For example, attention deficit/hyperactivity disor-

104. Ibid.   105. Ibid., 71.
106. Ibid., 80.

der (ADHD), according to the current consensus among professionals, is "brought about by some combination of genetic susceptibility and environmental factors."[107] Two of the environmental factors mentioned, "severe early emotional deprivation" and "familial psychosocial adversity," most likely stem from character flaws in one or both parents. It is not wise to improve the performance of children, argues the council, by relying on psychopharmacology. That sends the message that human problems are solved by chemicals and not by the proper moral formation and education. The council strongly recommends that parents, doctors, and educators rely mainly on moral education to help children improve their behavior and performance. In its opinion the spiritedness and restlessness of children may not be the sign of any disorder, but merely the prelude and raw material for higher performance. Sedating kids with Ritalin could bar the road to excellence. Not that Ritalin is never necessary for particularly troublesome and troubled children! But doctors must be wary of pressures exerted on them by insurance companies to use Ritalin, and parents must be careful not to succumb to the pressure imposed by school authorities and doctors to rely on Ritalin rather than more time-consuming methods of behavior modification—namely, character formation. "The beneficiaries of drug-induced good conduct may not be really learning self-control; they may be learning to think it is not necessary."[108] The liberty of children must not be repressed for the convenience of adults. As the council puts the matter, modifying behavior by drugs raises "significant worries about the prospects for benevolently enforced conformity, restriction of freedom, and perhaps even for the decline of genuine excellence."[109] The health of children should not be put at risk by stimulants such as Ritalin, whose long-term effects are still largely unknown.

The next topic the council addresses is "superior performance." To discuss this topic the council focuses on achieving excellence in sports, since it is really paradigmatic for most areas of human endeavor. The council, of course, acknowledges that life is not a game, but maintains "that things essential to sport—such as aspiration, effort, activity, achievement, and excellence—are essential also to many aspects of the good human life."[110]

The key question for the council is this: "Which biomedical interven-

107. Ibid.
109. Ibid., 91.
108. Ibid., 91–92.
110. Ibid., 107.

tions for the sake of superior performance are consistent with (even favorable to) our full flourishing as human beings, including our flourishing as active, self-aware, self-directed agents?"[111] There are three ways people's native powers and their activities can be improved: drugs, genetic modifications, and surgical procedures (including the implantation of very small mechanical devices). In this chapter the council focuses on performance-enhancing drugs, namely, the human growth hormone, EPO (erythropoietin, the agent used for "blood doping," the increased production of red blood cells, so as to increase the body's capacity to carry oxygen), and anabolic steroids. The majority of the chapter discusses the steroids. The council's overall evaluation of steroid use is negative because of its effect on the body and the human spirit. There is no disagreement about the long-term negative effects of steroids on physical health. Users run the risk of developing the following problems, among others: "fluid retention, high blood pressure, infertility, permanent cessation of growth in adolescents, and psychological effects from excessive mood swings to drug dependence."[112] The council's principal contribution to this discussion is probably its reflection on the damage done to the human spirit by the use of anabolic steroids. The council shows great respect for performance based on natural gifts and sustained practice or training. "The heart of *humanly* superior performance" is "the human being displaying in visibly beautiful action the workings of heart, mind, and body united as inseparably as the concave and the convex."[113] The council worries that drug-enhanced performance, often stemming from love of gain or recognition, is not quite real, shows disrespect for our embodiment, and compromises "our choosing and willing identity itself, since we are choosing to become less than normally the source or the shapers of our own identity."[114] In other words, excellence should be the result of our own desiring, striving, and cultivated gifts, and not largely the result of a drug injection. Still otherwise stated, we should improve our performance because of "what we do," not because of "what is done to us."[115] By these remarks the council is trying to engender respect for all those human qualities and activities that contribute to the attainment and maintenance of human dignity and human excellence, and to alert people to what is dehumanizing and undignified.

111. Ibid., 131.   112. Ibid., 137.
113. Ibid., 134.   114. Ibid., 150.
115. Ibid., 129.

In discussing superior performance the council makes two points about its relation to the good society. First, superior performance edifies and ennobles society: "it makes everyone better; it raises the spirits of a community; it nourishes the desire to be better and to do better, as individuals and as a people."[116] Secondly, the council believes that society could tolerate the use of anabolic steroids by certain individuals when the common good is at stake. In this perspective the following would make sense: "offering steroids to improve the strength of soldiers while rejecting them for athletes, offering steroids to improve the alertness of fighter-pilots while rejecting them for students, offering anti-anxiety agents to steady the hands of surgeons while rejecting them for musicians."[117] Of course, such drug-taking might benefit society, but possibly do harm to specific individuals. So, the council recommends great caution in asking individuals to risk their health for the sake of the common good. The model would seem to be the soldier who risks his life for the preservation of the community.

Shakespeare provides a good introduction to the council's next subject: the quest for ageless and healthy bodies. The bard says that one's final years are marked by "a moist eye, a dry hand, a yellow cheek, a white beard, a decreasing leg, an increasing belly...your voice broken, your wind short, your chin double, your wit single, and every part of you blasted with antiquity."[118] With this prospect in the offing, it is not surprising that people want to improve the quality and extend the length of healthy days. One expert quoted by the council even went so far as to say, "the real goal is to keep people alive forever."[119]

Without going into the three likely possibilities to retard aging mentioned by the council, I want to summarize its reflections about focusing on the prolongation of life, even to the point of seeking immortality on this earth. In response to these desires, the council emphasizes that the limited amount of time at our disposal makes us more serious about seeking and living the truth about human existence. The council believes that the sense of urgency imposed by a foreseeable death is probably what prompted the Psalmist to ask God to "teach us to number our days, that

116. Ibid., 152.

117. Ibid., 154.

118. William Shakespeare, *King Henry the Fourth*, part 2, act 1, scene 2, lines 179–83, quoted in President's Council on Bioethics, *Beyond Therapy*, 181.

119. President's Council on Bioethics, *Beyond Therapy*, 162.

we may get a heart of wisdom."[120] If people sense that they have a more or less endless future, or that their death is a long way off, they will not likely be serious about living well throughout their whole life.

The council notes that the increase in life expectancy from 48 to 78 in the United States between and 1900 and 2000 has led to a decline in the birth rate. In 1900 the birth rate was just above 30 per thousand population. In the height of the Baby Boom after World War II the rate was only 24.1; by 1965 it was 18.4 in the Unites States. The council's point in giving these statistics is this:

And so a world of men and women who do not hear the biological clock ticking or do not feel the approach of their own decline might have far less interest in bearing—and, more important, caring for—children. Children are one answer to mortality. But people in search of other more direct and immediate answers, or more to the point, people whose longer lease on life leaves them relatively heedless of its finitude, might very well be far less welcoming of children, and far less interested in making the sacrifices needed to promote human renewal through the coming of a new generation.[121]

It is somewhat controversial to maintain that there is a connection between "awareness of finitude" and "devotion to perpetuation." Not even all members of the council agree that such a connection exists. Without attempting to give any answers, the council does pose two more questions for consideration related to the effect of longer life on fidelity in marriage and family relations.

Would people in a world affected by age-retardation be more or less inclined to swear lifelong fidelity "until death do us part," if their life expectancy at the time of marriage were eighty or a hundred more years, rather than as today, fifty? And would intergenerational family ties be stronger or weaker if there were five or more generations alive at any one time?[122]

In my mind, the answer to the first question is most certainly no, since moral relativism has already dealt a blow to lifelong commitment.

Still another problem with age retardation is the possibility of becoming so wrapped up with living a long life that people become so anxious about potential health hazards that they don't focus on living well. In addition, if people live longer lives but in poor health without the prospect

120. Ibid., 188. 121. Ibid., 189.
122. Ibid., 190.

of a fatal illness to end their misery, then, as the council says, "pressures for euthanasia and assisted suicide might mount."[123]

Age retardation, of course, would also have significant effects on society. There would be fewer work openings for the young, fewer opportunities for advancement. It is also likely that there would be less innovation and adaptation in public and private institutions, as they would be controlled by older people for a longer time, who tend to be less inclined to take even prudent risks or to come up with new ideas.

The final observation of the council borders on the theological. "Only aging and death remind us that time is of the essence. They invite us to notice that the evolution of life on earth has produced souls with longings for the eternal and, if recognized, a chance to participate in matters of enduring significance that ultimately could transcend time itself."[124] In other words, the very imperfection and shortness of life generate longings in us for eternal things and move us to accomplish great things. Catholicism would describe those great accomplishments as the various way people can love God and neighbor more and more deeply.

Shakespeare once again provides a good introduction to the last topic addressed by the council: the happy soul. Macbeth asks a doctor to free his wife from the haunting memory of the guilt she feels because of the murder she committed:

> MACBETH: Canst thou not minister to a mind diseas'd
> Pluck from the memory a rooted sorrow,
> Raze out the written troubles of the brain,
> And with some sweet oblivious antidote
> Cleans the stuff's bosom of the perilous stuff
> Which weighs upon the heart
> DOCTOR: Therein the patient
> Must minister to himself.[125]

With the availability of new drugs painful memories could be erased from a guilty person's conscience, or significantly dulled, thereby removing a powerful incentive to acknowledge his wrongdoing and repent. Likewise, the anticipatory taking of drugs could prevent people from feeling pain when they do horrible things. The council also notes that the drugs could even dull the memories of injustice in the minds and

123. Ibid., 191.   124. Ibid., 200.
125. Ibid., 206–7.

hearts of good people, thereby causing them to be "too comfortable with the world, unmoved by suffering, wrongdoing or cruelty."[126] Without accurate memories, the moral responsibility of individuals deteriorates. "Without truthful memory, we could not hold others or ourselves to account for what we do and who we are. Without truthful memory, there could be no true justice or even the possibility of justice; without memory, there could be no forgiveness or the possibility of forgiveness—all would simply be forgotten."[127] All in all, drugs have the capacity to cut us off from the truth, and thereby are an obstacle to real happiness. Drugs could make us content with a shallow happiness, not the happiness that comes from aspirations for higher things, the cultivation of character, activity in the world, and our relations with others.

The council further argues that the sorrow we experience can make us "more attuned to the hardships of others, more appreciative of life's everyday blessings, more aware of the things and the people that matter most in our lives."[128] If St. Augustine had taken mood brighteners, he would not have felt appropriate sorrow when his mother died. The council actually presents Augustine's description of his sorrow over his mother's death as the mean between two extremes.

If his response to his mother's death had been hysterical, unremitting sorrow, we might think it excessive. And if he had been coldly indifferent, we would wonder at his lack of humanity. The sadness he actually felt was the humanly fitting response, the emotion called for and appropriate to the circumstances.[129]

In other words, experiencing measured sorrow at the right time makes us more of a human being. The contemporary desire to avoid even fitting sorrow as too much of a burden or as an interference in one's activities threatens to diminish "our appreciation of the depth of our love and of the one whose absence causes our pain."[130] In short, remembrance of the good and the bad in the proper way is essential to our humanity and happiness.

Speaking loosely, one might suggest that remembering well is *remembering at the right pitch:* neither too much, engulfing us in trivia or imprisoning us in the past, nor too little, losing track of life's defining moments or of knowledge needed

126. Ibid., 229.
128. Ibid., 258.
130. Ibid., 257.

127. Ibid., 232.
129. Ibid., 256.

for everyday life; neither with too much emotion, allowing past misfortunes to haunt or consume us, nor with too little emotion, recalling what is joyful, or horrible, or inconsequential, all with the same monotone affect.[131]

Related to the distortion of our memories through drugs is the distortion of our perception through the medicalization of understanding. "For example, a person who attributes his discontent or sadness to sickness may spare himself difficult self-examination and self-recrimination, as well as arduous attempts to change the way he lives."[132] Emotional and character problems are attributed to genes and neurochemicals. Spiritual achievement and the acquisition of a better character are not seen as relevant to happiness, which is seen either as a natural gift or the result of biotechnical manipulation.

In the final chapter the council reiterates previous themes, with a few clarifying additions. Space will only permit a partial summary. The council's main point is that the beneficiaries of biotechnology are in danger of losing a sense of human excellence. The council says that "the pursuit of an untroubled and self-satisfied soul may prove to be deadly to desire, if finitude recognized spurs aspiration and fine aspiration acted upon *is itself* the core of happiness."[133] Pursuing ageless bodies and factitiously happy souls is a distraction and even an obstacle, because their pursuit "could deprive us of the urge and energy to seek a richer and more genuine human flourishing."[134] Second, besides the loss of high aspirations and the achievement of wisdom and virtue, the council worries about the gradual loss of freedom. For example, parents will feel subtle pressure to medicate their children if that is the only way to remain competitive with drug-enhanced children. Third, "the absence of a respectful attitude is today a problem in some—though by no means all—quarters of the biotechnical world. It is worrisome when people act toward or even talk about our bodies and minds—or human nature itself—as if they were raw material to be molded according to human will."[135] If this attitude becomes sufficiently widespread, then people will gradually lose their sense that human beings have very great dignity. It is fair to say that the council published this book as a defense of human dignity. It is a remarkable achievement for a governmental commission or for any group of citizens, since, as Tocqueville wrote many years ago, Americans are not known for their in-

131. Ibid., 219.   132. Ibid., 261.
133. Ibid., 299.   134. Ibid.
135. Ibid., 289.

terest in theoretical questions. If American citizens and citizens of other countries reflected on the subject of biotechnology with the same depth as the President's Council, we would have less to fear from the uses of biotechnology.

Conclusion

While there is general agreement that the United States must address the issues of health care, energy policy, primary and secondary education, unstable credit markets, the repairing of roads and bridges, and the wars in Iraq and Afghanistan, there is not a firm consensus on the importance of maintaining traditional marriage, protecting life from conception until natural death, and making use of biotechnology without dehumanizing ourselves. I have tried to explain why Catholic social doctrine keeps the Catholic perspective on these three matters before the eyes of the public with a view to shaping the mores and inspiring the passage of good legislation.

PART 2

Civil Society and the Common Good

Three Mediating Institutions

CHAPTER 6

Civil Society and the Church

A healthy civil society makes an enormous contribution to the common good of the nation. It reaches into those areas of life that the law cannot or will not reach. The three most important agents of civil society are the Church, the family, and the university. The next two chapters will, accordingly, discuss these three pillars of society. The first section of this chapter, The Role of the Bishops, will explain how the United States Conference of Catholic Bishops (USCCB) has chosen to make its contribution to the political community, and then offer some reflections on its mode of engagement in the light of Catholic social doctrine. The second section will explain the role of the laity in the political and social order according to Vatican Council II and various papal documents. I will not specifically address how individual bishops might contribute to the common good, but will indirectly address their proper role by my reflections on the USCCB. The most important contribution that individual priests can make to the common good is to preach the fullness of the Catholic faith, including its countercultural aspects. As things stand, not a few priests in the United States are failing to give the laity a complete explanation of the faith from the pulpit. This is a quiet crisis in the Church. As one priest vocation director said to me, "It is hard to persuade young men to join a presbyterate that is reluctant to bear witness to the fullness of Catholic truth."

The Role of the Bishops

The ultimate end of the Church is the salvation of human beings, "which is to be achieved by faith in Christ and by his grace,"[1] and ful-

---

1. Vatican Council II, *Apostolicam actuositatem (Decree on the Apostolate of the Laity)*, no. 6; for all documents of Vatican Council II, see Walter M. Abbott, *The Documents of Vatican II* (New York: Guild Press, America Press, and Association Press, 1966), modified translation.

ly attained only in the afterlife.[2] Therefore, all the works of the Church
have as their goal "the sanctification of men and women and the glorification of God in Christ."[3]

The specific mission that Christ entrusted to his Church, according
to *Gaudium et spes (Pastoral Constitution on the Church in the Modern World)*, is not
in "the political, economic, or social order. The purpose which he set before her is a religious one."[4] Although the Church's mission is salvation
through sanctification, it nevertheless has much to offer life in the city.
Men and women receiving the message of salvation have the duty to imbue all temporal things with a Christian spirit. Out of the Church's religious mission, says *Gaudium et spes*, "comes a duty, a light, and forces which
can serve to structure and consolidate the human community according
to divine law."[5] "The mission of the Church in its full range," Avery Cardinal Dulles concludes, "may therefore be said to include not only the directly religious apostolate but also the penetration of the temporal sphere
with the spirit of the Gospel."[6] As the Catholic Church has an obligation
to foster peace and justice in the world, so popes and bishops rightfully
and regularly address political, economic, and social matters, but not just
like lay people.

At first glance it may seem that Vatican II is saying that the Church
does and does not have a proper mission in the political, social, and economic order. Cardinal Dulles explains the apparent contradiction:

To preach faith in Christ and to administer the sacraments are...proper to
the Church. The Church was established precisely in order that these activities
might be performed. But to erect a just and prosperous society is not...the
proper business of the Church. To contribute to such a society is, however,
a responsibility of Christians insofar as they are citizens of the earthly community. Unless they live up to their civic obligations they will be guilty in the
sight of God. All Christians whether clergy or laity, have duties as members
of the human community, but to penetrate secular professions and organiza-

2. Vatican Council II, *Gaudium et spes (Pastoral Constitution on the Church in the Modern
World)*, no. 40.

3. Vatican Council II, *Sacrosanctum concilium (Constitution on the Sacred Liturgy)*, no. 10,
modified translation.

4. *Gaudium et spes*, no. 42.

5. Ibid., no. 42, modified translation.

6. Avery Dulles, *The Reshaping of Catholicism: Current Challenges in the Theology of the Church*
(New York: Harper and Row, 1988), 147; Vatican II, *Apostolicam actuositatem (Decree on the
Apostolate of the Laity)*, 5.

tions with the spirit of the gospel is preeminently the responsibility or the laity.[7]

In other words, the laity act as leaven in the world in every aspect of their lives.

Distinguishing the duties of clergy from those of the laity has been difficult since the end of Vatican Council II. Right at the beginning of his papacy Pope John Paul II told bishops to pursue justice through evangelization,[8] to communicate Catholic social doctrine[9] and to avoid anything that "resembles political party spirit or subjection to this or that ideology or system."[10] "Secular duties and activities belong properly although not exclusively to laymen."[11] These duties include the prudent application of Catholic social principles to public policy. In making such prudential judgments on the basis of shared goals, "it happens rather frequently, and legitimately, so," says Vatican II's *Gaudium et spes*, "that with equal sincerity some of the faithful will disagree with others on a given matter."[12] Where Catholics may legitimately disagree with one another is the domain of partisan politics.

The United States Conference of Catholic Bishops

What about bishops engaging in partisan politics by taking positions on public policy? Since the mid-1960s the bishops' conference has been doing this on a regular basis. Is that the American way of communicating Catholic social doctrine, or does it resemble political party spirit? Surely, there are times when the principles of Catholic social doctrine may overlap with partisan politics as commonly understood. There are times when the necessity of combating clear evils will require bishops to enter the policy arena. For example, Catholic doctrine requires opposition to unjust wars, racism, the legalization of abortion. The question is whether ordinary partisan policy positions are appropriate for inclusion in episcopal pastoral letters or even in ordinary episcopal statements. In other

7. Dulles, *The Reshaping of Catholicism*, 148; Gaudium et spes, 43; Vatican II, *Decree on the Apostolate of the Laity*, 7.

8. John Paul II, *John Paul II in Mexico* (London: Collins, 1979), 80.

9. Ibid., 82.

10. John Paul II, *Journey in the Light of the Eucharist* (Boston: Daughters of St. Paul, 1980), 349.

11. *Gaudium et spes*, no. 43.

12. Ibid.

words, should the bishops endorse one out of several legitimate approaches to tax or welfare policy?

As I understand the arguments, the case for a social ministry focused on policy runs as follows. First, the U.S. Constitution gives all Americans, including bishops, the right to state their political opinions. Second, the simple proclamation of Catholic social principles is abstract and ineffective. No one will pay attention unless some policy is attacked or defended. Position-taking encourages people to reflect on the moral quality of their lives and moves them to action. Third, the root causes of injustice can be removed only by the right laws and structures.

Furthermore, law shapes the mores of the nation. Where would we be without the Civil Rights Act of 1964? That act certainly shows that policy removes evils. Fourth, Archbishop Rembert Weakland, chairman of the committee that wrote the economy pastoral of 1986, argued that the endorsement of specific, debatable policies in the letter is nothing new or extraordinary. He compared it on one occasion to the manner in which the Church specifies the duty to worship God by imposing a Sunday obligation. Weakland's position is shared by many revisionist moral theologians. Furthermore, a policy focus is simply the American way of being faithful to the exigencies of Vatican II and papal social teaching. Last, not seeking to benefit themselves, the bishops are not acting in a partisan manner.

In my judgment, these are not convincing arguments. The bishops should avoid a partisan policy focus in their pastoral letters unless it is required by Catholic social doctrine or the presence of clear evils. Theological reasons support this position. First, the presence of nonbinding statements or mere political opinions in pastoral letters confuses the laity and further erodes episcopal authority. A Vatican official commented on the partisan nature of the second draft of the U.S. bishops' pastoral letter on war and peace:

When bishops propose the doctrine of the church, the faithful are bound in conscience to assent. A serious problem arises on the pastoral level when bishops propose opinions based on the evaluation of technical or military factors. The faithful can be confused, their legitimate freedom of choice hindered, the teaching authority of bishops lessened and the influence of the church in society thus weakened.[13]

13. Jan Schotte, "A Vatican Synthesis," Origins 12 (1983): 691, 693.

The faithful will be confused because most Catholics will have great difficulty distinguishing binding from nonbinding statements, especially since information will come largely from the secular media, who often do not grasp the essentials of Catholic teaching or deliberately slant reports to promote political programs. Second, continuous teaching in the nonbinding mode leads to the opinion or even demand that the Church have a nonbinding category in the area of morals. This means that traditional Catholic teaching on moral matters, as expounded by the Magisterium, would be one opinion among many vying for acceptance. Cardinal Dulles also notes that the bishops must allow and even encourage dissent from their debatable political opinions. "The spirit of criticism and dissent thus unleashed can scarcely be prevented from spreading to strictly religious matters in which bishops have unquestionable authority in the church."[14] The laity, Cardinal Dulles implies, will have great difficulty drawing a line between proper and improper dissent from episcopal teaching. In other words, lay people may come to regard some authoritative Catholic teachings in the same light as ordinary political opinions. Third, the engagement of the Church in active partisan politics is not infrequently subsumed under the category of the prophetic mission of the Church. Calling nonbinding statements prophetic leads to a misunderstanding of Christianity itself. It is hard to imagine Amos or Isaiah saying to the Israelites, "These are my opinions with which you may legitimately disagree." Fourth, turning the episcopal conference into a lobby for good public policy necessarily diverts the attention of bishops from pressing internal problems in the Church, such as the seminaries, catechesis, moral theology, and dissent from the Church's Magisterium. Many young people are growing up with little knowledge of Catholicism, no sense of the Church, and a narrow understanding of their obligations toward the common good. Reading about the policy proposals of the U.S. bishops will have little, if any, educational value for Catholics, especially because most of the information will come from the secular media. Because devising detailed policy proposals takes a lot of time and energy, Cardinal Dulles asks,

Is it justified for [bishops] to go so far afield when many ecclesiastical matters, for which the bishops have inescapable responsibility, are crying out for greater attention? The impression is given that the bishops are more at ease in criti-

14. Dulles, *The Reshaping of Catholicism*, 178.

cizing the performance of secular governments than in shouldering their own responsibilities in the Church.[15]

Cardinal Dulles also notes that the bishops could be sending the wrong message to lay people by their heavy involvement in politics. "When the bishops devote so much attention to worldly affairs they can unwittingly give the impression that what is truly important in their eyes is not the faith or holiness that leads to eternal life, but rather the structuring of human society to make the world more habitable."[16]

The response to the theological critique of the bishop's mode of political activity should not be a call for the Church to withdraw from the public arena. Rather, the hierarchical Church should be encouraged to have an even deeper impact on American culture and public policy, but to do so as Church—not as a typical lobby, not in such a way as to create false impressions. In criticizing certain kinds of partisan involvement on the part of bishops, I am hoping to foster greater episcopal influence on all matters of public concern. In other words, if the bishops speak about public problems as religious leaders and not as politicians or ordinary citizens, they will be more effective in promoting peace and justice.

In order to clarify further what I believe Catholic social teaching expects from bishops in the public square, I will analyze three major initiatives taken by the USCCB: two during the year before the presidential election of 2004, and one in the fall of 2007. In the fall of 2003 the administrative committee of the USCCB issued and widely distributed in Catholic parishes, schools, and other organizations their quadrennial voters' guide for Catholics entitled *Faithful Citizenship: A Catholic Call to Political Responsibility*. In June of 2004 the bishops issued "Catholics in Political Life." A third document that I will examine is the 2007 edition of the bishops' quadrennial statement on the responsibility of Catholics in political and social life (1976 is the first year these statements were issued). The 2007 statement, much better than the one issued in 2003, was issued in the name of all the bishops, instead of by the administrative committee of the USCCB.

In mid-June of 2004 the USCCB distributed *Faithful Citizenship* to the Democratic and Republican Party platform committees. In its presentation of its document the USCCB's news release had this headline: "Bishops' Platform Committee Testimony Calls for Focus on Pursuit of the

15. Ibid., 176.
16. Ibid.

Common Good, Not Demands of Special Interests." As would be expected, the statement reminds U.S. citizens that the common good embraces the protection of life and the pursuit of social justice, peace, and human rights around the world. All Catholics should applaud the goals of the U.S. bishops.

While this Catholic call to political responsibility rightly focuses on the common good, it has nothing to say to or about pro-abortion Catholic politicians, fails to mention the president's power to appoint pro-life or pro-choice Supreme Court Justices, doesn't urge Catholic representatives and senators to oppose same-sex marriage, fails to distinguish clearly Catholic doctrine from partisan politics, doesn't show that the attainment of social justice depends on Catholics' knowing their faith and practicing virtue in every aspect of their lives, and gives the impression that Catholics exercise faithful citizenship simply by voting correctly. Worst of all, the committee's consistent ethic of life theory can easily be read by Catholics as giving them permission to vote for pro-abortion candidates if they support enough of the USCCB's statements on social justice, global solidarity, and war.

In the month of June 2004 the bishops addressed two omissions in *Faithful Citizenship*. On June 24 the president of the USCCB, Bishop Wilton Gregory, sent a letter to all bishops asking them to solicit support from their senators for the Federal Marriage Amendment. Early in July Bishop Gregory also sent a letter to the U.S. Senate requesting support of the same amendment. Because of public interest, the USCCB finally did address the subject of pro-choice Catholic politicians at their June meeting in a short statement published under the title "Catholics in Political Life." With the collaboration of Francis Cardinal George, Archbishop Charles Chaput and Bishop Donald Wuerl, the Task Force on Catholic Bishops and Catholic Politicians prepared this statement for the entire body of bishops. Since these reflections were not formally submitted to the platform committees of the Democratic and Republican parties, things not said in *Faithful Citizenship* are still significant. After my analysis of *Faithful Citizenship*, I will briefly summarize "Catholics in Political Life." Then, I will turn to the USCCB's 2007 statement pertaining to faithful citizenship.

The "consistent ethic of life" theory in *Faithful Citizenship* stands in contrast to a statement issued by all the bishops in 1998 bearing the title, *Living the Gospel of Life: A Challenge to American Catholics*. In that statement the bishops challenge all Catholics to defend the sanctity of life and argue incisively that being right on "social justice" issues *can never excuse a wrong choice regarding direct attacks on innocent human life.* Indeed, the failure to protect and defend life in its most vulnerable stages renders suspect any claims to the "rightness" of positions in other matters affecting the poorest and least powerful of the human community.[17]

Before the 2004 election Catholic Democrats in the House of Representatives prepared a "Catholic voting scorecard." The purpose of this scorecard was to show that Catholic House Democrats support more of the bishops' legislative priorities than their Republican counterparts. Democrats who support abortion and same-sex marriage may score higher than pro-life Republicans if they endorse a greater number of the bishops' policy positions. Of course, the Democrats' scoring card makes no distinction between USCCB positions based on Catholic doctrine and those based on debatable political preferences. Because the bishops themselves don't always carefully make this distinction, their political statement on faithful citizenship may actually be read as giving support to this latest Democratic initiative to attract Catholic voters. I wouldn't be surprised if the USCCB's "consistent ethic of life theory" didn't give Democrats the idea that they could minimize the effect of their pro-abortion stance by citing their support of the bishops' positions on social justice.

Within a short period of time two Church documents on faithful citizenship appeared, one issued by the Vatican Congregation for the Doctrine of the Faith on November 24, 2002, and the other, the one mentioned above, written by the USCCB's administrative committee and released in the fall of 2003. It was "developed under the leadership of [the USCCB's] Committees on Domestic and International Policy,"[18] in order to provide guidance for Catholic voters on the issues that should be kept in mind in the presidential election. In other words, the USCCB statement tells Catholics what kind of policy positions they should be supporting on a wide range of issues. While a few of these positions, such as the opposition to abortion and euthanasia, are required by Catholic doctrine, most are not, such as the support of affirmative action to over-

17. U.S. Catholic Bishops, *Living the Gospel of Life: A Challenge to American Catholics* (Washington, D.C.: United States Conference of Catholic Bishops, 1998), no. 23. This document is available on the web site of the USCCB under "Pro-Life Activities"; see http://www.nccbuscc.org/prolife/gospel.shtml.

18. United States Conference of Catholic Bishops Administrative Committee, *Faithful Citizenship: A Catholic Call to Political Responsibility* (Washington, D.C.: United States Conference of Catholic Bishops, 2003), copyright page.

come discrimination. These are simply debatable political opinions, as the bishops sometimes candidly admit.

The Vatican document entitled *Doctrinal Note on Some Questions Regarding the Participation of Catholics in Public Life* was issued to clear up misunderstandings and errors in the Catholic community about the way to participate in public life.[19] Unlike the USCCB document, it avoids endorsing positions with which the Catholic faithful may legitimately disagree and stays on the level of doctrine.

At first glance, many Catholics will regard the USCCB's *Faithful Citizenship* as a thoughtful, nonpartisan guide for voters. The bishops say they are exercising their responsibility to address the moral dimensions of public life and do so as pastors, not as partisan strategists. "A Catholic moral framework does not easily fit the ideologies of 'right' or 'left,' nor the platforms of any party. Our values are often not 'politically correct.'"[20] The bishops then call upon Catholics to be a community of conscience, to protect the dignity of the human person, and to promote the common good. In order to help Catholics do their civic duty the USCCB document poses ten questions for Catholics to consider as they make up their minds about the major issues facing the nation. Those questions are based on the bishops' formulation of seven themes in Catholic social teaching (mentioned in the "Introduction"), namely, (1) the life and dignity of the human person; (2) the call to family, community, and participation; (3) rights and responsibilities; (4) the option for the poor and vulnerable; (5) the dignity of work and the rights of workers; (6) solidarity; and (7) caring for God's creation. Protecting the life and dignity of the human person is at the top of the list because it is the sine qua non of a sound and moral democracy.[21]

On the basis of the aforementioned seven themes of Catholic social teaching, the USCCB comes up with four moral priorities for the public realm: protecting human life, promoting family life, pursuing social justice, and practicing global solidarity. Under the first rubric the bish-

---

19. Congregation for the Doctrine of the Faith, *Doctrinal Note on Some Questions Regarding the Participation of Catholics in Public Life* (November 24, 2002); this doctrinal note is available on the Vatican website under doctrinal statements of the Congregation for the Doctrine of the Faith; see http://www.vatican.va/roman_curia/congregations/cfaith/documents/rc_con_cfaith_doc_20021124_politica_en.html.

20. United States Conference of Catholic Bishops Administrative Committee, *Faithful Citizenship*, 7.

21. Ibid., 4–6.

ops mention their strong opposition to abortion, euthanasia, cloning, the targeting of civilians by states or terrorists, the abuses of biotechnology, the preventive use of force, the death penalty, the failure of the U.S. both to sign the treaty banning the use of anti-personnel land mines and the Comprehensive Test Ban Treaty, and the U.S. participation in "the scandalous global trade in arms."[22]

To promote family life the bishops endorse the legal protection of marriage "as a lifelong commitment between a man and a woman."[23] The bishops also call for just wages to those who support families, the protection and education of children, including the formation of their character in educational settings, the safeguarding of the parental right to choose private or public education for their children, and the enforcement of responsible regulations to protect children from pornography and violent material on television, the radio, and the Internet.[24]

The third and fourth priorities are social justice[25] and global solidarity.[26] Under the rubric of social justice the USCCB committee recommends the following: "jobs for all who can work," a living wage, the end of unjust discrimination at work, the right of all workers to organize, "economic freedom, initiative, and the right to private property," and welfare reform that doesn't cut programs and resources, and includes "tax credits, health care, child care, and safe, affordable housing." The committee further supports the work of faith-based groups as a partner with government, income security during retirement for the "low-and average-wage workers and their families," "affordable and accessible health care for all," the strengthening of Medicare and Medicaid, government aid for those suffering from HIV/AIDS and various addictions, affordable housing for all through contributions from the public and private sector, "food security for all," sufficient income for farmers, better treatment of farm workers, policies that "support sustainable agriculture" and respect the earth, better treatment of immigrants, quality education for all, more just salaries for teachers and administrators, and the provision of the typical public school services in private and religious schools. The bishops then call on the nation to address the culture of violence, especially in the media; they recommend tighter gun control measures, the end to the death penalty, and the continuation of the battle against discrimination,

22. Ibid., 17–19.
24. Ibid., 20–21.
26. Ibid., 26–28.

23. Ibid., 20.
25. Ibid., 22–26.

with the help of affirmative action programs. Finally, they urge "care for the earth and for the environment," attention to global climate change, energy conservation, and the development of new, clean energy sources.

Under the fourth priority, "practicing global solidarity," the USCCB urges the United States to take "a leading role in helping to *alleviate global poverty*," to make more efforts to promote *religious* liberty and other human rights around the world, and "to reverse the spread of *nuclear, chemical, and biological weapons,* and to reduce its own reliance on weapons of mass destruction by pursing progressive nuclear disarmament." The bishops further recommend more political and financial support for "appropriate United Nations programs, other international bodies, and international law," and they call upon the United States to adopt a more generous immigration policy, especially for those fleeing persecution. Finally, they urge the government to be a leader, "in collaboration with the international community, in addressing *regional conflicts* in the Middle East, the Balkans, the Congo, Sudan, Colombia, and West Africa." The USCCB places special emphasis on the U.S. role in helping to resolve the Israeli-Palestinian conflict with security for Israel, a state for the Palestinians, and peace for all. The bishops also urge the government, together with members of the international community, to persevere in working "to help bring stability, democracy, freedom and prosperity to *Iraq and Afghanistan.*"[27]

Although the USCCB doesn't list all its legislative priorities or give much detail about the issues they discuss, readers can still form a pretty good idea of where the bishops stand on the political spectrum. In terms of the sheer number of items the USCCB's agenda is more Democratic than Republican. But, in terms of its first two priorities, protecting human life and promoting family life, the USCCB's agenda favors Republicans over Democrats, unless Catholics think that opposition to the Bush administration's Iraq policy and its war on terrorism must take precedence over opposition to abortion and euthanasia. (The death penalty is supported by a majority of both Republicans and Democrats.) What conclusions does the bishops' administrative committee want Catholics to draw from reading their pre-election document?

The bishops offer their readers an overarching principle to guide them in the evaluation of all the issues, namely, the "consistent ethic of life."

27. Ibid., 29.

We do not wish to instruct persons on how they should vote by endorsing or opposing candidates. We hope that voters will examine the position of candidates on the full range of issues, as well as on their personal integrity, philosophy and performance. We are convinced that a consistent ethic of life should be the moral framework from which to address issues in the political arena.[28]

On the contrary, the USCCB does implicitly instruct voters, not by endorsing or opposing candidates, but by laying out its own policy positions and by suggesting that Catholics evaluate candidates for office in the light of those positions within the moral framework provided by "the consistent ethic of life," keeping in mind the character, the political vision, and past performance of the candidates.

What does this "consistent ethic of life" entail? Generally, it is a term used in social justice circles to describe the position that those who object to the taking of life at one stage or in one form must object to the taking of life at all stages and in all forms. Practically speaking, this means that those who oppose abortion should in practice oppose capital punishment and most wars. It is also generally understood to mean that Catholics should promote a respect-life attitude by supporting government spending on what are called the "social justice" issues, and embrace a host of progressive priorities. This is a position articulated by the late Cardinal Bernardin, the former Archbishop of Chicago, who argued in his much-discussed Fordham address of December 6, 1983, that a consistent ethic of life not only opposes abortion but also endorses policies designed to increase a people's well-being—that is, their quality of life. Cardinal Bernardin argued, "A quality of life posture translates into specific political and economic positions on tax policy, employment generation, welfare policy, nutrition and feeding programs and health care."[29]

Anyone who is consistently pro-life and on the side of justice should favor the kind of governmental policy that will help everyone, especially the poor. Reasonable Catholics, nevertheless, might disagree as to which policies will do the most good. So Cardinal Bernardin interprets "the consistent ethic of life" to mean both opposition to clear evils about which there is no dispute and the endorsement of specific positions on such matters as tax policy, about which there will inevitably and legiti-

28. Ibid., 11.
29. Joseph Cardinal Bernardin, "Call for a Consistent Ethic of Life," *Origins* 13, no. 29 (1983): 493.

mately be disagreement. *Faithful Citizenship* implicitly reflects the same interpretation of "the consistent ethic of life."

The bishops attempt to clarify what the "consistent ethic" requirement means by quoting from the Vatican *Doctrinal Note:*

A well formed Christian conscience does not permit one to vote for a political program or an individual law which contradicts the fundamental contents
of faith and morals. The Christian faith is an integral unity, and thus it is
incoherent to isolate some particular element to the detriment of the whole
of Catholic doctrine. A political commitment to a single isolated aspect of
the Church's social doctrine does not exhaust one's responsibility towards the
common good.[30]

Unfortunately, the bishops do not offer an explanation of this quotation.
They simply urge Catholics to adhere to moral principles, practice discernment, and make "prudential judgments based on the values of our
faith."[31] Then they mention the seven moral principles or themes of Catholic social teaching and explain their four moral priorities for public life.

The bishops comment on such a dizzying array of political issues that
their readers will be hard-pressed to distinguish which ones should have
priority for Catholics, especially when *Faithful Citizenship* argues that "some
Catholics may feel politically homeless, sensing that no political party
and too few candidates share a consistent concern for human life and dignity."[32] The bishops' administrative committee is apparently not heart-
ened—even though pro-choice-supporters are dismayed—by George
Bush's position on abortion. In other words, both the Republicans and
Democrats fail to measure up to the high standards of Catholic social
teaching. The message seems to be that each party is more or less equally
deficient.

When all is said and done, *Faithful Citizenship* may be interpreted by
Catholics as a permission to vote for a pro-abortion candidate if his position on other issues supports enough items on the USCCB's political
agenda. The Catholic faithful will receive an additional incentive to think
this way from pro-abortion Democrats who can display high marks on
their "Catholic voting scorecard." Did the bishops intend this state of af-

---

30. *Faithful Citizenship*, 12, quoting Congregation for the Doctrine of the Faith, *Doctrinal Note*, no. 4.
31. *Faithful Citizenship*, 12.
32. Ibid., 3.

fairs, one may ask? Surely not. Nevertheless, previous USCCB documents on faithful citizenship and political responsibility have been so interpreted by people with an interest in voting for liberal candidates, despite their pro-choice stance.

Many Catholics may interpret the "consistent ethic of life" to mean that a candidate who is against abortion, euthanasia, the destruction of embryos in research, cloning, and same-sex marriage does not deserve their vote if he or she supported the recent war in Iraq, believes in the death penalty, and doesn't support certain poverty programs. Put another way, Catholics might read the document to mean that a candidate who is adamantly "pro-choice" and a supporter of same-sex marriage might be worthy of their vote if he also favors generous anti-poverty legislation, minority rights, job training for poor and underprivileged, and increased educational opportunities for the poor, and opposes war and the death penalty. This is a likely scenario, because the USCCB doesn't explicitly argue that some evils are more serious than others and, therefore, should be addressed above all. While listing abortion and euthanasia as the first moral priorities for public life might incline some readers to take these evils more seriously than others, *Faithful Citizenship* avoids the dramatic language used both by John Paul II in his *Gospel of Life* about the culture of death and by the USCCB itself in statements specifically addressing the evil of abortion. Not noticing any special urgency, Catholics might also conclude that abortion is not that much of a priority if the pro-life candidate is judged to be the cause of X number of other evils, or insufficiently committed to the USCCB's positions on social justice and global solidarity.

My point will perhaps become clearer by taking a brief look at Michael Pakaluk's critique of Cardinal Bernardin's "seamless garment" or "consistent ethic theory." Pakaluk says it would make no sense to argue that the South before 1865 was unjust because of the institution of slavery and because the roads were not properly maintained in poorer regions. While the latter would be a problem, it would simply pale in relation to the evil of slavery. To think about the relation of abortion to other evils Pakaluk suggests that there are two ways of conceiving the evils of abortion.

The first is that abortion is a calamity, a moral catastrophe of the first order, like the Ukrainian famine or the Holocaust. On this view, legalized abortion constitutes a direct attack on the foundation of our society: it involves the destruction of the most fundamental human bonds and requires, perilously, the continued corruption of our legal and medical professions. Our immediate task as citizens is to work with an almost militant commitment…to remove this evil.[33]

According to this view, the primary duty of all citizens, especially Catholics, is do everything morally possible to oppose the evil of abortion. The second way of looking at abortion, argues Pakaluk, is to look at it as one of many evils threatening the polity. "These evils come and go over time; and…we simply have to do our best to bring about the best society that we can achieve."[34] According to this way of looking at things, faithful citizens may vote for pro-abortion candidates who seem to oppose more evils than pro-life candidates. "The seamless garment theory," argues Pakaluk, "gives no support to the first view, which follows logically from the very nature of abortion conceded by Bernardin, and encourages the second view, which is a formula for lukewarmness and apathy."[35] Unfortunately, *Faithful Citizenship* doesn't present abortion as a calamity of the first order, as the bishops do in some of their fine statements on human life. The document's focus on the "consistent ethic of life" reflects more Cardinal Bernardin's seamless garment theory than it does John Paul II's *Evangelium vitae (Gospel of Life)*.

Besides the problems posed by the USCCB's "consistent ethic of life" theory, *Faithful Citizenship*, unfortunately, has the potential of misleading Catholics in a number of other areas. In comparing the Vatican's *Doctrinal Note* with the bishops' statement, one immediately notices that the former understands better than the latter the distinction between Church teaching and partisan politics, the importance of bishops being pastors and not partisan strategists, the indispensability of the practice of virtue for the reform of the political order, the devastating effect of relativism on society and the political order, the hierarchy of evils in society, how imperative it is for the Church to oppose the legalization of same-sex marriage, and the necessity of giving directives to Catholic politicians. A comparison of papal social teaching and other USCCB statements with *Faithful Citizenship* reveals that the latter omits to mention the many ways citizens may help the poor and promote social justice besides having the right opinion on the issues and voting for the best candidates.

33. Michael Pakaluk, "A Cardinal Error: Does the Seamless Garment Make Sense?" *Crisis* 6, no. 10 (1988): 14.
    34. Ibid.
    35. Ibid.

Let us first look at the understanding of partisanship in *Faithful Citizenship*. The bishops realize that their own policy proposals may not always be the best way to realize their goals. That's why they openly state in various places that lay Catholics may reasonably disagree with their approach. They actually admit their partisanship in both their pastoral letters on war and peace (1983) and on the economy (1986). In the former they write, "At times we state universally binding moral principles found in the teaching of the Church; at other times the pastoral letter makes specific applications, observations and recommendations which allow for diversity of opinion on the part of those who assess the factual data of a situation differently."[36] In the latter they alert their readers to their partisanship by writing, "We know that some of our specific recommendations are controversial. As bishops, we do not claim to make these prudential judgments with the same kind of authority that marks our declarations of principle."[37] Given this admission, I am constantly baffled when they affirm that their conference is not partisan. In *Faithful Citizenship* the bishops say, "As an institution, we are called to be *political but not partisan. The Church cannot be a chaplain for any one party or cheerleader for any candidate.*"[38] The bishops seem to think that they can avoid the charge of partisanship as long as they don't endorse a candidate or a party. In fact, any time they endorse policy positions with which reasonable Catholics may disagree they are acting in a partisan manner. They are rightly political when they teach the whole faith, explain all of Catholic social teaching, call for the end of clear evils, and inspire an educated and virtuous laity to change the world.

Avery Cardinal Dulles, before he became a cardinal, directed attention to the bizarre claim made by the bishops that they are speaking as pastors when they

enter into technical realms such as counterforce targeting of military objectives,...the minimum wage law, progressive taxation and affirmative action. The bishops claim to be speaking as pastors, not as experts on military affairs,

36. National Conference of Catholic Bishops, *The Challenge of Peace: God's Promise and Our Response: A Pastoral Letter on War and Peace* (Washington, D.C.: United States Catholic Conference, 1983), i.

37. National Conference of Catholic Bishops, *Economic Justice for All: Pastoral Letter on Catholic Social Teaching and the U.S. Economy* (Washington, D.C.: United States Catholic Conference), xii.

38. *Faithful Citizenship*, 29.

economics or whatever. But when they make detailed applications of the kind I have mentioned, this distinction is hard to maintain.[39]

Let us recall the teaching of the Vatican's *Doctrinal Note*. Since there are various political opinions compatible with faith and the moral law, "it is not the Church's task, to set forth specific political solutions—and even less to propose a single solution as the acceptable one—to temporal questions that God has left to the free and responsible judgment of each single person."[40] There is a good reason behind this position. If bishops endorse debatable policy solutions to specific problems, "they stir up opposition to themselves within the church," says Cardinal Dulles, "and undermine their own authority to teach and govern." Since the end of Vatican Council II, the USCCB has continuously entered the world of partisan politics by making choices among policy proposals "that are held by sincere and intelligent Catholics."[41] It is true that the number of bishops appreciating the wisdom of Dulles's point does seem to be growing. As we will soon see, at least some of these bishops did have an influence on the content of the next document that was issued in the fall of 2007 to guide Catholics in the 2008 election.

Even though the bishops are obviously people of good will trying their best to benefit society, the USCCB's denial of partisanship is not a harmless mistake. If Catholics are convinced that bishops are never partisan, they may elevate the bishops' debatable policy proposals to the level of doctrine. Such a move will further skew the interpretation of "the consistent ethic of life." If a pro-choice candidate supports twenty five of the USCCB's policy proposals on social justice and global solidarity, won't many Catholics be induced to downplay his support of abortion in the light of his "non-partisan," Catholic positions on social justice?

A third problem with the USCCB's *Faithful Citizenship* is the failure to tell Catholics that faithful citizenship includes much more than voting for good public policy. *Faithful Citizenship* claims to be "a statement on the responsibilities of Catholics to society." In fact, it doesn't really address this large topic at all. It is simply a guide to the issues facing the nation in the election of 2004. If the USCCB had just spelled out the implications of the spiritual and corporal works of mercy, it would, indeed, have

39. Avery Dulles, "Religion and the Transformation of Politics," *America* 167, no. 12 (1992): 297.
    40. Congregation for the Doctrine of the Faith, *Doctrinal Note*, no. 3.
    41. Dulles, "Religion and the Transformation of Politics," 297.

a good beginning for a statement on how Catholics could contribute to the well-being of society. In no place does the USCCB call upon the laity to make a contribution to civil society, except through some kind of political action. The episcopal conference chooses not to point out its own belief, professed elsewhere, that civil society offers Catholics an opportunity to be good citizens at work, in their families and neighborhoods, and in their volunteer activities. Failure to make this point unwittingly gives Catholics the idea that they can be good citizens simply by supporting good public policy through their votes.

A document that really focused on the responsibilities of Catholics toward society would have approached their four priority issues in a more comprehensive way. For example, in the section on promoting family life, where the bishops call for the legal protection of traditional marriage, they could also have called upon Catholic clergy and laity to persevere in their efforts to prepare the young for marriage by educating them in the faith and by persuading them to practice chastity before and after marriage. Ignorance of the faith, pre-marital promiscuity, and cohabitation, as well as the practice of contraception in marriage, are obstacles to living out the Church teaching on the sacrament of matrimony. Here was a perfect opportunity to point out that the separation of sex from its essential connection to procreation through the practice of contraception has prepared the way for acceptance of same-sex marriage. The section on social justice could have made the point that two of the most effective, long-term solutions to the problem of poverty are intact families and the work of Catholic education in poor neighborhoods. There are Catholic schools throughout the country that have done a wonderful job educating the poor, both Catholic and non-Catholic. They could even do better with more resources.

A fourth, and most serious, omission in *Faithful Citizenship* is the failure to address Catholic politicians on the subject of abortion and same-sex marriage. Surprisingly, the USCCB doesn't take Catholic legislators to task for their persistent support of the right to abortion and for resorting to the subterfuge that they are personally opposed to abortion but wouldn't think of trying to persuade others to share their opinion. This is like a pre–Civil War politician saying, "I am personally opposed to slavery, but won't support a law banning slavery." At least, they could have spoken like Archbishop Charles Chaput of Denver, who said,

We've come a long way from John F. Kennedy, who merely locked his faith in the closet. Now we have Catholic senators who take pride in arguing for legislation that threatens and destroys life—and who then also take communion. The kindest explanation for this sort of behavior is that a lot of Catholic candidates don't know their own faith.[42]

Furthermore, the bishops neither call upon the Catholic politicians to oppose the legalization of "marriage" between persons of the same sex, nor do they alert Catholics in their document to the movement in the country to legalize same-sex marriage. This omission reveals a lack of political prudence, given the real possibility that the legalization of same-sex marriage will change the public understanding of marriage entirely. This is in stark contrast to the Vatican effort to provide specific guidelines to Catholic politicians in a statement issued on June 3, 2003, entitled *Regarding Proposals to Give Legal Recognition to Unions Between Homosexual Persons*. Catholic politicians are instructed to oppose any laws that give legal recognition to same-sex unions. If laws are passed giving such legal recognition, Catholic politicians must make their opposition known and work to have the laws repealed. The Congregation for the Doctrine of the Faith states its rationale for its position as follows:

Society owes its continued survival to the family, founded on marriage. The inevitable consequence of legal recognition of homosexual unions would be the redefinition of marriage which would become, in its legal status, an institution devoid of essential reference to factors linked to heterosexuality; for example, procreation and raising children.[43]

Still another problem with the USCCB's *Faithful Citizenship* is the treatment of the cultural crisis in the United States. In the very beginning of the text the USCCB says, "Our culture sometimes does not lift us up but brings us down in moral terms." The qualifier "sometimes" is explained in the next sentence: "Our world is wounded by terror, torn apart by conflict, and haunted by hunger."[44] Are these the primary ways in which our culture brings us down in moral terms? In my mind, Catholic social

42. Archbishop Charles Chaput, "How to Tell a Duck from a Fox: Thinking with the Church as We Look toward November," *Denver Catholic Register* (April 14, 2004); this article is available on the website of Priests for Life, at http://www.priestsforlife.org/magisterium/bishops/04-04-14chaputpoliticians.htm.

43. Congregation for the Doctrine of the Faith, *Regarding Proposals to Give Legal Recognition to Unions Between Homosexual Persons*, III, no. 8 (June 3, 2003).

44. *Faithful Citizenship*, 3.

teaching shows that the negative characteristics of American culture are, first and foremost, rampant relativism, materialism, and nihilism in all areas of life, "the culture of death," and the movement to undermine the understanding of marriage as a union between a man and a woman. Given the bishops' moral priorities, you would expect them to alert Catholics to those aspects of American culture that most seriously oppose their Catholic principles. For example, there is a mention, but no description, of the "culture of death" so eloquently drawn in Pope John Paul II's *Gospel of Life.*

In conclusion, let us return to the Vatican's point about what Catholics need to keep in mind in evaluating political issues. Its *Doctrinal Note* says that faithful citizenship requires all Catholics both to oppose clear evils such as abortion and euthanasia and to realize that the common good demands more than opposition to clear evils, although such opposition must never be omitted in the name of social justice concerns. Otherwise stated, Catholics may not legitimately argue that their pro-life stance in the form of opposition to abortion and euthanasia exhausts the Catholic contribution to the common good. The young must be adequately educated, jobs created, terrorism thwarted, the poor cared for. Under no circumstances, however, does a well-formed Christian conscience "permit one to vote for a political program or an individual law which contradicts the fundamental contents of morals."[45] Neither the Vatican nor the US-CCB explicitly says so, but this statement from the *Doctrinal Note* seems to mean that Catholics may not vote for a candidate whose political program is to protect the right to choose abortion, or to support the legalization of same-sex marriage and euthanasia, even if he or she seems to have good positions on the issues falling under the rubric of social justice.

While the USCCB missed an opportunity in *Faithful Citizenship* to contribute more to the political education of Catholics, especially Catholic politicians, the bishops addressed this lacuna in their meeting of June 2004. After the June meeting the USCCB issued "Catholics in Political Life," a two-page statement prepared by its Task Force on Catholic Bishops and Catholic Politicians, with the collaboration of two additional bishops and a cardinal, and then modified by the entire body of bishops during its meeting. This short statement, developed on the basis of its more extensive interim report, is obviously not the final word.

"Catholics in Political Life" makes the following points: (1) "If those

---

45. Congregation for the Doctrine of the Faith, *Doctrinal Note,* no. 4.

who perform an abortion and those who cooperate willingly in the action are fully aware of objective evil of what they do, they are guilty of grave sin and thereby separate themselves from God's grace." (2) "Those who formulate law...have an obligation in conscience to work toward correcting morally defective laws, lest they be guilty of cooperating in evil and in sinning against the common good." The bishops mention the legalization of abortion on demand as an example of a morally defective law. (3) The bishops "counsel Catholic public officials that their acting consistently to support abortion on demand risks making them cooperators in evil in a public manner." Note that they don't say that pro-choice Catholic politicians are definitely cooperating in evil or are in an objective state of sin. The bishops seem to imply that Catholic pro-choice politicians may not know that supporting the legalization of abortion is formal cooperation in evil. They then express the hope that the proper formation of their consciences will deter Catholic politicians from supporting the right to abortion. (4) All Catholics have an obligation to defend human life and human dignity in public life. (5) Catholic institutions should not honor Catholics who act against the fundamental moral teachings of the Catholic Church. (6) It is up to individual bishops to decide whether to deny communion to pro-choice Catholic politicians. (Of the 70 bishops who submitted an opinion to the task force, those opposing the denial of Holy Communion to pro-choice Catholic politicians prevailed by a margin of three to one.) (7) The bishops commit themselves to "to continue to *teach* clearly and help other Catholic leaders to teach clearly on our unequivocal commitment to the legal protection of human life from the moment of conception until natural death." (8) The bishops further recognize that they "need to do more to *persuade* all people that human life is precious and human dignity must be defended." To accomplish this goal the USCCB says that "more effective dialogue and engagement" with Catholic politicians is necessary. (9) "All must examine their conscience as to their worthiness to receive the Body and Blood of our Lord. This examination includes fidelity to the moral teaching of the Church in personal and public life."

These points in "Catholics in Political Life" fill a big gap in *Faithful Citizenship*, which had nothing to say about or to pro-choice Catholic politicians. The strong point of this statement is the commitment of bishops to persuade pro-choice Catholic politicians to recognize they are not in communion with the Church and to refrain from receiving the Eucharist out of a sense of integrity. One should not underestimate how important this point is. The weakness of "Catholics in Political Life" is its failure to appreciate the full import of Cardinal Ratzinger's memorandum to the USCCB, which was eventually released to the public. (It appears that the vast majority of the bishops didn't have a copy of the Ratzinger memorandum. They received, instead, an inaccurate summary of the memorandum.)

The head of the Vatican Congregation for the Doctrine of the Faith, now Pope Benedict XVI, encouraged pastors of pro-choice Catholic politicians to meet with them and explain that they should not receive communion until they put an end to "the objective state of sin" in which they have placed themselves by campaigning and voting for permissive abortion and/or euthanasia laws. If Catholic politicians refuse to be persuaded, and still seek to receive the Eucharist, "the minister of holy Communion must refuse to distribute it" (cf. Pontifical Council for Legislative Texts Declaration "Holy Communion and Divorced, Civilly Remarried Catholics" [2002], nos. 3–4). Cardinal Ratzinger adds that this is "not a sanction or penalty. Nor is the minister of Holy Communion passing judgment on the person's subjective guilt, but rather is reacting to the person's public unworthiness to receive Holy Communion due to an objective situation of sin." The cardinal's text clearly implies that the refusal to distribute communion to a pro-choice Catholic is not to be done for political reasons, for instance, to influence the outcome of an election, but only for religious reasons.

Ratzinger also addresses the pro-choice Catholic voter in an incisive paragraph appended to the end of his memorandum.

A Catholic would be guilty of formal cooperation in evil, and so unworthy to present himself for Holy Communion, if he were to deliberately vote for a candidate because of the candidate's permissive stand on abortion and/or euthanasia. When a Catholic does not share a candidate's stand in favor of abortion/euthanasia, but votes for that candidate for other reasons, it is considered remote material cooperation, which can be permitted in the presence of proportionate reasons.[46]

This is a very helpful clarification and will help Catholics form their conscience if their pastors can find a way to tell them about it.

While the USCCB statement does urge every bishop to meet with pro-

46. The one-page memorandum from Joseph Cardinal Ratzinger to Cardinal McCarrick can be found on the website of Priests for Life at http://www.tldm.org/news7/Ratzinger.htm.

choice Catholic politicians and work tirelessly to persuade them that their position contradicts Church teaching, one cannot but notice the reluctance of the American bishops to be more insistent with pro-choice Catholics by denying communion to them when the work of persuasion fails to achieve its end. By not following Cardinal Ratzinger's teaching on the theology of denying communion, the USCCB, in my judgment, has not done enough to unsettle pro-choice Catholics and Catholic politicians in their vincible or invincible ignorance. The overwhelming majority will continue to be pro-choice and to maintain that they are in full communion with the Catholic Church because they are able to receive the Eucharist.

At present, only a minority of bishops are likely to be lovingly insistent that pro-choice Catholic politicians may not receive communion if they refuse to be persuaded that their support for abortion is morally wrong. These bishops will greatly benefit the Church as they bear courageous witness to the Catholic faith. One can hope that this minority will eventually persuade their fellow bishops to see the wisdom of withholding communion as a last resort in order to bring about the conversion of pro-choice Catholic politicians.

Let us now turn to the 2007 quadrennial statement on the political responsibility of Catholics, which was issued under the signature of the entire body of bishops. The general secretary noted at the very end of the text that it "was developed by the chairmen, in consultation with the membership, of the Committees on Domestic Policy, International Policy, Pro-Life Activities, Communications, Doctrine, Education, and Migration of the United States Catholic Conference of Bishops (USCCB)." Despite being a document of many committees, it is a vast improvement over its immediate predecessor, thanks in some measure to the work of the USCCB's Committee on Doctrine in coordinating the input from all the participating committees and from individual bishops throughout the country. The Committee on Pro-Life Activities obviously had much more of an influence on the 2007 document than on the one issued in 2003, when the Committee on Domestic and International Policy wielded the most influence. It is still somewhat of a compromise document, because the USCCB's committees are representative of the split between liberal and conservative Catholics on questions of justice and the common good. I will not summarize the whole document, but will direct attention to its new tone, organization, and clearly stated priorities, and then I will suggest that a fuller explanation of some themes drawn from Catholic social doctrine should be included.

There are three parts to *Forming Consciences for Faithful Citizenship: A Call to Political Responsibility from the Catholic Bishops of the United States*. Part 1 (nos. 1–62), the most important part of the document, speaks of forming the consciences of Catholics for political life and presents, through an explanation of seven themes, what the Catholic Church has to say about the role Catholic social teaching should play in the public square. The seven themes are exactly the same ones discussed in the 2003 statement. Part 2 (nos. 63–88) applies the principles of Catholic social teaching to the issues arising in the areas of human life, family life, social justice, and global solidarity, also in the same way as the bishops did in 2003. The emphasis on forming consciences, however, is a completely new tack, especially in that it exhorts lay people to acquire the virtue of prudence. Part 3 (nos. 89–90) lists ten goals for political life in a way meant to challenge citizens, candidates, and public officials. This is a completely new tack as well. What's new in this quadrennial document goes a long way to remedy the deficiencies I just noted in the previous one.

In the very beginning of the introduction to Part 1 the bishops draw attention to the fact that "the right to life itself is not fully protected, especially for unborn children, the most vulnerable members of the American family" (no. 2). Right away the reader realizes that abortion is going to be a priority. Shortly afterward, they cite a very important statement from Vatican Council II's *Dignitatis humanae (Declaration on Religious Freedom)*, no. 6, on the relation between the practice of the faith and the attainment of justice. The declaration says, "society itself may enjoy the benefits of justice and peace, which result from [people's] faithfulness to God and his holy will." The bishops comment, "The work for justice requires that the mind and the heart of Catholics be educated and formed to know and practice the whole faith" (no. 4). This point may seem very obvious, but is hardly, if ever, mentioned by influential Catholics. Yet, the whole endeavor of Catholic social doctrine depends on the widespread practice of the entire Catholic faith—as already mentioned.

Toward the end of the introduction the bishops say that their purpose in writing "is to help Catholics form their consciences in accordance with God's truth" (no. 7). With a properly formed conscience, one oriented toward social charity, the lay faithful can more effectively participate in political life by voting and other means. Noteworthy is the bishops' point that voting does not by any means exhaust one's political responsibility. The service of the common good requires many different initiatives.

Quoting the *Catechism*, the bishops say that "'it is necessary that all participate, each according to his position and role, in promoting the common good. This obligation is inherent in the dignity of the human person.... As far as possible citizens should take an active part in *public life*'" (nos. 1913–15). The implication of this statement is that fulfilling duties is a way of being faithful to one's dignity. In other words, not carrying out duties in life is to act beneath one's dignity. So, dignity is not just an inalienable given, but a quality that is achieved by the way one lives. This is an observation that the USCCB does not make when it directly explains the meaning of human dignity.

The bishops also clearly distinguish their role in the public square from that of the laity. Quoting Pope Benedict XVI, the bishops explain that the "Church cannot take upon itself the political battle to bring about the most just society possible" (*Deus caritas est* [*God is Love*], no. 28); "the direct duty to work for a just ordering of society is proper to the lay faithful" (*Deus caritas est*, no. 29). The role of the Church is to form consciences by teaching Catholic social doctrine. The laity, then, enter into the political fray and work for the implementation of policies and laws that will promote justice.

The bishops next elaborate on the meaning of conscience and form the consciences of the lay faithful by exhorting them to acquire the virtue of prudence. A prudent person recognizes that there are some things that neither individuals nor society can do because they are *intrinsically evil*. "A prime example is the intentional taking of innocent human life, as in abortion and euthanasia" (no. 22). Other examples include genocide, racism, torture, "and the targeting of non-combatants in acts of terror or war" (no. 23). A prudent person also realizes that people must do good in the public square by choosing policies that will improve the economy, food distribution, health care, the chances of peace in Iraq. "The moral imperative to respond to the needs of our neighbors... is universally binding on our consciences and may be legitimately fulfilled by a variety of means" (no. 25). In other words, faithful Catholics may legitimately disagree on which policies will improve the economy or promote better health care. This has to be the case, since there are so many factors to be considered and such difficulty in grasping all the particulars that pertain to a good economy and good health care. Just because the work is difficult doesn't excuse people from helping those in need. As Thomas Aquinas noted, people will have various levels of abilities in discerning the positive initiatives that should be taken to promote the common good in the public square; all good people, however, should be able to recognize intrinsically evil actions.

To make sure they are not misunderstood, the bishops mention again that rejecting intrinsically evil actions and embracing a particular solution to the health-care problem are very different moral actions. "The direct and intentional destruction of innocent human life from the moment of conception until natural death is always wrong and is not just one issue among many. It must always be opposed" (no. 28). The bishops quote Pope John Paul II to reinforce their point: "'Above all, the common outcry, which is justly made on behalf of human rights—for example, the right to health, to home, to work, to family, to culture—is false and illusory if *the right to life*, the most basic and fundamental right and the condition for all other personal rights, is not defended with maximum determination' (*Christifideles laici* [*On the Vocation and Mission of the Lay Faithful in the Church and the Modern World*], no 38)." In other words, the virtue of prudence doesn't allow a faithful Catholic to say that a particular political candidate's policy proposals with respect to the economy, health care, and energy are so good that his acceptance of abortion and euthanasia, intrinsically evil actions, doesn't matter all that much. Respecting the right to life always remains a priority, even for the attainment of social and political rights. In addition, "A Catholic cannot vote for a candidate who takes a position in favor of an intrinsic evil action, such as abortion or racism, if the voter's intent is to support that position" (no. 34). Catholics may never approve of intrinsically evil actions for any reason whatsoever. There can be no exception to this principle.

The next question that naturally arises is this one: "Can Catholics vote for pro-abortion candidates, not because of their anti-life stance, but in spite of it, because they are right on so many other matters?" The bishops respond very carefully. "There may be times when a Catholic who rejects a candidate's unacceptable position may decide to vote for that candidate for other morally grave reasons. Voting in this way would be permissible for truly grave moral reasons, not to advance narrow interests or partisan preferences or to ignore a fundamental evil act" (no. 35). Unfortunately, the bishops do not elaborate on the meaning of *"grave moral reasons,"* but their previous remarks imply that Cardinal Justin Rigali was right to say in an interview with the *National Catholic Register,* "That is the core of the document—that the 'obligation to oppose intrinsically evil acts has a special claim on our consciences and actions.'" (Cardinal Rigali is actually quoting from no. 37 in the document.) The very designation of various actions as "intrinsically evil" marks them as calamities in the moral order. By speaking in this way the bishops have made crystal-clear that opposition to abortion and opposition to a particular economic or energy policy are of an entirely different order. While Catholics are not single-issue voters, "a candidate's position on a single issue that involves an intrinsic evil, such as support for legal abortion or the promotion of racism, may legitimately lead a voter to disqualify a candidate from receiving support" (no. 42). Reasonable Catholics may legitimately disagree about economic and energy policy, but not on what is intrinsically evil. To vote for a candidate who supports intrinsically evil acts, the bishops imply, requires very compelling reasons, a standard not easily met. Nevertheless, we all know that Catholics will interpret "grave moral reasons" in a variety of unpersuasive ways, even if the bishops were more explicit about their understanding of the term. In other words, many Catholics will vote for pro-choice candidates if they are perceived to have good policy suggestions, say, on global warming, energy policy, and the housing crisis.

In a short document the bishops could not elaborate that much on the seven themes of Catholic social doctrine that they mention. Nevertheless, they would do the laity a great service by clarifying the meaning of human dignity. As explained in chapter 1 of this book, the dignity of the human person is both a given and a goal, laboriously achieved over a lifetime. If Christians can act beneath their dignity by sinning, they can also live in accordance with it by practicing virtue in every aspect of their lives. In discussing the theme of family, the bishops specifically mention the harm of "permitting same-sex unions or other distortions of marriage" (no. 46). *Faithful Citizenship* of 2003 omitted this point in its discussion of the family.

The section on rights and responsibilities improves the 2003 document by laying stress on the importance of religious freedom and freedom of conscience. Following the lead of Pope John Paul II and Benedict XVI, the document says, "In a fundamental way, the right to free expression of religious beliefs protects all other rights" (no. 49). Given the various attempts on the part of governments around the world to restrict religious freedom, this is a very important addition.

I must say, however, that the bishops still give short shrift to the multiple duties people have. People are much more prone to think about public morality in terms of rights rather than duties. In order to redress this imbalance, the bishops need to explain how the fulfillment of duties is perfective of the human person.

The discussion on caring for God's creation is also an improvement on the 2003 treatment because it issues a particular challenge to individuals:

"We should strive to live simply to meet the needs of the present without compromising the ability of future generations to meet their own needs" (no. 54).

In the conclusion, the bishops draw attention to the limits of politics and to the importance of implementing the principle of subsidiarity. In its work to achieve the common good, the state is aided by the actors in civil society. "Building a world of respect for human life and dignity, where justice and peace prevail, requires more than just political commitment. Individuals, families, businesses, community organizations, and governments all have a role to play" (no. 57).

Part 2 explains how the bishops themselves apply Catholic social teaching to the major issues of the day under the rubrics of human life, family life, social justice, and global solidarity. There is not much difference between the 2003 and 2007 documents in this section, with a few exceptions. The bishops begin by explaining that some of their observations must be accepted by all Catholics because they involve fundamental moral principles; with respect to the application of some principles to the issues, the bishops acknowledge that others may legitimately apply the principles in a different way. "While people of good will may sometimes choose different ways to apply and act on some of our principles, Catholics cannot ignore their inescapable moral challenges or simply dismiss the Church's guidance or policy directions that flow from these principles" (no. 63). Earlier in the document they had said, "The judgments and recommendations that we make as bishops on specific issues do not carry the same moral authority as statements of universal moral teaching" (no. 33). These are important caveats, because lay Catholics may legitimately apply principles to many issues on the basis of their own well-formed conscience in ways that differ from positions taken by the USCCB. Despite the bishops' admission of diminished authority, I still think they are making a mistake by teaching in this nonbinding mode, for reasons already explained earlier in this chapter.

In the section on family life the bishops add a comment about coercive contraception programs and freedom of conscience. "We oppose contraceptive mandates in public programs and health plans, which endanger rights of conscience and can interfere with parents' rights to guide the moral formation of their children" (no. 71). The section on social justice contains an additional paragraph indicating that "the religious duty of stewardship" requires careful care of the earth (no. 87). In the section on global solidarity the bishops urge the United States not to support programs imposing contraception on the poor people of the world. "Our nation's efforts to reduce poverty should not be associated with demeaning and sometimes coercive population control programs; instead these efforts should focus on working with the poor to help them build a future of hope and opportunity for themselves and their children" (no. 88). This is an important addendum, given what is happening at international conferences throughout the world. Many actors in the international arena are seeking to impose contraception on the poor.

In the new third and final section of their 2007 document, the bishops list their ten goals for political life. The first three goals reflect the bishops' priorities revealed earlier in the document: (1) end the legalization of abortion; (2) avoid using violence to address fundamental problems: "a million abortions each year to deal with unwanted pregnancies, euthanasia and assisted suicide to deal with the burdens of illness and disability, the destruction of human embryos in the name of research, the use of the death penalty to combat crime, and imprudent resort to war to address international disputes" (no. 90); and (3) "Define the central institution of marriage as a union between one man and one woman, and provide better support for family life morally, socially, and economically so that our nation helps parents raise their children with respect for life, sound moral values, and an ethic of stewardship and responsibility" (no. 90). The other seven goals deal with such things as immigration, poverty, health care, discrimination, encouragement of all to pursue the common good, the use of military force, and human rights.

This 2007 statement is an immense improvement over its 2003 predecessor, which will, unfortunately, remain a beguiling alternative in the years to come for not a few Catholics. One thing is certain: on the campuses of Catholic universities the faculty with an orientation toward social justice is more likely to invoke the 2003 statement because of its reliance on the so-called consistent ethic of life. Many Catholics interpret this theory to mean that they can vote for the liberal agenda with a clear conscience, even though it includes support for same-sex marriage and the untrammeled right to choose abortion and other anti-life measures.

The Role of the Laity

The theology of the laity put forth by the Second Vatican Council, canon law, and Pope John Paul II is inspiring and challenging. *The Code of Canon Law* succinctly identifies the laity and explains its role in the Church. The Christian faithful are those who have been incorporated into Christ and the Church by baptism, and, therefore, share in Christ's priestly, prophetic, and royal office (*munus*). They have a duty to live a holy life, to promote the growth of the Church in holiness, and to work for the diffusion of the divine message of salvation throughout the world. In addition, sometimes the laity even has the right and the duty to alert the hierarchy about matters that pertain to the salvation of souls. Vatican II's *Lumen gentium* (*Dogmatic Constitution on the Church*) inspired the following words found in *The Code:*

In accord with the knowledge, competence and preeminence which they possess, [the Christian faithful] have the right and even at times a duty to manifest to the sacred pastors their opinion on matters which pertain to the good of the Church, and they have a right to make their opinion known to the other Christian faithful, all with due regard for the integrity of faith and morals and reverence toward their pastors and with consideration for the common good and the dignity of persons.[47]

The laity's second principal duty is both to be a leaven in the world by working for social justice and "to assist the poor from their own resources." More generally stated, "Each lay person in accord with his or her condition is bound by special duty to imbue and perfect the order of temporal affairs with the spirit of the gospel; he or she thus gives witness to Christ in a special way in carrying out those affairs and in exercising secular duties."[48]

Turning now to Vatican II's *Lumen gentium*, we find more detail about the role of the laity in the world. The most helpful text is the following: "Moreover, let the laity by their combined efforts remedy the customs and conditions of the world, if the mores therein are an inducement to sin, so that all things may be conformed to the norms of justice and may favor the practice of virtue rather than hinder it."[49] The effect of this kind of work is to imbue culture and human activity with morality, and to "better prepare the field of the world for the seed of the Word of God."[50] In other words, the laity is to work for the amelioration of the mores in every area of political, social and economic life. Where it is successful, people will more easily practice virtue in their everyday lives

47. *The Code of Canon Law*, canon 212.
48. Ibid., canon 225.
49. Vatican Council II, *Lumen gentium*, no. 36, modified translation.
50. Ibid.

and more readily let their lives be transformed by the word of God. Otherwise stated, holiness is more easily attainable in a good regime, as explained in chapter 2 of this book.

Another passage of *Lumen gentium* says the laity makes Christ known to others, especially by a life of faith, hope, and charity. Then it adds, "the layman is closely involved in temporal affairs of every sort. It is therefore his special task to illumine and organize these affairs in such a way that they may always start out, develop, and persist according to Christ's mind, to the praise of the Creator and Redeemer."[51] It is the distinctive task of lay people to renew the temporal order. Guided by the Gospel and the mind of the Church, and prompted by love, lay people act on their *own* responsibility and use their *own* particular competence to seek the justice of God's kingdom in all things—through family life and other mediating structures or voluntary associations, and through business, the trades, the professions, the institutions of the political community, international relations. As part of their duty to pursue holiness and to perfect the temporal order, married laity have duties toward their families. The married faithful are "to work for the upbuilding of the people of God through their marriage and their family.... Christian parents are especially to care for the Christian education of their children according to the teaching handed on by the Church."[52] Life in the family is especially crucial for the pursuit of holiness and the perfection of the temporal order. Catholic social teaching keeps saying, as goes the family, so goes the nation.

This task of renewing the temporal order is both difficult to execute *and* to conceive. Vatican II explains:

Affected by original sin people have fallen into very many errors about the true God, human nature and the principles of morality. As a consequence the mores and human institutions became corrupted, the human person himself held in contempt. Again in our own days not a few, putting an immoderate trust in the conquests of science and technology, fall into a kind of idolatry of temporal things, having become the slaves of them rather than the masters.[53]

Because of ignorance caused by sin, lack of education as well as the simple human inability to grasp complex concepts and situations, lay people often

51. Ibid., no. 31.
52. *Code of Canon Law*, canon 226.
53. Vatican Council II, *Decree on the Apostolate of the Laity*, no. 7, modified translation.

have a more or less limited understanding of what the renewal of the temporal order entails. What can be done to foster the stability of marriages, to raise exit requirements from public schools, to insure the education of the underclass in the nation's cities, to improve general education in the universities? What initiatives will help produce a consensus on the purpose of medicine among health-care professionals? Can anything be done to persuade lawyers and their clients not to press frivolous, immoral lawsuits?

Even when lay people achieve the requisite clarity for their work of renewal, they must still contend with opposition from others or with their own weaknesses caused by ignorance or by disordered passions, such as immoderate love of pleasure, gain, honor, and power, as well as fear of toil and laziness.

Despite the obstacles posed by ignorance and weakness, individual lay persons, dedicated to the pursuit of holiness, will always find ways to bring more order, harmony, and justice to family and social life, to the conduct of the trades, business, and the professions, to political life. Even when large-scale problems resist resolution, individual men and women can still be good husbands and wives, fathers and mothers, good doctors and plumbers, dedicated volunteers and active citizens.

In working for any kind of political and social reform, lay people would do well to keep in mind the prudent advice Thomas More gives in his *Utopia:*

[S]uggestions ought not to be made or advice proffered which you are sure will never be taken. . . . If erroneous beliefs cannot be plucked out root and all, if you cannot heal long established evils to your satisfaction, you must not therefore desert the state and abandon the ship in a storm, because you cannot check the winds. Nor should you force upon people strange and unaccustomed discourses which you know will have no weight with them in their opposite beliefs. But you should try and strive obliquely to settle everything as best you may, and what you cannot turn to good, you should make as little evil as possible. For it is not possible for everything to be good unless all men are good, and I do not expect that will come about for many years.[54]

More's stress on moderate expectations for reform is not at all cynical resignation to the status quo, but an invitation to reach for the possible with enthusiasm and serenity. Aiming too high could lead to the kind

---

54. Thomas More, *Utopia,* trans. Peter K. Marshall (New York: Washington Square Press, 1965), 33–34.

of revolutionary zeal that thrives on anger and hatred. The would-be reformers must be careful not to let anger at opponents devour their souls. Impatience with the way things are can lead to the sadness and despair of Goethe's Faust who, after renouncing hope and faith, exclaims "and cursed above all be patience." Commenting on this line, the theologian Romano Guardini wrote,

[Faust] is the ever-immature who never sees reality or accepts it as it is. Always he flies above it in his fancy. Always he is in a state of protest against his destiny, whereas the maturity of man begins with his acceptance of what is, of reality. Only this gives him the power to change and to re-shape it.[55]

Because of the ever-present temptation to give up when confronted with ignorance and sin, Guardini urges us to make this prayer: "Lord, have patience with me, and give me patience so that the possibilities granted to me may, in the short span of my life-time, those brief years, grow and bear fruit."[56]

In *Christifideles laici* Pope John Paul II talks about the renewal of the temporal order in a very concrete way, so that most Catholics could understand what the Church is teaching lay people about their specific vocation. He says, "*Charity toward one's neighbor,* through contemporary forms of the traditional spiritual and corporal works of mercy, represent the most immediate, ordinary and habitual ways that lead to the Christian animation of the temporal order, the specific duty of the lay faithful."[57] This is much less complicated than figuring out how to solve the malpractice insurance crisis, reform the legal profession, reestablish the Catholic identity of Catholic universities, apply just war principles to war with Iraq. For example, one of the corporal works of mercy that is only heeded by a few Catholics is "Visit the imprisoned." With some creative leadership from dioceses and parishes, many more Catholics would visit prisoners and help them with the problems of reentry when released from prison.

Back in 1998 Pope John Paul II was already aware that the laity was running up against obstacles in the fulfillment of its mission. In *Christifideles laici* the pope specifically mentioned two enticing temptations for the laity:

the temptation of being so strongly interested in Church services and tasks that some fail to become actively engaged in their responsibilities in the pro-

---

55. Romano Guardini, *The Virtues: On Forms of Moral Life* (Chicago: Henry Regnery, 1963), 32.

56. Guardini, *The Virtues,* 36.   57. John Paul II, *Christifideles laici,* no. 41.

fessional, social, cultural and political world; and the temptation of legitimiz-
ing the unwarranted separation of faith from life, that is, a separation of the
Gospel's acceptance from the actual living of the Gospel in various situations
of the world.[58]

Not many would disagree that vast numbers of the laity have succumbed
to these temptations. Instead of helping the laity resist the first temptation, pastors have been instructing and encouraging them to become active in some church ministry as the admired and privileged way of living
out their Catholicism more fully. (You must all have noticed that everything is a ministry these days.) At one holy Thursday Mass I attended
the pastor explained that the twelve people on the altar having their feet
washed were all active in some Church ministry. No one was chosen who
had brought Christ to the workplace in an extraordinary way or who had
evangelized the culture in some area of life. Homilists shy away from explaining how lay people can renew the temporal order. Instead, they mention how lay people can get more involved in Church ministries. The lay
responsibility for being a leaven in the world has become a dim memory
and is hardly known to young people today.

With so much discussion about the role of the laity in the Church
at the time of Vatican II, one might expect more progress in this area.
There are, of course, examples of individuals and groups doing wonderful things. In an article on the laity, Mary Ann Glendon mentioned
Communion and Liberation, the Community of St. Egidio, Focolare, the
Neo-Catechumenate Way, Opus Dei, and Regnum Christi. I constantly
hear stories about lay individuals exercising a quiet influence throughout
their lives. Nevertheless, one can't help but notice that most lay Catholics
are unaware of their opportunities to be a leaven in the world. A Catholic principal of a Catholic elementary school told a friend of mine that it
would be discrimination to prefer hiring a qualified Catholic rather than
a similarly qualified non-Catholic teacher. The principal added for good
measure that it would also be discrimination to ask a non-Catholic teacher to respect the mission of Catholic schools. Other principals have commented that with the departure of the sisters from the schools, lay people
couldn't hope to promote Catholicism very effectively.

At Jesuit universities there is a lot of talk about being "men and wom-
en for others." At first glance this would seem to be a way of overcoming

58. Ibid., no. 2.

the split between faith and life, of which John Paul II spoke. This exhortation is unfortunately not integrated into a complete presentation of the faith or accompanied by another exhortation to prepare oneself for service by ever-deeper conversion. Just before he died, Fr. Roy Davis, S.J., long-time dean at Georgetown University, said to me that the mode of presenting and understanding the meaning of "being for others" at Jesuit universities was usually not distinctively Catholic.

In the midst of the sexual-abuse crisis in the Catholic Church, some of the laity wants to ascend higher on the altar steps so that they might begin to share in the governance of the Catholic Church as a remedy for what they regard as the failure of many bishops to be true shepherds of the faithful. The newly constituted Voice of the Faithful has as its mission statement "to provide a prayerful voice attentive to the Spirit, through which the Faithful can actively participate in the governance and guidance of the Catholic Church." Especially noteworthy is that there is nothing in the mission statement about the role of the laity as a leaven of the world.

The separation of faith from life is a temptation to which many have already succumbed on principle. Avery Cardinal Dulles says that many Americans regard religion as a private matter.

Any effort by a church to say what is morally permitted, required or prohibited by the law of God in the spheres of politics, medicine, business or family life is resented as an intrusion into alien territory....Anyone who sees religion as determinative for secular activities is likely to be regarded as a fanatic. Teachers, businessmen, politicians or judges who let religion impinge in a major way on their professional activities are considered eccentric.[59]

The causes of the separation of faith from life are several. The most obvious explanation for the phenomena described by Dulles is the desire for acceptance and influence in the world of work. People in the business and the professional worlds don't want to be regarded as sectarian or out of step with the way things are done.

The question arises: why don't more Catholics resist the message that their faith is a private matter? My response looks at both internal and external factors. First, bishops, priests, catechetical leaders, Catholic schools on the primary and secondary level, and families have not done an adequate job in forming the young in the basics of the faith. Being only partially instructed, most parents are not able to impart a thorough and rig-

59. Avery Dulles, "Orthodoxy and Social Change," *America* 178, no. 21 (1998): 10.

orous formation in the faith. It is typical for Catholic college students not to know the meaning of such terms as Incarnation, redemption, Pentecost, and virtue. Hardly any can recognize that there are petitions in the Lord's prayer. With a poor formation in the faith, how could most Catholics recognize any improper separation of faith from life? Second, the instruction and formation in the faith at Catholic universities may succeed in a few institutions, but for the most part, are weak, absent or, in some cases, even detrimental. While one of my sons was a student at a Catholic university, a program run by the administration told students that "consent" was the principle of sexual morality. Nothing was said about the immorality of pre-marital sex.

A third reason people have trouble relating their faith to their work and other aspects of their daily lives is the difficulty of acquiring the kind of prudence required to make the proper connections. Being a good person does not necessarily give someone the ability to make the kind of prudential decisions that will benefit his fellow citizens. Aquinas's distinction between ordinary prudence and political prudence, as mentioned in chapter 3, helps to clarify my point. He says that everyone in the state of grace has sufficient prudence to do what is required for his own salvation, but not everyone has the political prudence to discern the requirements of the common good. Let us recall Aquinas's words: "There is also another diligence which is more than sufficient, whereby a man is able to make provision both for himself and for others, not only in matters necessary for salvation, but also in all things relating to human life; and such diligence as this is not in all who have grace."[60] The acquisition of such diligence may be acquired over time with the right kind of experience and instruction.

In the fall of 2002 I attended a funeral of a well-known and beloved physician in Scranton. J. Robert Gavin suddenly died at the age of 78, not having missed a day of work in 49 years because of illness. People stood in awe in the presence of this man's dedication to his patients. He still made house calls for the infirm, and it was not unusual to see him visiting hospital patients at 11:00 in the evening. As they say, prince or pauper received the same meticulous care from this Catholic physician. I don't think he needed any more than ordinary prudence to live his life as he did. But, good as this man was, he would not have been able to contribute to the solution of the malpractice-insurance crisis in Pennsylvania without the kind of political prudence of which Aquinas speaks. Dr. Gavin

60. Aquinas, *Summa theologiae*, II-II, qu. 47, a. 14, reply to obj. one.

may well have been gifted with political prudence, but he was too busy taking care of his patients to attend to the malpractice insurance crisis.

Still another reason for the separation between faith and life is the bad influence of lay Catholics in the limelight. Catholics have heard a steady drumbeat from Catholic politicians who say, "I am personally opposed to x but I will not impose my opinion on others, especially my religious opinions." Mary Ann Glendon's comment about this subterfuge is enlightening:

That slogan was the moral anesthesia that they offered to people who are troubled about moral decline, but do not know quite how to express their views, especially in public settings....It is a sinister doctrine that would silence only those moral viewpoints that are religiously based. But the anesthesia was very effective in silencing the witness of countless good men and women. And of course the slogan was a bonanza for cowardly and unprincipled politicians.[61]

That many Catholics could not see the problems with the slogan is surely another sign that their theological and political education is deficient. Even Catholic leaders were not able to show right away the deficiencies of the slogan by means of a few persuasive clarifications. Glendon explains,

Only in recent years have some Catholics, Protestants, and Jews stepped forward to point out that when citizens in a democratic republic advance religiously grounded moral viewpoints in the public square, they are not imposing anything on anyone. They are proposing. This is what is supposed to happen in our form of government—citizens propose, they give reasons, they deliberate, they vote.

In the last chapter we will discuss at length why religiously grounded viewpoints are discouraged in the public arena. Following in the footsteps of Locke, contemporary political theorists have tried to provide a theoretical justification for excluding religion from the public square.

Conclusion

Pope John Paul II believes that re-evangelization is necessary to overcome the secularization of societies all over the world. But he says there is a precondition for this ecclesial work. To imbue societies with a Christian spirit, "what is first needed is to *first remake the Christian fabric of the ecclesial*

61. Mary Ann Glendon, "The Hour of the Laity," *First Things*, no. 127 (2002): 27.

community itself present in these countries and nations." The problem is that Catholics are conforming to the spirit of the age; they are being evangelized by the culture. Glendon describes the crisis this way:

But the fact is that far too many American Catholic theologians, trained in nondenominational divinity schools, have received too little grounding in their own tradition. [This is a point developed compellingly by Fr. Matthew Lamb of Ave Maria University.] Far too many religious education materials are infused with the anger and disappointments of former priests and sisters who went to work in religious publishing houses because their training suited them for little else. And far too many bishops and priests have ceased to preach the word of God in its unexpurgated fullness, including the teachings that are most difficult to follow in a hedonistic and materialistic society.[62]

A moving literary presentation of the last point is found in *The Diary of a Country Priest*. The Dean of Blangermont tells the young priest that the Church is powerless to teach the Christian faithful among the petty bourgeoisie that they should moderate their greed for gain.

They may be more or less amenable to our teachings as far as, for instance, the errors of the flesh are concerned,…but what they call business appears to these industrious folk their special preserve, where hard work excuses everything, since to them work is a kind of religion. Each one for himself. That's their rule. And we are helpless; it will take years, centuries maybe to enlighten their minds and rid them of the feeling that business is in the nature of war with all the rights and privileges of real war.[63]

If Bernanos were writing today in the United States, he might very well have said through some priest that the Church must acknowledge its inability to challenge the invocation of personal autonomy by the faithful in matters pertaining to the culture of life and sexual ethics. Even if that were the case in general, there would always be individual bishops, priests, catechists, and religion teachers effectively doing that very thing.

Adequately formed laity may conceive of their mission as a leaven in the world in two ways, to uproot evil and do good in a positive way. Tolkien's *The Lord of the Rings* offers help in understanding the first aspect of the lay mission. In Part 3, *The Return of the King*, Gandalf explains that evil will not disappear if the Ring of Power is destroyed and Sauron is defeated, but must be defeated over and over again in every generation.

62. Ibid.
63. George Bernanos, *The Diary of a Country Priest* (New York: Macmillan, 1970), 62.

If [the Ring of Power] is destroyed, then, he will fall; and his fall will be so low that none can foresee his arising ever again....And so a great evil of this world will be removed. Other evils there are that may come; for Sauron is himself but a servant or emissary. Yet it is not our part to master all the tides of the world, but to do what is in us for the succor of those years wherein we are set, uprooting the evil in the fields that we know, so that those who live after may have clean earth to till. What weather they shall have is not ours to rule.[64]

Tolkien's vision is both inspiring and an education in moderation. It encourages people to realize that their success in uprooting evils will not only benefit themselves, but also future generations (e.g., a ban on cloning). But Tolkien's story also teaches that the victory over evil is never definitive on this earth. Hatred and injustice cannot be banned, as some social justice advocates naively hope. Bernanos is of the same opinion. His Curé de Torcy tells the younger country priest to give up his fixation about wiping out the devil. Then he adds:

What the Church needs is order, you've got to set things straight all the day long. You've got to restore order, knowing that disorder will get the upper hand the very next day, because such is the order of things unluckily—night is bound to turn the day's work upside down—night belongs to the devil.[65]

The positive task of the laity is to practice the spiritual and corporal works of mercy and to use whatever political prudence they have to ameliorate the various communities in which they live (e.g., in the family, at work, in society, and in the political order). While the amelioration is difficult and depends on favorable circumstances and rare qualities of souls, it can always be carried out in various ways.

Finally, the various attempts to keep Catholic views out of the public square must be resisted in every way possible by those Catholics who understand that Catholicism is not and cannot be a private matter. Theoretical arguments and political action are both necessary.

64. J.R.R. Tolkien, *The Lord of the Rings*, part 3, *The Return of the King* (New York: Ballantine, 1994), 160.
65. Bernanos, *The Diary of a Country Priest*, 16.

CHAPTER 7

Civil Society, the Family, and the
Principle of Subsidiarity

American liberal democracy has a constant need of citizens with competence and good character. "The American version of the democratic experiment," says Mary Ann Glendon, "leaves it primarily up to families, local governments, schools and workplace associations, and a host of other voluntary groups to teach and transmit republican virtues and skills from one generation to the next."[1] Both within and outside the Church many still look to families as "the principal setting for learning ordinary, decent behavior,"[2] despite the many serious difficulties they are experiencing in most societies. The proper nurture in the family will help individuals acquire the virtues necessary for marriage, work, and all their responsibilities in the community. When the family succeeds in its mission, the other aforementioned units of civil society can more effectively inspire citizens to make some contribution to the common good. Of course, the well-being of the family itself depends, as we have seen, on the contribution of the Church. All the talk in secular circles about what the family does for its members and for civilization clearly shows that the eminent roles assigned to the family by the Catholic Church are not unusual. There is, in fact, a whole chapter on the family in the *Compendium of the Social Doctrine of the Church*.

The first and longer part of this chapter will explain the gist of the Church's teaching on the family by closely analyzing John Paul II's *Familiaris consortio (On the Role of the Family in the Modern World)* and several speeches by Pope Benedict XVI, as well as parts of Vatican Council II, the *Catechism of the Catholic Church*, the *Compendium of the Social Doctrine of the Church*, and Cardinal Höffner's *Christian Social Teaching*.

1. Mary Ann Glendon and David Blankenhorn, eds., *Seedbeds of Virtue: Sources of Competence, Character, and Citizenship in American Society* (Lanham, Md.: Madison Books, 1995), 2.
2. Glendon and Blankenhorn, *Seedbeds of Virtue*, 13.

Pope John Paul II's *Familiaris consortio* discusses God's plan for marriage and the family in part 2 and then explains the four tasks of the family in part 3. These tasks are (1) to form a community of persons, (2) to serve life and educate children, (3) to contribute to the development of society, and (4) to share in the life and mission of the Church. The second and much shorter section of this chapter will deal in a general way with voluntary associations and the principle of subsidiarity.

As a quick introduction to thinking about the family, let us call to mind phrases used by the Church to describe it: "domestic Church," "the first community called to announce the Gospel," "sanctuary of life," "heart of the culture of life," "an intimate community of life and love," "communion of persons," "the first and vital cell of society," "a school of deeper humanity," and "the first school of those social virtues that every society needs." In public life the term "seedbeds of virtue" is often used to describe the family and other associations and groups in civil society. While the term is not used in official Church documents, it does convey part of the Church's thinking on the family. In *City of God* St. Augustine actually used the term "seedbeds of the city" to describe the community of husband and wife, since marriage provides generation for the earthly city and regeneration for the heavenly city.[3] In other words, the family provides citizens for society and Christians for this life and the next.

God's Plan for Marriage and the Family

Part 2 of *Familiaris consortio* begins by calling to mind the biblical teaching that God made human beings in his image. Since God is love (1 Jn 4:8) all people are created to love God and their neighbors. "Love is therefore the fundamental and innate vocation of every human being" (FC, no. 11). (That vocation can, of course, be lived in the celibate or married state.) What makes marriage possible is the differentiation of the sexes. A man and a woman can realize their vocation to love by pledging fidelity to one another in the marital bond, which is expressed by both a physical and personal self-giving. The former would not be possible without the bodily differences. In addition, "The total physical self-giving would be a lie," writes John Paul II, "if it were not the sign and fruit of a total per-

3. St. Augustine, *The City of God* (Baltimore: Penguin Books, 1972; New York: Modern Library, 1950), book XV, chap. 16.

sonal self-giving."⁴ In other words, the former pontiff is referring to the fact that a man and a woman can engage in sexual relations without really loving each other. But he is also implying that conjugal relations are an important way of fostering love in a marriage, because man is an embodied spirit. Pope Paul VI felicitously made this point in *Humanae vitae (On the Regulation of Birth)*: "Conjugal acts do not cease being legitimate if the spouses are aware that they are infertile for reasons not voluntarily caused by them; because these acts remain ordained to expressing [or signifying] and strengthening the union of the spouses" (*cum non cesset eorum destinatio ad coniugum coniunctionem significandam roborandamque).*⁵

Pope Benedict XVI discerns two basic teachings in his predecessor's famous catechesis on love, which was given for a five-year period between 1979 and 1984. First, "Marriage and the family are rooted in the inmost nucleus of the truth about man and his destiny." Because man is made in the image of God, his destiny is to love. Second, Christ teaches that the person's vocation to love is only achieved by a gift of self to others.⁶ In a later speech Pope Benedict even quotes directly from John Paul II's catechesis on love to make his point: "'man has been made in the image and likeness of God not only by his being human, but also by the communion of persons that man and woman have formed from the beginning.... They become the image of God, not so much in their aloneness as in their communion.'"⁷ This all means that the right understanding of marriage depends on knowing the nature of a human being and what God is like. Pope Benedict reinforced this point in his annual address to the Roman Curia in December of 2006. In reflecting on his trip to Valencia, Spain, to discuss marriage and the family, he exclaimed, "The visit to Valencia became for me a quest for the meaning of the human being."

Both John Paul II and Benedict XVI relate this theology of marital communion to the institution of marriage. The former says that the institution is "an interior requirement of the covenant of conjugal love," not

4. Pope John Paul II, *Familiaris consortio (On the role of the Christian Family in the Modern World)*, no. 11.

5. Pope Paul VI, *Humanae vitae (On the Regulation of Birth)*, translated by Janet Smith (New Hope, Ky.: New Hope Publications, no date), no. 12.

6. Cf. "Address of His Holiness Benedict XVI to Members of the Pontifical John Paul II Institute for Studies on Marriage and Family on the XXVth Anniversary of Its Foundation," May 11, 2006.

7. "Address of the Holy Father during the vigil of prayer in Valencia, Spain on July 8, 2006," quoting John Paul II's catechesis on love, November 14, 1979.

an arbitrary external form imposed by societal authorities (FC, no. 10). The latter reiterates John Paul II's thought and adds that the institution of marriage enables the personal consent or "yes" to marriage to "be a publically responsible yes," and is "an intrinsic requirement...of the depths of the human person." Both popes are implying that the mutual self-giving of marriage requires an external form to reinforce and express the personal commitment of the spouses.[8] The reinforcement is necessary because of ordinary human weakness. It is often hard for many to keep high-level commitments until death.

Pope John Paul II's next point is that marital consent followed by subsequent marital life proclaims in word and deed the most important teaching of revelation, "God Loves his people."[9] The bond between husband and wife "becomes the image and the symbol of the covenant which unites God and his people." When Israel becomes unfaithful, God remains faithful and remains united to his unfaithful people. This steadfast love is put forth in the Bible "as the model of the relations of faithful love which should exist between spouses."[10]

Pope John Paul II next explains that the "communion between God and his people finds its definitive fulfillment in Jesus Christ, the bridegroom who loves and gives himself as the savior of humanity, uniting it to himself as his body."[11] Jesus sends forth his Spirit, giving spouses the power to love one another as Christ loved all people by his Incarnation and Paschal mystery. Conjugal life in Christ is a sacrament, by means of which the spouses are bound together in an indissoluble relationship. The indissolubility of marriage means that the spouses are "the real representation, by means of the sacramental sign, of the very relationship of Christ and the Church."[12] Just as Christ remains ever faithful to the Church, so husband and wife should never abandon one another. Marriage points to the depth of the human person by requiring from the spouses Christlike love and is even a sign of God's action in the world by representing Christ's never-ending love for the Church. John Paul says that "spouses are therefore the permanent reminder to the church of what happened on the cross."[13]

8. Cf. "Address of His Holiness Benedict XVI to the Participants in the Ecclesial Diocesan Convention of Rome," June 6, 2005.

9. *Familiaris consortio*, no. 12.   10. Ibid.

11. Ibid., no. 13.   12. Ibid.

13. Ibid.

The foundation of the family is marriage, because the latter is "or-dained to the procreation and education of children, in whom it finds its crowning."[14] (At every appropriate moment Pope Benedict keeps repeat-ing that marriage is the foundation of the family, implicitly denying that a family can be formed in any other way.) While the possibility of spous-es achieving a communion of persons in marriage reveals the exalted dig-nity of human beings, the possibility of children resulting from spousal love reveals the extraordinary character of marriage. Conjugal love ren-ders spouses "capable of the greatest possible gift, the gift by which they become cooperators with God for giving life to a new human being."[15] Then the spouses receive the gift from God of being a sign of his love for their children. Through baptizing and educating their children in the faith, the family then builds up the Church.

The First Task of the Family

The family's mission for love entails four main tasks, the first of which is to form a community of persons. The *first* communion of persons, brought about and continuously developed over a lifetime by love, is the indivisible unity of husband and wife who become "one flesh" in their marriage, which oneness is made possible by the natural complementar-ity of man and woman. The communion of parents and children and the communion among relatives follows from the first communion between husband and wife.

The indivisible union is also indissoluble because, first, the mutual gift of husband and wife to each other can only achieve its perfection by a lifelong relationship in which spouses express their fidelity and grow in their union every day. A second reason marriage is indissoluble is on ac-count of the good of the children. Their total physical and spiritual care requires the lifelong presence and commitment of parents. The third rea-son for indissolubility is, of course, God's will that marriage be "a fruit, a sign and a requirement of the absolutely faithful love that God has for man and that the Lord Jesus has for the Church."[16] So, by living a good marriage until death, spouses not only help convey the central word of revelation that God loves his people and that Christ is eternally faith-ful to his Church, but also bear witness to the inestimable good of fidel-

14. Ibid., no. 14.   15. Ibid.
16. Ibid., no. 20.

ity and indissolubility. The possibility of this kind of witness confers on marriage an extraordinary dignity.

The communion between husband and wife naturally leads to children and then to communion between parents and children, brothers and sisters, family and grandparents. "A fundamental opportunity for building such a communion is constituted by the educational exchange between parents and children, in which each gives and receives."[17] At first glance, it may seem that parents do all or most of the giving, but they receive innumerable blessings by giving generously to their children. Eventually, many children recognize all that they have received and express their gratitude in such a way as to convince parents that their cup runneth over. That is because their children's *acceptance* of education, love, and truth from them is, indeed, a precious *gift in return*. Upon receiving all that he needs for his life without bringing in anything to the family, the small child comes to understand "what it means to be loved by God undeservedly."[18]

Cardinal Höffner makes a few other points about the relation of parents and children that complement Pope John Paul II's thought. He says that children long for the love of their mother and father and deserve parents who love each other.[19] The life of children is diminished when the family doesn't eat or pray together or have any social life at home together, as often happens in modern society. After quoting St. Augustine's statement about the family being "the seedbed of society," Cardinal Höffner says that "God has gifted the family with fruitfulness not only that the deceased may have successors, but also that the living may have companions."[20] Family members are companions in one way as the children are growing and in another as they grow up and found their own families. The love of siblings for one another as they grow up and after leaving the family is a great joy for parents.

Quoting Thomas Aquinas, the pope points out that the grace of Christ is "a grace of brotherhood,"[21] contributing to the communion of family members among themselves and with Christ. The family even constitutes a form of ecclesial communion and is thus appropriately named "the do-

---

17. Ibid., no. 21.

18. Joseph Cardinal Höffner, *Christian Social Teaching* (Bratislava: Lúc, 1997), 98.

19. Ibid., 103.

20. Ibid., 105–6.

21. *Familiaris consortio*, no. 21, quoting St. Thomas Aquinas, *Summa theologiae*, II-II qu. 14, a. 2, reply to obj. 4.

mestic Church."[22] In this community everyone contributes according to his talents and gifts, in such a way that all receive what they need: the aged, the young, the sick, and every other family member. When all build up the communion of persons the family becomes "a school of deeper humanity."[23]

At some time every family will experience tension, discord, and conflict. Sometimes, the forces of disunity could be very great because of selfishness and other vices. When this happens the pope recommends a commitment to reconciliation and recourse to the sacraments of reconciliation and Holy Communion.

Pope John Paul II sheds more light on what it means for a husband and wife to form a community of persons in his reflections on the so-called theology of the body, presented during his Wednesday audiences between 1979 and 1984. Genesis 2:24 says, "a man leaves his father and mother and cleaves to his wife and they become one flesh." In other words, comments John Paul II, "human beings, created as man and woman, have been created for unity."[24] According to him, Genesis implies that the strong bond of one-flesh unity established by the Creator "is without doubt the unity that is expressed and realized in the conjugal act."[25] To be one flesh is to be a *communio personarum*, a communion of persons, which means that husband and wife live with and, "even more deeply and completely," for one another.[26] Through their bodies they achieve a profound unity of their persons. In the pope's words, the human body "contains 'from the beginning' the 'spousal' attribute, that is, *the power to express love: precisely that love in which the human person becomes a gift* and—through this gift—fulfills the very meaning of his being and existence."[27] John Paul II goes so far as to say that the conjugal union, made possible by the Creator, "contains in itself a new and in some way definitive discovery of the meaning of the human body in its masculinity and femininity."[28] Otherwise stated, the male and female bodies are not interchangeable. In addition, when husband and wife bring a child into the world, they *"know each other reciprocally in the 'third,'*

---

22. *Familiaris consortio*, no. 21, quoting Vatican Council II, *Lumen gentium* (*Dogmatic Constitution on the Church*), no. 11.

23. *Familiaris consortio*, no. 21, quoting Vatican Council II, *Gaudium et spes*, no. 52.

24. Pope John Paul II, *Man and Woman He Created Them: A Theology of the Body* (Boston: Pauline Books and Media, 2006), 168.

25. Ibid., 167.   26. Ibid., 182.

27. Ibid., 185–86.   28. Ibid., 208.

originated by both."[29] Mutual dedication to the spiritual and physical well-being of their children enables the couple to grow in their knowledge and love of one another. Not that knowledge and love can't grow without children. But having children is the normal way for most married couples to deepen their one-flesh unity.

Today many people don't believe that this one-flesh unity is either possible or perhaps even desirable. The alternative is for two persons to make bodily contact in any way that pleases them. No one can say that one form of contact is better or more effective in bringing about whatever imperfect unity is possible for human beings. Autonomy rules and, therefore, the structure of the body is not indicative, and the division of the human species into male and female offers no guidance as to the proper form of sexual relations.

In commenting further on the one-flesh verse from Genesis, John Paul II has tried to persuade people that the achievement of one-flesh unity by spouses is both a gift from God and a human task. Genesis teaches that "God created man in his own image, in the image of God he created them; male and female he created them."[30] Because they are made in God's image, a man and a woman can choose to cleave to one another and achieve a communion of persons. In order to reach this goal spouses must remain united to God and love each other in the proper way. One of the greatest obstacles to this communion is lust, which inclines spouses to treat their own bodies and each other as objects of pleasure. Because of the loss of original innocence, spouses will also be subject to the temptation to treat each other as possessions and to exercise mutual domination. Genesis further indicates that the woman is more likely to be dominated in a marriage lived apart from God. Because of the sinfulness into which people fell after original sin, husband and wife "must reconstruct the meaning of the reciprocal disinterested gift with great effort."[31] They must not assume that this one-flesh unity can be achieved without great effort and God's grace.

After discussing what it means to form a community of persons in the family, Pope John Paul II then addresses some particular matters pertaining to the life of mothers, fathers, children, and the elderly. What the pope said about the role of women in society has attracted the most

29. Ibid., 211.
30. Gen. 1:27.
31. Pope John Paul II, *A Theology of the Body*, 216.

criticism. Recall his observation that the communion of husband and wife is rooted in the "natural complementarity that exists between man and woman."[32] In his *Letter to Women* John Paul II expands on this theme: "Womanhood and manhood are complementary *not only from the physical and psychological points of view,* but also from the ontological."[33] Over and over again the recent pope kept saying that the giving and receiving of love in a marriage was an image of the love in the Trinity. John Paul II also kept speaking about the "genius of woman." Women are especially inclined to be of service to others and to show respect for the dignity of every human being. For example,

Wherever the work of education is called for, we can note that women are ever ready and willing to give of themselves generously to others, especially in serving the weakest and most defenseless. In this work they exhibit a kind of *affective, cultural and spiritual motherhood* which has inestimable value for the development of individuals and the future of society.[34]

Women's physical motherhood develops their generous disposition "of paying attention *to another person,*" argues the late pope. "This unique contact with the new human being developing within her gives rise to an attitude towards human beings—not only towards her own child, but every human being—which profoundly marks the woman's personality."[35]

Let us return to *Familiaris consortio* for more light on the pope's thoughts regarding the motherhood of women. Pope John Paul II insists that mothers have a very important role to play at home, should be honored for what they do in the family by their husbands and by society at large, and should not be forced out of the home for economic reasons. "Society must be structured in such a way that wives and mothers are not in practice compelled to work outside the home, and their families can live and prosper in a dignified way even when they themselves devote their full time to their own family."[36] At the same time John Paul II argues that women should be able to work outside the home, if they so desire, and participate in public life. The pope's preference clearly seems to be that mothers choose to stay home with their children, if it is at all possible. He even thinks that society should find a way to give financial compensa-

32. *Familiaris consortio,* no. 19.
33. Pope John Paul II, *Letter to Women,* June 29, 1995, no. 7.
34. Ibid., no. 9.
35. Pope John Paul II, *Mulieris dignitatem* (*On the Dignity and Vocation of Women,* 1988), no. 18.
36. *Familiaris consortio,* no. 23.

tion to full-time mothers. In his *Letter to Families* John Paul II writes, "the 'toil' of a woman who, having given birth to a child, nourishes and cares for that child and devotes herself to its upbringing particularly in the early years, is so great as to be comparable to any professional work."[37]

Cardinal Höffner's position is the same. He believes that the spiritual gifts of the child must be awakened by the constant presence of a loving mother. Cardinal Höffner is relying on Aquinas's teaching that the goal of education is "to lead one to human perfection. The family is, so to speak, the second, spiritual womb in which the child born of the mother should mature to a moral personality or character."[38] The cardinal implies that this work of moral education is a full-time job.

Can John Paul II reasonably call for a new feminism and still prefer that mothers stay at home with their young children? Professor Laura Garcia begins to answer that question in an article entitled, "Can Feminism Acknowledge a Vocation for Women?" She notes that some understandings of complementarity could consign women to an inferior status, but an understanding of complementarity in accord with the mind of John Paul II would not do so. He affirms that men and women are equal in dignity, but have different gifts. Garcia asks, "*is there a greater responsibility for women in raising children* (if not greater, at least *substantive* in its demands and *different* from the demands on men)?" She answers, "it would certainly seem so."[39] Echoing the thought of Betsey Fox-Genovese, Garcia says that Christian women "must lead the way in recovering the virtues that will enable people to make sacrifices for each other, as mothers do for children."[40] She then adds, "And if women have a special responsibility for children, it is also clear that men have a special responsibility for women."[41] If women withdraw from their careers and public life to meet the needs of their children, they then deserve great support and honor from their husbands.

As for fathers, the pope recognizes that fathers have not been sufficiently involved in the education of children, and, therefore, encourages them to take up that responsibility enthusiastically. Fathers must see to

37. *Letter to Families*, February 2, 1994, no. 17.

38. Höffner, *Christian Social Teaching*, 101, my translation.

39. Laura Garcia, "Can Feminism Acknowledge a Vocation for Women?" in *The Church, Marriage, and the Family*, edited by Kenneth Whitehead (South Bend, Ind.: St. Augustine's Press, 2007), 151.

40. Ibid., 152.

41. Ibid., 152.

it that all members of the family develop their talents and strive toward perfection in union with other family members. Both the absence of a father's presence as well as tyrannical behavior, sometimes known as "machismo," cause problems for family members.

In speaking about children the pope emphasizes the great responsibility of parents toward their children. They have the vocation to insure their physical, emotional, spiritual, and intellectual formation. When children grow in wisdom and grace, they "offer their own precious contribution to building up the family community and even to the sanctification of their parents."[42] The pope desires great respect for the child, not only from the family, but from society at large. To make his point he quotes from his 1979 address to the United Nations. "Concern for the child, even before birth, from the first moment of conception and then throughout the years of infancy and youth, is the primary and fundamental test of one human being toward another."[43] Clearly he wants the legal prohibition of abortion throughout the world as a starting point, followed by other unmentioned initiatives to ensure the care and education of the young.

As for the aged, he urges better care of them in those cultures where they are neglected and an appreciation of the contribution they can make to the lives of children and to a felt sense of continuity between the generations.[44] As Pope Paul VI said, "the family is the place where the various generations come together and help one another grow wiser."[45]

Before going on to discuss the second task of the family, it will be helpful to explain why the Church believes that a marriage cannot take place between people of the same sex. They may be friends, but cannot enter into that communion of persons of which John Paul II has spoken in *Familiaris consortio.* Some advocates of same-sex marriage are saying, "But God or nature made people homosexual and, therefore, a gay couple should be entitled to the same marital privileges as a husband and a wife." Certainly the God who reveals himself in the Bible has never condoned the practice of homosexuality. On the contrary, biblical texts clearly indicate that it is a serious sin.[46] In the New Testament, I Corin-

---

42. *Familiaris consortio,* no. 26.

43. Ibid., quoting John Paul II, "Address to the General Assembly of the United Nations" (October 2, 1979), 21; *Acta Apostolicae Sedis* 71 (1979), 1159.

44. *Familiaris consortio,* no. 27.

45. Pope Paul VI, *Populorum progressio (On the Development of Peoples),* no. 36.

46. In the Old Testament, see the Sodom story in Genesis 19 and Leviticus 18:22 ("You shall not lie with a male as with a woman; such a thing is an abomination.")

thians 6:9 says, "Do not be deceived; neither fornicators, nor idolaters nor adulterers nor *malakoi* (men who are the receptive partners in homosexual acts) nor *arsenokoitai* (the active partners in male homosexual acts) nor thieves nor the greedy nor drunkards nor slanderers nor robbers will inherit the kingdom of God." I Timothy 1:9–10 teaches that "the law is not laid down for the just but for the lawless and disobedient, for the ungodly and sinners, for the unholy and profane, for those who kill their father or mother, for murderers, fornicators, *arsenokoitai* [sometimes translated as practicing homosexuals], kidnapers, liars, perjurers, and whatever else is contrary to sound doctrine." Finally, Romans 1:26–27 says, "For this reason God gave them up to dishonorable passions. Their women exchanged natural relations for unnatural, and the men gave up natural relations with women and were consumed with passion for one another, men committing shameless acts with men and receiving in their own persons the due penalty for their error." These are clear indications of biblical teaching on homosexuality, but still may not be understood today, because of various factors leading to invincible ignorance. People, of course, may do great harm to themselves and others when acting out of invincible ignorance. Therefore, the Church must increase her efforts to persuade Christians to accept the Biblical teaching on homosexuality.

The argument that people are born homosexual has attracted a considerable following today. A complete discussion of this theme is involved and beyond the scope of this chapter. I would simply say that there is no credible scientific evidence for a gay gene, although there may be some indirect genetic contribution to homosexuality. As one scientist argues, "Whatever genetic contribution to homosexuality exists, it probably contributes not to homosexuality *per se*, but rather to some other trait that the makes the homosexual option more readily available than to those who lack this genetic trait (as in the correlation between height and basketball)."[47] It is not as though one is destined to be a homosexual or a basketball player because a person possesses some particular trait. Other factors that merit investigation are intrauterine influences (the hormonal environment), the role of the family (especially parental abuse), childhood trauma in one's environment (e.g., rejection by same-sex peers), and choice.[48]

47. Jeffrey Satinover, "The Biological Truth about Homosexuality," in *Same-Sex Attraction: A Parents' Guide*, edited by John F. Harvey and Gerard V. Bradley, 14 (South Bend, Ind.: St. Augustine's Press, 2003), 14.

48. See Satinover's essay for an interesting discussion of these topics.

Whatever the effect of natural traits, intrauterine influences, the family, or the environment on one's sexual orientation, Catholic teaching holds that sex is only appropriate in a marriage between a man and a woman. The *Catechism of the Catholic Church* describes the homosexual inclination as "objectively disordered." Scripture, according to the *Catechism,* "presents homosexual acts as acts of grave depravity." The *Catechism* further teaches that homosexual acts are "contrary to the natural law. They close the sexual act to the gift of life. They do not proceed from a genuine affective and sexual complementarity. Under no circumstances can they be approved."[49]

Homosexual persons are called to live a chaste life and should be treated with respect by all and not be subject to unjust discrimination. "By the virtues of self-mastery that teach them inner freedom, at times by the support of disinterested friendship, by prayer and sacramental grace, they can and should gradually and resolutely approach Christian perfection."[50]

The Second Task of the Family

Procreation

The second task of the family is to serve life by bringing children into the world and educating them. John Paul II kept telling us that the family is the sanctuary of life, a safe haven for the unborn and children. It is "the place in which life—the gift of God—can be properly welcomed and protected against the many attacks to which it is exposed."[51] "In the face of the so-called culture of death the family is the heart of the culture of life."[52]

Pope John Paul II says that the Church helps the family to fulfill its mission as a safe haven by opposing government efforts to inhibit the freedom of parents to have children. The Church therefore condemns government action to impose on its citizens contraception, sterilization, and abortion, either by fiat or by establishing incentives—such as the promise of economic help to developing nations—to accept these anti-

49. *Catechism of the Catholic Church* (Vatican City: Libreria Editrice Vaticana, 1994), no. 2357.
50. Ibid., no. 2359.
51. Pope John Paul II, *Evangelium vitae (The Gospel of Life)*, no. 92.
52. Pope John Paul II, *Centesimus annus (On the Hundredth Anniversary of Rerum Novarum)*, no. 39.

life practices. These offensive practices should never be required in order to be eligible for foreign aid from nations or international organizations. In the words of the *Compendium of the Social Doctrine of the Church*, "All programs of economic assistance aimed at financing campaigns of sterilization and contraception, as well as the subordination of economic assistance to such campaigns, are to be morally condemned as affronts to the dignity of the person and the family."[53]

In a most obvious way the family fails to be a sanctuary of life when the unborn child is aborted. In a less obvious way the married couple acts against the life-giving purpose of marriage and the family by having recourse to contraception. Knowing that a Catholic married couple will be tempted to practice contraception, John Paul II summarizes the Church's teaching on birth regulation, largely drawing upon Paul VI's *Humanae vitae*, and urges theologians to make common cause with the hierarchical Magisterium in presenting the Biblical, ethical, and personalistic reasons behind the Church's teaching.

Drawing inspiration from Bishop Joseph Martino's pastoral letter on chastity as well as the writings of Pope John Paul II, I would respond to the pope's invitation with the following observations.[54] While only a minority fails to understand that adultery, lust, or addiction to pornography is a violation of marital chastity, many Catholics have not understood that the practice of contraception is intrinsically immoral and unchaste. The great Catholic writer Flannery O'Connor provides a thought-provoking comment on birth control in a 1959 letter to a friend. She writes, "The Church's stand on birth control is the most absolutely spiritual of all her stands and with all of us being materialists at heart, there is little wonder that it causes unease."[55] O'Connor's incisiveness is an attention-getting reminder that the purpose of marriage is both the communion of husband and wife through their union with God in view of salvation and the procreation of human beings destined for eternal life. Communion between human beings and eternal life in communion with the three persons of the Blessed Trinity! What could be more spiritual? By practicing

53. Pontifical Council for Justice and Peace, *Compendium of the Social Doctrine of the Church* (Vatican City: Libreria Editrice Vaticana, 2004), no. 234.

54. Joseph Martino, *Chastity: A Pastoral Letter*, December 8, 2004; this letter is available on the website of the Diocese of Scranton; see http://www.dioceseofscranton.org/Bishop's%20Pastoral%20Letters/Bishop'sLetteronChastity.asp.

55. Flannery O'Connor, *The Habit of Being*, ed., introduction by Sally Fitzgerald (New York: Farrar, Straus and Giroux, 1978), 338.

contraception, husband and wife no longer enter into or understand sexual union as God meant it to be. True sexual union between spouses or becoming one flesh is the image of the love that exists in the Trinity.

Because true sexual union is an image of the Trinity, *Humanae vitae* draws the following conclusion:

> There is an unbreakable connection between the unitive and the procreative meaning [of the conjugal act], and both are inherent in the conjugal act. This connection was established by God, and Man is not permitted to break it through his own volition.... And if both essential meanings are preserved, that of union and procreation, the conjugal act fully maintains its capacity for [fostering] true marital love and its ordination to the highest mission [*munus*] of parenthood to which man is called.[56]

Janet Smith summarizes Pope John Paul II's view of conjugal relations in simple but arresting language. The pope's point is that the very act of sexual intercourse says, "I wish to become wholly one with you and to accept the possibility of having children with you."[57] Still otherwise stated, the act of sexual intercourse says, "There's nothing of mine that is not yours." This is always the meaning of intercourse apart from any further intentions of the spouses. If this is the inherent meaning of sexual intercourse— its body language, so to speak—spouses should mean what they do. They cannot hold back their fertility without being dishonest. Contraceptive sex, then, is a lie because it falsifies the language of the body. "Uncontracepted" intercourse expresses a willingness to have a child with one's spouse and, therefore, to spend one's whole life with him or her. Love between parents and children, by its very nature, is meant to last a lifetime.

Contraception not only violates the procreative meaning of conjugal intercourse, but the unitive dimension as well. Conjugal acts must remain open and ordered to procreation if they are to be true acts of love. In making this argument *Humanae vitae* offers a response to those who contend that contraception is necessary in marriage in order to allow for the expression of love and the promotion of unity without fear of an unwanted pregnancy. To explain this teaching of *Humanae vitae* Pope John Paul II writes,

---

56. *Humanae vitae*, no. 12.

57. Janet Smith, *Humanae Vitae: A Generation Later* (Washington, D.C.: The Catholic University of America Press, 1991), 113; This ordinary language is Smith's way of summarizing the pope's basic point.

The conjugal act signifies not only love, but also potential fecundity, and therefore cannot be deprived of its full significance by artificial means. In the conjugal act it is not licit to separate the unitive aspect from the procreative aspect, because both the one and the other pertain to the intimate truth of the conjugal act: the one is activated with the other and in a certain sense by the other. Therefore, in such a case the conjugal act, deprived of its interior truth, because artificially deprived of its procreative capacity, ceases to be an act of love.[58]

In other words, since a loving union is what we seek through sexual relations, we are working against our desires when we use contraception. The union attained through authentic conjugal intercourse confirms the spouses' affection for each other and has a healing effect on their hearts and souls, often wounded by so many enemies of love in the world.

To summarize in the words of Professor Janet Smith, "Acts that destroy the power of human sexual intercourse to represent objectively the mutual, total self giving of the spouses are wrong."[59] This is what contraception does and, therefore, it is wrong. Because "it is an act that withholds from one's spouse one's fertility and all that it means,"[60] contraceptive sex doesn't signify or foster total self-giving. Professor Smith formulates the traditional natural law argument of *Humanae vitae* as follows: "It is wrong to impede the procreative power of actions that are ordained by their nature to assist God in performing his creative act that brings forth new life."[61] This is exactly what contraception is designed to do, and therefore is wrong.

When spouses cooperate with God to bring a new life into the world, everything changes. Husband and wife are called to live even more in service to one another and to sacrifice for the common good of the children and the family. In their conjugal love they imitate the life and love of the three persons in the Blessed Trinity. The love of the spouses for each other is so wondrous and such a great gift because it can bring into being a third person, thus closely imaging the Blessed Trinity.

When it is time for couples to put off having a child for periods of time, they can make use of natural family planning (NFP). Unlike unnatural methods of birth control, NFP is more a way of life than it is a

58. Pope John Paul II, *Reflections on "Humanae vitae"* (Boston: Pauline Books and Media, 1984), 33–34.

59. Smith, *Humanae Vitae: A Generation Later*, 110.

60. Ibid.   61. Ibid., 99.

method of limiting births. It is not the calendar rhythm method practiced by Catholics in the 1930s, 1940s and 1950s. Rather, NFP is a term used to describe medically sound, scientific methods that enable couples to determine *both* the woman's fertile *and* infertile phases, in view of conceiving a child *or* of postponing conception for reasons of responsible parenthood. The 99-percent efficacy rate of NFP in limiting births (an issue of great concern to Catholic couples in poor or Third World countries) is as successful as modern hormonal methods of contraception such as the birth control pill, without its harmful physical and spiritual side effects. The success rate of NFP in enabling couples to have a child is very high when both spouses are physically able to conceive.

Couples practicing NFP have marriages that rarely end in divorce. The divorce rate in our culture of widespread contraception is currently around 50 percent, while the rate of divorce among couples using NFP is less than 5 percent. The reason for this surprising statistic is that NFP fosters extraordinary communication between spouses and respect and regard for one another's dignity, and it helps spouses to keep their promise of total self-giving to one another. Without this total self-giving, couples will not be fully faithful to their marriage vow.

Communication is fostered as couples must regularly engage in their most important conversation: whether to try to co-create with God another human being destined for eternal life, or to postpone that joy for responsible reasons of health, finances, or age. Mutual respect for their dignity as persons is inherent in the spouses' recognition of their fertility as a gift. Contraception denies that truth and treats fertility as an inconvenience.

Finally, periodic abstinence, often necessary in the practice of natural family planning, is, perhaps, the thing most feared by contracepting couples. A simple reflection on the realties of married life, however, reveals that periodic abstinence is as much a reality for contracepting couples as it is for NFP couples, for reasons of illness, business travel, fatigue, and stress. The difference is in the attitude or mindset. Periodic abstinence becomes an opportunity for expressions of affection other than the conjugal act, and a challenge for couples to grow spiritually through the practice of discipline and virtue.

Besides teaching the wrongfulness of contraception, the Church also explains why the husband and wife should not have recourse to any of the artificial methods of reproduction, namely, any use of donor gametes, surrogate motherhood, artificial insemination (husband), in vitro fertilizatio (whether heterologous or homologous), and cloning. These methods are wrong because they fail to respect the dignity of the human person and the dignity of human procreation.[62] In vitro fertilization and cloning are more akin to manufacturing by technicians than begetting by a couple through conjugal relations.

The Family as Educator

Pope John Paul II begins his reflection on the educational duties of parents by quoting from Vatican Council II: "it devolves on parents to create a family atmosphere so animated with love and reverence for God and others that a well-rounded personal and social development will be fostered among the children. Hence, the family is the first school of those social virtues which every society needs."[63] Children learn from their parents "what it means to love and be loved, and thus what it actually means to be a person."[64] This education in truth, the virtues, and love is an education in holiness in view of salvation and of service to the common good of society, i.e., "the Christian transformation of the world."[65]

Nearly everyone knows that the Catholic Church has always regarded education in the family as a very serious obligation for parents.[66] In order to indicate how sublime this familial education really is, John Paul II quotes St. Thomas Aquinas's comparison of the ministry of priests to the parental education of children. "Some only propagate and guard spiritual life by a spiritual ministry and this is the role of the sacrament of orders; others do this for both corporal and spiritual life, and this is brought about by the sacrament of marriage by which a man and a woman join in order to beget offspring and bring them to worship God."[67] More specifi-

62. *Compendium of the Social Doctrine of the Church*, nos. 235–36; see also Congregation of the Doctrine of the Faith, *Donum vitae: Instruction on Respect for Human Life and Its Origin and on the Dignity of Procreation* (Boston: St. Paul Books and Media, 1987).

63. *Familiaris consortio*, 36, quoting Vatican Council II, *Gravissimum educationis (Declararation on Christian Education)*, 3; for all Documents of Vatican II, see Walter M. Abbott, ed., *The Documents of Vatican II* (New York: Guild Press, America Press, and Association Press, 1966).

64. *Centesimus annus*, no. 39.

65. *Familiaris consortio*, no. 36, quoting Vatican Council II, *Gravissimum educationis*, 3.

66. Vatican Council II's *Gravissimum educationis*, no. 3, says, "Since parents have conferred life on their children, they have a most solemn obligation to educate their offspring."

67. *Familiaris consortio*, no. 38, quoting St. Thomas Aquinas, *Summa contra gentiles*, vol. 4 (Notre Dame, Ind.: University of Notre Dame Press, 1975), 58.

cally, parents have the task of instructing and forming their children in faith and morals. This will include teaching children to know their faith, to pray, to receive the sacraments, and to live a holy life in the family, at work, and everywhere else.

If Christians are going to live a life of holiness in the midst of a secularized world, they must especially develop the proper attitudes toward freedom and the use of material goods. In John Paul II's words, "children must grow up with a correct attitude of freedom with regard to material goods, by adopting a simple and austere lifestyle and being fully convinced that 'man is more precious for what he is than for what he has.'"[68] In addition, the visible self-giving and mutual love of the parents is to be "the model and norm" for the children and other members of the household, such as grandparents living in the family. Children are further to learn that sexuality "manifests its inmost meaning in leading the person to the gift of self in love." By the latter point John Paul II shows what a positive attitude the Church has toward sexuality. It is the catalyst that many people need to embark on a life of love for their spouse and children. Formed in the habit of love, family members will then be able to love their friends and neighbors faithfully over the long run.

Pope Benedict XVI, of course, echoes the teaching of his predecessor on education, but adds his own personal touch. He puts emphasis on the importance of parents being close to their children and bearing witness to their faith and hope, which really echoes John Paul II's teaching that parents are "the model and norm" for their children. "The daily experience of closeness that is proper to love," says Pope Benedict, is necessary for parents to be effective educators of their children. The witness of mothers and fathers living their faith shows children that their parents are "personally involved in the truth" proposed.[69] In bearing witness to their faith and hope, parents teach children the greatness of their dignity by explaining their ultimate origin in God and their destiny to be a child of God. This kind of education requires a heavy time commitment on the part of parents. So Pope Benedict exhorts parents to find the necessary time: "To have time and to give time—this is for us a concrete way to learn to give oneself, to lose oneself in order to find oneself."[70] In oth-

68. *Familiaris consortio*, no. 37, quoting Vatican Council II, *Gaudium et spes*, no. 35.

69. "Address of His Holiness Benedict XVI to the Participants in the Ecclesial Diocesan Convention of Rome," June 6, 2005.

70. "Address of His Holiness Benedict XVI to the Roman Curia Offering them his Christmas Greetings," December 22, 2006.

er words, parents will also do themselves good by taking the time to do good for their children.

Parental education must counter the contemporary emphasis on the autonomy of the individual who creates his own values by will instead of discovering life-guiding truths through faith and reason. Pope Benedict says that "parents need gradually to give their children greater freedom, while remaining for some time guardians of their freedom." From the good example of parents children learn to be joyful, even in the midst of difficulties, and to love not only their relatives, but also their neighbors, near and far, as well. Children's joy in living will help them get through the difficulties life inevitably brings.

One last point from Pope John Paul II: he argues that not only the Church but also governments as well should do what they can to enable families to fulfill their educational mission. For example, the *Compendium* says that governments should not make it difficult for families to send their children to religiously affiliated schools. "The refusal to provide public economic support to non-public schools that need assistance and that render a service to civil society is to be considered an injustice."[71] If state-sponsored schools promote ideologies contrary to Catholic teaching the families must join together in associations in order to "help the young not to depart from the faith."[72]

The Third Task of the Family

The third task of the family, "the first and vital cell of society,"[73] is to participate in the life of society by bringing future citizens into the world and by educating them to practice the social virtues "that are the animating principle of the existence and development of society itself."[74] In other words, society needs families who not only bring children into the world, but also provide them with the kind of character formation and education that make them capable of love, friendship, and dedication to the common good. In John Paul II's words, "The very experience of communion and sharing that should characterize the family's daily life rep-

---

71. *Compendium*, no. 241.

72. *Familiaris consortio*, no. 40.

73. Vatican Council II, *Apostolicam actuositatem* (*Decree on the Apostolate of the Laity*), no. 11.

74. *Familiaris consortio*, no. 42; Vatican Council II's *Gravissimum educationis*, no. 3, says, "the family is the first school of those social virtues which every society needs."

resents its first and fundamental contribution to society."[75] John Paul II doesn't use the language of friendship, but, in my mind, it captures what he is getting at. The most excellent form of communion between members of a family is friendship based on the love known as agape. This is the self-sacrificing love that Christ has for his Church.

The Christian family teaches children what friendship is and persuades its members to be friends with one another. Friends within families can and will form friendships in their life outside the family. This is extremely important, because "friendship seems to hold states together," says Aristotle, "and lawgivers apparently devote more attention to it than justice.... When people are friends, they have no need of justice, but when they are just, they need friendship in addition."[76] Because the family is the school of the virtues and friendship, it is "the most effective means for humanizing and personalizing society."[77]

Virtuous family members capable of friendship will strive to be in solidarity with their fellow citizens, especially those most in need. Christian families will practice hospitality, do what they can before governmental authorities and nongovernmental organizations (NGOs) to "defend the rights and duties of the family," and, most generally stated, assume responsibility for promoting those aspects of the common good of which they are capable. Elaborating on family duties in *Evangelium vitae,* John Paul II said, "As the domestic church, the family is summoned to proclaim, celebrate and serve the Gospel of Life."[78] This is an extremely important duty, because there is so much support for such anti-life measures as abortion, euthanasia, and the killing of embryos in order to retrieve their stem cells.

In liberal societies lawgivers will not do much to promote friendship, so there is an even greater burden on the family to do so. Not that the government doesn't do anything. For example, in the United States the holidays of Thanksgiving Day, Memorial Day, Veterans Day, and the national celebrations of Mother's Day and Father's Day remind citizens ei-

75. *Familiaris consortio,* no. 43. In *Christifideles laici (On the Vocational Mission of the Lay Faithful in the Church and the Modern World),* no. 40, John Paul II says, "the human person has an inherent social dimension which calls a person from the innermost depths of self to *communion* with others and to the *giving* of self to others."

76. Aristotle, *Nichomachean Ethics,* trans. Martin Ostwald (New York: Macmillan, 1962), cf. 1155a20–30.

77. *Familiaris consortio,* no. 43.

78. *Evangelium vitae (The Gospel of Life),* no. 92.

ther of their family connections or of their connections to one another as citizens. Abraham Lincoln issued an executive order in 1863 establishing the last Thursday of November as the day for all Americans to celebrate Thanksgiving Day. His words are instructive.

It has seemed to me proper that [God's mercies on the war-torn nation] should be solemnly, reverently and gratefully acknowledged, as with one heart and voice, by the whole American people. I do, therefore, invite my fellow-citizens…to set apart and observe the last Thursday of November next as a day of thanksgiving and prayer to our beneficent Father.…And I recommend to them that, while offering up the ascriptions justly due to Him for such singular deliverances and blessings, they do also with humble penitence for our national perverseness and disobedience commend to their tender care all those who have become widows, orphans, mourners, or sufferers in the lamentable civil strife in which we are unavoidably engaged, and fervently implore the interposition of the Almighty hand to heal the wounds of the nation, and to restore it…to the full enjoyment of peace, tranquility and union. In testimony whereof I have hereunto set my hand and caused the seal of the United States to be affixed.[79]

Note that President Lincoln didn't order American citizens to celebrate Thanksgiving Day, but invited them to do so. He also invited them to look after widows, orphans, mourners, and other sufferers, just as John Paul invited families to be hospitable in every way and to attend to the needs of others, especially children, the poor, and anyone not reached by the protective net of government services. Lincoln further invited Americans to pray and to show their gratitude to God on Thanksgiving Day, thereby recommending that citizens maintain a strong connection and friendship with God, thus indirectly supporting Christian teaching.

Especially because of all the suffering experienced by families throughout the world, John Paul II likewise forcefully states that society and government should respect all the political and economic rights necessary for the family to fulfill its mission. For example, men and women need religious liberty, the freedom to marry and educate their children, housing, work, the right to form associations, and the right to emigrate.[80] In a later

---

79. Mary Keys, *Aquinas, Aristotle, and the Power of the Common Good* (New York: Cambridge University Press, 2006), 222, quoting the *New York Times* (October 4, 1863), front page.

80. Cf. *Familiaris consortio*, no. 46, for a complete list of the rights mentioned by John Paul II.

document, John Paul II said, "As the fundamental nucleus of society, the family has the right to the full support of the state in order to carry out fully its particular mission. State laws, therefore, must be directed to promoting its well-being, helping it to fulfill its proper duties."[81] The ultimate reason the state should help the family is *the priority of the family over society and over the State.... The family, then, does not exist for society or the State, but society and the State exist for the family.*"[82]

Pope Benedict uses almost the exact same language as John Paul II in referring to the family as "the vital cell and pillar of society," but adds that this is true both for believers and nonbelievers alike. Healthy families benefit society when parents educate children "to the full measure of their humanity. The experience of being loved by their parents helps children to become aware of their dignity as children." When people live in accordance with their dignity, social and political life is more just and pleasant. When the family does its job, it is a leaven in the culture and counters the "destructive predominance" of relativism, especially by its witness and public commitment to defend "the inviolability of human life from conception until its natural end."[83]

In addition, Pope Benedict keeps repeating his view that there should be no legal recognition of de facto unions (cohabitation) or homosexual unions (gay marriage). He also points out that "vast areas of the world are suffering from the so-called 'demographic winter,' with the consequent gradual ageing of the population." Married couples are having too few children to replace the population, especially in Europe.

The following sentence from the conclusion of *Familiaris consortio* sums up the Church's position on the contribution of the family to society: "The future of humanity passes by way of the family."[84]

The Fourth Task of the Family

The fourth task of the family, "the community of life and love," is to share in the life and mission of the Church. It believes the word of God and becomes an evangelizing community. John Paul II goes so far as to

81. Pope John Paul II, "World Day of Peace Message," 1994, no. 5.

82. *Compendium*, no. 214.

83. "Address of His Holiness Benedict XVI to the Participants in the Ecclesial Diocesan Convention of Rome," 6 June 2005.

84. *Familiaris consortio*, no. 86.

say that "the future of evangelization depends in great part on the church of the home."[85] He no doubt makes this dramatic statement because lay witness to the truth of Christianity and to the presence of God's love will not be effective unless enough family members persuade one another to seek holiness.

The family, founded on marriage, partakes in the dignity of being "a sign and meeting place of the loving covenant between God and man, between Jesus Christ and his bride, the Church."[86] The family receives the love of Christ in the Church and then communicates this love to one another and to neighbors. Whatever spiritual riches the family receives, it shares. Through a life of love, manifested over a lifetime, the family participates in the prophetic, priestly, and kingly mission of Jesus Christ. "The apostolic mission of the family is rooted in Baptism and receives from the grace of the sacrament of marriage new strength to transmit the faith, to sanctify and transform our present society according to God's plan."[87] The family, argues John Paul, "has a special vocation to witness to the paschal covenant of Christ by constantly radiating the joy of love and the certainty of the hope for which it must give account."[88] In short, the family does what the Church does: it preaches the Word by speech and deeds, lives from the sacraments, and exercises the service of charity.[89]

The family not only draws strength from the sacrament of marriage, but also from the sacraments of the Eucharist and reconciliation. A sacramental marriage, says Pope Benedict XVI, "confers greater splendor and depth on the conjugal bond and more powerfully binds the spouses."[90] Marriage gives specific duties to family members in order to live out the universal call to holiness; the Eucharist provides "the foundation and soul of its 'communion' and its 'mission,'" and reconciliation promotes repentance and mutual pardon, which are so continuously necessary for its well-being, within the family. After discussing the benefit of the sacraments, John Paul II lays a great deal of stress on the prayer with-

---

85. Ibid., no. 52.

86. Ibid., no. 51.

87. Ibid., no. 52.

88. Ibid.

89. Cf. Pope Benedict XVI, *Deus caritas est* (*God is Love*), no. 25: "The Church's deepest nature is expressed in her three-fold responsibility: of proclaiming the word of God (*kerygma-martyria*), celebrating the sacraments (*leitourgia*), and exercising the ministry of charity (*diakonia*)."

90. "Address of His Holiness Benedict XVI to the Participants in the Plenary Assembly of the Pontifical Council for the Family," May 13, 2006.

in the family. "Only by praying together with their children can a father and mother—exercising their royal priesthood—penetrate the innermost depths of their children's hearts and leave an impression that the future events in their lives will not be able to efface."[91] John Paul II reminds Catholics that the Church encourages families to meditate on the word of God, to say morning and evening prayers, the divine office, and the rosary, and to have devotion to the Sacred Heart.

John Paul II makes a special point of encouraging parents to persevere in the education of their children with courage and serenity in the face of the difficulties and opposition they encounter. The pope no doubt realizes that the negative aspects of the culture will often have a deep effect on the souls of their children. The pope also encourages parents to provide the kind of education children need in order to live out the vocation they have received from God. Pope Benedict XVI has also commented on the role the family plays in helping the young to discern their vocation. On the Feast of the Holy Family he referred to the story of the twelve-year-old Jesus who leaves Joseph and Mary to go to the temple, where he attends to his Father's affairs. Benedict XVI says that this episode in the Gospel "reveals the most authentic and profound vocation of the family: that is to accompany each of its members on the path of the discovery of God and of the plan that he has prepared for him or her."[92]

Civil Society and the Principle of Subsidiarity

The *Compendium* describes civil society "as the sum of the relationships between individuals and intermediate social groupings, which are the first relationships to arise and which come about thanks to 'the creative subjectivity of the citizen.'"[93] While the family and the Church are the principal seedbeds of virtue in civil society, innumerable associations also make a contribution to civil society. The Church and the family are the most important institutions because they teach the faith and morality, the practice of which has such a good effect on society. In Leo XIII's words, "if human society is to be healed, only a return to Christian life and practices will heal it." He says this because religion addresses the root

91. *Familiaris consortio*, no. 60.
92. Pope Benedict XVI, "Angelus," December 31, 2006.
93. *Compendium*, no. 185, partly quoting John Paul II, *Sollicitudo rei socialis (On Social Concern)*, no. 15.

causes of political problems. That's why the Church is so important and why Tocqueville called religion the first of our political institutions. It is especially through the family that the influence of religion is felt.

As for the other institutions of civil society, think of primary and secondary schools, universities, hospitals, social service agencies, unions, and political parties, and consider what they do for a community and what more they could do. Catholic social thought treats the subject of associations in civil society or mediating institutions under the concept of subsidiarity. The classic description of this concept is found in Pius XI's *Quadragesimo anno.*

Just as it is gravely wrong to take from individuals what they can accomplish by their own initiative and industry and give it to the community, so also it is an injustice and at the same time a grave evil and disturbance of right order to assign to a greater and higher association what lesser and subordinate organizations can do. For every social activity ought of its very nature to furnish help to the members of the body social, and never destroy and absorb them. The supreme authority of the state ought, therefore, to let subordinate groups handle matters and concerns of lesser importance, which would otherwise dissipate its efforts greatly.... Therefore, those in power should be sure that the more perfectly a graduated order is kept among the various associations, in observance of the principle of "subsidiarity function," the stronger social authority and effectiveness will be and the happier and more prosperous the condition of the state.[94]

"*On the basis of this principle,*" explains the *Compendium,* "*all societies of a superior order must adopt attitudes of help ('subsidium')—therefore of support, promotion, development—with respect to lower-order societies.*"[95] This means that Catholic social thought wants to see everyone contributing to the well-being of civil society: individuals, families, the Church, voluntary associations, and the state. The larger entities are to support and encourage the smaller ones, so that the initiative, freedom, and responsibility of all will be in play. This important principle of political philosophy promotes contributions of everyone to the common good of society. Of course, it will not always be clear when a larger association or the government should take over a function that individuals or smaller groups cannot manage. Discernment in all difficult cases depends on the political prudence of the decision

94. Pius XI, *Quadragesimo anno (On Reconstruction of the Social Order),* nos. 79–80.
95. *Compendium,* no. 186; emphasis in *Compendium.*

makers. Since they will inevitably possess various levels of prudence, or none at all, there will always be disagreements among citizens about the best way to proceed. In contemporary society many don't want government to give any support to religiously affiliated schools, even if they are able to help the poor in the inner city. In other cases, matters may be so complex that open-minded people of good will not be able to come to an agreement about the wisdom of relying on the state, the federal government, or a private association for an adequate solution.

"*The principle of subsidiarity . . . is imperative,*" says the *Compendium*, "*because every person, family and intermediate group has something original to offer to the community.*"[96] The participation of all in the life of society is not just a democratic desideratum, but a logical implication of human dignity. Men and women realize their dignity by contributing to the common good of society through their active participation in its life. Of course, the active participation of citizens also ensures the smooth working of democracy and is "*one of the major guarantees of the permanence of the democratic system.*"[97]

One might also say that God really suggested the idea of subsidiarity to us by allowing everyone to participate in the work of redemption.

96. Ibid., no. 187.
97. Ibid., no. 190.

CHAPTER 8

Civil Society, the Catholic University, and Liberal Education

Catholics need Catholic universities in order to receive a thorough liberal education that includes the serious study of philosophy and theology in addition to the other usual subjects. Without this kind of education it is very hard to understand thoroughly the principles and implications of Catholic social doctrine (CSD). As mentioned in my introduction, CSD uses the disciplines of theology, political philosophy, literature, history, political science, economics, sociology, and natural science. Liberally educated Catholics with a knowledge and love of their faith, including CSD, can make a significant contribution to the promotion of justice in the workplace, the political order, and civil society.

In order to show the importance of a Catholic liberal education, this chapter will first present Pope John Paul II's vision of a Catholic university through an analytic summary of the pope's influential 1990 apostolic constitution, *Ex corde ecclesiae (Apostolic Constitution on Catholic Universities)*. In the second half of the chapter I will turn to a much-discussed address of the former Jesuit superior general, the Rev. Peter-Hans Kolvenbach, S.J., on educating students to justice. Fr. Kolvenbach delivered this adddress at Santa Clara University on October 6, 2000. I will conclude with my thoughts on educating students to love justice, properly understood.

The analysis of Fr. Kolvenbach's address will reveal some of the problems that Catholic universities will face in their attempt to teach the main themes of Catholic social thought, especially justice. Catholic universities are tempted to downplay the role of faith in their work for justice, to neglect the study of masterworks dealing with questions of justice and the common good, to avoid the theoretical inquiry into the meaning of justice, and simply to identify justice with the current agenda of secular progressives. There is so much talk in Catholic universities about justice and often so little light shed on its meaning. It makes one think of Tocqueville's oft-quoted observation at the very beginning of the second volume of his masterpiece: "Less attention, I suppose, is paid to philosophy in the United States than in any other country of the civilized world."[1] Americans are just not that interested in theory.

Ex corde ecclesiae

Pope John Paul II's *Ex corde ecclesiae* (hereafter EC) describes the kind of Catholic university America and individual Catholics need. It poses an enormous challenge to Catholic universities, but not in the way many people imagine. Presidents of Catholic universities, the Association of Catholic Colleges and Universities (ACCU), and the media have focused on the following EC requirements for Catholic colleges and universities: "the *institutional* fidelity of the university to...the teaching authority of the Church in matters of faith and morals,"[2] the accountability of Catholic universities to the local bishop (actually already required by *The Code of Canon Law*, canons 808 and 810), a mandate for Catholic theologians, and the necessity of hiring enough faithful Catholics as faculty and administrators to keep an institution Catholic. Acceptance of these requirements would, it is argued, imperil institutional autonomy, academic freedom, state and federal grants, student loans, and standing in the eyes of the prestigious secular universities of the United States. At first glance, these EC exigencies seem formidable in the American context. Actually, they are not nearly as formidable as the challenge posed by John Paul II's vision of the Catholic university.

EC is a relatively short document: 37 pamphlet pages. It has a brief introduction, followed by part I, on "Identity and Mission," part II, on "General Norms," and a one-page conclusion. The six-page introduction begins with the assertion that the Catholic university is born from the heart of the Church. In other words, the Catholic university emerged from the life of the Church and helps the Church accomplish her mission.

EC begins to describe the purpose of Catholic higher education in these words:

It is the honor and responsibility of a Catholic university to consecrate itself without reserve to *the cause of truth*,...the whole truth about nature, man and

---

1. Alexis de Tocqueville, *Democracy in America*, tr. George Lawrence (New York: Harper Collins, 1969), 429.
2. Pope John Paul II, *Ex corde ecclesiae (Apostolic Constitution on Catholic Universities)*, no. 27.

God....By means of a kind of universal humanism a Catholic university is completely dedicated to the research of all aspects of truth in their essential connection with the supreme truth, who is God.[3]

In a university dedicated to truth, philosophy and theology play an architectonic role in reconciling the claims of faith and reason and in promoting the integration of the various university disciplines.

In the early Church, St. Augustine promoted a dialogue between faith and reason in his *Confessions* and *City of God*. According to Father Ernest Fortin, A.A.,[4] a former theology professor at Boston College, the medieval university was originally created for this purpose:

that of reconciling the truths that come to us from divine revelation with the philosophical wisdom of Greece and Rome....By and large, the new institution sought to promote the twin goals of classical education, namely the formation of the human being and the citizen, but with the understanding that these goals would henceforth be subordinated to the larger goal of forming Christians. These three terms sum up the ideals to which it was dedicated: "humanity," "civility," and "Christianity"—*humanitas, civilitas, Christianitas.*[5]

"It is interesting to note," writes Auxiliary Bishop John Dougherty of Scranton, "that Vatican II proposes the same concrete goals for Christian education as the medieval university: *humanitas* and *civilitas* from a Christian perspective."[6] Vatican II's exact words are these: "True education promotes the formation of the human person in view of his final end and, simultaneously, in view of the good of the societies of which he is a member and in the duties of which, as an adult, he will have a share."[7] In other words, true Catholic education prepares people to receive the gift of sal-

3. Ibid., no. 4.

4. A.A. refers to the Augustinians of the Assumption, a congregation founded in France by Fr. Emmanuel D'Alzon in the nineteenth century. Known also as the Assumptionists, this congregation of priests and brothers founded Assumption College in Worcester, Massachusetts.

5. Ernest L. Fortin, "Thomas Aquinas and the Reform of Christian Education," in *The Birth of Philosophic Christianity: Studies in Early Christian and Medieval Thought*, vol. 1 of *Collected Essays*, edited by J. Brian Benestad (Lanham, Md.: Rowman and Littlefield, 1996), 236.

6. Bishop John Dougherty, "From the Heart of the Church: The Catholic University for the Third Millennium," in *A Compendium for Catholic Higher Education Officials*, edited by Mo Fung (Falls Church, Va.: Cardinal Newman Society, 1998), 7.

7. Vatican Council II, *Gravissimum educationis (Declaration on Christian Education)*, no. 1; for all Vatican Council II documents, see Walter M. Abbott, ed., *The Documents of Vatican II* (New York: Guild Press, America Press, and Association Press, 1966).

vation and to contribute to the good of the communities in which they live throughout their lives.

The truth is sought and taught, says John Paul, so that the young and all those learning to think rigorously "may act rightly and thus better serve human society."[8] Truth, right behavior, better service! Nowadays, service to others is often presented as the distinguishing characteristic of a Catholic university, but without linking that service to the prior task of seeking the truth and achieving some order in one's soul through prayer, a sacramental life, acceptance of the Catholic creeds, and the practice of Christian morality. It seems naive to me, and even Pelagian, to think that Christlike service can be informed and embraced without a foundation in Christian doctrine and a basis in learning. As I constantly told my seminary students, serving others often requires knowledge, laboriously acquired. Some used to tell me that they didn't need a lot of knowledge, since they were going to be focused on pastoral ministry, as though communicating the truth of the faith was not a part of their ministry.

EC also argues that consecration to the cause of truth is the university's way "of serving at one and the same time both the dignity of man and the good of the Church."[9] The search for truth, in addition, brings to light the relationship between faith and reason. It is through this encounter between the Gospel message and all the fields of knowledge accessible to reason that the Church is able "to institute an incomparably fertile dialogue with people of every culture."[10] It is a testimony to Pope John Paul II that he continually promoted dialogue with the religions of the world, ancient and modern philosophers, and contemporary cultures in order to facilitate access to the whole truth about the most important things.

Still another benefit resulting from the search for truth is the ability "to evaluate the attainments of science and technology in the perspective of the totality of the human person."[11] This sounds reminiscent of Vatican II's emphasis on the primacy of persons over things in *Gaudium et spes (Pastoral Constitution on the Church in the Modern World)*. At any rate, John Paul II clearly wants philosophy and theology to evaluate scientific discoveries and their technological applications in the light of the good of individuals and the common good of society. For example, scholars at Catholic universities should be contributing to the national debate on stem-cell research and cloning.

8. *Ex corde ecclesiae*, no. 2.   9. Ibid., no. 4.
10. Ibid., no. 6.   11. Ibid., no. 7.

To accomplish its mission to search for the truth the universities have to engage in "continuous renewal," says John Paul. "Such renewal requires a clear awareness that, by its Catholic character, a university is made more capable of conducting an impartial [or disinterested] search for truth, a search that is neither subordinated to nor conditioned by particular interests of any kind."[12] This is a very important and thought-provoking statement and no doubt puzzling to most Americans, including Catholics, and especially intellectuals. A common opinion is that secular universities enjoy complete freedom to study the various disciplines, while Catholic universities, if they are really Catholic, have to exercise caution so as not to run afoul of Church teaching. A more probing look reveals this fact: the tyranny of political correctness and/or some narrow perspective often hinders open-minded study in some disciplines. For example, note the following tendencies in the disciplines: law and political science are studied without any attempt to deal with the question of justice; psychology assumes that human beings are conditioned by genes or the environment; philosophy cultivates the kind of critical thinking that cannot ever arrive at truth, but must keep raising questions; theology balks at the notion that it can't be properly done without reference to Church teaching; many departments of English insist on reading literature through the prism of some contemporary philosophical or political theory, and much social science accepts the fact-value distinction. This means that social science can deal with facts, but not say anything about values, that is to say, about what is just and unjust, good or bad.

A Catholic university in line with EC would not uncritically accept the reigning paradigm for studying a particular discipline. It would study a subject in a way most fruitful for the acquisition of the truth. If EC is correct, it doesn't make sense to argue that an institution must first become a university and then address its Catholic identity. The faith and the grand Catholic tradition can actually help scholars gain a critical perspective on the weaknesses inherent in popular approaches to the study of the various disciplines. David Schindler, the editor of *Communio*, goes so far as to say, "I do not think there can be a genuine Catholic university today without a thorough reflection on and revision of the current self-understanding of the disciplines."[13] Assumptions about the nature of the

12. Ibid.

13. "Going to the Heart: An Interview with Dr. David L. Schindler," conducted by Mo Fung, in *A Compendium for Catholic Higher Education Officials*, 31.

human person and of community life implicit in the disciplines may not be compatible with the teaching of Jesus Christ. No believing Christian, for example, could accept the denial of freedom by some schools of modern psychology or the neglect of justice by professors of law and politics.

The pope concludes his introduction by revealing his conviction "that a Catholic university is without doubt one of the best instruments that the Church offers to our age, which is searching for certainty and wisdom."[14] The Catholic university aids the Church in its mission of bringing the Gospel message to the world by finding "cultural treasures, both old and new" through its research and teaching. John Paul is also convinced that "Catholic universities are essential to [the growth of the Church] and to the development of Christian culture and human progress."[15] These are high hopes and surely place enormous demands on the universities. Later sections of EC will shed more light on what the pope means by these general statements.

Part I of EC begins with a list of the four essential characteristics of every Catholic university. It is taken word for word from the 1972 document of the Second International Congress of Delegates of Catholic Universities.

1. A Christian inspiration not only of individuals but of the university community as such;

2. A continuing reflection in the light of the Catholic faith upon the growing treasury of human knowledge, to which it seeks to contribute by its own research;

3. Fidelity to the Christian message as it comes to us through the Church;

4. An institutional commitment to the service of the people of God and of the human family in their pilgrimage to the transcendent goal which gives meaning to life.[16]

The Catholic university must have these characteristics, EC maintains, if it is to address the great questions of society and culture. Following *Gaudium et spes*, EC uses the word "culture" to indicate two things. "The word *culture* in a general sense indicates all those things by which man refines and unfolds his various gifts of body and soul." Culture includes, for example, those customs and institutions by which man "renders social life

---

14. *Ex corde ecclesiae*, no. 10.

15. Ibid., no. 11.

16. Ibid., no. 12.

more human both within the family and the whole civil community."[17]
Thus culture refers to those qualities of soul that perfect a person's character and his mind, as well as those mores and laws that promote the
good of every person. The second sense of culture is not clearly explained
by *Gaudium et spes,* but it is surely a derivative and secondary sense. It refers
to the "great experiences and spiritual desires" conserved in the works of
men and women over time. "Hence it follows that human culture necessarily has a historical and social aspect and that the word *culture* often
takes on a sociological and ethnological sense."[18] There will necessarily
be a plurality of cultures, given that various peoples will differ in the way
they establish laws, customs, and juridical institutions and cultivate the
arts and sciences. Some will do this better than others. So it will be natural to speak of richer and poorer cultures.

In order for the university to do its proper work, EC says that it "enjoys institutional autonomy" and "guarantees its members academic freedom, while safeguarding the rights of individuals and the community,
within the demands of the truth and the common good."[19] Many would
be surprised to realize that this emphasis on the freedom of the Catholic university is a theme of EC; they would not be surprised that the pope
elevates truth and the common good to the level of guidelines for the exercise of freedom. If interpreted sanely, this is a very good recommendation. Actually, every university limits speech in the name of rights, some
notion of truth, and some version of the common good. When limitations are imposed in the name of the Zeitgeist or political correctness,
university life surely suffers.

Research in a Catholic university necessarily includes "(a) the search
for an *integration of knowledge,* (b) *a dialogue between faith and reason,* (c) *an ethical
concern, and* (d) *a theological perspective."* The first task is very difficult because
of "the growing compartmentalization of knowledge within individual
academic disciplines."[20] With the help of philosophy and theology, "university scholars will be engaged in a constant effort to determine the relative place and meaning of each discipline within the context of the vision
of the human person and the world that is enlightened by the Gospel,
and therefore by faith in Christ, the *logos,* as the center of creation and of
human history."[21] This is an excellent solution to all the partial or erro-

17. Ibid., endnote no. 16, quoting *Gaudium et spes,* no. 53.
18. Ibid.   19. *Ex corde ecclesiae,* no. 12.
20. Ibid., no. 16.   21. Ibid.

neous perspectives put forth by the experts in the various disciplines, but it requires the kind of liberal education and openness not readily found in the contemporary university. How many faculty members look to philosophy and theology for help in understanding the limits of their disciplines?

In one university I have had an ongoing conversation with some psychologists who believe that all human beings are conditioned by genes and/or the environment. On several occasions I suggested that they read Aristotle's *De Anima*, Augustine's *Confessions,* and anything of Shakespeare. I made the point that they should at least consider prominent alternatives to their assumptions about the lack of freedom in human beings. They feel no need to read anything prior to the twentieth century. We have made progress, they implicitly argue. But how can scholars make credible judgments about progress in the understanding of freedom when they are unfamiliar with positions that contradict their own, especially those put forth by great thinkers of the past?

Part of the task of integrating knowledge "is to promote *dialogue between faith and reason,* so that it can be seen more profoundly how faith and reason bear harmonious witness to the unity of all truth."[22] John Paul's point is that truly scientific research "in accord with moral norms" will never conflict with faith. And if it does, it becomes incumbent on both sides to resolve the conflict.

"Research in a Catholic university is always carried out with a concern for the *ethical* and *moral implications* both of its methods and of its discoveries," especially "in the areas of science and technology."[23] It is the knowledge of the human person given by Christ that is the ultimate ethical criterion.

John Paul expects theology to play "a particularly important role in the search for a synthesis of knowledge as well as in the dialogue between faith and reason." He also believes that it "serves all other disciplines...not only by helping them to investigate how their discoveries will affect individuals and society but also by bringing a perspective and an orientation not contained in their own methodologies."[24] To do theology effectively in this mode, theologians would need immense learning in several disciplines, especially philosophy, in addition to the various areas of theology.

22. Ibid., no. 17.   23. Ibid., no. 18.
24. Ibid., no. 19.

In the last part of this section John Paul quite logically argues that "every Catholic university...has a relationship to the Church that is essential to its institutional identity."[25] It should be in communion with the local Church and the universal Church in matters of faith and morals. "Each institution participates in and contributes to the life and mission of the universal Church, assuming consequently a special bond with the Holy See by reason of the service to unity which it is called to render to the whole Church."[26] Members of the university promote unity by seeking truth and by living in communion with the Trinity and with the Church, the only solid bases for bringing people together.

As a logical consequence of the university's relation with the Church, bishops "should be seen not as external agents but as participants in the life of the Catholic university."[27] This, of course, is one of those statements that have troubled Catholic university presidents. It doesn't mean that bishops participate in the internal governance of universities, but it does indicate that they are to participate in the promotion and strengthening of a university's Catholic identity. University presidents don't mind having dinner and informal conversation about Catholic identity, but authoritative episcopal interventions are another matter altogether. Ever since the late 1960s or early 1970s, presidents of Catholic universities have become virtual monarchs. It seems to me that they can pretty much run their universities as they see fit, as long as they don't endanger the financial stability of their institutions. According to university bylaws, they are, in principle, answerable to a board of trustees. But if they happen to be members of religious orders, board members will usually show them a great deal of deference. This is a new situation. Jesuit presidents used to be appointed by their religious superiors and owed an account of their stewardship to them. That accountability came to an end when Catholic universities turned over their institutions to boards of trustees, the majority of whose members were laymen and -women.

After thirty years of near-complete autonomy, presidents are understandably not eager to share any authority with the local bishop. I once saw a picture of an outgoing Jesuit president playfully pulling back the

25. Ibid., no. 27.

26. Ibid.

27. Ibid., no. 28, quoting John Paul II, Address to Leaders of Catholic Higher Education, Xavier University of Louisiana, September 12, 1987; *Acta apostolicae sedis* 80, no. 4 (1988): 764.

mace he was handing over to the new Jesuit president at his inauguration. He might not have been playing. It's hard to give up so much authority and go back to being an ordinary person. There are very human reasons for presidents to keep bishops off their campuses.

Most U.S. bishops seem quite happy not to have any juridical connection with the Catholic universities in their dioceses. In fact, the American bishops drew up a document in 1996 to implement EC that celebrated the trust between university and Church authorities, but contained no juridical statutes. Despite being passed by a vote of 224 to 6, the Vatican told the bishops in very polite language that their document was not acceptable. They produced another application with the requisite juridical provisions, approved it on November 17, 1999, and submitted it to the Vatican Congregation for Catholic Education. On June 7, 2000, the National Conference of Catholic Bishops announced that the Vatican had approved their application document.

If the pope had not written EC, Catholic college presidents and deans of Catholic schools of law and medicine would probably not have to worry about the opinions and judgments of the local ordinary. What the pope has done is to introduce something analogous to the American system of checks and balances. EC reinforces the local bishop's right and duty to pay attention to the identity and mission of the Catholic university in his diocese. University presidents, in principle, have to give an account to someone besides the board of trustees, who may or may not exercise judgment independent of presidential influence. Even from a purely secular point of view, this new arrangement makes sense. Power is checking power, a time-honored principle in the American way of doing things. Whether individual bishops will use their powers of persuasion to help Catholic institutions of higher learning become or remain Catholic remains to be seen.

Independent oversight of Catholic universities will always be necessary, but especially today, when so many Catholics feel free to determine the meaning of Catholicism without reference to authoritative sources. The presidents who cannot see any wisdom in the new arrangements, however, can take consolation in the fact that most bishops will not be eager to make their presence felt in the life of Catholic universities located in their dioceses.

Even when bishops intervene in the life of the universities, no one should underestimate the power of the latter to resist wise advice and heartfelt admonitions. As EC says, "The responsibility for maintaining and strengthening the Catholic identity of the university rests primarily with the university itself."[28] No bishop can keep a university Catholic if its administrators and faculty are determined to secularize it. Of course, under canon law a bishop can always publicly declare that an institution may no longer call itself Catholic, but such a declaration is very unlikely.

Turning now to the section entitled "The Mission of Service of a Catholic University," I will just focus on a few points. The Catholic university has a duty to study the roots and causes of *"serious contemporary problems"* such as "the dignity of human life, the promotion of justice for all, the quality of personal and family life…and a new economic and political order that will better serve the human community at a national and international level."[29] In addition, in the light of "the predominant values and norms of modern society," the Catholic university, in certain situations, "must have the courage to speak uncomfortable truths which do not please public opinion, but which are necessary to safeguard the true good of society,"[30] and even "try to communicate to society those *ethical and religious principles which give full meaning to human life."*[31] Another EC formulation of this point is in the brief section on the Gospel and culture. Catholic universities will attempt to discern the positive and negative aspects of diverse cultures and "seek to discern and evaluate both the aspirations and the contradictions of modern culture, in order to make it more suited to the total development of individuals and peoples."[32]

This EC invitation to speak uncomfortable truths will be very difficult for Catholic universities that ardently desire to be accepted by public opinion and by their peers at secular universities. Some of these uncomfortable truths are Catholic teachings on the relation of law and morality, abortion, euthanasia, suicide, the death penalty, divorce, contraception, homosexuality, extramarital sexual relations, and relativism, as well as teachings on liberal education, the Catholic way of doing theology, marriage, family life, virtues, and the necessity of practicing virtue as a means of realistically promoting social justice and the common good. In order to accomplish this task of speaking uncomfortable truths, the Catholic university cannot become enamored of the Zeitgeist or take its bearings by the way contemporary society defines its needs. On the contrary, as Fr. Ernest Fortin says, a Catholic education provides students with "standards of judgment that ultimately are independent of the regime and the

28. *Ex corde ecclesiae*, part II, article 4, no. 1.
29. Ibid., no. 32.					30. Ibid.
31. Ibid., no. 33.					32. Ibid., no. 45.

pervasive influence of its principles." (By regime Fortin means the total way of life of a society, as reflected in the laws, mores, tastes, and opinions of a particular society.) In other words, the Catholic university teaches students to evaluate all aspects of the society in which they live on the basis of transpolitical standards, standards shaped by faith and sound reasoning, uninfluenced by the reigning opinions of the day.

Today, it is so much more likely that Catholic universities will succumb to the reigning opinions, especially of secular intellectuals, because they are not doing a good job of preserving alternative opinions through the study of the grand Catholic tradition, ancient and foreign languages, and masterworks of philosophy and theology. The new director of the graduate theology program at Ave Maria University and a former theology professor at Boston College, Fr. Matthew Lamb, has shown that the majority of Catholic theologians teaching in Catholic universities today have not received a thorough training in Catholic theology. Here is an example of what he has to say.

The so-called non- or inter-denominational Divinity schools are actively attracting Catholics. Catholic departments with doctoral programs in theology tend to hire the graduates of these Protestant programs. Ten years ago Notre Dame had 65% of its theology faculty with non-Catholic doctorates; Boston College had 55%. Today a preliminary survey finds Notre Dame with 75% of its faculty with non-Catholic degrees; Boston College has 65%. This is a dangerous situation for two reasons. First, as the Deans of all the Divinity Schools would tell you, they cannot form their students in Catholic philosophical and theological traditions. At most, Catholic students there can get some courses in this or that Catholic theologian. This means that they have a very inadequate Catholic philosophical and theological education. They do not know what they do not know. Secondly, as a result, there has been a drastic lowering of standards for specifically Catholic scholarship and Catholic formation in such areas as classical languages, ancient and medieval philosophical traditions, doctrinal, systematic, and moral theology. The graduate programs in theology at a Notre Dame or Boston College look much the same as they do at Chicago or Yale or Harvard.[33]

Without a deep knowledge of the Catholic philosophical and theological traditions Catholic universities will not be in a position to speak "un-

33. Matthew Lamb, "Life of the Mind and Life of Faith: The Context of *Ex corde ecclesiae*," an unpublished lecture at St. Mary's University in Orchard Lake, Michigan in October of 2001.

comfortable truths" to contemporary society or to maintain their Catholic identity, for that matter. It would, of course, be risky for untenured faculty members or an unemployed graduate student to publish what Fr. Lamb wrote. Academic freedom only goes so far in the modern Catholic university. Everyone knows that a professor at most Catholic universities would be on much safer ground publishing a critique of papal teaching on Catholic morality than criticizing the ignorance and dissent of Catholic theologians.

Other major points in this section of EC are on pastoral ministry and evangelization. "Pastoral ministry is that activity of the university which offers the members of the university community an opportunity to integrate religious and moral principles with their academic study and non-academic activities, *thus integrating faith with life.*"[34] Students and other university members will be encouraged to pray, to receive the sacraments, to know the elements of their faith, and to put it into practice in every aspect of their lives. The pastoral ministry team will especially encourage students and teachers "to become more aware of their responsibility toward those who are suffering physically or spiritually."[35] The desire to promote social justice in a university must "be shared by its teachers and developed in its students."[36] This, of course, implies that a Catholic university has a duty to form its students in virtuous habits.

EC concludes this section on identity and mission with the statement that "each Catholic university makes an important contribution to the Church's work of evangelization. It is a living *institutional* witness to Christ and his message."[37] The teaching, research, and professional training should all be decisively affected by the Catholic faith. For example, professional training is to "incorporate ethical values and a sense of service to individuals and to society."[38]

The General Norms of *Ex corde ecclesiae*

We now turn to part II, EC's general norms, which "are based on, and are a further development of, *The Code of Canon Law* [specifically canons 817–84], and the complementary Church legislation."[39] These are valid for all Catholic universities in the world. EC also requires that these

---

34. *Ex corde ecclesiae*, no. 38.   35. Ibid., no. 40.
36. Ibid., no. 34.   37. Ibid., no. 49.
38. Ibid.   39. Ibid., part II, art. 1, no. 1.

general norms "be applied concretely at the local and regional levels by episcopal conferences." The application document is to be in conformity with *The Code of Canon Law* and, "as far as possible, civil law." By the latter statement EC implies that a Catholic university may not be able to accept some provisions of the civil law.

All Catholic universities must incorporate into their governing documents both the general norms of EC and any other requirements specified in the application document drawn up by the USCCB. Then they must submit their governing documents to the competent ecclesiastical authority for approval. How this will work out in practice remains to be seen.

The essence of the norms (listed in seven articles under the title "Part II: General Norms") are as follows: (1) All aspects of life at a Catholic university must be informed by "Catholic ideals, principles and attitudes." (2) University authorities must establish a link with the Church, at least by a voluntary, institutional commitment. (3) "Every Catholic university is to make known its Catholic identity, either in a mission statement or in some other appropriate document, unless authorized otherwise by the competent ecclesiastical authority." (4) "Freedom in research and teaching is recognized according to the principles and methods of each individual discipline, so long as the rights of the individual and of the community are preserved within the demands of the truth and the common good." (5) "The responsibility for maintaining and strengthening the Catholic identity of the university rests primarily with the university itself." (6) The competent authority at the university is bound by canon 810 of *The Code of Canon Law*, which says: "It is the responsibility of the authority who is competent in accord with the statutes to provide for the appointment of teachers to Catholic universities who, besides their scientific and pedagogical suitability, are also outstanding in their integrity of doctrine and probity of life; when these qualities are lacking they are to be removed from their positions in accord with the procedures set forth in the statutes." (7) "The conference of bishops and the diocesan bishops concerned," according to section 2 of the same canon, "have the duty and right of being vigilant that in these universities the principles of Catholic doctrine are faithfully observed." (8) "All Catholic teachers are to be faithful to, and all other teachers are to respect, Catholic doctrine and morals in their teaching." (9) EC further points out that, according to canon 812, "It is necessary that those who teach theological disciplines in any institute of higher studies have a mandate from the competent ecclesiastical authority." (10) "In order not to endanger the Catholic identity of the university...the number of non-Catholic teachers should not be allowed to constitute a majority within the institution." (11) "The education of students is to combine academic and professional development with formation in moral and religious principles and the social teachings of the Church." (12) "The program of studies for each of the various professions is to include an appropriate ethical formation in that profession." (13) "Every Catholic university is to maintain communion with the universal Church...the Holy See," and the local bishop. (14) The local bishop has the duty to make sure that Catholic universities in his diocese preserve and strengthen their Catholic identity. "If problems should arise concerning the Catholic character, the local bishop is to take the initiatives necessary to resolve the matter, working with the competent university authorities in accordance with established procedures and, if necessary, with the help of the Holy See." (15) "A Catholic university is to promote the pastoral care of all members of the university community, and to be especially attentive to the spiritual development of those who are Catholics." (16) In order to address contemporary societal problems and to strengthen their identity, Catholic universities are to cooperate among themselves. (17) Catholic universities should further cooperate, "when possible and in accord with Catholic principles and doctrines," with non-Catholic universities, government programs, and with "programs of other national and international organizations."[40]

Adhering to these norms is difficult, because, as everyone is beginning to recognize, Catholics today no longer share the same faith. They don't even agree on the sources one should consult to discern authentic Catholic teaching. It used to be scripture, tradition, and the Magisterium or the teaching authority of the Church. It still is for a number of Catholics, but not for many others. Dissenting theologians and their followers don't describe a faithful Catholic in the same way as the pope and bishops do. This causes disunity in the communion to which all Catholics are called. The Catholic novelist Walker Percy directs attention to the problem by writing that the choice for Catholics is "either Rome or California."[41] Cardinal Ratzinger said in his book-length interview, *The Salt of*

40. Ibid., cf. part II, articles 1–7.

41. I found this quotation from Walker Percy in a piece written by Richard John Neuhaus for *Commonweal* on November 19, 1999. Neuhaus reported that Percy had used that expression in a letter written to *Commonweal*. Since Percy died on May 10, 1990, the letter had been written quite a few years before Neuhaus quoted from it.

the Earth, that Catholics now form two churches in one Church.[42] This is an untenable situation. Still another way to appreciate the disunity in the Church is to take note of the fact that the majority of Catholics no longer regularly attend Mass and receive the sacraments. In short, we have a situation in which many Catholics, especially the more educated, feel free to concoct their own version of Catholicism. The Church is reproached as a judgmental scold if she insists on calling the faithful to live in the splendor of truth.

The EC norms, of course, establish the much-maligned juridical connection between Catholic universities and the Church. The presidents had protested to the Vatican that they were trustworthy and always willing to dialogue. We don't need law among colleagues and fellow Catholics, they seem to be saying. In my mind, these presidents seem to have forgotten that we have bodies and passions. Individuals are mortal; the work of the Church goes on to the end of time. Even the best human beings succumb to irrational passions at times and may occasionally embrace the spirit of the age in order to be accepted, or because they believe it is true. Institutions need some protection from the lapses of their leaders. Is it not true that the presidents would never conduct a number of internal matters in their own universities without binding legal contracts, no matter how friendly their relationships? If there is Church law governing marriage, surely there can be a place for law governing less intimate relationships, such as that between a Catholic university and the Church. In his defense of a juridical connection Father Lamb quotes from addresses Cardinal George gave at Georgetown University and to all the Catholic colleges in Illinois. The Cardinal of Chicago said at Georgetown, "A sacramental Church makes invisible relationships visible; and law is one way of making purposes and relationships public." In Illinois he added, "The Church is a sacramental sign. In that kind of Church, purpose is made visible in law."[43]

Law helps to give some stability to the character of an institution. But as Tocqueville argued in his great work on America, *Democracy in America*,

42. Joseph Cardinal Ratzinger, *The Salt of the Earth: Christianity and the Catholic Church at the End of the Millennium, an Interview with Peter Seewald* (San Francisco: Ignatius Press, 1997), 243. "And in the Catholic Church herself there are, in fact, very deep ruptures, so much so that one sometimes really has the feeling that two Churches are living side by side in one Church."

43. Quoted from Matthew Lamb, "Life of the Mind and Life of Faith: The Context of *Ex corde ecclesiae*."

the law depends on mores. The law governing Catholic universities needs support from the dedication to truth and holiness of administrators, faculty, trustees, and students. As mentioned, the Catholicity of an institution will depend on the understanding and will of its members. The juridical connection to the Church will, however, help them stay on track and will always be necessary because of human weakness. As C.S. Lewis said, every age has its characteristic blind spots, for which, I believe, law can provide some remedy. Today, most Catholic universities are having trouble understanding and working out the relationships between freedom and truth, preserving the liberal arts, and protecting themselves against the pressures and invitations to secularize their way of life.

The general norms of course have implications for student life and the content of the curriculum. In accepting EC the Catholic university will commit itself to form Catholic students in the Catholic way of life. This has enormous implications for the offices of student life, campus ministry, and even instruction in the classroom. (Just think of the much-publicized drinking problem, the casual acceptance of premarital sex, and the low attendance at Sunday Mass that characterize most college campuses.) In order to seek the truth and carry on a dialogue with the various ways of looking at the most important things, students and faculty need a curriculum that includes not only the traditional disciplines, but also serious study of masterworks or great books, especially works of theology, philosophy, literature, art, and history. Without studying the deepest thinkers of the past, faculty and students will almost necessarily look at things from the perspective of the current reigning opinions. The laborious task of "unlearning," of really thinking for oneself, requires meditation on the works of the great authors. EC, I must add, does not specifically recommend the study of masterworks, or languages, for that matter, but both these activities, in my judgment, are necessary if the Catholic university is going to carry out effectively its proper mission. Without some knowledge of the political philosophers mentioned in the introduction and in several chapters, a student's grasp of Catholic social thought will be incomplete.

The pope concludes his apostolic constitution with this dramatic statement:

The mission that the Church, with great hope, entrusts to Catholic universities holds a cultural and religious meaning of vital importance because it concerns the very future of humanity. The renewal requested of Catholic universities will make them better able to respond to the task of bringing the message of Christ to man, to society, to the various cultures.[44]

This remark shows the enormous respect and high expectations that John Paul has for Catholic universities.

Keeping *Ex corde* in mind, let us now turn to the Rev. Peter-Hans Kolvenbach's address at Santa Clara in the fall of 2000 in order to understand some of the problems Jesuit universities are facing in their new dedication to justice and in their attempt to make Catholic social thought better known.

Fr. Kolvenbach's Santa Clara Address

During the conference at Santa Clara University on the commitment to justice in American Jesuit higher education,[45] the Rev. Peter-Hans Kolvenbach, the general of the Society of Jesus at the time, articulated the question facing the conference participants in these words: "How can the Jesuit colleges and universities in the United States express faith-filled concern for justice in what they are as Christian academies of higher learning, in what their faculty do, and in what their students become?" Fr. Kolvenbach then said that his remarks would help conference participants formulate a response to this key question.

In his address Fr. Kolvenbach first explains that the Thirty-second General Congregation of the Society of Jesus (henceforth GC 32), held in 1975, declared that "the overriding purpose of the Society of Jesus, namely 'the service of faith,' must also include 'the promotion of justice.'" The latter is henceforth to guide every single Jesuit and every Jesuit work, not just Jesuits working in the so-called social apostolate. The Jesuit General can claim that work for justice is a "new direction" for the Society, because he believes GC 32 is endorsing a new understanding of justice, one focused predominantly on changes in the political and social order. Fr. Kolvenbach explains that the word "promotion" has the "connotation of a well-planned strategy to make the world just." Because St. Ignatius wanted love expressed in words and deeds, "fostering the virtue of justice in people was not enough," says Kolvenbach. "Only a substantive jus-

---

44. *Ex corde ecclesiae*, conclusion.

45. This address is available at http://www.creighton.edu/CollaborativeMinistry/ justice.html/html. Unfortunately, there are no page numbers in the online version. So, I cannot give precise references to Kolvenbach's text.

tice can bring about the kinds of structural and attitudinal changes that
are needed to uproot those sinful oppressive injustices that are a scandal
against humanity and God." While "substantive justice" is not a term
used in the Catholic philosophical or theological tradition, Fr. Kolvenbach seems to mean that view of social justice prevalent in many Catholic
circles, which is not understood to be a virtue, but a set of political and
social conditions brought about by law and public opinion.

   Fr. Kolvenbach's reference to needed "attitudinal changes," on the other hand, seems to imply some kind of interior transformation in the souls
of individuals. Since Fr. Kolvenbach acknowledges that attitudinal changes are indispensable in the struggle against injustice, he is implicitly directing his readers' attention to the virtues. Christian virtues are all about
transforming hearts and inclining people to do the right thing, including
work for good public policy.

   In reading about the newness of the Jesuit promotion of justice, I
couldn't help but think of the many Jesuits who labored to instill the
virtue of justice in the lives of an untold number of individuals since
the time of Ignatius. I also thought of the Jesuit educational institutions
that did an admirable job explaining the nature of justice and the common good to their students, with beneficial consequences for the life of
society. Surely, many Jesuit alumni throughout the world have made the
world more just because of their Jesuit education. Obviously, Fr. Kolvenbach knows better than I the great work done by Jesuits to promote faith
and justice in the last 470 years. The promotion of justice advocated by
Fr. Kolvenbach and GC 32, therefore, can only be reasonably described as
a "new direction" in a limited sense, insofar as the Society of Jesus is directed to focus on making the world more just through the promotion of
structural changes in the political and social order.

   The Vatican response to GC 32's decree 4 on faith and justice seemed
to understand it to be breaking new ground, but was critical in two important respects. Writing on behalf of Pope Paul VI, J. Cardinal Villot,
the secretary of state, said "the promotion of justice was unquestionably
connected with evangelization,"[46] but then quoted from a papal address
to the 1974 synod of bishops in order to show that decree 4 didn't make
all the proper connections. The key passage quoted by Villot reads, "Hu-

---

46. Letter of the Cardinal Secretary of State to Father General, Pedro Arrupe, S.J.,
May 2, 1975, in *Documents of the 31st and 32nd General Congregations of the Society of Jesus* (St. Louis: Institute of Jesuit Sources, 1977), 547.

man development and social progress in the temporal order should not be extolled in such exaggerated terms as to obscure the essential significance which the Church attributes to evangelization and the proclamation of the full Gospel."[47] Cardinal Villot then added, "This applies to the Society of Jesus in a special way, founded as it was for a particularly spiritual end and supernatural end. Every other undertaking should be subordinated to this end and carried out in a way appropriate for an Institute which is religious, not secular, and priestly."[48]

The second criticism of the decree at least implied that distinctions between the roles of the clergy and the laity in the promotion of justice were not sufficiently clarified. "Moreover, we must not forget that the priest should inspire lay Catholics, since in the promotion of justice theirs is the more demanding role. The tasks proper to each should not be confused."[49] Pope Paul VI and Cardinal Villot undoubtedly understood that the promotion of justice recommended by GC 32 would necessarily involve the Jesuits and their institutions in the kind of lobbying for social reform that would be more properly and efficiently carried out by the laity. In other words, Paul VI was asking the Society of Jesus to think more carefully about the way it was planning to promote justice. Not that Paul VI had anything against making the world more just through good law and public policy! This is especially the role of the laity, not that of religious orders, whose work for the salvation of souls provides the indispensable foundation for the promotion of justice. On the basis of these two criticisms I would have to conclude that Pope Paul VI thought that GC 32 was attempting to give the Society of Jesus a new direction without an adequate compass.

Fr. Kolvenbach's Santa Clara address was also critical of GC 32's decree on justice: "Just as in 'diakonia fidei' (the service of faith) the term faith is not specified, so in the 'promotion of justice,' the term justice also remains ambiguous." The General Congregation meant an "almost ideological" form of social justice, he argues, as well as the Gospel understanding of justice "which embodies God's love and mercy." The ambiguity lies in GC 32's decision not "to clarify the relationship" between the two forms of justice. Despite the ambiguity about the meaning of justice, Fr. Kolvenbach nevertheless says that GC 32 maintained its radicality by simply juxtaposing the service of faith and the promotion of justice.

47. Ibid., 547.   48. Ibid., 548.
49. Ibid.

This adds another ambiguity: the uncertain relationship between faith and justice. The inability to clarify this relationship is one of the great failings of American Catholicism since the end of Vatican Council II. By no means is this omission peculiar to the Jesuit leadership in 1975.

Fr. Kolvenbach's forthright admission that the Society of Jesus has taken a new direction on the basis of an ambiguous notion of justice is a helpful clarification, as is his acknowledgment that in the last 25 years "the promotion of justice has sometimes been separated from its wellspring of faith." Two extremes emerged in the Jesuits, he argues. On the one hand, "Some rushed headlong towards the promotion of justice without much analysis or reflection and with only occasional reference to the justice of the Gospel. They seemed to consign the service of faith to a dying past." (This admission shows that Cardinal Villot's comments were right on target.) On the other hand, "Those on the other side…gave the impression that God's grace had to do only with the next life, and that divine reconciliation entailed no practical obligation to set things right on earth." In short, according to Fr. Kolvenbach, Jesuits displayed an uninformed promotion of justice and an incomplete proclamation of the faith. This kind of candor from the highest authority of any organization is rare. I don't know, however, if Fr. Kolvenbach's analysis is completely accurate. I have never seen any evidence in American scholarship to support his claim that Jesuit academics or Jesuits in other pastoral ministry have *argued* in the last 25 years that fidelity to God entails "no practical obligation to set things right on earth" by loving one's neighbor and hungering for justice. That Jesuits and other Christians may not have *acted* directly or indirectly to promote justice is another matter! As for the headlong rush of some Jesuits "towards the promotion of justice without much analysis or reflection," this should not be surprising if the Jesuit leadership gave them an ambiguous notion of justice as their lodestar.

Fr. Kolvenbach's address prompted me to take a closer look both at the famous decree 4 of GC 32 and at selected decrees of the Thirty-fourth General Congregation, promulgated on September 27, 1995. I cannot do justice to them in this chapter, but will simply direct attention to several passages, which shed more light on Fr. Kolvenbach's talk. GC 32 does say that "Injustice must be attacked at its roots which are in the human heart by transforming those attitudes and habits which beget injustice and foster the structures of oppression."[50] This dovetails nicely with Fr. Kolven-

50. Thirty-second General Congregation, decree 4, no. 32.

bach's emphasis on the necessity of "attitudinal changes." But GC 32 also sounds like a utopian political tract in making the following judgment about the world:

it is now within human power to make the world more just—but we do not really want to.... We can no longer pretend that the inequalities and injustices of our world must be borne as part of the inevitable order of things. It is now quite apparent that they are the result of what man himself, man in his selfishness, has done.[51]

The solution to the problem is to "preach Jesus Christ and the mystery of reconciliation" and to exert an influence on the economic, social, and political structures of the world, which influence must be understood as "service according to the Gospel." GC 32 writes as though the political importance of uprooting selfishness is a new discovery and not a long-standing biblical teaching, eloquently expounded in the fifth century by St. Augustine. Because of the persistence of sin and ignorance and the failures of Christian persuasion, human efforts to make the world more just will more or less succeed depending on the extent and depth of conversion.

GC 34 reaffirms the teaching of GC 32, but with added nuance. Like Fr. Kolvenbach it admits that "the promotion of justice has sometimes been separated from its wellspring of faith." In seeming response to Pope Paul VI and other critics, it firmly links faith and justice, though without sufficient explanation. "In the light of Decree 4 and our present experience, we can now say explicitly that our mission of the service of faith and the promotion of justice must be broadened to include, as integral dimensions, proclamation of the Gospel, dialogue, and the evangelization of culture."[52] This General Congregation emphasizes the indispensability of evangelization and faith in the work of justice, quoting part of the Formula of the Institute on the purpose of the Society: "'to strive especially for the defense and propagation of the faith and for the progress of souls in Christian life and doctrine.'"[53] While the aim of the Jesuit mission is the service of faith, "the integrating principle of [the] mission is the inseparable link between faith and the promotion of the justice of the Kingdom."[54] GC 34 argues for the evangelization of cultures, "since the roots

---

51. Ibid., no. 27.

52. *Documents of the Thirty-fourth General Congregation of the Society of Jesus* (St. Louis: Institute of Jesuit Resources, 1995), decree 2, no. 20.

53. Ibid., no. 32.   54. Ibid., no. 34.

of injustice are embedded in cultural attitudes as well as economic structures."[55] The dialogue recommended is with people in other religious traditions.

After looking at various Jesuit approaches to faith and justice, we can now turn to Fr. Kolvenbach's application of the new thinking to the field of education. He first quotes Fr. Arrupe's well-known statement delivered at the 1973 International Congress of Jesuit Alumni of Europe:

Today our prime educational objective must be to form men for others (now men and women for others and also with others); men who will live not for themselves but for God and his Christ, for the God-man who lived and died for all the world; men who cannot even conceive of love of God which does not include love for the least of their neighbors; men completely convinced that love of God which does not issue in justice for men is a farce.

While not initially well received, Fr. Arrupe's focus on "men and women for others," according to Fr. Kolvenbach, provoked thought and the eventual transformation of Jesuit educational institutions. Another statement considered influential by the Jesuit General is that made by Fr. Ignacio Ellacuria in 1982 at Santa Clara University. That statement reads in part, "the university should be intellectually present where it is needed: to provide science for those who have no science; to provide skills for the unskilled; to be a voice for those who do not have the qualifications to promote and legitimate their rights." Fr. Ellacuria further affirms that the university must pursue academic excellence "in order to solve complex social problems." Fr. Kolvenbach sees these two statements guiding the Jesuit university between the Scylla of a "disincarnate spiritualism" and the Charybdis of a "secular social activism."

Fr. Kolvenbach points out that the great divide between the haves and the have-nots "has its root cause in chronic discrepancies in the quality of education." While this deprivation of the poor remains a fact of life, because of science and technology "human society," argues Fr. Kolvenbach, "is able to solve problems such as feeding the hungry, sheltering the homeless, or developing more just conditions of life," but, nevertheless, fails to do so for an obvious reason. "Injustice is rooted in a spiritual problem, and its solution requires a spiritual conversion of each one's heart and a cultural conversion of our global society so that humankind, with all the powerful means at its disposal, might exercise the will to

55. Ibid., no. 42.

change the sinful structures afflicting our world." This statement is, first of all, a reminder that the cause of injustice is disorder in the soul, which can only be remedied by the practice of all the virtues, including justice. A conversion of the culture, of course, will depend on enough individuals undergoing conversion and practicing the virtues and, therefore, is an enormous task that may or may not be successful. This emphasis on conversion also implies that every effort to educate people in the faith has implications for the promotion of justice in society.

In the last part of his paper Fr. Kolvenbach spells out ideal characteristics of Jesuit higher education manifested in three complementary dimensions of university life: "in who our students become, in what our faculty do, and in how our universities proceed." The goal of education is to form the "whole person" of the students, "intellectually and professionally, psychologically, morally and spiritually." This has been the goal for 470 years. Today's whole person, however, "is different from the whole person of the Counter-Reformation, the Industrial Revolution, or the 20th Century." In the future the whole person must be educated to be in "solidarity" with others, "especially the disadvantaged and oppressed." Fr. Kolvenbach's remark seems to imply that education to solidarity with others was a concern missing from prior Jesuit education. I do not understand how this implication can be true. Jesuit institutions worth their salt had to give this kind of education, albeit under other names, such as love of neighbor, justice, and the common good. Since Fr. Kolvenbach surely knows this, he must believe that today's situation is so different from past ages that the old Jesuit education to justice, however well delivered, could not have encompassed the kind of solidarity needed today in response to contemporary injustice.

According to Fr. Kolvenbach, the best way to teach solidarity to students is through "contact" rather than "concepts." The Jesuit General believes that personal involvement with the poor and marginalized and the experience of the injustice others suffer "is the catalyst for solidarity, which then gives rise to intellectual inquiry and moral reflection." He further believes that campus ministry is especially able to instill compassionate solidarity in students, so that they will "choose and act for the rights of others." Other helpful educational tools are hands-on courses and all the service programs sponsored by Jesuit universities, which "should not be optional or peripheral, but at the core of every Jesuit university's program of studies." While these suggestions will no doubt reinforce Jesuit commitment to solidarity, they are already accepted by those interested in promoting the Jesuit identity on campus. Unfortunately, Fr. Kolvenbach says nothing about the kind of curriculum and courses that would help students understand the meaning of justice, solidarity, and the common good. He may, of course, presume that good curricula are already in place or that it is not his role to address curricular questions. He writes, however, as though experiences outside the classroom are the main ingredients of educating students to solidarity. In my judgment, Jesuit universities in the United States could benefit from hearing Fr. Kolvenbach and every Jesuit General explicitly endorse the study of such great authors as Plato, Augustine, Shakespeare, and Lincoln as aids for helping students to understand and love solidarity. Upon sufficient reflection most students will recognize that Lincoln would not have understood the problem of slavery better if he simply visited plantations instead of spending a lot of time steeping himself in scripture and Shakespeare. Didn't Martin Luther King make better arguments against legally sanctioned racial discrimination because he was well-versed in scripture and the tradition of natural law?

I believe that the authoritative promotion of the serious study of masterworks is necessary to convince many that the way to the heart is often through the mind. Combining a serious liberal education with personal experience of the needs of others is a good way to graduate students who will intelligently fulfill their responsibilities toward their neighbor and the wider world. But this is still not sufficient for educating students to a love of justice. As Father Kolvenbach said in the beginning of his address, the education to faith cannot be omitted. (Why he says so little about faith is, then, puzzling.) According to the logic of Fr. Kolvenbach and the teaching of the Thirty-fourth General Congregation, students need an education in the whole faith, including doctrine, morals, sacraments, and prayer. Unless the faith takes root in the souls of students, they will not sustain a commitment to justice through their lives. Consequently, instruction in the faith and exhortation to practice it in every aspect of life must accompany social-justice projects. In addition, education to justice must not remain focused exclusively on such things as Third World debt and the suffering of the poor in developing countries. Young people need to learn about being just in their everyday lives as students and then as employees and citizens after they graduate. They need to see that living justly depends on the practice of the other cardinal virtues, namely, courage, temperance, and prudence. The habitual practice of justice toward one's immediate neighbors is the sine qua non of an education to promote justice away from home and neighbor. Finally, students must come to see that justice includes a broader range of subjects than they ever imagined. For example, GC 34, in a text to which we referred in chapter 5, teaches that the Jesuit mission to promote justice includes the life questions:

Human life, a gift of God, has to be respected from its beginning to its natural end. Yet we are increasingly being faced with a "culture of death" which encourages abortion, suicide and euthanasia; war, terrorism, violence, and capital punishment as ways of resolving issues; the consumption of drugs; turning away from the human drama of hunger, AIDS, and poverty. We need to encourage a "culture of life."[56]

Fr. Kolvenbach's thought on the mission of the faculty starts off on a promising note: "Their mission is tirelessly to seek the truth and to form each student into a whole person of solidarity who will take responsibility for the real world." As an aid for this mission, Fr. Kolvenbach encourages all faculty to engage in an interdisciplinary dialogue. Then he suggests that every discipline, besides pursing its own proper subject matter, must cultivate "moral concern about how people ought to live together." How this could be done by faculty in every discipline without incompetent speculation and thought-killing moralizing is not explained. Many faculty at comprehensive Jesuit universities no longer have the kind of broad and deep education that would enable them to address questions pertaining to the common good of society.

To promote justice, all faculty at Jesuit universities, argues Fr. Kolvenbach, "need an organic collaboration with those in the Church and in society who work among and for the poor and actively seek justice." Where feasible, faculty should gravitate toward "projects of the Jesuit social apostolate" such as "poverty and exclusion, housing, AIDS, ecology and Third World debt." Professors absolutely need such partnerships, Fr. Kolvenbach maintains, in order to do research on justice and to teach solidarity to their students. That some faculty could profitably choose to concentrate all their efforts on studying the best books on justice and solidarity doesn't enter into Fr. Kolvenbach's description of life at Jesuit universities.

The third dimension of Jesuit higher education concerns the character and procedures of universities. The character is the mission to serve faith and to promote justice. This was first done by "affirmative action for mi-

56. Ibid., decree 3, no. 8.

norities and scholarships for disadvantaged students." More telling, argues Fr. Kolvenbach, is hiring and promoting for mission. He concludes by urging Jesuit institutions "to shed university intelligence" on social reality and "to use university influence to transform it." This latter recommendation is in accord with Fr. Kolvenbach's vision of an activist university focused on devising and promoting policy solutions to the world's political, economic, and social problems.

In the conclusion to his talk, Fr. Kolvenbach summarizes the "high ideals and concrete tasks" of Jesuit universities in the following words from Pope John Paul II's *Ex corde ecclesiae:* "The dignity of human life, the promotion of justice for all, the quality of personal and family life, the protection of nature, the search for peace and political stability, a more just sharing in the world's resources, and a new economic and political order that will better serve the human community at a national and international level." This, of course, is a very appealing vision. My question is what kind of a university is more likely to achieve these goals: one following the description of Fr. Kolvenbach in his address or one much more focused on the right kind of curriculum taught by full-time scholars, a good number of whom are inspired by Catholicism.

Jesuit universities owe a debt of gratitude to the Jesuit General for admitting that the Jesuits have been relying on both an ambiguous concept of justice and an unspecified understanding of faith, and that they have not clarified the relation between the service of faith and the promotion of justice, but have even tended to separate the two. Fr. Kolvenbach has also done a service by emphasizing the unfashionable view that injustice is rooted in a spiritual problem. This is the teaching of Augustine, Aquinas, and many others, downplayed or rejected today in favor of "social justice," which is incorrectly interpreted to mean that good public policy (usually left-leaning policy) is enough to change the unjust structures of the world. The General's emphasis on forming students to solidarity is continually necessary because of the prevailing individualism in today's culture. Students need an education that directs their minds and hearts to the common good. Having a personal experience of injustices will serve students well if accompanied by rigorous courses requiring mastery of the great thoughts on justice, solidarity, and the common good.

As a response to Fr. Kolvenbach's address, many Jesuit universities will emphasize service learning, work among the poor and oppressed, advocacy of public policy, and other similar initiatives. I would suggest that they also make sure that many of their graduates have a deep understand-

ing of faith, justice, and the other virtues. It is virtue that produces the attitudinal changes desired by Fr. Kolvenbach. Second, universities should
encourage theologians and philosophers to clarify the notion of justice
upon which the Society of Jesus is staking its future. Leaving the understanding of justice ambiguous will ultimately harm the Jesuits and the
cause of justice at their institutions. In order to do this work properly,
the Jesuits should also clarify the meaning of faith and its relation to the
promotion of justice. Furthermore, serious dedication to justice depends
on the *practice* of the whole faith, including prayer and the reception of the
sacraments. Otherwise stated, order in the soul of individuals is the basis of a just society. As St. Augustine argues in his *Confessions,* people are
moved to action by what they love. If Christians love their faith and take
delight in it, they will continually try to be just. With the proper education and favorable opportunities, zealous Christians will transform the
world. Finally, the language of Fr. Kolvenbach's talk could be interpreted
as support both for diminishing the theoretical dimension of the Jesuit
university and for hiring activist faculty who share those political opinions deemed most likely to promote whatever ambiguous notion of justice happens to prevail at a particular Jesuit institution.

I believe that Fr. Kolvenbach has a more scholarly vision of the Jesuit university than he puts forth in this address. He may have thought it
was unnecessary to reiterate what he considers to be obvious: namely, that
universities are, first of all, places of scholarly inquiry before they become
advocates of social justice. In the present climate, however, dedication to
the promotion of justice in American Jesuit universities could easily give
short shrift to the laborious effort to understand all the various aspects
of justice, especially social justice, in favor of a social activism not informed by thoughtful inquiry.

Conclusion: Educating People to Love Justice

It is no easy task to educate students or the body politic to know,
much less to love, justice, despite all the talk about ethics in recent years.
Ethics courses abound in colleges, and at least one ethics course is offered
in law schools, medical schools, and business schools. The professional
schools often present students with dilemmas to study and resolve. The
premise behind these courses is that knowledge of cases and principles
as well as critical thinking skills are the linchpin of an ethical education.

Universities hope to turn out ethical professionals both by exposing students to the various ethical challenges and dilemmas in their professions and by teaching them to think critically on the basis of certain principles.

Augustine would find something missing in these efforts because of his understanding of what really moves people to act. That understanding is unmistakably revealed in one of the key passages in the *Confessions*, where he says:

Oil poured over water is borne on the surface of the water, water poured over oil sinks below the oil: it is by their weight that they are moved and seek their proper place. Things out of place are in motion: they come to their place and are at rest. My love is my weight I am carried, wherever I am carried by my love.[57]

Before his conversion Augustine was carried along by contradictory loves: desire for truth and wisdom and desire for sexual pleasure; desire for honor and acceptance by his friends and desire for acceptance by God. He aspires to real friendship, but opts for "unfriendly friendships," that is to say, friendships that lead him, as a sixteen-year-old, to behave badly in deference to peer pressure. Shortly before his conversion he longs to unite his will to God's will, but still prays, "Grant me chastity and continence, but not yet"; and he says to Alypius that the unlearned are more successful in seeking God than we are with our *"doctrinae sine corde"* (heartless learning).[58] He knows that he should turn back to God with his whole heart and soul, but can't make the decision to move himself. Finally, his love for higher things drives out the love for the lower things, and he is able to overcome the paralysis in his soul. He responds to that mysterious voice repeating, *"tolle lege, tolle lege"* (take and read, take and read)[59] and picks up St. Paul's Epistle to the Romans and reads, "Make not provision for the flesh in its concupiscences."[60] This exhortation touches him and he is able to abandon his bad loves and turn wholeheartedly toward God.

In order to shed more light on what happened to Augustine during his gradual conversion, I would like to highlight two excerpts from his sermons. Here is the first:

Think of ordinary human love; think of it as the hand of the soul. If it is holding one thing, it can't hold another. To be able to hold something it's giv-

---

57. St. Augustine, *The Confessions* (Indianapolis, Ind.: Hackett, 1993), XIII, 9.
58. Ibid., VIII, 8.   59. Ibid., VIII, 12.
60. Ibid., quoting Romans 13:13.

en, it must let go of what it is already holding....God says to you, "Here, hold what I am giving you." You are reluctant to let go of what you were holding already; you cannot receive what is being offered you.[61]

Augustine hadn't been able to receive God's word and grace because of what he was clutching in the hand of his soul: lust, self-satisfaction, desire for honor, love of being accepted and praised by his friends, the desire not to accept responsibility for his sins, disdain for the simplicity of sacred scripture.

The second excerpt reads: "Do not remove cupidity or desire, but change it....*Transfer your love.* Break your fetters to earthly goods; bind yourself to the creator. Change your love, change your fear. Only good and bad loves make good and bad morals."[62] Ever the passionate man, Augustine did not quash his desires, but redirected them to God and then was able to stop loving himself and others badly.

Becoming more receptive, both by letting go of destructive desires and by developing new desires for truth and every other good thing, brought Augustine out of the depths of self-destruction into the light. Augustine goes so far as to say that we become what we love. "A human being is such as his love. If you love the earth, you will be earth. Do you love God? Will you be God? What may I say? I don't dare speak on my own authority. Let us hear Scripture: 'You are all gods and sons of the most high.'"[63] Love, then, unites us with whom we love. We become identified with what we love. Consequently, we will acquire self-knowledge through the observation of our loves.

If we ask Augustine how a person may come to love God, his answer is clear. He says, "Inquire where a person gets the ability to love God from, and absolutely the only discovery you will make is that it is because God has first loved him. He has given us himself, the one we have loved; he has given us what to love with."[64] This answer, of course, means that

61. St. Augustine, *Sermons,* part III, vol.4 (New York: New City Press, 1992), sermon 125: 258.

62. St. Augustine, *Sermo Denis XIV,* in *Miscellanea Agostiniana,* vol. I (Rome: Tipographia Poliglotta Vaticana, 1930–1931), 66–67 (my translation).

63. St. Augustine, *Tractatus in epistulam Joannis ad Parthos,* 11,14; see the English translation, St. Augustine, *A Select Library of Nicene and Post-Nicene Fathers of the Christian Church,* vol. 7, *Tracts on the First Epistle of John,* edited by Philip Schaff and Henry Wace, Second Series (1890ff; New York: Eerdmans, 1956).

64. St. Augustine, *Sermons,* part III, vol. 2 (New York: New City Press, 1990), sermon 34, p. 166.

Christian faith is at the basis of the love of God. We know by faith that God has demonstrated his love by sending his Son to liberate us from sin and death through his death on the cross and resurrection. So, whatever clears the way for faith and causes it to grow is the sine qua non of the generation of new and better loves. For example, in the *Confessions* Augustine describes how the study of philosophy, the overcoming of his prejudices against scripture, the dispelling of his ignorance about the Catholic Church, the prayers and other efforts of his mother and friends, and his own personal sufferings all helped him to come back to the faith of his childhood.

What does all this mean for educating students to take justice seriously? Simply stated, the hands of their souls must be free to receive the love and knowledge of justice, as well as the knowledge of faith and the other virtues. If we are all carried by our loves, Augustine is perfectly logical in arguing that Christians must be educated to know and love all the virtues. The personal experience of suffering by the innocent is one way of generating a love for justice. Two other approaches to the same end are indispensable: an education to know and love the whole faith, including the creeds, the Church and the sacraments, morality, and prayer; and an education to ponder the thoughts of great authors on matters pertaining to justice and injustice. As John Paul II has argued, the way to the heart is often through the mind. Think of the influence of Solzhenitsyn's *Gulag Archipelago* in weaning French intellectuals from their love of communism.

Augustine's concept of love not only explains what moves individuals to act, but also helps to understand the behavior of nations. Recall Augustine's second definition of a republic: "a fellowship of a multitude of rational beings united through sharing in an agreement about what it loves....It is a better people if it agrees in loving better things; a worse one if it agrees in loving worse things."[65] If Augustine is correct, the mores of the citizens are the crucial determinant. If the mores are corrupt, citizens will not support social reform at home or abroad, unless their self-interest is somehow engaged. Citizens who have a disordered love of goods and freedom will not be inclined to support public initiatives requiring self-sacrifice and the practice of the virtues. So, anything done to elevate the loves of citizens will be a contribution to justice in a particular society. This means that individuals, families, schools, universities, vol-

---

65. St. Augustine, *The City of God*, book XIX, chapter 24. Translation from Augustine, *Political Writings*.

untary groups, churches, political persuasion, and wise laws will all contribute to forming and deforming the loves of citizens. Whatever these citizens love will decisively affect the attainment of justice in a particular society.

So, if universities want students to become citizens focused on justice in everything they do, they must educate them to love what is good. This is no easy task because, as Augustine argues in the *Confessions,* we want what we love to be the truth.[66] It takes great effort and God's grace to let truth determine our loves. In addition, to carry out this vision universities will have to hire professors who love their faith and love their students.

66. St. Augustine, *Confessions,* X, 23.

PART 3

Private Property and the Universal Destination of Goods

CHAPTER 9

The Economy, Work, Poverty, and Immigration

The first part of this chapter will present the basics of Catholic teaching on the economy and work. These two subjects belong together because the economic system of a country exists to provide the framework in which work takes place and exercises a great influence on all employers and employees. Pope Leo XIII set the tone for the Catholic approach to this subject with his defense of the right to acquire private property, especially through work, and his forceful reiteration of the long-standing Catholic teaching on the obligation to put one's talents and resources at the service of others. Without using the phrase, Leo XIII was arguing for the universal destination of goods, the great theme of Pope John Paul II. He teaches that *"the foundation of the universal destination of the earth's goods"* is God's gift of the earth to the whole human race. To make this a reality people need private property, the knowledge required for work, and a deep sense of their duty to share with others. Without embracing generosity people cannot enter into "solidarity and communion with others" and, therefore, lapse into alienation.

A man is alienated if he refuses to transcend himself and to live the experience of self-giving and of the formation of an authentic human community oriented toward his final destination, which is God. A society is alienated if its forms of social organization, production, and consumption make it more difficult to offer this gift of self and to establish this solidarity between people.[1]

The second part of this chapter focuses first on the challenge of poverty and on what should be done for individuals who can't support themselves through work. The principle of the universal destination of all goods guides all welfare initiatives and private charity as well as the sec-

1. Pope John Paul II, *Centesimus annus* (*On the Hundredth Anniversary of Rerum novarum*), no. 41.

315

ond related subject: immigration. This same principle is also at the basis of a sustainable environment, the subject of the next chapter.

The Economy

What Catholic social doctrine (CSD) can say about the economy and economics is limited to moral principles, but significant nonetheless. It sets broad goals, but doesn't get into the kind of detail that many would desire. Even though some goals will be unattainable at the present time, they nevertheless offer guidance for improvement strategies. The lack of detail is deliberate in order to allow Catholics the freedom to apply the principles of CSD to many and varied situations. As Pope Leo XIII said on one occasion about the possible contents of *Rerum novarum,* "If I gave my approval to particular points on matters essentially economic, I would be restricting the liberty of men in an area where God left them entirely to themselves."[2]

The *Compendium of the Social Doctrine of the Church* says that the economy has as its purpose "the development of wealth and its progressive increase, not only in quantity, but also in quality; this is morally correct if it is directed to man's overall development in solidarity and to that of the society in which people live and work."[3] Goods and services must be in sufficient quantity and quality to serve the needs of all citizens. Good business enterprises respect the dignity of workers, produce a good product or service without damaging the environment, make a sufficient profit, pay a just wage, and create an atmosphere in which their workers can develop as persons and live in solidarity with one another, while making a genuine contribution to society by their work. Businesses, of course, cannot consistently deliver these goods unless business leaders are not only competent, but also people of good character. The mere pursuit of self-interest is not sufficient to ensure the just management of a business or the success of a nation's economy.[4] This became painfully evident during the recent economic crisis in the United States,

In *Laborem exercens (On Human Work),* Pope John Paul II argues that the

2. Quoted from Eduardo Soderni, *The Pontificate of Leo XIII,* trans. Barbara Barclay Carter (London: Burns, Oates and Washburne, 1934), vol. I, 67.

3. Pontifical Council for Justice and Peace, *Compendium of the Social Doctrine of the Church* (Vatican City: Libreria Editrice Vaticana, 2004), no. 334.

4. For a discussion of this point see my appendix on Pope Benedict's third encyclical, *Caritas in veritate.*

best way to evaluate the justice of an economic system is to determine whether workers receive a just wage. Remuneration for work is the way that most people "can have access to those goods which are intended for common use: both the goods of nature and manufactured goods."[5] It is also through their wages and benefits that workers have access to necessary services. In other words, it is through wages that most people are able to participate in the universal destination of material goods, the ultimate goal of any economy. In sum, a good economic system must give people the opportunity to support themselves and their families, and make provision for unemployment compensation and some kind of a social security system when people can no longer work.

As for the shape or political framework of the most desirable economic system, Church teaching stays within its competence by drawing out the general implications of the relevant moral principles. Freedom of initiative, the possibility of acquiring private property, respect for subsidiarity and solidarity, and other moral principles have persuaded the Church to reject collectivism and individualism. According to the *Catechism*, "The Church has rejected the totalitarian and atheistic ideologies associated in modern times with 'communism' or 'socialism.' She has likewise refused to accept in the practice of 'capitalism,' individualism and the absolute primacy of the law of the marketplace over human labor."[6] With respect to the Church's attitude toward contemporary capitalism, John Paul II's *Centesimus annus (On the Hundredth Anniversary of Rerum Novarum)* provides the clearest answer possible. The Church is in favor of a free economy provided it is reasonably regulated, because it "is the most efficient instrument for utilizing resources and effectively responding to needs."[7] What cannot be accepted is a capitalistic system "in which freedom in the economic sector is not circumscribed within a strong juridical framework, which places it at the service of human freedom in its totality and sees it as a particular aspect of that freedom, the core of which is ethical and religious."[8] A good economy, argues *Gaudium et spes (Pastoral Constitution on the Church in the Modern World)*, both respects and promotes the dignity of the human person and the welfare of everyone in society. The *Compendium* adds, "It would not be acceptable to achieve economic growth at the ex-

5. Pope John Paul II, *Laborem exercens (On Human Work)*, no. 19.
6. *Catechism of the Catholic Church* (Vatican City: Libreria Editrice Vaticana, 1994), no. 2425.
7. *Centesimus annus*, no. 34.
8. Ibid., no. 42.

pense of human beings, entire populations or social groups, condemning them to indigence."[9] These remarks imply that CSD will always find the free economy to be somewhat deficient. Yet, CSD also makes clear that it is the best alternative available, the one most open to beneficent influence by law and the mores, the one most likely to be "a service to the common good and to integral human development."[10]

What exactly the reasonable regulation of the economy entails cannot be specified in that much detail. The state has to steer a middle path between individualism and collectivism. To stay on the broad middle path it must above all respect the principle of subsidiarity. This means, you will recall, that the state must not do what individuals and intermediate associations are able to accomplish on their own. The state intervenes to give help to individuals and associations when they are unable to do what is necessary for the common good. "Public control," argues John Paul II, "upholds the principle of the common destination of material goods." Examples of good public control guaranteeing the dignity of work given by John Paul II are "a solid system of social security and professional training, the freedom to join trade unions and the effective action of unions, the assistance provided in cases of unemployment, [and] the opportunities for democratic participation in the life of society."[11]

Another guideline for state intervention in the economy suggested by CSD is acting within the parameters established by the principle of solidarity. "Solidarity without subsidiarity, in fact can easily degenerate into a 'Welfare State,' while subsidiarity without solidarity runs the risk of encouraging forms of self-centered localism."[12] The Catholic approach to economics keeps showing the importance of defending freedom and promoting concern for the common good on the part of individuals, associations, and the state. For example, individuals and groups can use their purchasing power to influence the way a company does business. Keeping charity for their neighbors in mind, buyers can look not only to price and quality, but also to "the presence of fair working conditions in the company as well as the level of protection of the natural environment in which it operates."[13] The leaders of states should persuade citizens to commit a certain portion of the gross national product to the relief of poverty and the care of the sick in the developing nations of the world.

9. *Compendium of the Social Doctrine of the Church*, no. 332.
10. Ibid., no. 348.   11. *Centesimus annus*, no. 19.
12. *Compendium of the Social Doctrine of the Church*, no. 351.
13. Ibid., no. 359.

In rejecting unregulated capitalism, CSD is taking issue with the claim of Adam Smith and John Locke that private interest by an invisible hand produces public benefits. Otherwise stated, the old liberalism of Smith and Locke held that the competition of people's selfish interests in the marketplace would necessarily contribute to the common good of society. Experience with the operation of capitalism has shown that is not true. In the nineteenth century many European workers suffered immensely from this laissez-faire approach to economics. In rejecting communism and so-cialism CSD denies that the collectivization of property necessarily leads to justice in society. Marx was especially hopeful that the abolition of private property would necessarily bring about a just state of affairs in society. The history of communism in the twentieth century shows that CSD was right to reject communist collectivism.

Besides apt public regulation of the economy, consumers and produc-ers need the kind of education that will enable them to distinguish real needs from "artificial new needs." That is to say, an economic system pro-vides a framework for economic activity, but doesn't offer guidance to people about what to produce and what to consume. John Paul notes that some *"consumer attitudes* and *life styles"* can damage people's "physical and spiritual health." The family, Church, and the institutions of civil society must create a culture and provide the kind of education that save people from destructive economic choices. Specifically, people must be persuad-ed to embrace ways of life "in which the quest for truth, beauty, goodness and communion with others for the sake of common growth are the fac-tors which determine consumer choices, savings and investments."[14]

John Paul II is trying to persuade individuals to avoid being led astray by the civilization of consumerism and to learn to live their lives in soli-darity with others. Let us now recall how John Paul II defines solidarity. "It is *a firm and persevering determination* to commit oneself to the *common good;* that is to say the good of all and of each individual, because we are *all* re-ally responsible *for all."*[15] Even before the mention of solidarity and the universal destination of material goods in papal social encyclicals, Pope Leo XIII provided insight on these concepts in his famous social encycli-cal, *Rerum novarum,* reference to which we made in chapter 1.

Whoever has received from the bounty of God a greater share of goods, whether corporeal and external, or of the soul, has received them for this pur-

14. *Centesimus annus,* no. 36.
15. Pope John Paul II, *Sollicitudo rei socialis (On Social Concern),* no. 38.

pose, namely, that he employ them for his own perfection and, likewise, as a servant of Divine Providence, for the benefit of others. "Therefore, he that hath talent, let him constantly see to it that he be not silent; he that hath an abundance of goods, let him be on the watch that he grow not slothful in the generosity of mercy; he that hath a trade whereby he supports himself, let him be especially eager to share with his neighbor the use and benefit thereof."[16]

Pope Leo XIII made this plea for generosity after his ringing defense of the right to private property. Everyone has the right to enjoy the fruits of private property, but also has the obligation to contribute to the common good of society with his time, talents, and resources.

While the Church is very realistic in defending the right of people to acquire material goods, she doesn't hesitate to emphasize the duty of Christians to be generous. Knowing how difficult this can be in a liberal society that encourages people to use their resources for their own benefit, CSD highlights what the book of Tobit says about resisting the temptation to regard material things as more important than redemption, grace, and generosity: namely, "'prayer with fasting and almsgiving' (cf. Tb 12:8)—prayer against the 'desire to rule and to be important,' fasting against 'the desire to enjoy,' and almsgiving against the 'desire to have' (cf. *Gaudium et spes*)."[17] So, Catholic social doctrine holds that the possession of material goods is only really beneficial for individuals if they are generous with their goods and talents, promote the common good, and always keep in mind that "a person has more worth for what he is than for what he has."[18]

The Church has put a lot of emphasis on virtue, generosity, solidarity, and the common good because contemporary culture induces people to be overly preoccupied with the pursuit and enjoyment of material things. In fact, Church teaching has always put the emphasis on the interior transformation of the individual as the best way to effect transformations in society. "The Fathers of the Church," the *Compendium* notes, "insist more on the need for the conversion and transformation of the consciences of believers than on the need to change the social and politi-

---

16. Pope Leo XIII, *Rerum novarum*, 36, quoting St. Gregory the Great, *Homelia In Evangelium* 9, no. 7 (Patrologia Latina 76, 1109B).

17. Joseph Cardinal Höffner, *Christian Social Teaching* (Bratislava: Lúc, 1997), 145–46.

18. Vatican Council II, *Gaudium et spes* (*Pastoral Constitution on the Church in the Modern World*), no. 35; for all Vatican II documents, see Walter M. Abbott, ed., *The Documents of Vatican II* (New York: Guild Press, America Press, and Association Press, 1966).

cal structures of their day."[19] This approach makes sense in every era, because a society or an economy will never be just unless individuals are virtuous. This has been the constant teaching of the Church at least since
the time of St. Augustine.

The Church obviously believes that a system of private ownership of
goods is the most likely way to ensure what Pope John Paul II frequently called the universal destination of material goods.[20] This, of course,
means that society and government must try to arrange things so that everyone has sufficient goods to live a human life. Vatican II's *Gaudium et spes*
expresses the same thought in slightly different terms: "Of its nature private property also has a social function which is based on the law of the
common purpose of goods."[21] So private property with generosity brings
together the best aspects of capitalism and socialism or communism: the
use of freedom guided by a legitimate concern for oneself and by solidarity with others.

Aristotle and Aquinas no doubt provided the principal source of inspiration for the teaching on the importance of private property for a society. In arguing against having possessions in common, Aristotle says
that people will work harder and quarrel less if they can acquire their
own property. Having property also enables people to be generous to
their friends and to their fellow citizens. "It is a very pleasant thing to
help or do favors for friends, guests, or club mates; and this requires that
possessions be private."[22] Private possessions will serve the common good
if citizens receive a good character formation. "It will be through virtue
that 'the things of friends are common,' as the proverb has it, with a view
to use."[23] For Aristotle, of course, it is the job of the legislators to make
sure that the citizens receive the requisite education to virtue.

Following the thought of Aristotle, Aquinas says that there are three
reasons people should have their own possessions. First, they will be more
solicitous for what is their own. When things are held in common, everyone is tempted to let the other guy take care of things. Second, there is
more order in society and less confusion if people take care of their own
things. Last, people are more likely to live in peace and to avoid quarrels

19. *Compendium of the Social Doctrine of the Church*, no. 328.

20. *Centesimus annus*, nos. 30–41.

21. *Gaudium et spes*, no. 71.

22. Aristotle, *The Politics*, tr. Carnes Lord (Chicago: University of Chicago Press,
1984), 1263b5.

23. Ibid., 1263a30.

over possessions if they have their own things. The use of possessions is another matter entirely. To make his point Aquinas quotes I Timothy 6:17–18, "As for the rich of this world,...they are to do good, to be rich in good deeds, liberal and generous." So when it comes to use, things are not simply our own but, in various ways, others have a claim on them.[24]

Pope Leo XIII's *Rerum novarum* developed Aquinas's teaching by affirming that the law of nature or natural law includes the sacred right to acquire property as one's own and to possess it "by stable and perpetual right."[25] This natural right is even stronger when vested in man as the head of a family. It is further indirectly sanctioned by divine law, because the seventh commandment strictly forbids taking what belongs to another. Furthermore, argues Leo, "the practice of all ages" has protected this right because it helps people to live together in peace and tranquility. Because the right to private property has been so beneficial to nations, civil laws have protected it "even by the use of force." Leo further argues that it is perfectly suited to human nature by allowing people to make provision for their needs and those of their families through the use of their reason. Protecting this right, in addition, takes into account that most individuals need the incentive of self-interest to be industrious about producing goods and rendering services, which are so important for the success of an economic system.

Just like Aquinas, Pope Leo XIII, as mentioned, also adds that the exercise of the right to acquire land and other property must be complemented by the strict duty to use one's goods and talents for the benefit of others. By proclaiming this duty Leo XIII hopes to protect poor people from being neglected or abused by those who successfully exercised their right to acquire property. Leo also wants the law to be so framed "that the largest possible number of people among the masses of population prefer to own property."[26] The law providing for tax deductions on mortgage interest, for example, gives people an incentive to buy their own homes.

Cardinal Höffner's *Christian Social Teaching*, drawing on Vatican Council II and papal social writings, enumerates five positive reasons to maintain private property.[27] First, the freedom and independence afforded by private property corresponds to the dignity of the human person

---

24. St. Thomas Aquinas, *Summa theologiae*, II-II, qu. 66, art. 2.
25. *Rerum novarum*, no. 11.   26. Ibid., no. 65.
27. Höffner, *Christian Social Teaching*, 169.

and to "well-ordered self-love." Second, private ownership serves to create separate realms of responsibility within an economy. Individuals and associations have their own separate responsibility for the use of their goods. Third, private ownership enables husband and wife to take care of their own family. Fourth, economic exchange establishes connections among the people of a nation and among the nations of the world. Cardinal Höffner notes, "the Christian tradition has pointed again and again to the fact that God's providence has distributed wealth and natural resources unequally among the peoples in order to tie a band of love around the people of different lands and races."[28] Fifth, Cardinal Höffner quotes Clement of Alexandria to explain that the possession of private property enables people to be generous toward one another: "Where would the possibility be of sharing with others, if no one possessed anything any longer? How can one ask and receive and borrow, if there is no one who has and gives and lends?"[29]

Cardinal Höffner also gives five reasons that the abolition of private property would have negative consequences for society. First, "the community of goods leads to laziness and disinclination to work, since each seeks to shift his or her work on to others." Second, in a society where goods are in common there would be disorder, since people would not have clear responsibilities. Third, the community of goods would cause social unrest, since administrative functionaries would most likely take a greater share of goods than the ordinary workers. Fourth, concentrating the community of goods in the hands of the few would give them enormous power and the temptation to misuse it. Fifth, "a centrally administered community of goods threatens the freedom and dignity of man." The cardinal notes that private property upholds human dignity by protecting his freedom. "The economic dependence on the collective entails a lack of political, cultural, and religious freedom."[30]

Work

The principal way of acquiring private property and participating in an economy is, of course, through work. To understand the perspective of CSD on work we turn to Pope John Paul II's *Laborem exercens* (henceforth LE) and several other pertinent Catholic sources.

28. Ibid., 170.   29. Ibid.
30. Ibid., 170–71.

In many ways work is not going very well. Capital is often used and moved without sufficient regard for the impact on workers. Corporations increasingly dismiss long-time employees for the sake of the bottom line, even if their workers have given loyal, competent service. When people are fired, stories recount how they are abruptly notified and escorted out of the building so they can't destroy property or steal information. Too many workers are now employed on a part-time basis with low salaries, few or no benefits, and no job security. Many people don't have well-paying, full-time jobs. Many high-salaried workers are wretchedly busy and take little time for rest on Sunday or during their vacations. A number of CEOs and their accountants have been exposed as dishonest, causing great financial loss to employees and investors. With the economic crisis of 2008–09 many people have lost their jobs or suffered a cut in pay. And prosperity itself has introduced a whole set of woes into American life!

The attitude of many workers toward their jobs is often not very good. Many people don't choose their jobs out of a desire to serve the common good or because they love to do their work well. Consequently, people are so pleased to meet workers who love their jobs and do them competently, especially when they need some product or service. Loyalty to employers is becoming a foreign concept, since salary is to the worker as the bottom line is to employers. Many Christians do not see their work as an integral part of their Christian life. It is simply something they must do to earn a living. If people can still get paid without fulfilling all their assigned duties, many would say, "so much the better."

John Paul II's LE reintroduces a Christian attitude toward work that will only be fully persuasive to people who have embraced Christianity. The pope's thought could still be at least partially attractive to people of other faiths and to people with just plain common sense if they can accept some of the Christian teachings on human dignity, the virtues, the family, and the common good. Because Pope John Paul II believes that his encyclical could conceivably get a wide hearing, he addresses it not only to bishops, priests, religious, and the Catholic laity, but also to all men and women of good will.

Biblical Teachings

The Church has learned from Genesis, according to John Paul II, that "work is a fundamental dimension of man's existence on earth....Man is the image of God partly through the mandate received from his Creator to subdue, to dominate, the earth. In carrying out this mandate, man, every human being, reflects the very action of the Creator of the universe."[31] In fact, through work he participates not only in the act of creation, but also in that of redemption.[32] In other words, human beings partly show themselves to be the image of God by carrying out their work in an "objective sense." That means cultivating the earth in accord with God's will through such tasks as agriculture and carpentry. John Paul II goes so far as to say, "The knowledge that by means of work man shares in the work of creation constitutes the most profound *motive* for undertaking it in various sectors."[33]

Workers participate in the work of Christ's redemption of humanity when they "put up with the difficult rigors of work in union with Jesus."[34] In accepting the cross of work the Christian "finds a small part of the Cross of Christ and accepts it in the same spirit of redemption in which Christ accepted His cross for us."[35] By these remarks John Paul II is implying that collaborating with the Son in his work of redemption is as profound a motive for working well as the opportunity to participate in the work of creation.

In carrying out their work Christians have a duty to exercise stewardship over the earth, which entails both negative and positive duties. Christians are not to pollute the air, water, or soil while doing their work, and they should be mindful about preserving the earth's resources for future generations as far as possible.

"*Work has a place of honor,*" says the *Compendium*, "*because it is a source of riches, or at least of the conditions for a decent life, and is, in principle, an effective instrument against poverty* (cf. Pr. 10: 04)."[36] While work is sometimes painful and toilsome because of the effects of sin, it enables people to earn their living, to found a family, and make contributions to society and to the poor in particular. St. Paul, in fact, tells Christians that they have a duty to work and to be generous to those in need.

In its section on the biblical view of human work the *Compendium* also includes some comments by the fathers of the Church because of their close connection to biblical teaching. The *Compendium* summarizes some of the fathers' teachings in this way: "By means of work, man governs the

31. *Laborem exercens*, no. 4.
32. *Compendium of the Social Doctrine of the Church*, no. 263.
33. *Laborem exercens*, no. 25.
34. *Compendium of the Social Doctrine of the Church*, no. 263.
35. *Laborem exercens*, no. 27.
36. *Compendium of the Social Doctrine of the Church*, no. 257.

world with God; together with God he is its lord and accomplishes good things for himself and for others."[37] According to St. Irenaeus, people's work and industriousness actually enable them to make creation more beautiful.[38]

The *Compendium* highlights the importance of pausing from work to observe the Sabbath rest by calling it "the apex of biblical teaching on work." This commandment deters people from becoming slaves to work either of their own free will or by force. It is especially meant to protect the poor from exploitation and to give people the opportunity to worship God, to be with family members and friends, and to serve others. Jesus performed healings on the Sabbath to show that this day of rest "is his, because he is truly the son of God, and that is the day on which men should dedicate themselves to God and others."[39] Consciousness of this teaching is much diminished in the lives of Christians. The culture has almost turned the Sabbath into a clone of every other day, while Christians don't seem to visit relatives and friends as much as they used to do.

While the teaching of Jesus encourages everyone to work well, he also says that work must be kept in perspective. "For what does it profit a man, to gain the whole world and forfeit his life" (Mk. 8:36). Jesus also teaches people not to be anxious about their work. "When people are worried and upset about many things, they run the risk of neglecting the kingdom of God and his righteousness (cf. Mt 6:33), which they truly need."[40]

The Objective and Subjective Sense of Work

After discussing the biblical view of work Pope John Paul II begins his systematic treatment of work by discussing the objective and subjective sense of work. In the objective sense work refers to the various tasks that have to be accomplished to keep a society in existence: agriculture, industry, education, services. The pope draws attention to the role that technology is playing today for good and for ill. While technology increases the quantity and often improves the quality of goods, it can create serious problems for the worker,

---

37. Ibid., no. 265.

38. Ibid., no. 266, summarizing St. Irenaeus, *Adversus haereses: St. Irenaeus of Lyons against the Heresies*, tr. Dominic J. Unger, rev. John J. Dillon (New York: Paulist Press, 1992), 5, 32, 2.

39. *Compendium of the Social Doctrine of the Church*, no. 261.

40. Ibid., no. 260.

as when the mechanization of work "supplants" him, taking away all personal satisfaction and incentive to creativity and responsibility, when it deprives many workers of their previous employment, or when, exalting the machine, it reduces man to the status of its slave.[41]

Pope John Paul II's inspiring vision of work for the people of the world focuses primarily on the subjective sense of work, that is to say, on persons doing their work, not the particular tasks they perform. The pope's source of inspiration for his "Gospel of Work" is the hidden life of Jesus as a carpenter. Made in the image of God, the human being is a person whose work contributes to the perfection of his humanity. Jesus' life as a carpenter introduced an alternative to the view prevalent in the ancient world that manual labor was unworthy of a free man. The fact that Jesus devoted most of his life to manual labor shows that "the basis for determining the meaning and importance of work is not primarily the kind of work being done but the fact that the one who is doing it is a person. The sources of the dignity of workers are to be sought primarily in the subjective dimension, not in the objective sense."[42] It really doesn't so much matter what you are doing, but the way the task is carried out is crucial.

Before he became Pope Benedict XVI, Joseph Cardinal Ratzinger directed attention to the humble work of Brother Konrad. "Those who were able to observe the inexhaustible patience, the steadfastness, and the kindness with which Brother Konrad performed his duty as porter day after day, saw the image of God illumined in him."[43] Brother Konrad, a Capuchin friar, was the hospitable doorkeeper in the Capuchin monastery at Altotting, Germany, for about forty years. He died in 1894 and was canonized in the 1930s. His attentiveness to his duties and his way of receiving pilgrims made him a saint. The example of saints like Konrad shows every kind of worker that his or her task can lead to saintliness. In my own university I have seen maintenance and secretarial tasks performed with such competence and kindness that the faculty are edified. In my own department we routinely say among ourselves that the departmental secretary, Marie Gaughan, walks on water. She sets a tone that is inspiring to us all.

41. *Laborem exercens*, no. 5.
42. Ibid., no. 6.
43. Joseph Cardinal Ratzinger, *Co-Workers of the Truth: Meditations for Every Day of the Year* (San Francisco: Ignatius Press, 1992), 219.

Contributions of Work to Personal Dignity, Family, and Nation

By way of summarizing his thought on the subjective sense of work, Pope John Paul II discerns three "outstanding goods" gained by work. The first good, of course, is the benefit to the human person from the practice of the virtue of industriousness: "for virtue as a moral habit, is something whereby man becomes good as man."[44] Through work, which is a *bonum arduum*, persons perfect themselves, build up their lives, and express as well as *increase* their God-given dignity. In John Paul II's words, "[Work] is not only good in the sense that it is useful or something to enjoy; it is also good in the sense that it is worthy, that is to say, something that corresponds to man's dignity, that expresses that dignity and increases it."[45] (Remember our discussion of the *achievement* of human dignity in chapter 1.) John Paul adds that it is through love for their work that persons perfect themselves.[46] The pope makes a special point of recognizing the work of women to take care of their homes and to raise their children, often without receiving proper recognition from society and even from their own families.

Besides being a road to holiness or perfection, "work constitutes a foundation for the formation of *family life*."[47] This is the second outstanding good of work. Work provides the material necessities of family life, and it is an important means whereby the family provides its members with an education, which is one of the main purposes of the family. In the pope's words, "Work and industriousness . . . influence the whole *course of education* in the family, for the very reason that everyone 'becomes a human being' through, among other things, work, and becoming a human being is precisely the main purpose of the whole process of education."[48] Mothers and fathers work both within and outside the family, and they teach their children to do the same in accordance with their age level. One of the main tasks of children, of course, will be to develop their talents through their schoolwork.

The third area where work achieves outstanding goods is that of the great society to which everyone belongs by virtue of cultural and historical links. Through their work human beings can contribute to the com-

---

44. *Laborem exercens*, no. 9.
46. Ibid., no. 11.
48. Ibid.

45. Ibid.
47. Ibid., no. 10.

mon good of the society in which they live. This is a simple, but often neglected, truth. Catholic teaching in the United States does not emphasize
that work well done is a significant contribution to the common good. If
porters and other workers in everyday positions behave like Brother Konrad, if doctors teach us how to stay healthy or cure diseases, if carpenters
build good houses, if teachers motivate students to develop their talents,
if managers honestly keep a business going and show respect for their
workers, it is easy to see how the common good is promoted by day-to-
day work. When a Lance Armstrong, after waging a painful battle with
cancer, performs incredible feats riding a bicycle in the Tour de France
(seven victories in a row), cancer patients all over the world are given a lift
and added courage to fight their own battles. Exhorting others by word
and/or example to be intent on recovering their health is an eminent contribution to the common good.

In short, men and women work out of self-love, desire for sanctification, love for their families, their neighbors, their country, people in other
countries, and, of course, God. As John Paul II puts it in *Laborem exercens,*
"man must work out of regard for others, especially his own family, but
also for the society he belongs to, the country of which he is a child, and
the whole human family of which he is a member" (no. 16). In *Centesimus
Annus* John Paul II said, "More than ever, work is work *with others* and *work
for others:* it is a matter of doing something for someone else."[49] In short, it
is a part of one's vocation in life.

Given this vision of human work it is not surprising to read that John
Paul II considers work as "a *key,* probably *the essential key* to the whole social question, if we try to see that question really from the point of view
of man's good."[50] To address the social question through work is to make
life more human. Otherwise stated, it is work that promotes the physical, material, and spiritual well-being of all. That goal can only be approached and achieved by the competent and dedicated work of a nation's
citizens, which is directed toward the realization of many and varied
goals.

Work done with the proper attitude always builds up the kingdom
of God, contributes to the goods of "human dignity, brotherhood and
freedom," and may contribute to earthly progress. Quoting *Gaudium et
spes* and seemingly responding to Marx's critique of religion, John Paul II

49. *Centesimus Annus,* no. 31.
50. *Laborem exercens,* no. 3.

says, "the expectation of a new earth must not weaken but rather stimulate our concern for cultivating this one.... To the extent that [earthly progress] can contribute to the better ordering of human society, it is of vital concern to the Kingdom of God."[51] The good of work done for Christ is not destroyed if it fails to accomplish its goals for reasons outside the control of the worker, but Christians should always aim to accomplish good things in the community by their work because doing so contributes to the common good.

Of course, to approach work as John Paul suggests requires faith, industriousness, and the other virtues. In no other way could a person participate in the life and mission of Jesus Christ and thereby achieve personal holiness and work for the common good. At the end of his encyclical John Paul gives Christians the most persuasive reason to cherish and love work. Through it Christians participate in the redemptive work of Jesus Christ. "By enduring the toil of work in union with Christ crucified for us, man in a way collaborates with the Son of God for the redemption of humanity. He shows himself a true disciple of Christ by carrying the cross in his turn every day in the activity that he is called upon to perform."[52]

The Priority of Labor over Capital

The priority of labor over capital and of the person over things naturally follows from the pope's observations on the subjective sense of work. Still another argument for this priority is the origin of much capital from labor. For capital not only includes natural resources, but also all the means produced by labor to develop these resources. "Thus *everything that is at the service of work*, everything that in the present state of technology constitutes its ever more highly perfected 'instrument,' *is the result of work*."[53]

Pope John Paul II has put forth his vision of work not only to promote Christian perfection, but also in order to influence the theory and practice of contemporary liberalism and capitalism. He knows that the philosophic and economic theories of the eighteenth century as well as "the *economic and social practice* of that time" caused an opposition to develop between labor and capital. More specifically, that opposition was caused by an error of economism, "that of considering human labor solely according to its economic purpose," which he calls an error of materialism.

51. Ibid., 27, quoting *Gaudium et spes*, no. 39.
52. *Laborem exercens*, no. 27.   53. Ibid., no. 12.

Referring to this time as "the period of primitive capitalism and liberalism,"[54] he warns that the same error "can nevertheless be repeated in other circumstances of time and place, if people's thinking starts from the same theoretical or practical premises."[55] In fact, the root cause of the error will not be overcome, according to the pope, unless the present era embraces "adequate changes both in theory and in practice, changes *in line with* the definite *conviction of the primacy* of the person over things, and of human labor over capital."[56] This seems to be a delicate way of saying that the theories about labor and the practice of employers today are often not sufficiently respectful of the working person.

In order to protect workers from being exploited by unjust employers, John Paul II reiterates the Church's longtime support of unions as well as the right to strike. He says that unions are "to secure the just rights of workers within the framework of the common good of the whole of society."[57] The pope also mentions that unions must take care not to act against the real interests of workers by acting against the common good through a variety of actions, including unnecessary strikes.

The Workplace

For things to go well in the workplace, workers need to appreciate and realize the three outstanding goods of work: the achievement of dignity or virtue, the foundation of the family, and the constitution of society. By working dutifully a person practices virtue and thereby perfects his dignity, provides the conditions for the foundation and flourishing of the family, and contributes to the common good of various communities, including that of the workplace and society at large. If the three goods are not sufficiently appreciated, then the leaders at work must try to show individual workers how desirable these goods are, how important they are for everyone's happiness and for the achievement of goals sought in a particular workplace.

In *Mater et magistra (On Christianity and Social Progress)* Pope John XXIII said about the workplace: "Every effort should be made that the enterprise become a community of persons in the dealings, activities, and standing of all its members." For this to happen, the relations among employers, managers, and employees must be characterized by "mutual re-

---

54. Ibid., no. 13.
56. Ibid.
55. Ibid.
57. Ibid., no. 20.

spect, esteem, and good will." It also means that "the workers may have a say in, and may make a contribution toward, the efficient running and development of the enterprise."[58] Productive, dedicated workers will naturally win the esteem and respect of hardworking colleagues, and, when consulted, be able to contribute in various ways to the success of an enterprise. Even well-meaning managers, however, may not recognize the benefit of encouraging participation or may lack the wisdom to implement different modes of participation. Hard work, active participation in the mission of the workplace, and accountability for one's productivity and participation are the keys to personal happiness at work and to the success of the overall enterprise. When individuals are trying to get out of work or fail to see the importance of their role at work, the community of workers will necessarily fall short of its goals.

Two important means of showing respect for the dignity of workers and encouraging their participation are to offer them the opportunity for development through training and education and to upgrade the responsibilities of the capable and diligent when feasible. Of course, pay increases for self-development and performance would also improve morale. In the Christian workplace some other measures would be desirable, such as time for common prayer and accommodations for those with personal or family problems. Appropriate encouraging words at the right time can go a long way in maintaining a happy workplace.

Determining a Just Wage

Let us now turn to some considerations on the determination of a just wage put forth by several moral theologians. These considerations are an attempt to apply the principles of CSD to an important matter in the lives of nearly everyone.

In *La dottrina sociale cristiana* (1966) Pietro Pavan and Teodoro Onofri list six principles to determine a just wage: Pay for work

1. "Must be sufficient to ensure what's necessary and fitting for the worker."

2. "Must be sufficient to procure what is necessary and fitting for the support of a family."

3. "Must be proportionate to the productivity of the work of each company."

---

58. Pope John XXIII, *Mater et magistra (On Christianity and Social Progress)*, no. 92.

4. "Must be in harmony with the requirements of the common good."

5. "Must allow the worker the possibility of acquiring property."

6. "Must allow the worker to satisfy the more noble human aspirations."[59] (E.g., participating in public life and having sufficient resources to educate children according to their capacities).

Principles one, two, five, and six should be the goals of every employer and economic system. Principles three and four not only indicate guidelines for determining to what extent an employer is justified in not reaching the target goals, but also suggest that employers have a duty to insure the productivity of their firms and that knowledgeable citizens have a similar duty to contribute to the common good of their country. I would argue that employers need knowledge, resources, and virtue to promote productivity and to reward employees according to their just deserts. The shape of the common good allowing for the attainment of the target goals is more difficult to articulate, but would include such elements as the following: an education that adequately prepares workers to be productive (career-oriented education as well as various levels of liberal education), education to virtue in the family as well as control of inflation, and suitable interest rates. International competition would also affect every nation's economy for good or ill.

A similar approach to that of Pavan and Onofri is found in a book by Michael Naughton and Helen Alford, O.P., entitled *Managing As If Faith Mattered: Christian Social Principles in the Modern Organization.* They argue that the Christian social tradition requires three tests in the determination of a just wage: "'Is it a *living* wage?' (the test based on the principle of need). 'Is it an *equitable* wage?' (the test based on the principle of contribution). 'Is it a *sustainable* wage?' (the test based on the principle of economic order)."[60]

In discussing the living wage Naughton and Alford point out that both German and Japanese corporations spend much more money on training programs for their workers than their American counterparts. When it comes to apprentices, the Germans spend seventeen times as much as companies in the United States.[61] It is not surprising, then, that many

---

59. Pietro Pavan and Teodoro Onofri, *La dottrina sociale cristiana*, 3rd ed. (Rome: An. Veritas Editrice, 1966), 156–59.

60. Helen J. Alford, O.P., and Michael J. Naughton, *Managing As If Faith Mattered: Christian Social Principles in the Modern Organization* (Notre Dame, Ind.: University of Notre Dame Press, 2001), 130.

61. Ibid., 133.

American workers lack the skills and knowledge to do the kind of work that would pay them a living wage. In the light of this situation Naughton and Alford make two proposals that go to the heart of the matter: managers should redesign jobs so that they require more knowledge and skill and then find a way to retrain workers to do them. In this way workers below the living wage could really earn their pay raises. When managers are able to accomplish these two goals, workers will also receive more satisfaction in their jobs because of their increased skills and self-management of their careers. "By training employees in necessary skills, organizations in effect 'push' knowledge, information and decision making down to lower levels of the organization," which is a way of observing the principle of subsidiarity.[62] In order for the two proposals to be practicable, managers must teach and workers must learn. Managers need to care enough about their employees so that they are willing to go to the trouble of redesigning work and instituting training programs. If managers succeed, they will also contribute to the overall productivity of their firms and thereby promote their self-interest as well.

An equitable wage, Naughton explains, is *"the measure of the contribution of an employee's productivity and effort within the context of the existing amounts of profits and resources of the organization."*[63] Two of the principal obstacles to the payment of an equitable wage are the limitation of incentive programs to top executives and the great disparity between employee and executive compensation. It is only fair that all those who contribute to the economic success of a company should profit accordingly. Devising some system of pay for performance would contribute to the attainment of an equitable wage. Executives and managers must often rely on the expertise of their employees in an economy based so much on knowledge. Therefore, it is only right that knowledgeable and high-performing employees share equitably in the profits of their company.

Sustainable wages depend on "the economic health of the organization as a whole"[64] and on fidelity to ethical and legal norms. Obviously, companies have to make enough money to pay a living wage and an equitable wage. If a company experiences some kind of a crisis because of market conditions, then sacrifices will have to be made. When just some employees are made to bear the burden of the necessary sacrifices, morale will suffer and justice will often not be observed. Naughton and Alford point

---

62. Ibid., 135.   63. Ibid., 149.
64. Ibid.

out that some companies will emerge stronger from a crisis if all employees make proportionate sacrifices and the lowest-paid are protected from falling below a living wage. Sometimes companies will pay lip service to ethics, but reward those managers who improve the bottom line, even if they act unethically to do so. This kind of leadership can have a devastating effect on company morale, leading to lower productivity.[65]

Employers and managers should be intent on preparing their workers to do jobs that can pay a living wage. This educational work will not only require virtue, but also various kinds of business skill. Second, an emphasis on education at all levels is crucial, since access to good jobs depends on receiving an appropriate education. Pope John Paul II makes this point in *Centesimus Annus:*

Many people, perhaps the majority today, do not have the means which would enable them to take their place in an effective and humanly dignified way within a productive system in which work is truly central. They have no possibility of acquiring the basic knowledge which would enable them to express their creativity and develop their potential. They have no way of entering the network of knowledge and intercommunication which would enable them to see their qualities appreciated and utilized.[66]

Besides a just wage, workers also need benefits such as health insurance, a pension, and compensation for injuries sustained at work. In the Unites States alone there are millions of part-time and full-time workers who don't have any health insurance or a private pension. These cost-cutting measures, putting people in a very difficult position, cry out to be addressed by individuals, associations, and government.

Work and Contemporary Culture

Let us now take a brief look at work in the light of the current state of liberalism and in relation to Catholic teaching on the common good. Contemporary liberal culture, if my assessment is accurate, is not hospitable to the Christian way of approaching work. In fact, the culture is so influential in the lives of many that they can't even begin to grasp what John Paul II is saying about work. Hence, the pope's call to change the culture, addressed especially to bishops and other Christian leaders, must be more effectively heeded. Presently, the currents of liberalism affect American

65. Ibid., cf. 143–48.   66. *Centesimus annus,* no. 31.

Catholics in the way they move other American citizens. In sum, liberalism tends to promote individualism, the separation of rights from duties, the loosening of commitments in families and at work, undue sympathy for the principle of autonomy and "the culture of death," more deference to reigning opinions than to Church authority, the reception of revealed religion as opinion, and understanding morality more in terms of rights and values than virtues. All these trends are an obstacle to the Christian vision of work, especially to seeing work in relation to the common good.

Despite the unfavorable climate created by the reigning liberal culture, the Catholic Church can still put forward its vision of the common good in some detail as a beacon for individual Catholics. If Catholics really understood the grand vision of the common good in Catholic teaching, many would approach their work with renewed understanding and enthusiasm, knowing what could be accomplished by work, even apparently insignificant work. So informed, they would also understand the importance of working to reform liberal culture though their jobs or by means of volunteer work. They would also understand that the achievement of their dignity through work depends on the continuous struggle both to become competent and to practice the virtues.

Poverty

CSD is crystal-clear about the obligation toward the poor. Christians are obliged to have "a love of preference for the poor" or a preferential option for the poor, which Pope John Paul II defined as a *"special form* of primacy in the exercise of Christian charity."[67] This means much more than having the right opinion on welfare. A genuine love of the poor must include efforts to help people to get out and/or stay out of poverty. Welfare is important as a temporary measure for those on the road to self-support and as a permanent subsidy for people who cannot, for various legitimate reasons, obtain or hold a job.

Fr. Raniero Cantalamessa says that we must keep the poor before our eyes and let them "get under our skin."[68] We must take notice of the poor with our heart. "The question is to let them into our hearts, so that they stop being someone else's problem rather than ours and become a kind of family problem."[69] In order to acquire the proper attitude people should develop the habit of self-denial and keep constantly in mind that to wel-

---

67. *Sollicitudo rei socialis,* no. 42.
68. Raniero Cantalamessa, *Poverty* (New York: Alba House, 1997), 3.
69. Ibid., 4.

come the poor is to welcome Christ. "For parents, children are a constant reason to do without things, to give up something, to make savings—in a word, to be poor."[70] When we are poor in some way, we are more likely to perceive the poor with our heart, to see Christ. If we pray for guidance, the Spirit will let us know what we are to give up and how we might benefit the poor in our state of life. Fr. Cantalamessa tells the story of a rich businessman who went to a cloistered nun and asked how he might serve the poor. After praying for a time, realizing that he had the money, she said, "'Well, go and open another factory and give jobs to some more workers!' And that's what he did."[71]

I have long thought that the provision of education to the poor may be the most important means of getting vast numbers out of poverty. Special attention should be given to public schools in areas of poverty so that poor children may receive the kind of education that will free them from the cycle of poverty. Whether governments do or do not assume any responsibility for educating the poor, individuals, associations, and churches should always try to find ways to do so. For example, private programs have arranged for college graduates to devote several years teaching the poor in inner-city schools. Catholic schools in the big cities have educated a great number of poor children, both Catholic and non-Catholic. Everyone knows that Catholic schools and other religiously affiliated schools can and do help the poor. It is high time, therefore, for more accommodation in church-state laws. At the very least government should find a way to provide funding to poor children whose families want them to attend a private school, religiously affiliated or not.

Because divorce often plunges children into poverty, another effective measure to overcome it is to help people marry well and stay together. This is especially the role of the churches, but properly framed laws can also help. For example, laws that diminish the incidence of divorce will prevent some children from slipping into poverty. As things stand, the marriage laws in the states do not discourage divorce at all. On the contrary! Since the law is a pedagogue, it should tell stories of fidelity between spouses and loving care of children, and it should make divorce more difficult. With some help from the law more couples will work out their difficulties and, thereby, give their children a better chance to avoid becoming mired in poverty.[72]

70. Ibid., 56.   71. Ibid., 86.

72. Mary Ann Glendon's 1987 book, *Abortion and Divorce in Western Law: American Fail-*

While attending an NEH seminar in 1980 I committed to memory one of Wilson Carey McWilliams's obiter dicta. He said something to this effect: "We should give some kind of a tax break to people who don't move. We move too much in America," he said, "and that breaks up community." From this comment I inferred that we should find some way in our tax, marriage, and welfare laws to encourage people to think well of marriage, to marry, and to stay together. For example, some kind of tax break could be given to couples who remain married.

The several states could do more both to mandate adequate child support in case of divorce and to develop effective means of enforcing child support. Currently, many children often don't receive adequate support after a divorce takes place.

Continued opposition to the legalization of euthanasia is still another important means of serving the poor. I believe that the poor will be the first casualties of legalized euthanasia. Not a few insurance companies and hospitals will welcome euthanasia as a cost-cutting device.

The Catholic community must find a way to change attitudes in the culture toward partnership between religious institutions and government. For example, Catholics should continue to work at persuading citizens that some financial support of religiously affiliated schools will serve the common good. In addition, Catholics should have no hesitation in persuading their fellow citizens that lifelong fidelity in marriage and openness to procreating and educating children are goods of the highest order.

The Catholic community should also encourage a public morality of generosity. We should find a way to make John F. Kennedy's appeal attractive once again: "Ask not what your country can do for you, ask what you can do for your country." If many more Catholics took this advice to heart, the needs of American citizens would be addressed more creatively and effectively, especially those of the poor.

Immigration

Closely related to the themes of work, poverty, and the universal destination of goods is immigration. Throughout the world many people emigrate from their countries looking for work opportunities. Because of the demographic winter or birth dearth in Europe, immigrants are especial-

---

ures, *European Challenges* (Cambridge, Mass.: Harvard University Press), is eloquent and informative on this subject.

ly needed both to do the necessary day-to-day work and to support the vast social welfare systems of European countries. Writing in 2006, Mary Ann Glendon notes:

The combination of low birth rates and greater longevity is already bringing the health-care and social-security programs of welfare states into crisis. Social welfare systems were constructed in the late nineteenth and early twentieth centuries on the basis of a proportion of nine, or in some cases, seven active workers for every active pensioner. Now Europe is approaching three workers per retiree, and those retirees are living much longer.[73]

The United States also needs immigrants to fill open jobs or jobs that Americans don't want to do, but our situation is a far cry from that of Europe, because our birth rate hovers around 2.1 babies per woman, the exact rate a nation needs for population replacement. Europe as a whole has a much lower rate, with Spain, Italy, and Greece in the 1.3 range.

The *Compendium of the Social Doctrine of the Church* doesn't have a lot to say about immigration, but does offer some helpful reminders that might be overlooked in the heat of discussions about immigration. *"Immigration can be a resource for development rather than an obstacle to it."*[74] This is because they do necessary jobs that the local labor force is either unwilling or unable to do. Second, care must be taken that immigrant workers are not exploited, but rather enjoy the same rights as everyone else. In addition, appropriate steps should be taken to help them become integrated into society. For example, immigrants should be welcomed as neighbors and educational opportunities be made available for their children. Fourth, *"the right of reuniting families should be respected and promoted."*[75] Fifth, the countries from which people emigrate should endeavor to create jobs so that people will have the choice to stay home if they so desire. Last, established unions should do what they can to help immigrants secure fair compensation for their work. This, of course, would expand the solidarity of unions to workers outside their usual constituency. The *Compendium* wisely refrains from indicating how their recommendations could be implemented. So many factors will have to be taken into consideration by the institutions and individuals who decide to extend a welcoming hand to immigrants and their families.

Mary Ann Glendon mentions some reasonable concerns that people

73. Mary Ann Glendon, "Principled Immigration," *First Things*, no. 164 (2006): 23.
74. *Compendium of the Social Doctrine of the Church*, no. 297.
75. Ibid., no. 298.

have about immigration. Labor economists agree that the employment of immigrants "has somewhat reduced the earnings of less educated, low-wage workers." Taxpayers, especially in states bordering Mexico, will have to assume more burdens to support schools and social services for immigrants and their families. Terrorists could also slip into the country along with the immigrants seeking jobs. People might also fear that immigrants could jeopardize the cultural cohesion and stability of local communities. Finally, the question of widespread illegal immigration looms large in the discussion, because, as Tocqueville noted, "there is not a country on Earth where legal values play a more prominent role in the nation's conception of itself than in the United States."[76] Glendon implies that the United States will have to deal fairly with all of our illegal immigrants and find a way to curtail illegal immigration. Many people will balk at accepting immigrants if they enter the country illegally.

Two unreasonable concerns come from those who object to outsiders on principle and to those radical environmentalists and population controllers who object to immigrants on the grounds that they will consume resources. Glendon comments, "What unites that loose coalition in what I call an 'iron triangle of exclusion' is their common conviction that border controls and abortion are major defenses against an expanding, threatening, welfare-consuming, and non-white underclass."[77] For making this comment, Glendon paid a price. An unnamed foundation had promised Glendon to support her work while on unpaid leave from Harvard University, but reneged when they read the sentence quoted above. Commenting on this event, Glendon said, "It turned out that their idea of protecting the environment included keeping out immigrants and keeping poor people from having children."[78]

In 2003 the U.S. and Mexican bishops issued a joint pastoral letter on the problem of immigration entitled *Strangers No Longer: Together on the Journey of Hope.* It listed five principles which guide the bishops in their work on behalf of immigrants: (1) "Persons have the right to find opportunities in their homeland"; (2) "Persons have the right to migrate to support themselves and their families," when there are insufficient opportunities at home; (3) "Sovereign nations have the right to control their borders," but the affluent and powerful nations have an obligation to facilitate migration; (4) "Refugees and asylum seekers should be afforded protection";

76. Glendon, *"Principled Immigration,"* 25.   77. Ibid.
78. Ibid.

(5) "The human dignity and human rights of undocumented migrants should be respected."[79] Glendon lists these five principles and then suggests a sixth drawn from Pope John Paul II's *Sollicitudo rei socialis (On Social Concern)*, namely, "that solidarity imposes duties on the disadvantaged as well as the advantaged." The previous pope stressed that immigrants shouldn't just passively enjoy their rights, but actively seek to promote the good of all. This papal teaching expresses respect for the dignity of immigrants by recognizing that, like everybody else, they need to make a contribution to society in order live a fully human life.

The American and Mexican bishops make policy proposals on the basis of their five principles and call on the faithful to be hospitable and welcoming to immigrants. For example, they suggest creating more employment opportunities in Mexico and modifying the laws so as to reduce the long waiting time for immigrant workers and families to be reunited. Of course, they also call for the establishment of a legalization program for undocumented immigrants. As pastors of immigrants, the bishops pledge efforts to evangelize them and to provide access to religious services.

Glendon rightly notes that moving "from the level of principle to specific programs and policies will require enormous dedication, intelligence, creativity, and goodwill on the part of all concerned."[80] I could not agree more, because the reasonable and unreasonable concerns that people have need to be carefully considered and answered. These efforts would be difficult in any circumstances, but are even more so because of the strong passions of many participants in the immigration discussion.

79. U.S. and Mexican Catholic Bishops, *Strangers No Longer: Together on the Journey of Hope* (Washington, D.C.: United States Conference of Catholic Bishops, 2003) nos. 34–38.
80. Glendon, "Principled Immigration," 26.

CHAPTER 10

Safeguarding and Sustaining
the Environment

To safeguard and sustain the environment is a work for every locale and nation, and a momentous task for the whole world. The *Compendium of the Social Doctrine of the Church* says, "Modern ecological problems are of a planetary nature and can be effectively resolved only through international cooperation capable of guaranteeing greater coordination in the use of the earth's resources."[1] This chapter will first explain the basic approach to the environment of the neo-Malthusian movement because of the influential framework of analysis it has provided. Then we will turn to the approach of Catholic social doctrine, which has the potential of being more effective than the extreme positions advocated by some neo-Malthusians.

It is common today to speak of the safeguarding or sustainability of the environment. While the former term is readily understandable, the latter is not. Sustainability is still a word unknown to most people. The word "sustain" is derived from the Latin *sustineo,* meaning to hold up, to support, to maintain. Citing a 1965 source, *The Oxford English Dictionary* (OED) first says that sustainable means that something is "capable of being maintained at a certain level." If something is maintained or sustained like economic growth or per capita income, it is kept in existence over an indefinite period of time. In its 2002 edition, the OED, citing sources no earlier than 1980, gave the following definition of sustainable in relation to ecology: "of, relating to, or designating forms of human economic activity and culture that do not lead to environmental degradation, especially the long-term depletion of natural resources." This definition actually captures the most common use of the word "sustainability" today. It generally refers to the ongoing maintenance of (1) the economy, (2) the environment, and (3) society.

1. Pontifical Council for Justice and Peace, *Compendium of the Social Doctrine of the Church* (Vatican City: Libreria Editrice Vaticana, 2004), no. 481.

While much has been written about sustainable environments and economies, very little has been done by sustainability advocates to explain the concept of a sustainable society. This is quite understandable, since it is a highly philosophical topic requiring an approach from many different angles. It is the kind of thing usually discussed by political philosophers, political theorists, and theologians, usually with different terminology, such as justice, social justice, the common good, or the good society. These subjects must be addressed, because the environment and the economy depend on a sustainable society and vice versa. Recall our discussion of justice and the common good in earlier chapters. My subsequent comments about the environment will draw upon conclusions reached in those chapters.

In order to study sustainability issues it is most important to keep in mind the number of people in the world as well as population trends. Everyone agrees that replacement level population is 2.1 children per woman. The extra .1 makes up for children who don't live long enough to procreate. No one knows for sure what the population will be in 2050, but the United Nations regularly presents its projections to the public. In its *World Population Prospects* 2008 Revision (Executive Summary), the population division of the Department of Economic and Social Affairs of the United Nations Secretariat estimated that the population of the world, at 6.8 billion in 2008, would be 7 billion by late 2011.[2] Between 2005 and 2009, the world added 79 million people annually. The UN has offered a low, medium, and high estimate of the population in 2050; the high estimate is more than 9 billion people. The birth rate in the developed nations—now estimated at 1.64 children per woman—would cause a huge decline in population, were it not for their constant immigration rate. Even with immigration, the more developed nations are only expected "to increase slightly from 1.23 billion in 2009 to 1.28 billion in 2050."[3] Without immigration the population would tumble to 1.15 billion.

Between 2005 and 2010 twenty-five countries, mostly located in Southern and Eastern Europe, have had fertility rates below 1.5 children per woman. The world fertility level "is expected to fall from 2.56 children per woman in 2005–2010 to 2.02 in 2045–2050."[4] In the least developed nations the pro-

2. UN Department of Economic and Social Affairs, Population Division, "World Population Prospects: The 2008 Revision, Executive Summary"; available at http://esa.un.org/unpd/wpp2008/pdf/WPP2008_Executive-Summary_Edited_6-Oct-2009.pdf.

3. "World Population Prospects," 7.

4. Ibid., 9.

jections for 2050 are a decline from today's 4.39 to 2.41 children per woman. In the other developing countries the projected dip is from 2.46 children per woman to 1.93.[5] The UN population division thinks that life expectancy in the world as a whole will increase from age 68 in 2005–2010 to 76 in 2045–2050. During the same time period, people's life spans in the developed countries will increase from 77 to 83, in the least developed countries from 56 to 69 (as long as HIV/AIDS is contained), and in the rest of the developing world from 66 to 74. Of course, with the decline of fertility rates comes the ageing of the population. Even in the developing world the percentage of persons over 60 is expected to rise from 8 percent today to 20 percent by 2050. In the developed world that figure will rise from 21 percent of the population today to 33 percent. "Globally, the number of persons aged 60 years or over is expected to almost triple, increasing from 737 million in 2005 to nearly 2 billion by 2050."[6] In the developed countries older persons will outnumber children two to one by 2050.

One of the primary reasons for the growth in the world's population from 1.6 billion in 1900 to 6.5 billion in 2006 is not only the fertility rate, but also the health explosion over the last 100 years. All over the world, even in the least developed nations, life expectancy has dramatically increased. In 1900 it was around 30 in the whole world; today it is about 68. People are just not dying as early as they used to die.[7]

In his book *Fewer: How the New Demography of Depopulation Will Shape Our Future*, Ben Wattenberg draws attention to what seem to be irrefutable population facts. A declining and graying population in Europe will cause serious problems. "For example," writes Wattenberg, "lots of old people and relatively few younger people mean that nations cannot meet their pension obligations without increasing taxes or lowering benefits."[8] With a policy of "pay as you go," state-run programs depend on enough people working to meet their obligations. Even in the United States, with a growing population, there is still a problem. In 1955 "there were nearly 9 workers for every retiree; today there are only 3.3. Under current projections, the ratio will fall to 2 workers for every retiree by 2035."[9] A fortiori

---

5. Ibid.   6. Ibid., 8.

7. Nicholas Eberstadt, "Population, Resources, and the Quest to 'Stabilize Human Population': Myths and Realities," in *Global Warming and Other Eco-Myths* (Roseville, Calif.: Prima Publishing, 2002), 74.

8. Ben J. Wattenberg, *Fewer: How the New Demography of Depopulation Will Shape Our Future* (Chicago: Ivan R. Dee, 2004), 88.

9. Ibid., 120.

European governments will face even greater difficulties meeting their pension obligations. Because of fewer workers, states will also have difficulty paying for seniors' health care.

Other problems caused by the demographic implosion noted by Wattenberg are less economic growth and prosperity and a decline in military power. Business needs enough customers to thrive and nations enough citizens to mount an adequate defense against enemies, such as terrorists. Because of Europe's population decline, the Unites States will have to assume more responsibility for defending itself and victims of aggression.

Wattenberg comments on the necessity of people for prosperity by using the example of the United States. "The nation with the largest population explosion in history," explains Wattenberg, "has been the United States, going from 4 million to nearly 300 million in 210 years while becoming the world's most prosperous nation."[10] Not that every nation could duplicate what the United States has done, but the American experience shows that no one can say that an increase in population necessarily causes a decline in the standard of living.

Still another problem is the imbalance between males and females in China and India. There is going to be a bride shortage in these countries, because in the year 2000 China had a ratio of 118 males to 100 females, while India's ratio was 108 to 100 in 2001. Wattenberg doesn't say so, but there are other Asian countries where there is a similar problem. His great concern is that young men will be deprived of founding a family. Other consequences of the imbalance between girls and boys, not mentioned by Wattenberg, are also very serious. If a great number of men are unable to find a marriage partner, they are likely to aggravate social and political problems such as prostitution, the transmission of STDs, and civil unrest.

The Context for Catholic Social Doctrine on the Environment: The Neo-Malthusian Movement

The most visible part of the sustainability movement is made up of people commonly known as neo-Malthusians because of their great emphasis on reducing the population and on stressing the inevitability of scarcity due to overpopulation. Their most striking characteristic is an apocalyptic and, many would say, alarmist tone. Whether the neo-Malthusians are ex-

10. Ibid., 58.

aggerating the dangers we face is the question to be decided. They certainly sound a loud alarm and, at first glance, *seem* to be alarmists.

Economist Maria Sophia Aguirre regards the neo-Malthusians as the most visible players in the sustainability movement. "It is clear that the neo-Malthusian perspective has become the most popularized and widespread vision of the population-resources-environment debate, especially in media and policymaking circles."[11] Journalists and TV programs have certainly done a lot to convince Americans that they should be quite worried about global warming, population growth, and other environmental developments. Al Gore, a classic neo-Malthusian, in his movie *An Inconvenient Truth*, "suggests, for example, that Greenland's ice cap is in danger of melting, which in turn would cause the jet stream to shut down."[12]

The contemporary neo-Malthusians can trace their ancient origins back to an essay Thomas Malthus wrote in 1798 entitled, "An Essay on the Principle of Population As It Affects the Future of Society." His followers came to be known as Malthusians; those who have adapted his thought to contemporary times are appropriately called neo-Malthusians. Malthus believed that the population grows exponentially, while food production can only sustain "arithmetic growth." Simply stated, that means that the demand for food over the centuries will greatly exceed the supply because of the inevitable exponential population growth. The neo-Malthusians believe that the demand for every resource will greatly surpass the supply and put unsustainable demands on the environment unless population growth is stopped.

The more immediate origins of the contemporary sustainability movement are Garrett Hardin's article, "The Tragedy of the Commons," Paul Ehrlich's *The Population Bomb* (1968), and the Club of Rome's 1972 *The Limits to Growth* and Earth Day in April of 1970. Hardin argued against society's practice of allowing people to make free use of natural resources.[13] Ehrlich, known especially for his advocacy of drastic population control, predicted that hundreds of millions of people were going to starve in the 1970s because of overpopulation. The Club of Rome was a group of

11. Maria Sophia Aguirre, "Sustainable Development: Why the Focus on Population?" 17; paper presented at the Harvard-MIT Conference on International Health, March 10–12, 2000; cf. http://faculty.cua.edu/aguirre.

12. Kevin Shapiro, "Global Warming: Apocalypse Now?" *Commentary* 122 (2006): 45.

13. Hardin's article will be discussed later in the chapter. On November 21, 2008 a conference was held at Adrian College in Adrian, Michigan, to celebrate the fortieth anniversary of Hardin's article. It is obviously still having an influence.

European industrialists who published a study "claiming to demonstrate that American industry, by maintaining the American standard of living, was making the planet unlivable for everyone else."[14]

The celebration of the first Earth Day on April 22, 1970, gave the environmental movement a concrete beginning to which one can point. Twenty million people participated in some way. Senator Gaylord Nelson, the prime organizer of this Earth Day, said that "the important objective and achievement of Earth Day" was forcibly to "thrust the issue of environmental quality and resource conservation into the political dialogue of the nation."[15] Many environmental laws were passed in the 1970s, including the 1970 amendments to the Clean Air Act. In addition, the Environmental Protection Agency (EPA) opened its doors on December 2, 1970. It must be noted that not all participants in the first or subsequent Earth Days share all the views of Hardin, Ehrlich, and the Club of Rome.

The neo-Malthusian sustainability advocates received some help in their efforts to draw attention to the necessity of population control from the 1994 World Conference on Population and Development held in Cairo, Egypt, but not nearly as much as they wished. A great deal of time was spent discussing whether abortion should be accepted as a method of family planning. Despite pressure from the United States and others, the final document said no, but not enough time was devoted to sustainable development.

Population controllers did decide to introduce the language of reproductive rights as a way to combat overpopulation, thinking that most people would respond better to rights talk, which is the preferred moral language of public discourse. Austin Ruse explains,

Their thinking went that if everyone demanded and received their "reproductive rights," as defined by the UN, then fertility rates would continue to decline. So, under the guidance and support of UNFPA [the UN Population Fund, formerly the UN Fund for Population Activities], the United Nations began the international call for reproductive rights at the Cairo conference on Population and Development in 1994.[16]

14. Midge Decter, "The Nine Lives of Population Control," in *The Nine Lives of Population Control*, edited by Michael Cromartie (Washington, D.C.: Ethics and Public Policy Center; Grand Rapids, Mich.: Eerdmans, 1995), 9.

15. Cf. United States Environmental Protection Agency, "Earth Day '70: What It Meant," available at http://www.epa.gov/history/topics/earthday/02.htm.

16. Austin Ruse, "Overpopulation Is a Myth," in *Population: Opposing Viewpoints*, edited by Karen F. Balkin (Farmington Hills, Mich.: Greenhaven Press, 2005), 29.

This new language, however, has not eclipsed the old language of population control, because some leaders in the sustainability movement don't believe that the voluntary exercise of rights is, or ever will be, sufficient to reduce the population enough. Population control through coercive measures will be necessary.

Yesterday's and Today's Model Neo-Malthusians

Paul Ehrlich's *The Population Bomb* tried to persuade Americans that they needed drastic measures to reduce the population in order to prevent depletion of food and other resources. "One plan often mentioned involves the addition of temporary sterilants to water supplies or staple food."[17] Realizing that people wouldn't accept such drastic measures, Ehrlich suggested that the government give people incentives through tax policy not to have children. For example, families with two children would have an extra $600 added to their taxable income for each child. Families with more than two children would pay $1,200 for each additional child. He further recommended the imposition of luxury taxes on various baby products, such as cribs and diapers. He also suggested that government give "responsibility prizes" to couples for each five years of marriage they remained childless, and for men who had a vasectomy before siring two children. In addition, Ehrlich wanted federal laws guaranteeing the right to abortion and the right to voluntary sterilization, and he advocated sex-education programs in the schools that would teach students about the need for birth control and explain the various contraceptive techniques.

Through legislation and education Ehrlich expected that within a generation people could be enjoying sexual activity, "mankind's major and most enduring recreation,"[18] while having fewer and healthier children. "The population should be relatively free of the horrors created today by divorce, illegal abortion, venereal disease, and the psychological pressures of a sexually repressive and repressed society."[19] Ehrlich noted that the Catholic Church might pose some obstacles to his plan to reduce premature death in the world by curbing population growth. "Unless the Pope does a complete about face [sic], I think we can count on continuing and effective Catholic support for raising the death rate."[20] Ehrlich did derive hope from his perception that many Catholics would not observe their

---

17. Paul Ehrlich, *The Population Bomb* (New York: Ballantine Books, 1968), 122.
18. Ibid., 126.   19. Ibid., 127.
20. Ibid., 131.

Church's teaching on birth control. He urged all biologists to teach that contraception is more desirable than abortion and that the latter is often more desirable than childbirth. Ehrlich actually regarded the Catholic problem as more amenable to a solution than the one posed by the belief of businessmen that a prosperous economy depends on population growth. He noted with relief, however, that a few distinguished economists believed that the GNP could grow without an increase in population.

With respect to the forced sterilizations that took place in India under Mrs. Gandhi, Wattenberg noted that neo-Malthusian Paul Ehrlich criticized the United States "for not supporting *mandatory* sterilization of all Indian men with three or more children." He quotes Ehrlich as saying, "'We should have volunteered logistic support in the form of helicopters, vehicles, and surgical instruments. We should have sent doctors.... Coercion? Perhaps, but coercion in a good cause.'"[21]

Thirty-seven years after Ehrlich wrote, Lester Brown published *Plan B 2.0: Rescuing a Planet Under Stress and a Civilization in Trouble* (2006), a revised edition of an earlier work published in 2003. Brown is the president of the Earth Policy Institute and winner of the prestigious MacArthur fellowship, as well as the recipient of the United Nations Environment Prize and Japan's Blue Planet Prize. His work is one of the best single-volume introductions to the contemporary Neo-Malthusian perspective. There is no mention of abortion, but some dramatic statements on the necessity of birth control. For example, he calls upon public officials to convince people they should have no more than two children. "The time has come for world leaders—including the Secretary General of the United Nations, the President of the World Bank, and the President of the United States—to publicly recognize that the earth cannot easily support more than two children per family."[22] At the very least, Brown is most likely implying that these leaders should use their "bully pulpit" to raise people's consciousness about the necessity of limiting the size of their families for the sake of the survival of civilization.

In the last chapter Brown summarizes his solution to the cataclysm he says we are facing.

We know that sustaining progress depends on restructuring the global economy, shifting from a fossil-fuel-based, automobile-centered, throwaway econ-

21. Wattenberg, *Fewer*, 47.

22. Lester R. Brown, *Plan B 2.0: Rescuing a Planet under Stress and a Civilization in Trouble* (New York: W. W. Norton, 2006), 130.

omy to one based on renewable sources, a diverse transportation system, and a comprehensive reuse/recycle materials system. This can be done largely by restructuring taxes and subsidies. Sustaining progress also means eradicating poverty, stabilizing population, and restoring the earth's natural systems.[23]

In Brown's mind we need something akin to a Marshall Plan with a national leader like Winston Churchill to persuade the world to recognize the coming environmental cataclysm and to embrace the kind of solutions suggested by himself. Only concerted, sustained action can prevent the cataclysm. Terrorism is a threat, but "not even close to being the top threat facing our early twenty-first century civilization. Population growth, climate change, poverty, spreading water shortages, rising oil prices, and a potential rise in food prices that could lead to unprecedented political instability are the leading threats."[24]

The present use of fossil fuel is already causing global warming, "generating social stress in the form of crop-shrinking heat waves, ice melting, rising seas, and more destructive storms."[25] As the developing world makes progress, more and more fossil fuels are used for energy sources. This is an unsustainable situation, especially because of rapid economic development in India and China. The only alternative is to use energy sources derived from the wind, the sun, and the earth, namely, wind turbines, solar cells, and geothermal energy. These three energy sources can be used to generate electricity. The only vehicles that have a future are gas-electric hybrid cars that draw their electrical power from wind turbines.

Brown's book takes his readers from the prospect of impending cataclysm to a kind of utopia where all the world's problems can be solved by the Plan B budget. Brown is not concerned that people with a bad character may have the capacity to subvert his plan or that, with the best will in the world, some problems may prove to be intractable. In addition, he does not consider the argument that parts of the world may need a higher fertility rate in order to ensure sufficient productivity. Population growth is a problem anywhere it happens.[26]

The neo-Malthusians say that because of overpopulation and high

23. Ibid., 250.   24. Ibid., 252–53.
25. Ibid., 252.

26. A third edition of Brown's book was published by W. W. Norton in 2008 under the title *PLAN B 3.0: Mobilizing to Save Civilization.* The same publisher brought out the fourth edition in 2009 under the title *Plan B 4:0: Mobilizing to Save Civilization* (New York: W. W. Norton, 2009).

consumption people are using too much fresh water, polluting it as well as the air, land, and sea, taking too many fish from the ocean, consuming too much food, dangerously diminishing the supply of crop land and forests, causing global warming and the rise of sea levels, generating unemployment and more homelessness because of insufficient housing, triggering a loss of a great number of plant and animal species, exhausting the supply of fossil fuels and every other natural resource, causing poverty (which, in turn leads to environmental damage by such practices as overfarming and cutting down needed forests), reducing our standard of living, and straining "the capacity of governments to provide basic social services, such as education and welfare, for each citizen."[27]

Global Warming

Let us take a closer look at one of the more visible results of overpopulation and the high level of consumption that the neo-Malthusians discern: global warming. Many environmentalists claim that the emission of greenhouse gases (carbon emissions, CO_2) produced by the burning of fossil fuels such as oil and coal is the cause of excessive global warming. Rising global temperatures, they contend, cause the melting of arctic ice, the prolongation of the melting season in Antarctica, rising seas, more powerful and more numerous hurricanes and tornadoes, floods, and crop-shrinking heat waves. The solution to these problems is to phase out our dependence on fossil fuels by using solar energy, wind turbines, and hybrid cars. Scientists agree, according to Lester Brown, that we have to cut carbon emissions by 70 percent to stabilize the climate.

Sustainability advocates realize that people might ask whether scientists agree among themselves about the cause of global warming. Various business leaders have expressed skepticism about the necessity of stricter controls on carbon dioxide emissions, claiming that the science is uncertain. Writing in *Science* magazine, Naomi Oreskes says there is overwhelming scientific consensus that human behavior affects climate change. "For example, the National Academy of Sciences report, *Climate Change Science: An Analysis of Some Key Questions,* begins, 'Greenhouse gases are accumulating in Earth's atmosphere as a result of human activities, causing surface air temperatures and subsurface ocean temperatures to rise.'"[28] Other groups who say that the "evidence for the human modi-

27. Brown, *Plan B 2.0,* 48.
28. Naomi Oreskes, "The Scientific Consensus on Climate Change," *Science* 306 (December 2004): 1686.

fication of climate is compelling"[29] are the Intergovernmental Panel on Climate Change ("created in 1988 by the World Meteorological Organization and the United Nations Environmental Program"), The American Meteorological Society, the American Geophysical Union, and the American Association for the Advancement of Science. Oreskes doesn't mention whether any of these societies attempt to determine how significant the human contribution to global warming is or to what extent natural causes enter into the equation.

Al Gore's film *An Inconvenient Truth* is entirely devoted to the problem of global warming, caused by the emission of greenhouse gases. He reports the alleged fact that the ten hottest years scientifically measured have occurred in the last ten years. The year 2005 was the hottest on record so far. Scientists also report that CO_2 emissions are projected to keep on rising, with no end in sight. It is unethical, Gore argues, not to do anything about these emissions, because they imperil civilization itself.

Gore further considers the objection that scientists don't agree on the fact or danger of global warming. In response, he notes that a recent study of 928 peer-reviewed scientific articles revealed that every single scientist considered global warming a serious problem; there is simply no disagreement among scientifically educated people. It is also not true that we have to decide between the environment and the economy. Gore says that doing the right thing for the environment will benefit the economy. One example he gives to prove this point is that Toyota and Honda are much more prosperous than American automakers, and the average miles per gallon of their fleet of cars is much higher than that of American cars.

Proposed Solutions: Reliance on Self-interest and Coercion
(No Place for Conscience)

The question naturally arises of how to reduce the rate of population growth and the level of consumption in view of promoting sustainable development. There is no unanimity as to the remedies. The neo-Malthusians tend to suggest the following measures: legislation, tax incentives, appeals to people's self-interest and enlightened self-interest, restrictions on immigration, and the formation of communities whose animating principle is respect for the environment. Some of these sustainability advocates openly favor instituting coercive contraception to bring down the growth rate of the population in the Third World. The

29. Ibid.

strategy is to tie the reception of economic aid to the acceptance of the coercive contraception.

Loosely formed communities, based on dedication to sustainability, convey to their members by various means that a progressive, enlightened person makes a commitment to population control, reduces consumption, recycles, lowers the thermostat during the winter to the low sixties or high fifties Fahrenheit, turns off or lowers the air conditioning, encourages people to buy hybrid automobiles and to drive less, turns off lights, walks the stairs instead of taking the elevator, doesn't use more napkins than necessary, grows a garden, creates a compost. In other words, sustainability groups convey to people the attitudes and behaviors characteristic of the committed environmentalist. This is a kind of conscience formation, but is perhaps more appropriately called consciousness raising. One professor recently told me that she attempts to educate her students or raise their consciousness by removing all aluminum cans and plastic bottles from the wastebasket before the beginning of each class. She glowers at the students, puts the cans and bottles in the recyclable containers, and then washes her hands. No words need be spoken.

To encourage behavior that promotes sustainability, neo-Malthusians pay little or no attention to the role that Judaism or Christianity might play through their moral teachings on conscience and the practice of virtue. In fact, some, like Ehrlich, as we have already seen, criticize Christian churches that oppose contraception and abortion. The traditional formation of conscience was dealt a severe blow in environmental circles by Garrett Hardin in his "The Tragedy of the Commons," the previously mentioned address, given on June 25, 1968, to the Pacific division of the Association for the Advancement of Science. It appeared shortly thereafter as an article in *Science* magazine. At the time Hardin was a professor of biology at the University of California in Santa Barbara. Professor Hardin forcefully argues that people should not be allowed to ruin the commons by their ill-advised free choices. "Freedom in a commons brings ruin to all."[30] People should not be allowed the "freedom to breed" as they see fit. The Universal Declaration of Human Rights errs, he declares, in granting individuals the right to choose the size of their family. Then, he says, "It is a mistake to think that we can control the breeding of mankind by an appeal to conscience."[31] He further adds

30. Garrett Hardin, "The Tragedy of the Commons," *Science* 162 (1968): 1244.
31. Ibid., 1246.

354 The Universal Destination of Goods

that society can't reasonably expect individuals to exercise self-restraint in the commons (i.e., with respect to the earth's natural resources) for reasons of conscience. In fact, it would be foolish for some to follow their conscience while others, heedless of conscience, did damage to the commons in the pursuit of their self-interest. The only solution is coercion, mutual coercion, to be exact, "mutually agreed upon by the majority of the people affected."[32] Even temperance can be coerced by using the coercive device of taxing. Why would people disinclined to follow their conscience agree to coercive solutions to save natural resources from the destructive effects of human freedom? Hardin implies that the only reason is and should be self-interest. Hardin calls conscientious people "simpletons" who restrain themselves while others freely exploit the commons. In other words, people should be moral as long as they can be sure that other people are, too. Hardin doesn't address the difficulty of persuading men and women that it is in their self-interest to allow themselves to be coerced to do what is beneficial for the public good.

Back in 1967 Kingsley Davis also made a plea to supplement voluntary family planning with effective measures. He says, "The industrialized countries have had family planning for half a century without acquiring control over either the birthrate or population increase."[33] What's holding the population control movement back is the reluctance of liberal intellectuals to embrace the coercive measures they do in the economic and social realms. "Put the word *compulsory* in front of any term describing a means of limiting births—*compulsory sterilization, compulsory abortion, compulsory contraception*—and you guarantee violent opposition."[34] Davis's hope was that educated liberals would begin to accept coercion in the area of reproduction. Forty years after he wrote, compulsory sterilization and abortion have been tried in India and China. Today there seems to be great support among many people in the West for the implementation of coercive measures, by means of such instruments as taxation and tax incentives, to promote contraception, sterilization, and abortion in the Third World. Some intellectuals would even support legal penalties for violating government policy on the number of children allowed in each family.

In 1989 Garrett Hardin wrote another article on population control

32. Ibid., 1247.
33. Kingsley Davis, "Population Policy: Will Current Programs Succeed?" in *Population Puzzle: Boom or Bust*, edited by Laura E. Huggins and Hanna Skandera (Stanford, Calif.: Hoover Institution Press, 2004), 333.
34. Ibid., 333.

and asked this question: "So what are the chances that American society
as a whole can achieve population control by voluntary means?" His answer is simple. "Essentially zero, at present."[35] Hardin believes that some
kind coercion or economic incentive is absolutely necessary. As examples,
he suggests that we agree to allow the dependency deduction only for
one or two children. Another possibility is to give monetary rewards to
women between the ages of twelve and twenty for not getting pregnant.
"The control of all is achieved by *mutual coercion, mutually agreed upon.*"[36]
That should be the governing principle. Right now we don't know exactly where it will lead, but one way or another population control requires
coercion or offers that people can't refuse. Hardin professes ignorance of
what these measures will be, but in the meantime, he says, "*we must bring
immigration virtually to an end and do so soon.*"[37]

China, of course, has been pursuing a one-child policy since 1970. In a
white paper issued in 2000 the Information Office of the People's Republic of China justified China's policy by noting its favorable consequences.
Decreasing the birth rate has contributed to world peace, a more developed national economy, a higher standard of living, better health care, a
higher percentage of children attending school and college, delayed marriages, more women in the workforce (46.5 percent in 1999), better provisions for the retired, conservation of natural resources, and the protection of the environment. The white paper also mentions that China has
worked closely with governments, international institutions, and NGOs
on "reproductive health, adolescent education, emergency contraception, male participation in family planning, and so on."[38] This vague-
sounding statement implies that the Chinese government has received
help in planning and carrying out its one-child policy. The paper concludes by expressing the hope that China's way of controlling population
growth will prove to be a beacon for the world. "The successful implementation of China's population and family planning program has provided useful experience and lessons for others."[39] Noteworthy is omission
of any reference in the white paper to the compulsory nature of China's

35. Hardin, "There Is No Global Population Problem: Can Humanists Escape the
'Catch 22' of Population Control?" in *Population Puzzle Boom or Bust?* 338.
36. Ibid.
37. Ibid., 339.
38. Information Office of the State Council of the People's Republic of China, excerpt from "White Paper on Information 2000," in *Population Puzzle Boom or Bust?* 274.
39. Ibid.

one-child policy, forcing women pregnant with a second child to undergo an abortion.

Not too long ago, a professor of philosophy at Ithaca College, Carol Kates, vigorously defended Hardin's line of thought, "mutual coercion mutually agreed upon." She doesn't believe that the turn toward "reproductive rights" at Cairo in 1994 was the right move. Economic development and empowering women with "better educational and economic opportunities" will not, she argues, sufficiently and quickly bring down the fertility rate. Respecting women's right to procreate as they see fit is not a luxury we can afford. (This is an interesting conflict between the feminist emphasis on freedom and the neo-Malthusian focus on effective population control.) It is "misguided and harmful" to substitute a women's rights agenda for effective population control. Coercion is just more effective than relying on respect for human rights.

Reducing population to a sustainable level (at some desirable level of consumption), would obviously require a major global effort, not merely to subsidize and distribute effective modern contraceptives, but to offer incentives and impose penalties to influence fertility, manipulate institutional variables, aggressively counter pronatalist cultural values, and, very likely, impose coercive limits on reproductive liberty.[40]

Kates realizes that she has an uphill battle to realize her agenda, since it is opposed by many liberals and conservatives. "[T]he strange alliance of religious conservatives, feminists, 'progressive' liberals, and free market ideologists now poses a threat to the environment and human welfare."[41] The religious conservatives oppose abortion and contraception, progressive liberals are unwilling to override personal liberties, and the free-market economists think that the remedy for poverty is economic and political liberty. Kates favorably quotes David Pimentel's view that the ideal population for the world would be two billion. Attaining this optimum level would require limiting each couple to an average of 1.5 children for 100 years. Kates also wants to reduce consumption throughout the world, but offers no suggestions as to how to realize this goal. The visible sustainability movement doesn't look to the Judeo-Christian tradition for any help in protecting the environment, because Jews and Christians are trained to follow their well-formed conscience. That is widely regarded as

40. Carol Kates, "Aggressive Population Control Policies Should Be Supported," in *Population: Opposing Viewpoints*, 136.
41. Ibid., 142.

a totally ineffective way of generating the requisite attitudes and behavior, since it is too dependent on chance. In addition, some environmentalists see the Bible as the primary cause of today's ecological problems. Back in 1967 Lynn White, a science historian, published "Historical Roots of Our Ecological Crisis," in which he made an influential case for that position. White contends that "Christianity is the most anthropocentric religion the world has seen." God made man in his image and gave human beings dominion over the animals and told them to subdue the earth. "Christianity, in absolute contrast to ancient paganism and Asia's religions (except, perhaps, Zoroastrianism), not only established a dualism of man and nature but also insisted that it is God's will that man exploit nature for his proper ends." Genesis inculcated an "exploitative mentality" by its command to subdue or master the earth and "exercise dominion over every living thing," and thus ensured devastation to the environment.

In addition, Christianity actually gave birth to modern science and technology by its teaching about man's transcendence and mastery over nature. Joined together, science and technology, argues White, "give mankind powers which, to judge by many of the ecological effects, are out of control. If so, Christianity bears a huge burden of guilt."[42]

Catholic Approaches to Sustaining the Environment

In a remarkable essay on Christianity and the environment Ernest Fortin draws attention to "the Bible's profound admiration for the splendor and orderliness of nature."

Psalm 8 speaks of the heavens not simply as the work of God's hands but as the work of his "fingers," thereby stressing its surpassing delicacy. Psalm 100 dwells on the solicitude of a loving God who looks after all his creatures, both human and subhuman, providing for each its shelter and its food in due season; trees for birds to nest in, high mountains for wild goats, rocks as a refuge for badgers, bread to strengthen our hearts and wine to gladden them.[43]

The Bible encourages people to admire God's handiwork and to be good stewards of what has been entrusted to them. While vacationing in the mountains of the Aosta Valley Pope Benedict XVI said, "Driven by the

42. Lynn White, "Historical Roots of our Ecological Crisis," *Science* 155 (1967): 1203–07.
43. Ernest L. Fortin, *Human Rights, Virtue, and the Common Good: Untimely Meditations on Religion and Politics*, vol. 3 of *Collected Essays*, edited by J. Brian Benestad (Lanham, Md.: Rowman and Littlefield, 1996), 114.

heartfelt need for meaning that urges them onwards, people perceive the mark of goodness, of beauty and of divine Providence in the world that surrounds them and open themselves almost spontaneously to praise and prayer."[44] The reference to Providence refers to the way God makes the earth provide for the needs of his creatures. The perception of goodness, beauty, and Providence should engender a profound attitude of respect toward the environment.

We show our gratitude to God for the gift of the earth by admiring his creation and by exercising a prudent stewardship. That means that the Bible surely supports the reasonable demands of the environmental movement. Fortin even discerns a profound reason that human beings must take care of the earth. Because the Bible urges respect for life and forbids the unjust taking of anyone's life "it follows that they are not to destroy or inflict unnecessary damage on the physical environment needed to sustain life."[45] Love of life should translate into respect and care for the environment. Pope John Paul II stresses the obligation of all to observe the moral laws governing our relation with the environment. In *Evangelium vitae (The Gospel of Life)* he quotes what he said in *Sollicitudo rei socialis (On Social Concern)* on the subject: "when it comes to the natural world, we are subject not only to biological laws but also to moral ones, which cannot be violated with impunity."[46]

Despite the obvious links between personal immorality and damage to the environment, questions about the disorder in people's souls are not raised very often. There is a great reluctance to say that a person's use of his freedom is just wrong. While a cardinal, Joseph Ratzinger addressed this problem in his second book-length interview, *Salt of the Earth*. He said,

[T]he pollution of the outward environment that we are witnessing is only the mirror and the consequence of the pollution of the inward environment, to which we pay too little heed. I think this is also the defect of the ecological movements. They crusade with an understandable passion against the pollution of the environment, whereas man's self pollution of his soul continues to be treated as one of the rights of his freedom.[47]

---

44. Pope Benedict XVI, *Angelus*, July 17, 2005.

45. Fortin, *Human Rights, Virtue, and the Common Good*, 114.

46. Pope John Paul II, *Sollicitudo rei socialis (On Social Concern)*, no. 34.

47. Joseph Cardinal Ratzinger, *Salt of the Earth: The Church at the End of the Millennium, an Interview with Peter Seewald* (San Francisco: Ignatius Press, 1997), 230–31.

Cardinal Ratzinger implies that the defense of the continuous misuse of freedom is a serious obstacle to addressing the very real environmental problems.

The solution to environmental problems is not to make ecology a kind of religion, but to inculcate the kind of attitude toward the natural world recommended in the Bible and to link the concepts of freedom and truth. If the freedom of individuals, businesses, associations, and government is not guided by a public morality, grounded in truth, there will be no real solution either to the pollution of the environment or to the exhaustion of limited natural resources. If the freedom to pursue comfort, health, and safety is without significant moral limits, then people will not have any scruples about damaging the environment in the pursuit of their desires.

Summary of Catholic Teaching on
Sustaining the Environment

The summary of Catholic social teaching on the environment in the *Compendium of the Social Doctrine of the Church* is very brief and remains on a general level. Nevertheless, what is said provides valuable guidance for Catholics and reveals some of the disagreements with neo-Malthusian perspectives.

Quoting Pope John Paul II, the *Compendium* says, "'it is the relationship man has with God that determines his relationship with his fellow human beings and with his environment.'"[48] With a right relationship with God, persons love one another, are grateful for the gift of creation, and exercise stewardship over the environment. This stewardship avoids two extremes: the unconditional domination and manipulation of nature and the worship of nature. *"A correct understanding of the environment prevents the utilitarian reduction of nature to a mere object to be manipulated and exploited. At the same time, a correct understanding does not absolutize nature and place it higher in dignity than the human person."*[49] Moral considerations always govern man's relationship to the environment. The *Compendium* also notes that the reconciliation of human beings and the world with God is brought about by the death and resurrection of Jesus Christ. *"The whole of creation participates in the renewal flowing from the Lord's Paschal Mystery,* although it still awaits full liberation from corruption."[50] In other words, the sins of men and women can have

48. *Compendium*, no. 464, quoting John Paul II, "Address to Participants in a Convention on 'The Environment and Health'" (March 24, 1997), 5.

49. *Compendium*, no. 463.   50. Ibid., no. 455.

a negative effect on the environment. For example, the immoderate love of gain could induce individuals to be heedless of the damage their work could cause to the environment. Without giving examples, the *Compendium* also says that people's sins have brought corruption and disorder into the work of creation. Perhaps it is implying that such things as famines and hurricanes are ultimately the result of human sins.

To address environmental problems the international community and individual states must use juridical means to regulate the production of goods and to protect ecosystems. Legislation, of course, is not sufficient. It must be accompanied by positive changes in the way people think and act on their own. *"Serious ecological problems call for an effective change of mentality leading to the adoption of new lifestyles,* 'in which the quest for truth, beauty, goodness and communion with others for the sake of the common good are the factors that determine consumer choices, savings and investments.'"[51] In other words, there is no effective solution to environmental degradation unless individuals practice virtue in their daily lives, a theme of our earlier chapters.

The *Compendium* makes a point of stressing that the Church doesn't have a quarrel with science and technology per se, because they can help in the work to promote the development of peoples and to overcome disease and hunger. The Church will only raise objections to their immoral use.

With respect to global warming and climate change, the *Compendium* doesn't endorse a particular position, since any endorsement depends on the perception of the facts, about which there is some dispute. It simply reminds producers and consumers "to develop a greater sense of responsibility for their behavior."[52] When the U.S. bishops addressed the subject of global climate change in 2001 they also made a point of directing people's attention to the needs of the people in the developing nations. They said, "Action to mitigate global climate change must be built upon a foundation of social and economic justice that does not put the poor at risk or place disproportionate and unfair burdens on developing nations."[53] In other words, they are implying that there is no way to

51. Ibid., no. 486, quoting John Paul II, *Centesimus annus (On the Hundredth Anniversary of Rerum novarum)*, no. 36.

52. *Compendium*, no. 470.

53. National Conference of Catholic Bishops/United States Catholic Conference, *Global Climate Change: A Plan for Dialogue, Prudence, and the Common Good* (Washington, D.C.: United States Conference of Catholic Bishops, 2001); see http://www.nccbuscc.org/sdwp/international/globalclimate.shtml.

cut drastically the use of fossil fuels without causing immense economic problems. When nations take steps to address global warming, they must be attentive to the trade-offs.

The developing nations are blamed for the level and growth of their population, while the developed nations are responsible for most of the greenhouse gas emissions. "Affluent nations such as our own have to acknowledge the impact of voracious consumerism instead of simply calling for population and emissions control from people in poorer nations."[54] What the developing nations need is economic development and widespread education rather than coercive population control. "We should promote a respect for nature," according to the bishops, "that encourages policies fostering natural family planning and the education of women and men rather than coercive measures of population control or government incentives for birth control that violate local cultural and religious norms."[55] It may seem out of place for the bishops to discuss population control in their statement on climate change, but they believe this discussion is wholly appropriate, because the neo-Malthusian sustainability advocates regularly call for population control as an effective way to address global warming. As we have seen, the neo-Malthusians reason that fewer people mean fewer greenhouse gases in the atmosphere. The bishops argue that self-restraint, a spirit of sacrifice, and a sense of stewardship by people in the developed nations could really help mitigate the effects of global warming brought about by man-made CO_2. They reason that less consumption means fewer greenhouse gases.

The *Compendium* does take a rather specific position on the economy as a whole as a way to safeguard the environment.

An economy respectful of the environment will not have the maximization of profits as its only objective, because environmental protection cannot be assured solely on the basis of financial calculations of costs and benefits.... Seeking innovative ways to reduce the environmental impact of production and consumption of goods should be effectively encouraged.[56]

In other words, the bottom line cannot be the final consideration of individuals and businesses. While producing and consuming, businesses and individuals must take into account the common good, of which a sustainable environment is an integral part.

54. Ibid. 55. Ibid.
56. *Compendium*, no. 470.

Let us now turn to some specific themes in Catholic social doctrine that both put some flesh on the bare bones of the *Compendium* on the environment and respond to some of the positions taken by the neo-Malthusians.

Stewardship, Solidarity, and Sin

Edward Wilson, professor emeritus of biology at Harvard University and self-described secular humanist, believes that the Christian teaching on stewardship is solidly based and could be very useful to the secular environmental movement. That is why he wrote an open letter to an imagined Southern Baptist pastor soliciting his help, conceding that "environmental activists cannot succeed without you and your followers as allies."[57] There just aren't enough activists. So, Wilson concludes, "Those who for religious reasons, believe in saving Creation, have the strength to do so through the political process; acting alone secular environmentalists do not. An alliance between science and religion in an atmosphere of mutual respect, may be the only way to protect life on earth."[58] Wilson is writing because he believes that some pastors are not motivating their flock to exercise stewardship over the environment.

While Lynn White argues that Christianity is responsible for damage to the environment, Christian teaching holds that every Christian has a serious obligation to exercise stewardship over the environment. The biblical command to "subdue the earth" and "exercise dominion over every living thing" is not an invitation to wreck ecological damage, but rather a command to exercise stewardship over God's gifts. When the Bible uses the words "mastery" or "dominion" "it is always in its primary sense, the *dominus* or master being the one who rules his subordinates for the good of the whole rather than for his own private good."[59] This means that Christians must use the earth in such a way as to avoid waste and damage. They should always endeavor to preserve the commons in the measure possible.

White also errs not only in thinking that Genesis gave human beings carte blanche in their dealings with the environment, but also in ascribing the origin of modern science to Christianity. Francis Bacon clearly

---

57. Edward O. Wilson, "Apocalypse Now," *The New Republic* 235, no. 4781 (2006): 18.

58. Ibid.

59. Ernest Fortin, "The Bible Made Me Do It: Christianity, Science and the Environment," in *Human Rights, Virtue and the Common Good*, 124.

explains that modern science, without Christian influence, arose as an alternative to ancient science. The aim of modern science is not to contemplate nature, but to perform experiments on it in order to acquire the kind of knowledge that would lead to the relief of man's estate. In other words, scientists aim to become "masters and possessors" of nature in view of providing longer life, health, comfort, and prosperity to humanity. "The Moderns, not Ancients," explains Ernest Fortin, "are the ones who put nature on the rack and thereby set up an adversarial relationship between the investigator and the object of his investigation."[60] Pope Benedict notes that the benefits provided by modern science eventually gave rise to "*faith in progress*," replacing faith in Jesus Christ as the way to recover what was lost by man's sin in Paradise.[61] Nevertheless, the Church supports modern science because of the benefits it provides, as long as it doesn't contradict moral principles, as it does, for example, when scientists extract stem cells from embryos, thereby killing them.

In his 1990 World Day of Peace Message Pope John Paul II elaborated on the Christian explanation for ecological damage. The sin of Adam and Eve not only alienates them from God, but also subjects all human beings to alienation from one another and from the earth itself. "When man turns his back on the Creator's plan," writes John Paul II, "he provokes a disorder which has inevitable repercussions on the rest of the created order. If man is not at peace with God, then earth itself cannot be at peace." John Paul II supports this theological interpretation of environmental problems with an appeal to scripture. Because of the evil people do, Hosea says "'Therefore the land mourns and all who dwell in it languish, and also the beasts of the field and birds of the air and even the fish of the sea are taken away'" (Hos 4:3).[62]

Some damage to the environment is not due to sin or the disorder in people's souls, but to harsh necessity. Sometimes the poor in the developing nations are, in fact, coerced by circumstances to exhaust the capacity of the soil or to clear away forests in order to create more arable land. That is why the fight against worldwide poverty is an important part of the effort to save the environment, and thus an aspect of steward-

---

60. Ibid.

61. Benedict XVI, *Spe salvi (On Christian Hope)*, no. 17.

62. World Day of Peace Message, *Peace with God the Creator, Peace with All of Creation*, no. 5 (January 1, 1990); see http://www.vatican.va; go to Papal Archives, Pope John Paul II, messages and then World Day of Peace.

ship, broadly understood. Consequently, Pope John Paul II points out the Christian conviction that "the ecological crisis reveals the *urgent moral need for a new solidarity,* especially in relations between the developing nations and those that are highly industrialized."[63] With respect to the poor this means that individuals, churches, intermediary groups, NGOs, and governments must find ways to mitigate poverty to the extent possible. Such action is an aspect of solidarity because it serves the common good.

Other ways the well-off people in the industrialized world can contribute to the common good are by personally moderating their consumption. "Simplicity, moderation and discipline, as well as a spirit of sacrifice must become part of everyday life," Pope John Paul II argues.[64] The emphasis on these virtues has been a constant theme of the Church since the very beginning of Christianity because of their beneficent influence on the whole person. Now they happen to qualify as green measures, since they benefit the environment.

A whole series of agents play a role in educating citizens to be good stewards by taking responsibility for the maintenance of the environment: the family, churches, schools, NGOs, governmental organizations, and society as a whole. They, of course, will deliver different kinds of education. Churches emphasize how love of God and neighbor requires care for the environment. Governments educate citizens through legislation and tax incentives. Primary and secondary schools could make students aware of environmental problems, while universities could investigate their causes and proposed solutions. One of the fine contributions Catholic universities could make is to show that the accurate description of problems and their solutions depend upon a number of agents and factors that are not usually mentioned in the sustainability movement, such as the family, character formation, a moderate way of life, freedom from ideological prepossession, respect for life, rejection of abortion, euthanasia, and contraception, and an aesthetic appreciation of nature. About the last John Paul II says that "our very contact with nature has a deep restorative power [and] the contemplation of the magnificence of nature imparts peace and serenity.... The relationship between a good aesthetic education and the maintenance of a healthy environment cannot be overlooked."[65]

63. Ibid., no. 10.

64. Ibid., no. 13. By solidarity the former pontiff means a *"firm and persevering determination* to commit oneself to the *common good"* (*Sollicitudo rei socialis,* no. 38).

65. Ibid., no. 14.

On the Importance of the Family and
Education for Sustainability

The education to respect nature and the environment and to love one's neighbor takes place primarily in the family. Growing up in New York City during the 1950s, I was exposed to the Catholic culture generally informing the family life of typical Catholics. My schoolmates and I learned at home not to waste food and never to litter, even before there were fines for doing the latter. These habits were so ingrained in many Catholics that even if they were to abandon their faith, many probably would not throw litter out of a car window. The willingness and effort to love one's neighbor intelligently moves Christians not to do damage to the commons.

The Catholic economist Maria Sophia Aguirre has made the case that as the family goes, so go the economy and the environment. She relies on a number of studies to argue that the family is best at developing human, social, and moral capital. By human capital economists mean all those skills that enable workers to participate in the economic life of their country. By social capital they mean those qualities that enable workers to cooperate among themselves. Moral capital is a term used by economists to refer to the qualities that make for a good character. The family prepares and motivates children to receive the education outside the home that they need to participate in their economic and social life. Children from healthy families do much better in school than those children from dysfunctional families. The development of moral and social capital depends initially and most importantly on the family, without which schools and churches will not be able to do much in most cases. In short, a healthy family is the place where human beings develop physically, emotionally, intellectually, and spiritually.

Aguirre also notes that family life encourages moderation in the consumption of resources and goods. "What moderation would there be in consumption and spending if there were no family?"[66] The love of one's own can induce people to make sacrifices that they might not be willing to make otherwise. Not many people will moderate their consumption, for example, if they are told that limiting their use of energy is necessary to slow down global warming. If Aguirre is right about the voluntary

66. Maria Sophia Aguirre, "The Family and Economic Development: Socioeconomic Relevance and Policy Design," paper delivered at Doha Conference Preparatory Sessions in Geneva, Switzerland, August 23–25, 2004: 4; see http://faculty.cua.edu/aguirre.

moderation induced by good family life, then she has found the solution to the problem with which the neo-Malthusians struggle. They desperately and urgently call for moderate consumption but, as we have seen, their leaders rule out the appeal to conscience and rely only on enlightened self-interest or coercion to motivate people. (I am sure that some neo-Malthusians break ranks and turn to conscience in their work.)

When families sit down together to have a meal, the conversation of children with their parents builds a stronger relationship. Empirical evidence suggests, argues Aguirre, that everything pertaining to the total development of children goes better when there are family dinners and worse without them. The evidence reveals that poor relations between children and parents cause a decline not only in the physical and psychological health of children, but also in their academic performance and in their ability to get along with their peers. Watching many hours of TV is a significant factor in causing obesity in both children and adolescents, which then further contributes to poor academic performance and increases the cost of health care.[67] If Aguirre is right, then you can say that sustainable economic growth really depends on family dinners, because so many good things necessarily accompany those dinners. In Aguirre's words, "Frequent family meals enhance human, moral, and social capital, the existence of which are necessary conditions for sustainable economic growth."[68]

Because the family is so important in preparing the young for education, and, thus, for developing an economy, Aguirre wants government and society to do what they can to meet the needs of families.[69] Whether the economy aids the family, will, of course, depend on what government and society do. For example, businesses in society may or may not make it easier for mothers and fathers both to work for them and raise children.

Aguirre also holds the unconventional view that an economy cannot run well for the long term simply on self-interest. "An economy that is based exclusively on profit and selfish individualism could be successful for a period of time, but it would not last (among other things because it will not produce enough population without which, no economy is possible)."[70] Aguirre implies that selfish individualists will bring few or no

67. Aguirre, "Family Dining, Diet and Food Distribution: Planting the Seeds of Economic Growth," paper presented at "Excellence in the Home," 2006 Conference, London, May 8–9, 2006, 12–13.
68. Ibid., 18.   69. Ibid., 7.
70. Ibid.

children into the world. Her implicit assumption is, of course, that with too few people no economy can thrive.

On the Role of Conscience

Aguirre's reflections on character formation in the family strongly confirm that conscience has an important role to play in the quest for sustainability. One way to see quickly the importance of conscience is to take another look at Joseph Cardinal Ratzinger's oft-reprinted essay on "Conscience and Truth,"[71] which is a challenge to Garrett Hardin's contention that a person is a fool to act on conscience when others don't.

In Cardinal Ratzinger's perspective, if conscience enables people to act in accord with truth or the way things are, it makes no sense to follow Hardin's advice. Why should anyone do evil or follow an erroneous path because other people decide to hurt themselves and others by their neglect of conscience? To live according to human dignity requires people to form their conscience and to act in accordance with it. Not to do so is to act beneath human dignity.

The *Catechism of the Catholic Church* confirms Cardinal Ratzinger's perspective. It says, "Conscience is a judgment of reason whereby the human person recognizes the moral quality of a concrete act that he is going to perform, is in the process of performing, or has already completed."[72] The judgment of a well-formed conscience puts people in contact with the way things are, and thus enables them to distinguish good from evil. Without conscience people cannot be at peace with God, with their fellow human beings, or with the environment.

Population Control through the Imposition of Condoms

Catholic teaching is open to the regulation of births, but not by immoral means such as contraception and sterilization. The Catholic Church is especially opposed to the imposition of contraception on individuals or on a whole nation. To appreciate why the Church finds imposed contraception so abhorrent, I would like to turn to an essay written on events in Uganda.

In "AIDS, Condomization, and Christian Ethics," Emmanuel Ka-

71. See Joseph Ratzinger, "Conscience and Truth," in *Crisis of Conscience*, edited by John M. Haas (New York: Crossroad, 1996), 1–20; this essay was originally published in *Catholic Conscience: Foundation and Formation: Proceedings of the Tenth Bishops' Workshop*, ed. Russell Smith (Braintree, Mass.: Pope John Center, 1991).
72. *Catechism of the Catholic Church*, no. 1778.

tongole discusses the emphasis in the West on condoms to fight AIDS. Fr. Katongole is an African priest from the archdiocese of Kampala in Uganda and professor in the Divinity School at Duke University. Professor Katongole prefaces his remarks with an observation on the UN Cairo conference of 1994. He says that Africans reacted negatively to the Western position that the growing population of Africa was the main reason for the poverty of African and other Third World nations. Katongole judged that "a number of Africans rightly suspected that the conference was an attempt by the West to avoid confronting issues of economic justice in a global economy unfairly skewed to the advantage of the North."[73]

The enthusiasm for condoms and their use, argues Professor Katongole, has become a cultural symbol of postmodern Africa. To make his point he describes the changing face of billboards in Uganda. In the mid-1980s the billboards said, "Love Faithfully. Avoid AIDS." In the early 1990s it was "Love Carefully" and then in the mid-1990s "Use a Condom to Avoid AIDS." Love disappears and protection is everything; "the other is a potential danger against whom you need protection."[74] The two later advertisements, of course, reflect the view that people in an intimate sexual relationship cannot really trust one another. Life-long commitment to one's partner is not regarded as a live option. All there seems to be is mutual use of one another and mutual defensiveness. "Viewed in this manner, the 'protector' condom is both an expression and a way of managing the radical suspicion that has already inserted itself at the core of this most intimate of human relationships."[75] Katongole believes that not trusting anyone will eventually lead Africans to be self-destructive. "One who is unwilling to trust anyone sooner or later discovers that one cannot even trust oneself."[76]

As many have noticed, the Western nations have expressed their impatience with African countries for not more aggressively promoting the condomization of the populace. Many Westerners just regard closing the condom gap as the best technical solution to the AIDS problem, which is ravaging many African countries. If African leaders were to criticize condomization as cultural imperialism or a deepening of Africa's problems, the reaction would be one of incredulity. How could the slowing

73. Emmanuel M. Katongole, *A Future for Africa: Critical Essays in Christian Social Imagination* (Scranton, Penn.: University of Scranton Press, 2005), 38.

74. Ibid., 41.   75. Ibid.

76. Ibid.

down of HIV infection through the use of condoms not be a wonderful idea? Professor Katongole attempts to provide an answer in the remaining parts of his essay. He first notes that the prevalence of AIDS is intimately linked to the other major problems of African nations: poverty, corrupt governments, insufficient employment, malnutrition, widespread diseases, and a general lack of hope. In the midst of their deprivation and loss of hope a number of Africans will gravitate toward sex as a pleasurable activity in the midst of so many woes. The condom becomes a means to that end, but also a symbol of the despair and nihilism gripping the population. The condom facilitates playful or debonair nihilism. With the condom people can mutually use one another sexually, dispose of the condom, and then dispose of one another. Professor Katongole explains, "For disposability, not simply of goods, but of relationships and particular attachments of any kind, seems to be the hallmark of postmodern society."[77] Condomization is really about popularizing a form of sexual activity that has nothing to do with an irrevocable commitment to another person. As one Ugandan condom commercial says, "this feels so good!" Professor Katongole comments, "While it is one thing to live in a world where there are no serious or stable commitments and where relationships and partners are disposable, to think that this is a good thing too (one that feels so good) is the ultimate sign of despair."[78] Katongole doesn't enter into the argument of whether the use of condoms will effectively prevent the transmission of HIV/AIDS, the only concern of the West. He fears that the focus on condomization will further undermine the Africans' sense of their dignity as human beings and promote shallow and even destructive human relationships. Katongole is really implying that the loss of human dignity is worse than the loss of health.

Condomization cannot save Africa, argues Professor Katongole. It is a path of despair and cynicism, encouraging people to use one another and to avoid making commitments in a stable marriage.[79] Katongole recommends the practice of the Christian faith as the best way to address the despair threatening Africans because of their serious problems. It is the Eucharist that can give Africans a renewed sense of their own dignity and the possibility of genuine love between human beings.

During Pope Benedict's flight to Africa in March of 2009 a journalist reiterated a common complaint against the Church's position on AIDS:

77. Ibid., 43.   78. Ibid.
79. Ibid., 45.

it is "not realistic and not efficacious." The pope responded, "I would say that the problem of AIDS cannot be overcome with advertising slogans. If the soul is lacking, if Africans do not help one another, the scourge cannot be resolved by distributing condoms; quite the contrary, we risk worsening the problem." Pope Benedict proposed, instead, a twofold solution: "the humanization of sexuality" so that people treat each other with respect and "friendship" with those suffering from the AIDS virus, including a willingness to make personal sacrifices on their behalf. The reaction to this statement was swift, intense, and intolerant. The governments of Belgium, France, and Germany, as well as the *New York Times*, the *Washington Post*, the World Health Organization, and the British medical journal *Lancet* all expressed their utter dismay and scorn for the pope's remarks.

Support for the pope's statement came from a seemingly unlikely source: the Center for Population and Development Studies at Harvard University. The Center's Edward C. Green, the director of the AIDS Prevention Research Project, said about condom use in Africa, "We have found no consistent associations between condom use and lower HIV-infection rates, which 25 years into the pandemic, we should be seeing if this intervention was working." In fact, Green argues that the best studies indicate an association "between greater availability and use of condoms and higher (not lower) HIV-infection rates."[80] These studies also show that the reduction of multiple and concurrent sexual partners is the most effective way to reduce the infection rate. Green believes that condoms may not be as effective as people expect, because condom users are prone to take risks, believing they are protected.[81]

Another way to appreciate the wisdom of the pope's remarks is to reflect on the alternatives of an HIV-infected husband who has no moral objections to the use of condoms. The most reasonable and loving thing to do would be to avoid conjugal relations with his wife in order to protect her from any chance of infection. Abstinence, not condoms, offers 100 percent protection against infection by HIV.

Pope Benedict's reasonable comments on condoms were not only roundly dismissed as wrongheaded and even immoral, but also con-

<hr />

80. Edward C. Green, Interview by Kathryn Jean Lopez, March 19, 2009, National Review Online; see http://article.nationalreview.com/388934/from-saint-peters-square -to-har. Green's testimony is particularly interesting because he is not against the use of condoms. He even believes that condoms have worked in the brothels of Thailand and Cambodia, but definitely not in Africa.

81. See Green's "The Pope May Be Right," *Washington Post* (March 29, 2009), A15.

demned as an improper papal interference in the culture and politics of the world's nations. In other words, governments and NGOs are attempting to inhibit the religious freedom of the pope and the Catholic Church. They want to suppress the input of Catholics on matters pertaining to the common good of nations. Unfortunately, this is a trend that has been developing for some time now. Recently, even some Catholics are joining the secular movement to keep the Church out of the public square, on the grounds that anything less is both a violation of the separation of the church from the state and a distortion of genuine religion, which is falsely understood as a wholly private affair.

Concluding Remarks

Catholic social teaching on the environment is in tension with some of the key principles of the neo-Malthusian sustainability advocates. They have raised interesting questions, but have provided too many wrong answers. The evidence seems to indicate that in many countries the fertility rate needs to increase, not decrease, especially in Europe. The history of the United States shows that population growth and high fertility rates do not necessarily cause poverty, deplete resources, or destabilize governments. Bringing about a reduction of the population through coerced contraception, sterilization, or abortion is a blow to human dignity.

While the Catholic Church has a clear position on condoms and contraception, it does not have a teaching on the ideal number of people in the world or in a particular nation. Its teaching on justice would imply that nations should at least strive to have as many people as necessary for its well-being. Since there will necessarily be disagreements among citizens about the ideal number of people in their country, Catholics should examine the evidence proposed by reliable demographers and then make a prudent judgment based on the evidence.

The explicit or implicit embrace of voluntary abortion is not only a violation of the equality liberal democracies are designed to protect, but also an intrinsic evil. Rejecting any appeal to conscience and dismissing the Christian tradition as an obstacle to a sustainable environment are suicidal, as Edward Wilson implies in his open letter to the imagined Southern Baptist pastor. Indifference or antagonism toward religion and the neglect of the character formation of children within the family are a rejection of the most important civilizing influences in the lives of a nation's citizens.

The neo-Malthusians need to ask themselves again whether it can be morally justified to promote their cause through coercive contraception, coercive abortion, infanticide in China, euthanasia, and the destruction of embryos in the search for disease cures. While only a few of the neo-Malthusians trumpet their support of these practices, none seem to raise any objections to them. They seem to know that publicly embracing these positions will not increase their chances of converting people to their cause. The more ideologically driven among them, like Hardin and Ehrlich, don't hesitate to express their belief in coercion. Others, when pressed on their opinion of various kinds of coercion, would most likely say that one way or another, the population has to be reduced. The implications of this somewhat vague response are acceptance of some kind of coercive contraception through various kinds of incentives, continued support for the right to abortion, and even unreasonable limits on immigration.

It is unlikely that a democratic majority in the United States will agree to submit to coercion in the area of "reproductive rights," as desired by Hardin, Ehrlich, and their disciples. Americans like their freedom too much at the present time to impose compulsory sterilization or mandatory abortion on themselves after a couple has one child. American society would take a gigantic step toward despotism by accepting compulsion in the area of contraception. The latter would be foreign to the tradition of liberty in America and to the teachings of the Judeo-Christian tradition, but, alas, could perhaps be made more palatable for a future generation by financial incentives. Some Americans, foundations, and international NGOs, unfortunately, do support coercive reproductive policies for the less-developed nations. This is an authoritarian violation of human rights, smacking of eugenicism, unworthy of a people in the developed nations, who claim to respect freedom and equality.

There is nothing in neo-Malthusian thought that would lead them not to support the right to voluntary abortion. It is simply a part of their general orientation. In their minds, support of abortion is just a way to exercise responsibility toward the environment and to live in the light of the earth's limited resources. In fact, they seem more interested in abortion as a form of population control than as a way to empower women, which is uppermost in the minds of feminists and defenders of individual autonomy. So the right to abortion is a means to an end, and not an end in itself for the neo-Malthusians. They don't have much regard for freedom when it gets in the way of their two principal goals: population control and reduction of consumption.

Scarcity of most natural resources is not yet a problem, but could conceivably become one if people's ingenuity can't come up with alternatives to a dwindling supply of a resource—such as oil—as it has so many times in the past. Global warming merits an unbiased attention to the ascertainable scientific facts, but doesn't call for hysteria. Finding a way to be more efficient in the use of energy in our production and consumption makes sense from every point of view. Becoming less dependent on fossil fuels, especially oil in the Middle East, by developing alternative sources of energy would significantly contribute to the independence of the United States.

The call for moderation of consumption is probably the best idea of the neo-Malthusians, but they have no idea how to persuade Americans to accept this self-restraint. In fact, the whole sustainability movement seems to be at a loss as to how to reduce consumption other than to say that it is in our self-interest to do so, and that government should give people incentives to cut back. This is not surprising when Christianity has trouble convincing people to moderate their love of money and material goods. Missing from the statements of the sustainability advocates is the recognition that persuading people to reduce their consumption on a wide scale is a daunting enterprise, especially because of the widespread loss of deep spiritual convictions in the body politic. Without family or religious reasons the vast majority of people will not limit their consumption.

Neo-Malthusian advocacy, it is important to note, has become more or less an ersatz religion. These radical environmentalists look at those who disagree with their environmental strategies as heretics. When people make a kind of religion out of the quest for sustainability, they ascribe religious certitude to convictions that should be open to change or modification if new evidence surfaces or if the situation changes. For example, the decline of the birth rate in Europe is so steep that an unbiased look at the situation would cause a person to recognize that Europe has a serious problem. Such a realization has not yet occurred to any prominent neo-Malthusian, despite the fact that the evidence of a birth dearth in Europe is overwhelming. For example, European governments are giving financial incentives to women in order to induce them to have children. France has offered women $960 per month for a year if they will have a third child. Austria has offered their women "450 Euros a month for three years for a first birth." In Italy the Prodi government has established a Ministry of Family to address the low birth rate.[82]

82. Elisabeth Rosenthal, "Europe, East and West wrestles with falling birth rates," *International Herald Tribune* (September 3, 2006), 4.

The objectivity of the science upon which the neo-Malthusians rely needs to be examined very carefully. Nearly everyone knows that the scholarship of university humanities departments is not always disinterested. Less well known is the bias and political correctness sometimes involved in scientific research. My colleagues in the science departments tell me that research purporting to show that human beings are making a significant contribution to global warming is much more likely to be funded than research that shows that the anthropogenic factor is more modest. Writing in *Commentary*, Kevin Shapiro says, "Scientists skeptical of the importance of anthropogenic warming have testified that it is difficult to publish their work in prestigious journals; when they do publish, their articles are almost always accompanied by rebuttals."[83] So, the subjects of scientific investigation, and sometimes the results, are affected by the political climate.

The interest in sustainability gives us the opportunity to think about everything that contributes to a sustainable community as a whole or a sustainable democratic polity: genuine faith and rightly formed conscience, shared ethical principles, good character in individuals, the moderation of consumption for the sake of one's soul and the common good, ethical and competent government, good culture, intact marriages, healthy families, education for all, the protection of civil rights and liberties, good health and health care, work to eliminate poverty, opportunities for employment, sound industry and agriculture, social security, safety nets, a reliance on the spiritual wisdom of cultures, and the promotion of justice. In drawing attention to the above-mentioned themes, I am contending that, according to Catholic social doctrine, the present sustainability movement is too narrowly conceived. The movement must address such themes in a sensible way if it hopes to be successful.

83. Shapiro, "Global Warming: Apocalypse Now?": 146.

PART 4

The International Community and Justice

CHAPTER 11

The International Community

A chapter on the international community is a near-impossible task. There are so many topics and such limited space. In order to facilitate my task I will put off the subject of just war principles until chapter 12. This present chapter will focus on the fundamental principles that should animate the international community. It will begin with a selective summary of Pope John Paul II's subtle address to the United Nations on October 5, 1995 (already partially treated in chapter 2 to explain the meaning of the common good). The second section will explore what the *Compendium of the Social Doctrine of the Church* (2004) says about the international community. The chapter will then explain carefully Pope Benedict XVI's address to the United Nations delivered on April 18, 2008, and then turn to Mary Ann Glendon's explanation of the Universal Declaration of Human Rights (1948), about which Pope Benedict had important things to say in his UN address. Finally, I will recount what the Holy See said at the international conference on women in Beijing sponsored by the United Nations (1995). This section will show how Catholics put Catholic social teaching into practice in the international arena. My appendix on Pope Benedict's third encyclical, *Caritas in veritate* (*On Integral Development in Charity and Truth*), will present the pope's comprehensive vision of integral development and the means that would have to be adopted to make it more of a reality throughout the world. These varied sources, taken together, reveal the main points of Catholic social doctrine as it relates to the international community.

Pope John Paul II at the United Nations—October 5, 1995

Pope John Paul II begins his speech, as mentioned in chapter 1, by referring to the UN's Universal Declaration of Human Rights as "one of the highest expressions of the human conscience of our time" (no. 2).[1]

---

1. Pope John Paul II's UN address is available online at the Vatican website under the category of speeches in 1995; see http://www.vatican.va.

The reason for this high praise is that the nations of the world can and do appeal to the Declaration as a kind of universal public morality, both a standard accepted by the member nations of the UN in 1948 and a goal to be achieved. Cardinal Dulles points out that the "principles of the Declaration have been built into many international treaties and into new constitutions of states in Africa, Asia, Latin America and Europe. Its influence was crucial in the peaceful elimination of apartheid in South Africa."[2] The Jesuit cardinal also notes, however, that the implementation of the Declaration has by no means been achieved throughout the world, as is shown by the incidence of repression, torture, and genocide in various states.

It is, of course, obvious to many that the Declaration is violated in countries throughout the world. Much less well known is its insufficient philosophical foundation. In his address to the Diplomatic Corps in January of 1989, the pope drew people's attention to this fact: "[T]he 1948 Declaration does not contain the anthropological and moral bases of human rights that it proclaims." Of course, the basis of rights in the Declaration is dignity, but the exact content of dignity and its foundation are not addressed by the Declaration's framers. Without a solid philosophical foundation, dignity and rights are subject to erosion and rejection. Some contemporary scholars today scoff at the concept of dignity as hollow, useless, and stupid. Mary Ann Glendon says, "The human rights project will rest on shaky foundations unless and until philosophers and statespersons collaborate on the business that the [Declaration's] framers left unfinished."[3]

Aware of the lacuna in the Declaration, Pope John Paul II looks to the Catholic intellectual tradition for help. Expanding upon the teaching of the Declaration, John Paul II says that there is a universal moral law written in the heart of every individual, which is the foundation for dignity, rights, and duties (nothing resembling this statement is found in the Universal Declaration). You could then say that rights are rooted in the nature of the human person, a nature shared by all people who have ever lived. Recognizing a shared human nature and human rights for all is the basis for what the pontiff calls the "international politics of persuasion"

2. Avery Cardinal Dulles, *Human Rights: The United Nations and Papal Teaching* (New York: Fordham University Press, 1998), 11.

3. Mary Ann Glendon, *Traditions in Turmoil* (Ann Arbor, Mich.: Sapientia Press, 2006), 337.

(no. 3). Without this shared recognition, there is no basis for persuasion in the international arena. In short, John Paul II is appealing to natural law—though the term itself is never mentioned—as the foundation for dignity, duties, and rights. The pope is implicitly inviting thoughtful people to take another look at the natural law as an important resource for the international community.

John Paul II goes on to discuss the universal aspiration for freedom in the individuals and nations of the world. The events of 1989, by which the nations of Eastern Europe achieved their liberation without violence, were a sign that *"the quest for freedom cannot be suppressed. It arises from a recognition of the inestimable dignity and value of the human person"* (no. 4). While World War II was fought and the United Nations founded to protect the rights of nations, their violation, nevertheless, took place immediately after the war, when the Soviet Union enslaved so many nations. John Paul II was especially sensitive to these events because the nation of Poland also lost its freedom. The pope thinks the nation (the word is derived from the Latin *nasci*, meaning to be born) is an extremely important community because it bears the culture of its people. That culture is so precious because, as in the case of Poland, it not only "enables a nation to survive the loss of political and economic independence" (no. 8), but also enables a people to live on a high level. John Paul II explains,

For different cultures are but different ways of facing the question of the meaning of personal existence. And it is precisely here that we find one source of the respect which is due to every culture and every nation: *every culture is an effort to ponder the mystery of the world and in particular of the human person: it is a way of giving expression to the transcendent dimension of human life.* The heart of every culture is its approach to the greatest of all mysteries: the mystery of God (no. 9).

Because the culture of nations is so important, so are the rights of nations. In John Paul II's mind, the international community has insufficiently addressed the rights of nations, limiting its attention to the rights of individuals. He explains, "The Universal Declaration of Human Rights...spoke eloquently of the rights of persons; but *no similar international agreement has yet adequately addressed the rights of nations*" (no. 6). In the pope's mind, nations have a right to their culture, language, and to a way of life in harmony with the "truth about man." The culture of a nation is not an absolute and may be criticized if it tramples on the dignity of the human person. Yet, a nation's right to develop its culture remains.

Our respect for the culture of others is therefore rooted in our respect for each community's attempt to answer the question of human life. And here we can see how important it is to safeguard *the fundamental right to freedom of religion and freedom of conscience,* as the cornerstones of the structure of human rights and the foundation of every truly free society. No one is permitted to suppress those rights by using coercive power to *impose an answer* to the mystery of man (no. 10).

This stress on the importance of religious freedom in the international arena is a constant theme of CSD and strongly emphasized by Pope Benedict XVI.

After speaking of human rights and freedom for more than half his speech, Pope John Paul II dramatically shifts gears and begins to talk about the right use of freedom, not a popular subject in the public square of liberal democracies. He indicates the transition by addressing the audience as "Ladies and Gentlemen!" and then says, "The basic question which we must all face today is the *responsible use of freedom,* in both its personal and social dimensions" (no. 12). Freedom must take its bearings by truth; otherwise it deteriorates into a destructive license. If powerful leaders don't let truth guide their use of freedom, then the likely consequences are caprice and the unbridled arrogance of power. It is only when people exercise their freedom in the light of the moral law written in their heart that freedom has a future in the world. What he recommends on two occasions in his speech is that people of the world use their freedom to acquire "wisdom and virtue" (nos. 4, 18). Still another way John Paul II tries to communicate to his listeners what he means is by this sentence: "Whatever diminishes man—whatever shortens the horizon of man's aspiration to goodness—harms the cause of freedom" (no. 16). Linking freedom to truth, goodness, solidarity, love, wisdom, and virtue was a constant theme of John Paul II's long pontificate.

The pope next gives a prominent example of the misuse of freedom, namely, the reliance on the ethic of utilitarianism. This leads nations to do what is to their advantage, not what is good: for instance, tyrannizing over less powerful nations and taking unfair advantage of the developing nations. What the world needs, he argues, is an ethic of solidarity, which would incline people to help others in their pressing needs brought about by poverty, hunger, disease, and lack of education. People in the world's nations also have to overcome their fear of one another and the fear that there might not be a future if nations are unable to resist the temptation to be destructive. "The answer to the fear which darkens human existence

at the end of the twentieth century is the common effort *to build the civiliza-*
tion of love, founded on the universal values of peace, solidarity, justice, and
liberty" (no. 18). The pope promises that the Church will use its religious
liberty not only to work for the salvation of all, but also to be a tireless
advocate of solidarity throughout the world. The Church cannot do otherwise, because part of its mission is to forge unity among the peoples of
the world.

What Pope John Paul II tries to do in this speech is to moderate the
fascination with "autonomy," the guiding principle of modernity. "It is
one of the great paradoxes of our time that man, who began the period
we call 'modernity' with a self-confident assertion of his 'coming of age'
and 'autonomy,' approaches the end of the twentieth century fearful of
himself, fearful of what he might be capable of, fearful for the future"
(no. 16). The principle of autonomy has been an obstacle to understanding that freedom cannot stand on its own, but, for the sake of solidarity
and the common good, must be understood in relation to truth and love.
Throughout his papacy John Paul II tried to help people understand the
permanent validity of this premodern principle.

The *Compendium of the Social Doctrine of the Church*

While John Paul II focused on the subjects of dignity, rights, and their
philosophical foundation, the culture and rights of nations, and freedom
in its relation to the truth, the *Compendium* provides an abbreviated summary of Catholic social teaching on the international community in a
chapter of the same name. The focus of this chapter is on bringing about
the unity of nations through the Church, morality, and law, along with
considerations on promoting development in the developing nations.

The *Compendium* begins with the biblical teaching on the unity of the
human family. The main point on this subject in the New Testament is
that in Christ

racial and cultural differences are no longer the causes of division (Rom 10:12;
Gal 3:26–28; Col 3:11). *Thanks to the Spirit, the Church is aware of the divine plan of unity
that involves the entire human race* (Acts 17:26), a plan destined to reunite in the mystery of salvation wrought under the saving Lordship of Christ (Eph 1:8–10) all
of created reality, which is fragmented and scattered (no. 431).

From the day of Pentecost the Church has the mission of restoring the
unity of the human family lost at the tower of Babel. Christianity teach-

es that full unity is only achieved in Christ. In preparation for that unity the Church and other international actors work for "the *universal* common good, which is the common good of the entire human family" (no. 432).

Echoing John Paul II's UN speech, the *Compendium* says that what makes unity possible among the nations of the international community is the applicability of the same moral law that governs the lives of individuals. It is a *"universal moral law,* written on the human heart" (no. 436). This law applies to all because everyone shares the same human nature, which does not change over time. All men and women also enjoy the same dignity and have the same natural inclination to form associations. The *Compendium* reminds us that not only persons but also peoples have the "natural inclination...to establish relations among themselves" (no. 433). For these relations to be productive they must be based on "truth, justice, active solidarity, and freedom" (no. 433).

The relations among nations are governed not only by the moral law, but also by juridical arrangements and international law. Each nation remains sovereign, but that sovereignty is not absolute.[4] The main task of international law is to "'ensure that the law of the more powerful does not prevail'" (no. 439).[5] This, of course, means that nations are not free in an international juridical order to do whatever their interests dictate; sovereignty is then limited by justice. The *Compendium* also reiterates John Paul II's remark that "there is still no international agreement that adequately addresses 'the rights of nations.'" It does not explain what would be the content of such an agreement (no. 435).

Reiterating the teaching of Pope John XXIII, Paul VI, Vatican Council II, and John Paul II, the *Compendium* calls for the voluntary establishment of a universal public authority by the nations of the world that would have sufficient power to deal with worldwide problems, now multiplied and complicated by the fact of globalization. It should not be a "global super-state," and it should help individual nations carry out their responsibilities. *"Political authority exercised at the level of the international community must be regulated by law, ordered to the common good and respectful of the principle of subsidiarity"* (no. 441). This proposal has been part of Catholic social teaching since the time of Pope John XXIII, but was not emphasized by

4. In his UN speech Pope Benedict XVI also explains why the sovereignty of nations must be limited.

5. Pontifical Council for Justice and Peace, *Compendium of the Social Doctrine of the Church* (Vatican City: Libreria Editrice Vaticana, 2004); the *Compendium* is quoting John Paul II's "Message for the 2004 World Day of Peace," 9.

Pope John Paul II and was mentioned by Pope Benedict XVI in his third encyclical, *Caritas in veritate*. In present circumstances, I cannot imagine how such a proposal could be reasonably implemented. One might regard the International Criminal Court as a modest beginning.

Last, the *Compendium* addresses the subject of poverty and the insufficient development in the developing nations, "'the one issue that most challenges our human and Christian conscience'" (no. 449).[6] A part of one illuminating paragraph shows an acute awareness of this vast problem.

Among the causes that greatly contribute to underdevelopment and poverty, in addition to the impossibility of acceding to the international market, mention must be made of illiteracy, lack of food security, the absence of structures and services, inadequate measures for guaranteeing basic health care, the lack of safe drinking water and sanitation, corruption, precariousness of institutions, and of political life itself. There is a connection between poverty and, in many countries, the lack of liberty, the lack of possibilities for economic initiative, and the absence of a national administration capable of setting up an adequate system of education and information (no. 447).

Free-market mechanisms alone cannot address these problems, although the spirit of initiative is crucial; in fact, it is "the fundamental basis of all social and economic development in poor countries" (no. 449). The spirit of initiative must be accompanied by the practice of justice, solidarity, and universal charity and respect for the principles of subsidiarity and the universal destination of all goods. The *Compendium* implies that the practice of the above-mentioned virtues by the people who can do something about development will lead to effective initiatives.

There are several points pertaining to the international community that appear outside the chapter devoted explicitly to that subject. In a chapter on the promotion of peace, the *Compendium* says that "[a]ttempts to eliminate entire national, ethnic, religious or linguistic groups are crimes against God and humanity and those responsible must answer for them before justice" (no. 506). As examples, it mentions the genocides of the twentieth century: those of the Armenians, Ukrainians, and Cambodians, as well as those in Africa and the Balkans. "Among these, the Holocaust of the Jewish people, the Shoah stands out: 'the days of the *Shoah* marked a true night of history, with unimaginable crimes against God and

6. *Compendium*, quoting John Paul II, "Message for the 2000 World Day of Peace," 14.

humanity.'"[7] In the light of these horrendous events the *Compendium* states the responsibility to protect in these words: "*The international community as a whole has the moral obligation to intervene on behalf of those groups whose very survival is threatened or whose basic human rights are seriously violated.*"[8]

In a chapter on the family the *Compendium* takes aim at those who insist on forcing sterilization and contraception on people. "*All programs of economic assistance aimed at financing campaigns of sterilization and contraception, as well as the subordination of economic assistance to such campaigns, are to be morally condemned as affronts to the dignity of the person and the family*" (no. 234). The Church must keep reiterating this remark, because the radical environmentalists are laying great stress on the importance of finding ways to pressure people to limit births by means of contraception.

Pope Benedict XVI at the United Nations—April 18, 2008

On April 18, 2008, Pope Benedict XVI gave an address to the General Assembly of the United Nations. He began by saying that the peoples of the world look to the UN as a "'center for harmonizing the actions of nations in the attainment of these common ends' of peace and development (cf. *Charter of the United Nations*, article 1.2–1.4)." The UN should build solidarity among nations in view of promoting lasting peace and sustained development in the member nations.

The ideals that should guide international relations, "the desire for peace, the quest for justice, respect for the dignity of the human person, humanitarian cooperation and assistance," are actually the founding principles of the UN and the aspirations of all reasonable people. In order to realize these ideals the UN establishes binding international rules and structures "capable of harmonizing the day-to-day unfolding of the lives of peoples." The pope clearly implies that there still isn't enough cooperation among the nations of the world to solve problems that "call for interventions in the form of collective action by the international community." Examples of problems calling for collective action on the part of international leaders are "questions of security, development goals, reduction of local and global inequalities, protection of the environment, of resources, and of the climate." The pope says that he is especially think-

---

7. *Compendium*, no. 506, quoting John Paul II, Address at the *Regina Coeli* (April 18, 1993), 3.

8. Ibid., no. 506.

ing of countries in Africa and similarly situated countries throughout the world. While the pope calls the international community to collective action, he does not mention Catholic social teaching pertaining to the establishment of a worldwide public authority.

The rules and structures governing international relations properly limit freedom when necessary to achieve the common good. People must come to realize that they have freedom not only to exercise their rights, but also to fulfill their duties. As an example, the pope says that scientific research and technological application of scientific knowledge must be guided by the dutiful following of ethical principles. Otherwise, the sacred character of life, the dignity of the human person and the family will be harmed. Unfortunately, the pope does not give any examples to illustrate his point. On the basis of his other writings I infer that he is, at least, referring to embryonic stem cell research, which necessarily destroys life.

A most important duty of each nation is to exercise the "responsibility to protect" its own citizens from genocide, ethnic cleansing, starvation, and epidemics. When individual nations are not able or are unwilling to exercise their responsibilities toward their citizens, the international community has the obligation to intervene, first by diplomatic means, and with force if there is no other alternative. (Rules for just use of force, of course, apply.)

The Security Council of the UN officially endorsed this "responsibility to protect" on April 28, 2006. Pope Benedict endorses the responsibility of individual nations and the international community "to protect" persecuted individuals. It is when individual nations fail to fulfill their responsibilities toward their citizens that the international community "must intervene with the juridical means provided by the United Nations Charter and in other international instruments." The pope further argues that individual nations cannot legitimately invoke national sovereignty to ward off international intervention if they are unable or unwilling to exercise their duty to protect citizens.

The international acceptance of the responsibility to protect implies that the rights of human persons are ultimately more important than the sovereignty of individual nations. In other words, there is a universal morality that can be invoked in carefully defined circumstances as justification for overriding the sovereignty of nations when they fail to protect their citizens. For example, I would suggest that some international force could have intervened to stop the 1994 Rwanda genocide. Whether a par-

ticular genocide can be stopped has to be a prudential judgment of the
international community and individual nations with the power to intervene. As I write, the genocide in the Sudan continues despite diplomatic
efforts.

Pope Benedict points out that the responsibility to protect is really
nothing new, but "was considered by the ancient *ius gentium* as the foundation of every action taken by those in government with regard to the
governed." The foundations of this principle are, first, the person created in the image of God, "second, the desire for the absolute and third,
the essence of freedom." The pope is surely implying that the human
person has such dignity from his freedom and aspiration for God that
he deserves protection by the international community when his nation
fails him. It was actually the gross violation of human dignity during
World War II that led to the founding of the United Nations.

Pope Benedict next discusses the Universal Declaration of Human
Rights in the year of its sixtieth anniversary. The pope notes that it was
adopted by the nations of the world, according to its preamble, as a "common standard of achievement," that is to say, as an ideal to be realized
over time by the nations of the world. The pope recognizes that the Declaration's language of rights has become the common way of discussing
universal principles of morality and is now "the ethical substratum of international relations. At the same time, the universality, indivisibility, and
interdependence of human rights all serve as guarantees safeguarding human dignity." Pope Benedict says that rights are universal because natural
law, present and accessible in every culture, is their foundation. Respect
for rights, he argues, promotes the common good, part of which is justice,
development, and security. "The promotion of human rights remains the
most effective strategy for eliminating inequalities between countries and
social groups, and for increasing security." The pope has such high hopes
from the protection of rights because of their foundation in natural law,
which requires each person to show respect for the rights of everyone else
by practicing the virtues. In other words, natural law doesn't just teach individuals to assert their own rights, but to work for the promotion of the
rights of all.

The pope next points out that rights will be weakened and even under-
mined if they are simply regarded as established by legislation. Rights are
on a firmer foundation when they are regarded as a way to explain what
justice is. In the pope's judgment, "The Universal Declaration has...rein-
forced the conviction that respect for human rights is principally rooted

in unchanging justice, on which the binding force of international proclamations is also based." This is why the Holy See has lavished such praise on the Declaration. It provides the rudiments of a universal morality, "a commonly held sense of justice," that the world so desperately needs. In other words, even without any philosophical inquiry people have a sense that respecting human rights is the right and just thing to do.

As a further explanation of the universal applicability of rights, Pope Benedict invokes the thought of Augustine of Hippo, who "taught that the saying: *Do not do to others what you would not want done to you* cannot in any way vary according to the different understandings that have arisen in the world." The pope implies that putting Augustine's teaching into practice is tantamount to respecting people's rights.

Pope Benedict next takes up the theme of religion and makes two points. First, people with a deeply religious vision of life will be inclined to establish a social order "respectful of the dignity and rights of the person." Genuine religious belief produces a conversion of heart, "which then leads to a commitment to resist violence, terrorism and war, and to promote justice and peace." In other words, order in the soul or conversion of heart or the practice of virtues is necessary to bring about a just social order in which people respect rights and fulfill their duties. This is the constant teaching of St. Augustine, St. Thomas, and modern Catholic social doctrine, as mentioned in previous chapters.

Pope Benedict's second point about religion is that the right to religious freedom is one of the most important human rights. He says, "The full guarantee of religious liberty cannot be limited to the free exercise of worship, but has to give due consideration to the public dimension of religion, and hence to the possibility of believers playing their part in building the social order." I would note that whereas various Muslim lands curtail the free exercise of worship, Western countries often try to confine religion to the private sphere. In the United States religious believers are not infrequently criticized as violating the separation of church and state when they bring their faith to bear on public affairs. Secularists want a naked public square, one in which religion has no effect on the great issues of the day. Pope Benedict notes that religious believers not only speak out on public affairs, but also contribute to the well-being of their countries by providing education, health care, and various kinds of social services for the poor and marginalized.

In his concluding paragraphs Pope Benedict formally expresses the solidarity of the Catholic Church with the United Nations in its role as a sign of unity among all the nations of the world and as "an instrument of service to the entire human family." He promises to keep making available to the United Nations the Church's experience "of humanity." The Church especially bears witness to "the transcendent nature of the human person," the recognition of which is crucial for solving the world's problems. In Pope Benedict's words, "Recognition of this dimension must be strengthened if we are to sustain humanity's hope for a better world and if we are to create conditions for peace, development, cooperation, and guarantee of rights for future generations." Unfortunately, the pope didn't have the time to elaborate on the reason he stresses this point. In my mind, he had to be thinking of the biblical teaching that all human beings are created in the image and likeness of God. Once that is truly recognized, people carry themselves with a new dignity and realize that they must work for a better world in order to show respect for their own dignity. In other words, a person who does not respect the rights of others acts beneath his own dignity. If the transcendent nature of the human person is not acknowledged, then people can neglect the needs of others without pangs of conscience.

Catholics can see in the pope's brief talk his desire to persuade the nations of the world that there is a universal morality binding on all the peoples and nations of the world. This universal morality has its basis both in natural law and in sound religious belief. Even nonreligious people, the pope implies, have the capacity to recognize the universal applicability of human rights and duties. The human rights enumerated in the *Declaration* indicate the kinds of things that all should desire for their fellow human beings throughout the world. Catholics, in particular, have the duty to promote respect for human rights and the performance of duties in every country throughout the world. They should encourage the lawmakers in their own countries and NGOs to benefit the poor and oppressed abroad whenever possible. In this work they should especially support effective Catholic organizations, such as Catholic Relief Services. Of course, discernment is crucial for knowing what to say or do in order to benefit those in need throughout the world.

As a kind of follow-up to his April UN address, Pope Benedict sent a message on June 2, 2008, to the participants attending a conference on food security organized by the United Nations Food and Agricultural Organization (FAO). In attendance were the Secretary General of the UN and heads of state and government. The pope elaborated on points that he touched on briefly in his UN address. His main point was that people suffering from lack of food "must be helped to gradually become capable of satisfying their own needs for sufficient and healthy nutrition." He, of course, recommended effective political action to address hunger in the world, but he also urged governments and the UN officials "to cooperate in an ever more transparent manner with the organizations of civil society committed to filling the growing gap between wealth and poverty." Among those organizations would be the Catholic Church, other churches, and NGOs. This recommendation is a good example of taking seriously the principle of subsidiarity, which "is the coordination of society's activities in a way that supports the internal life of the local communities."[9] When the principle of subsidiarity is respected, every group in society is given the chance to make a contribution to the resolution of public problems.

The pope also added that a deep-rooted conviction about human dignity in the movers and shakers of the world would incline them to make things happen in the face of seemingly overwhelming odds. In the pope's words, "If, therefore, respect for human dignity had effective influence at the negotiation table, in making decisions and accomplishing them, it would be possible to rise above otherwise insurmountable obstacles and it would eliminate, or at least diminish, the disinterest in the good of others."[10] This observation is a good example of the ethics that Catholic social doctrine brings to the world of practical affairs. Unless motivated by respect for human dignity, leaders are unlikely to persevere in seeking solutions to the problem of world hunger when confronted by overwhelming difficulties. Pope Benedict concludes his remarks by noting that the Holy See takes part in international affairs in order "to encourage every People to share the needs of other Peoples, placing in common the goods of the earth that the Creator has destined for the entire human family." This, of course, is a reference to the principle of the universal destination of goods so amply explained by Pope John Paul II in his encyclical *Centesimus annus* (*On the Hundredth Anniversary of Rerum novarum*), nos. 30–43. Acceptance of this principle is an expression of the willingness to enter into solidarity with those in need.

On July 6, 2008, the day before the meeting of the heads of state and government of the G8 member countries (Canada, France, Germany,

9. "Address of His Holiness Benedict XVI to the Participants in the 14th Session of the Pontifical Academy of Social Sciences," May 3, 2008.
10. Translation modified on the basis of the original Italian.

Italy, Japan, Russia, the United Kingdom, and the United States), Pope
Benedict took the occasion of his weekly *Angelus* to deliver a strong exhortation to the government leaders. "I address the participants in the Meeting at Hokkaido-Toyako asking that they make the center of their delib-
erations the needs of the weakest and poorest people." In particular he
urged that all necessary measures be taken in order "to put an end to the
scourges of extreme poverty, hunger, disease and illiteracy which still affect such a large part of humanity." This recommendation also explains
what the pope means in his UN address by speaking of a concerted effort to promote development. As we have seen from the pope's previous
speeches, he does not expect governments to do everything; the institutions of civil society, including the Church, also have their contribution
to make. The pontiff, however, knows that some things must be accomplished by political action on the national and international level.

Glendon on the Universal Declaration of Human Rights

Let us now turn to some writings of Mary Ann Glendon, a prominent
Catholic legal scholar, for guidance in giving an in-depth analysis of the
Universal Declaration of Human Rights, with close attention to its relation to Catholic social doctrine (CSD). For our purposes what is especially important is to understand how CSD might support and complement the Declaration, and shore up its foundations.

The General Assembly of the United Nations (58 nations at the time)
approved the Declaration on December 10, 1948, with no negative votes,
but with eight abstentions (Byleorussia, Czechoslovakia, Poland, Saudi
Arabia, South Africa, the Soviet Union, Ukraine, and Yugoslavia). The
Declaration "is the most important reference point for cross-cultural discussion of human freedom and dignity in the world today,"[11] says Glendon at the beginning of one of her articles on the subject. It reflects input
from the Orient (especially China), Latin America, Europe, the United
Kingdom, the United States, the Soviet Union, many smaller countries,
and from the tradition of CSD, especially through the input of Charles
Malik, a Lebanese philosopher who was on the subcommittee of the UN
Commission on Human Rights, which drafted the Universal Declaration
of Human Rights.

The Declaration is composed of a preamble and 30 articles. The pre-

11. Glendon, *Traditions in Turmoil*, 315.

amble begins with the "recognition of the inherent dignity and of the equal and inalienable rights of all members of the human family" and proclaims that recognition of human dignity and rights are "the foundation of freedom, justice and peace in the world." Dignity and rights are recognized rather than conferred by some legal document. So, they exist prior to what any state or international organization says about them. Glendon notes that the proclamation of the universality of human rights is repudiating a "longstanding view that the relation between a sovereign state and its own citizens is that nation's own business."[12] Recall that Pope Benedict made much of this fact. The Declaration does not say why people have dignity and rights. In other words, no philosophical foundation is offered for the recognition of dignity and rights, presumably because the member nations of the UN could not come to an agreement on this important subject.

The member nations of the UN "pledged themselves to achieve, in cooperation with the United Nations, the promotion of universal respect for and observance of human rights and fundamental freedoms" (Preamble). Since fulfillment of this pledge depends on a widespread understanding and acceptance of these rights and freedoms, the "General Assembly proclaims This Universal Declaration of Human Rights as a common standard of achievement for all peoples and nations." To this end the General Assembly calls upon every individual and "every organ of society" (not only the state, but all the elements of civil society, such as families, schools, churches, synagogues, mosques, and other mediating institutions) to "strive by education and teaching to promote respect for these rights and freedoms and by progressive measures, national and international, to secure their universal and effective recognition and observance, both among the Member States themselves and among the peoples of the territories under their jurisdiction" (Preamble). These few statements about education in the preamble reveal that the UN understood that much effort would be required all over the world for the Declaration's recognition of dignity and rights to become a reality on the ground among the peoples of the world. The UN clearly recognized that its high goals depended on help from member states and the institutions of their civil societies.

After the preamble, articles 1 and 2 begin, says Glendon, "with a statement of what all human beings have in common."[13] Article 1 reads, "All

12. Ibid., 322.
13. Ibid., 323.

human beings are born free and equal in dignity and rights. They are endowed with reason and conscience and should act toward one another in a spirit of brotherhood." The endowment with reason and conscience and the duty to act in a brotherly manner seem to be a partial explanation of what it means to have dignity. Otherwise stated, human beings act in accordance with their dignity when they recognize and use reason, form their consciences, and fulfill unspecified duties toward their fellow citizens. This article implies that human dignity is both a given and an achievement realized by the fulfillment of duties, including the respect of people's rights. "Article 2's emphatic statement of the anti-discrimination principle," says Glendon, "underlies the principle of universality."[14] Every person on the face of the planet is entitled to respect for his or her rights. It is then wrong to invoke any principle of discrimination to exclude anyone.

Glendon divides the remaining 28 articles into five groups: articles 3–11 list personal liberties; articles 12–17 enumerate "the rights of the individual in relation to others and to various groups"; articles 18–21 focus on the "spiritual, public and political liberties"; articles 22–27 present social, economic, and cultural rights; and articles 28–30 describe rights and duties of individuals with respect to their own countries and the international order.[15]

Article 3 says that "Everyone has the right to life, liberty and security of person." This is the fundamental right among the personal liberties. Other rights specify what this fundamental right includes. No one shall be made a slave, subjected to torture, arbitrary arrest, detention, or exile. Everyone is equal before the law and shall have the right to a remedy from a national tribunal "for acts violating the fundamental rights granted him by the constitution or the law." Articles 10 and 11 specify the rights of citizens when they are accused of crimes. Commenting on these personal liberties as a whole, Glendon says they were crafted to protect individuals from aggression.[16]

Glendon says the second group of rights (articles 12 through 17) "includes the right to be free from arbitrary interference with one's 'privacy, family, home, or correspondence' and from arbitrary attacks upon one's 'honor and reputation'; freedom of movement and the right of return; the right to political asylum; the right to a nationality; provisions on marriage and the family; and the right to own property." The article on the

14. Ibid., 324.   15. Ibid., 322.
16. Ibid., 324.

family includes the right to found a family, equal rights of the spouses (not a widespread right in the national legislation of 1948), and the duty of society and the state to protect the family, "the natural and fundamental group unit of society."[17]

The spiritual, public, and political rights enumerated in articles 18–21 include the right to freedom of thought, opinion, association, and assembly; the right to religious freedom, including the right to show the public relevance of one's faith alone or in association with others, and the right to change one's religion; the right to participate in the government of one's own country, "directly or through freely chosen representatives"; and the right to participate in elections by secret vote.

At the time the social and economic rights listed in articles 22 through 27 were very important to many nations, not just the Soviet Union. Glendon explains,

Much of what is contained in Articles 23 and 24 were the common stuff of labor legislation in most liberal democracies (decent working conditions including paid vacations and limits on working hours; protection against unemployment; the right to form and join unions). Less widely recognized, however, were Article 23's "right to work" and its "equal right to equal pay for equal work" without discrimination; Article 25's elevation of social welfare principles into a universal right to [a] decent standard of living; and Article 26's right to education.[18]

Article 22, a kind of preamble to the rights that follow, contains important observations on their importance and realization. It says that economic, social, and cultural rights are "indispensable" for upholding the "dignity" of individuals, and they are to be realized "through national effort and international co-operation and in accordance with the organization and resources of each state." This qualification injected into the Declaration a note of realism, which helped assure its acceptance by the nations of the world.

About the last three articles on the relation of the individual to society, Glendon says that they "address certain conditions that are prerequisite to the realization of the rights and freedoms enumerated in the Declaration."[19] The first condition is the kind of "social and international order in which the rights and freedoms set forth in this Declaration can be ful-

17. Ibid.   18. Ibid., 325.
19. Ibid., 326.

ly realized." The second condition is the fulfillment of duties by individuals toward the communities in which they live, and the third condition
is carefully circumscribed limitations on rights. As examples, Article 29
mentions "such limitations as are determined by law solely for the purpose of securing due recognition and respect for the rights and freedoms
of others and of meeting the just requirements of morality, public order
and the general welfare in a democratic society." Glendon makes much of
the significance of the last three articles:

> In the view of Cassin [the primary drafter of the Declaration] and others,
> it had to be made clear that the responsibility for protecting human rights
> belonged not only to the nation-states, and international organizations, but
> to persons and groups below and above the national level. The Declaration
> was thus ahead of its time in recognizing the importance for human free-
> dom of a wide range of social groups, beginning with families, and extending
> through the institutions of civil society, nation states, and international orga-
> nizations.[20]

In other words, it is not just the state that is the first line of defense of human rights in the world, but as Cassin wrote, "'respect for human rights
depends first and foremost on the mentalities of individuals and social
groups.'"[21] Glendon adds, "After all, rights emerge from culture, cannot
be sustained without cultural underpinnings, and, to be effective, must
become part of each people's way of life."[22] This, of course, means that
effective respect for human rights depends on what families, schools, and
churches and other religious institutions do to shape the character of individuals in every part of the world.

By way of concluding remarks, Glendon suggests that dignity may be
the ultimate value in the Declaration. The word appears five times, twice
in the preamble and once in articles 1, 22, and 23. While the Declaration
doesn't attempt to explain fully what the word means, it does say in article 1, as mentioned, that human beings are "endowed with reason and conscience" and are to "act toward one another in a spirit of brotherhood."
Dignified human beings do not just assert their rights. They are also social and political beings with duties to fulfill. As Glendon explains, everyone is portrayed "as situated in families, communities, workplaces, associations, societies, cultures, nations, and an emerging international order."[23]

---

20. Ibid., 327.   21. Ibid., 328.
22. Ibid., 331.   23. Ibid., 329.

In mentioning that "Everyone has duties toward the community," article 29 implies that the fulfillment of duties is an integral aspect of a person's dignity. Glendon also thinks that the Declaration is promoting solidarity among human beings by surrounding the list of rights by articles 1 and 29, where duties are emphasized.

In a subsequent essay Glendon looked more closely at dignity as the foundation of rights and commented on a sentence in one of my writings about the twofold nature of human dignity in Christian teaching. I had written that dignity "is both a given and an achievement or an end to be gradually realized." Glendon notes that if dignity is a goal to be realized by overcoming sin and practicing virtue, then you can't simply say that dignity always provides a foundation for rights. She explains,

From a Christian point of view, the resolution of this dilemma may be that human rights are grounded in the obligation of everyone to perfect one's own dignity, which in turn obliges one to respect the "given" spark of dignity of others whatever they may have done with it. In other words, it may be our own quest for dignity (individually and as a society) that requires us to refrain from inflicting cruel punishments on criminals, or from terminating the lives of the unborn and others whose faculties are underdeveloped or dormant.[24]

Glendon adds that many shared Jacques Maritain's view that the effectiveness of the Declaration would depend on whether or not a "culture of human dignity develops." Glendon further adds her conviction that, since religion is the heart of culture, it will ultimately "be up to the religions to demonstrate whether they are capable of motivating their followers to fulfill their own calling to perfect their own dignity, and in so doing to respect the dignity of fellow members of the human family."[25]

Because the Catholic Church has a great tradition of upholding the dignity of the human person, it is making a contribution to the protection of rights whenever it effectively teaches the faith. That it could be more effective, no one would deny. Besides the churches, other seedbeds of civic virtue are families, schools, and various other mediating institutions. They can also move people to act in accordance with their dignity and, thus, respect the rights of others.

---

24. Ibid., 346; I also quote these sentences at the very end of chapter 1 to affirm that respect for dignity properly understood is the foundation of rights.
25. Ibid., 347.

The Holy See at Beijing—1995

As an example of how the Catholic Church makes very specific contributions to the well-being of the international community, let us now examine what the Holy See tried to do for the women of the world at the 1995 UN Women's Conference in Beijing. Mary Ann Glendon was the head of the Holy See's twenty-two-member delegation. She presented the two formal interventions of the Holy See and then wrote her own personal report on the conference. Examining these documents will reveal some basic difficulties the women of the world are facing, especially in the developing countries, and what international actors are and are not doing to help them.

The Holy See's statement at the opening of the UN Women's Conference in Beijing, made in the light of preparatory conference documents, described the needs of women and mentioned ways in which they are being ill-served. Many women are being denied a right to education and to adequate health care. Two-thirds of the world's vast illiterate population is women; of all the children not receiving primary education, 70 percent are girls. These facts are most significant because people are increasingly recognizing that "investment in the education of girls is the fundamental key to the later full advancement of women."[26] The "feminization of poverty" is, to a great extent, the result of poor, or no, education. The Holy See mentions that law and culture may also prevent women from taking their place in the economic life of their countries.

International organizations focus on health care with respect to sexuality, but devote inadequate attention to the problems of poor nutrition and unsafe drinking water. In addition, "Conference documents," says the Holy See, "are not bold enough in acknowledging the threat to women's health arising from widespread attitudes of sexual permissiveness."[27]

With respect to the transmission of life, the Holy See defends the teaching of the Catholic Church on family planning against various objections, especially the belief that natural methods of spacing births are too demanding for people. The Holy See responds, "But no way of ensuring deep respect for human life and its transmission can dispense with self-discipline and self-restraint, particularly in cultures which foster self-indulgence and immediate gratification." It also stresses the importance

26. Ibid., 294.
27. Ibid., 295.

of husbands learning to share the duties of responsible procreation, recognizing that this "will only be achieved through a process of changing
attitudes and behavior."[28]

The Holy See also joins other nations in condemning coercion in the
methods of birth control. No examples are given, but one immediately
thinks of China's policy of forcing women to have abortions after they
have one child. The Holy See addresses the question of abortion by taking note of the consensus in the international community "that abortion
should not be promoted as a means of family planning and that all efforts
must be made to eliminate those factors which lead women to seek abortions." In its own name the Vatican calls upon women throughout the
world to "take the lead in the fight against societal practices which facilitate the irresponsibility of men, while stigmatizing women, and against
a vast industry that extracts its profits from the very bodies of women,
while at the same time purporting to be their liberators."[29]

The Holy See commends the conference for drawing attention to the
widespread violence against women and girls throughout the world, even
in the developed nations. It also asks that more be done to eliminate child
prostitution, the slave trade in children, the sale of children's organs, female genital mutilation, and child marriages.

The Holy See concludes by arguing that respecting and promoting the
full dignity of women will benefit all of humanity. "The freer women are
to share their gifts with society and to assume leadership in society, the
better are the prospects for the entire community to progress in wisdom,
justice and dignified living."[30]

At the concluding session of the conference, Glendon presented the assessment of the Holy See's delegation. Glendon's statement praises what
the conference documents said "on the needs of women in poverty, on
strategies for development, on literacy, and education, on ending violence
against women, on a culture of peace, and on access to employment, land,
capital, and technology." Glendon also noted that conference statements
on these matters correspond closely to Catholic social teaching.

The delegation of the Holy See presented two major criticisms of the
conference's final documents. First, argued Glendon, their tone was sometimes characterized by "individualism," causing, for example, a neglect of
what the Universal Declaration of Human Rights said about "the special

28. Ibid., 295–96.   29. Ibid., 296.
30. Ibid., 297.

care and assistance" (article 25) motherhood needs. Under the influence of "an impoverished, libertarian rights dialect," women are left, so to speak, alone with their rights. The Holy See clearly would have liked more statements about the obligations people and institutions have with respect to women. Second, the final documents neglect the health needs of women and the higher education of their minds.

Surely we can do better than to address the health needs of girls and women by paying disproportionate attention to sexual and reproductive health. Moreover, ambiguous language concerning unqualified control over sexuality and fertility could be interpreted as including societal endorsement of abortion and homosexuality. A document that respects women's dignity should address the health of the whole woman. A document that respects women's intelligence should devote at least as much attention to literacy as fertility.[31]

Catholic scholars have noted that international conferences often try to secure endorsement of the right to abortion, or, failing that, sufficiently ambiguous language to justify reading it into the text at a later date. That "international standard" is then presented to individual nations as something to adopt in their constitutions or legislation. The Holy See is trying to make people aware of this ruse.

Shortly after the Beijing conference Mary Ann Glendon wrote a personal assessment of the final conference documents and pointed out various developments in the international area that are hurting women, and which the Holy See is continuously trying to address. The results of the conference were mixed. Glendon first explained how Beijing's Program for Action had many provisions "consonant with Catholic teachings on dignity, freedom and social justice."[32] For example, it recognized that females were targeted for abortion in various countries and that abortion was not acceptable means of promoting family planning; it made people aware of "the connection between the feminization of poverty and the disintegration of the family"; it also came up with strategies to address the problems and suffering women experience from violence, poverty, illiteracy, and lack of access to education and employment; it also noted the "relation between environmental degradation to scandalous patterns of production and consumption."

Glendon next explained the Holy See's objections both to the Beijing

31. Ibid., 300.
32. Ibid., 307–8; see the first half of page 308 in Glendon's book for details on the nature of the agreement between Beijing's document and Catholic social teaching.

document and to positions taken by various participants at the conference. "As at Cairo, the Holy See was concerned that language on sexual and reproductive 'health' would be used to promote the quick-fix approach to getting rid of poverty by getting rid of poor people."[33] Glendon noted that some foundations present at the Beijing conference were tying the reception of their funds to programs that coercively promoted abortion, sterilization, and the use of contraceptives dangerous to the health of women. Giving priority to these measures instead of development, health care, and education, argued the economist-philosopher Amartya Sen, causes "negative effects on people's well-being and reduce[s] their freedoms."[34]

A block of 15 nations in the European Union pressed for the acceptance of five approaches to women's needs that directly contradicted the principles of Catholic social teaching. The EU nations first wanted to pluralize the word "family" in the documents in order to give legal standing to "alternative lifestyles" such as same-sex unions. Second, the EU wanted to omit the word "motherhood" unless it "appeared in a negative light."[35] Third, the EU coalition "sought to remove all references to religion, morals, ethics, or spirituality, except where religion was portrayed as associated with intolerance or extremism." In particular one EU negotiator argued that "ethics have no place in medicine." The EU team didn't want to provide for religious freedom or respect for conscience in the context of education. Fourth, the coalition showed indifference to the parent-child relationship by removing "all recognition of parental rights and duties." Finally, the EU wanted to remove all references to human dignity in the Beijing documents, even though this concept is so important in the Universal Declaration of Human Rights. Glendon explains, "To eliminate dignity is to undermine the concept that human rights, including equality, belong to all men and women by virtue of their inherent worth as human beings, rather than existing at the whim of this or that political regime."[36] The five approaches recommended by the EU revealed that the European nations were thinking and speaking as though they didn't have any Christian roots whatsoever. Moreover, Glendon points out, "the EU negotiators' stances on these matters were at variance with similar provisions in most of their own national constitutions and with the underlying

33. Ibid., 309.
34. Glendon, quoting Sen, in *Traditions in Turmoil*, 310.
35. Glendon, *Traditions in Turmoil*, 304.
36. Ibid., 305.

principles for their own family assistance programs."[37] Glendon came to the conclusion that the EU was so interested in promoting the sexual and reproductive rights of women that it was willing to pass over other time-honored principles in international documents, especially those prominent in Catholic social teaching.

While the affluent nations made much of their commitment to sexual rights and population control, they were not forthcoming with commitments of resources to poor women. "In defiance of evidence that economic development and women's education lead to lowered fertility rates, the developed countries made it clear that they wanted population control on the cheap."[38] Glendon was also mystified why Third World representatives didn't speak up much for the needs of women in their countries.

In conclusion, Glendon warned that actors in the international community will continually try "to make abortion a fundamental right" and "to depose heterosexual marriage and child-raising from their traditionally preferred positions."[39] They will also use the language of rights to advance an agenda not respectful of rights long considered fundamental—"exemplified at Beijing by the emphasis on formal equality at the expense of motherhood's special claim to protection, and by the elimination of most references to religion and parental rights."[40] Glendon is also sure that people will keep trying to divorce rights from duties, to absolutize their favorite rights at the expense of fundamental rights (as, for example, those in the Universal Declaration), to invent new vague rights, and will argue that we should envision the rights-bearer "as radically autonomous and self-sufficient," with no obligations to anyone.

Conclusion

The *Compendium of the Social Doctrine of the Church* indicates the building blocks of an international community in one illuminating sentence: "*The centrality of the human person and the natural inclination of persons and peoples to establish relationships among themselves are the fundamental elements for building a true international community, the ordering of which must aim at guaranteeing the effective universal common good.*"[41] So, promoting the dignity, rights, and duties of the human person and various forms of solidarity among the peoples of the earth is

37. Ibid.
39. Ibid.
41. *Compendium*, no. 433.

38. Ibid., 311.
40. Ibid., 310–11.

the most important task of the actors in the international community. These actors are, for example, the UN, the agencies of the UN, the Holy See, indigenous churches, international agencies, nongovernmental agencies like Catholic Relief Services, the affluent nations, and the developing nations. In setting forth a vision of the international community, Catholic social doctrine provides guidance not only for Catholics, the Catholic church, and Catholic institutions, but also for everyone else participating in the life of the international community. The various actors will all be able to promote human dignity, solidarity, and the universal common good in various ways.

   "The diplomatic service for the Holy See, the product of an ancient and proven practice," the *Compendium* explains, *"is an instrument that works not only for the freedom of the Church (libertas Ecclesiae) but also for the defense and promotion of human dignity, as well as for a social order based on the values of justice, truth, freedom and love."*[42] We just saw how the Holy See tried to benefit the women of the world at the Beijing conference. The present and previous pope brought Catholic social teaching directly to the nations of the world through the UN. Recall Pope John Paul II's visit to the UN in October of 1995, when he reminded the nations' representatives that freedom had to be understood and exercised in the light of truth. In April of 2008 Pope Benedict XVI, as we just recounted, tried to persuade the world's nations to continue to take seriously the UN Universal Declaration of Human Rights, because it upholds the rudiments of a universal morality, and to recognize that this common morality applies to every individual, institution, and nation. He said that universal morality in the form of natural law is the solid foundation of human dignity and human rights. For the peoples of the world to recognize the centrality of the natural law for assuring respect for the rights that all desire, more scholarly work is necessary, along with dialogue with public leaders on the meaning and foundation of natural law.

   On the basis of Pope Benedict's UN speech, Glendon's reflection on the Universal Declaration of Human Rights, her account of the Holy See's impact at Beijing, and the chapter on international community in the *Compendium of the Social Doctrine of the Church,* we can see the clear outlines of Catholic social doctrine on international matters. That doctrine doesn't put forth specific solutions to the world's problems, but tries to propose the principles that, if accepted, would lead to good solutions to the world's problems. These principles can be briefly summarized and

42. Ibid., no. 445.

understood more completely in the light of what was said in previous chapters. They are as follows: the sacredness of all life, the grave wrong of abortion, the importance of the traditional family, the foundation of rights and duties in the dignity of the human person, respect for rights and the fulfillment of duties as the path to genuine solidarity, the necessity of providing access to education and work, especially for women, limitations on the sovereignty of nations on the basis of "the responsibility to protect" citizens from their rulers' abuse of power, respect for religious freedom, recognition of the political and social benefits flowing from the practice of sound religious belief, and the promotion of integral development coupled with respect for the environment.

CHAPTER 12

Just-War Principles

One of the most urgent tasks of Catholic social teaching is to keep the principles of the just-war doctrine before the eyes of government leaders and citizens. This chapter lays out the fundamental tenets of just-war principles and shows the roots of these principles in the thought of Augustine and Aquinas. Familiarity with the thought of Augustine on peace is especially important in order to understand both the necessity for a just-war teaching and the preconditions for a just peace.

St. Augustine

Augustine argues that the practice of justice preserves the peace. He understands justice primarily as order in the soul of individuals, which contributes to the proper ordering of society, and thus to peace. Ernest Fortin's summary of Augustine's reflection on justice is helpful:

It exists when the body is ruled by the soul, when the lower appetites are ruled by reason, and when reason itself is ruled by God. The same hierarchy is or should be observed in society as a whole and is encountered when virtuous subjects obey wise rulers, whose minds are in turn subject to the divine law.[1]

This means that citizens and rulers must strive to achieve order in their soul by the practice of all the virtues. So, Augustine is talking about justice as a general virtue that encompasses all the virtues that produce order in the soul.

Augustine's description of peace in *The City of God* is closely related to his definition of justice.

---

1. Ernest Fortin, *Classical Christianity and the Political Order: Reflections on the Theologico-Political Problem*, vol. 2 of *Collected Essays*, edited by J. Brian Benestad (Lanham, Md.: Rowman and Littlefield, 1996), 7; Cf. St. Augustine, *The City of God* (Baltimore: Penguin Books, 1972; New York: Modern Library, 1950), book XIX, chap. 21.

Thus, the peace of the body is the ordered proportion of its parts. The peace of the irrational soul is the ordered repose of the appetites. The peace of the rational soul is the ordered agreement of knowledge and action.... The peace between a mortal man and God is an ordered obedience, in faith, under the eternal law.

The peace among human beings is ordered concord. The peace of the household is an ordered concord concerning commanding and obeying among those who dwell together. The peace of the city is an ordered concord concerning commanding and obeying among the citizens. The peace of the heavenly city is a fellowship perfectly ordered and harmonious, enjoying God and each other in God. The peace of all things is the tranquility of order [*tranquilitas ordinis*].[2]

Augustine is arguing that the achievement of peace in the city and among nations depends heavily on the dispositions in the souls of rulers and ruled. Peace within individuals is disrupted when they fail to act according to their knowledge of the good and indulge disordered appetites. Concord in the family or the city is, of course, disrupted by the disordered passions in the souls of individuals. For example, the inordinate desire for pleasure, power, gain, glory, honor, or revenge could lead individuals to disrupt the concord of the household or the city. The peace between man and God depends on obedience to God's will. Peace among human beings also depends on the universal obedience to God's will. Insofar as human beings disobey God, they will be at odds with each other. The very first pages of Genesis emphasize this point with unmistakable clarity. Cain's killing of Abel quickly follows Adam's and Eve's disobedience of God. John Paul II reflects on this truth in his 1995 encyclical *Evangelium vitae (The Gospel of Life)*.[3]

Political communities cannot be rightly ordered if individuals, especially the leaders, don't have order in their souls produced by the practice of virtues. What caused World War II in Europe, if not the disorder in the soul of Adolph Hitler? Hitler's lust to dominate and his hatred of the Jews led to terrible consequences for vast numbers of people, especially the Jews. What is the principal cause of Al Qaeda's terroristic acts, if not the disordered passions of its leaders and members?

I believe it is a misreading of Augustine to think that *tranquilitas ordi-*

2. St. Augustine, *Political Writings*, tr. Michael W. Tkacz and Douglas Kries, ed. Ernest L. Fortin and Douglas Kries (Lanham, Md.: Rowman and Littlefield, 1994), 153–54.
3. Pope John Paul II, *Evangelium vitae (The Gospel of Life)*, nos. 7–10.

nis refers only to a stable and ordered political community that can be achieved without justice in the souls of individuals. Augustine, of course would recognize that the desire for gain or the threat of force might induce a bad state or an individual tyrant to forsake evil public purposes. So, a "peace process" might yield some results, even if no effort is made to overcome the vices of the principal antagonists in a conflict. But any peace process will have great difficulty in forging a peace between bitter enemies, if the anger and hatred of many individuals do not lessen. Given Augustine's understanding that peace within and among nations depends on peace or order in the souls of individuals, it comes as no surprise that Augustine believes that war will never disappear from the face of the earth. Because of sin, war is inevitable. The sin or disorder in the souls of individuals leads one state to make war on another. In the words of Ernest Fortin: "However much one may dislike and regret it, war is unavoidable, not because good men want it, but because it is not within their power to avoid it altogether, since it is imposed on them by the wicked."[4] Augustine has no doubt that wicked people will always threaten the peace. Of course, they may be more or less numerous or more or less able to disturb the peace in certain periods of time. In some moments of history peaceful nations may be able to keep the wicked in check by the judicious use of force.

Augustine believes that the evil purposes of the wicked must be resisted out of love, love for them and their victims. Summarizing Augustine's position, Fortin writes, "nothing is more injurious to mankind than that evildoers should be given free reign to prosper and use their prosperity to oppress the good."[5] Obviously, unjust aggressors are resisted so that they cannot overthrow nations and inflict harm on innocent people. But they are also resisted to stop them from doing harm to themselves by doing evil to others. Evil people receive a benefit when their license for wrongdoing is wrested away.

When, however, men are prevented, by being alarmed, from doing wrong, it may be said that a real service is done to themselves. The precept "Resist not evil" was given to prevent us from taking pleasure in revenge, in which the mind is gratified by the sufferings of others, but not to make us neglect the duty of restraining men from sin.[6]

4. Fortin, *Classical Christianity and the Political Order*, 46.
5. Ibid.
6. St. Augustine, *Letter 47*, 5, quoted from Herbert A. Deane, *The Political and Social Ideas of St. Augustine* (New York: Columbia University Press, 1963), 164.

Augustine's advice to political leaders on war follows logically from his position on the love required of political leaders. In letter 138 Augustine says, "If this earthly republic kept the Christian precepts, wars themselves would not be waged without benevolence, so that, for the sake of the peaceful union of piety and justice, the welfare of the conquered would be more readily considered."[7] Augustine wants political leaders to protect the innocent from unjust aggression, and he wants the victorious leaders to benefit the souls of the conquered who disrupted the peace. In a similar vein, he says in a letter to Boniface, the Roman governor of the province of Africa:

Be a peacemaker, then, even by fighting, so that through your victory you might bring those whom you defeat to the advantages of peace....Let necessity slay the warring foe, not your will. As violence is returned to one who rebels and resists, so should mercy be to one who has been conquered or captured, especially when there is no fear of a disturbance of peace.[8]

Augustine wants political leaders to declare war only out of *necessity* and to show love to their enemies by resisting their evildoing and by showing mercy after they have been conquered. Necessity means there is no other way of protecting innocents and resisting aggressors. As a way of inculcating in leaders a reluctance to see necessity where there is none, Augustine tells leaders to look at just wars as lamentable necessities.

They say, however, that the wise man will wage only just wars—as if, mindful that he is human, he would rather lament that he is subject to the necessity of waging just wars. If they were not just, he would not be required to wage them, and thus he would be free of the necessity of war. It is the iniquity on the part of the adversary that forces a just war upon the wise man.[9]

If leaders reluctantly come to the conclusion that lethal force has to be used to protect their community and to restrain evildoers, then they are less likely to lie to themselves and declare a war to be necessary when it clearly is not.

Augustine's recommendation to leaders even goes so far as to ask them to lament the existence of all iniquity, even when it doesn't require a decision to go to war.

7. St. Augustine, *Political Writings*, 209.
8. Ibid.
9. St. Augustine, *The City of God*, tr. Tkacz and Kries, book XIX, chap. 7.

Even if it did not give rise to the necessity of war, such iniquity must certainly be lamented by a human being since it belongs to human beings. Therefore, let anyone who reflects with sorrow upon these evils so great, so horrid, and so savage, confess that he is miserable. Anyone, however, who either permits or considers these things without sorrow in mind is certainly much more miserable, since he thinks himself happy, because he has lost human feeling.[10]

Augustine is asking a lot of political leaders. If they rise to this standard, there will be many fewer wars.

Augustine realizes that he has to justify his position on the permissible use of lethal force against evildoers by finding a basis in the New Testament. He points out that the New Testament writings show that soldiers serving in the military were recognized as pleasing to God. In response to the Roman centurion who expressed his belief that he could heal his paralyzed servant, Jesus said, "Amen, I say to you I have not found such faith in Israel" (Mt 8:8–10). If Jesus disapproved of the profession of arms, Augustine implies, surely he would have said something to the soldier. Augustine also mentions the centurion Cornelius, to whom an angel said, "Cornelius, your alms have been accepted and your prayers heard" (Acts 10:4). In letter 138 Augustine says,

Indeed, if Christian teaching condemned all wars, then the advice given in the Gospel to the soldiers asking for salvation would have been to throw down their arms and quit the military completely. What they were told, however, was "terrorize no one, accuse no one falsely, and be content with your pay" (Lk 3:14). With these words,...[John the Baptist] commands them to be content with their own pay; he certainly does not prohibit them from serving as soldiers.[11]

Augustine interprets this statement of John to be the mind of Christ.

If the teaching of Jesus allows just wars to be fought, that doesn't mean that political leaders and soldiers fighting in a just war need not worry about their attitudes and dispositions during the war. Augustine explains: "The desire for harming, the cruelty of revenge, the restless and implacable mind, the savageness of revolting, the lust for dominating, and similar things—these are what are justly blamed in wars."[12] In other words, belligerents must observe various norms while fighting in a just war. In later times such norms will be discussed under the rubric of *ius in bello*.

10. Ibid.   11. St. Augustine, *Political Writings*, 209.
12. Ibid., 221–22.

In summary, Augustine set the stage for the development of just-war doctrine by his rich notion of peace, his understanding of war as inevitable because of sin, and his teaching that rulers have an obligation to protect their fellow citizens from unjust attack, even by the judicious use of force. These Augustinian themes remain an important part of modern Catholic teachings on just war, to which we now turn.

Thomas Aquinas and Contemporary Just-War Theorists

John Courtney Murray provides a good introduction to thinking about war by posing two questions. "First, what are the norms that govern recourse to the violence of war? Second, what are the norms that govern the measure of violence to be used in a war? In other words, when is war rightful, and what is rightful in war?"[13] Today, theologians ask, "when is there a *ius ad bellum?*" and "what is *ius in bello?*" Thomas Aquinas, of course, did not make this specific distinction.

Aquinas first introduces us to his thought on war by treating it under the rubric of charity in the second part of the *Summa theologiae.*[14] Unjust war is an offense against charity. Soldiers fighting in a just war are practicing charity, since they put their lives on the line in order to protect the innocent and preserve the common good.

The great thirteenth-century theologian tells us that three things are necessary for a war to be just: a decision by a sovereign authority, a just cause, and a rightful intention. These categories are still used today, although a just cause is usually listed first. The criterion of a competent public authority means that private individuals cannot declare war or summon others to fight in a war. Aquinas gives three reasons for this position. Private parties have the option of asking their superiors or even the sovereign for a redress of their grievances. It belongs to the lawful ruler alone to protect the commonweal, both against internal disturbances and foreign enemies. To that end the ruler may punish evildoers and even use lethal force when necessary. James Turner Johnson provides an interesting explanation of why competent authority came first for Aquinas and other medieval theorists. Many private individuals were claiming the authority to use arms, which "led to a high level of social violence and fragment-

---

13. John Courtney Murray, "War and Conscience," in *A Conflict of Loyalties: The Case for Selective Conscientious Objection,* ed. James Finn (New York: Pegasus, 1968), 21.

14. St. Thomas Aquinas, *Summa theologiae,* II-II, qu. 40.

ed—often unjust—rule by local warlords or armed gangs." Second, the question arose whether the pope and diocesan bishops had the authority to use armed force. Thomas followed the canonists of the late twelfth and thirteenth centuries in holding that only the sovereign rulers of sovereign political entities had the authority to use armed force.[15]

In his own name Johnson offers additional reasons that a competent authority is so important. "The requirement that there must be a right authority for the use of force means that we must inquire whether there is any authority who can control the employment of force so as to limit its effects, and behind that to inquire as to the breadth and depth of popular support this authority possesses."[16] Johnson is referring not only to the head of a legitimate government, but also to the heads of revolutionary groups.

John Courtney Murray recommends an initial deference to a war decision made by the competent political authorities. "In the just-war theory it has always been maintained that the presumption stands for the decision of the community as officially declared. He who dissents from the decision must accept the burden of proof." Murray objects to the view that the spirit of just-war principles "'demands that every war be opposed until or unless it can be morally justified in relation to these principles.'" This especially makes sense when people are not conversant with just-war principles. "The citizen is to concede the justness of the common political decision, made in behalf of the nation, unless and until he is sure in his own mind that the decision is unjust, for reasons that he in turn must be ready convincingly to declare."[17] Even though Murray advocated deference to authority, he was in favor of legalizing selective conscientious objection, with the proviso that the objector give an account of his reasons before "a competent panel of judges."[18] Such a requirement, he thought, could raise the level of political discourse in the country and, in my mind, could help political leaders keep in mind relevant moral norms in their decisions about war. Murray's position both serves to heighten respect for political authority and to encourage thoughtfulness on the part of citizens.

Thomas explains the criterion of just cause by citing a passage from

15. James Turner Johnson, *Morality and Contemporary Warfare* (New Haven, Conn., and London: Yale University Press, 1999), 46–47.

16. Johnson, *Can Modern War Be Just?* (New Haven, Conn., and London: Yale University Press, 1984), 24.

17. Murray, "War and Conscience," 27.

18. Ibid., 28.

Augustine: "A just war is wont to be described as one that avenges wrongs, when a nation or state has to be punished, for refusing to make amends for the wrongs inflicted by its subjects, or to restore what it has seized unjustly."[19] Self-defense is, of course, the third criterion of a just cause. Johnson summarizes Aquinas's understanding of just cause "in terms of three responsibilities" of political leaders: "to maintain order by defending against internal wrongdoing and external attack, to restore justice by punishing those responsible, and to retake any persons, properties or powers wrongly seized by evildoers."[20]

Today, international law seems only to recognize self-defense as a just cause. Yet, Johnson wisely notes that the two other reasons still enter into the determination of a just cause, although under the rubric of self defense. He explains: "A retaliatory second strike, for example, would classically have been called 'punishment for evil'; today it is categorized as 'defense.' The use of force to retake Kuwait from Iraq would have classically been called 'retaking something wrongly taken'; in the language of contemporary international law, however, it was 'defense' against 'armed attack' that remained in progress so long as Iraq occupied Kuwait."[21]

The question naturally arises as to whether the just cause of self-defense includes a preemptive strike. Yes, it does, but great caution is needed. In 1967 Israel correctly determined that their enemies were about to attack and, arguably, did the right thing by taking preemptive measures to protect their citizens. The United States launched a preemptive attack against Iraq in March of 2003 because the administration determined that Saddam Hussein had weapons of mass destruction (WMD) and was planning either to use them or to pass them on to terrorists. It turned out that Mr. Hussein was not hiding WMD.

The determination of a just cause also requires a comparison of the regimes in nations about to go to war. Writing when the Soviet Union was still in existence, William O'Brien gave an illustrative example. "Specifically one must ask whether the political-social order of a country like the United States is sufficiently valuable to warrant its defense against a country like the Soviet Union, which, if victorious would impose its political social order on the United States."[22] One could also ask whether

19. Aquinas, *Summa theologiae* II-II, qu. 40, a. 1.
20. Johnson, *Morality and Contemporary Warfare*, 48.
21. Ibid., 31.
22. William V. O'Brien, *The Conduct of Just and Limited War* (New York: Praeger, 1981), 20.

the regime of South Vietnam was good enough to merit a defense by the United States. That scholars have answered both yes and no to that question indicates that recognizing a just cause will not always be easy.

Other criteria entering into the determination of a just cause are proportionality of ends, last resort, and reasonable hope of success. Only leaders with political prudence will be good at assessing these criteria. Everyone in the state of grace has sufficient prudence to work out his salvation, but not necessarily the political prudence that would enable a leader to do what is best for the common good. Let us recall Aquinas's thought on the matter: "there is also another diligence which is more than sufficient whereby a man is able to make provision both for himself and for others, not only in matters necessary for salvation, but also in all things relating to human life; and such diligence as this is not in all who have grace."[23] What this means is that even leaders of enormous good will may not be astute enough to determine whether it is right or wrong to use armed force in a particular situation.

"The concept of proportionality [or proportionality of ends] in just war tradition," explains Johnson, "means the overall balancing of the good (and evil) a use of force will bring about against the evil of not resorting to force. It begins with the recognition that a loss of value has already occurred (the just cause) prior to the consideration whether force is justified to restore that value."[24] O'Brien insists that "calculation of proportionality between probable good and evil must be made with respect to all belligerents, affected neutrals, and the international community as a whole before initiating a war and periodically throughout a war to reevaluate the balance of good and evil that is actually produced by the war."[25] Paul Ramsey notes that this calculation is very difficult and can be violated both by acts of omission and commission. "But, of all the tests for judging whether to resort to or participate in war, this one balancing an evil or good effect against another is open to the greatest uncertainty. This, therefore, establishes rather than removes the possibility of conscientious disagreement among prudent men."[26] As Aquinas implies, some people are better at making a prudential decision when many

23. Aquinas, *Summa theologiae*, II-II, qu. 47, a. 14.

24. Johnson, *Morality and Contemporary Warfare*, 35.

25. O'Brien, *The Conduct of Just and Limited War*, 28.

26. Paul Ramsey, *The Just War: Force and Political Responsibility* (New York: Charles Scribner's Sons, 1968), 195.

variables have to be considered. Ramsey even refers to the principle of proportionality as the "principle of proportion or prudence."[27]

The criterion of reasonable hope of success doesn't mean that you necessarily have to win the war. Prudent political leaders may realize that even in defeat an important good could be retained or achieved. A stalwart, heroic resistance could bear witness to beliefs and inspire future generations. But it would be imprudent to undertake a defensive war that could only end in defeat, with no prospect of achieving any worthwhile goals. Only leaders with refined political prudence could rightfully make the decision to put their people at risk in a no-win situation.

The requirement that war be a last resort means that "every reasonable peaceful alternative should be exhausted."[28] I would put the emphasis on "reasonable." Prudence can determine that some alternatives are unreasonable or fruitless without actually trying them. This criterion is a logical corollary that war should only be undertaken as a lamentable necessity.

The third major condition for a just war is right intention. Aquinas says the belligerents should intend to promote good or to avoid evil. Then, he quotes two passages from Augustine to indicate more specifically what kinds of things should be avoided and promoted. "True religion looks upon as peaceful those wars that are waged not for motives of aggrandizement, or cruelty, but with the object of securing peace, of punishing evildoers, and of uplifting the good."[29] The second passage indicates only what attitudes are to be avoided. "The passion for inflicting harm, the cruel thirst for vengeance, an unpacific and relentless spirit, the fever of revolt, the lust of power, and such like things, all these are rightly condemned in war." In order to have the kind of intention required by Aquinas, political leaders and the body politic would have to possess various virtues in order to stay focused on pursuing a just peace without succumbing to the temptation of indulging disordered passions. For example, it would have been wrong for President George W. Bush to declare war on Iraq because Saddam Hussein made plans to kill his father. O'Brien further explains right intention by adding that just belligerents must prepare themselves for reconciliation after the fighting is over and

27. Ramsey, "Is Vietnam a Just War?" in *War in the Twentieth Century: Sources in Theological Ethics*, edited by Richard B. Miller (Louisville, Ky.: Westminster/John Knox Press, 1992), 189.
28. O'Brien, *The Conduct of Just and Limited War*, 33.
29. Aquinas, *Summa theologiae*, II-II, qu. 40, art. 1.

maintain the virtue of charity toward their enemies throughout the conflict and in the aftermath. This, at least, means that you don't fight the war in such a way as to make reconciliation impossible or very difficult. For example, you don't use disproportionate force or weapons of mass destruction, and you don't act in such a treacherous way as to undermine all possibility of trust on the part of your enemy after the conclusion of the war.

The proper conduct of the war or *ius in bello* depends on observing the principle of proportion and the principle of discrimination. O'Brien succinctly explains the former in two brief sentences.

In summary, the principle of proportion deals with military means at two levels: (1) tactically, as proportionate to a legitimate military end, *raison de guerre*; and (2) strategically, as proportionate to the just-cause ends of the war, *raison d'état.* The definition of *legitimate military end* and the calculation of the proportionality of means to such an end is a matter of the preexisting standards set by the international law of war and of judgments of reasonableness in the light of accepted practices.[30]

Johnson says that "proportionality of means" means "avoiding needless destruction to achieve justified ends."[31] Otherwise stated, "Proportionality imposes a further positive obligation to seek to accomplish justified military objectives by the least destructive means."[32] Weapons of mass destruction would violate the principle of proportionality and the principle of discrimination, as well.

The principle of discrimination requires belligerents to avoid "direct, intentional harm to non-combatants."[33] The *Catechism* quotes Vatican II to explain this principle with this frequently cited statement: "Every act of war directed to the indiscriminate destruction of whole cities or vast areas with their inhabitants is a crime against God and man, which merits firm and unequivocal condemnation."[34] Many would argue that the carpet bombing of German cities in World War II by Great Britain and the U.S. and the atomic bombing of Hiroshima and Nagasaki violated the principle of discrimination. Johnson rightly points out that the inten-

30. O'Brien, *The Conduct of Just and Limited War*, 42.
31. Johnson, *Morality and Contemporary Warfare*, 36.
32. Ibid., 157.
33. Ibid., 36.
34. *Catechism of the Catholic Church* (Vatican City: Libreria Editrice Vaticana, 1994), quoting Vatican Council II, *Gaudium et spes*, no. 80.

tional killing of the innocent has now become standard policy in many conflicts. "Intentional, direct targeting of civilians has been the pattern in much warfare since World War II, and it is a particular problem in the form that armed conflicts have taken since the end of the Cold War."[35] For a long time the United States and the Soviet Union targeted their strategic nuclear weapons against one another's population centers. Contemporary terrorism is directed at noncombatants on purpose.

Michael Walzer gives a thought-provoking account of the terror bombing that the British decided to inflict on the civilian population in German cities between 1942 and April of 1945. These bombing raids killed about 300,000 people—most of whom were civilians—and seriously wounded another 780,000. The attack on Dresden alone killed 100,000 in the spring of 1945. The purpose of this kind of bombing was to undermine German morale and thus shorten the war and, ultimately, save lives. Arthur Harris, chief of the Bomber Command, argued that the bombing of German cities "was the only force in the West...which could take offensive action...against Germany, our only means of getting at the enemy in a way that would hurt at all."[36] Harris thought that the destruction of German cities was the only thing that could stop Hitler. Another motive for the bombing of German cities was revenge for the German bombing of Coventry and other British cities. Walzer mentions that, according to many historians, Churchill had to satisfy the British desire for revenge in order to maintain their fighting spirit. But opinion surveys done as late as 1944 revealed that a majority of the British thought their bombers were only attacking military targets. Since evidence was available indicating that this was not the case, Walzer judges that British saw "what they wanted to believe."

By mid-1942 the Russian and American participation in the war offered other ways of fighting the war besides the bombing of cities. Winston Churchill grants this, but still said, "All the same, it would be a mistake to cast aside our original thought...that the severe, ruthless bombing of Germany on an ever-increasing scale will not only cripple her war effort...but will create conditions intolerable to the mass of the German population."[37] Walzer maintains that Churchill only had "second thoughts" about this policy after the devastating bombing of Dresden.

35. Johnson, *Morality and Contemporary Warfare*, 120.
36. Michael Walzer, *Just and Unjust Wars: A Moral Argument with Historical Illustrations* (New York: Basic Books, 2000), 258.
37. Ibid., 261.

To the argument that the terror bombing would shorten the war and save lives, Walzer echoes just-war teaching in saying, "the deliberate slaughter of innocent men and women cannot be justified simply because it saves the lives of other men and women."[38] He also notes that the British bombing policy "had further consequences: it was the crucial precedent for the fire-bombing of Tokyo and other Japanese cities and then for Harry Truman's decision to drop atomic bombs on Hiroshima and Nagasaki."[39]

The Jesuit theologian John Ford reflected on the bombing of German cities by the British and American bomber commands in his famous 1944 article, "The Morality of Obliteration Bombing." He conclusively shows that both Great Britain and the United States violated the principle of discrimination by targeting the civilian populations of ninety German cities with obliteration bombing, otherwise known as area bombing. His explanation of the key term is as follows:

Obliteration bombing is the strategic bombing, by means of incendiaries and explosives, of industrial centers of population in which the target to be wiped out is not a definite factory, bridge, or similar object, but a large area of a whole city, comprising one-third to two-thirds of its whole built-up area, and including by design the residential districts of workingmen and their families.[40]

Ford quotes American and British leaders to show that they intended to launch direct attacks on civilians. For example, on May 10, 1942, Churchill, reflecting on the bombing of innocent civilians, said:

The civilian population of Germany have an easy way to escape from these severities. All they have to do is leave the cities where munition work is being carried on, abandon the work [as if the majority were engaged in it] and go out into the fields and watch the home fires burning from a distance. In this way they may find time for meditation and repentance.[41]

Ford cites statements by the bishops of France and the Primate of Belgium, Cardinal Van Roey, respectively calling upon the British and Americans to stop the indiscriminate bombing of civilians in France and Belgium. For example, the French hierarchy made this statement in May of 1944:

38. Ibid., 262.   39. Ibid., 255.
40. John C. Ford, "The Morality of Obliteration Bombing," *Theological Studies* 5 (1944): 267.
41. Ibid., 274.

Almost daily we witness the ruthless devastation inflicted upon the civilian population by air operations carried out by the Allied Powers. Thousands of men, women and children who have nothing to do with war are being killed or injured; their homes are wiped out; churches, schools and hospitals are destroyed....We are convinced that it should be possible to distinguish with greater care between military objectives and humble dwellings of women and children with which they are surrounded.[42]

Ford's judgment: "It is fundamental in the Catholic view that to take the life of an innocent person is always intrinsically wrong, that is, forbidden by natural law."[43]

The only thorny question, Ford argues, is this one: "*Who are to be considered non-combatants in a war like the present one?*" Some military leaders claim that they can now attack civilians, "because modern industrial and economic conditions have changed the nature of war radically and made them all aggressors."[44] Other arguments used to justify direct attacks on civilians are military necessity, reprisals, "the enemy did it first," "the situation is abnormal," and the "whole nation is the aggressor, and not just the army." In a country like the United States Ford estimates that at least three-fourths of the population have nothing to do with the war effort and, therefore, should not be attacked. Ford also rejects the argument that relying on the principle of double effect could justify the bombing of German civilians. By quoting authoritative government sources, Ford shows that the terrorization of civilians was the direct object of Allied bombing policy and not the indirect effect of attacks on military targets. Ford's conclusion, "now I contend that it is impossible to make civilian terrorization or the undermining of civilian morale, an object of bombing without having a direct intent to injure civilians."[45] Even if the killing of civilians were an indirect effect of the bombing, there is no proportionate reason that could justify the evil of civilian deaths, not the shortening of the war, nor the saving of soldiers' lives. "The alleged proportionate cause," Ford concludes, "is speculative, future and problematical, while the evil is definite, widespread, certain and immediate."[46]

Many moralists distinguish carefully the direct, intentional killing of noncombatants from unintended harm to civilians resulting from attacks on military targets. The so-called "collateral damage" is justifiable

42. Ibid., 266.
44. Ibid., 281.
46. Ibid., 302.

43. Ibid., 272.
45. Ibid., 294.

if belligerents are only intending to hit military targets and take reasonable measures to avoid the killing of civilians and the destruction of their property. If the principle of noncombatant immunity could never be violated, even unintentionally, no just war could ever be fought, for war will always bring about some civilian casualties. In classic just-war theory, what is crucial is the intention not to directly attack noncombatants and the adoption of military means that can be controlled. In other words, weapons to be avoided are "broadly destructive or incapable of consistent discriminating use even under the best of conditions. Heavy megatonnage nuclear and thermonuclear weapons fall into the first category, while chemical and bacteriological weapons fall into the latter."[47] If these weapons have long-term effects, such as the spread of radiation, the moral case against them is even stronger.

In thinking about the principle of noncombatant immunity, moralists necessarily make use of the principle of double effect. The direct intention of a belligerent is to hit a military target. That is a morally good act in a just war. An unintended, though foreseen, consequence of his action is the killing of innocent civilians. So, there is a double effect of his action, one intended, the other unintended. This is a justifiable action if the belligerent only intends to hit the military target, does his best to avoid hitting innocent civilians, and simply tolerates the inevitable collateral damage. Killing civilians cannot be part of his intention and not the means to accomplish his end. The good achieved, the striking of the military target, must outweigh the unintended evil, namely, the death of civilians. In other words, "the good effect must be sufficiently desirable to compensate for the allowing of the bad effect."[48]

The emergence of revisionist or proportionalist moral theology has induced some theologians to look at the principle of discrimination in another way. The essence of the revisionist approach is to look for a proportionate reason rather than to distinguish a direct from an indirect intention. Nothing is intrinsically evil in itself. The revisionist argues that a person can do "evil" to achieve good for a proportionate reason. So, a belligerent can kill civilians during wartime if there is a "proportionate reason." According to the revisionists, there is no need to make use of the direct-indirect distinction. It is right to attack the military target if there

47. Johnson, *Can Modern War Be Just?* 71.

48. F. J. Connell, "Principle of Double Effect," *New Catholic Encyclopedia*, vol. 4 (1981), 1021.

is a proportionate or commensurate reason for killing innocent civilians as well. This is one of the positions determined to be incompatible with Catholic teaching by Pope John Paul II in his encyclical *Veritatis splendor* (*The Splendor of Truth*).

The revisionist perspective, introducing a sea-change in moral theology, increases the difficulty of discerning a proportionate reason for tolerating the death of innocent civilians. When the principle of double effect is observed, certain kinds of actions are ruled out a priori before the deliberation about proportionality even begins. According to that principle,

(1) The act itself must be morally good or at least indifferent. (2) The agent may not positively will the bad effect but may merely permit it. If he could attain the good effect without the bad effect, he should do so. (3) [T]he good effect must be produced directly by the action, not by the bad effect. Otherwise, the agent would be using a bad means to a good end, which is never allowed. (4) [T]he good effect must be sufficiently desirable to compensate for the allowing of the bad effect.[49]

Observing the first three requirements of the principle of double effect automatically eliminates some alternatives that could come to the mind of a person attempting to discern a proportionate reason for an action. These requirements are really rules of prudence to be welcomed and followed by a prudent person. Discernment in difficult circumstances is easier when the range of alternatives is reduced by following reliable guidelines. The revisionist perspective increases the chances of erroneous judgment about the presence of a proportionate reason for permitting a bad effect to occur.

Applying the Just-War Ethic

In 1993 the American bishops[50] published a statement in which it briefly addressed the difficulty of applying just-war criteria.

Moral reflection on the use of force calls for a spirit of moderation rare in contemporary political culture. The increasing violence of our society, its growing insensitivity to the sacredness of life and the glorification of the technology of destruction in popular culture could invariably impair our soci-

49. Ibid.
50. The United States Conference of Catholic Bishops was known as the National Conference of Catholic Bishops when this statement was issued.

ety's ability to apply just-war criteria honestly and effectively in time of crisis.

In the absence of a commitment of respect for life and a culture of restraint, it will not be easy to apply the just-war tradition, not just as a set of ideas, but as a system of effective social constraints on the use of force.[51]

The bishops talk about the culture because they know that the opinions of citizens will affect the way political leaders make decisions about war and peace. Given the reality of abortion, surreptitious euthanasia, and the lack of restraint with respect to sex, alcohol, and money, many citizens will not be in a position to reflect carefully about the use of lethal force. Back in the 1960s John Courtney Murray observed: "the American attitude toward war has tended to oscillate between absolute pacifism in peacetime and extremes of ferocity in wartime."[52] As examples of ferocity, he mentioned the fire bombing of Tokyo, the atomic bombing of Hiroshima and Nagasaki, and the saturation bombing of German cities. Murray contends that Americans easily put aside *ius in bello* in seeking the defeat of Japan and Germany. Recently, Jean Bethke Elshtain remarked that just-war thinking presupposes a certain kind of citizen, "one attuned to moral reasoning and capable of it; one strong enough to resist the lure of seductive enthusiasms of violence; one laced through with a sense of responsibility and accountability; in other words, a morally formed character."[53] To sum up what the bishops Murray and Elshtain are saying: citizens in a democratic nation need to be virtuous and capable of moral reasoning in their political discourse. This is a high standard, which will surely not always be met. What could save a democratic nation from violating *ius ad bellum* and *ius in bello*? I would suggest the quality of its leaders. But since the election of such leaders will not always happen, a nation will fail, at times or often, to grasp and apply just-war principles. This is a sobering thought.

George Weigel has argued that "the just war tradition remains alive in our national cultural memory."[54] Certainly, it does inform American mores, but there have been violations of just-war teachings in America's wars and there will be more in the measure that education and character

51. National Conference of Catholic Bishops (NCCB), *"The Harvest of Justice Is Sown in Peace: A Reflection of the National Conference of Catholic Bishops on the Tenth Anniversary of The Challenge of Peace;* available at http://www.usccb.org/sdwp/harvest.shtml.

52. Murray, "War and Conscience," 20.

53. Jean Bethke Elshtain, "Just War as Politics: What the Gulf War Told Us About Contemporary American Life," in *But Was It Just? Reflections on the Morality of the Persian Gulf War* (New York: Doubleday, 1992), 46.

54. George Weigel, "Moral Clarity in a Time of War," *First Things*, no. 129 (2003): 21.

formation are deficient. One form of education is that given by the president from his "bully pulpit" and other spokesmen for the nation. Writing about the morality of the first Gulf War, Elshtain addressed the question of the many unintended civilian deaths caused by errant bombing in Baghdad. She rightly commented, "this tragedy should have been addressed by the President and our military spokesmen in language of deep regret and acknowledgment of responsibility—a responsibility ironically magnified precisely *because* our bombs were so smart."[55] I vividly remember the wild cheering when President George H. W. Bush addressed Congress shortly after the first Gulf War ended. There was no mention of regret for the unintentional killing of civilians. By his silence President Bush passed up a valuable opportunity to educate the citizenry by apologizing for killing Iraqi civilians while attacking military targets. Saying such things from the heart on momentous occasions would teach many Americans a valuable lesson about the just-war ethic and help ensure its preservation.

In writing about the first Gulf War Elshtain brought up another important topic: the role of women soldiers in war. She expressed misgivings about sending young mothers off to the war zone, separating them from their infants and young children. "A society that puts the needs of its children dead last," she writes, "is a society 'progressing' rapidly toward moral ruin."[56] Even Israel, Elshtain points out, exempts married women from all military service. Israel does have women soldiers, but they don't participate in combat on land, sea, or in the air. In the first Gulf War American women were in the war zone but didn't participate in combat, although an NBC/*Wall Street Journal* poll revealed that "74 percent of women and 71 percent of men...favored sending women on combat missions."[57] Sixty-four percent of Americans were, however, against sending mothers of young children into combat. Given the emphasis on rights, equality of opportunity, careerism, and individualism in American culture, it is not surprising to see a majority of Americans in favor of giving women the opportunity to earn their spurs by participating in combat. The desire of sixty-four percent of Americans to spare mothers of young children from combat showed that the culture had not completely overwhelmed common sense. Even during the second war with Iraq, Americans reacted differently when women soldiers were taken prisoner. Today new mothers will be deployed in the war zone, but still not in ground

55. Elshtain, "Just War as Politics," 51.   56. Ibid., 58.
57. Ibid., 57.

combat. Women, however, are now eligible to fly attack planes and attack helicopters.

In his third book-length interview Cardinal Ratzinger made pointed comments about the growing tendency to recruit women as soldiers.

Personally it still horrifies me when people want women to be soldiers just like men, when they, who have always been the keepers of the peace and in whom we have always seen a counterforce working against the male's willingness to stand up and go to war, now likewise run around with submachine guns, showing that they can be just as warlike as men.[58]

Ratzinger implies that to have about half the human race as a force for peace is a good thing for nations. Excepting women from combat is a reminder that fighting in a war, however just, is an exceptional and undesirable activity. Even though soldiers can do righteous deeds by participating in a just war, they do not hope and pray that all their friends and relatives can join them. War is always a lamentable necessity, even when it is a righteous deed.

One last point. The responsibility of applying the just-war ethic belongs to political leaders, not religious authorities. The latter can lay out the principles and even make a judgment about their application, but political leaders must assume the final responsibility for particular judgments about whether to go to war and how to fight it. George Weigel explains:

If the just war tradition is indeed a tradition of statecraft, then the proper role of religious leaders and public intellectuals is to do everything possible to clarify the moral issues at stake in a time of war, while recognizing that what we might call the "charism of responsibility" lies elsewhere—with duly constituted public authorities, who are more fully informed about the relevant facts and who must bear the weight of responsible decision-making and governance. It is simple clericalism to suggest that religious leaders own the just-war tradition in a singular way.[59]

Pacifism and Conscientious Objection

Vatican II's *Gaudium et spes* addresses the subject of pacifism in two oft-quoted passages.

58. Joseph Cardinal Ratzinger, *God and the World: A Conversation with Peter Seewald* (San Francisco: Ignatius Press, 2002), 82.
59. Weigel, "Moral Clarity in a Time of War," 27.

We cannot fail to praise those who renounce the use of violence in the vindication of their rights and who resort to methods of defense which are otherwise available to weaker parties too, provided that this can be done without injury to the rights and duties of others or of the community itself.[60]

It seems right that laws make provision for the case of those who for reasons of conscience refuse to bear arms, provided however, that they accept some other form of service to the human community.[61]

Vatican II recognizes that some individuals "for reasons of conscience" cannot personally participate in the defense of their country by bearing arms. This is a legitimate and praiseworthy moral choice for individuals to make, argues Vatican II, as long as their conscientious decision doesn't harm other individuals or the community itself. The Council further argues that "it seems right" (*aequum videtur*) that the laws allow individuals to be conscientious objectors to all wars, provided that they perform some other service for the community. It is interesting to note that Vatican II takes pains to qualify its endorsement of conscientious objection in two ways: it must not do injury to other individuals or to the political community, and the conscientious objectors must perform some kind service for their fellow citizens. If members of the armed forces are "agents of security and freedom on behalf of their people," then it is fitting and necessary for conscientious objectors likewise to serve their country in some way. In no way does Vatican II call into question the right of a state to defend itself from unjust attack. Immediately after expressing its approval of state-sanctioned conscientious objection, Vatican II reaffirms Church teaching on the legitimacy of just defense.

As long as the danger of war remains and there is no competent and sufficiently powerful authority at the international level, governments cannot be denied the right to legitimate defense once every means of peaceful settlement has been exhausted. Therefore, government authorities and others who share public responsibility have the duty to protect the welfare of the people entrusted to their care and to conduct such grave matters soberly.[62]

The question naturally arises today whether Vatican II authorizes conscientious objectors to believe as Catholic doctrine that no state may legitimately defend itself with armed force against an unjust attack. The answer is clearly no.

60. Vatican Council II, *Gaudium et spes (Pastoral Constitution in the Modern World)*, 78.
61. Ibid., 79.   62. Ibid.

The Council doesn't make clear in what circumstances conscientious objection of some individuals would pose a danger to others or to the nation itself. Noteworthy too is the Council's way of endorsing the legalization of conscientious objection. It "seems right" for government to exempt conscientious objectors from military service by law. Vatican II doesn't *urge* governments to enact such legislation. The *Catechism of the Catholic Church*, however, does encourage governments to grant exemption to military service in these words: "Public authorities should make equitable provision for those who for reasons of conscience refuse to bear arms."[63]

In line with Vatican Council II, the *Catechism* doesn't teach that it is acceptable for a Catholic to believe that the state is forbidden to defend itself with force of arms against an unjust attack. Official Church teaching only recognizes the right of individuals to recuse themselves from bearing arms for reasons of conscience. The Council and the *Catechism* expect conscientious objectors to serve their country in some other way when they are unable to bear arms. Catholic citizens are, however, encouraged to use just-war criteria to determine whether or not a particular war is justified. The very existence of just-war doctrine implies that in some instances Catholics will have to refuse to fight in what they deem to be unjust wars. This is what is called selective conscientious objection, and is the necessary consequence of just-war reasoning. By endorsing the concept of a just war, Vatican II implicitly gives moral approval to selective conscientious objection, but doesn't call for its legalization or even mention it by name.

In the 1960s the National Advisory Commission on Selective Service took up as one of its topics the question of selective conscientious objection (SCO). Only a minority on the commission, including John Courtney Murray, S.J., as mentioned, voted in favor of its legalization. Commenting on the minority report, Paul Ramsey made several revealing observations on implementing legal provisions for SCO in the United States. "Its acceptability depends first of all upon whether there exists in the ethos of this country a moral consensus or doctrine on the uses of military force" that could be used in determining the statutory grounds on which individuals could base their objections to a particular war the United States was waging or planning to wage.[64] Ramsey be-

63. *Catechism of the Catholic Church*, no. 2311.

64. Paul Ramsey, "Selective Conscientious Objection: Warrants and Reservations," in *A Conflict of Loyalties: the Case For Selective Conscientious Objection*, edited by James Finn (New York: Pegasus, 1968), 39.

lieves this moral consensus is indispensable as a basis for deliberation and judgment. Without it the decisions of individuals would be arbitrary or simply the result of partisan political judgments. He believes that no nation should exempt its citizens from participating in a particular war for merely "political" reasons.

One of the main reasons Congress will not and should not legalize SCO, according to Ramsey, is the disappearance of common theological and philosophical principles in the nation and within religious communities.

The first [trend] is the steady erosion, for at least three or four decades, of shared basic convictions concerning normative structures in social ethics having for religious people final theological warrant. There has been a flight from the use of rational principles of analysis, and a lack of political philosophy or norms governing our deliberation upon moral questions. This means that there can be no fundamental moral consensus among or within the religious communities of our nation....The name of the game is casuistry without principles, decision-making that is believed to be more responsible because situations are so unique that there are no relevant, specific norms.

Writing in the late 1960s, Ramsey believed that the "refinement in moral judgment" would be very rare in the discussion of every moral matter, "including the morality of war." As a result individuals appearing before a government panel to argue their case for the status of SCO would hardly be in a position to elevate the discourse of the nation, either on the decision to go to war or on war conduct. Ramsey hoped that SCO were possible in the United States, because thoughtful individual objectors to a particular war would engender "the state's acknowledgment of some transcendence over its particular decisions on the part of this juridical order, resident within its own body politic, even when it does not agree or think it possible to act in accord with these claims."[65] In other words, public recognition of well-thought-out conscientious objection to a particular war would remind political leaders and the entire body of citizens that policy and laws are subject to transcendent moral norms. That kind of reminder is important for the health of political life.

Murray's endorsement of SCO was not without some caveats. Like Ramsey, he is concerned about the ignorance of selective conscientious objectors. They could have an erroneous conscience, which will have to

65. Ibid., 73–74.

be respected by the government if SCO is legalized. Consequently, Murray argues that "the political community cannot be blamed for harboring the fear that if the right to selective objection is acknowledged in these sweeping terms [necessary deference to decisions of an erroneous conscience], it might possibly lead to anarchy, to the breakdown of society, and to the paralysis of public policy."[66] The only way SCO would work, Murray argues, is if there were enough "political and moral discretion" in the body politic. The consciences of citizens would have to be formed and informed. Murray doesn't say, like Ramsey, that such discretion doesn't exist on a wide scale in America, but he does say: "To cultivate this power of discretion is a task for all of us."[67]

In 1968, three years after the close of Vatican Council II, the U.S. bishops expressed their approval of conscientious objection, and then called for the legalization of selective conscientious objection, although with none of the caveats mentioned by Ramsey and Murray.

We...recommend a modification of the Selective Service Act making it possible, although not easy, for so-called selective conscientious objectors to refuse—without fear of imprisonment or loss of citizenship—to serve in wars which they consider unjust or in branches of service (e.g., the strategic nuclear forces) which would subject them to the performance of actions contrary to deeply held moral convictions about indiscriminate killing. Some other form of service to the human community should be required of those so exempted.[68]

In 1971 and 1983 the bishops reiterated their support of conscientious objection and their call for the legalization of selective conscientious objection.

When people decide to become conscientious objectors, they could still logically believe that their country could defend itself in a just war. An analogy may clarify this point. Individuals can both believe that it is right for them to live a life of celibacy and right for others to enter into the state of matrimony. Likewise, people can believe that it would be wrong for them to participate in a just war because of their chosen way of life, but right for others because it is their way of fulfilling duties to God and country. Thomas Aquinas taught both that war can be just under certain conditions and that bishops and priests cannot participate in just wars be-

66. Murray, "War and Conscience," 30.   67. Ibid.

68. National Conference of Catholic Bishops, "Human Life in Our Day," in *Pastoral Letters of the American Hierarchy*, vol. 3. 1962–1974, edited by Hugh J. Nolan (Washington, D.C.: National Conference of Catholic Bishops, United States Catholic Conference, 1983–1984), no. 152: 704.

cause of their way of life. He first argues that "warlike pursuits are full of unrest, so that they hinder the mind very much from the contemplation of Divine things, the praise of God, and prayers for the people, which belong to the duties of the cleric." Second, he says that it is not fitting for clerics to shed blood, even in a just war, because they have the duty to enact the memorial of Christ's death and resurrection. He adds that it is "more fitting that they should be ready to shed their blood for Christ, so as to imitate in deed what they portray in their ministry." Aquinas gives a third reason in a reply to an objection. He says, "Although it is meritorious to wage a just war, nevertheless it is rendered unlawful for clerics, by reason of their being deputed to works more meritorious still. Thus the marriage act may be meritorious; and yet it becomes reprehensible in those who have vowed virginity, because they are bound to a greater good."[69] If clerics should be exempt from military service because of their work, one could argue that the same exemption should be extended to lay persons who make special commitments to follow Christ more closely in some way. The Church could then teach that there is a special kind of life that goes along with being a pacifist, that is, a greater-than-average dedication to the highest level of perfection demanded by the Gospel.

What about Catholic conscientious objectors who deny that there is such a thing as a justifiable use of force by a state? It seems to me that Catholics should not embrace absolute pacifism, because of the Church's long-standing support of the just-war ethic. To deny a state the moral authority to defend with military force its own people or innocent victims in other countries from unjust attack is a failure to love one's neighbor. It may also be an implicit denial that sin can have devastating effects if not resisted by force of arms when the conditions for a just war are met. (At other times the effects of sin will have to be borne with patient endurance, as the Bible teaches.) Third, the acceptance of both absolute pacifism and the just-war ethic as authentic Catholic teaching lends support to those theologians who advocate the legitimacy of dissent from long-standing Catholic moral teaching by means of proportionalism or historicism. If Church leaders on the local level ever taught that Catholics can rightfully believe that the just-war ethic is either moral or immoral, soon revisionist theologians and others would reasonably say, "Why not say the same thing about contraception, same-sex marriage, divorce?"

69. Aquinas, *Summa theologiae*, II-II, qu. 40, art. 2.

The Tension between Catholic
Social Doctrine and the Proponents
of Religion as a Private Affair

The most obvious source of tension between Catholic social doctrine and American liberal democracy is the emphasis on autonomy in contemporary culture. Many people just want to create their own values without being bothered with the teachings of natural law or revealed religion. When the Catholic Church calls abortion, euthanasia, premarital sex, gay marriage, and cloning immoral, the relativists bristle. They wonder why anyone or any institution would dare try to "impose values" on their fellow Americans. They may think the Church is irrelevant, but recognize her right to teach faith and morals. Today, however, there is a group of liberal theorists who think that religion is a private affair and shouldn't be a presence in the public square. The first part of this chapter will explain the thought of these theorists, who have already had a significant effect on the opinion-makers in the culture. In order to explain why liberal theorists insist on describing religion as a private affair, I will briefly examine John Locke's *A Letter Concerning Toleration* and then turn to the writings of several contemporary liberal theorists: John Rawls (through the eyes of Michael Sandel), Stephen Macedo, and William Galston.

The liberal insistence that religion is a private affair is a very old opinion. It goes back at least to Locke's *Epistola de tolerantia (A Letter Concerning Toleration)*, published in 1689. Locke's liberalism requires religion and the Church to stay out of the affairs of the commonwealth. I do not propose to summarize his arguments, but only to mention a few of his points that will shed light on the contemporary attempt to limit the influence of religion, to impair its transmission, and even to transform its content.

Locke argues that the commonwealth should be constituted solely for the purpose of preserving and advancing civil goods, namely, life, liberty, bodily health, comfort, and the various forms of wealth.[1] One condition for the realization of this end is the establishment of the proper relation between the commonwealth and the Church (i.e., absolute separation between the two institutions). "The church itself is absolutely separate and distinct from the commonwealth and civil affairs. The boundaries on both sides are fixed and immovable."[2] Locke achieves this clear-cut separation by defining each institution in such a way that their respective ends are mutually exclusive. The commonwealth attains and preserves civil goods and the Church works for the salvation of souls. To realize its purpose, the Church will be absolutely free both to propose speculative doctrines for belief and to observe those forms of worship that are judged helpful unto salvation. By describing religion most frequently (no less than thirty times) as belief in doctrines or dogmas or faith or opinions, and as belief in, and observance of, forms of worship or rites, Locke theoretically excludes religion from the domain of civil affairs. Without harm to the state, people may freely embrace the doctrines and worship of their choice. Beliefs and worship are to have no effect on civil life. As Locke puts it, "In this society [i.e., the Church] nothing is or can be done that relates to the possession of civil or earthly goods."[3]

Locke, of course, knows that neatly separating the concerns of church and state is not so simple. He tacitly concedes the dubious validity of the absolute distinction between them by his remarks on religiously grounded moral actions. Locke admits that practical doctrines and some forms of worship have as their consequence moral actions that can affect the end of the state. In the case of conflict the government should not tolerate any moral actions that are "contrary to the good morals which are necessary for the preservation of civil society."[4] Clearly, Locke implies that the business of the commonwealth and the Church are not so distinct as he proclaimed elsewhere. Nevertheless, he spends a good deal of his *Letter* making a seemingly impressive case for the absolute separation of church and state.

Locke goes further than recommending toleration of one religious group or Church by another. He asserts that "Mutual toleration among Christians…is the chief distinguishing mark of a [or the] true church."[5]

---

1. John Locke, *Epistola de Tolerantia (A Letter Concerning Toleration)*, tr. J. W. Gough (Oxford: Clarendon Press, 1968), 67.

2. Ibid., 85.

3. Ibid., 117.

4. Ibid., 131.

5. Ibid., 59.

This implies that two or more groups of Christians exhibit the chief mark of a true Church when they tolerate each other. Another implication is that the true Church or churches would probably not insist on orthodoxy, but rather emphasize toleration of dissenters. Locke's dogmatic statement is remarkable, given that neither scripture, nor tradition, nor the Magisterium teaches such a doctrine. How could Locke fail to mention belief in the Trinity, the Incarnation, and redemption or at least love of God and neighbor as chief distinguishing marks? Locke's statement could, of course, be interpreted in a way that does not break with traditional Christian convictions. Christians getting along with each other in a spirit of love has always been regarded as a sign of true Christianity. In John's Gospel we read that Christians are recognized by the love they show each other. In other New Testament passages Christians are urged to bear with one another's faults. Mutual toleration could then be read as a new way of expressing this venerable teaching. It is more likely, however, that Locke is giving a new interpretation of the Christian religion in order to promote his political ends. Mutual toleration among Christians contributes to peace and prosperity.

Political theorist Stephen Macedo makes reference to Locke's extraordinary comment on toleration in a few illuminating sentences. "So toleration (the basic liberal virtue) is in the first instance defended as a religious mandate....Strikingly, the principal theme of much of the *Letter* is that Christ and the Gospels command toleration."[6] Striking indeed! How convenient for Locke that Christ and the Gospels mandated the practice of toleration, the mainspring of political liberalism. Locke knew that the success of his liberalism depended upon the support of private beliefs and practices.

Locke does favor religiously grounded morality insofar as it contributes to the good order of his kind of state. "At the last judgment, God will reward everyone according to his merit, that is according as he promoted the public good [security of life, liberty, and property], peace and piety, sincerely and according to law or justice and right."[7] Locke surely has in mind the transformation of Christian morality into a code of behavior that is subordinate to the ends of the state. Traditional Christian

6. Stephen Macedo, "Transformative Constitutionalism and the Case of Religion: Defending the Moderate Hegemony of Liberalism," *Political Theory* 26, (1998); page 7 in Proquest.

7. Locke, *Epistola de Tolerantia*, 36 (modified translation).

teaching states that God will reward man according to the degree of his love for God and neighbor. This love may or may not promote the public good sought by a particular commonwealth. Locke's commonwealth, with its emphasis on gain and security, is in tension with the Christian emphasis on detachment from material goods and trust in God. Thus, traditional Christian moral teaching would not promote the public good exactly as Locke understands it. Christian moral teaching, therefore, has to be transformed to help ensure the success of Locke's new regime.

Locke prudently provides for situations in which the wrong kind of religiously grounded morality would be taken seriously. He lays down a hard-and-fast rule: no religious doctrines with practical consequences "incompatible with human society, and contrary to the good morals which are necessary for the preservation of civil society, are to be tolerated by the magistrate."[8] Religiously grounded moral actions are to be clearly *subordinate* to the ends of the commonwealth. To deemphasize this crucial subordination, Locke quickly adds that the advocacy of illegal moral actions by a church would be rare. "For no sect is likely to reach such a degree of madness as to think fit to teach, as doctrines of religion, things which manifestly undermine the foundations of society, and are therefore condemned by *the judgment of all mankind*" (my emphasis).[9] From Locke's perspective the possibility of conflict between church and state will be reduced in the measure that people come more and more to accept the exclusive role of belief and worship for the attainment of salvation; and in the measure that Christian morality is subtly transformed from a "faith working through love" into a code of behavior that promotes Lockean civil goods. In my mind, *le sage* Locke was not averse to redefining Christianity in a way that might be plausible to Christians and singularly beneficial to his political aims.

Three hundred-plus years after Locke, liberalism continues to find various ways to keep religion and churches out of the public square. Supreme Court decisions, political theories such as Rawls's political liberalism, the self-limitation of theologians and churches in addressing public problems, and the typical American understanding of religion as a private affair have all contributed to the separation of religion and politics.

In reflecting on Alan Wolfe's *One Nation, After All*, a sociological survey of Americans, Jean Bethke Elshtain noticed that the middle-class respon-

8. Ibid., 131.
9. Ibid.

dents to Wolfe's survey "begin by viewing religion as a private matter to be discussed only reluctantly." She notes with dismay that many people really want religion "reduced to a purely private role." The separation of church and state is now interpreted by many to mean that society should be secularized. Elshtain adds,

> To a good many of the middle-class respondents in the book, public expression itself is forcing something on someone else: you have already crossed a line because you are supposed to keep quiet about what you believe most strongly.... Consider the remarks of Jody Fields, one of Wolfe's respondents. "If you are a Hindu and you grew up being a Hindu, keep it to yourself.... Don't impose your religion, and make me feel bad because I do this and you do that." I submit that is not tolerance at all but, rather an intolerance of religious pluralism: if one changes Hindu to Jew in the comment that becomes clearer.[10]

Locke, of course, would be pleased with middle-class Americans who think like Jody Fields.

Back in 1983 I attended a summer seminar, sponsored by the National Endowment of the Humanities, on biomedical ethics given by a religious ethicist. After a short time I realized that nothing theological was going to be said. The leader of the seminar and all the participants, whether theologians or philosophers, all talked the same language, and it wasn't in the least theological. My experience was not unique. One of America's most insightful bioethicists, Leon Kass, has noted the paucity of theological reflection by theologians on bioethical issues: "Most religious ethicists entering the public practice of ethics leave their special religious insights at the door and talk about 'deontological vs. consequentialist,' 'autonomy vs. paternalism,' 'justice vs. utility,' just like everybody else."[11] Kass also notes that the nonreligious mainstream in the field regard theological insights "as hopelessly parochial or sectarian."[12] To be a player and to be taken seriously, religious ethicists conclude that they must limit themselves to the reigning philosophical language and concepts.

Following in the footsteps of Locke, contemporary political theorists have tried to provide a theoretical justification for excluding religion from the public square. Michael Sandel provides a nice summary of the liberal

10. Jean Bethke Elshtain, "How Should We talk?" *Case Western Reserve Law Review* 49 (1999): 744.
11. Leon Kass, "Practicing Ethics: Where's the Action," *Hastings Center Report* (January/February, 1990): 7.
12. Ibid., 6.

project to set up a government that "should be neutral among compet-
ing conceptions of the good life. Despite their various accounts of what
rights we have, rights-oriented liberals agree that the principles of justice
that specify our rights should not depend for their justification on any
particular conception of the good life."[13] In other words, liberals believe
that "rights can be identified and justified in a way that does not presup-
pose any particular conception of the good."[14] This is, of course, an extraordinary claim that we can adequately understand justice without appealing to some notion of the good or to our ends as human beings.
Sandel's questions about this project reveal its far-reaching implications.
"[In reflecting on justice] why must we 'bracket,' or set aside, our moral
and religious convictions, our conceptions of the good life? Why should
we not base the principles of justice that govern the basic structure of society on our best understanding of the highest human ends?"[15]

In *Political Liberalism* John Rawls, for example, argues that there are neutral principles of justice on which everyone can and should agree. These
indisputable principles of justice, he argues, can be determined without
relying on any theological and philosophical views of the good, about
which there is and always will be reasonable pluralism. Once accepted,
these so-called neutral principles of justice establish the parameters within which citizens are to make moral arguments about public matters. Just
as there is an absolute separation between the affairs of the Church and
the commonwealth for Locke, so for Rawls there is an absolute separation between justice and conceptions of the good, whether theological or
philosophical. Sandel's most serious objection to this political arrangement is cogent. "According to the ideal of public reason advanced by political liberalism," writes Sandel, "citizens may not legitimately discuss
fundamental political and constitutional questions with reference to their
moral and religious ideals. But this is an unduly severe restriction that
would impoverish political discourse and rule out important dimensions
of public deliberation."[16]

Rawls and his defenders would reply that neutral principles of justice
would prevent people of different religious and philosophical conviction
from disrupting the constitutional and political order with their inter-

13. Michael Sandel, review of *Political Liberalism*, by John Rawls, *Harvard Law Review* 107
(1994): 1766.
14. Ibid., 1767.　　　　　　15. Ibid., 1772–73.
16. Ibid., 1776.

minable arguments and would enable them to cooperate for the common good. Rawls is assuming that "the exercise of human reason under conditions of freedom will *not* produce disagreements about justice." Even a cursory glance at political reality indicates that Rawls's position cannot be true. As Sandel says,

Consider, for example contemporary debates about affirmative action, income distribution and tax fairness, health care, immigration, gay rights, free speech versus hate speech, and capital punishment, to name a few. Or consider the divided votes and conflicting opinions of Supreme Court justices in cases involving religious liberty, freedom of speech, privacy rights, voting rights, the rights of the accused, and so on. Do not these debates display a "fact of reasonable pluralism" about justice?[17]

Consider how Rawls's principles of justice work in practice with respect to abortion. Government neutrality on abortion would mean that the political values of toleration and women's equality would prevail, and that any moral and religious convictions about the origin of life and the status of the embryo would be bracketed. That is to say, it would not be appropriate or permissible to argue against the legality of abortion on the basis of some comprehensive moral or religious viewpoint. So a neutral principle of justice would require the toleration of a woman's right to choose abortion and would not allow Catholic doctrine on abortion to be debated in the public arena. Sandel explains,

In the debate about abortion rights, those who believe that the fetus is a person from the moment of conception and that abortion is therefore murder could not seek to persuade their fellow citizens of this view in open political debate. Nor could they vote for a law that would restrict abortion on the basis of this moral or religious conviction.[18]

The bracketing or exclusion of these comprehensive views in the public arena would extend to all matters pertaining to justice and rights.

Rawls argues that "the ideal of public reason" requires the exclusion of all comprehensive religious and moral views from the affairs of the commonwealth. Sandel lays out the implications of this position.

According to this ideal [of public reason], political discourse should be conducted solely in terms of "political values" that all citizens can reasonably be

17. Ibid., 1783.
18. Ibid., 1790.

expected to accept. Because citizens of democratic societies do not share comprehensive moral and religious conceptions, public reason should not refer to such conceptions.[19]

This very narrow understanding of public reason would keep the Church out of the public square.

Just as Locke erected sharp boundaries between Church and commonwealth by narrow and questionable descriptions of both institutions, so too does Rawls separate religion from the political order by a narrow and questionable description of what counts as "public reason," and by limiting the teachings of the Church to the private realm. From the point of view of the Catholic Church and other churches as well, Rawls's political theory unduly restricts religious freedom. As Jean Bethge Elshstain says, "But a private religion makes no sense. One must have public expression of a faith in order for it to be faith."[20]

If Rawls's theory were accepted by religious believers, it would lead to a transformation of their faith into something other than it is. Theologian Stanley Hauerwas is famous for pointing out that churches and religious believers sometimes imprudently accept the place carved out for them by political liberalism and then address political questions on the world's terms, and not on the basis of their own teachings. In reviewing Hauerwas's work, Thomas Hibbs directs attention to the theologian's problems with the language of the pro-life movement: the right to life instead of the gift of life, as taught by scripture. Hibbs explains, "Right-to lifers may thereby gain a hearing in the public realm, but they also distort the distinctively Christian understanding of human dependence—and thus unwittingly reinforce the notion that our humanity consists in our prized autonomy, our self-conscious independence from others."[21] I would add that many Catholics are much more comfortable using the language of rights in addressing public questions than the language of virtue. Political liberalism leads to a "liberal monism," to use Elshstain's phrase. All political participants are induced in various ways to use the same language: rights, toleration, fairness, values.

Not only do individuals, groups, and churches voluntarily trim their religious teachings under the influence of political liberalism, but some

19. Ibid., 1789.
20. "How Should We Talk?" 744.
21. Thomas Hibbs, "Stanley Hauerwas's Pacifism: The Radical Gospel," *The Weekly Standard* 7, no. 34 (2002): 38.

political theorists are intent on inducing churches and their adherents to reshape their teachings so that they are more compatible with Rawls's understanding of "public reason." A good example of this tendency can be found in the writings of Stephen Macedo. He wants religions to be transformed so that they are more in harmony with political liberalism. He notes with satisfaction the liberalizing effect that American democracy has had on the Catholic Church, making it

a positive and in many instances decisive force for liberalization around the world. The indirect, educative effects of American liberal democracy may have altered, in this way, not only the beliefs of American Catholics but also the official doctrine of the Roman Catholic Church itself, and thereby the beliefs of Catholics around the world. This story represents a dramatic triumph of the spirit of transformative constitutionalism.[22]

This kind of transformation operates indirectly on the sentiments and thoughts of believers and is, therefore, not oppressive in the traditional sense. Parents are indirectly induced not to educate their children in, say, an Aristotelian or Augustinian understanding of politics. Children so raised would develop a view of citizenship at odds with the liberal one, "which we have good reason to see as the best conception available."

We have good reason to hope that there will be fewer families raising such children in the future. We should, therefore, preserve liberal institutions, practices, rituals, and norms that psychologically tax people unequally, for if that has the effect of turning people's lives—including their most "private" beliefs—in directions that are congruent with and supportive of liberalism, thank goodness it does. This is what transformative constitutionalism is all about."[23]

Macedo also calls this approach "the 'moderate hegemony' of liberal public values." He doesn't understand himself to be introducing a new approach to the problem of religion in America. Macedo reminds his readers that "on Herberg's account, the three great religions of America have...followed...at least the basic imperatives of liberalism in America."[24]

22. Stephen Macedo, "Transformative Constitutionalism and the Case of Religion: Defending the Moderate Hegemony of Liberalism," *Political Theory* 26, no. 1 (February 1998): 56–80; see also http://www.jstor.org/stable/191869; page 9 in Proquest.

23. Ibid.; page 13 in Proquest.

24. Ibid.; page 10 in Proquest. Will Herberg wrote a well-known book on religion in

In reflecting on how educational vouchers work in practice, Macedo shows how a liberal regime might induce religious institutions to transform themselves. Voucher plans in Milwaukee and Cleveland require participating private schools "to admit voucher students on a random basis and to excuse voucher students from compulsory religious exercises."[25] Macedo applauds the likely results of these public requirements on religiously affiliated schools.

The school's affiliation with the particular sponsoring religious community may be somewhat muted, even attenuated, or at least revised as a consequence; religious references in the curriculum may become more ecumenical, or else perhaps robust expressions of sectarianism will tend to be confined to certain voluntary aspects of the curriculum.[26]

Commenting on this reflection by Macedo, Michael McConnell writes, "In other words, private religious schools would be forced by the internal pressure of a diverse student body to soften, and perhaps abandon, their religious identity and message."[27] I don't think that Macedo wants religious schools to "abandon" their religious identity, but he definitely would like to see it watered down in case of conflict with political liberalism. What he especially desires from religious schools is indoctrination in the core values of political liberalism, because he knows that the survival of liberalism depends on educating citizens to practice the liberal virtues. Macedo also knows that liberal civic education, given in a public or religious school, "is bound to have the effect of favoring some ways of life or religious convictions over others." Macedo's comment on this fact: "So be it."[28]

Macedo's political liberalism not only confines religion to the private sphere, but also recommends modifying the content of religions that don't accept their confinement to the private sphere, or whose teachings can't accommodate the fundamental principles of political liberalism.

America entitled *Protestant, Catholic and Jew: An Essay in American Religious Sociology* (1960; Chicago: University of Chicago Press, 1983).

25. Michael W. McConnell, "Religion and Civic Education: The New Establishmentarianism," *Chicago-Kent Law Review* 75 (2000): 470.

26. Stephen Macedo, "Religion and Civic Education Constituting Civil Society: School Vouchers, Religious Nonprofit Organizations, and Liberal Public Values," *Chicago-Kent Law Review* 75 (2000): 437.

27. McConnell, "The New Establishmentarianism," 471.

28. Macedo, "Liberal Civic Education and Religious Fundamentalism: The Case of God v. John Rawls?" *Ethics* 105 (April 1995): 485.

This modification or transformation would be affected by the pervasive influence of liberal principles on the minds and hearts of religious believers.

A liberal thinker who is more tolerant of religion and religious diversity is William Galston. Not surprisingly, Macedo believes that Galston "seems…to go well beyond giving 'diversity its due' when he advances an interpretation of liberalism as the 'Diversity State,' a state that affords 'maximum feasible space for the enactment of individual and group differences, constrained only by the requirements of liberal social unity.'"[29] Throughout the 1990s William Galston continued to write about the requisite conditions for the viability of the liberal state. His fundamental principles have not changed. He still believes that a liberal regime is "a community of subcommunities," which is unified on the basis of core principles inculcated by public and private education and enforced by law.[30] While Galston allows more space for religion and churches in the public square, he recommends silence on certain matters, any imposition of which would infringe on the religious liberty of Catholics, other Christians, and people of other religious persuasions.

While allowing considerable diversity in the subcommunities, a liberal community, Galston admits, does have a distinctive influence on the lives of most individuals, families, groups, and churches. In other words, individuals are free in principle to choose a way of life, but liberal public principles exercise a gravitational pull on people's day-to-day life. Galston's description of liberalism's influence is imaginative and, in my mind, quite accurate.

To understand this dimension think of the social space constituted by liberal political principles as a rapidly flowing river. A few vessels may be strong

29. Ibid., 470, n. 8.

30. For example, Galston argues that the liberal state properly aims to protect human life, to ensure the development of every citizen's basic capacities, and to promote social rationality, "the kind of understanding needed to participate in the society, economy, and polity." In the name of these goals the state would rightly prohibit human sacrifice by the Aztecs and mistreatment of the young by any individual or group. It could also prevent any kind of private or public education from hindering the development of "social rationality"; cf. William Galston, "Two Concepts of Liberalism," *Ethics* 105 (April 1995): 525; see also my article for a more complete list of the goods Galston believes are accepted by citizens in a liberal polity; J. Brian Benestad, "William Galston's Defense of Liberalism: Forging Unity Amid Diversity," in *Liberalism at the Crossroads: An Introduction to Contemporary Liberal Political Theory and Its Critics*, edited by Christopher Wolfe and John Hittinger (Lanham, Md.: Rowman and Littlefield, 1994), 172.

enough to head upstream. Most, however, will be carried along by the current. But they still choose where in the river to sail and where along the shore to moor. The mistake is to think of the liberal regime's public principles as constituting either a placid lake or an irresistible undertow. Moreover, the state may seek to mitigate the effect of its public current on the navigation of specific vessels whenever the costs of such corrective intervention are not excessive.[31]

For example, the shape of liberalism today inclines people to think more about their rights than their duties. In cultural matters liberalism pulls people to "embrace an expansive notion of personal autonomy." Galston observes that the "idea of autonomy becomes a hyper-expansive notion of individual choice, which is the closest thing to an inviolable norm that now exists in American culture."[32] Galston even notes that liberal public principles contribute to the generation of pluralism *within* various churches.[33] For example, even Catholicism, once known for great unity among believers, now has to deal with individual Catholics deciding that "x" number of Catholic teachings (such as those on divorce, assisted suicide, and same-sex marriage) are not compatible with their thinking or way of life.

Galston points out that some liberal theorists, such as Amy Gutmann and Stephen Macedo, want to intensify the pull of liberal principles through law, political rhetoric, and civic education. For example, they argue that public education should induce all students to engage in a Socratic questioning of the way of life handed on to them by their parents. Galston opposes this approach, arguing that public education should only inculcate the core beliefs and virtues needed for the viability of the liberal state. Galston's guiding principle is the "maximum feasible accommodation of diverse ways of life, limited only by the minimum requirements of civic unity."[34] In one of his major scholarly articles Galston says that "liberal societies can and must make room for individuals and groups whose lives are guided by tradition, authority, and faith."[35] For example, Catholic hospitals should not be forced to do abortions; the Boy Scouts should remain free to choose their own leaders; and the Amish rightfully enjoy

31. Galston, "Two Concepts of Liberalism," 530.

32. Galston, "Contending with Liberalism: Some Advice for Catholics," *Commonweal* 127, no. 7 (2001): 13.

33. Galston, "Expressive Liberty, Moral Pluralism, Political Pluralism: Three Sources of Liberal Theory," *William and Mary Law Review* 40 (1999): 880.

34. Ibid., 902.

35. Ibid., 889–90.

the government-granted privilege of keeping their children out of school after the eighth grade (Macedo objects to this exemption granted by the Supreme Court).[36] Galston calls the attempt to impose liberal norms on individuals and groups "exclusionary liberalism" or "liberal imperialism."[37] "At the heart of the liberal democratic settlement," Galston argues, "is a principled refusal to allow religions to engulf the political order, or politics to invade and dominate religion."[38] Acceptance of the core liberal beliefs and virtues by all groups prevents religious tyranny, and the renunciation of liberal imperialism creates breathing space for individuals and groups.

Maximum feasible accommodation not only carves out space for revealed religions, but also serves to benefit the liberal state in the long run. Galston believes that the beliefs and virtues taught by the revealed religions will, for the most part, contribute to the viability and unity of the liberal state by supporting its core principles and requisite virtues. Galston welcomes opposition to such tendencies as individualism, egoism, and unthinking conformity to reigning public opinions. He even says that Catholics "must reject...versions of liberalism" that "embrace skepticism or relativism about the human good;...downplay the role of the state or seek to exclude faith-based arguments from public discourse; [or]...emphasize the prerogatives of the state at the expense of family and associational autonomy."[39] Galston is willing to tolerate whatever teachings that he thinks might unduly burden liberal regimes, all the while trying to persuade groups and churches not to oppose core liberal principles. He specifically urges Catholic social thinkers both to critique "the expansive and unnuanced account of personal autonomy that is the long pole in a number of liberal theoretical tents these days" and to oppose "exclusionary liberalism."[40] But he also urges Catholics not to use theology or natural law to "impose" on non-Catholics their views on abortion, assisted suicide, or homosexuality. He reasons, "Catholics may be affronted by a legal code that permits acts they view as abominable. But in circumstances of deep moral diversity, the alternative to enduring these affronts is even worse."[41] Galston does not advert to the fact that Cath-

36. Galston, "Two Concepts of Liberalism," 516.
37. Galston, "Contending with Liberalism: Some Advice for Catholics," 14.
38. Galston, "Expressive Liberty, Moral Pluralism, Political Pluralism," 905.
39. Galston, "Contending with Liberalism: Some Advice for Catholics," 15.
40. Ibid.
41. Ibid.

olic social thinkers may see, for example, the legalization of physician-assisted suicide as just one more improper use of choice, and consequently may rightfully attempt—arguably on the basis of Galston's principles—to "persuade" their fellow Americans not to go the way of Oregon and Washington. At any rate, Galston believes the advantages of "maximum feasible accommodation" will outweigh the disadvantages by a wide margin, despite the problems that may arise from improper advocacy on the part of the churches or anyone else.

As a second major theme, Galston addresses the requirements of civic unity in a good liberal community. Galston never tires of reiterating his conviction that a liberal community must be established and maintained. It cannot be a good community if citizens abuse their liberty, think only of their rights, and fail to maintain strong bonds in the family, neighborhoods, and voluntary associations. Galston is especially worried about relativism gaining a foothold in the lives of so many citizens.

This new morality—do what you choose, when you choose, without fear of legal coercion or social disapproval—is an experiment without precedent in human history. Perhaps it will succeed; I doubt it. At some point, we will be called upon for sacrifices that we can't pay others to make on our behalf. And then we will see whether the self-protective nonjudgmentalism Wolfe so ably describes constitutes an adequate basis for a free society.[42]

Galston is referring to the work of sociologist Alan Wolfe, who published his findings about America's moral condition several years ago in *One Nation, After All*. From his conversations with middle-class Americans over a two year period, Wolfe found that they are willing to be personally accountable, but reluctant to make judgments about what anyone else is doing or to assume responsibility for righting what they see as wrongs in society. On the basis of the evidence presented by Wolfe, Galston says that the sociologist "pulls his punches" in not raising "far more serious questions."

A choice-based conception of social life leads to instrumental bonds, a cult of conflict avoidance, an absence of real engagement, and a loss of seriousness. Worst of all it is hard to see how this new morality provides any basis for sacrifice, in either personal or civic life. Marriages are ended when they become

---

42. Galston, Review of *One Nation, After All*, by Alan Wolfe, *The Public Interest*, no. 133 (Fall 1998): 116–20.

inconvenient; religions are selected like new fashions in the mall and then cast aside when they cease to meet our personal needs.[43]

In Galston's mind this level of morality is insufficient to build and maintain a good liberal community. Consequently, Galston addresses America's moral deficiencies in many of his writings and proposes helpful solutions.

Like a growing number of other public intellectuals, Galston argues that families, public schools, voluntary associations, and churches can become more effective seedbeds of good habits, virtues, and salutary beliefs.[44] To that end he advocates public support for the two-parent family, public discouragement of divorce and teen pregnancy, parents taking responsibility for giving a moral education to their children, a limited character formation in the public schools (as needed by a good liberal community), respect for religion, including its contribution to the public square, and a reinvigoration of civic associations. Galston would like to see marriage preparation mandated by the state and carried out by faith-based institutions.[45] He would further welcome the repeal of no-fault divorce laws, which have contributed to the high rate of divorces. And Galston would like all citizens to understand the difference between asserting a right and doing what is right. In his mind there has been too much "rights talk" and not enough talk about personal and social responsibilities. He also expresses "grave doubts" about the encouragement of gambling by the state. Galston believes that the rising popularity of gambling "not only reflects but also reinforces a loss of confidence in hard work as a source of social advancement."[46] Doing productive work is one of the ways citizens contribute to the viability of the liberal state.

Galston's expectations of colleges and universities reveal still another facet of his sustained effort to shore up a liberal community. He wants all colleges to transmit "the principles, beliefs, and virtues that liberal societies (indeed, all societies) require for their perpetuation."[47] He also wants

43. Ibid.
44. Galston, "A Public Philosophy for the 21st Century," *The Responsive Community* (Summer 1998): 21.
45. Cf. Galston, "Divorce American Style," *The Public Interest* 124 (Summer 1996): 12–26.
46. Galston, "Gambling Away Our Moral Capital," *The Public Interest* 123 (1996): 58–71.
47. Galston, "Moral Inquiry and Liberal Education in the American University," *Ethics* 110 (July 2000): 814.

them to make a "gentlemanly liberal education" available, which "equips talented individuals to exercise farsighted and public spirited leadership within the framework of an established order."[48] Those capable of such an education are the "natural aristoi," men and women of talent and virtue. Galston himself, of course, is one of those men who has received such an education and has dedicated his life to promoting the good of civil society and the liberal state.

Galston admires and cherishes the liberal state because it enables people of different points of view to live together in relative peace and harmony. But there is an even more profound reason for his admiration and affection. Galston describes himself as a value pluralist and a political liberal. According to value pluralism, "there is no summum bonum that enjoys a rationally grounded priority for all individuals."[49] Otherwise stated, "Contrary to the teachings of classical philosophical and theological traditions, human nature does not prescribe a single, generally valid model of human flourishing or perfection."[50] Therefore, it would never be right for the state to impose on citizens any one model of a dominant good. On the other hand, value pluralism "is not the same as relativism. Philosophical reflection supports what ordinary experience suggests—a nonarbitrary distinction between good and bad."[51] Hence, Galston believes that the minimal perfectionism of the liberal state can be defended on objective grounds: it is a true account of human beings in society. Galston is really saying that reason can arrive at a certain number of basic truths valid for all human beings, but is incapable of discerning a *summum bonum* for all. In other words, Galston claims to know that neither reason nor faith can legitimately say that human nature "prescribe[s] a single, generally valid model of human flourishing or perfection."[52] Of course, Galston's definitive position on the limits of reason and faith presupposes a philosophical vision as grand as that of Kant. To deny that neither reason nor faith can discern a *summum bonum* is implicitly a claim to possess an extraordinary degree of knowledge.

While continuing to admire what Galston is trying to do for liberal society, I am not at all persuaded that he has made good arguments for

48. Ibid., 816.

49. Galston, "Value Pluralism and Liberal Political Theory," *American Political Science Review* 93 (1999): 770.

50. Ibid., 772.   51. Ibid., 770.

52. Ibid., 772.

his assertions about the limits of faith and reason. I am surprised that he didn't confess an inability to evaluate the claims of the classical theological traditions nor argue that faith would be required to accept the teachings of revelation about the highest good. He has only shown me that his view of a smooth-running liberal polity requires the avowal of an incapacity to know the *summum bonum* on the part of philosophers, theologians, Church authorities, and political leaders. Galston seems to believe that lives lived without aspirations for a *summum bonum* would offer protection against religious and political tyranny. Secondly, Galston's public commitment to the Democratic Party may generate some blind spots, as would a similar commitment to the Republican Party. For example, he really has nothing significant to say about "the culture of death" in America. On the other hand, his political principles led him to break with the mainstream of the Democratic Party on at least two significant issues. Galston deplored the Democratic Party's decision not to allow Governor Robert Casey to speak at the 1992 Democratic Convention. "I protested against it to no avail. I believe the Democratic Party has made a serious and indeed historic mistake in turning *Roe v. Wade* into a litmus test for party leadership."[53] Recently, Galston also pointed out that he "published an article…recommending a carefully monitored national voucher experiment."[54] This position, contrary to the platform of the Democratic Party, does fit in with his belief that faith-based groups can serve public purposes.

Conclusion

The few writings examined in this essay clearly show that some prominent liberal theorists, especially Rawls and Macedo, want to keep religion out of the public square in order to promote peace and harmony. What they recommend is an undue restriction on religious liberty, with harmful consequences both for churches and civil society. The Catholic Church, for example, has to give public witness to the sacredness of human life and is obliged to call upon public authorities to prevent the killing of unborn children. If churches are not allowed to speak on all matters pertaining to justice, then civil society has less of a chance of arriving at a more complete understanding and practice of justice.

53. Galston, "Contending with Liberalism: Some Advice for Catholics," 15.
54. Ibid., 14.

The Rawlsian position on justice should prompt religious believers and philosophers to insist, in season and out of season both, that justice cannot be understood apart from theological and philosophical views of the good, and that there are no "neutral" principles of justice upon which everyone does and should agree. This liberal position on the neutrality of justice unduly narrows the concept and prematurely cuts off political discussion among the citizens of a nation.

To accept the liberal proposition that religion is a private affair is also to narrow the scope of political philosophy and theological ethics and to reduce the depth and breadth of religion. We have seen that the privatizing of religion goes hand in hand with the establishment of principles of justice that are sundered, at least in theory, from comprehensive views of the good. That religious liberty is curtailed is too obvious to merit any more comment.

Galston is very aware that Rawlsian political liberalism unduly narrows religious liberty and, therefore, argues for maximum feasible accommodation of religion out of respect for religion and desire to promote the good of liberal regimes. Galston knows that religions generally promote the practice of the virtues necessary for the survival of liberal regimes. But even this most accommodating liberal doesn't want the Catholic Church to argue against the legalization of abortion.

Locke's argument for toleration and Macedo's argument for the moderate hegemony of liberalism should alert believers to the ever-present danger of their faith being transformed and truncated in order to serve the ends of the liberal state. The self-censorship of typical American believers, described by Wolfe and Elshtain, and the avoidance of theological language and concepts by religious ethicists and social activists, as reported by Kass and Hauerwas respectively, should make believers aware that liberal regimes are able to induce changes in the practice of religious believers without using the law or any other palpable force.

The liberal theorists' desire to keep religion out of the public square is a sign of respect for the power of religious truth to be persuasive. They rightly fear the disruptive influence of religious fanaticism and religiously inspired utopian politics. But the fear of Catholics criticizing abortion laws, proposals to legalize same-sex marriage, and cultural trends is unreasonable and short-sighted. A Catholic critique of policy and culture can be carried out in a way respectful of liberal democratic regimes, as is clearly shown by Pope Benedict's third encyclical, *Caritas in veritate.*

Pope Benedict XVI has been continually proclaiming that churches and individual believers require religious freedom in the public square; all must be accorded freedom to follow their conscience and never forced to act against it. In *Caritas in veritate* the pope made use of his religious freedom to offer the world a vision of development which, if accepted, could transform the lives of millions throughout the world.[55]

55. See the appendix for an in-depth analysis of *Caritas in veritate* (*On Integral Development in Charity and Truth*).

Pope Benedict XVI's *Caritas in veritate*

In the introduction I explained that Catholic social doctrine (CSD) helps people to know what love and justice require in the various circumstances of life, knowledge that would escape many without instruction. It is worth taking a second look at St. Augustine's statement on the difficulty of being faithful to the commandment to love one's neighbor in everything one does. He wrote, "From this commandment, arise the duties pertaining to human society, about which it is difficult not to err."[1] In other words, it is easy for human beings to love one another badly, both in personal encounters and in devising proposals for the common good of society. Pope Benedict's new encyclical, dated June 29, 2009, builds on the earlier CDF *Instruction* by emphasizing that love has to be guided by truth. "'Caritas in veritate' (*On Integral Development in Charity and Truth*) is the principle around which the Church's social doctrine turns." (no. 6). Both faith and reason discern the truth by which love takes its bearings.

In a speech on the new encyclical Cardinal Tarcisio Bertone directed people's attention to a text recently published by the International Theological Commission entitled "The Search for Universal Ethics: A New Look at Natural Law."[2] The commission summarizes what St. Thomas Aquinas says about the three natural inclinations of every human person, the third of which is "the inclination to know the truth about God and to live in society." Bertone rightly interprets the universal presence of this inclination to mean that "truth and love are essential requirements of every person and deeply rooted in his being." Seeking these goods for oneself is, then, a requirement of the natural law for every person and a sine qua non of solving the current economic

1. St. Augustine, *The Catholic and Manichaean Ways of Life (De Moribus Ecclesiae Catholicae et de Moribus Manichaeorum)* (Washington, D.C.: The Catholic University of America Press, 1966), no. 49:40.
2. Cardinal Tarcisio Bertone, "It Is Also Possible to Do Business by Pursuing Aims that Serve Society," speech delivered on *Caritas in veritate (On Integral Human Development in Charity and Truth)* to the Italian Senate on July 28, 2009.

crisis. The implication of Bertone's interpretation is that without truth and love no one can be happy and no one can effectively address societal problems.

People who love in truth live in accordance with their dignity and effectively promote justice and contribute to the common good. You could even say that they perfect their dignity and help others do the same.[3] In *Populorum progressio (On the Development of Peoples)* Pope Paul VI said that justice is "the minimum measure" of love, and, therefore, is love's first task. But love demands more. "The *earthly city* is promoted not merely by relationships of rights and duties [required by justice], but to an even greater and more fundamental extent by relationships of gratuitousness, mercy and communion" (no. 6). People motivated by gratuitousness and mercy are grateful for the opportunity to love and give of themselves without expecting anything in return, realizing that they have benefitted from other people's gratuitous love. They are happy to be "instruments of God's grace, so as to pour forth God's charity and weave networks of charity" (no. 5). Later in the encyclical Pope Benedict explains that participants in economic life must not only be just, but also live a life of gratuitousness in their work.

Love in truth requires an exceptionally generous commitment to the good of individuals and to the common good of peoples in accordance with the multiple vocations of persons and their opportunities in life. To love in truth on the macro level is to keep in mind that unless the common good is achieved, many individuals will be unable to perfect their dignity or to realize their integral development.[4] For example, without good family life and good education from kindergarten through college (both important aspects of the common good), the young will usually fail to achieve their perfection. So, for example, whatever is done to shore up the family and improve education is an example of love in truth.

The theologian pope reminds us that "Truth, in fact, is *lógos* which creates *diá-logos*, and hence communication and communion" (no. 4). Exchanging words that put us in contact with reality or the way things are can forge bonds of unity among people. Sharing in the truth, people are able to overcome their erroneous opinions engendered by the cultures in which they live and enter into productive conversation with their fellow citizens and with those of other nations. "Practicing charity in truth helps people to understand that adhering to the values of Christianity is not merely useful but essential for building a good society and for true integral development" (no. 4). In other words, the practice of real Christianity is always beneficial to the perfection of every person and the complete well-being of every regime.

3. See chapter 1, where the notion of perfecting one's dignity is explained at length.
4. Please see chapter 2 for further clarification of this point.

Pope Benedict insists that love and truth cannot be separated. It is, in fact, the genius of CSD to keep the two together, with the truth of faith and reason guiding the practice of love. "Without truth, without trust and love for what is true, there is no social conscience and responsibility, and social action ends up serving private interests and the logic of power" (no. 5). A conscience that does not take its bearing by truth is really not a conscience, but simply the product of a person's will, and not the judgment of reason.[5] In addition, a conscience not guided by truth doesn't come into contact with reality

Drawing upon Pope Paul VI's 1967 encyclical *Populorum progressio*, Pope Benedict, guided himself by love in truth, offers the world a vision of development that is richer and more complete than the common understanding. He reminds us of Paul VI's teaching that "life in Christ is the first and principal factor in development."[6] This means that integral development should aim at the "greatest possible perfection" for every single person, in addition to overcoming poverty, disease, unemployment, and ignorance. This kind of development, of course, needs the contributions of people motivated by love in truth. Otherwise, they would never think that working for development means bringing Christ into people's lives.

Chapter 1, entitled "The Message of *Populorum progressio*," is entirely devoted to reflecting on the implications of saying that "life in Christ is the first and principal factor of development." Inspired by Vatican Council II's vision of the Church serving the world by truth and love, Pope Paul VI makes two important points in his 1967 encyclical on development. First, when the Church is faithful to her threefold mission of proclaiming the Word, celebrating the sacraments and performing works of charity,[7] she is also *"engaged in promoting integral human development"* and is thus serving the world in the best way possible (no. 11). In other words, the Church helps people develop a life in Christ by teaching the truth, communicating God's love in the sacraments and living that love in her works of mercy. Second, *"authentic human development concerns the whole of the person in every single dimension"* (no. 11). In other words, it must include the material, intellectual, and spiritual needs of the person.

Throughout the rest of the encyclical Pope Benedict will gradually unfold the meaning of authentic or integral development. If life in Christ is the crucial determinant, then it is no surprise that Paul VI and Benedict XVI will affirm that development requires the "greatest possible perfection" of the hu-

5. See the introduction for a fuller account of Pope Benedict's thoughts on conscience.

6. See Paul VI, *Populorum progressio (On the Development of Peoples)*, no. 16.

7. See Pope Benedict XVI, *Deus caritas est (On Christian Love)*, nos. 19–25, for his reflections on these three activities, which constitute the life of the Church.

man person (no. 18). The achievement of this goal requires religious and political freedom, a transcendent vision of the human person, the help of God, and a personal sense of responsibility as well as solidarity and charity toward one's neighbors. This means that people should take upon themselves the responsibility of pursuing their own development or perfection and should help others do the same. When individuals attend to the development of others in solidarity and charity, they will necessarily also contribute to their own integral development. Neglect of the development needs of others would cause one to live beneath his or her dignity. So, the love of self and others, guided by truth and the virtue of charity, is, as Paul VI taught, "the principal force at the service of development" (no. 13). You could also say that a life of charity perfects the dignity of the human person. This is because charity properly understood is Christ's charity, which, affirms Paul VI, *through works of justice, peace and development, is part and parcel of evangelization* (no. 15). In other words, evangelization is not just the proclamation of the Word, but living it in works of justice, peace, and development.

While charity is the most important factor in promoting development, Paul VI also had "a keen sense of the importance of economic structures and institutions" (no. 17). Pope Benedict agrees, but insists here and elsewhere that people should never think that the establishment of any structures or institutions guarantees success. This is the error of certain modern political philosophers, discussed by Pope Benedict in his *Spe salvi (On Christian Hope)* and in a speech delivered in Brazil on May 13, 2007, to the bishops of Latin America and the Caribbean.[8]

Both Paul VI and Benedict XVI insist that people must not entrust "the entire process of development to technology alone" (no. 14). Pope Benedict also directs our attention to the opposite extreme of those who would support "the upsurge of ideologies that would deny *in toto* the very value of development, viewing it as radically anti-human and merely a source of degradation" (no. 14). This attitude leads both to the rejection of deriving benefit from scientific discoveries and their technological applications, and to the goal of "'being more,'" that is to say the perfection of one's person through love and truth. Benedict XVI says this rejection of integral development would be in the name of an impossible and undesirable "return to humanity's natural state" (no. 14). This sounds like a rejection of Rousseau's looking to a supposed natural state of humanity for guidance in shaping his political philosophy. For Pope Benedict the rejection of integral development "indicates a lack of trust in man and God" (no. 14). In other words, to reject development is to

8. See the introduction for a discussion of Pope Benedict's reflections on this point.

refuse the gifts that God wants to give us and to deny that human beings are able and willing to promote one another's proper development.

Pope Benedict also tried to overcome the split between life ethics and social ethics, or what has come to be known as social justice, by pointing to Paul VI's *Humanae vitae (On the Regulation of Birth*, the encyclical on marriage and contraception. Ironically, both in some Catholic and secular circles opposition to abortion is not considered to be a requirement of social justice. To show the absurdity of defending justice and peace while promoting contraception and abortion, Pope Benedicts quotes from John Paul II's *Evangelium vitae (The Gospel of Life)*: "'a society lacks solid foundations, when, on the one hand, it asserts values such as the dignity of the person, justice, and peace, but then, on the other hand, radically acts to the contrary by allowing or tolerating a variety of ways in which human life is devalued and violated, especially where it is weak or marginalized'" (no. 15).[9] How can people, especially Catholics, speak passionately of social justice and the dignity of the human person without embarrassment, when they have no problem with *Roe v. Wade,* which allows the killing of unborn children for the whole nine months of pregnancy?

Citing Paul VI's 1975 apostolic exhortation *Evangelii nuntiandi (On Evangelization in the Modern World)*, Pope Benedict affirms that evangelization must include work for peace, justice, and development. These three works, in fact, are "'part and parcel of evangelization'" (no. 15).[10] Right after making this point, Paul VI warns that work for development and liberation sometimes reduces the mission of the Church to a this-worldly project.

We must not ignore the fact that many, even generous Christians...would reduce [the mission of the Church] to a man-centered goal; the salvation of which she is the messenger would be reduced to material well-being. Her activity, forgetful of all spiritual and religious preoccupation, would become initiatives of the political or social order. But if this were so, the Church would lose her fundamental meaning.[11]

This is a caveat with which Pope Benedict wholeheartedly agrees, but chose not to mention at this point in the encyclical. I cite it so that Pope Benedict's connection between evangelization and development cannot be misunderstood. Still today, many people, including Christians, are inclined "to reduce [the Church's] mission to the dimensions of a simply temporal project."[12]

9. Pope John Paul II, *Evangelium vitae (The Gospel of Life)*, no. 101.
10. Pope Benedict quotes the following sentence from *Evangelii nuntiandi (On Evangelization in the Modern World)*, no. 31: "Between evangelization and human advancement—development and liberation—there are in fact profound links."
11. Pope Paul VI, *Evangelii nuntiandi*, no. 32.
12. Ibid.

In other words, a narrow view of social justice is embraced that has little or no connection to the Church's mission to be an instrument of salvation for all.

At the end of this first chapter Pope Benedict also directs attention to Paul VI's thoughts about the three reasons the work for development fails in the world. The will "often neglects the duties of solidarity"; the mind "does not always give proper direction to the will"; and more important than deficient thinking, "brotherhood" or solidarity "among individuals and peoples" doesn't develop. These reasons direct attention to the underlying theme of the encyclical *Caritas in veritate.* The mind needs to attain the truth in order to love correctly, and the will needs the determination and fire to carry out what the mind correctly perceives.

Deficient thinking would, of course, include counsel to rely exclusively on structures and institutions to promote development, the failure to see the importance of charity and truth, the rejection of technology altogether, not seeing the link between social ethics and life ethics, not realizing that openness to new life is required by development, and the inability to grasp that integral development includes "being more" or life in Christ for every single person in the world. The rich understanding of development is "the central message of *Populorum progressio,* valid for today and for all time" (no. 18).[13]

Chapter 2, "Human Development in our Time," is different from the previous two chapters in that it focuses to a significant extent on describing the contemporary economic and cultural situation. In responding to the situation, Pope Benedict puts forth a few more perennial elements of CSD in addition to a number of contingent judgments. As mentioned in the introduction, the 1986 *Instruction on Christian Freedom and Liberation* by the Congregation for the Doctrine of the Faith also sheds light on the different levels of teaching found in *Caritas in veritate* by distinguishing between permanently valid principles and "contingent judgments" in CSD (no. 72). The latter may or may not be suitable for overcoming the current economic crisis.

Pope Benedict refers first to the economic damage done by "badly managed and largely speculative financial dealing," extensive migration of peoples, and "unregulated exploitation of the earth's resources" (no. 21). Other perceived problems are inequalities within and among nations, corruption of "the economic and political class" in both rich and poor countries, and the refusal of people in rich countries to share knowledge, especially pertaining to health care (no. 22). Mere economic development has been stressed to the neglect of integral development (no. 23). The "new context of international trade and finance, which is characterized by increasing mobility of financial capital and

13. See no. 8 for the connection between life in Christ and development.

means of production, material and immaterial" has decreased the power of individual states, since they are less able to deal with the effects of international trade and finance (no. 24).

Other characteristics of the contemporary situation are *"the downsizing of social security systems"* in order to be more competitive in the market, the mobility of labor causing psychological instability and extra problems in planning for marriage and family life, the difficulties labor unions are experiencing in effectively representing the interests of workers (no. 25), the tendency to promote relativism by viewing all cultures as equal, "substantially equivalent and interchangeable" (no. 26), and the existence of structural causes of world hunger and food insecurity.

In addition, Pope Benedict discerns as problems the promotion and the imposition of contraception, sterilization, and abortion; the legalization of euthanasia in some places and the constant advocacy of expanding legal access to euthanasia; the denial of religious freedom in various parts of the world; and the practice of killing in the name of God, especially by terrorists (no. 29). The pope maintains that all these practices, especially violence, pose serious obstacles to integral development. Pope Benedict further notes that the state at times places serious obstacles in the way of integral development by imposing "practical atheism," and that the developed countries sometimes export a "reductive vision of the person" to the developing nations. This is evident when the mere economic model of development overwhelms the rich traditions in the poor countries.

In response to the contemporary situation Pope Benedict proposes more insights from CSD. He begins by explaining what Pope Paul VI expected from development. "He understood the term to indicate the goal of rescuing peoples, first and foremost, from hunger, deprivation, endemic diseases and illiteracy" (no. 21). This goal requires the opportunity of all peoples to participate in the international economy on equal terms; second, it means providing education to the peoples of every nation, including a formation in solidarity; third, it means "the consolidation of democratic regimes capable of ensuring freedom and peace." This description of development focuses on those aspects that are readily understood, except for solidarity. Call to mind John Paul II's definition of solidarity. It is a virtue that inclines a person to have *"a firm and persevering determination* to commit oneself to the *common good;* that is to say to the good of all and of each individual, because we are *all* really responsible *for all.*"[14] The highest good, of course, is the formation of the life of Christ in each individual. Because this is the Catholic belief, no one should be surprised to read the pope's

---

14. Pope John Paul II, *Sollicitudo rei socialis (On Social Concern)*, no. 38.

next comment on development: "Yet it should be stressed that *progress of a merely economic and technological kind is insufficient.* Development needs above all to be true and integral" (no. 23).

Having established the full meaning of true and integral development, Pope Benedict mentions practical measures that must be embraced in order to achieve the minimum level of development: the acceptance of labor unions as a way to foster cooperation on the local and international level, the establishment of economic institutions that will have the possibility of eliminating world hunger, the cultivation of "a public conscience that considers *food and access to water as universal rights of all human beings, without distinction or discrimination*" (no. 27), helping people to realize that "[o]penness *to life is at the center of true development*" because it strengthens the moral fiber of a nation, and maintaining or establishing the right to religious freedom. The latter two recommendations are quite controversial in various circles, since many people see abortion as a way of ensuring that fewer individuals will be sharing in the world's resources. Religious freedom does not exist in many countries of the world and is in danger of being curtailed in both the United States and Europe.

To address further the complicated issue of integral development, Pope Benedict next makes some very important comments on the relation between love and knowledge. Persons whose work for development is guided by love in truth recognize that interdisciplinary study is necessary to acquire all the requisite knowledge. Their love moves them to acquire that knowledge. As Paul VI affirmed in *Populorum progressio,* "'the individual who is animated by true charity labors skillfully to discover the causes of misery, to find the means to combat it, to overcome it resolutely'" (no. 30).[15] CSD provides valuable help because it is, of necessity, interdisciplinary. "It allows faith, theology, metaphysics and science to come together in a collaborative effort in the service of humanity" (no. 31). The study of CSD, then, enables people to acquire wisdom about the most important things and knowledge of all the practical measures that must be taken to bring about the full range of development.

Some other practical measures suggested by Pope Benedict are as follows: prioritizing "*the goal of access to steady employment* for everyone" (no. 32), preventing disparities of wealth from developing in a "morally unacceptable manner" (no. 32), not reducing the meaning of culture to its technological dimension, thinking more deeply about "*the meaning of the economy and its goals*" (no. 32), avoiding the imposition of the kind of tariffs that would prevent poor countries from exporting their products to rich countries, and the very big goal of guiding globalization by charity in truth so as to avoid causing more division among the peoples of the world (no. 33).

15. Pope Benedict is quoting *Populorum progressio,* no. 75.

Chapter 3 is entitled "Fraternity, Economic Development and Civil Society." This chapter is remarkable because of Pope Benedict's thoughts on the effects of original sin and the desirability of "gratuitousness" in the economic realm. The pope first quotes the *Catechism*, 407: "'Ignorance of the fact that man has a wounded nature inclined to evil gives rise to serious errors in the areas of education, politics, social action and morals'" (no. 34). Then, he mentions two errors that people are making today: thinking that evil can be eliminated by human effort alone and that "the economy must be shielded from 'influences' of a moral character" (no. 34). The consequence of these errors has been the establishment of political, social, and economic systems that have been unable to deliver justice because they "trample upon personal and social freedom" (no. 34). This failure, in turn, leads to a loss of hope, which is indispensable in the work for the high goal of integral development. "Hope encourages reason and gives it the strength to direct the will" (no. 34). Recall Benedict's previous comment that a deficient will is one of the causes of underdevelopment in the world. Without hope, charity, which is a virtue of the will, cannot effectively sustain a commitment to achieve integral development.

Pope Benedict's emphasis on the necessity of practicing "gratuitousness" in civil society has left commentators on the encyclical wondering what this means in practice. We know that what is gratuitous is bestowed freely, not in response to any claim or merit. The pope tells us that "The human being is made for gift." Then, he adds that the *"principle of gratuitousness"* is "an expression of fraternity" (no. 34). Gratuitousness connotes friendship, solidarity, and charity; it "fosters and disseminates solidarity and responsibility for justice and the common good among the different economic players" (no. 38). Invoking gratuitousness, then, is just another way of saying that human beings cannot achieve the perfection of their dignity, imitate Jesus Christ, and contribute to the common good, unless they freely give themselves in service to others in all areas of their life. The necessity of gratuitousness also means that no economy will ever function properly if the participants lack this quality. As Pope Benedict explains, "[I]n *commercial relationships* the *principle of gratuitousness* and the logic of gift as an expression of fraternity can and must *find their place within normal economic activity.* This is a human demand at the present time, but is also demanded by economic logic. It is a demand both of charity and truth" (no. 36). In other words, you don't have to accept Catholic teaching to realize at the present time that participants in the economy must avoid dishonesty and live in solidarity, brotherhood, and mutual trust. In the pope's mind, because that trust no longer exists, the economy is in grave difficulty.

After highlighting the principle of gratuitousness, Pope Benedict explains that there are really three prongs to a viable and just economy: a free market in which people enjoy equal opportunity and respect contracts, just laws, political action to redistribute wealth, and, most importantly, the spirit of gift or the principle of gratuitousness (no. 37). This means that economic behavior in a free market is regulated by law, commutative justice, and the personal virtues of the participants. The pope highlights the point that the presence of gratuitousness, or freely embraced solidarity, is necessary for the attainment of justice. Neither the free market nor the laws, then, can assure justice, especially commutative justice, but only the virtuous qualities of the economic players. Pope Benedict is really saying that the market-plus-state binary model is not sufficient to produce a just and productive economy. Otherwise stated, the economy cannot function well simply on the basis of self-interest and state intervention, however intelligent. The market and politics absolutely need virtuous participants, but that poses a serious problem. There is no market for gratuitousness, "and attitudes of gratuitousness cannot be established by law" (no. 39). From Pope Benedict's other writings one could infer that these gratuitous attitudes could only be generated in the family, the school, and the Church. At any rate, the pope's position on the principle of gratuitousness is an enormous challenge and a wake-up call to every economy in the world. Without virtuous participants the economy won't deliver the goods people need at a just price.

In addition to stressing the importance of virtue for a sound economy, Pope Benedict also suggests that businesses adopt a totally different mode of management. "[B]usiness management cannot concern itself only with the interests of the proprietors, but must also assume responsibility for all the other stakeholders who contribute to the life of the business: the workers, the clients, the suppliers of various elements of production, the community of reference" (no. 40). Attentiveness to the interests of all the stakeholders would increase the long-term sustainability of the business enterprise. The pope questions the justice of business managers being responsible only to the shareholders.[16] He also suggests finding ways of benefitting the local community where capital was initially generated instead of sending it abroad without thought of what effect such an action would have.

In the latter part of chapter 3 Pope Benedict reminds his readers of his predecessor's teaching on work and then offers some observations on improving the effectiveness of political authority and the beneficence of globalization. Work is an "*actus personae*" by means of which a person supports himself and his family and promotes the common good of the nation, thereby contributing to the realization of his own dignity.

16. Some would argue that managers are, in practice, not even deferential to shareholders.

To address the complicated economic problems of the day the pope argues that we need vigorous political authority on local, national, and international levels. To be more effective at promoting a productive and just economy, governments must cooperate with each other, and international aid should be targeted in such a way as to consolidate "constitutional, juridical and administrative systems in countries that do not yet fully enjoy these goods" (no. 41).

Globalization is a term used to describe the growing interconnection among the economies and peoples of the world. Quoting John Paul II, Pope Benedict says that the fact of globalization "'is neither good nor bad. It will be what people make of it'" (no. 42).[17] The pope hopes that it will be possible to *"steer the globalization of humanity in relational terms, in terms of communion and the sharing of goods"* (no. 42). More precisely, Pope Benedict wants solidarity to keep growing among all people, and he desires globalization to be so directed that it results in a "large-scale redistribution of wealth on a world-wide scale" (no. 42).

Chapter 4 announces three subjects: "The Development of People, Rights and Duties, The Environment." It begins with the countercultural affirmation that unless duties take precedence over rights, the latter can get out of control and become *"mere license"* (no. 43). That is to say, some people in affluent countries, not guided by duties, now feel justified in defending a "'right to excess,' and even to transgression and vice" (no. 43). When duties are the primary moral counter, they set limits to rights and ensure more respect for the genuine rights of individuals and peoples. If enough people are guided by their duties, they will be moved to do something about "the lack of food, drinkable water, basic instruction and elementary health care in areas of the underdeveloped world and on the outskirts of large metropolitan centers" (no. 43). The priority of duties over rights is not widely accepted in liberal democracies and has not even been a prominent theme in CSD, though it has been mentioned several times.

The recognition and fulfillment of duties will contribute to integral development, as will responsible procreation in a family founded on marriage between a man and a woman. Marriage and the family, unencumbered by the tyranny or restrictive policies of the state (e.g., through the imposition of contraception or abortion) "correspond to the deepest needs and dignity of the human person" (no. 44). It is crucial for society that individuals come to understand that the purpose of sexuality is both to forge a one-flesh unity between spouses and to procreate. Society suffers a blow when people look at sexuality just as a form of entertainment, paying scant or no attention to the

17. Pope Benedict is quoting John Paul II, "Address to the Pontifical Academy of Social Sciences," April 27, 2001.

two high goals of marriage. The procreation of children is immensely important for any society because of the need for a sufficient number of workers.

The decline in births, falling at times beneath the so-called "replacement level," also
puts a strain on social welfare systems, increases their cost, eats into savings and
hence the financial resources needed for investment, reduces the availability of qualified laborers, and narrows the "brain pool" upon which nations can draw for their
needs. Furthermore, smaller and at times minuscule families run the risk of impov-
erishing social relations, and failing to ensure effective forms of solidarity (no. 44).

Spouses who work at forming a one-flesh unity will necessarily promote solidarity in their families, at work, and in all the communities in which they in-
teract.

When individuals are educated to recognize and fulfill their duties in the
family, at work, and everywhere else, the economies of the world will receive
the most important boost they need: virtuous participants in economic life.
As Pope Benedict teaches, "The economy needs ethics in order to function
correctly" (no. 45). Ethics, then, is not only important for an economy to be
just, but also to be productive.

After asserting the importance of ethics for economic life Pope Benedict
briefly touches on the great contribution that CSD can make to the foundation and generation of ethical principles. It "is based on man's creation 'in
the image of God' (Gen 1:27), a datum which gives rise to the inviolable dignity of the human person and the transcendent value of natural moral norms"
(no. 45). Pope Benedict could only be referring to the natural law, morality
that, in principle, all could grasp by the use of reason and observe with the
help of grace. The dignity of the human person and the natural law are "two
pillars" that must be accepted by business ethics in order to retain "its distinctive nature" (no. 45). In addition, Pope Benedict is also implying that ethics
rests on the knowledge of who man is. In other words, it makes all the difference in the world for ethics that man is made in the image of God.

Next, Pope Benedict XVI briefly discusses the importance of discussing a
new type of business oriented toward the so-called "'civil economy' and the
'economy of communion'" (no. 46). This is not a "'third sector'" designed to
complement public and private companies, but "a broad new composite reality embracing the private and public spheres, one which does not exclude
profit, but considers it a means for achieving human and social ends" (no. 46).
The pope expresses the hope that these kinds of businesses will grow in every
country of the world. Unfortunately, he does not give more detail on the precise shape of these new kinds of companies. It is, however, clear that they have
ethics built into their very constitution.

Before beginning a long discussion on the environment in relation to development, Pope Benedict quotes Pope Paul VI's statement on the responsibility of every person for his or her development with the help of those who can give it: "'The peoples themselves have the prime responsibility to work for their own development. But they will not bring this about in isolation'" (no. 47).[18] The reason CSD keeps repeating this point is fidelity to the principle of subsidiarity. CSD holds that every person, group, and government should be actively promoting integral development.

Pope Benedict begins his discussion of environmental matters with an important observation about two extreme attitudes that people have toward the environment: either considering it "more important than the human person," a kind of "untouchable taboo," a reflection of "neo-paganism or a new pantheism"; or abusing it with "total technical dominion over nature" (no. 48). Both attitudes are serious obstacles to development and, in my judgment, quite common today. The proper attitude is the desire to "exercise a *responsible stewardship over nature*" (no. 50). This means using natural resources in such a way as to provide for everyone on the planet with attention to the needs of future generations and without doing harm to the environment. The pope stresses the need for a "worldwide redistribution of energy resources" (no. 49). This kind of stewardship is the responsibility of individuals, groups, companies, and the various levels of government, including the international community. Companies and states exercise responsible stewardship when they don't hoard nonrenewable energy resources and when individuals moderate their consumption of natural resources, avoiding hedonism and consumerism. Echoing Pope John Paul II's teaching, Pope Benedict says that what is really needed is the adoption of a way of living "'in which the quest for truth, beauty, goodness and communion with others for the sake of common growth are the factors which determine consumer choices, savings and investments'" (no. 51).[19] Living this way is really an exercise in solidarity, since moderation in the consumption of resources necessarily will redound to the benefit of others.

In order to protect nature, the decisive factor is the "*overall moral tenor of society.*" To preserve that moral tenor, especially important is the protection of life. Otherwise stated, environmental ecology depends on "human ecology." Human life must be protected from conception until natural death. "If there is a lack of respect for the right to life and to a natural death, if human conception, gestation and birth are made artificial, if human embryos are sacri-

18. Pope Benedict is quoting Pope Paul VI, *Populorum progressio*, no. 77.

19. Pope Benedict is quoting Pope John Paul II, *Centesimus annus (On the Hundredth Anniversary of Rerum novarum)*, no. 36.

ficed to research, the conscience of society ends up losing the concept of human ecology and, along with it, that of environmental ecology" (no. 51). This is another point that is not on the screen of the world's liberal democracies, which keep talking about respect for the environment while maintaining the right to kill unborn children for research and for any other reason. What is hardly understood today is that "Our duties towards the environment are linked to our duties towards the human person considered in himself and in relation to others" (no. 51). If there is a widespread lack of respect for the human person, born or unborn, there is really no hope of assuring respect for the environment or of encouraging lasting moderation in the use of resources.

Chapter 5, entitled "The Cooperation of the Human Family," ranges from the highly theoretical themes of faith, reason, truth, and charity, religious freedom, natural law, and education to reflections on international tourism and the establishment of a world public authority. The pope's treatment of the theoretical themes is a continuation of his previous reflections found in *Deus caritas est (On Christian Love)* and in his various addresses.

Because the existence of religious freedom in the world is precarious on account of fundamentalism and secularism, but necessary for seeking truth and promoting development, Pope Benedict directs our attention to its meaning, great importance, and its particular benefits. He first makes clear that religious freedom doesn't mean "religious indifferentism, nor does it imply that all religions are equal" (no. 55). It does mean freedom from state interference and freedom to live one's faith in both the private and public realms. "The Christian religion and other religions can offer their contribution to development *only if God has a place in the public realm*, specifically in regard to its cultural, social, economic, and particularly its political dimensions" (no. 56). With religious freedom Christians and other religious believers can bring to bear the truths of their faith on the issues of the day. They can also enter into dialogue with each other in order to see better the public implications of their faith, cooperate among themselves, and, in addition, they can bring their faith into conversation with reason, including political reason. This latter dialogue is very important so that reason and faith can mutually purify each other and contribute to integral development. Before becoming pope, Joseph Cardinal Ratzinger discussed this mutual purification of faith and reason with Jürgen Habermas on January 19, 2004. Then he took up this most important theme in his first encyclical, *Deus caritas est.* Pope Benedict is fully aware that both reason and faith can go astray. In this encyclical, as an example of faith going astray, Pope Benedict mentions that "some religious cultures in the world today...do not oblige men and women to live in communion, but rather cut them off from one another in a search for individual well-being" (no. 55). The pope consistently teaches that Christians work in the Church for the salvation of all.

In the midst of cultural and religious diversity, even serious religious differences, what enables people to dialogue and cooperate fruitfully with each other, is the natural law or the universal moral law that all people can discern and observe with their reason. "[I]t insures that the multi-faceted pluralism of cultural diversity does not detach itself from the common quest for truth, goodness and God. Thus adherence to the law etched on human hearts is the precondition for constructive social cooperation" (no. 59). Discernment of the natural law can also move the developed nations to rediscover the "oft-forgotten virtues which made it possible for them to flourish throughout their history" (no. 59), and can enable the developing nations to hold on to the truth in their traditions when tempted to neglect them in the face of the way of life promoted by today's technological civilization. In short, the natural law is an agent of unity within and among nations because it gives all access to truth, which "unites spirits and causes them to think in unison" (no. 54).

Reason directed by Christian revelation can discern the transcendent worth of the human person and can reflect deeply on the *"category of relation."* "As a spiritual being, the human creature is defined through interpersonal relations. The more authentically he or she lives these relations, the more his or her own identity matures. It is not by isolation that man establishes his worth, but by placing himself in relation with others and with God" (no. 53). This observation, of course, relates closely to the theme of gratuitousness and solidarity previously discussed. Human beings can only seek the perfection of their dignity through the proper kind of giving and receiving. The opposite of being in relation would be isolation and alienation. The pope calls the former "one of the deepest forms of poverty a person can experience" (no. 53). Rejection of God's love would plunge a person into the worst isolation and alienation possible.

One of Pope Benedict's greatest hopes from the dialogue between faith and reason is to "render the work of charity more effective within society" (no. 57). That could happen because faith and reason together can discern the truths that guide the practice of charity. To illustrate his point Pope Benedict explains that the principle of subsidiarity is a "particular manifestation of charity and a guiding criterion for fraternal cooperation between believers and non-believers" (no. 57). To affirm that respecting the principle of subsidiarity is a way of loving one's neighbor is a brilliant observation that I have not previously found in the body of CSD (no. 57). Intermediate associations and the state offer aid to human persons so that they can participate in the life of society and make their contribution to the common good, an eminent form of charity. In other words, people practice charity by observing the principle of subsidiarity, since they show respect for the dignity of others by putting them in a better position to practice charity themselves. Since charity or "reciprocity" is the "heart of what it is to be a human being" (no. 57), subsidiarity is much more than a principle of government; helping people to love is an eminent contribution to their salvation and hence to integral development.

As a governing principle, subsidiarity does, however, make an important contribution. It facilitates participation of all citizens in the life of society, protecting them from the "all-encompassing welfare state" (no. 57), and guiding the governance of globalization so that political authority does not become overbearing. To work well, subsidiarity must not be divorced from the principle of solidarity. As Pope Benedict says, *The principle of subsidiarity must remain closely linked to the principle of solidarity and vice versa,* since the former without the latter gives way to social privatism, while the latter without the former gives way to paternalist social assistance that is demeaning to those in need" (no. 58). When the two principles remain linked together, economic aid "must be distributed with the involvement not only of the governments of the receiving countries, but also local economic agents and the bearers of culture within civil society, including local Churches" (no. 58). The yoked principles also require giving developing nations the opportunity to sell their products in the international market, and to help them improve and adapt their products, as is necessary to satisfy the demand. Subsidiarity ensures that those receiving aid are also helped to become agents of charity themselves.

Besides providing a counterbalance to subsidiarity, solidarity also requires nations to provide greater access to education, understood as classroom instruction, vocational training, and the "complete formation of the person." The latter, of course, is not possible, unless educators have a solid knowledge of human nature. "The increasing prominence of a relativistic understanding of that nature," argues Pope Benedict, "presents serious problems for education, especially moral education, jeopardizing its universal extension" (no. 61). Part of the person's formation is, of course, an education to exercise social responsibility as a consumer. This is also a theme taken up earlier in the encyclical.

Toward the end of this fifth chapter Pope Benedict takes up the subjects of international tourism, migration, work and unions again, finance, the reform of the United Nations, and the establishment of a world political authority. The pope discourages the kind of tourism that is sexually immoral, consumerist, and hedonistic. He briefly summarizes Pope John Paul II's appeal for "'a global coalition in favor of "decent" work'" (no. 63),[20] and urges unions to

20. See Pope John Paul II, Jubilee of Workers, "Greeting after Mass," May 1, 2000.

look after "exploited and unrepresented workers" (no. 64). He then argues that "the entire financial system has to be aimed at sustaining true development" (no. 65). To this end he says that financiers must "rediscover" and maintain sound ethics to guide their important work. By this remark Pope Benedict is certainly implying that the unethical actions of financiers contributed to the economic crisis of 2008–2009.

Lastly, Pope Benedict argues for the legal establishment of a world political authority focused on the common good, whose form would reflect guidance from the principles of subsidiarity and solidarity. Clearly, Pope Benedict wants the kind of stratified authority that would take input from the nations of the world and not be a threat to act in a despotic manner. He thinks that this radical step is urgently needed in order to accomplish the following goals: *"To manage the global economy; to revive economies hit by the crisis; to avoid any deterioration of the present crisis and the greater imbalances that would result; to bring about integral and timely disarmament, food security and peace; to guarantee the protection of the environment and to regulate migration"* (no. 67). In addition, a properly constituted world political authority would be able to implement the principle of the *"responsibility to protect."*[21]

At the present time conditions don't exist that would allow for the establishment of a world political authority on the basis of subsidiarity, solidarity, and the common good. The Catholic Church and other organizations would first to have to make these principles better known and widely accepted before any kind of suitable world political authority could be reasonably established.

Chapter 6, on "The Development of Peoples and Technology," returns to the theme of integral development. The pope's most striking statement is the following: *"Development must include not just material growth but also spiritual growth,"* since the human person is a 'unity of body and soul,' born of God's creative love and destined for eternal life" (no. 76). This means that the nations of the world cannot adequately pursue the development of their peoples unless they understand the richness of human nature or what it really means to speak of the dignity of the human person. As St. Augustine argued, human beings are made for God and are restless until they rest in him. "When he is far away from God, man is unsettled and ill at ease. Social and psychological alienation and the many neuroses that afflict affluent societies are attributable in part to spiritual factors" (no. 76). So, the developing nations must be careful not to imitate the typical narrow understanding of development that prevails among affluent peoples. The spiritual and moral welfare of every individual in every nation must always be kept in mind in the work for development in the developing nations. This, of course, implies that the affluent nations must come

21. See Chapter 11 for a discussion of the "responsibility to protect."

to a deeper understanding of the spiritual needs of the human person. Unless this spiritual renewal takes place in Europe and the United States, the developing nations, in my judgment, are likely to imitate the narrow understanding of development that prevails in Western societies.

A second point is that the development of a people depends on the integral development of every single individual. One cannot be content with the mere prosperity of a nation as a whole. This makes perfect sense, given the spiritual meaning of development. Even the material side of development, however, "*is impossible without upright men and women, without financiers and politicians whose consciences are finely attuned to the requirements of the common good*" (no. 71). The integral development of individuals can never simply be the result of impersonal forces such as the removal of tariffs, financial engineering, or the opening up of markets. These and other actions are necessary, but not sufficient. Financiers and politicians acting according to high ethical standards for the high goal of integral development are necessary for the complete good of individuals.

Related to the theme of development is that of technology. Pope Benedict first directs attention to the good that technology can do. It "enables us to exercise dominion over matter, to reduce risks, to save labor, to improve our conditions of life" (no. 69). In addition, through technology man "forges his own humanity," and responds to God's command "*to till and keep the land*" (no. 69, cf. Gen 2:15). Technology, however, also has a dark side. Through globalization it could replace the destructive influence of political ideologies and "become an ideological power that threatens to confine us within an *a priori* that holds us back from encountering being and truth" (no. 70). Technology is very harmful in the hands of people who understand freedom as "total autonomy." Under the influence of that intoxication people pursue what seems useful and efficient without looking to moral norms for guidance in making choices. "When technology is allowed to take over, the result is confusion between ends and means, such that the sole criterion for action in business is thought to be the maximization of profit, in politics the consolidation of power, and in science the findings of research" (no. 71).

It is especially in the area of bioethics that technology must take its bearing by faith and reason. As mentioned previously by Pope Benedict, faith and reason must work together or they are likely to go astray. The greater danger in the area of bioethics is that "*reason without faith is doomed to flounder in an illusion of its own omnipotence*" (no. 74). Reason is tempted to approve whatever biotechnology is able to do, whether that is in vitro fertilization, embryonic stem cell research, or cloning.

Technological development has given the media more power to influence people for good or ill. Because the pope recognizes the media's power to have a *"civilizing effect"* by affecting people's fundamental attitudes in a profound way, he argues that "they need to focus on promoting the dignity of persons and peoples, they need to be clearly inspired by charity and placed at the service of truth, of the good, and of natural and supernatural fraternity" (no. 74). The media can, furthermore, bring about "the growth in communion of the human family" when they inspire people to undertake a "common search for what is just." These are, of course, extraordinary goals for the media, seemingly out of reach unless a new understanding of dignity, charity, fraternity, and the good could become persuasive to journalists and radio and television personnel. Pope Benedict reveals his full awareness of this enormous challenge when he says in a subsequent paragraph that cultural viewpoints exist that deny human dignity, leading to acceptance of in vitro fertilization, destruction of embryos through research, abortion, euthanasia, and "systematic eugenic programming of births" (no. 75). Because these practices foster "a materialistic and mechanistic understanding of human life" (no. 75), we should be not surprised that many people in the developed nations fail to be moved by the plight of those people living in degrading situations.

Pope Benedict concludes this chapter with an apt but unusual comment on truth and love. "All our knowledge, even the most simple, is always a minor miracle, since it can never be fully explained by the material instruments that we apply to it. In every truth there is something more than we would have expected, in the love that we receive there is always an element that surprises us" (no. 77). He then compares the height to which truth and love take us to the heights of integral development, which requires a spiritual dimension, as mentioned several times in the encyclical.

The conclusion is very short and to the point. We cannot possibly succeed at bringing about the integral development of individuals and peoples unless we have a relationship with God, in which we are receptive to his gifts. "The greatest service to development, then, is a Christian humanism that enkindles charity and takes its lead from truth, accepting both as a gift from God" (no. 78). Christian humanism, of course, develops as a result of people's relation to God. "Openness to God makes us open towards our brothers and sisters and towards an understanding of life as a joyful task to be accomplished in a spirit of solidarity" (no. 78). When you genuinely worship God, you want to love your neighbors so as to do good for them. Genuine love wants to take its bearings by truth. Being aware of God's immense love gives us patient endurance in our work for justice and development. "God gives us the strength to fight and suffer for love of the common good, because he is our All, our greatest hope" (no. 78).

The work for development requires Christians to pray for "truth-filled love," *caritas in veritate*. Pope Benedict expresses the hope that all people will learn to ask God specifically "for the grace to glorify him by living according to his will [necessarily a request for truth-filled love], to receive the daily bread that we need, to be understanding and generous towards our debtors, not to be tempted beyond our limits and to be delivered from evil" (no. 79). In his book *Jesus of Nazareth* Pope Benedict reflects deeply on the last petition of the Lord's Prayer, "deliver us from evil." Citing St. Cyprian, he says that after praying that ultimate petition, "'there is nothing further for us to ask for.'" You are protected against anything the devil and the world can throw at you. Pope Benedict also says that "the last petition brings us back to the first three: In asking to be liberated from the power of evil, we are ultimately asking for God's kingdom, for union with his will and for the sanctification of his name."[22] So, in the work for development we must attend to our spiritual life and rely on "God's Providence and mercy" (no. 79).

In the very last paragraph Pope Benedict concludes with a request that Mary "protect and obtain for us, through her heavenly intercession, the strength, hope and joy necessary to dedicate ourselves with generosity to the task of bringing about the "'*development of the whole man and of all men*'" (no. 79).[23] This last word reminds us of Pope Benedict's initial point that integral human development requires "life in Christ...[as] the first and principal factor of development" in every single human being (no. 8).

As a last word, I would simply say that *Caritas in veritate* is proposing a Christian humanism to improve the productivity, ethics, and dignity of the economic life of nations. The practice of the virtues by all participants in modern economies, the pope argues, is more important for a functioning market than the pursuit of self-interest or any set of structures devised by policy makers.

22. *Jesus of Nazareth* (New York: Doubleday, 2007), 166, 167.
23. Pope Benedict is quoting *Populorum progressio*, no. 42.

Bibliography

Abbott, Walter M., ed. *The Documents of Vatican II.* New York: Guild Press, America Press, and Association Press, 1966.

Aguirre, Maria Sophia. "The Family and Economic Development: Socioeconomic Relevance and Policy Design." Paper delivered at Doha Conference Preparatory Sessions in Geneva, Switzerland, August 23–25, 2004.

———. "Family Dining, Diet and Food Distribution: Planting the Seeds of Economic Growth." Paper presented at "Excellence in the Home" 2006 Conference, London, May 8–9, 2006.

———. "Sustainable Development: Why the Focus on Population?" Paper presented at the Harvard-MIT Conference on International Health, March 10–12, 2000.

Alford, Helen J., O.P., and Michael J. Naughton. *Managing As If Faith Mattered: Christian Social Principles in the Modern Organization.* Notre Dame, Ind.: University of Notre Dame Press, 2001.

Ambrose, St. *De officiis. Oxford and New York: Oxford University Press, 2001.*

Aquinas, St. Thomas. *Collationes in Decem Praeceptis,* I, line 27, edition critique avec introduction et notes par Jean-Pierre Torrell. In *Revue des sciences philosophiques et théologiques* 69 (1985): 5–40, 27–63.

———. *Commentary on Aristotle's Nichomachean Ethics.* Translated by C. I. Litzinger. Notre Dame: Dumb Ox Press, 1993.

———. *Disputed Questions on Virtue.* Translated by Ralph McInerny. South Bend, Ind.: St. Augustine's Press, 1999.

———. *In Duo Praecepta Caritatis et in Decem Legis Praecepta. Prologus, Opuscula Theologica,* II, no. 1129. Edited by Raymundi A. Vercudo and Raymundi M. Spiazzi. Torino: Marietti, 1954.

———. *On Kingship, to the King of Cyprus.* Toronto: Pontifical Institute of Medieval Studies, 1982.

———. *Summa contra gentiles.* Vol. 4. Notre Dame, Ind.: University of Notre Dame Press, 1975.

———. *Summa theologica.* 3 vols. New York: Benziger Brothers, 1947.

Aristotle. *Nichomachean Ethics.* Translated by Martin Ostwald. New York: Macmillan, 1962.

———. *The Politics.* Translated by Carnes Lord. Chicago: University of Chicago Press, 1984.

Augustine, St. *The Catholic and Manichaean Ways of Life (De Moribus Ecclesiae Catholicae et de Moribus Manichaeorum).* Washington, D.C.: The Catholic University of America Press, 1966.

————. *The City of God*. Baltimore: Penguin Books, 1972; New York: Modern Library, 1950.

————. *The Confessions*. Indianapolis, Ind.: Hackett, 1993.

————. "Letter 138, to Marcellinus." In *Augustine: Political Writings*, edited by Douglas Kries and Ernest Fortin, 209–10. Indianapolis, Ind.: Hackett, 1994.

————. *On Free Choice of the Will*. Indianapolis and New York: Bobbs Merrill, 1964.

————. *Political Writings*. Translated by Michael W. Tkacz and Douglas Kries. Edited by Ernest L. Fortin and Douglas Kries. Indianapolis, Ind.: Hackett, 1994.

————. *Sermo Denis XIV*. In *Miscellanea Agostiniana*. Vol. I. Rome: Tipographia Poliglotta Vaticana, 1930–1931.

————. *Sermons*. Part III, vol. 4. New York: New City Press, 1992.

————. *Tractatus in epistulam Joannis ad Parthos*.

————. *A Select Library of Nicene and Post-Nicene Fathers of the Christian Church*. Vol. 7, *Tracts on the First Epistle of John*, edited by Philip Schaff and Henry Wace. Second Series. 1890ff. Reprint, New York: Eerdmans, 1956.

Austen, Jane. *Persuasion*. New York: Viking Penguin, 1986.

Benestad, J. Brian. *The Pursuit of a Just Social Order: Policy Statements of the U.S. Catholic Bishops, 1966–1980*. Washington, D.C.: Ethics and Public Policy Center, 1982.

————. "Review Essay on Leon Kass's *Life, Liberty and the Defense of Dignity: The Challenge for Bioethics* and *Toward a More Natural Science: Biology and Human Affairs*." *National Catholic Bioethics Quarterly* 5, no. 3 (Autumn 2005): 631–45.

————. "William Galston's Defense of Liberalism: Forging Unity Amid Diversity." In *Liberalism at the Crossroads: An Introduction to Contemporary Liberal Political Theory and Its Critics*, edited by Christopher Wolfe and John Hittinger, 172. Lanham, Md.: Rowman and Littlefield, 1994.

Bernanos, George. *The Diary of a Country Priest*. New York: Macmillan, 1970.

Bernardin, Joseph Cardinal. "Call for a Consistent Ethic of Life." *Origins* 13, no. 29 (1983): 491–95.

Bertone, Tarcisio Cardinal. *L'Etica del Bene Commune nella Dottrina Sociale della Chiesa*. Vatican City: Libreria Editrice Vaticana, 2007.

Boston Globe. "The Price of Vouchers." Editorial, June 28, 2002.

Bradley, Gerard V. "Same-Sex Marriage: Our Final Answer?" In *Same-Sex Attraction: A Parents' Guide*, 127. South Bend, Ind.: St. Augustine's Press, 2003.

Bradley, Gerard V., and J. F. Harvey, eds. *Same Sex Attraction: A Parents's Guide*. South Bend, Ind.: St. Augustine's Press, 2003.

Budziszewski, J. *What We Can't Not Know: A Guide*. Dallas: Spence, 2003.

————. *Written on the Heart: The Case for Natural Law*. Downers Grove, Ill.: Intervarsity Press, 1997.

Brown, Lester R. *Plan B 2.0: Rescuing a Planet Under Stress and a Civilization in Trouble*. New York: W. W. Norton, 2006.

————. *Plan B 4.0: Mobilizing to Save Civilization*. New York: W. W. Norton, 2009.

Calvez, Jean-Yves. "Social Justice." In vol. 13 of the *New Catholic Encyclopedia*, 242–44. Washington, D.C.: The Catholic University of America, 1967.

———. *The Social Thought of John XXIII: Mater et Magistra.* Translated by George J.M.McKenzie. Chicago: Regnery, 1965.

Calvez, Jean-Yves, and Jacques Perrin. *The Church and Social Justice.* Chicago: Regnery, 1961.

———. *Église and Societé économique: L'enseignment social des papes de Leon XIII à Pie XII 1878–1958.* Paris: Aubier, 1959.

Cantalamessa, Raniero. *Poverty.* New York: Alba House, 1997.

Carlen, Claudia, ed. *The Papal Encyclicals: 1740–1981.* 5 vols. Ann Arbor: Pierian, 1981.

Center for the Study of Catholic Higher Education. *The Enduring Nature of a Catholic University: Commemorating the Anniversary of Pope Benedict XVI's Address to Catholic Educators on April 17, 2008.* Manassas, Va.: Cardinal Newman Society, 2009.

Cessario, Romanus. *Introduction to Moral Theology.* Washington, D.C.: The Catholic University of America Press, 2001.

Chaput, Archbishop Charles. "How to Tell a Duck from a Fox: Thinking with the Church as We Look toward November." *Denver Catholic Register* (April 14, 2004).

———. *Render Unto Caesar.* New York: Doubleday, 2008.

Charles, Rodger. *An Introduction to Catholic Social Teaching.* San Francisco: Ignatius, 1999.

———. *Christian Social Witness and Teaching: The Catholic Tradition from Genesis to Centesimus Annus.* Leominster: Gracewing, 1998.

———. *The Social Teaching of Vatican II, Its Origin and Development: Catholic Social Ethics, an Historical and Comparative Study.* San Francisco: Ignatius Press, 1982.

Chesterton, Gilbert K. *Orthodoxy.* Garden City, N.Y.: Doubleday Image, 1989.

Christie, Agatha. "Wasps' Nest." In *Hercule Poirot's Casebook.* New York: Dodd, Mead, 1984, 814.

Chrysostom, St. John. *Six Books on the Priesthood.* Crestwood, NY: St. Vladimir's Seminary Press, 1984.

Clark, Homer H. *The Law of Domestic Relations in the United States.* 2nd ed. St. Paul, Minn.: West Publishing, 1998.

Coelho, Juan Souto. *Doctrina Social de la Iglesia: Manual Abreviado.* Madrid: Biblioteca De Autores Cristianos, 2002.

Connell, Francis. J. "Principle of Double Effect." In vol. 4 of *New Catholic Encyclopedia,* 1981.

Connery, John R. *Abortion: The Development of the Roman Catholic Perspective.* Chicago: Loyola University Press, 1977.

Coulter, Michael L., Stephen M.Krason, Richard S.Myers, and Joseph A.Varacalli, eds. *Encyclopedia of Catholic Social Thought, Social Science, and Social Policy.* 2 vols. Scarecrow Press, 2007.

Cronin, John F. *Catholic Social Principles: The Social Teaching of the Catholic Church Applied to American Economic Life.* Milwaukee: Bruce Publishing, 1950.

———. *Christianity and Social Progress: A Commentary on Mater et Magistra.* Baltimore: Helicon, 1965.

Crosson, Frederick. J. "American Reflections on a Century of Catholic Social Teaching." In *One Hundred Years of Philosophy,* edited by Brian J.Shanley. Washington, D.C.: The Catholic University of America Press, 2001.

Curran, Charles. E., and Richard McCormick, eds. *Official Catholic Social Teaching.* New York: Paulist Press, 1986.

Davis, Kingsley. "Population Policy: Will Current Programs Succeed?" In *Population Puzzle: Boom or Bust,* edited by Laura E. Huggins and Hanna Skandera, 333. Stanford, Calif.: Hoover Institution Press, 2004.

D'Azeglio, Luigi Taparelli. *Saggio teoretico di diritto naturale appoggiato sul fatto.* 2 vols. Palermo, 1840–1843.

Deane, Herbert A. *The Political and Social Ideas of St. Augustine.* New York: Columbia University Press, 1963.

Decter, Midge. "The Nine Lives of Population Control." In *The Nine Lives of Population Control,* edited by Michael Cromartie, 9. Washington, D.C.: Ethics and Public Policy Center; Grand Rapids, Mich.: Eerdmans, 1995.

De Koninck, Charles. *De la primauté du bien commun.* Québec: Editions de l'université Laval, 1943.

de Tocqueville, Alexis. *Democracy in America.* Edited by Harvey C. Mansfield and Delba Winthrop. Chicago: University of Chicago Press, 2000.

———. *Democracy in America.* Translated by George Lawrence. New York: Harper Collins, 1969.

Di Noia, J. Augustine and Romanus Cessario, eds. *Veritatis Splendor and the Renewal of Moral Theology.* Huntington, Ind.: Our Sunday Visitor, 1999.

Documents of the 31st and 32nd General Congregations of the Society of Jesus. St. Louis: Institute of Jesuit Sources, 1977.

Documents of the Thirty-Fourth General Congregation of the Society of Jesus. St. Louis: Institute of Jesuit Resources, 1995. Decree 3, no. 8, p. 42.

Doeflinger, Richard. "Experimentation on Human Subjects and Stem Cell Research." In *Moral Issues in Catholic Health Care.* Wynnewood, Penn.: St. Charles Borromeo Seminary, 2004.

Dougherty, Bishop John. "From the Heart of the Church: The Catholic University for the Third Millennium." In *A Compendium for Catholic Higher Education Officials,* edited by Mo Fung, 7. Falls Church, Va.: Cardinal Newman Society, 1998.

Dulles, Avery Cardinal. *Church and Society: The Lawrence J. McGinley Lectures 1988–2007.* New York: Fordham University Press, 2008.

———. "Human Rights: The United Nations and Papal Teaching," in *Church and Society: The Lawrence J. McGinley Lectures 1988–2007.* New York: Fordham University Press, 2008.

———. *Magisterium: Teacher and Guardian of the Faith.* Naples, Fla.: Sapientia Press, 2007.

———. "Orthodoxy and Social Change." *America* 178, no. 21 (1998): 8–17.

———. "Religion and the Transformation of Politics." *America* 167, no. 12 (1992): 296–301.

———. *The Reshaping of Catholicism: Current Challenges in the Theology of the Church.* New York: Harper and Row, 1988.

———. *The Splendor of Faith: The Theological Vision of Pope John Paul II.* New York: Herder and Herder, 2003.

Bibliography

Dunn, John. *Locke.* New York: Oxford University Press, 1984.

Dwyer, Judith A., and Elizabeth L. Montgomery, eds. *The New Dictionary of Catholic Social Thought.* Collegeville, Minn.: Liturgical Press, 1994.

Eberstadt, Mary. "The Vindication of Humanae Vitae." *First Things,* no. 185 (2008): 35–42.

Eberstadt, Nicholas. "Population, Resources, and the Quest to 'Stabilize Human Population': Myths and Realities." In *Global Warming and Other Eco-Myths,* 74. Roseville, Calif.: Prima Publishing, 2002.

Ehrlich, Paul. *The Population Bomb.* New York: Ballantine Books, 1968.

Elshtain, Jean Bethke. "How Should We Talk?" *Case Western Reserve Law Review* 49 (1999): 744.

———. "Just War as Politics: What the Gulf War Told Us About Contemporary American Life." In *But Was It Just? Reflections on the Morality of the Persian Gulf War,* 46. New York: Doubleday, 1992.

Ferree, William. *The Act of Social Justice.* Dayton: Marianist Publications, 1951.

———. *Introduction to Social Justice.* New York: Paulist Press, 1948.

Finnis, John. *Natural Law and Natural Rights.* Oxford: Clarendon Press, 1980.

———. *Nuclear Deterrence: Morality and Realism.* New York: Oxford University Press, 1987.

Foley, Michael. P., and Douglas Kries, eds. *Gladly to Learn and Gladly to Teach: Essays on Religion and Political Philosophy in Honor of Ernest Fortin.* Lanham, Md.: Lexington Books, 2002.

Ford, John C. "The Morality of Obliteration Bombing." *Theological Studies* 5 (1944): 267.

Fortin, Ernest L. "The Bible Made Me Do It: Christianity, Science and the Environment." In *Human Rights, Virtue and the Common Good,* vol. 3 of *Collected Essays,* edited by J. Brian Benestad, 124. Lanham, Md.: Rowman and Littlefield, 1996.

———. *Collected Essays.* Edited by J. Brian Benestad. 3 vols. Lanham, Md.: Roman and Littlefield, 1996.

———. *Ever Ancient, Ever New: Ruminations on the City, the Soul, and the Church.* Vol. 4. Edited by Michael Foley. Lanham, Md.: Rowman and Littlefield Publishers, 2007.

Fox-Genovese, Elizabeth. *Feminism Without Illusions: A Critique of Individualism.* Chapel Hill: University of North Carolina Press, 1991.

Fuchs, Joseph. *Moral Demands and Personal Obligations.* Translated by Brian McNeil. Washington, D.C.: Georgetown University Press, 1995.

Galston, William A. "Contending with Liberalism: Some Advice for Catholics." *Commonweal* 127, no. 7 (2001): 13.

———. "Divorce American Style." *The Public Interest* 124 (Summer 1996): 12–26.

———. "Expressive Liberty, Moral Pluralism, Political Pluralism: Three Sources of Liberal Theory." *William and Mary Law Review* 40 (1999): 880.

———. "Gambling Away Our Moral Capital." *The Public Interest* 123 (1996): 58–71.

———. *Liberal Pluralism: The Implications of Value Pluralism for Political Theory and Practice.* New York: Cambridge University Press, 2002.

———. *Liberal Purposes: Goods, Virtues, and Diversity in the Liberal State*. New York: Cambridge University Press, 1991.

———. "Moral Inquiry and Liberal Education in the American University." *Ethics* 110 (July 2000): 814.

———. "A Public Philosophy for the 21st Century." *The Responsive Community* (Summer 1998): 21.

———. Review of *One Nation, After All*, by Alan Wolfe. *The Public Interest*, no. 133 (Fall 1998): 116–20.

———. "Two Concepts of Liberalism." *Ethics* 105 (April 1995): 525

———. "Value Pluralism and Liberal Political Theory." *American Political Science Review* 93 (1999): 770.

Garcia, Laura. "Can Feminism Acknowledge a Vocation for Women?" In *The Church, Marriage, and the Family*, edited by Kenneth Whitehead, 145–53. South Bend, Ind.: St. Augustine's Press, 2007.

George, Robert P. *The Clash of Orthodoxies*. Wilmington, Del.: ISI Books, 2001.

———. *In Defense of Natural Law*. Oxford: New York: Oxford University Press, 1999.

———. "Law and Moral Purpose." *First Things*, no. 79 (2008): 22.

———. *Making Men Moral: Civil Liberties and Public Morality*. Oxford: Clarendon Press, 1993.

———. "Same-sex Marriage and Moral Neutrality." In *Homosexuality and American Public Life*, edited by Christopher Wolfe. Dallas: Spence, 1999.

George, Robert P., and Christopher Tollefsen. *Embryo: A Defense of Human Life*. New York: Doubleday, 2008.

Gleason, Philip. *Catholicism in America*. New York: Harper and Row, 1970.

Glendon, Mary Ann. *Abortion and Divorce in Western Law: American Failures, European Challenges*. Cambridge, Mass.: Harvard University Press, 1987.

———. "For Better or For Worse? The Federal Marriage Amendment Would Strike a Blow for Freedom." *Wall Street Journal*, editorial page, February 25, 2004.

———. "The Hour of the Laity." *First Things*, no. 127 (2002): 23–29.

———. "Principled Immigration." *First Things*, no. 164 (2006): 23–26.

———. *Rights Talk: The Impoverishment of Political Discourse*. New York: Free Press, 1991.

———. *Traditions in Turmoil*. Ann Arbor, Mich.: Sapientia Press, 2006.

———. *A World Made New: Eleanor Roosevelt and the Universal Declaration of Human Rights*. New York: Random House, 2001.

Glendon, Mary Ann, and David Blankenhorn, eds. *Seedbeds of Virtue: Sources of Competence, Character, and Citizenship in America Society*. Lanham, Md.: Madison Books, 1995.

Goerner, Edward A. *Peter and Ceasar: The Catholic Church and Political Authority*. New York: Herder and Herder, 1965.

Goldwin, Robert A. "John Locke." In *History of Political Philosophy*, 3rd ed., edited by Leo Strauss and Joseph Cropsey, 476–512. Chicago: University of Chicago Press, 1986.

Gormally, Luke, ed. *Issues for a Catholic Bioethic: Proceedings of the International Conference to Celebrate the Twentieth Anniversary of the Foundation of the Linacre Centre*. London: Linacre Center, 1999.

Grasso, Kennneth. L., Gerard V. Bradley, and Robert P. Hunt, eds. *Catholicism, Liberalism, and Communitarianism: The Catholic Intellectual Tradition and the Moral Foundations of Democracy.* Lanham, Md.: Rowman and Littlefield, 1993.

Green, Edward C. "The Pope May be Right." *Washington Post,* March 29, 2009, A15.

Gregory the Great. *Pastoral Care.* New York: Newman Press, 1978, 1950.

Grisez, Germain. *The Way of the Lord Jesus.* Vol. 1, *Christian Moral Principles.* Chicago: Franciscan Herald, 1983.

———. *The Way of the Lord Jesus.* Vol. 2, *Living a Christian Life.* Quincy, Ill.: Franciscan Press, 1993.

———. *The Way of the Lord Jesus.* Vol. 3, *Difficult Moral Questions.* Quincy, Ill.: Franciscan Press, 1997.

Guardini, Romano. *The Virtues: On Forms of Moral Life.* Chicago: Regnery, 1963.

Guerra, Marc D. "Beyond Natural Law Talk: Politics and Prudence in St. Thomas Aquinas's on *Kingship.*" *Perspectives on Political Science* 31, no. 1 (Winter 2002): 9–14.

———. *Christians as Political Animals: Taking the Measure of Modernity and Modern Democracy.* Wilmington, Del.: ISI Books, 2010.

Haas, John, ed. *Crisis of Conscience.* New York: Crossword, 1966.

Hardin, Garrett. "There Is No Global Population Problem: Can Humanists Escape the 'Catch 22' of Population Control?" In *Population Puzzle Boom or Bust,* edited by Laura E. Huggins and Hanna Skandera, 338. Stanford, Calif.: Hoover Institution Press, 2004.

———. "The Tragedy of the Commons." *Science* 162 (1968): 1244.

Harvey, John F. *The Homosexual Person—New Thinking in Pastoral Care.* San Francisco: Ignatius, 1987.

———. *The Truth About Homosexuality: The Cry of the Faithful.* San Francisco: Ignatius, 1996.

Haughey, John C., ed. *The Faith that Does Justice.* New York: Paulist Press, 1971.

Heckel, Roger. *General Aspects of the Social Catechesis of John Paul II: The Use of the Expression 'Social Doctrine' of the Church.* Vatican City: Pontifical Commission on Justice and Peace, 1980.

Hehir, J. Bryan. "Social Justice." In *The Harper Collins Encyclopedia of Catholicism,* edited by Richard P. McBrien, 1203–05. San Francisco: Harper Collins Publishers, 1995.

Herberg, Will. *Protestant, Catholic and Jew: An Essay in American Religious Sociology.* 1960. Reprint, Chicago: University of Chicago Press, 1983.

Hibbs, Thomas. "Stanley Hauerwas's Pacifism: the Radical Gospel." *The Weekly Standard* 7, no. 34 (2002): 38.

Hittinger, John. P. *Liberty, Wisdom, and Grace: Thomism and Democratic Political Theory.* Lanham, Md.: Lexington Books, 2002.

Hittinger, Russell. *A Critique of the New Natural Law Theory.* Notre Dame, Ind.: University of Notre Dame Press, 1987.

———. *The First Grace: Rediscovering the Natural Law in a Post-Christian World.* Wilmington, Del.: ISI, 2003.

———. "Natural Law as 'Law': Reflections on the Occasion of *Veritatis Splendor.*" *American Journal of Jurisprudence* 39 (1994): 1–32.

Höffner, Joseph Cardinal. *Christian Social Teaching.* Bratislava: Lúc, 1997.

Hogan, Frances X., and Marianne. Rea-Luthin. "Exporting Death or Offering Compassion: Vignettes of the American Experience with Physician-assisted Suicide." In *The Dignity of the Dying Person: Proceedings of the Fifth Assembly of the Pontifical Academy for Life,* edited by Juan Correa and Elio Sgreccia, 378. Vatican City: Libereia Editrice Vaticana, 2000.

Hunt, Robert P., and Kenneth L. Grasso, eds. *John Courtney Murray and the American Civil Conversation.* Grand Rapids, Mich.: Eerdmans, 1992.

Information Office of the State Council of the People's Republic of China. Excerpt from "White Paper on Information 2000." In *Population Puzzle Boom or Bust?* edited by Laura E. Huggins and Hanna Skandera, 274. Stanford, Calif.: Hoover Institution Press, 2004.

Irenaeus, St. *Adversus haereses: St. Irenaeus of Lyons against the Heresies.* Translated by Dominic J. Unger; revisions by John J. Dillon. New York: Paulist Press, 1992.

John of the Cross, St. *The Ascent of Mount Carmel,* book 1, chap. 14. in *Collected Works of St. John of the Cross.* Translated by Kieran Kavanaugh and Otilio Rodriquez. Washington, D.C.: Institute of Carmelite Studies, 1973.

Johnson, James Turner. *Can Modern War Be Just?* New Haven, Conn., and London: Yale University Press, 1984.

———. *Morality and Contemporary Warfare.* New Haven, Conn., and London: Yale University Press, 1999.

Kant, Immanuel. *Perpetual Peace and Other Essays.* Indianapolis, Ind.: Hackett, 1983.

Kass, Leon R. *Life, Liberty, and the Defense of Dignity: The Challenge for Bioethics.* San Francisco: Encounter Books, 2002.

———. "Practicing Ethics: Where's the Action." *Hastings Center Report* (January/February, 1990): 7.

——— *Towards a More Natural Science: Biology and Human Affairs.* New York: Free Press, 1985.

Kates, Carol. "Aggressive Population Control Policies Should Be Supported." In *Population: Opposing Viewpoints,* edited by Karen F. Balkin, 136. Farmington Hills, Mich.: Greenhaven Press, 2005.

Katongole, Emmanuel M. *A Future for Africa: Critical Essays in Christian Social Imagination.* Scranton, Penn.: University of Scranton Press, 2005.

Kelly, George A. *Inside My Father's House.* New York: Doubleday, 1989.

Keys, Mary. *Aquinas, Aristotle, and the Promise of the Common Good.* New York: Cambridge University Press, 2006.

———. "Personal Dignity and the Common Good: A Twentieth Century Thomistic Dialogue." In *Catholicism, Liberalism, and Communitarianism: The Catholic Intellectual Tradition and the Moral Foundations of Moral Foundations of Democracy,* edited by Kenneth L. Grasso, Gerard V. Bradley, and Robert P. Hunt, 173–95. Lanham, Md.: Rowman and Littlefield, 1995.

King, Martin Luther, Jr. "Letter from Birmingham City Jail." In *A Testament of Hope: The Essential Writings of Martin Luther King Jr.,* edited by James Melvin Washington, 289–302. San Francisco: Harper and Row, 1986.

Krason, Stephen M. *The Public Order and the Sacred Order: Contemporary Issues, Catholic Social Thought, and the Western-American Traditions.* Lanham, Md.: Scarecrow Press, 2009.

Kraynak, Robert. P. *Christian Faith and Modern Democracy: God and Politics in the Fallen World.* Notre Dame, Ind.: University of Notre Dame Press, 2001.

Kreeft, Peter. *The Philosophy of Tolkien: The Worldview Behind* The Lord of the Rings. San Francisco: Ignatius Press, 2005.

La Farge, John. *The Race Question and the Negro: A Study of the Catholic Doctrine on Interracial Justice.* New York and Toronto: Longmans, Green, 1945.

Lamb, Matthew. "Life of the Mind and Life of Faith: The Context of *Ex Corde Ecclesiae.*" Unpublished lecture at St. Mary's University in Orchard Lake, Michigan, in October of 2001.

Lamb, Matthew, and Matthew Levering, eds. *Vatican II: Renewal Within Tradition.* New York: Oxford University Press, 2008.

Lawler, Ronald, Joseph Boyle, and William E. May. *Catholic Sexual Ethics: A Summary, Explanation, and Defense.* Huntington, Ind.: Our Sunday Visitor.

Lay Commission on Catholic Social Teaching and the U.S. Economy. *Toward the Future: Catholic Social Thought and the U.S. Economy: A Lay Letter.* New York: Rowman and Littlefield, 1985.

Letter of the Cardinal Secretary of State to Father General, Pedro Arrupe, S.J. May 2, 1975 in *Documents of the 31st and 32nd General Congregations of the Society of Jesus.* St. Louis: Institute of Jesuit Sources, 1977. 547.

Lewis, Clive Staples (C. S.). *The Abolition of Man.* New York: Collier, 1962.

———. *The Screwtape Letters.* New York: Macmillan, 1961.

———. *The Weight of Glory and Other Addresses.* Revised edition. New York: Macmillan, 1980.

Locke, John. *Epistola de Tolerantia (A Letter Concerning Toleration).* Translated by J. W. Gough. Oxford: Clarendon Press, 1968.

Lubac, Henri de. "The Authority of the Church in Temporal Matters." In *Theological Fragments.* San Francisco: Ignatius, 1989.

———. *Catholicism: Christ and the Common Destiny of Man.* Translated by Lancelot C. Sheppard and Sister Elizabeth Englund. San Francisco: Ignatius Press, 1988.

———. *Splendor of the Church.* Translated by Michael Mason. New York: Sheed and Ward, 1956.

Macedo, Stephen. "Religion and Civic Education Constituting Civil Society: School Vouchers, Religious Nonprofit Organizations, and Liberal Public Values." *Chicago-Kent Law Review* 75 (2000): 437.

———. "Transformative Constitutionalism and the Case of Religion: Defending the Moderate Hegemony of Liberalism." *Political Theory* 26 (1998): page 7 in Proquest.

Machiavelli, Niccolo. *The Prince.* Translated and introduced by Harvey C. Mansfield, Jr. Chicago: University of Chicago Press, 1985.

Mahoney, Daniel J. *Aleksandr Solzhenitsyn: The Ascent from Ideology.* Lanham, Md.: Rowman and Littlefield, 1998.

———. "The Moral Foundations of Liberal Democracy." In *Public Morality, Civ-*

ic Virtue and the Problem of Modern Liberalism, edited by T. William Boxx and Gary M. Quinlivan, 25. Grand Rapids, Mich.: Eerdmans, 2000.

Malik, Charles, ed. The Challenge of Human Rights: Charles Malik and the Universal Declaration. Oxford: Oxford Center for Lebanese Studies, 2000.

Manent, Pierre. The City of Man. Translated by Marc LePain. Princeton, N.J.: Princeton University Press, 1998.

———. An Intellectual History of Liberalism. Translated by R. Balinski. Princeton, N.J.: Princeton University Press, 1994.

———. Modern Liberty and Its Discontents. Edited by Daniel Mahoney. Lanham, Md.: Rowman and Littlefield, 1998.

———. Tocqueville and the Nature of Democracy. Translated by John Waggoner. Lanham, Md.: Rowman and Littlefield, 1996.

Manzoni, Alessandro. The Betrothed. New York: Viking Penguin, 1987.

Maritain, Jacques. Confession de foi. New York: Editions de la maison francaise, 1941.

———. I Believe. New York: Simon and Schuster, 1939.

———. Man and the State. Chicago: University of Chicago Press, 1951.

———. The Person and the Common Good. Translated by John J. Fitzgerald. Notre Dame, Ind.: University of Notre Dame Press, 1947.

Markus, Robert A. Saeculum: History and Society in the Theology of St. Augustine. Cambridge: Cambridge University Press, 1970.

Martino, Joseph. Chastity: A Pastoral Letter, December 8, 2004. See http://www.dioceseofscranton.org/Bishop's%20Pastoral%20Letters/Bishop'sLetteron(-)Chastity.asp.

Massaro, Thomas. Living Justice: Catholic Social Teaching in Action. Lanham, Md.: Rowman and Littlefield, 2008.

May, William E. Catholic Bioethics and the Gift of Human Life. 2nd ed. Huntington, Ind.: Our Sunday Visitor, 2008.

———. Introduction to Moral Theology. 2nd ed. Huntington, Ind.: Our Sunday Visitor, 1994.

McConnell, Michael W. "Religion and Civic Education: The New Establishmentarianism." Chicago-Kent Law Review 75 (2000): 470.

McInerny, Ralph. Ethica Thomistica: The Moral Philosophy of Thomas Aquinas. Rev. ed. Washington, D.C.: The Catholic University of America Press, 1997.

———. "The Principles of Natural Law." American Journal of Jurisprudence 25, no. 1 (1980): 1–15.

———. St. Thomas Aquinas. Notre Dame, Ind.: University of Notre Dame Press, 1977.

———. Thomism in an Age of Renewal. Notre Dame, Ind.: University of Notre Dame Press, 1966.

McIntyre, Alasdair. After Virtue. Notre Dame, Ind.: University of Notre Dame Press, 1981.

Messner, Johannes. Social Ethics: Natural Law in the Western World. Revised. edition. Translated by J. J. Doherty. London: B. Herder, 1965.

Montcheuil, Yves de. Problèmes de Vie Spirituelle. Paris: Editions de L'Epi, 1961.

More, Thomas. *Utopia.* Translated by Peter K. Marshall. New York: Washington Square Press, 1965.

Murray, John Courtney. "The Issue of Church and State at Vatican II." *Theological Studies* 27 (December 1996): 580–806.

———. "The Problem of Religious Freedom." *Theological Studies* 25 (December 1964): 503–75.

———. "War and Conscience." In *A Conflict of Loyalties: The Case for Selective Conscientious Objection,* edited by James Finn, 19–30. New York: Pegasus, 1968.

———. *We Hold These Truths: Catholic Reflections on the American Proposition.* New York: Sheed and Ward, 1960.

Nathanson, Bernard N. *The Hand of God: A Journey from Death to Life by the Abortion Doctor Who Changed His Mind.* Washington, D.C.: Regnery, 1996.

Nathanson, Bernard N., and Richard N. Ostling. *Aborting America.* Garden City, N.Y.: Doubleday, 1979.

Nell-Breuning, Oswald von. "The Drafting of Quadragesimo Anno." In *Readings in Moral Theology No. 5: Official Catholic Social Teaching,* edited by Charles Curran and Richard McCormick. New York: Paulist, 1986.

———. *Reorganization of Social Economy: The Social Encyclical Developed and Explained.* New York: Bruce, 1936–1937.

———. "Social Movements." In *Sacramentum mundi: An Encyclopedia of Theology,* vol. 6, edited by Karl Rahner, et al., 98–116. New York: Herder and Herder, 1970.

Neuhaus, Richard J. *The Catholic Moment: The Paradox of the Church in the Modern World.* San Francisco: Harper and Row, 1987.

———. "The Public Square." *First Things,* no. 56 (October 1995): 83.

Newman, Jeremiah. *Foundations of Justice: A Historico-critical Study in Thomism.* Cork, Ireland: Cork University Press, 1954.

———. *Principles of Peace: A Commentary on John XXIII's "Pacem in Terris."* Oxford: Catholic Social Guild, 1964.

Novak, Michael. *Catholic Social Thought and Liberal Institutions: Freedom with Justice.* New Brunswick, N.J.: Transaction, 1989.

———. *Freedom with Justice: Catholic Social Thought and Liberalism.* San Francisco: Harper and Row, 1984.

———. *Moral Clarity in the Nuclear Age.* New York: Thomas Nelson, 1983.

———. *The Spirit of Democratic Capitalism.* Lanham, Md.: Madison Books, 1982.

———. *To Empower People: From State to Civil Society.* 2nd ed. Washington, D.C.: American Enterprise Institute, 1996.

O'Brien, William V. *The Conduct of Just and Limited War.* New York: Praeger, 1981.

O'Connor, Flannery. *The Habit of Being.* Edited and with an introduction by Sally Fitzgerald. New York: Farrar, Straus and Giroux, 1978.

Oreskes, Naomi. "The Scientific Consensus on Climate Change." *Science* 306 (December 2004): 1686.

Pakaluk, Michael. "A Cardinal Error: Does the Seamless Garment Make Sense?" *Crisis* 6, no. 10 (1988): 10–14.

Pangle, Thomas. *The Rebirth of Classical Political Rationalism: An Introduction to the Thought of Leo Strauss.* Chicago: University of Chicago Press, 1985.

Paulhus, Normand. *The Theological and Political Ideals of the Fribourg Union.* Ann Arbor, Mich.: University Microfilms, 1983.

———. "Uses and Misuses of the Term 'Social Justice' in the Roman Catholic Tradition." *Journal of Religious Ethics* 15 (1981): 261–82.

Pavan, Pietro, and Teodoro Onofri. *La dottrina sociale cristiana.* 3rd ed. Rome: An. Veritas Editrice, 1966.

Percy, Walker. *Signposts in a Strange Land.* Edited by Patrick Samway. New York: Noonday Press, 1992.

Pieper, Joseph. *Faith, Hope, Love.* San Francisco: Ignatius Press, 1997.

———. *The Four Cardinal Virtues.* Notre Dame, Ind.: University of Notre Dame Press, 1966.

Pinckaers, Servais. *Sources of Christian Ethics.* Translated from the 3rd ed. by Sr. Mary Thomas Noble. Washington, D.C.: The Catholic University of America Press, 1995.

———. *The Sources of Christian Ethics.* Washington, D.C.: The Catholic University of America Press, 1995.

Plato. *The Laws.* Translated by Thomas L. Pangle. Chicago: University of Chicago Press, 1988.

———. *The Republic.* 2nd ed. Translated by Allan Bloom. New York: Basic Books, 1968.

President's Council on Bioethics. *Beyond Therapy: Biotechnology and the Pursuit of Happiness.* New York: Regan Books/HarperCollins, 2003.

———. *Human Cloning and Human Dignity: The Report of the President's Council on Bioethics.* Foreword by Leon Kass, Chairman. Washington, D.C.: Public Affairs, 2002.

Rahner, Hugo. *Church and State in Early Christianity.* San Franciso: Ignatius, 1992.

Ramsey, Paul. "Is Vietnam a Just War?" In *War in the Twentieth Century: Sources in Theological Ethics,* edited by Richard B. Miller, 189. Louisville, Ky.: Westminster/John Knox Press, 1992.

———. *The Just War: Force and Political Responsibility.* New York: Charles Scribner's Sons, 1968.

———. "Selective Conscientious Objection: Warrants and Reservations." In *A Conflict of Loyalties: the Case for Selective Conscientious Objection,* edited by James Finn, 31–77. New York: Pegasus, 1968.

Ratzinger, Joseph Cardinal. *Christianity and the Crisis of Cultures.* Introduction by Marcello Pera. Translated by Brian McNeil. San Francisco: Ignatius, 2006.

———. *Church, Ecumenism and Politics.* New York: Crossroad, 1988.

———. "Conscience and Truth." In *Crisis of Conscience,* edited by John M. Haas, 1–20. New York: Crossroad, 1996.

———. *Co-Workers of the Truth: Meditations for Every Day of the Year.* San Francisco: Ignatius Press, 1992.

———. *Credo for Today: What Christians Believe.* San Francisco: Ignatius Press, 2009.

————. "Culture and Truth: Reflections on the Encyclical," *Origins* 28, no. 36 (1999): 627.

————. "Glaube, Wahrheit und Kultur: Reflexionen im Anschluss an die Enzyklika *Fides et Ratio*," unpublished text made available to the public, 18.

————. *God and the World: A Conversation with Peter Seewald.* San Francisco: Ignatius Press, 2002.

————. *Introduction to Christianity.* Translated by J.R.Foster. New York: Herder and Herder, 1973; Crossroad, 1988. Now published by Ignatius Press.

————. *Jesus of Nazareth.* New York: Doubleday, 2007.

————. Memorandum to Cardinal McCarrick. *Priests for Life* website. See http://www.tldm.org/news7/Ratzinger.htm.

————. *The Nature and Mission of Theology: Essays to Orient Theology in Today's Debates.* San Francisco: Ignatius Press, 1993.

————. *Pilgrim Fellowship of Faith: The Church as Communion.* San Francisco: Ignatius Press, 2005. Contains bibliography of Joseph Ratzinger.

————. *The Salt of the Earth: Christianity and the Catholic Church at the End of the Millenium—An Interview with Peter Seewald.* San Francisco: Ignatius Press, 1997.

————. *Theological Highlights of Vatican II.* New York: Paulist Press, 1966.

————. *Truth and Tolerance: Christian Belief and World Religions.* San Francisco: Ignatius Press, 2004.

————. *Values in a Time of Upheaval.* New York and San Francisco: Crossroad and Ignatius Press, 2006.

————. "Vérité du Christianisme." *La documentation catholique*, no. 2217 (Jan. 2, 2000): 29.

————. *What It Means to Be a Christian.* San Francisco: Ignatius Press, 2006. German original published in 1966.

Ratzinger, Joseph, with Vittorio Messori. *The Ratzinger Report: An Exclusive Interview on the State of the Church.* San Francisco: Ignatius, 1985.

Rice, Charles. *Fifty Questions on the Natural Law.* San Francisco: Ignatius Press, 1993.

Riley, Patrick G.D., ed. *Keeping Faith: Monsignor George Kelly's Battle for the Church.* Front Royal, Va.: Christendom, 2000.

Rommen, Heinrich A. *The Natural Law: A Study in Legal and Social History and Philosophy.* Translated by Thomas R.Hanley. Indianapolis: Liberty Fund, 1998.

————. *The State in Catholic Thought: A Treatise in Political Philosophy.* Westport, Conn.: Greenwood, 1970.

Rosenthal, Elisabeth. "Europe, East and West, Wrestles with Falling Birth Rates." *International Herald Tribune*, September 3, 2006, 4.

Royal, Robert. *Catholic Martyrs of the Twentieth Century.* New York: Crossroad, 2000.

————. *The Virgin and the Dynamo: Use and Abuse of Religion in Environmental Debates.* Grand Rapids, Mich.: Eerdmans, 1999.

Ruse, Austin. "Overpopulation Is a Myth." In *Population: Opposing Viewpoints*, edited by Karen F.Balkin, 29. Farmington Hills, Mich.: Greenhaven Press, 2005.

Ryan, John A. "The Concept of Social Justice." *Catholic Charities Review* 18, no. 4 (1934): 313–15.

————. *Distributive Justice*. New York: Macmillan, 1942.

————. *Social Doctrine in Action: A Personal History*. New York: Harper and Brothers, 1941.

————. "Social Justice and the State." *Commonweal* 30 (1939): 205–6.

Ryan, John A., and Francis J. Boland. *Catholic Principles of Politics*. New York: Macmillan, 1941.

Sandel, Michael J. *Liberalism and the Limits of Justice*. Cambridge: Cambridge University Press, 1998.

————. Review of *Political Liberalism*, by John Rawls. *Harvard Law Review* 107 (1994): 1766.

Satinover, Jeffrey. "The Biological Truth about Homosexuality." In *Same-Sex Attraction: A Parents' Guide*, edited by John F. Harvey and Gerard V. Bradley, 14. South Bend, Ind.: St. Augustine's Press, 2003.

Schall, James V. "On the Place of Augustine in Political Philosophy: A Second Look at Some Augustinian Literature." *Political Science Reviewer* 23 (1994): 128–65.

————. "Reason, Revelation, and Politics: Catholic Reflections on Strauss." *Gregorianum* 62, no. 2 and 3 (1981): 349–66 and 467–98.

————. *Revelation and the Foundations of Political Philosophy*. San Francisco: Ignatius, 1987.

————. *Roman Catholic Political Philosophy*. Lanham, Md.: Lexington Books, 2004.

————. "The Uniqueness of the Political Philosophy of Thomas Aquinas." *Perspectives in Political Science* 26 (Spring 1997): 85–91.

Schindler, David L. "Going to the Heart: An Interview with Dr. David L. Schindler," conducted by Mo Fung. In a *Compendium for Catholic Higher Education Officials*, edited by Mo Fung, 31. Falls Church, Va.: Cardinal Newman Society, 1998.

————. *Heart of the World, Center of the Church: Communio Ecclesiology, Liberalism, and Liberation*. Grand Rapids, Mich.: Eerdmans, 1996.

Shakespeare, William. *King Henry the Fourth*. Part 2, act I, scene 2, lines 179–83.

Schotte, Jan. "A Vatican Synthesis." *Origins* 12 (1983): 691–95.

Shapiro, Kevin. "Global Warming: Apocalypse Now?" *Commentary* 122 (2006): 45.

Shaw, Russell. *To Hunt, to Shoot, to Entertain: Clericalism and the Catholic Church*. San Francisco: Ignatius Press, 1993.

Shields, Leo. "The History and Meaning of the Term Social Justice." Ph.D. diss., Notre Dame University, 1941.

Shell, Susan. "The Liberal Case Against Gay Marriage." *The Public Interest*, no. 156 (2004): 3–16.

Simon, Julian L. *Theory of Population and Economic Growth*. New York: Basil Blackwell, 1986.

————. *The Ultimate Resource*. 2nd ed. Princeton, N.J.: Princeton University Press, 1998.

Simon, Yves. R. *Philosophy of Democratic Government*. Chicago: University of Chicago Press, 1951.

Smith, Janet. *Humanae Vitae: A Generation Later*. Washington, D.C.: The Catholic University of America Press, 1991.

Smith, Janet, and Christopher Kaczor. *Life Issues, Medical Choices: Questions and Answers for Catholics.* Cincinnati, Ohio: St. Anthony Messenger Press, 2007.

Smith, Russell, ed. *Catholic Conscience: Foundation and Formation: Proceedings of the Tenth Bishops' Workshop.* Braintree, Mass.: Pope John Center, 1991.

Soderni, Eduardo. *The Pontificate of Leo XIII.* Translated by Barbara Barclay Carter. London: Burns, Oates and Washburne, 1934, vol. 1:67.

Steichen, Donna. *Ungodly Rage: The Hidden Face of Catholic Feminism.* San Francisco: Ignatius, 1991.

St. John of the Cross. *The Ascent of Mount Carmel.* Book 1, chap. 14. In *Collected Works of St. John of the Cross,* translated by Kieran Kavanaugh and Otilio Rodriquez. Washington, D.C.: Institute of Carmelite Studies, 1973.

Strauss, Leo. *The City and Man.* Chicago: University of Chicago Press, 1964.

————. *Natural Right and History.* Chicago: University of Chicago Press, 1953.

————. *Political Philosophy: Six Essays by Leo Strauss.* Edited by Hilail Gildin. New York: Bobbs Merrill, 1975.

————. *Studies in Platonic Political Philosophy.* Edited by T. Pangle. Chicago: University of Chicago Press, 1983.

————. *Thoughts on Machiavelli.* Chicago: University of Chicago Press, 1958.

————. *What Is Political Philosophy? and Other Studies.* Glencoe, Ill.: Free Press, 1959.

Tessitore, Aristede. *Reading Aristotle's Ethics: Virtue, Rhetoric, and Political Philosophy.* Albany, N.Y.: SUNY Press, 1996.

Tierney, Brian. *The Idea of Natural Rights: Studies on Natural Rights, Natural Law, and Church Law 1150–1625.* Grand Rapids, Mich.: Eerdmanns, 1997.

Tolkien, John R. R. *The Lord of the Rings.* Part 3, *The Return of the King.* New York: Ballantine, 1994.

UN Department of Economic and Social Affairs, Population Division. *World Population Prospects: The 2008 Revision, Executive Summary.* Available at http://esa.un.org/unpd/wpp2008/.

UN General Assembly. *Universal Declaration of Human Rights.* Lake Success: UN Department of Public Information, 1949.

————. *Universal Declaration of Human Rights.* Final Authorized Text. New York: UN Department of Public Information, 1952.

Vorgrimler, Herbert, ed. *Commentary on the Documents of Vatican II.* Vol. 5. New York: Herder and Herder, 1969.

Walzer, Michael. *Just and Unjust Wars: A Moral Argument with Historical Illustrations.* New York: Basic Books, 2000.

Wattenberg, Ben J. *Fewer: How the New Demography of Depopulation Will Shape Our Future.* Chicago: Ivan R. Dee, 2004.

Wegemer, Gerard B. *Thomas More on Statesmanship.* Washington, D.C.: The Catholic University of America Press, 1996.

Wegemer, Gerard B., and Stephen Smith, eds. *A Thomas More Source Book.* Washington, D.C.: Catholic University of America Press, 2004.

Weigel, George. *Building the Free Society: Democracy, Capitalism, and Catholic Social Teaching.* Grand Rapids, Mich.: Eerdmans, 1993.

————. *The Final Revolution: The Church and the Collapse of Communism.* New York: Oxford University Press, 1992.

————. "Moral Clarity in a Time of War." *First Things*, no. 129 (2003): 21.

————. *Tranquilitas Ordinis.* New York: Oxford University Press, 1987.

————. *Witness to Hope: The Biography of Pope John Paul II.* New York: Cliffe Street Books, 1999.

Weigel, George, and Robert Royal. *A Century of Catholic Social Thought: Essays on Rerum Novarum and Nine Other Key Documents.* Washington, D.C.: Ethics and Public Policy Center, 1991.

White, Lynn. "Historical Roots of our Ecological Crisis." *Science* 155 (1967): 1203–07.

Wilken, Robert. *The Spirit of Early Christian Thought: Seeking the Face of God.* New Haven, Conn.: Yale University Press, 2003.

Will, George. "Implacable Enemies of Choice." *Washington Post*, June 28, 2002.

Wilson, Edward O. "Apocalypse Now." *The New Republic* 235, no. 4781 (2006): 18.

Woytla, Karol. (Pope John Paul II). *Love and Responsibility.* New York: Farrar, Straus, and Giroux, 1981.

————. *Sources of Renewal.* San Francisco: Harper and Row, 1980.

Church Documents

In addition to the Church documents listed here, see the speeches given by popes Benedict XVI and John Paul II during their travels both within and outside of Italy. Other accessible sources are the Sunday Angelus, the Wednesday audiences, and speeches given once a year such as the World Day of Peace Message.

The statements of the Catholic bishops of the United States issued in the last decade will be listed under "United States Conference of Catholic Bishops," the name of the episcopal conference since July 1, 2001. I will also indicate the other names under which the bishops as a conference have issued statements between 1966 and July 1, 2001: National Conference of Catholic Bishops (NCCB), United States Catholic Conference (USCC), and Catholic Bishops of the United States. See note 1 in the introduction for information on the change of names.

Benedict XVI. "Address to the General Assembly of the United Nations," April 18, 2008.

————. *Caritas in veritate*, 2009.

————. *Deus caritas est*, 2005.

————. *Sacramentum caritatis*, 2007.

————. *Spe salvi.* 2007.

Catechism of the Catholic Church. Vatican City: Libreria Editrice Vaticana, 1994.

Catholic Bishops of the United States. *A Century of Social Teaching: A Common Heritage, A Continuing Challenge.* Washington, D.C.: United States Conference of Catholic Bishops, 1990.

————. *Living the Gospel of Life: A Challenge to American Catholics.* Washington, D.C.:

United States Conference of Catholic Bishops, 1998. Available at http://www
.nccbuscc.org/prolife/gospel.shtml.

———. *Sharing Catholic Social Teaching: Challenges and Directions.* Washington, D.C.: United States Conference of Catholic Bishops, 1998.

Code of Canon Law. Latin-English edition. Washington D.C.: Canon Law Society of America, 1983.

Congregation for Catholic Education. *Guidelines for the Study and Teaching of the Church's Social Doctrine in the Formation of Priests, 1988.* Vatican City: Polyglot Press; Rome: Congregation for Catholic Education, 1988.

Congregation for the Doctrine of the Faith. *Declaration on Euthanasia,* May 5, 1980.

———. *Dignitas personae.* 2008.

———. *Doctrinal Note on Some Questions Regarding the Participation of Catholics in Public Life,* November 24, 2002.

———. *Donum Vitae: Instruction on Respect for Human Life and Its Origin and on the Dignity of Procreation.* Boston: St. Paul Books and Media, 1987.

———. *Instruction on Christian Freedom and Liberation,* 1986.

———. *Regarding Proposals to Give Legal Recognition to Unions Between Homosexual Persons,* June 3, 2003.

John Paul II. "Address to the General Assembly of the United Nations," October 2, 1979. Reprinted in *Acta Apostolicae Sedis* 71 (1979), 1159.

———. "Address to the General Assembly of the United Nations," October 5, 1995. Published as "The Fiftieth General Assembly of the United Nations: Address of His Holiness John Paul II." *Origins* 25, no. 18 (October 19, 1995): 299–314.

———. "Address to Leaders of Catholic Higher Education," Xavier University of Louisiana, September 12, 1987. Published in *Acta apostolicae sedis* 80, no. 4 (1988): 764.

———. *Centesimus annus.* 1991.

———. *Christifideles laici.* 1989.

———. *Dives in misericordia.* 1980.

———. *Dominum et vivificantem.* 1986.

———. *Evangelium vitae.* 1995.

———. *Ex corde ecclesiae.* 1990.

———. *Familiaris consortio.* 1981.

———. *Fides et ratio.* 1998.

———. *John Paul II in Mexico.* London: Collins, 1979.

———. *Journey in the Light of the Eucharist.* Boston: Daughters of St. Paul, 1980.

———. *Laborem exercens.* 1981.

———. *Letter to Families,* February 2, 1994.

———. *Letter to Women,* June 29, 1995.

———. *Man and Woman He Created Them: A Theology of the Body.* Boston: Pauline Books and Media, 2006.

———. *Mulieris dignitatem.* 1988.

———. *Novo millenio ineuente.* 2001.

———. *Redemptoris hominis.* 1979.

———. *Redemptoris mater.* 1987.

———. *Reflections on "Humanae vitae."* Boston: Pauline Books and Media, 1984.

———. *Sollicitudo rei socialis.* 1987.

———. *Tertio millenio adveniente.* 1995.

———. *Veritatis splendor.* 1993.

John XXIII. *Mater et magistra.* 1961.

———. *Pacem in terris.* 1963.

Leo XIII. *Rerum novarum.* 1891.

National Conference of Catholic Bishops. *The Challenge of Peace: God's Promise and Our Response: A Pastoral Letter on War and Peace.* Washington, D.C.: United States Conference of Catholic Bishops, 1983.

———. *A Decade After Economic Justice for All.* Washington, D.C.: United States Conference of Catholic Bishops, 1995.

———. *Economic Justice for All: Pastoral Letter on Catholic Social Teaching and the U.S. Economy.* Washington, D.C.: United States Conference of Catholic Bishops, 1986.

———. *"The Harvest of Justice is Sown in Peace: A Reflection of the National Conference of Catholic Bishops on the Tenth Anniversary of The Challenge of Peace."* Available at http://www.usccb .org/sdwp/harvest.shtml.

———. *Pastoral Letters of the United States Catholic Bishops.* Edited by Hugh Nolan. Vol. 1: 1792–1940. Vol. 2: 1941–1961. Vol. 3: 1962–1974. Vol. 4: 1975–1983; vol. 5: 1983–88. Washington, D.C.: United States Conference of Catholic Bishops, 1989.

National Conference of Catholic Bishops/United States Catholic Conference. *Global Climate Change: A Plan for Dialogue, Prudence, and the Common Good.* Washington, D.C.: United States Conference of Catholic Bishops, 2001. See http://www.usccb.org/ sdwp/international/globalclimate.shtml.

Paul VI. *Evangelii nuntiandi.* 1975.

———. *Humanae vitae.* Translated by J.Smith. New Hope, Ky.: New Hope Publications, no date.

———. *Octogesima adveniens.* 1971.

———. *Populorum progressio.* 1967.

Pius XI. *Quadragesimo anno.* 1931.

———. *Divini redemptoris.* 1937.

Pius XII. *The Feast of Hope: The Christmas Messages of Pius XII.* Edited by V.Yzermans. St. Meinrad, Ind.: Grail Publications, 1956.

Pontifical Council for Justice and Peace. *Compendium of the Social Doctrine of the Church.* Vatican City: Libreria Editrice Vaticana, 2004.

———. *Compendium of the Social Teaching of the Church.* Washington, D.C.: United States Conference of Catholic Bishops, 2005.

United States Conference of Catholic Bishops. *Faithful Citizenship: A Catholic Call to Political Responsibility.* Administrative Committee. Washington, D.C.: United States Conference of Catholic Bishops, 2003.

———. *Forming Consciences for Faithful Citizenship. Washington, D.C.: United States Conference of Catholic Bishops, 2007).*

U.S. and Mexican Catholic Bishops. *Strangers No Longer: Together on the Journey of Hope.* Washington, D.C.: United States Conference of Catholic Bishops, 2003.

Vatican Council II. *Documents of Vatican II.* Edited by Walter M. Abbott. New York: Guild Press, America Press, and Association Press, 1966.

———. *Apostolicam actuositatem.* 1965.

———. *Dignitatis humanae.* 1965.

———. *Gaudium et spes.* 1965.

———. *Gravissimum educationis.* 1965.

———. *Lumen gentium.* 1964.

———. *Sacrosanctum concilium.* 1963.

Index

Abigail, 125–26, 146

abortion: Catholics' duty to oppose, 238–40; and environmental concerns, 371; as first moral priority for public life, 228–29, 234, 240–41; and genetic screening, 184, 202–3; influence of culture on acceptance of, 91; justifications for, 192; as kinship violation, 182–83; law on, 180; as murder, 191; and Nazism, 180–81; under neutral principles of justice, 433; pharmaceutical products for, 184; and potential educational role of law, 173; in rights culture, 55; U.N. Women's Conference in Beijing, 397–400; and violence, 181; voting decisions on, 227–29, 234

Abortion and Divorce in Western Law (Glendon), 172

absolutizing of rights, 54–58

acceptance of faith, 10

Adam and Eve, 404

Adorno, Theodore, 16, 23

Africa, population control imposed in, 367–71

age retardation, 206–8

Aguirre, Maria Sophia, 346, 365–66

After Virtue (MacIntyre), 116

"AIDS, Condomization, and Christian Ethics" (Katongole), 367–68

Alford, Helen, 333–34

Ambrose, 116, 123, 125–26

America: rights-based culture of, 30–31; rights tradition of, 54–58; Tocqueville's insights on, 27–30, 57, 282, 296–97, 340

"America the Beautiful" (Bates and Ward), 31–32

anamnesis (remembrance), 21

ancient vs. modern thought, 23–27

anger, 126

Aquinas, Thomas: anger, 126; authority of

Catholic social doctrine, 9; charity, 119, 120, 124, 127; civil law, 64, 171; the common good, 82, 83, 162, 239; on disorder of the soul, 156; divine reason, 65–68; division of possessions, 60; faith, 118–19; family, 259–60, 271; just society, 93, 96; justice, 12, 64, 143–47, 152; just-war principles, 408–12; love of God, 119–20; meekness, 126; natural inclinations, 66–68, 447; natural law teaching of, 49; patience, 123; private possessions, 321–22; reason, 71; role of state, 23, 85; social justice not discussed by, 151, 161–62; sorrow, 123; suicide, 193; temperance, 124–25; virtue, 115, 116–19, 122, 126–28, 158, 250; war, 425–26

Aristotle: on disorder of the soul, 156; effect of habits on perception, 68–69; intellect and will, 127; justice, 147–48; just society, 93; private possessions, 321; the regime, 24, 92; social justice not discussed by, 151; virtue, 23

armed forces, legitimacy of, 407

Armstrong, Lance, 329

Arrupe, Pedro, 303

artificial reproduction, 184, 201–2

Ashcroft, John, 194

assisted suicide, 207–8

attention deficit/hyperactivity disorder (ADHD), 203–4

Augustine: on accountability of the soul, 141; and armed forces, legitimacy of, 407; authority of Catholic social doctrine, 9; charity, 121; conscience, 21; culture, 105, 387; on disorder of the soul, 156; early life of, 122, 309–10, 311; faith and reason, 29, 283; family, 255; on habits, 69; human beings made for God, 463; just society, 12, 23, 93, 96; just war principles, 403–8, 410, 412; love as motivator, 308, 309–12;

Church, State, and Society: An Introduction to Catholic Social Doctrine was designed and typeset in Centaur by Kachergis Book Design of Pittsboro, North Carolina. It was printed on 50-pound Natural Offset and bound by Sheridan Books of Ann Arbor, Michigan.

CPSIA information can be obtained
at www.ICGtesting.com
Printed in the USA
FFHW021427250819
54436986-60150FF

9 780813 218014